CITIES IN REVOLT

BOOKS BY CARL BRIDENBAUGH

The Beginnings of the American People:

I VEXED AND TROUBLED ENGLISHMEN, 1590-1642

II NO PEACE BEYOND THE LINE:
The English in the Caribbean, 1624-1692
[In preparation]

CITIES IN THE WILDERNESS:
The First Century of Urban Life in America, 1625-1742

PETER HARRISON, FIRST AMERICAN ARCHITECT

THE COLONIAL CRAFTSMAN

SEAT OF EMPIRE:
The Political Role of Eighteenth-Century Williamsburg

MYTHS AND REALITIES:
Societies of the Colonial South

MITRE AND SCEPTRE:
Transatlantic Faiths, Ideas, Personalities, and Politics, 1689-1775

REBELS AND GENTLEMEN:
Philadelphia in the Age of Franklin (co-author)

GENTLEMAN'S PROGRESS:
Dr. Alexander Hamilton's Itinerarium, 1744
(edited, with an Introduction)

CITIES

IN REVOLT

Urban Life in America, 1743–1776

Carl Bridenbaugh

OXFORD UNIVERSITY PRESS
LONDON   OXFORD   NEW YORK

OXFORD UNIVERSITY PRESS

Oxford   London   New York
Glasgow   Toronto   Melbourne   Wellington
Cape Town   Salisbury   Ibadan   Nairobi   Lusaka   Addis Ababa
Bombay   Calcutta   Madras   Karachi   Lahore   Dacca
Kuala Lumpur   Hong Kong   Tokyo

For ARTHUR MEIER SCHLESINGER

Preface to the Oxford
Paperback Edition

As NOTED in the original preface, publishing considerations caused me to drop the notes and references to this volume. Now, fifteen years later, these have been restored with the hope that they will prove of use to scholars, some of whom have raised questions about certain statements in the text. Here are my authorities. The opportunity for a new edition has permitted me to correct such errors as I have found in the text. The illustrations, which did not appear in an earlier paperback issued by another publisher, are again included. Thus, this Oxford paperback edition provides the readers, for the first time, with the complete volume as the author wrote it. My thanks are due to the Oxford University Press for their generosity in making this kind of an edition possible.

C. B.

Providence
August 1970

Preface

THE AMERICAN REVOLUTION is looked upon today as not merely the leading event of the nation's history but, in its ultimate consequences, as one of the most momentous happenings of the last three centuries. It was an overt expression of the profound material and mental transformation which, beginning in western Europe and the British Isles in the seventeenth century, produced by the middle of the eighteenth century in nearly all departments of life the revolt against monarchy, aristocracy, and authority that we call modern times. As members of the Atlantic civilization, the American colonies of England responded promptly, receptively, and decisively to the forces of the new age. Just as this great revolt had its origins in the principal cities of Europe, so its various manifestations first appeared in the five largest cities in the English colonies—Boston, Newport, New York, Philadelphia, Charles Town.

This book is not a history of the American Revolution. It is rather a study of the locale and the conditions in which the uprising took place and of the people who participated in it. Much of the story of the movement for independence is deliberately omitted. Sentiment for the break with the mother country was a long time developing, and it is here contended that in these cities, at least, signs of the divergence between loyal colonialism and a new American nationality are discernible after 1743; though naturally no such clear understanding was vouchsafed to the citizens, who, like most people, were often blind to the significance of what was happening in their lives. Firmly convinced that it is people who make history, I have tried to portray them in their physical environment performing their daily economic and social activities, and also to analyze and describe what may be termed the public mind, as it expressed itself in many ways and at the several levels of the city population.

Constant comparisons are made with the developments in the cities of contemporary Europe. Colonial cities did not, of course, equal or approach such impressive capitals as London, Paris, or Rome in size or culture, but they did more than match the provincial cities of Europe, especially those in the British Isles.

Cities in Revolt is designed as an independent volume, but it also continues to the end of the colonial period the history of American urban life that I began in 1938 with *Cities in the Wilderness: The First Century of Urban Life in America, 1625–1742.*

As the writing of this book progressed, adequate treatment of the increased complexity of colonial urban life demanded a longer volume than was originally planned. Any pruning would have meant the elimination of entire topics and would have decreased the usefulness of the study. Faced with the necessity of cutting somewhere to meet publication considerations, I regretfully decided to omit the notes and references. Their form would have been identical with those in *Cities in the Wilderness*. It is my hope to issue these separately for the use of scholars. In quotations the familiar eighteenth-century shorthand abbreviations are expanded, and frequently italicized words are printed in ordinary roman type when no emphasis was intended. The illustrations are a special feature of this work, for they not only supply documentation for many statements, but have been carefully selected to fortify and extend the text. They are an integral part of the book.

Historical writing, like scientific research, no longer remains within the competence of a single individual; more and more it is becoming a co-operative undertaking. In the preparation of this volume I have been what the eighteenth century would have called "the Grand Beneficiary" of the labors of many bibliographers, archivists, editors, and historians, who have made my journey into the colonial period both easier and more enjoyable than it would have otherwise been. I am happy to be able to thank them collectively here. There are, however, certain students, friends, and associates to whom especially my gratitude goes out. The criticisms of Douglass Adair are always wise, stimulating, and kindly. For suggesting or making available materials I want to thank Stephen J. Riley of Boston; Miss Carolyn Jakeman of Cambridge; Clifford K. Shipton of Shirley; Miss Mary T. Quinn, Lawrence C. Wroth, the late Bruce M. Bigelow, and Clifford P. Monahon of Providence; Herbert S. Brigham and Mrs. Peter Bolhouse of Newport; Miss Dorothy C. Barck, R. W. G. Vail, and Wayne Andrews of New York; Philip White of Columbia University; Miss Lois V. Given, J. Harcourt Givens, R. Norris Williams, and Barney Chesnick of Philadelphia; Robert H. Land of Washington; Mrs. Fraser Neiman, Lester J. Cappon, and A. Lawrence Kocher of Williamsburg; Miss Virginia Rugheimer of Charleston; J. H. Easterby of Columbia; and Raymond P. Stearns of Urbana. Miss Rena Vassar, Lawrence A. Harper, Kenneth M. Stampp, and Lawrence and Adrienne Koch Kegan of Berkeley; Dr. Ernest Caulfield of Hartford; and Brooke Hindle of New York have performed special and deeply appreciated services for me.

For gracious permission to use copies of paintings or other illustrative matter in their possession I desire to acknowledge the officials of the National Portrait Gallery and the Guildhall Library at London; the American Antiquarian Society, the John Carter Brown Library, the Boston Museum of Fine Arts, the Cleveland Museum of Art, the New York Historical Society, the Frick Art Reference Library, the Historical Society of Pennsylvania, the South Carolina Archives Department, the Yale University Art Gallery, the Henry E. Huntington Library; and in particular Mrs. Frederick H. Horlbeck, the Countess Lâzlo Széchényi, and Charles E. Peterson.

Funds needed for travel, research, and preparation of the manuscript were generously made available by the Social Science Research Council, the Institute of Early American History and Culture, and the Institute of Social Sciences and President Robert Gordon Sproul of the University of California.

And to Roberta Herriott Bridenbaugh for her intelligent criticism and countless hours of devoted and painstaking labor in the research, revision, and final writing of *Cities in Revolt* I can give no adequate form of recognition.

CARL BRIDENBAUGH

Berkeley, January 1955

Contents

Illustrations

Part One

WAR, EXPANSION, AND PROSPERITY, 1743–1760

CHAPTER 1

The Urban Prospect

COMING THROUGH THE NARROWS into the lower harbor of New York at midafternoon on an October day in 1753, the passengers in the ship *Arundel*'s barge caught their first glimpse of the city crowding the southern tip of Manhattan Island. Sir Danvers Osborne, newly appointed Royal Governor, and his entourage shared simultaneous sensations of amazement and delight; so impressed was the Governor's secretary, Thomas Pownall, that, taking out his notebook, he made a hasty sketch of the distant prospect, to which he later added a pen picture: "This populous and well built Town with the Fort in front, with the many steeples of its Churches, the Turret of the Stadthouse and 'Change dispersed amidst its buildings, and the multitude of Shipping with which it is thronged perpetually, makes a very striking appearance and alltogether as fine and as pleasing a View as I ever saw." [1]

The cities of America have always fascinated European visitors. In the middle of the eighteenth century, however, astonishment and approval animated most of them upon their first sight of any of the five metropolises of the English colonies—Boston, Newport, New York, Philadelphia, Charles Town. Nurtured on fuzzy concepts and much misinformation about the New World, they could scarcely have been prepared for what they saw as they sailed into any one of the five harbors, for it was not the anticipated wilderness of tall trees, fierce animals, and red savages, but, rather, rising centers of civilization, cities as busy, as large, and as sightly as any but the great capitals of Europe. Boston, exclaimed the Reverend Andrew Burnaby, had much of the air of the best provincial cities of England! Charles Town and Newport elicited similar compliments from other travelers, but the "grandeur and perfection" of Philadelphia, achieved in barely threescore and ten years, the allotted span of a man's life, seemed unparalleled to Swedish Peter Kalm in 1748. "And yet," he declared, "its natural advantages, Trade, riches and power, are by no means inferior to those of any, even of the most ancient towns in Europe."

Perennially evoking the interest and admiration of contemporaries, to modern observers, these cities of the Atlantic seaboard assume a promi-

[1] In the eighteenth century *town* was synonymous with *city*, and I follow this usage.

3

nent place among the wonders of the eighteenth century. More than any of the provincial urban centers of western Europe, they display the unfolding, working out, and institutionalizing of the ideals and aspirations of the Age of Enlightenment. They symbolize above all else the revolt that was transforming the century. How this came about is the theme of this book.

II

As urban America entered upon its second century of existence, external conditions of a world-wide as well as of a local nature silently and inexorably determined its future, for the cities lay in the center, not on the periphery, of Western civilization. Since 1713 the great European powers had remained more or less at peace, but from 1743 to 1760 there was to be no peace; the period opened in war and in war it closed. For six years only (1748–54) did the colonies enjoy a partial surcease from hostilities; and even then, in the Caribbean, essential trading continued in what was in truth our first cold war.

In the life of the five seaports throughout these seventeen years, war, not peace, was normal. England's struggle with Spain and France deranged but at the same time stimulated their commercial activities; it also created or aggravated problems within the cities and, in several instances, actually altered their appearance. Upon communities already rapidly growing, the conflict acted as a forced draft to produce unprecedented physical expansion and economic prosperity. Likewise the Anglo-French struggle for North America invigorated and sharpened the intellects of the townsmen, impelling them to scientific and cultural undertakings which, if peace had obtained, would have come much more slowly. Nor was the effect of this ferment felt solely by what the age called "the better sort"; the "middling and inferior sorts" responded to a degree seldom realized and, in so doing, laid the groundwork of an urban revolt not merely in politics but in all spheres of life, which portended so much for the future.

It was in this period that mobility became a salient and constant feature of American life. Although enemy warships and privateers added new dangers to the tedious crossing of the tempestuous Atlantic, the immigration of Palatine Germans, Scotch-Irish, English, and Scots, despite temporary lulls, increased steadily, serving to swell the population of both city and farm. In fact the well-known growth of the rural hinterland of the colonies, in numbers and extent, provides a fundamental explanation of the urban expansion. In these years, moreover, many a countryman, yielding to the age-old attraction of the city, joined the small but highly significant migration from country to town and further contributed to American mobility. As both city and country prospered, the inevitable and familiar resentment between the two forms of society intensified and received open acknowledgment in newspaper and pamphlet.

Improved communications with the mother country, partly normal and partly in response to war needs, speeded the transfer of European ideas and culture to the colonies. This accelerating transit of civilization is evident in the whole range of urban activities and was primarily caused by the coming of the British Army and by the steady stream of immigrants arriving on these shores. The citizens kept abreast of the age in most fields of endeavor and, in their success in solving the urban problems of living together, occasionally moved ahead of it. In this particular old judgments must be revised.

Notwithstanding the prevalence of wartime conditions between 1743 and 1760, and in some measure because of them, the combined populations of the five urban centers increased by 19,509 in contrast with the population increase in rural America, which, as our first demographer pointed out in 1755, doubled every twenty-five years. This was not remarkable, but the more significant fact was that the urban accretion of thirty-six per cent in less than twenty years was markedly greater than the growth of contemporary commercial cities in England during this pre-industrial age.

POPULATION OF COLONIAL CITIES, 1743–1760		
	1743	1760
Philadelphia	13,000	23,750
New York	11,000	18,000
Boston	16,382 *	15,631 *
Charles Town	6,800	8,000
Newport	6,200	7,500
	53,382	72,881

* Actual census

Philadelphia and New York passed Boston in numbers, but in the Northern colonies there appeared the first signs of the rise of secondary towns to meet the local needs of an increasing, rural population. Such centers as Portsmouth in New Hampshire, Salem in the Bay Colony, Providence in Rhode Island, New Haven, New London, and Hartford in Connecticut, and Albany in New York province now became small cities and took on many of the attributes of urban life.

The new forces—mobility, growth, and improved communication—taken in conjunction with the maturing and mellowing effects of a century of urban life in the colonies, presaged rapid and profound changes.

That these were exciting times and often as bewildering as our own for the city folk of English America one senses immediately as one reads through their private correspondence and their public prints.

III

New or drastically altered conditions created by mounting populations and expanding physical areas strained the already existing agencies of city government to the limit, and in two cases forced important reforms upon the authorities. The basic difficulties derived from the need for new or additional municipal services and from the inability of local governments to finance them. The solutions arrived at reflect the experiences in the British Isles during the same period, where cities were also beginning to grow rapidly and where forms of borough control inherited from earlier centuries were also proving woefully inadequate. Colonial borrowings of English municipal institutions were, however, never slavish copies; rather they were adaptations to American conditions made in the light of over a hundred years of urban experience on this side of the Atlantic. And in most instances, furthermore, the colonial assemblies proved more liberal than Parliament in granting necessary powers, even though they were no more willing to confer them upon already existing municipal bodies.

The two New England communities continued to operate under the town-meeting plan with its executive and administrative agency, the familiar board of selectmen. The democratic features of this form of local government made it sensible of public wants, and the system proved its worth by being the most flexible and therefore the most congenial to the American situation and ideally suited to the times. As the town meetings of Boston and Newport, working efficiently, early supplied the best available public services, the citizens of those towns willingly paid their taxes, and no major changes in powers or procedures were required in these years.

Boston continued to be the best-regulated colonial city. Since every male rated for an estate of twenty pounds could vote, its town meeting was as popular a body as existed anywhere in this age: attendance varied from 250 to 450. Every March the meeting chose nearly two hundred officials—from hogreeve and "Informer" to selectman. Nowhere in the entire world did so large a number of the populace participate in the government of their city as elected officers. Serving without salary in the capacity of constable, assessor, or clerk of the market proved exceedingly onerous; consequently many of the gentry refused, preferring to pay the fines exacted for this relief, with the result that tradesmen of the middle rank performed most of the work. On occasions when one of the latter pleaded a reasonable excuse, he was released from his obligations without penalty. The gentry saw to it, however, that the key offices of moderator, selectmen, town clerk, and overseers of the poor went to merchants, gentlemen, or lawyers only.

Swearing in the town's officials and approving all bylaws and ordinances passed by Boston's Town Meeting were prerogatives of the Court of General Sessions of Suffolk County. These supervisory powers, and others vested in the county court, were at the root of exasperating and inefficient delays which vexed the Selectmen constantly. In 1744 the town debated a long time and then decided against submitting a petition to the General Court of Massachusetts urging the creation of a selectmen's "Court of Record" to try offenses against the bylaws. When several of the most distinguished lawyers of Boston undertook to revise and codify the town's ordinances in 1756, the Court of General Sessions held up ratification and publication until the town met its objections. Then in 1758 the justices cited the Selectmen to appear in court because they had refused to renew Mary Clapham's tavern license upon finding her guilty of "misrule." In a stinging reply, the Selectmen insisted that the court had power to confer licenses only upon those recommended to them. The justices backed down.

Boston's success in providing urban facilities surpassing those of the other four cities was achieved in the face of many obstacles: a stable population, declining commerce, heavy taxes, inflation, deflation, and war. The only sources of revenue besides taxes were small sums from fines and the rental of town properties, but these availed little in a time of soaring municipal costs. Finally in 1757 the General Court raised £3,500, which it loaned to Boston for three years at six per cent to discharge its debts—a loan that had to be extended for three more years in 1760. The town obtained additional moneys in 1759 by borrowing from private citizens at five per cent, to be deducted from taxes, in order to support the Alms House. At the close of this period the levy on the "Estates Real and Personal" of Bostonians amounted to 13s. 6d. in the pound, or 67 per cent! Small wonder that Thomas Hutchinson should brag that "the People hitherto have chearfully submitted to an amazing burthen of Taxes every Year and seem disposed still to exert themselves until the great design of the War is effected."

Increased urbanization of the thickly inhabited portions of the Newport community led five hundred freeholders of "the wood's part" to seek division of the town in 1741. Resistance by the Town Meeting, which feared loss of taxable lands and polls, prompted the petitioners to appeal to the Assembly, arguing that no common bonds existed between rural folk and merchants and tradesmen. They won their point and, despite loud objections, Middletown was set off from Newport in August 1743.

Confronted with far fewer obstacles than Boston, Newport's local government pursued an unobtrusive course. Enjoying an autonomy denied others, this town could tax as it saw fit. Its comparative isolation, homogeneous population, and smaller size were other factors. The Town Council, composed year after year of the same merchants, usually met at Jonathan Nichol's tavern and conducted local administration with precision and dispatch. It also probated wills. Only about twenty-five to thirty-five men were required for other offices, and not until 1749 did the town think it necessary to appoint three citizens "to Inspect into Nucences" and report them to the Grand Jury. Uncontrolled inflation and high prices presented a constant need to readjust fees and fines, and the constables experienced added difficulties in collecting town rates. The rift between town and country opened by this currency issue gradually widened and, by the time of the Revolution, ended Newport's leadership of the colony.

In the Middle colonies the medieval English chartered corporation, made up of a mayor, a recorder, aldermen, and common council, directed the affairs of the two large cities, New York and Philadelphia. The Montgomerie Charter of 1731 provided for an open corporation at Manhattan, one in which the "freemen" of each ward voted annually for an alderman and a councilman. The mayor, recorder, and aldermen also sat as the Mayor's Court, which, as in most English boroughs, exercised extensive judicial authority in civil cases. Because the number of freemen increased steadily, the city government had to be more responsive to public opinion in respect to services offered and its own judicial activities than contemporary English closed corporations. When the acute situation developing out of the extraordinary growth of its population in these war years is considered, New York was more than adequately governed.

The same could not be said for its neighbor on the Delaware. The Philadelphia Corporation closely resembled that of New York with the significant exception that it was of the closed type, and, because of this power of self-perpetuation, the Mayor and Common Council aroused the suspicions of the legislature and popular hostility. As early as 1712 when granting the city much-needed powers of taxation, the Pennsylvania Assembly provided that a board of six assessors, elected each year by inhabitants possessing fifty pounds lawful estate, should join with the Corporation in setting sums necessary for payment of the public debts, construction and repair of streets, wharves, markets, and like purposes. The frequent reluctance of the Corporation to work in harmony with the assessors so protracted the laying and collecting of taxes that certain citizens petitioned the Assembly to authorize still another board of commissioners to work with the assessors; city officials persuaded the Governor to veto the bill in 1740. Public dissatisfaction with their aristocratic and inefficient form of government continued to plague Philadelphians for many years.

After 1743 the financial predicament grew worse. The plight of the Corporation seemed beyond all hope when it could not even collect fines and rents due. Twice it desperately sought to escape the dilemma by purchasing large blocks of lottery tickets; the first time paid off. More and more the members sensed their collective inadequacy. It became very difficult to induce anyone to serve as mayor, even on the two occasions when a salary was offered; nominees would rather pay fines than serve. Alderman Morris actually hid out in Bucks County in 1747 to avoid receiving notice of his election. Moreover the mayor was, by custom, required to give his associates a handsome banquet each year, and not until James Hamilton gave £150 to the treasury in lieu of the entertainment was this tradition inherited from Merrie England broken. Selection of Philadelphia's leading citizen as a councilman in 1748 and his elevation to alderman in 1751 marked the advent of a craftsman to the board but produced no change in policies; the records reveal that Benjamin Franklin was not constant in attendance at meetings. As the suburban areas north and south of the city built up, friction arose about conflicting jurisdictions over such matters as the care of the poor and the extension or building of streets.

Philadelphia was experiencing the same growing pains as the towns in the mother country. That the familiar English system of administering newly developed services by boards elected by the taxpayers was worked out earlier on the Delaware than in the leading cities of the British Isles can be explained by the absence of an entrenched corporation burdened by tradition, by the willingness of the Pennsylvania Assembly to correct abuses in its capital, but most of all by the mobilizing of public opinion as war conditions and unprecedented expansion aggravated old and generated new urban problems. There is genuine irony in the fact that in the one instance when the Mayor and Common Council, seeking to ensure greater public safety by strengthening the night watch and lighting the streets, applied pressure on the Assembly, the forthcoming authority had to be shared with an elected board of wardens. Through the agency of these boards, which were elected on a much narrower franchise than the New Yorkers exercised, the people of Penn's "green countrie town" were able to ease somewhat its transformation into the metropolis of colonial America.

At Charles Town even more anomalous governmental arrangements existed. Early in the century the city became the center from which the richest planters ruled the province—a city state in which the state ruled the city. As the capital grew into a large community and faced the usual urban situations, its inhabitants deplored the absence of an independent and rationalized local administration. Prior to 1712 the Assembly governed the town directly by designating commissioners drawn from the Commons House to supervise the execution of each act pertaining to Charles Town. Provisions for filling vacancies in a commission were often mentioned in the acts, but when there were none, either the Governor made appointments, or the remaining commissioners chose members of their own house. This practice prevailed until the War for Independence and gave the Assembly direct administrative control of local affairs. Busy assemblymen could not, however, be expected to make Charles Town's welfare their principal concern, especially if they did not happen to be personally interested residents of the town.

Living in St. Philip's Parish, the people of Charles Town, in accordance with the policy of the established Church of England, came under the supervision of a vestry. Every year at Easter, balloting took place for two church wardens and seven vestrymen, beside some twenty or thirty parish officers to administer fire, workhouse, market, weights and measures, highway, and other regulations. Lest this annual election seem democratic, as has been maintained, it should be noted that between 1745 and 1759 only those resident Anglicans who possessed a town house and land valued at sixty pounds proclamation money exercised the parish franchise. Newspaper accounts of the elections frequently announced the presence of "inhabitants and freeholders of the parish . . . and of such parishioners as thought proper to attend," but only qualified Charlestonians could actually participate in the written vote. There was very little democracy in this dispensation. Such a limited electorate did, however, place leading and public-spirited gentlemen in the more important offices: in 1744 prominent merchants like John Crokatt and John Scott were chosen wood-measurers, and twelve years later Henry Bedon, Peter Leger, and Gabriel Guignard were designated packers.

Charles Town was never accorded strictly municipal courts, for all of the judicial agencies of the province above the justices of the peace were located in the capital. When, in 1756, the Governor commissioned eighty-five justices for Berkeley County, the list included nearly every important merchant and planter living in the city. These gentlemen licensed taverns, advertised strays, and dealt with the usual civil and criminal small causes. All serious cases went before the Court of General Sessions, which, until 1772, served all of South Carolina. Periodical presentments of abuses and grievances covering the entire colony were made to the court by a Grand Jury, but since the jurors were drawn from the vicinity, it devoted a major share of its attention to local matters. Sooner or later, under a series of able and influential foremen such as Gabriel Manigault and Thomas Smith, the Grand Jury singled out just about everything that was wrong with the community, whether with the behavior of its people, with its institutions, or with the lack of them, even going so far in 1745 as to criticize the court itself for ignoring former presentments. If ever pressure for reform and better integration of the miscellany of authorities that passed for local government in Charles Town should be forthcoming, it would probably emanate from the public spirit of this sole agency for popular protest.

As local officials tried to contend with the forces of change and expansion in the five cities, two conditions developed which had appeared intermittently in the past but which would henceforth permanently characterize the American urban scene. These were the sharp cleavage between town and country interests, and the prevalence of political evils within the cities.

The colonial assemblies provided the stages on which the urban-rural conflict was dramatized. Even though all sectional differences quickened and deepened, taxation seemed to be the overt issue. Superior numbers in the assemblies enabled rural interests to force the greater incidence upon the cities. Boston's pleas for tax relief met with no success. The New York Assembly raised the city's portion of the provincial tax to nearly fifty per cent in 1744 because the rural members claimed that the city would be the beneficiary of contemplated defense expenditures. The next year the quota was permanently fixed at one third of the total, whereas previously it had never exceeded one quarter; and only stout resistance by the Council saved Manhattan from having to pay forty-four per cent of the entire colony's levy in 1746. In reply to a letter in the *New York Post Boy* pointing to the injustice of making a merchant pay forty to fifty pounds in property taxes yearly at the same time that he was expending four hundred to five hundred pounds in duties on goods imported, Robert R. Livingston defended untaxed real property in "Reasons against a Land Tax," which argued the nexus between property and class interests as cogently as James Madison later did in the classic *Federalist* No. 10.

The rural debtors of Rhode Island employed the more subtle device of taxing Newport creditors by issue after issue of paper money. Desperate mercantile protests accurately predicting the pernicious effects on the trade of the whole colony failed to stop the presses. This impasse was rendered more distasteful to Newport by the notorious Ward-Hopkins struggle for the governor's office, which, beginning in 1757, was only ended by the urgency for united action against the mother country in 1770. At the core of this contest lay the fact that Stephen Hopkins represented a rising Providence, the town that would soon successfully challenge the leadership of Henry Ward's Newport.

The inability of the urban centers to make their numbers and wealth count in provincial councils widened the breach between town and country. New York City had only four representatives out of a total of twenty-seven; yet it contained one fifth of the entire population of the colony. By joining forces with the city of Albany, it strengthened the urban cause, but the alliance could not defeat unfriendly legislation. Over at Philadelphia in 1752 the citizens importuned for additional representatives, alleging that the growth of the community made it "both equitable and necessary." Not only did the Assembly ignore their pleas, but in 1759 the provincial collector laid a tax on the Corporation that exceeded its annual income. The end of the period came with Philadelphia still having but two members in the Assembly, though by taxables it would have been entitled to four, and by taxes paid, to seven and a half members. Here, indeed, was a real source of conflict, one that would go on echoing down through American history to our own day.

Conversely, because Charles Town was the focal point of the Low Country gentry, who neglected with fine impartiality the mass of its citizens and the host of new settlers to the westward, it was the upcountry, the Cheraws, that in 1752 produced the first protest, a demand for court facilities beyond the limits of the city. Thus arose an issue that was not to be resolved before it merged with the larger controversy over separation from the mother country in 1775.

Within each city the inhabitants divided over social and economic questions, into the many and the few. They did not have the elaborate machinery and carefully framed programs of a later day; rather did they split into unorganized "factions" when contention spread. Nevertheless these party beginnings are of great importance, and contemporaries recognized them for what they were. "The parties in Massachusetts-Bay at present," wrote Dr. William Douglass in 1749, "are not the Loyal and Jacobite, the Governor and the Country, Whig and Tory, or any religious sectary denominations, but the Debtors and Creditors." The truth of this assertion later found an echo in John Adams's statement that "this country, like all others, has been a theatre of parties and feuds for near two hundred years."

The upper class of every city very largely controlled the municipal government and ran it in a way to preserve the interests of the gentry, even through the town meetings of Boston and Newport. But the demagogue made his appearance with popular and representative institutions and stood ready to pit numbers against wealth. As early as 1744, Philadelphia newspapers began to carry political advertisements like those of Mordecai Lloyd soliciting the office of sheriff, and of his rival, Nicholas Scull, who shrewdly printed appeals in German as well as in English. Three years later in the public prints at Manhattan all four candidates for the Assembly flatteringly addressed the freeholders as "Gentlemen" when they begged for their "Votes and Interest." Questionable political activities by aldermen in wards other than their own in connection with a ferry franchise called forth condemnation in the New York press: the Recorder was labeled "a most roaring genius." William Livingston, "The

Independent Reflector," frequently considered the "Practice of making Interest for Elections, and intoxicating the People to influence their Voices, with equal Grief and Indignation." A treat usually meant a bribe, especially with the recently arrived and thirsty members of the middle and lower classes. Religious interests played a large part in Newport's town meeting: in 1758 Ezra Stiles believed that fully a third of the voters were "silenced by Connexions."

New economic and social pressures, products of growth, taxed all municipal facilities and authorities between 1743 and 1760. Boston and Newport met the shock more satisfactorily than the other cities because of the flexibility of the town-meeting system and because of their freedom from provincial controls; whereas the corporations of New York and Philadelphia were too rigid to cope with the great and complex problems confronting them. Charles Town, hampered by administrative chaos, was unable to supply itself with much-wanted services. Soon, too, English cities encountered the same problems, though they were fortunately remote from the conflicts with Spain and France which so agitated and complicated colonial urban existence. During these years the important question was whether the constituted authorities of the five American communities could adjust to the painful process of becoming large cities. It was not merely a local problem, however, but one that involved the whole Atlantic civilization.

IV

The most obvious sign of urban expansion in this period was the impressive amount of construction going on in every city. New York, Boston, and Newport—each over a century old—had acquired something of the miscellany of structures, old and new, which so delighted Dr. Johnson with contemporary London. Even at Charles Town and Philadelphia newness began to give way to the mellowness of age. Over and beyond the peculiarity of terrain and location, national tastes in architecture and varying ideas of town planning imparted to each community an individuality that became more evident as the years went by. Save at Newport, size brought about a development of specialized areas: warehouses and lofts along the waterfronts; shopping and market centers; and retreats in newly opened suburbs for those who could afford them. Unquestionably the five cities were more than mere clusters of buildings.

As the Quaker City's population moved past Boston's, additional buildings were needed to shelter it. The 1,500 dwellings of 1743 became 2,300 a decade later, and 2,969 in 1760. Although it was imperative to replace many that Dr. Hamilton described as "mean and low and much decayed," some of the jerry-built, crude, and unsightly wooden structures from the first days of settlement still stood. Age could be found nestling conspicuously close to modernity as evidenced by the advertisement of "a Frame and Log House, 20 Foot by 23" on Wicaco Lane near George Mifflin's beautiful mansion.

Carpenters and masons produced houses of all sizes and descriptions through these years, for in spite of wars the fashionable vice of all classes was building. In the *American Magazine* the Reverend William Smith censured his fellow citizens: "Building is one gulph of expence scarce fathomable. Additions, alterations, decorations are endless. 'Tis one eternal scene of pulling down and putting up." Peter Kalm had the impression in 1748 that most of "the Houses make a good appearance." Some of them were made of wood, like the one offered for sale by Thomas James on Lombard Street, but by 1754 Israel Acrelius had reported that they were of brick and were two or three stories high. Tile and slate were replacing cypress shingles for roofing; and their additional weight forced the strengthening of party walls that formerly had been extremely thin.

Real-estate values mounted in the heart of the town, where all lots had narrow fronts and considerable depth. Some artisans erected relatively large buildings, using the extra space for their trades and taking in lodgers to earn a little more income. Most houses stood right on the street, with only enough room in front for a little porch before the door and a cellar entrance. In the rear, one often discovered separate kitchens, usually of brick and occasionally two stories high. Typical of the medium-sized establishments was Thomas Barton's, situated at the upper end of Front Street on a lot "20 Feet in Front, and 100 in Depth, 3 Stories high, with 3 Rooms on the first Floor and Fireplaces in each; the Front Room painted a fine Blue, the middle-Room a Slate Colour, and the rest a Chocolate Colour. This House," said the advertisement, "is likewise furnished with a large Stone Kitchen, and a spacious Cellar, good Water and a free open Air; it commands a fine Prospect, and is very fit for a private Gentleman, Shop-Keeper, or Tradesman."

The addition of nearly fifteen hundred domiciles did not keep pace with the demands of Philadelphians. Genuine urban crowding existed in the oldest parts of the city, where Middle and Mulberry wards contained 238 and 488 houses respectively, the latter being the section where most of the artisans and newly arrived Palatines lived. In the congested areas, warehouses, merchants' countinghouses, or the dwellings of artisans, who conducted trades in them, lined the streets, and a few large residences might be seen. This cramming in of buildings on narrow lots necessitated the use of party walls, and on some streets block after block was solid, reminding Thomas Pownall of Cheapside, because nearly every house had a pent roof above the base story and a "little flip of a window to

PLATE 1 · *George Whitefield preaching, 1742. by John Wollaston*

Engraving after Charles Willson Peale, *Columbian Magazine*, 1778

PLATE 2 · *The State House, Philadelphia, ca. 1775. Designed by Edmund Woolley*

The two sheds were for visiting Indian delegations. In the foreyard are two pumps and rows of posts to protect pedestrians from Chestnut Street traffic.

light a closet by the side of the chimnies." What was probably the first large row of houses in any American city was "the Fourteen Chimnies" put up one hundred feet back from the west side of Fifth Street above Sassafras (Race) in 1759. Philadelphia's expansion did not follow the founder's plan, for instead of moving westward beyond Tenth Street toward the Schuylkill, people went north and south for over a mile along the Delaware in search of greater convenience for business purposes. It was also cooler near the river.

Although most of the new houses, irrespective of size or cost, were erected by those who intended to occupy them, many merchants with spare funds ventured into urban properties, and, as a rule, readily secured tenants. Samuel Powel, known as the "rich carpenter," became the foremost colonial operating builder; at his death in 1756 he left his son and namesake over ninety houses profitably rented. In 1760 Andrew Burnaby learned that "Houses are so dear, that they will let for £100, currency, per annum" and well-situated lots not over thirty by one hundred feet brought one thousand pounds sterling. Indubitably rents were high, but of course such a place as "the little Brick Tenement in Mulberry Street" was rented by Dr. Samuel Preston Moore to Ann Newell for four pounds a year, and others let for as low as eight pounds; in general, however, Burnaby's figure is right. Despite good earnings from rentals, some property-owners preferred to lease their lands, allowing others to put up the buildings and taking their profits on relatively high ground rents, in the meantime trusting that the lots would appreciate in value. Either way it is manifest that Philadelphia real estate represented a large amount of saved capital, and that a large proportion of the income of well-to-do citizens came from this source.

For the first time in our history, building construction was accompanied by improvements that ensured more comfortable living. Some measure of protection from the intolerable heat of a Philadelphia summer was had by hanging "awnings of painted cloth or duck" over shop windows and doors, and Dr. Alexander Hamilton remarked on the large number of balconies on the houses, "where sometimes the men sit in a cool habit and smoke." Almost every dwelling had a bench on either side of its front door, where the occupants lolled on sultry summer nights. But these were mere palliatives. "We have had excessive hot weather now near two weeks," Benjamin Franklin wrote to Susanna Wright in 1753 from his new house at Second and Sassafras streets. "This Town is a mere Oven. . . . I languish for the Country, for Air and Shade and Leisure, but Fate has doom'd me to be stifled and roasted and teased to death in a City."

Experiments in the heating of houses during the cold winters turned out more efficaciously. Well-plastered brick and stone structures were weather-tight, but the large, old-fashioned fireplaces and chimneys permitted most of the heat to go up the flues. In due course the masons learned that smaller chimneys and shallow fireplaces with curved breast-plates would throw the heat out into the rooms. Early in the eighteenth century stoves of one sort or another had been made in France, Germany, and Holland, and several types had been brought to Philadelphia. They all consumed too much costly wood and, furthermore, failed to warm the entire room. About 1740 Benjamin Franklin improved upon them, and his friend Robert Grace, the ironmaster, cast the plates for the new stoves. They commanded immediate approval, and, to aid Grace in marketing them, the printer wrote and published in 1744 *An Account of the New-Invented Pennsylvanian Fire-Places,* which listed fourteen advantages over other heaters and supplied two excellent diagrams by Lewis Evans, as well as directions to the masons for connecting one with a chimney. Grace's products also had the virtue of being much cheaper than Dutch tile stoves, and Philadelphians bought them eagerly. New Yorkers soon learned about them and they too installed them in their houses. But all comforts seem relative to a spoiled modern: "How warm our Stove Rooms seem in Winter," the inventor told a Bostonian, whose ink still froze on his desk, "and yet the highest they ever rais'd my Thermometer was to 56."

From the East River, New York appeared to be wholly a seaport, with a skyline formed by 250 warehouses, distilleries, and sugarhouses, broken here and there by the spire of some church or the cupola of a public building; but within the town, residences predominated. Although New York did not receive as many immigrants as Philadelphia, the requirements of the British armed forces created a great demand for houses, which increased from 1,140 in 1743 to about 2,600 by 1760.

Some observers thought it "the pleasantest and best built City in all British America." Old residences in the Dutch style, of brick and wood, and from one to three stories high, stood with their stepped gable ends toward the street. Toward the end of the period one visitor noticed that the "New Houses have been built in a more modern taste and many of the Gabel-ends of the old houses, just as is done in Holland, have been new fronted in the Italian stile"; another stranger, as late as 1759, commenting on the outsides of the houses, thought them "very fine," the builders "being very fond of scalloping and painting."

Everyone agreed that New York was a more compact city than Philadelphia, which covered twice as much ground. High urban rents produced lucrative returns for such men as Stephen and Nicholas Bayard, who owned so many tenements that they could advertise ten of them at once in 1746. Thomas Dongan leased thirty city lots for twenty years in 1759 to Thomas White for a building speculation, which turned out very well. The Corporation also engrossed large tracts of land which it was able to lease at good prices. Pownall thought the average annual rent ran around twenty-five pounds, but a small house like that on Golden Hill occupied by Anthony De Milt, mason, let for fifteen.

Early in the period Newport also added many new buildings, spreading along the harbor's edge and gradually moving up the hill, where picturesque windmills silhouetted against the sky. James Birket, in 1750, found the newly developed part of the town called "the Point" to be "laid out in Squares and pretty well built." In fact, travelers generally commended the beauty of the little community. The Colony House and Godfrey Malbone's residence were the only brick structures; the rest were of frame construction, "well built." Because of the reverses of the Old French War and also because the population was fairly well sheltered, not one house a year was erected between 1750 and 1760. In the last year, however, the physical assets of Newport consisted of 888 dwellings, 6 windmills, 439 warehouses and other buildings.

Newporters did not erect private houses on the scale of those in the larger cities. Few rose above three stories, and nearly all had ample yards and gardens surrounding them. The little city had not yet become congested, though double houses appeared in more crowded parts, like one on Easton's Point that James Rogers sold in 1759. The Rhode Islanders lived comfortably in their little dwellings, which, as Birket described them, were "as well furnished as in Most places you will meet with, many of the rooms being hung with printed Canvas and paper etc., which looks very neat. Others are well wainscoted and painted as in other places." By the late fifties, too, merchants like Peter Bours could supply any townsman with a "Handsome Philadelphia Fire-Stove."

The two other American cities experienced public disasters which destroyed much of their housing and greatly altered their appearance. The Boston of 1743 showed the effects of its eight "great fires." Many medieval structures, like Paul Revere's house, still survived in the North End; around the Town Dock stood numerous brick or plaster two-story buildings with high-peaked slate roofs erected following the fire of 1679; three-story brick houses with garrets, flat roofs, and balustrades rose from the ruins of 1711 along Cornhill and around the State House. Conglomerate as the city was upon close examination, seen from the harbor it was truly impressive, with buildings stretched out all the way from Charlestown Ferry to Roxbury Neck.

In the forties a Bay Town census showed 1,719 dwellings and 166 warehouses. Experiencing steady employment, the building trades had constructed many new buildings and replaced old ones by 1760. In the Massachusetts community, unlike Philadelphia and New York, engrossing of real estate proved impossible; properties changed hands more frequently. Even so, there were not enough houses to go around, and many a family had to share its dwelling with one or more others, especially in the older sections filled with poorer people. The better residences, such as one George Tilley described, customarily had "eight rooms, seven of them fire-rooms, with a Number of convenient Closets and a good Cellar; four of the said Rooms is cornish'd, and the House is handsomely painted throughout; one of the Rooms is painted Green, another Blue, one Cedar and one [in imitation of] Marble; the other four a Lead colour; the Garrets are . . . handsomely plaistered; the House has twenty Sash-Windows to it and is pleasantly situated on Pleasant Street, near the Hay-Market."

When it came to household comforts, Bostonians enjoyed all that were available. In August 1743 Richard Clarke announced that those who desired "Hearths . . . against the next Winter Season" might have them if they ordered promptly, and soon there were others supplying stoves of Franklin's design. Improvements in lighting houses also were introduced early at Boston. In 1744 "Train or Lamp-Oyl" was sold by the barrel, and before long President Holyoke burned whale oil in his study lamp over at Cambridge. In a primitive ballyhoo advertisement James Clemens claimed, not without some truth, that spermaceti candles exceeded "all others for Beauty, Sweetness of Scent when extinguished; Duration . . . Dimensions of Flame, nearly four Times more, emitting a soft easy expanding Light, bringing the Object close to the Sight, rather than causing the Eye to trace after them as all Tallow Candles do."

Ill fortune befell the Bay Town again on March 20, 1760, when the worst fire of the entire colonial period swept over it, leaving the center of the city a shambles. Nearly four hundred houses, warehouses, and smaller buildings were consumed, and there was much bitter truth in the assertion of the *Boston Post Boy* that, coming as it did "after the exhaustion of war," the fire determined that "this once flourishing Metropolis must long remain under its present Desolation." The leading citizens were not so depressed as to be indifferent to the rebuilding that started immediately, for within ten days the provincial government joined with the Selectmen in prohibiting the erection of any new structures in the burned area that failed to meet their specifications for dimensions and materials. The rise of the Boston phœnix was to be carefully supervised.

Calamity attended Charles Town at both the opening and the closing of the period. In 1740 the Southern community had been gutted by a fire that destroyed nearly all of its seventeenth-century buildings. Manfully the inhabitants went about reconstructing, and within a decade they had made real progress, though all too often wise regulations requiring new buildings to be of stone or brick, and forbidding any on the wharves, were relaxed or ignored. No wooden shingles could be used after December 20, 1745. Within ten years Governor James Glen could inform the Board of Trade that along the Bay alone one hundred lots contained eighty-four new structures, including the establishments of fifty merchants, numerous artisans, four widows, and a dancing master, besides six taverns and a dram shop. Many residences went up throughout the town, most of them of brick: some for modest tradesmen who conducted their crafts at home, others grand town houses for prominent citizens like Captain Henry Frankland and Chief Justice Benjamin Whitaker. Double houses became more common, and the scarcity of accommodations bred high rents that forced families of the inferior sort to live together.

On September 15, 1752 the most destructive hurricane ever known in the South struck the Carolina capital about nine o'clock in the morning, and in two hours "reduced this Town to a very melancholy situation." All the vessels in the harbor blew ashore, all wharves and warehouses on them washed away, and many buildings lost their roofs. "Nothing was now to be seen but ruins of houses, canows, wrecks of pettiauguas and boats, masts, yards, incredible quantities of all sorts of timber, barrels, staves, shingles, household and other goods, floating and driving, with great violence thro' the streets, and round about the Town." Many persons drowned; others died under falling walls and beams. Broughton's Battery was beaten to pieces, and on the land side of Charles Town the new curtain line, built of stone four or five feet thick, was badly damaged. Worst of all, the hurricane demolished five hundred houses; out of two hundred on White Point, scarcely one remained standing. Two weeks later another great wind blew up, but it caused little damage other than frightening the populace and impeding their progress in clearing up the debris of the first storm. Because of its misfortunes, Charles Town alone of the five cities in 1760 gave the impression of complete newness. The *American Gazetteer* reported that the houses were "large, some of brick, but more of timber and generally sashed, and let at excessive rates."

These were the years when Englishmen began to adorn their cities with costly public buildings in the classical mode introduced to London in the previous century and carried on in the eighteenth by the Earl of Burlington and his protégés. Bath is only the most celebrated of the provincial centers, because the thousands who went there to take the waters talked and wrote about the architecture of the elder John Wood. More important for the age was the completion in 1743 at still-medieval Bristol, the second city of England, of Wood's noble Exchange, whose Palladian purity and splendor of detail not only stimulated further building in that city but awakened in others a desire for civic magnificence. Within a decade after 1750, for example, the merchants in the great slave-trading seaport of Liverpool had raised several new churches, an exchange, and the new Drury Lane Theatre in Williamson Square. Although the five American colonial capitals had not yet amassed enough wealth to emulate the elaborate and expensive structures of London, they did acquire contemporaneously many public buildings rivaling those of other British cities, and the lanthorns and cupolas taken with the spires of many places of worship gave to each of the towns of the New World an individual skyline.

The public buildings of Newport excelled in architectural distinction. As the period opened, Richard Munday's Colony House, with its mile-long vista from the upper end of the Parade, was brought to completion. But it was the arrival of Peter Harrison at this time that signalized the coming of age of colonial urban architecture. In 1749 he designed and erected the lighthouse at Beaver Tail on Conanicut Island in the harbor. With a charming little Doric temple, which he built for the Redwood Library the next year, the Palladianism of the Earl of Burlington came to America, and thereafter the academic manner held sway in Newport as Peter Harrison anticipated the classicism of Thomas Jefferson; even his Fort George of 1754 followed "classical" lines. Between March 1759 and July 1760 this "ingenious English gentleman" made three more designs for his adopted town: in 1759 the Anglican accommodated the Congregation of Sephardic Jews with a plan for a synagogue which many authorities today consider to have the most exquisite interior of any house of worship in this country; at the behest of the Proprietors of the Long Wharf he produced a "very elegant" design for the now famous Brick Market House; and the third commission came from the Freemasons for "a very pretty building" for their hall, which was "to serve also occasionally for an Assembly-room." The first two were not finished in the period, and the last never rose above its foundations because funds ran out.

St. Philip's Church at Charles Town, which survived the great fire of 1740, was the city's only public building until the opening of the new brick barracks in 1746. When the parish of St. Philip's was divided, a new church was needed, and a plausible case can be made from circumstantial evidence for Peter Harrison as the architect of the city's most celebrated edifice. Begun in 1752, St. Michael's was not opened for services until 1761. Across the street from the new church, another "State House" and a new market house began to rise in 1753, helping to make the intersection there at Broad and Meeting streets one of the most impressive in the colonies. As described by Dr. James Milligen, the State House, which has long since disappeared, was "a large commodious Brick Building. The South Front is decorated with four 2/3 Columns of the Composite Order, whose Capitals are highly finished, supporting a large angular Pediment and Cornice; it consists of two Stories besides the [mansard] Roof; on the lower are the Court-Room, the Secretary's Office, and Apartments for the House-Keeper; one is for the Governor and Council, the other for the Representatives of the People, with Lobbies and Rooms for their Clerks; the Room, called the Council-Chamber, appears rather crouded and disgusting, than ornamental and pleasing, by the great Profusion of carved Work in it; in the upper Part of the House or Roof is a large Room for the Provincial Armory."

The citizens of Boston held their first meeting in the great hall that the painter John Smibert designed for Peter Faneuil's gift to the town late in 1742. Six years later an acid Anglican critic, after approving of the city's sightly brick mansions, burst out: "but to the Honour and Glory of the Lord; their Churches are of Clap board and Shingle." Actually many of them were of brick, and the next year, 1749, saw the beginning of the only cut-stone church in English America. The façade of King's Chapel was designed by Peter Harrison to be as impressive as any in Georgian London, but the parishioners could not afford to put up the majestic spire intended to crown his efforts. Its plain sides and small lower windows gave it a military look which provoked that punning divine Mather Byles to say "he had often heard of the Canons of the Church, but never had seen the Port-holes before." The edifice was not completed until 1754, and at about that same time the brothers Deblois dedicated a temple to the Muses, best known as "Concert Hall." This was "a very neat . . . Building," whose second floor was "elegantly finished in the Corinthian style and handsomely ornamented" for use as a music or dancing room and for polite entertainments like the famous assembly rooms of English cities.

In the colonial metropolis on the Delaware, construction of the State House from the plans of Edmund Woolley had begun in 1736, though he did not finish the tower until 1750. It was the central unit of a most imposing group of civic buildings; in fact Ezra Stiles thought it the most magnificent he had ever seen. Followers of the Reverend George Whitefield built the first tabernacle for an evangelist in this country at Fourth near Arch Street in 1740. The great size of the New Building, as it was always called, made it a show place and the usual scene of public gatherings for the next nine years. The trustees of the projected Academy of Philadelphia purchased the New Building in 1750 for £775 and altered its interior to suit the needs of collegiate living. Erection of a well-proportioned two-story brick market house on Second Street at Pine in 1745 and of "a good assembly-room" by the Freemasons at about the same time provided the city with additional public buildings. Ten years later a carpenter-builder, Quaker Samuel Rhoads, prepared plans for the new Pennsylvania Hospital. The design called for east and west lateral wings joined by a larger "center house" with a dome, each unit to be architecturally and functionally complete in itself. At the beginning, only the T-shaped east building was put up, and the patients were moved in on December 17, 1756. Rhoads's Pennsylvania Hospital was the most ambitious piece of construction in the colonies, and, completed, it would have rivaled similar English projects in both monumentality and magnificence. It testified to the architectural maturity and soaring ambition of colonial cities.

Domestic housing absorbed New York's energies until 1752, and then, like the other cities, she too began to put up buildings for civic purposes. When the old, decayed, wooden building where the merchants met daily was to be replaced, a new brick structure with a gambrel roof and cupola was built overlooking the dock at the foot of Broad Street. Consisting of a large meeting room over an arcade, it incorporated the universal features of English mercantile exchanges. The same year St. George's Chapel with its 175-foot steeple was completed after a "modern" plan. Near "the new and handsome building called the Workhouse" in the Fields on Broadway beyond the "Pallisadoes" appeared a three-story brick jail, which Andrew Burnaby pronounced as fine a prison as he had ever seen. These, and new barracks large enough for a regiment, were suitable public buildings, but the pride of Manhattan was King's College. Its designer was Robert Crommelin, a merchant who had also planned St. George's Chapel and who must henceforth be ranked with Peter Harrison and Samuel Rhoads among the foremost architects of urban America. Work on it commenced in 1756 and by May 1760 had gone far enough to allow the faculty and students to occupy their quarters and to move an Englishman to exclaim that when finished it would be "the most beautifully situated of any college . . . in the world." Nor was this mere hyperbole, for the location of King's on the Church Farm in the West Ward on the banks of the mighty Hudson was undeniably superb.

The inexorable demands of war during these years markedly affected urban profiles as each city acquired some kind of fortification and military works. Although Charles Town had long been a walled city, as soon as war with Spain broke out in 1739, provincial authorities began construction of a new "Curtain-Line" before the Bay and other defenses along the Ashley River. Next they condemned all sheds and warehouses on the wharves east of the curtain line that might encumber the town's defenders. By 1743 two new forts or bastions were finished, and there were two more abuilding across the harbor. Such works proved exceedingly costly, and skilled labor was nearly as scarce as trained engineers. Several years later, Peter Henry Bruce, a military engineer of the Vauban school, arrived and prepared a report on the state of fortifications for the Governor and Council. Among other things, he recommended cutting a canal behind the city from the Cooper to the Ashley, because an island would be easier to defend. The high cost of labor, shortage of lime and stone, and other difficulties recommended substitutions for the plan for a canal; so in place of it, "great numbers of Hands" worked diligently digging a moat, erecting brick barracks, a bombproof, new magazine, an armory, another bastion, and several more works. With the Peace of Aix-la-Chapelle, the Carolinians thankfully dropped all defense efforts and indifferently permitted the valuable fortifications to fall into disrepair. When hostilities began anew, restoration and new construction were resumed "with forwardness" under the Swiss engineer and alchemist Gerard de Brahm, who strengthened existing bastions and added three more for 130 pieces of artillery by 1756. But it was the same old story. Seven batteries protected Charles Town from attack by sea, but the defenses on the land side remained unfinished until the War for Independence brought new threats to the Southern city.

Less elaborate works sufficed for the Northern cities. To protect the vulnerable harbor of Newport, the Assembly set about restoring crumbling Fort George on Goat Island opposite the Long Wharf and requested new cannon from England. "The rocks in their harbours are the best security," was Dr. Hamilton's sarcastic verdict, "for the fort . . . is the futiest thing of that nature ever I saw." However, Peter Harrison prepared new plans and, with his brother Joseph, superintended the reconditioning of the fort in 1745. As in the case of Charles Town, peace spelled neglect, and when war broke out again in 1754, the works on Goat Island were in a sad state. To the ten thousand pounds appropriated by the Assembly, Newport itself added five thousand more, that Peter Harrison might have ample funds to redesign and rebuild the fort. The new Fort George, with ravelins, redoubts, revetments, and the whole panoply of the engineer's art worked out from John Muller's well-known manual, was perhaps as skillfully planned as any on the western side of the Atlantic when it was begun in 1755. Work proceeded with incredible slowness, but folded up with lightning speed after the fall of Quebec in 1759.

Castle William in Boston Harbor was by far the strongest defense provided for any of the three other cities. Commodore Charles Knowles greatly reinforced it by adding a heavy battery during King George's War, and the Bostonians further protected themselves by erecting the North Battery near Thornton's shipyard and the South Battery at the foot of Fort Hill. They also fortified Boston Neck, where they set up gates to block the only road leading into the town. Since Fort George at New York could not alone defend that city, the Assembly provided additional batteries at Red Hook and some works on the quays along the East River. The older part of the city was shut off from its suburbs by a palisade, which was defended by six blockhouses covering the four gates, and which ran from near the East River at St. James Street across the island to the North River a little above Warren Street. At Philadelphia the boldness of the French raiders who sailed into Delaware Bay to seize merchant ships and to plunder ashore finally broke down Quaker opposition to a defense effort late in 1746. Under the leadership of Benjamin Franklin, the middle class forced both the Quaker and the proprietary gentry in 1747 to permit a lottery for raising three thousand pounds to construct a battery on Attwood's Wharf and the Great Association Battery just south of the city where Wicaco Lane reached the river. Thus did all five towns wear a martial air throughout most of this period.

One ordinarily thinks of the suburban movement of the present century as being of recent origin, and it will come as a surprise to many that the flight from the city began in the first half of the eighteenth century—and for the same reasons as today. The differences were in degree only. Just as Londoners moved westward from the City in search of quiet, better air, comfort, lower rents, and more room for display, so did Philadelphians cross the northern and southern bounds of the metropolis in a perennial search for the "green" the founder had hoped to preserve within, for it was a "countrie towne" no longer. Crowding of buildings in the center of town, lack of space for gardens, humid summer dog days, dust, filth, and disagreeable odors from tanneries and other establishments, all encouraged the suburban drift. That greatest of townsmen, Benjamin Franklin, even moved from High Street to Second and Sassafras, grumbling that "the din of the Market increases upon me; and that, with frequent interruptions, has, I find, made me say some things twice over."

For a time the choice residential section had been Society Hill, which lay along the river south of Spruce Street. "The buildings increase very fast towards the south end of the town," Franklin told a distant friend in 1750, "and many of the principal merchants now live there." Buildings spread below South Street into the district known as Southwark, a suburb that owed its rapid development to the Shippen brothers and Joseph Wharton, owners of large properties that they had cut up into lots and offered to sell or lease on "ground rents forever." It was through their influence also that the Corporation provided the new Second Street Market in 1745 to supply the neighborhood and, perhaps also, to help move their real estate. The Northern Liberties likewise built up rapidly. Robert Meade disposed of forty acres in 1749, and several other people broke up farms and sold them off in building lots to artisans who settled along North Second Street. Soon small houses appeared in the neighborhood of Spring Garden, and the tiny villages of Kensington and Ball Town developed as shipbuilding centers with ways, anchor forges, ropewalks, and the homes of those who worked on the vessels. The residents of the northern parts and the Northern Liberties, who had petitioned the Assembly as early as 1746 to remove the powder house from the area because its presence prevented the disposal of their property and the building of a market, got their wish with the Callowhill Market. Real-estate promotion drew both the well-to-do and the middle class toward the periphery of the city at the same time that congested urban conditions urged them outward.

The suburban movement at Boston was largely confined to members of the mercantile aristocracy who sought the kind of life that attached to every country gentleman in England or America. Many Bostonians established seats at Dorchester, Roxbury, Milton, Medford, and other nearby towns easily reached by carriage or boat. A few miles up the Charles River lay Cambridge, which developed into a unique suburb in the forties when the Vassalls, Apthorps, Lees, Inmans, and Lechmeres came out from Boston to join the Phipses and Brattles in forming a wealthy and exclusive pro-Anglican group in the environs of Harvard College. By 1760 they were boldly building, from Peter Harrison's plans, lovely little Christ Church within sight of the college yard. Overland communication with Boston through Roxbury or by the Charlestown Ferry enabled these gentlemen to pursue trade and yet live graciously in the country fashion. "What could be prettier, for instance, than the village of Cambridge, near Boston?" inquired Arthur Browne. "Its colleges, its scattered mansions, most of them splendid, the seats of rich West Indians whose health had induced a change of clime, surrounding a smooth and verdant lawn, and rising up peeping through thick clumps of wood, perhaps exceeded in beauty the prettiest village in England."

Extension of already existing settlement characterized the suburban growth of Newport and New York. Here, as at Boston, the gentry alone moved outward, leaving behind them the middle and inferior ranks. Both Rhode Island and Manhattan came to be dotted with country estates, and over on Long Island, fanning out from the village of Brooklyn, were more seats of Yorkers. Charles Town, so often an exception to generalizations about the other cities, witnessed an influx of people rather than the reverse, for the newly-rich planting gentry desired nothing so much as to escape from the lonely, rural, fever-infested Low Country for a taste of the man-made town.

Part of the housing problem and always a matter for public concern was a plentiful supply of firewood and other fuel at a price all townsfolk could afford. With the progress of cultivation in the countryside near the five ports, the woods rapidly receded and many of them disappeared entirely. Because hickory and oak burned slowly and gave out much heat, they usually commanded the highest prices and became scarce. The only substitutes known were imported Newcastle and Welsh coal, on which the freight was very high.

The constantly shrinking supply and rising cost of firewood, which had to be cut in "the Eastern Parts" and shipped by water, posed a real dilemma for the people of Boston. As a small vessel with three hands and carrying thirty cords of wood could make only fifteen trips annually, supplying firewood to sixteen thousand people the year round was a large and formidable operation. Besides, the charcoal needed by blacksmiths and braziers and for heating artisans' shops consumed large quantities of fuel. Woodcutters in Maine suffered from enemy and Indian attacks, and the expedition to Louisburg in 1745 took off many of them along with boatmen and their vessels. Finally, to make things worse, the Royal Navy press gangs raided the wood boats so often that many frightened crews refused to go near the Bay Town. Substantial craftsmen, shipwrights, blacksmiths, and sugar-bakers imported large amounts of coal until the supply was cut off by French privateers.

Bostonians set about determinedly to end the fuel shortage. One of the most powerful arguments for the capture of Louisburg was that the rich mines of Cape Breton could be made to supply the city with "sea coal." In 1747 the Selectmen persuaded Commodore Knowles at Louisburg to allow the Yankees to dig coal and ship it to Boston, and the Town Meeting, hoping to ensure an ample supply, resolved not to hire ships but to leave the trade open to everyone. The same year Governor William Shirley of Massachusetts provided military protection for woodcutters on "the Eastern Frontiers." Frugality in the consumption of fuel was urged by authorities, who also took measures against frauds in measurement of cordwood and against exorbitant prices. When the snow fell, sleds brought wood and provisions from the hinterland to relieve the shortage; one day in January of 1760 "upwards of one thousand" arrived. The fuel problem proved a permanent one for Boston and undoubtedly served among other causes in keeping down its population.

New York's firewood came either from Long Island or the Hudson and Raritan valleys, safe sources all, but during the wars and cold spells the supply was short. Even though as many as fifty wood boats arrived at Manhattan in a single day, they were not enough, for a medium-sized household consumed fifty or more cords of "good walnut wood" annually. In 1747 the price had risen as high as "40s/58s a cord," a price the newspapers said was "never equalled here before." Kalm observed in 1748 that "in many parts of the town coal is used both for kitchen fires and in other rooms, because it is considered cheaper than wood." Vessels returning from England and Holland without freights often brought Newcastle coal as ballast. Impressment of boat crews in the harbor after 1754 created a serious fuel shortage that was felt even by the military. To deter price-gouging, the *New York Mercury* began publishing the price of firewood in 1757. James Parker of the *New York Gazette* perceived the real source of the high prices when he pointed out that within forty miles of the city wood was much scarcer than two decades earlier, and that one had to go five times the distance from the boat landings to get it than previously. He thought that the best solution lay in developing coal mines near Shrewsbury, New Jersey, where he incidentally owned property. Then in 1760, not to add fuel to the fire but to harass the shivering citizenry still further, many wood boats shunned the city because the crews were afraid of catching the smallpox then raging in the town.

Of the three largest cities, Philadelphia had the least trouble in procuring fuel; most of the preferred walnut and hickory came from the Delaware Valley by boat to Budd's or Emlen's wharves. Growing population made such demands, however, that wood became both scarce and expensive; economy as much as improved heating inspired Franklin to devise his stove. Much burning of bricks for new buildings and the ravenous appetites of nearby iron furnaces added to the threat of a dangerous shortage. By 1760 the cost of wood was so great that the *Pennsylvania Gazette* demanded local regulation of prices charged by boatmen and carters for firewood.

Plenty of fuel could be had at Charles Town and Newport. Many Ashley River planters kept their slaves at work in off seasons cutting wood, which wood-boat patroons took to the city. Dr. Lionel Chalmers, in addition to his medical practice, carried on a large firewood trade, and Joseph Shute delivered Newcastle coal at the buyer's door for £5. 10s. a ton, "ready Money." But here, as elsewhere, prices rose and the poor, particularly, felt the pressure by 1759. At Newport wood came from the Narragansett Bay area in abundance; but even so, Joseph Harrison supplied artisans at Newport as well as at Boston with "sea coal." As in the past, fraudulent cording of wood continued to vex the purchasers. At Town Meeting in 1749 seven measurers were elected and given power "to set any person to cord wood when they think fit," but conditions grew worse instead of better. A correspondent of the *Newport Mercury* wrote in 1758: "I am credibly inform'd that it is the Practice of some Wood-sellers amongst us, to defraud their Customers of a great Part of their Measure, which with the Iniquity of some Boatmen, greatly enhances the Price. As the Poor generally sustain these Hardships (for the Rich may have a Supply upon good Terms in a proper Season) the Voice of Humanity, not to mention the Dictates of Religion, cry aloud for Redressing these manifest Impositions, and insufferable Grievances." Two years later a remonstrance from the lower class that retailers engrossed the supply of firewood, raised the price exorbitantly, and would sell only for coin, forced the Town Meeting to issue an ordinance against forestalling; it also ensured fair measures by awarding all short sticks to the poor. Indeed, it was time to act, for one householder who used fifteen cords each winter testified that he actually got only eleven out of the fifteen he bought.

V

Construction and maintenance of streets, lanes, and alleys and the attendant regulations and financial problems pertaining to the rapid expansion of each city absorbed much of the time of municipal bodies. In New York and South Carolina the provincial assemblies also had much to say about the streets of their towns. Everywhere new roads were laid out and old ones extended into newly built areas; in many instances narrow thoroughfares required widening, especially in Boston, where the Selectmen had sometimes to resort to eminent domain. Special officials—called surveyors in New England and New York, regulators at Philadelphia, and commissioners in Charles Town—supervised the highways, reported on their state of repair, and took action against householders and builders who encroached on or encumbered the streets. Dangers resulting from increased traffic in populous communities called for consideration. The achievement of the colonial cities in facing and solving these problems was remarkable for the times; because they did not have the accretion of centuries to combat, they often led the British Empire in both priority and quality of highway improvements.

Availability of funds dictated the success or failure of urban thoroughfare enterprises. In addition to raising large sums by local taxes, Boston secured passage of a provincial law taxing all carriages by the number of wheels for five years to defray the cost of a highway across the Neck. Likewise the Commons House of South Carolina voted £550 to improve the streets of Charles Town in 1758. Ordinarily, however, communities had to bear the charges themselves, and the simplest way seemed to require each householder to perform or provide a stipulated amount of labor on the streets annually. Charlestonians who failed to comply faced a heavy fine, but Newporters neglected their four days' service without compunction; the fine was so low that they would rather pay it than give the time. A real burden fell on the humble people of Manhattan, whom provincial law required to work two days a year on the Kingsbridge and Bloomingdale roads outside the city's limits or pay a large forfeit. The rich man, who daily deepened "the Ruts with his Gilded Chariot," might blithely pay his fine, but a half crown was a formidable sum to a poor widow. Commenting on the costs of the roads, William Livingston figured that the four thousand work days thus given were worth five hundred pounds, but considering that one hundred pounds would pay for a good job, pertinently inquired what the surveyors did with the remaining four hundred. At Philadelphia, indecision, indolence, and the inability of the members of the Corporation to agree resulted in a distressing street problem throughout the period.

Sir Christopher Wren made provisions for drainage for London after the great fire of 1666, but no other city in the British Isles provided it-self with sewers before the middle of the next century. Shortly after 1700 the people of Boston and New York had begun to underdrain their streets with "common shores" or sewers, laid about ten feet deep, into which water from indoor pumps discharged. Underground drains con-tinued to be laid at Boston, and persons opening the street to connect with the sewers had to have permits from the Selectmen and repair the streets afterwards. "The Common Shewer" running under Broad Street in New York was arched with stone in 1747, and the next year the Corporation allowed a group of subscribers to build another near the Fly Market. That diligent uncoverer of Manhattan nuisances William Livingston deplored "the continual Evacuations of the Sewers at the Slip and Meal Markets" in 1755, calling for the filling in of Rotten Row because of "the putrid Stench arising from that Sink of Corruption." Al-though all night soil was carried through the streets in ordure tubs after ten o'clock and never poured into the sewers, Gotham's drainage system remained unsatisfactory. A similar situation obtained over at Phila-delphia, where in October 1749 the Grand Jury presented the need to repair the sewer in Chestnut Street and the gutters of several other streets as a common nuisance. Citizens constructed new sewers in sev-eral parts of the city, while the Corporation bestirred itself to provide a brick arch under Third Street to drain the Almshouse grounds. Provin-cial authorities at Charles Town supplied funds for the extension of the Broad Street sewer and laying of new ones for Queen and Elliott streets, as well as setting regulations about connecting drains; but it is doubtful if the city was adequately underdrained. As much of Newport lay on the side of a hill, the water ran off quickly in gutters, and further drainage seemed unnecessary, but in the flat new development at Easton's Point, except for the common sewers that had been constructed before 1743, the town failed in its obligations.

Once having laid out new streets, officials of every city except Charles Town applied themselves to the costly business of paving them. Not only did paving ease the passage of traffic and eliminate much dust in dry weather and mud holes in wet, but in many ways it contributed directly to the health of the public. It had been undertaken with considerable success at Boston, Newport, and New York after 1700, but between 1743 and 1760 such advances were made everywhere that the colonial cities could well serve as models for those communities in Britain that awoke to the need for paved streets only after the mid-century, when Parliament authorized local commissions to tax and undertake such im-provements. If, as Beatrice and Sidney Webb maintain, the outstanding municipal achievement of London and the provincial towns between 1750 and 1790 was the durable new stone paving laid down, then Americans could pardonably take pride in their Northern cities. "The town is very conveniently laid into Streets which are paved with Stone," recorded a stranger in Boston in 1748. In the one year of 1757 over sixteen thousand yards on Boston Neck were paved with stone and gravel at a cost of three thousand pounds. New York's paved streets, instead of having side gutters, sloped toward the center, where a "water course" drained the surface. James Birket thought the streets of both cities narrow but well paved, and ten years later Burnaby reiterated these sentiments.

The exigencies of wartimes and financial strains aggravated by inflation held up paving projects at Newport. A lottery was proposed in 1747, but fell through; then in 1752 the Assembly, "being well informed of the great necessity of paving the streets of Newport, and more especially, that leading from the colony house," revived the lottery. Concurrently loaded carts and trucks were prohibited from using and thereby damaging the new surface before the Colony House. The town proceeded to pave the balance of Queen and Thames streets, running true to Rhode Island form by gambling to the sum of £1,504 in lottery tickets, which it covered by a new tax levy. Five years later the directors of the lottery turned over £5,885 to the Town Treasurer, which, even in inflated currency, enabled Newport to pave most of its important streets, lanes, and alleys.

The streets "are regular, pretty, and most of them are fifty feet . . . broad. . . . Some are paved, others not," Peter Kalm wrote while at Philadelphia in 1748. To him surfacing seemed "less necessary since the ground is sandy, and therefore soon absorbs the wet." Many inhabitants did not agree, however. The Grand Jury inveighed against "a great Slough in Kings Street," open sewers, the lack of gutters on Arch and Vine streets, and the need for much more paving; as late as 1754 Thomas Pownall marveled that in this bustling metropolis "there are remaining in some of the streets, the stumps or roots of some of the original Pine-Trees." Finding both the Corporation and the assessors inadequate, the citizens sent a petition to the Assembly in 1758 "setting forth the absolute Necessity of paving the Streets," and pointing to the absence of any public moneys for the purpose. The solution there, also, was a lottery, which yielded £2,250 to pay for the first paving strips in the middle of the streets.

A movement for cleaner streets naturally accompanied the agitation for better paving and other highway improvements. It is remarkable that in the colonial cities public interest in the removal of filth and rubbish did not focus exclusively on "making the passage through out our streets and lanes, safe, easy, and commodious," as did John Spranger and most other Englishmen, but also considered safeguarding the public health, for this was long before anyone understood the germ theory of disease. The 1731 ordinances of Manhattan were sufficient, and all that the

Mayor and Common Council had to do was to supervise the carters in the regular collection of the dirt people swept before their houses. In 1744 the street-cleaning law was published in the newspapers, and forty separately printed notices were posted in public places. One winter the sheriff notified the citizenry to clean up all filth in front of their houses, stables, and kennels as a health precaution. New Yorkers could have taken satisfaction in pointing out to British military men stationed in their town in 1746 that the rules proposed in "Parliamentary Motions" for paving and cleansing streets in the mother country, as recently published in the *Post Boy,* had long been in effect at Gotham. Bostonians could also be proud of the "decency and Clean-ness" of their community and of the fact that their twelve scavengers made money for the town by selling loads of the dirt and filth collected.

Charles Town made real progress in street cleaning despite the failure of the Assembly to provide pavements. As early as 1744 the Grand Jury had called for a public scavenger, but not until 1750 did a comprehensive highway act pass, which provided resident commissioners, headed by Gabriel Manigault, to administer it. They appointed a man to see to cleaning, filling up, or repairing all streets, drains, and sewers at the charge of the owners of the land or houses on the streets designated. Once or more every week dirt was carted away, and again the abutters on each street were assessed for the cost. An additional law of 1755 set a twenty-shilling fine for inhabitants who fouled a way after it had been cleaned, and within two years another law directed the scavengers to remove all obstructions or encumbrances from the thoroughfares. Although five hundred pounds of the annual parish tax went for hiring street-cleaners, Timothy's *Gazette* came out for better thoroughfares by printing a piece purporting to be "The Remonstrance of the Streets of Charles Town against the Inhabitants." "We are too narrow," complained the streets, "and you people allow a Number of little, narrow, dirty and irregular Alleys and Lanes to be opened up under pretense of private convenience, negligently leaving us dirty, poluting the air, and a disgrace to the capital of a great and flourishing province."

The deplorable condition of the streets of Philadelphia more closely resembled those of Westminster, Bristol, Liverpool, and Manchester than those of New York or Boston in 1750. Mayor Thomas Lawrence blamed the populace for "heaping great Piles of Dirt and Filth near the Gutters, so that the same is raised two and three Feet above them, thereby stopping the Water courses, and in consequence thereof, occasion[ing] an intollerable Stench at this Season, whereby Distempers will in all probability be Occasioned." His proclamation fruitlessly ordered every householder to clean before his door. Six months later the Grand Jury turned its attention to "the extreme Dirtiness of the Streets, for want of Paving," informing the Court of Quarter Sessions that the city could no longer afford such "deep and miry" thoroughfares that strangers "who otherwise commend our Regularity, make it their first Observation." Apparently the collecting of wood ashes was the only service, and that was privately conducted by William Ashe and Joseph Baker for a small fee. In 1754 another jury report, delivered by a trades-man, Isaac Searle, but written in the hand of Printer Franklin, de-manded provincial relief and some action on paving and keeping the streets clean. No lasting program was forthcoming, for in 1754 Colonel Henry Bouquet exploded to Richard Peters: "I never Saw anything but dirt and dust in and about your Town."

Stray animals roamed the streets of the cities frightening townsfolk and producing all manner of annoyances. Swine made good scavengers where street-cleaning service was poor, but they often caused more trouble than they were worth. Newporters particularly suffered from peregrinating hogs, and also from horses, cows, and sheep, which me-andered about the streets and impeded traffic. After 1745, town officers impounded all animals at large, awarding stray pigs to the "seizors," and in 1748 Newport concerted with neighboring Middletown and Portsmouth "concerning creatures [feeding] in the highway." Phila-delphia's pound-keeper and county ranger seem to have kept stray ani-mals at a minimum, but in the streets of Charles Town the ubiquitous hog shared the opprobrium with goats until a law of 1746 provided that all animals running at large be forfeited, killed, and given to the poor. Clearing the streets of objectionable creatures sometimes worked a hard-ship on New York's poor. Widow "Deborah Sl . . . e" complained bitterly in 1744 about the law prohibiting the keeping of swine in the city, insisting that pigs made the best collectors of garbage, "which now must be thrown into the Streets." Besides being denied the raising of pork in her back yard, she said she could not get any dung for the medicine she gave to the poor that had evoked so much praise from physicians! If hogs must go, quoth the irate dame, why not also banish cats and dogs?

The widow's point was well taken, for the canine nuisance plagued every town. In 1744 the democratic Town Meeting of Newport ordered that no one who did not possess current money or real estate valued at one thousand pounds could keep any "Bull, Mastiff, Spaniel, or Water Dogg or any other Dogg above the size of Lapp Doggs" under the pen-alty of death for the beast and a forty-shilling fine for the owner. Phila-delphians branded the plethora of dogs "a great and dangerous Nui-sance." The opinion of their Manhattan neighbors was printed in the *Independent Reflector* in 1753: "It appears, Sir, from the most accurate Calculation, that we have in this City, at Least a Thousand Dogs; I do not mean of the human kind. . . . These Creatures are a perfect Nui-sance . . . and with respect to Forty-Nine in Fifty, answer not one valuable purpose in Life." At a penny a day per dog, food alone costs their masters £1,520. 16s. 8d. each year. What a sum to save for the poor, insisted the writer, "Shadrach Plebianus," and what a relief from their filth, fierceness, and incessant howling!

The comfort and safety of "foot passengers" was an equal factor with the expediting of commercial traffic in forcing local officers to concern themselves with street improvements. In 1760 Andrew Burnaby noted the crowded streets of Philadelphia, nearly every one of which had rows of water beeches, locusts, elms or lime trees on either side, as did Broadway in New York, which formed an agreeable shade and produced "a pretty effect." The streets of the New England towns were often shaded, but no planned setting out of trees was attempted on them. Property-owners at Boston had to pave a certain portion of the street, and part of it was set off by white painted posts to protect both the pavement and the passer-by. New York also used posts, but occasionally had regular sidewalks, like the one on Broad Street. Its slowness in paving notwithstanding, Philadelphia had sidewalks that called forth universal praise from visitors. Many "trottoirs" were of brick, but Kalm noted that "in most of the streets is a pavement of flags, a fathom or more broad, laid before the houses, and four-foot posts put on the outside three or four fathoms apart. . . . Under the roofs are gutters which are carefully connected with pipes, and by this means, those who walk under them when it rains . . . need not fear being wetted." His approval suggests the absence of such advantages for the pedestrian in the towns with which he was familiar, at home and abroad.

The most important change in urban habits, and one that profoundly differentiated them from rural folkways, was in the night life of the towns. With each new year, more men and women went out after dark, and some measure of protection had to be accorded them. That the first successful move for lighting streets occurred at Philadelphia may be attributed in part to the wretched conditions encountered on its unpaved and unlighted ways. Quaker John Smith and other public-spirited citizens met at Widow Pratt's tavern on December 21, 1749 to lay plans for putting lamps before their own doors and hiring a lamplighter to tend them. Many residents must have joined in this voluntary scheme, for the next year Birket reported that the city "only wants the Streets to be Paved to make it appear to advantage, for there is few Towns, if any, in England that are better Illumined with Lamps and those of the best Sort." Meanwhile, far from content with voluntarism, Philadelphians agitated for an act of Assembly for regulating the night watch and "enlightening the streets, lanes, and alleys . . . and for raising money on the inhabitants" for the same. The act, passed in February 1751, granted the needed powers, not to the Corporation, but to a new ad hoc board of six elected wardens, who were to meet once a year in

November and "erect, put up and fix" as many lights as were deemed sufficient and to contract with lamplighters. The new whale-oil lamps were lighted for the first time late in September 1751. A wise provision set a forty-shilling fine for anyone damaging the lamps, and shortly after their installation the alert city watch procured the fining of a young blade for heaving an apple at one of the lights. Thereafter Philadelphia gladly paid taxes for the best lighting of any city in the Empire.

Throughout English America newspapers reported this achievement, and in the Northern cities authorities were spurred on to take similar action. Many residents of Newport, "out of a public Spirit," procured and put up "Glass Lamps" at their own expense outside their houses and shops. When some "evil Minded Persons" broke several, the Rhode Island Assembly passed a law in 1752 ordering a public whipping with twenty lashes or a fifty-shilling fine, or both, for any future vandalism. About the same time New York set a huge fine, twenty pounds, to discourage tampering with the new lamps erected by private citizens, inspired perhaps by an incident wherein "several daring Rakes" took some of them and hid them at the Meal Market. As soon as this law was passed, the *Gazette* reported a marked increase in the number of lamps put up, and tradesmen did a good business in "Globe Street Lamps." "Damnifying or breaking" street lamps in Boston entailed a forfeiture of five pounds and costs for the first offense and ten pounds for the second; and the law seems to have proved effective in protecting the lights.

The urban traffic problem is an old one. In the days before the automobile the horse and cart furnished an equally genuine threat to the safety of pedestrians. Back and forth through city streets coursed horsemen, gentlemen's chaises and chariots, a variety of tumbrils, carts, trucks, and great wagons drawn by from one to eight horses or oxen, and large numbers of packhorses, plus numerous laborers pushing wheelbarrows and countless porters carrying parcels large and small. Colonial streets provided little protection to citizens who did not stay on the sidewalk, and often not even there. When the careless driver of a lumbering oxcart ran over "a pleasant young Child" in 1743, the beasts and cart were confiscated by the government as a warning, but everywhere children died under hoofs and wheels; nor were their elders spared by galloping horsemen, reckless carters, or racing gentlemen whose equipages smashed into other vehicles on the streets.

Most of the accidents resulted from speeding. Often at Philadelphia there were collisions between chaises and the heavily loaded wagons "continually going with flour and wheat to the ships." During winter months highway hazards multiplied as sleighs appeared on the streets: a Philadelphia "Slay," exclaimed a West Indian, "goes at a prodigious Speed. All Ranks of people Covet this kind of Travelling . . . whilst the Snow lies upon the ground." In January 1750 he joined a party with two sleighs which drove the eight miles to Germantown for dinner in only forty minutes! To curb such threats to life and limb, nearly every community had severe penalties against galloping and trotting, as well as regulations requiring all carters to guide their horses on foot while passing through the streets. New York's action came after the "two Moor Princes" killed a five-year-old child during a display of "either their Dexterity or Ignorance on Horseback." Since over half of the population of Charles Town was black, the dominant whites severely regulated the handling of carts by Negroes and absolutely forbade them to ride horses within the city. "Coaches, Charriots and Chairs" blocked St. Philip's Church gate so often on Sundays that the South Carolina Assembly in 1750, the first occasion in American history, empowered the vestry to deal with the parking problem. When Newport officials grew lax in handling speeders, a private citizen offered a reward to whoever would identify certain of them, and he bluntly expressed the hope that the authorities would take steps to check such offenses.

Sometimes it was the rider who suffered at the hands of pedestrians. One Boston woman died as a result of being struck on the temple by a ball from a gun "imprudently fired by a lad . . . shooting at a mark on a Tree" while she was driving through the street in a chaise. Throwing or firing squibs in the streets caused so many accidents that all towns passed ordinances against it, and Charles Town had to deal with boys who threw stones at tied cocks. Indeed, there were life, excitement, and danger aplenty in city streets.

The clatter and clangor in the principal streets of the colonial towns disturbed the peace of mind of even those most intent on their business, and the sounds reverberated from sunrise to sunset. In Philadelphia the steady procession of country wagons down High (or Market) Street to the wharves guaranteed a dissonance composed of wagoners' shouts and curses, cracking of whips, and clanking of heavy chains, in addition to the loud rumble of iron-tired wheels over cobblestone pavements. Passing traffic in King Street so interrupted the debates and proceedings of the Great and General Court of Massachusetts that in 1747 it forbade all vehicles to go on either side of the State House during its sessions, and, because Boston drivers persisted in ignoring the injunction, later had iron chains hung to close the street when it convened. Even so well-adjusted a townsman as Benjamin Franklin resented "the whole Fraternity of Noise," but it was serious young John Adams, fresh from the country quiet of Braintree, who most eloquently pictured the urban distractions: "Who can study in Boston Streets? I am unable to observe the various objects that I meet, with sufficient precision. My eyes are so diverted with chimney-sweepers, sawyers of wood, merchants, ladies, priests, carts, horses, oxen, coaches, market-men and women, soldiers, sailors; and my ears with the rattle-gabble of them all, that I cannot think long enough in the street, upon any one thing, to start and pursue a thought. I cannot raise my mind above this crowd of men, women, beasts, and carriages, to think steadily. My attention is solicited every moment by some new object of sight, or some new sound. A coach, cart, a lady, or priest, may at any time, by breaking a couplet, disconnect a whole page of excellent thoughts."

In a public park, to be found in three of the five towns, a colonial could find some relief as well as pleasure, fresh air, and green grass. Boston Common dated back to the previous century, and discussions on its care and precautions against misuse by townsfolk or their cattle came up in town meetings throughout the years. Beyond the Mall lay the common pastures, where in 1753 the Selectmen added a third town bull. The following year Thomas Hancock received permission to plant lime trees before his new mansion farther up Beacon Hill "to beautify the Common." The Parade at Newport at this time ceased to be a grazing area as more and more town houses and the better sort of taverns appeared in the neighborhood of the Colony House. The railed-in Bowling Green proved a blessing to New Yorkers who passed the evening hours there or in "the fine gardens and terrace walks" close by Fort George, from which there was a delightful view of the bay. South of High Street and west of Tenth lay the Philadelphia Commons, a cleared area where the inhabitants diverted themselves. For the most part, however, small boys and the town kine claimed the Commons as their own, save on such occasions as that in October 1749 when the entire community turned out to see the robbers Fielding and Johnson hanged on the public gallows. Erection of the Pennsylvania Hospital on the Commons in 1756 led to noticeable improvement of the environs.

VI

The five seaports drew their remarkable vigor from sea-borne commerce. For this reason projects for the care and improvement of means of travel and communication and of waterfront facilities came up for constant consideration, regulation, and substantial expenditures.

In colonial law a ferry crossing any stream or body of water was considered part of "a public passage," and as an extension of a highway. Inasmuch as each of the towns was situated where one or more rivers entered the ocean, maintenance of several ferries developed into a vital urban service. A very lively and real picture of the role the ferry played in facilitating not only communication between a city and its immediate surroundings but also intercity exchange emerges from the *Itinerarium* of Dr. Alexander Hamilton of Annapolis, who leisurely journeyed north-ward with his servant and two horses in 1744. As he neared the Quaker City he had to ferry across the Schuylkill River; before he could reach New York he had to cross from Perth Amboy to Staten Island, to Long Island, and then back to Manhattan. Similarly, upon reaching Nar-ragansett Bay, he took two boats to get to Newport and a third to leave Rhode Island. At Boston only did he arrive without using a ferry, though when he departed for Salem he had to take either the Charles-town or Winnisimet ferry. This was the common experience of all co-lonial travelers, though they failed to hand on a newsy journal such as this genteel Scot left to posterity.

Passengers alone, however, did not make up even half of the ferry traffic. Cattle, sheep, hogs, poultry, and varieties of produce going to market accounted for the bulk of it, and market wagons and other ve-hicles for the rest. Farmers dwelling near the cities were the greatest users of the ferries, and they often protested against prescribed rates. Those living across the Schuylkill from Philadelphia in 1749 insisted that they were "People of low Circumstances" and petitioned the As-sembly to reduce by half the rates charged on James Coultas's High Street Ferry. On the other hand, ferry-keepers everywhere could charge only such tariffs as the laws allowed in posted schedules. Coultas peti-tioned the Assembly against any reduction, on the reasonable grounds that his new slips, wharves, and widened causeways, in addition to the constant attendance of three flats and several smaller boats "for the Ex-pedition of Passengers," involved heavy outlays. His was the busiest crossing in the colonies, because the vast hinterland stretching out from the city continuously stepped up its overland shipments to the markets and wharves. One of the few acceptable contributions of the Phila-delphia Corporation was its maintenance of sheds on the west bank of the Schuylkill "for the better Accommodation of the Country People who come down with Teams and Waggons loaded with Hemp, Flour, Wheat, and other Grain that requires Shelter in rainy Weather." Like most colonial ferries, that at High Street had a tavern to provide shelter and entertainment for travelers overtaken by darkness or storms. Ample custom and the presence of two competing ferries encouraged good service. "The Ferry boats at Schuylkill . . . are the most convenient I ever saw," Thomas Pownall insisted in a detailed description of 1755. In 1749 the Charlestown Ferry at Boston kept three boats to carry pas-sengers and milk to market and three more for horses, wagons, and lumber; and one of each continually crossing the river.

Ferry passages often turned out to be extremely hazardous. Most boats had flat bottoms without keels, and now and then frightened horses got out of control and capsized them, but bad weather and high seas produced most of the accidents. In places like New York Bay, small vessels known as passage boats were used to sail the long distance to Staten Island and Perth Amboy, and it took real courage to cross from New York to New Jersey in any but the calmest weather. At Newport and Boston the ferries also had to traverse fairly long stretches of open water. The full details of each occasion when a boat capsized or was "overset" as given in the papers would make it appear that colonial printers took an almost ghoulish pleasure in reporting them.

Of all the facilities furnished by these cities, those along the waterfronts seemed most essential to contemporaries; and where municipal action was lacking, the private enterprise of merchants supplied them. For shipping—in great vessels or small, foreign, coastal, and local—determined the economic well-being of each port; and wharves, quays, docks, slips, cranes, and warehouses to handle shipping and cargo had to be built as tonnage mounted. Local conditions profoundly influenced the nature of waterfront improvements up and down the Atlantic coast; likewise interesting regional variations in dockside nomenclature occurred.

Prior to 1743 both of the New England seaports had acquired all the wharves and docks they needed. Henceforth replacements and repairs concerned the merchants more than construction of new landing places; for, beyond minor regulations, their town meetings inclined to leave such matters in private hands. Boston did maintain and supervise the Town Dock for small craft, but its far-famed Long Wharf continued under the control of those who built it. This great pier ran out into the harbor a distance of 2,100 feet, according to Birket's measurements. Ships tied up along its south side and discharged their cargoes into the commodious stores lining the north side. Boston had several other large wharves in addition to a considerable number of small ones. In 1749 Thomas Hancock and three other merchants built a row of wooden warehouses 160 feet long, 18 feet wide, and 14½ feet stud, on Clarke's Wharf, and four years later the Davis brothers erected a wharf 400 feet long at a cost of one thousand pounds sterling.

Fresh from the West Indies in 1750, James Birket was taken with Newport's superb harbor. "They have abundance of good wharves which extend the whole length of the Town where vessels of any burthen can Load, discharge or heave down without the help of Lighters, which renders it an Excellent Scituation for trade and more Especially as it is so near the Sea that vessels are out or in, in a Moment." Ezra Stiles measured the wharfing in 1761 and found that the city had 177,791 "superficial feet." Among others, Godfrey Malbone, Josiah and Benjamin Brown, and Abraham Redwood owned several large and capacious wharves with stores on them, as warehouses were then called, but the Long Wharf was Newport's chief waterfront attraction. Jutting out 2,011 feet from the foot of Queen Street, it had a right angle in the middle of the north side connecting with Water Street on the Point and a drawbridge to allow boats to enter the largest and safest small-craft basin in America.

More waterside construction took place at Philadelphia than anywhere else. Here, as in other cities in the days before steam pile-drivers, most wharves consisted of square wooden casements, bolted or notched at the corners, and filled with stone, gravel, and earth. The Corporation, often so inefficient and complacent, had an excellent record for erecting and managing numerous public wharves. Sometimes it leased them to individuals for a period of years; at other times it permitted a private person like Samuel Powel to build a wharf and enjoy the profits from it provided it was kept in good repair. Nearly every considerable merchant had his own pier with one or more warehouses on it, because wharfage and storage yielded a good income. Thomas Richie, in 1755, charged Francis Rawles and others sums ranging from twelve shillings to ninety-nine pounds for using his wharf and docking equipment. Meredith's, Fishbourn's, Lawrence's, Mifflin's, and Willing's were only the better known among the sixty-six wharves along the Quaker City's two miles of frontage on the Delaware in 1760.

The Mayor and Common Council of New York controlled all water lots four hundred feet beyond low-water mark but failed to provide their city with all the facilities it needed. Also, their propensity to favor members with grants provoked much public criticism. Quays, or wharfing parallel to the shore, were favored for handling of ships, and few piers were built out into the water. There were times, consequently, while ships were loading or unloading, that others had to lie out in the roadstead awaiting a berth. Most large ships moored at Hunter's and Burnet's quays on the East River, where only six minor wharves had been built before 1760. The public-owned Great Dock at the foot of Broad Street, Beekman's, Coenties, and Peck's slips accommodated the many small craft—fishing, oyster, wood, and market boats—from Connecticut, Long Island, and New Jersey. Ice floes and high spring tides proved so destructive to piers in the North River that Ellison's was the only one of importance; as a result most Hudson traffic went around to the East River quays. Presumably the facilities sufficed for shipping needs, because Birket relates that all vessels could load and discharge cargoes at them without the aid of lighters. In general, however, it may be said that in these years New Yorkers had not supplied themselves with waterfront improvements adequate to the needs of so busy a port, nor did the ones they had compare favorably with those of the other colonial cities.

Governor James Glen wrote to the Board of Trade from Charles Town in 1751: "Notwithstanding we have few ships of our own, Cooper river appears sometimes a kind of floating market, and we have Numbers of Canoes, Boats and Pettygues [periaguas] that Ply incessantly Bringing down the Country Produce to Town and returning." To handle these small vessels and the great ships of the annual rice fleet as well as the constant traffic from the Caribbean and the North, Charlestonians in 1743 had eight well-built "bridges," as they called their wharves. On some of them were roomy warehouses for storing barrels of rice, and on the Bay, the street paralleling the harbor, there were at least thirteen more. Most Boston coasters used Captain Frankland's new wharf, formerly Rhett's, and on Motte's Bridge rice planters found well-equipped cooperages to supply them with barrels and hogsheads. Messrs. Roper, Gibbes, and Beresford were among those who constructed new bridges to meet the demand for more shipping berths. But this Southern city's fine harbor facilities were almost entirely ruined by the hurricane of 1751, and the painful process of rebuilding had to be undertaken. In 1756 the sea was dammed out from Granville's Bastion to Broughton's Battery along the Cooper.

Some measures to improve harbors and make them less dangerous to shipping had to be taken by the cities. The magistrates of New York and Philadelphia occasionally had to have the docks cleaned and freed of mud and silt, and in 1750 the province of New York passed an act to provide "able Pilots" to bring ships up from Sandy Hook to Manhattan. Masters of vessels tying up at Charles Town's wharves were carefully regulated so as not to incommode periaguas and canoes docking with rice, and an official was appointed to watch over such matters and to see to it that all boats unlading more than twenty barrels of rice had at least one white man in attendance. Charlestonians also recognized the need to regulate their bar pilots in 1747 but could get no official action from the provincial government; they did succeed, however, in persuading it to set out copper-sheathed buoys at the bar in 1753. The colonial assemblies also arranged for setting buoys to mark the channels leading into the other ports.

One of the great aids to Atlantic coast navigation came with the erection of lighthouses at the entrances of three of the harbors. Boston Light, which dated from 1716, was operated by the province of Massachusetts, and when the structure burned in 1751, the colony set up a "large Ship's Lanthorn" as a temporary beacon until a new stone lighthouse could be built. Plans made in 1738 for a lighthouse at the southern end of Conanicut Island to guide ships into Newport harbor at night were frustrated by the outbreak of the war with Spain, and not until August 1749 did Beaver-Tail Light go into service. All ships and coasters entering Narragansett Bay had to pay a fee for the support of the light and its keeper—wood, stone, and sand boats excepted. When this lighthouse burned to the ground in 1753, newspapers all along the seaboard notified mariners of the loss. A new light arose at the same spot in less than two years; costing £4,500 Rhode Island currency, it was a beautiful, three-story structure with a great whale-oil lanthorn designed by the former sea captain Peter Harrison of Newport. A lighthouse and dwelling on Lone (Bedloe's) Island was the first to serve vessels approaching New York, and was operating by 1753. Although Governor Glen told the Commons House of South Carolina in 1749 that Charles Town's harbor entrance badly needed a lighthouse, no action was taken.

VII

The remarkable expansion of the five colonial cities, brought about by an influx of population between 1743 and 1760, radically altered the external appearance of each. Despite the prevalence of war most of the time, and in part because of it, master builders and artisans were kept busily employed putting up new dwellings, with the result that the number of buildings nearly doubled everywhere, save at Boston, where a stabilized population improved its housing by replacement or repair. Along extended or new thoroughfares, increasingly better drained, paved, and cleaned, also arose sightly new brick or frame churches and dignified public buildings, whose towers seen from a distance lent to every city an individual aspect. Mariners making for Charles Town always strained for their first glimpse of its only landmark, St. Philip's steeple, while those heading for Boston sighted the masses of Fort, Beacon, and Copp's hills before they could distinguish the spires of its many meeting houses. To reach the three other ports one had to enter a harbor or sail up a river and thus come upon them rather suddenly. Two miles of busy wharves with a background of steeples characterized the leading city, Philadelphia. By comparison, Newport on its hill looked small, but shipshape. The first sight of Manhattan was Fort George, and not until the ship swung into the East River did the four- and five-storied houses come into view.

Upon closer scrutiny this uniqueness grew more pronounced. New York and Boston were old communities, built without any prearranged plan, with streets "irregularly disposed, and in general, too narrow," except in newly opened sections. Behind its ramparts, Charles Town, like Philadelphia, had been laid out in a gridiron design with broad streets and lanes in contrast with casually growing Newport, originally a town of two long streets parallel to the waterside, but now developing a more "regular" part at Easton's Point.

With vision and ingenuity colonial townsmen had met and solved many of the problems of urban expansion. Although here again local individuality displayed itself, and "acts of God" occasionally retarded improvements, the citizens uncovered their civic wants and loudly if not always effectively made their voices heard in public councils. By 1760 these five communities exhibited a physical completeness still lacking in English provincial cities. Not until 1749 did Parliament pass the act permitting taxation for highway improvements hailed by the historian of Liverpool as the beginning of "the regular progress of the town in wealth, extent, and civilization." This in part explains the astonishment of visitors to the colonial towns. "The nobleness of the town surprised me more than the fertile appearance of the country," exclaimed a naval officer at New York in 1756. "I had no idea of finding a place in America, consisting of near 2,000 houses, elegantly built of brick, raised on an eminence and the streets paved and spacious, furnished with commodious keys and warehouses, and employing some hundreds of vessels in its foreign trade and fisheries—but such is this city that very few in England can rival it in its show."

CHAPTER 2

The Fortunes of War

ALTHOUGH THE AMERICAN COLONIES were overwhelmingly rural, it was nevertheless the commercial activities of the cities that ensured the economic well-being of the country. The primary role of the seaports was to effect the exchange of colonial products for manufactured goods in international commerce; and when war interrupted normal traffic, city merchant and country farmer alike suffered. The years of King George's and the French and Indian wars were no exception. Governor Thomas of Pennsylvania argued this point to the Assembly in 1744 when he tried to persuade that body to erect defenses against the French privateers that were coming into Delaware Bay: "This whole City, indeed, in some way or other, depends upon the Merchant, and if he cannot trade to Advantage, it will be soon very sensibly felt by the Whole. Even the Farmer, who is too apt to consider the Landed and Trading Interest in Opposition to each other, must confine his Produce to the Consumption of his own Family, if the Merchant is disabled from exporting to foreign Markets."

By 1743 each of the cities had worked out ways of conducting profitable trade within the limits set by the British acts of trade and navigation and further dictated by its geographical position and the nature of the staples produced by the agricultural population of its hinterland. Such an accommodation to the requirements of empire and environment, always delicately balanced at best, became extremely precarious under war conditions. Philadelphia and New York, on the whole, benefited mightily; Charles Town held its own; Newport experienced ups and downs; but Boston, whose early commercial pre-eminence had given her such an advantage, never recovered from a decline that set in after 1735, and, when the fall of Quebec came, was surpassed by both Philadelphia and New York in prosperity and in numbers.

Philadelphia merchants succeeded in finding outlets for wheat, flour, bread, biscuit, pork, beef, beer, butter, iron, flaxseed, lumber, and furs —staples produced in abundance by Pennsylvania and adjoining provinces. To the British and foreign West Indies, the British Isles, Holland, Portugal, the Wine Islands, and even as far away as Leghorn in the Mediterranean, they dispatched cargoes in Delaware-built ships manned by provincial crews, and the vessels returned laden with the molasses, rum, sugars, salt, mahogany, and wines desired by colonists all along the Atlantic coast. An extensive traffic in foodstuffs and forest products with the Caribbean islands gave Philadelphia its most remunerative business, for there her mariners and supercargoes took on not only tropical products but also either good hard cash or bills of exchange on London. They also found profits in clandestine trading with the Dutch at Curaçao and St. Eustatius and with the French sugar islands. Moreover, Philadelphia's importations of English manufactured goods were always much smaller than those of Boston and New York, for the presence in the interior of Pennsylvania of numerous skilled artisans as well as many in the city reduced the need to import certain British articles. Consequently the task of procuring money or bills of exchange to pay for them did not so greatly trouble Quaker merchants. Furthermore they enjoyed an especially lucrative traffic in servants and convicts such as no other city had.

Less known and less extensive, though of prime significance to the city's prosperity, was its intercolonial commerce, which exceeded that of any of the other ports. To the southward Philadelphia sent supplies of locally produced and marketable staples, for aside from a few commodities that were mere adjuncts, South Carolina so confined herself to rice- and indigo-growing that Charles Town was compelled to import large quantities of foodstuffs and other colonial items. Samuel Powel sent "Burlington pork, which is the best," Pennsylvania flour, and Philadelphia bread in exchange for rice, turpentine, "superior Carolina Soal leather," and occasionally potatoes and oranges. Here again the real advantage of this trade lay in the fact that Quaker shippers sent down more than they brought back, and cash payments made up the difference. Re-exporting of Carolina produce paid so well that Powel and Thomas Willing laid plans to operate a small vessel regularly on the Charles Town route.

Pennsylvania ships likewise coasted to the northward, calling at nearly every port. New York and Philadelphia more or less complemented each other, but the latter enjoyed the heavier balance of trade with Boston. The Bay City procured much of its flour and some pork and beef from the Delaware, and when in 1756 Governor Morris of Pennsylvania laid an embargo on foodstuffs, the Boston Selectmen requested him to allow two or three ships to come to Boston, "as provisions are much wanted in this Town." Newporters also purchased Pennsylvania articles and, having none to return, paid for them in cash. New England skippers came to Philadelphia for wheat, flour, corn, and pork, Powel explained to a correspondent in 1747, "but they are at so great a loss for any Commodities to send here, for purchasing, that their Vessels come generally empty, or if they bring New England Rum . . . it will seldom yield more than their own Money, and often not so much, so that they are obliged to pay for what they buy chiefly in bills [of] Exchange on England or Silver or Gold. Necessity obliges them to deal with us, but we have no occasion of any Goods they have."

When shortsighted Pennsylvanians first conceived the idea of "protection" and clamored for an impost on trading in 1758, the "Watchman" wisely pointed out that a tariff would fetter the city's business, adding that "Trade much delights in Freedom and Ease." The Yankees understood this only too well. They read with envy in 1760 of the ships that sailed up the Delaware from "Great Britain, the West Indies, every part of North-America, the Madeiras, Lisbon, Cadiz, Holland, Africa, the Spanish Main, and several other places," as well as of the departure within a single fortnight in July of 134 sail.

The commerce of New York was much smaller than that of Boston or Philadelphia at the outbreak of King George's War. The value of its imports of British, European, and East India goods from the mother country in 1744 was only £54,957, but as the two wars brought in unparalleled boom times, they rose to £267,130 in 1750 and £480,106 a decade later. Up to 1750 most "European Goods" arrived via Boston or Philadelphia, but thereafter ships brought them directly from London and the outports. Because New York's exports were negligible, payments for such large purchases had to be accumulated by trading elsewhere. As William Alexander wrote to his cousin: "In the Trade between London and this place if any thing is gained it is generally in the goods from London and very seldom on what we ship from hence." To procure needed bills of exchange and coin, Manhattan merchants shipped quantities of wheat, corn, flour, barreled meats, and lumber to the West Indies, traded profitably outside the Empire with Amsterdam, built up a provision exchange for wines with the Madeira and Canary islands, and with the Guinea Coast for slaves. Twenty vessels left in 1753 for Ireland with flaxseed worth £17,500. The New Yorkers imitated their Philadelphia neighbors by trafficking in foodstuffs with the New England cities and Charles Town; and they seem to have developed an even larger rice re-export business than Philadelphia, but the total volume of their trade never became so great.

Despite every effort of the merchants of Manhattan, returns were hard to get, and they complained frequently of "the present Stagnation of Trade." They projected such schemes as cutting in on the Nova Scotia fisheries with the hope of averting "the utter Ruin of the City," which ran on credit "much beyond any in North-America." In a promotional vein comparable to that used by modern chambers of commerce, the *Independent Reflector* devoted a whole issue in 1755 to New York's alleged advantages over Philadelphia as a port. Then Mars came to the rescue, and New York became the center of British military operations in North America, first waxing prosperous, ultimately almost vulgarly rich on government contracts, privateering, and illegal trade—war babies all. And when the Continental phase of the Anglo-French conflict ended in 1760, no colonial city had so completely and permanently profited.

The flow of commerce in and out of Charles Town was controlled by its two staples, rice and indigo. In common with the entire Western World, South Carolina experienced a depressed economy from 1743 to 1749, and because it was geared to rice, the low price of that commodity hurt everyone. Although the rice crop got better every year, the exports, which had been 73,416 barrels in 1743, fell to 61,522 in 1751; with the upswing of business activity, the number of barrels of rice exported in 1760 attained the high figure of 101,359. Fortunately, at the low point of the cycle, satisfactory indigo was produced, and an initial high price gave shippers an article for exchange. Deerskins, too, continued to be a primary export until about 1750.

The falling off of rice exports and the difficulties of developing other commodities during a period of high interest rates (loans brought ten per cent) curtailed the Southern capital's growth. The two or three hundred British ships a year never carried off the entire rice crop, and Charlestonians used the surplus, along with a few other local items, to pay for the foodstuffs, rum, beer, sugars, and colonial manufactures they purchased from Northern cities. Governor James Glen regretted this excess of imports over exports, for by such means "we are kept low in circumstances." He also complained that the coastal trade with Philadelphia and New York was "draining us of all the little money and bills that we could gather from other places."

The fact that the hinterland of the two New England ports produced no staples suitable for exchange with Europe placed their merchants at a decided disadvantage and everlastingly tested their ingenuity and resourcefulness. As in the other cities, trade pivoted on the West Indies. To Barbados alone in 1755 Boston and Newport shipped an estimated one hundred thousand pounds sterling worth of merchandise. The bewildering variety of these cargoes and the small quantities of each article bear witness to the critical absence of New England staples.

Rhode Island's commerce endured in spite of a chronic unfavorable balance of trade with the three largest colonial ports. Since the previous century Newporters had always imported most of their goods from Boston. They partially continued in this economic bondage, but in the forties John Banister and others valiantly opened a direct connection with London, being "fully Convinc'd" that it offered "the only method to make them selves Independent of the Bay Government, to whom they have a mortal aversion." Although they reduced purchases from Boston, they accomplished this merely by shifting their custom to New

Artist unknown. Courtesy of the New-York Historical Society, New York City

PLATE 3 · *A View of New York, Showing Privateers in the East River,
ca. 1756–57*

*In the detail from the center (above) the quays, a market, and the stepped
gables of several old Dutch buildings can be identified.*

Richard Newſham, *of* Cloth-Fair, London, *Engineer,*

AKES the moſt uſeful and convenient Engines for quenching FIRES, which carry a conſtant Stream with great Force, and yet, at Pleaſure, will water Gardens like ſmall Rain. All impartial Men of Art and Ingenuity will allow this, and the moſt Prejudic'd ceaſe objecting, when they ſee how compleatly the whole Contrivance is adapted to the Uſe intended. He hath play'd theſe Engines before His MAJESTY and the Nobility at St. *James*'s, with ſo general an Approbation, that the largeſt was inſtantly order'd to be left for the Uſe of the Royal Palace aforeſaid: And as a farther Encouragement, (to prevent others from making the like Sort, or any Imitation thereof) His MAJESTY has *ſince* been graciouſly pleas'd to grant him His Second Letters Patent, for the better ſecuring his Property in this, and ſeveral other Inventions for raiſing Water from any Depth, to any Height requir'd. The largeſt Size will go through any Paſſage one Yard wide, in compleat working Order, without taking off, or putting on, *any Thing*, which is not to be parallel'd by *any other Sort* whatſoever: One Man can quickly and eaſily move about the largeſt Size in as little Compaſs of Ground as it takes up to ſtand in, and it is work'd by Hands and Feet, or by Hands only. Thoſe by Suction feed themſelves from a Canal, Pond, or Well, *&c.* or out of their own Ciſterns, as Opportunity offers: They are far leſs liable to Diſorder, much more durable than any extant, and play off large Quantities of Water, at the Diſtances under-mention'd, either from the Engine, or a Leather Pipe, or Pipes, of any Length requir'd, (the Screws all fitting each other) *This* the **cumberſome Squirting-Engines**, which take up four times the Room, cannot perform, nor do they throw one 4th Part of their Water on the Fire, at the like Diſtances, but loſe it by the Way; neither can they uſe a Leather-Pipe with them to much Advantage, whatever Neceſſity may call for. The Four largeſt Sizes go upon Wheels, and the Two others are carried like a Chair. Their Performances are as follow, and their Prizes fix'd very reaſonable, (tho' ſome may think otherwiſe, becauſe his Inventions are ſecur'd to him by Letters Patent) he having a due Regard to the publick Good, as well as his own Profit, both in theſe, and divers other Inventions, for ſeveral Purpoſes, which he has been the Inventor of, either for the Uſefulneſs, or Diverſion of Gentlemen.

Number of Sizes.	What Quantity of Water the Ciſterns hold in Gallons.	Quantity diſcharg'd per Minute in Gallons.	At what Number of Yards Diſtance.	Price without Suction.	Price with Suction.
1ſt.	30		26	18 *l.*	20 *l.*
2d.	36	30	28	20	23
3d.	65	36	33	30	35
4th.	90	65	36	35	40
5th.	120	90	40	45	50
6th.	170	120	40	60	70
		170			

Machina perfecta eſt, qua non præſtantior ulla | Mutatam cernis naturam: ſurgit in altum
Aſſervare domos, & aquas haurire profundas. | Artibus unda novis; dum flamma coacta recumbit.

PLATE 4 · *Broadside advertising Richard Newsham's Fire Engines*

Every colonial city purchased one or more of these pieces of equipment.

York and Philadelphia rather than by dealing directly with England.

Through the daring of her merchants, who realized that only by a relentless search for cargo could they survive, Newport somehow managed to prosper and to make payments for imports from the other American cities, New York in particular. Commerce with London and Liverpool grew, but it did not provide a way out; several avenues legitimately led to the British West Indies and distant Africa, as well as along the Atlantic coast. At the end of forbidden sea lanes, the teas of Amsterdam and the molasses of Curaçao and the French Caribbean exerted a fatal attraction for Newport merchants. Rhode Island and nearby Connecticut did supply limited quantities of certain products desired in the islands; the famous Narragansett horses turned most of the sugar mills in the Caribbean. Skippers sold in one port what they had bought in another, always hoping to turn a profit no matter how small. "Thus," one observer reported, "with the money they get in Holland, they pay their merchants in London; the sugars they procure in the West Indies, they carry to Holland, the slaves they fetch from Africa they send to the West Indies, together with lumber and provisions, which they get from the neighboring colonies; the rum that they distill they export to Africa; and with the dry goods, which they purchase in London, they traffic in the neighboring colonies. By this kind of circular commerce they subsist and grow rich."

As so many unfavorable balances had to be righted by proceeds from coastal freights, many ships of small tonnage suitable for coasting in all waters were built at Rhode Island for local mariners. With them, Newport's merchants drove a huckstering trade that earned them the label of "the Dutchmen of America." In the little sloop *Elizabeth,* of about thirty tons, Captain John Bryer carried down to Charles Town a typical assortment of Rhode Island goods and items picked up along the way: Pennsylvania and New York flour and bread, cheese, butter, rum, beer, sugars, apples, onions, cranberries, whale blubber, tables, cordage, "Hops by the bag," and, of course, "New England Primmers." Cheap furniture made in Newport, New England axes and locally forged anchors, sea coal from Nova Scotia, and slaves from the coast of Guinea always found ready sale at New York, Philadelphia, and Charles Town. Toward 1760, fish and candles became important items in the cargoes. Precarious at best, this mode of trading suffered severely during the wars, and Newporters turned greedily to privateering, with dreams of enormous profits, and then, eventually, to traffic with the enemy.

Boston was the only city not to experience an increase in population and commercial expansion before 1760. The coinciding of a very complex series of events explains this phenomenon. From its founding in 1630 until about 1735, Boston had always been the mart town of the English colonies. Priority had given her merchants control of virtually all of the coastwise and West India traffic and a major share of that with the mother country. The rise of the other four cities, however, meant the end of this commercial hegemony, and, lacking staples of her own, she faced serious problems of economic readjustment. Additional difficulties confronted the Yankees when King George's War broke out. At sea and in the Canadian expeditions of this and the succeeding war, the city suffered a crippling loss of manpower and had to support numerous widows at public expense. Successive epidemics carried off members of both sexes and all classes. Mounting taxes for the care of the poor and for necessary municipal improvements, as well as the high cost of fuel, not only proved increasingly burdensome but impelled many of the middle and lower classes to move elsewhere. To make matters worse, Philadelphia and New York merchants demanded money or bills of exchange for the provisions so essential to Boston's existence, and Newporters transferred much of their trade to Manhattan. With the "Change of Medium" in Massachusetts from paper money to specie in 1749, Boston's trade in English goods with Rhode Island and Connecticut "almost wholly" dried up. North and east of Cape Cod the press gang's seizures of seamen from coasters and wood boats started a flight of mariners to Newport. Finally a runaway inflation in the forties, followed by a deflation just as serious in the fifties, capped the economic woes of this unfortunate community, bringing on civil strife and leaving behind a legacy of bitterness that would eventually have momentous consequences. One thing above all is certain, the cries of the Town Meeting for relief in its "great distress" were genuine.

At the same time that Boston was reeling under these blows, secondary New England ports were beginning to compete with the town: Newbury and Portsmouth took away shipbuilding; Salem and Newport threatened in the West India trade; Lynn and neighboring villages wrested the butchering and leather trades from Boston artisans; Medford poached on the rum industry; Providence, via the Blackstone Valley, deprived her of commerce with Norfolk County and the interior.

The principal lubricant of the Bay Town's commerce was rum. With it the merchants purchased fish at Newfoundland, which in turn they exchanged in the English and French islands of the Caribbean for molasses, sugars, coin, or bills. Some Yankee captains returned, their boats laden with molasses for the distillers of Medford and Boston; others carried sugars to London to swap for manufactured articles; a few sold both cargo and vessel in England and came home as passengers.

This commercial routine was not enough, however, if the city was to flourish, and Boston merchants performed wonders in the face of what must have looked like wholly frustrating circumstances. In 1743 they took off £600,000 worth, or one sixth, of the total British exports to the plantations, which articles, together with the goods and produce at home and from nearby New England areas, they peddled up and down the coast on an even greater scale than their Newport competitors. Old hands at trying all ports to force a trade, Bostonians never balked at small undertakings. Into the hold of many a tiny sloop went lumber from Maine, whale oil and bone from Nantucket, Medford rum, axes and ironware from Norfolk and Plymouth counties, small boats and oars from Newbury, woodenware from Essex County, leather from Suffolk, along with many articles fabricated by artisans of the city itself—spermaceti candles, shoes, cheap furniture, fine cabinetwork, and a variety of carriages and harness. Everywhere one encountered Massachusetts masters with surprisingly miscellaneous cargoes ready to bargain shrewdly and often sharply in any kind of exchange. When Mayo Greenleaf let go the *Triton*'s anchor in the lower James in 1753, he had on board a typical cargo: ten hogsheads of salt, five thousand bricks, seven barrels of fish, "some Iron and Wooden ware," five hogsheads of rum, two barrels of sugar, three hogsheads of "melasses," and "one Riding Chair" to trade for the sweet-scented or oronoco tobacco of Virginia. A month later at Motte's Wharf in Charles Town, Atherton Haugh advertised to truck from the sloop *Desire* "good train oil and blubber, and two light New-England made chairs, one of them having curtains to draw over in bad weather." Since the Bay Town merchants had no staples to sell, it is little wonder that Boston newspapers never published lists of commodity prices as did those of other cities, and the prices charged or paid for the dozens of items in their ventures were, after all, trade secrets.

The romantic and dramatic part that sea-borne commerce of the colonial cities played has always attracted the attention of writers, while their more prosaic but nevertheless vital roles as collection and distribution points for a constantly widening interior have been neglected. The hinterland population grew astonishingly, principally because of a high birth-rate, but in certain areas heavy immigration accounted for much of it. Each year a larger agricultural surplus for export became available, enabling the rural inhabitants to increase their purchases of European goods in keeping with wartime tendencies toward greater consumption of luxuries. In varying degrees each city broadened its sphere of interior trading, sometimes at the expense of one of the others; and the overseas commerce of all rested directly on this traffic.

The principal factor in Philadelphia's rise to colonial pre-eminence was its widespread trade with the fertile and expanding country stretching out from the city in all directions. From these outlying parts the merchants took off grain, flour, lumber, limestone, bricks, barreled meats, flaxseed, and many other marketable items. Long in control of the trade of West New Jersey and the Delaware Valley, such merchants as John Reynell, Samuel Powel, Samuel Coates, and William Allen now intensified their activities. Either by granting generous credit or by forming partnerships, they financed many country stores, which gave them a favored position in dealing with rural settlers. The amount of credit accorded and the size of the stocks of some of these stores are really surprising. In the six years after 1745, John Reynell sold £1,176 worth of linen and other cloth to one storekeeper at Horsham in Bucks County. Myer Levy came up from Surinam in 1756, and ten Philadelphia mercantile houses set him up in business at Spotswood in East New Jersey. When he absconded four years later, he carried away goods valued at £2,300.

Not content with trafficking solely with the immediately adjacent country, ambitious men reached out for more distant business. In 1750 Dr. Thomas Graeme urged on the Penns the founding of a town at the forks of the Delaware (Easton), because this "point would necessarily become the focus of Trade not only for the Inhabitants therein and all above them, and for 20 miles below them, but for all that part of the Jerseys that lye over against" the river, and would divert Jersey flour from the wagon trade to New Brunswick by providing cheaper water carriage to Philadelphia. Among John Lownes's best customers were Melchior Wiener of Baltimore County, who usually paid him in "100 wt. chees," and Robert Evans, who remitted in good Maryland bar iron. Collins & Emlen conducted a store in "Pardnership" with John Wilson at Joppa in the same colony, and also with Samuel Harris on the Susquehanna, to whom they gave an initial shipment of six hundred pounds in goods. Soon much of the Maryland grain trade north of Annapolis was controlled from Philadelphia.

The exploitation of the Quaker City's hinterland induced the growth of numerous towns to serve as auxiliary centers. Most were small places like Trenton and Wilmington on the Delaware; or Charlestown, established by Davey & Carson at the head of the Northeast River in 1746 in expectation of tapping wheat, flour, and flaxseed shipments for at least three pennies a bushel less than in the city, and where convicts and servants might be imported w.thout "any risque" if the other articles became scarce. The enterprise of the Hollingsworth family built up a thriving little entrepôt at Head of Elk (Elkton, Maryland) to handle exchanges between the Delaware and Chesapeake valleys. In the forties, only eight miles from Philadelphia, the village of Germantown began to grow under the impetus of its tanneries, stocking manufacture, and the Wissahickon millers, its 2,800 people making it the third largest town in Pennsylvania.

"Lancaster is a growing town and making money," reported Thomas Pownall in 1754. By the end of the period it probably rivaled Germantown in size and exceeded it in importance. It was destined to be the chief town of inland America. Prosperity arose not alone from Lancaster's position as a market town for a rich countryside, but because it early became the point of departure for Germans and Scotch-Irish immigrants journeying southward to Maryland and Virginia and also for fur traders who pushed along trails with pack trains as far west in Ohio as Pickawillany on the Great Miami. Many artisans set up shop in the town to cater to these early migrants, but it was a group of enterprising Philadelphia merchants who turned the hamlet into a pulsing trading center and rigidly managed its economic activities. Levy & Franks, and Baynton, Wharton, & Morgan of Philadelphia opened branch offices to facilitate their fur-trading interests. George Dillwyn maintained a branch drygoods shop under the name of Whitelock & Dillwyn in Queen Street, Lancaster. Thomas Wharton used the bilingual *Lancastersche Zeitung* as soon as it appeared, in 1752, to advertise his insurance office at the metropolis. When the paper ceased publication within a year, Philadelphia newspapers began to carry Lancaster advertising regularly. Excellent wagon communication over the sixty-mile road between the two places enabled such Lancaster gentlemen as Edward Shippen to enjoy the luxury of imported tea, McCall's Fayal Wines, or a "generous Malaga," and a barrel of Rhode Island oysters.

The ramifications of the city's back-country connections continued to become more and more complex despite the wars. After 1745 Philadelphia newspapers contained notices of attractive farm property "as rich as any land in Conestoga Manor" for sale in Augusta County, Virginia, near the Shenandoah River, and in Ninety-Six Township near the Savannah River in South Carolina, both "very convenient for settlement," and the latter available on seven years' credit with only a twenty-five per cent down payment. Such opportunities enticed immigrants southward by the hundreds, and before long they sent their produce back. When the French cut off the peltry traffic in 1755, more and more drovers came up the "Great Philadelphia Wagon Road" from South Carolina and intermediate points, passing through Lancaster on their way, to fattening farms near the great city. As Gottlieb Mittelberger discovered, everyone "sends his annual surplus . . . to be sold there"; Philadelphia had indeed come to dominate a very wide area, and it offered the best instance of the emergence of a form of the metropolitan economy that marked such a definite break with the past.

Boston merchants sought to traffic with interior New England towns in order to compensate for the losses in the West Indian and coastwise trade. This necessitated cultivating new or larger markets for European goods and taking in exchange whatever was offered by a region that produced no substantial surplus of crops. Massachusetts, Connecticut, and New Hampshire towns were fast growing, and in them Boston met with considerable success. Newport continued to be the biggest customer, and, overland to Rhode Island, quantities of goods were sent in carts, which brought back molasses. New London exchanged Connecticut pork and grains for hardware and dry goods through resident merchants like Joseph Chew and Joseph Coit, who represented Apthorp & Gardiner and other houses of the Bay Town. One of the largest inland traders was Thomas Hancock, who commenced with bookselling and then graduated as a prosperous general merchant. His sales to a shopkeeper of Lancaster, Massachusetts, in May 1750, totaled £29. 18s. 4d. in silk, ribbons, crepe, buttons, necklaces, combs, and paper, for which he accepted farm produce. Samuel Hardcastle at the Three Nuns and Comb, who carried a very complete line of hardware, announced in 1754 that "all shopkeepers and country traders may be furnished by sending a letter as if present themselves," thereby inaugurating a mail-order service that soon had many imitators. The Amorys opened a branch shop in Salem, as did several other Bostonians; but the truly lucrative exploiting of interior New England had to await the close of the Old French War.

When the period began, New York's commercial sphere extended only to western Long Island, the Hudson Valley, and the Jersey shore, but at its end Manhattan merchants had crossed provincial boundaries to stake out new claims so successfully that the *Independent Reflector* exulted: "Connecticut on the East, and New Jersey on the West, are fertile and well cultivated Colonies, and thro' natural Necessity, must always contribute their Aids in rendering this City a plentiful Mart, because their Exports cannot with equal Ease be conveyed to any other Port of considerable Traffick." Printer Hugh Gaine published *The Tradesman's Director: or the London and Country Shopkeeper's Useful Companion,* composed of lists of English manufactures and the best makers of them for the benefit of local merchants ordering for country stores. From Manhattan, James Beekman dealt with country stores up the Hudson at Kingston and Albany, at Rye, and at Elizabeth Town and Shrewsbury in East Jersey. In 1751, with apparent effort, John Martin of New Rochelle wrote to him: "Be plas to sand ma two paşa of Irish Camblad and youl Blig your frind," while from Albany came a request for him "Pleas to Get us three Matrases Made by the Man that lives almost opesit to you." Philip Cuyler not only supplied goods to shopkeepers in the Hudson Valley, but started a correspondence at Schenectady and "Kanajoharie," where in 1757 he reminded William Seeber, Jr., that "it is now upwards of two Years since you had that dozen Gauz Handks. which think time you discharge."

Profits wrung from the new opportunities afforded by King George's War facilitated the expansion of trading zones, and during the fifties enabled New Yorkers to pare down Boston's market for European articles at Newport and work out a reciprocal traffic that suited them both. Gerardus Beekman informed John Channing at Newport in February 1749 that "as soon as the Ice breakes away [so] that Creeks and rivers are open'd and the Country Store Keepers can come to town for a supply," Rhode Island rum should rise in price. Sugar, molasses, rum, and spermaceti candles from Metcalf Bowler and Solomon Southwick were sold at New York by Beekman, who in turn sent them Esopus flour and pork along with such imported luxuries as a bolt of satin for Mrs. Bowler. Dutch tea smuggled into Manhattan always met with a good sale, and Philip Cuyler sent many chests of it to Robert Crooke, Joseph Wanton, and other Newporters at prices Bostonians could not meet with teas legally imported from England. New York merchants managed to steal most of the New London and Norwich business away from the Bay Town in 1755, though the size of the trade was less than that with Rhode Island. Proximity via Long Island Sound was a real advantage at New Haven, too, notwithstanding Beekman's heartfelt conviction that "7/8 of the people in New England has proved to be [so] d—d ungrateful cheating, that I am almost afraid to trust any Connecticut man tho' he's well recommended from others."

In a very real sense, the Yorkers were *arrivistes,* and their gains frequently went to their heads. William Livingston boasted immoderately in 1753 of his city's advantage in having the Hudson avenue rather than the costly "Highroads" leading out of Philadelphia, and when he turned to Boston, he could not refrain from unctuously blaming its decline on the luxury that brings ruin to empires. New York feeds Massachusetts and has fewer poor than any other colony because of its modest life. Boston, he sneered, has "more Shew than Substance, Pomp than Riches." Within a few years, only Charles Town would rival New York in riches and conspicuous display.

The tribute Newport had to pay to Manhattan and Boston for importations from Europe was largely made up of cash and items drawn from her West India and coastal ventures. This was partially supplemented by profits from trading in Rhode Island and nearby Connecticut. European manufactures procured direct from England or from Boston found their way from Newport warehouses to Providence, Hartford, New London, and such inland towns as Lebanon and Colchester. Jacob Richardson & Company and Wickham & Deblois advertised hardware and dry goods in Boston newspapers for the benefit of "country customers" living in Worcester County and the Blackstone Valley. But any great extension of inland trade was foredoomed. In 1750 Dr. William Douglass accurately predicted Rhode Island's commercial future: "Newport . . . is of easy and short Access, being near the Ocean, but for that Reason not so well scituated for inland Consumption; Providence is about 30 miles farther up Narragansett-Bay inland, therefore in a few Years must be their principal Place of Trade."

An unusual coastal formation of sea islands and a convenient system of sheltered waterways made Charles Town the natural entrepôt of Low

Country South Carolina, for by means of sounds, inlets, rivers, and creeks communication was open to small boats throughout the year. The region from the Pedee on the north to St. Simon's Island on the south, and reaching about sixty miles inland to the edge of the Pine Barrens, plus the valley of the Savannah as far up as Augusta, comprised the hinterland of the Southern capital until 1755. Throughout the Low Country one found "storekeepers" acting independently, or as agents for city merchants, or for resident English factors, in assembling rice and indigo shipments and in disposing of necessaries and luxury articles to the planters. James Mathews & Company at Pon Pon Bridge and Charles Lyon of Goose Creek seldom saw a cash transaction in their establishments, each sale being for "country produce" and therefore merely a matter of bookkeeping. John Cooper of Elliott Street, Charles Town, a dealer in Madeira and Vidonia wines who preferred direct trading, announced in 1759 that "Letters and Orders from the country" would be filled and the wine shipped promptly, adding as a come-on that he would refund fifteen shillings per dozen on empty bottles returned.

Threats of French and Spanish attacks and fear of Indian reprisals slowed the development of the back country west of the Pine Barrens until 1755, but thereafter settlement spread so rapidly that by 1760 the Low Country suddenly became aware of its potentialities for trade. By way of the Pedee, small craft ascended as far as the Cheraws to bring down the interior's flour and enable Charlestonians to reduce imports from Philadelphia and New York. Christopher Gadsden and John Crawford maintained stores at Cheraw Hill, and in 1760 Ancrum, Lance & Loocock began to advertise "Fine Carolina Flour" from Pine Tree Hill on the Wateree. Only the absence of mills prevented upcountry farmers from freeing the Charles Town market from dependence on Northern flour.

Charles Town continued to monopolize the lucrative trade with the Cherokee and other tribes, and, until the middle of the century, dressed deerskins accounted for sixteen per cent of its exports to England. After Augusta was founded in 1735, many traders located there, together with such city merchants as Robert Pringle and Macartan & Campbell. The latter firm carried "all sorts of Indian Trading" goods and accepted deerskins, beaver pelts, or "Georgia Currency" in payment. This was a large and profitable traffic, which from 1743 to 1760 provided these dealers with an annual average of over two hundred thousand pounds of deerskins for export, some of which had been brought from the Ohio country or the valley of the Arkansas River nearly a thousand miles to the westward.

After 1743 an astonishing amount of intra-province and intercolonial communication stemming from the economic and social necessities of a busy and gregarious people took place on this continent, an exchange of goods and ideas that steadily and increasingly tightened the bonds of colonial union. No concept about the last thirty-five years of the colonial period is more demonstrably erroneous than the one that the colonies were isolated one from another in thought and in deed, that travel by land was infrequent, and that even by water there was more intercourse from one to the mother country than from colony to colony. Actually the exact opposite was true. Common economic and social experience and points of view had to precede political union, and these the colonial cities supplied by so persistently improving the means of communication and travel that many more Americans went to and fro in their extensive new country than did those fabled travelers the Europeans in their own lands.

Intercity relations vastly improved despite the wars. Packet vessels ran between towns with freight and passengers on something approaching fixed schedules. From New York, sloops regularly sailed up Long Island Sound to Newport and Connecticut towns; yachts and smaller craft ascended the Hudson to Albany, and numerous "passage boats" plied back and forth to Staten Island and East Jersey as far as New Brunswick. The Schermmerhorns, based at Charles Town as well as at Manhattan, operated the earliest and most regular long-distance packet, though Philadelphians dispatched vessels periodically to both Charles Town and Rhode Island. New York and the Quaker City also led in establishing the first transatlantic packets. In 1755 New York assumed its position, never relinquished, as the principal entrepôt for England when the British government inaugurated monthly fast-sailing packets from Falmouth to Manhattan.

In the pursuit of trade with the countryside beyond the environs of the cities, easy water transport from nearby localities was widely employed and gave rise to secondary towns where produce could be gathered for transfer to larger ports. Regular boat service from Boston to Lynn commenced as early as 1746. Similarly, periaguas and canoes ran up the Ashley and Cooper or behind the Sea Islands to gather shipments of rice and indigo for Charles Town; while Savannah soon grew as the collection and distribution center of Georgia because of its connection by sloop with the South Carolina metropolis. From Lewes to Trenton up and down both shores of the Delaware and into its many tributary navigable rivers and creeks went multifarious shallops, yachts, and "flats" carrying goods to and from its great emporium. In the fifties above Trenton Falls as far as the Minnisink Range, shallow-draft Durham boats, so called from the place of their origin, took on cargoes of barreled flour or meats, and bar or pig iron for Philadelphia. Stage boats from the city to Burlington and Borden's Town connected with stagecoaches for Perth Amboy, and other boats went down the river to Reedy Island, whence coaches set out for Annapolis after 1756. As a result, villages and towns such as Marblehead, Salem, Providence, New London, New Haven, Albany, Perth Amboy, New Brunswick, Trenton, Burlington, Salem, Bristol, Wilmington, and Savannah grew along with the large centers and shared in their prosperity. By 1760 some of them even showed signs of rivaling the older communities.

Overland communication and travel between major cities was an accepted feature of colonial life, as Dr. Hamilton's journal of his Northern tour in 1744 with its serio-comic review of life along the highroad vividly demonstrates. Travelers of all ranks made their contribution to the emergence of an intercolonial solidarity that the rulers in the mother country little suspected. The growth of inland population astounded the provincials themselves, as it generated pressing demands for improved traveling conditions and communication—for roads, ferries, bridges, better navigation, transportation, and postal service. Henceforth colonial assemblies listened to petitions from town and country and, recognizing their validity, frequently acted upon them. Military needs pointed in the same direction. Consequently these seventeen years witnessed the laying out of the main lines of the American inland system of communications as they would be until the coming of the canal and railroad. In the *South Carolina Almanack* for 1756, one could find a description of the main highway from Savannah northward and eastward to Boston and faraway Portsmouth—the present U.S. routes 17 and 1.

Travel between Boston and Newport had been relatively heavy since 1736, when the first stage line over the seventy-mile route was opened. Jonathan Foster of Boston commenced a weekly carrier service in 1745, guaranteeing to carry goods and transact business for his patrons, and Mathew Pate of Newport immediately provided him with the competition needed to ensure good service. In 1757 Robert Pate, apparently Mathew's son and successor, announced that he would accommodate passengers with "good Horses and Chairs" as well as carry parcels.

Highways in Massachusetts and Rhode Island were adequate for the demands of this traffic, and for sleighs in winter. Those of New York, New Jersey, and Pennsylvania were generally acceptable, but the "rough roads" of Connecticut were proverbially bad. Dr. Hamilton, familiar with English highroads, found little to complain about in the colonies, and the evidence is that American thoroughfares comp red more than favorably with the wretched roads of the British Isles before the advent of Telford and Macadam. Building of roads and improvements in existing highways characterized the era. Aided by subscriptions, John Dalley of Kingston, New Jersey, surveyed the road from Trenton to Perth Amboy in 1745, erecting "durable Marks" every two miles and at all crossroads to assist travelers; soon thereafter he extended his work to cover the entire route from Philadelphia to New York and published a map showing its principal features. Roads out of Charles Town for many miles were exceptions to the rule in the South, for they were very good and heavily traveled.

A considerable volume of freight, in addition to passengers, moved across New Jersey between Philadelphia and New York. The route began and ended by water, and in between, connecting stages, eventually four of them, bridged the distance between the ports. The first stage ran twice a week from New Brunswick to Trenton in 1744. With the partnership of O'Brien, Richards, & Borden in 1751, an entire trip came under one general management: by boat to Amboy, thence overland by wagon to Borden's Town on the Delaware, and downstream by boat to Philadelphia—a route claimed by them to be forty-eight miles shorter than that by way of New Brunswick. By 1756 a "Multiplicity of Business," despite the entry of several competitors into the traffic, encouraged Daniel O'Brien to keep two boats in service from New York to Amboy to connect with the stage to Burlington, with which he was now associated. Joseph Borden and the Richards brothers thereupon commenced a newspaper campaign to win this business back, promising to make the stage trip from their town to Amboy in one day; and about the same time one Daniel opened a line from Cooper's Ferry across from Philadelphia to Middletown and Sandy Hook. Emulating the success of these stage lines, John Hughes & Company inaugurated one from the lower Delaware to the headwaters of the Chesapeake, connecting with passage boats from Philadelphia and Annapolis in 1757. Three years later George Honey drove his stage weekly to Lancaster, thereby making possible passenger travel in and out of the metropolis in all directions.

The most important and heavily thronged highway in all America was the Great Philadelphia Wagon Road running west to Lancaster, then turning southward to York, winding on into the Valley of Virginia, and finally debouching through a gap onto the Carolina Piedmont. Over this road coursed swelling trains of Scotch-Irish and German immigrants, afoot, on horseback, or driving two- and four-wheeled horse or oxcarts on their way in search of new lands and homes. Important towns and villages grew out of this migration.

The sixty miles of this great inland highroad between the metropolis and Lancaster were crowded with vehicles and travelers most of the year. Tons of produce from the four bountiful interior counties were conveyed to the Wissahickon mills and Delaware wharves by "Dutch Waggons." Lewis Evans thus described them in 1753: "the Oeconomy of the Germans has since Taught us the method of bringing this produce to Market, from the remotest part at small Expence. Their Method is this, ev'ry Farmer in our province almost has a Waggon of his own, for the Service of his Plantation, and likewise horses for Tillage; in the Spring and Fall of the Year . . . they load their Waggon and furnish themselves and beasts with provender for the Journey. The Waggon is their Bed, their Inn, their everything; many of them will come one hundred and fifty Miles without Spending one Shilling." In addition, professional wagoners drove back and forth between Philadelphia and Lancaster regularly, carrying freight and performing customary services. Contemporaries thought the province had nine thousand wagons in 1760; the arrival of sixty in one day in Philadelphia occasioned no comment. Riding out the Germantown road as far as Chestnut Hill in May 1755, Daniel Fisher declared that he was "almost choked with the Dust raised by the wagons, etc., I met," and soon public leaders called attention to the work of the Dublin Society in advocating the use of gravel "Close and firm" as a road surface and pointed to the abundance of gravel in Pennsylvania. Wagoners like Daniel Morgan, who learned his trade in the colony, were a rough lot, often refusing to give way to other vehicles, and inspired Christopher Saur to instruct his countrymen in road courtesy through the *Pensylvanische Berichte:* that empty wagons coming from the city should always turn aside, otherwise "so machen sich Teutsche bey den Englishen stinckent."

II

At any time in the eighteenth century a person trading overseas incurred great risks; at best he found it a speculative enterprise, with none of the stability attending business in our own day—nor could he fall back on the guarantees of government. Colonial merchants found it hard to win a fortune amid the vicissitudes of wind, wave, and war, particularly the last, and the period was one of incessant strife, opening with a maritime struggle against the Spanish that broadened in 1744 to include French menaces on both sea and land and not ending for the inhabitants of the American cities until General Amherst took Montreal in 1760.

Let no reader assume that actual fighting was alien to the townsman. Every ship fortunate enough to make one of the harbors brought stories of the *guerre de course* conducted so fiercely and so effectively by the Spanish and French. Boston and Newport went all out in King George's War, and the dismal failure and callous mismanagement of the British campaign against Cartagena aroused bitterness in New England. Only one Yankee out of ten ashore and afloat survived the horrible experience in the West Indies. When the provincial troops returned from Jamaica early in 1743, a Boston newspaper summed up the anguish of the town: "It is a very melancholy Reflection, that of the five hundred Men sent from this province in five Vessels at the first Embarkation, besides Recruits sent at sundry Times since, (not to mention two or three hundred sent from Rhode Island) there should not be a sufficient Number left to employ one Vessel to bring them home." Tales of discrimination between "the European and American Land Forces" by British officers aroused the ire of the colonials. In fact the very use of the label *American* in the communiqués spread the resentment that was beginning to find expression in New England. As a counter to such condescension, however, the colonials never ceased talking about the display of military ineptitude they knew so well at first hand.

In striking contrast, the mighty New England effort in the successful reduction of the fortress at Louisburg in 1745 and the consequent elimination of Gallic commerce-destroyers fired the Yankees' self-esteem, fostered overconfidence in their martial prowess, and even commanded admiration at Manhattan and on the Delaware:

> *Britannia strove a Carthagena to gain,*
> *While numbers perish'd on the wat'ry Main;*
> *And Wentworth's Forces languish'd ev'ry Day,*
> *'Till Rum and Fevers swept whole Hosts away.*

But Louisburg proved that in valor:

> *. . . the British Breed*
> *In Western Climes their Grandsires far exceed,*
> *And that New England Schemes the Old surpass,*
> *As much as solid Gold does tinkling Brass;*
> *And that a Pepp'rell's and a Warren's Name,*
> *May vie with Marlb'rough and a Blake for Fame.*

War struck at Philadelphia through its shipping. "Our Vessels are Reduced to about one Third of the number we had belonging to the Port att the Beginning of the Spanish war, since when we have had lost and taken that we know off about Sixty Sail," Samuel Powel of Philadelphia wrote to a London correspondent in 1745, and "if the War Continues att Least it must make our City grow very Poor."

King George's War may have come to an end in Europe in 1748, but not so in the Caribbean; inhabitants of New York in 1750 declared that their "Channel of Trade to the West Indies is almost blocked up"; Governor James Glen told a similar tale about Charles Town when privateers out of St. Augustine continued to cruise off the Carolina coast for prizes. As late as 1752 a Spanish *guardacosta* manned by a French crew seized a vessel bound from Jamaica to Charles Town off Mole St. Nicholas. Among six English ships detained at the Mole in January 1753 were three from New York and one from Philadelphia. Tired of calling on the mother country in vain, the colonials, in 1753, began to regard all Spaniards taken in *guardacostas* as pirates, and a Jamaica admiralty court so judged them; but complaints from the Spanish minister brought orders against the practice from London.

Victory in this war meant greater safety, glory, and satisfaction for the Northern colonies—but at a heavy price. Economic dislocation and unprecedented expenditures, a Bostonian reminded his fellows in 1748, had been augmented by "the prodigious Hardships we daily suffer, by the Diminution of the most useful part of our Inhabitants, particularly in two fatal Expeditions. By these and other Means I suppose we have lost, in the Compass of three Years, near one fifth of our Males; and the most of these in the Flower of Youth." The return of Louisburg to France in 1748, however justifiable the reasons, served only to convince the colonists that they were regarded as expendable. When the news of the evacuation of the island of Rattan and the embarkation of the troops for Jamaica in August 1749 reached Boston, the colonial press poured forth its bitterness: "O rare Peace! O f..mous Management! Farewel Trade! Farewel Honour!—Well, if the Sacrifice of Cape-Breton and Rattan prove us bad Politicians, they will at least prove us good Christians; for it may be truly said (our Enemies being Judges) that we don't Sacrifice that which cost us nothing."

When the final contest with France unofficially began in the Ohio country, townsmen, familiar with the war at sea, tended to look upon it as an inland extension of the maritime struggle that had never ceased. Soon, however, the stunning defeats at Great Meadows and the Monongahela were chronicled in detail by the Philadelphia press, followed by eyewitness accounts and tales of chilling horror by survivors of the Indian raids, which came closer and closer to the thickly settled portions of the western frontiers. Preparations for defense took place on all sides. Military or naval activities disrupted the normal life of the cities; fortifications again became matters of public concern; and even in peace-loving Philadelphia the local levies paraded, and Quaker citizens, fearful for their "liberties," debated whether these were more compromised by the French or by the first militia law of Penn's province. Charlestonians, ever alert for an attack from Florida or a rising of the Acadian refugees, mounted a military guard every night.

The events of the French and Indian War took an extra toll from Boston. Understandably people were war-weary before the conflict officially broke out. "Our Troops for Nova Scotia hope will Embark this week," sighed Stephen Greenleaf in 1755, "for tho' they Scatter some Money in Town, yet we grow very tired of them, and think it high time they should be on Duty." A year later he told a Newport acquaintance that "trading seems under great discouragement here, notwithstanding our navigation in general has been more successful than for many years past." He thought they had but one way to save themselves, and that was to retrench their expensive living. Nevertheless, inspired by Governor Shirley, Boston put forth the greatest war effort in money and taxes of all America. The unrestrained joy with which other colonies greeted the final reduction of Louisburg in 1758 by Amherst and Boscawen was tempered at the Bay Town by some inhabitants with long memories. Doubtless recalling their own abortive triumph of 1745 as well as heavy losses to Louisburg privateers of fishermen and merchant sailors from the Grand Banks all the way south to Boston Light, they had little stomach for making overmuch of this second conquest, and that by British regulars too. The doings of the press gang and insurance premiums of "thirty Guineas percent" on voyages to London only added to their gloom. No testimony to the effect of the war on the city's well-being is more pointed than the bankruptcy notices of twenty-eight merchants, shopkeepers, and master craftsmen published in the *Boston Evening Post* at the very time of the second capture of Louisburg and before the Privy Council disallowed the Massachusetts law permitting this form of relief to hard-pressed citizens, because "not a tenth part of its Creditors are resident" in the province.

It would be difficult to overrate the effect of the Anglo-French struggle upon the American cities, particularly upon their economic life. Defense of the colonies was an important consideration in the commercial thinking of the mother country, which until 1740 had always shouldered the entire burden. Then when numerous calls for help against depredations by enemy privateers cruising out of Louisburg, Havana, and the French West Indies came from the colonists, England not only invited but urged and cajoled them into sharing the defense with men, ships, and money. In so doing she called into being a relationship that created tensions and uncovered differences between herself and her colonies which relentlessly moved from a state of annoyance to one of profound irritation, and eventually to irreconcilability.

Partly in response to the calls of the mother country and in part the desire to "annoy our enemies," but most of all because of the shifting of normal channels of commerce and the hope of restoring their dwindling fortunes, merchants turned to private warfare. Letters of marque and private war vessels were needed to protect English and colonial shipping against French and Spanish corsairs, but it was the lure of huge and quick profits that drew seafarers of all ranks into privateering.

Although every city ventured into the game, New York was easily the leading privateer port. " 'Tis certain the Spirit of Privateering has prevailed greatly in this City, and but few of those fitted out here, have returned home empty, in comparison to those from other Places," commented the *New York Post Boy*. Between 1743 and 1748 at least thirty-one privateers fitted out at Manhattan, and the courts condemned seventy-nine of the prizes brought in. When King George's War ended, nine vessels were still cruising, and seven new ones were preparing to sail, for the New York privateers often paid handsome shares to their crews and built fortunes for their owners. The sight of four letters of marque standing up the harbor convoying six captures laden with valuable cargoes and thousands of pounds of specie in August 1744 could not but evoke "the general acclamation of the Public," and likewise when the daring of Captain John Burgess, whose undermanned *Royal Catherine* took *Le Mars* with 157 Frenchmen after only three broadsides off Sandy Hook, was known, all New York enthusiastically approved the Corporation's gift of a gold box containing the freedom of the city along with pieces of plate from the merchants.

When fighting began again in 1754, New York once more authorized the issuance of privateering commissions, and by the time the official declaration of war was made in June 1756, Manhattan venturers had twelve privateers either ready or preparing, and by November the *Mercury* reported nineteen cruising, five in the harbor, three on the stocks, and one expected from London. Over thirty went out the next year, more were building, and fourteen prizes estimated at £100,000 had been brought in. Indeed, all Gotham was ready to cruise for fame and fortune. The activity reached its height in 1759 when forty-eight ships were commissioned, manned by 5,670 seamen under the command of such fighters as Captain Robert Troup, David Fenton, Isaac Sears, and Alexander McDougall. James De Peyster, with an interest in eleven privateers, Waddell Cunningham and Lawrence Kortright in ten each, and many others in four to seven ships, grew rich. Prize courts condemned captures made from Barbados northward, and in Gotham taverns auctioneers passed the bottle to stir up bidding on vessels and cargoes. Competent authority states that many venturers doubled their investments during the war. Even lawyers raked in fees from mariners like George Sutton, who made his will in favor of his landlady, Sarah Egan, before he went to sea.

In the light of profitable beginnings in the early part of the century, Newport found privateering especially congenial, and when Captain Griffiths's schooner returned from the Caribbean in 1743 with reports of one prize netting each sailor five hundred pieces of eight, the rush to sign on for cruises began, and more than twelve hundred joined up in 1744. Rhode Island shipyards rang with activity as merchants hurriedly fitted out ships, hoping they too would clear £10,000 sterling. During King George's War a total of fifty-two commissions were issued. When John Banister, Philip Wilkinson, Sueton Grant, Daniel Ayrault, and, the leader of them all, Godfrey Malbone, sought crews, they capitalized on the fears Boston sailors had of the navy's press gang and encouraged them to "fly to Rhode Island to avoid it." When Governor Shirley tried to procure enough men for the Cape Breton expedition, he protested that "there are at this time many hundreds of foreign seamen daily walking the Streets of Newport, whilst scarce one is to be found in Boston," and he had to resort to press warrants. Although such "brisk and brave

Rhode Islanders" as Godfrey Malbone and Henry Collins made fortunes out of this business, Dr. Douglass concluded that as a group "they had bad Success," and it is clear that even with fewer vessels commissioned, New York was the greater gainer.

The major role in privateering during the French and Indian War has generally been accorded to Newport, and her citizens have been accused of preferring prize money to imperial welfare. Rhode Island actually issued thirty-five commissions to Newport ships before 1760, and about one third of the capital's adult males, including slaves, went a-cruising. Although an occasional rich prize was taken, most merchants, such as Metcalf Bowler, the Malbones, and the Champlins, had little to show but "Ill success" for their ventures. Henry Collins, leading local patron of culture in former times, came to complete ruin from privateering.

Boston also caught the fever in 1744, and nine vessels were fitted out. The tremendous effort required by the Louisburg enterprise, however, sapped all energies at the same time that Newport drained Boston's manpower. Two of the Bay's topping gentry, Edmund Quincy and Edward Jackson, earned a rich return from their letter-of-marque sloop *Bethel,* whose glorious encounter with the *Jesus, Maria, and Joseph* yielded a prize of over 471,000 milled dollars; a parade of armed sailors escorted 163 chests of silver and gold from the wharf to Quincy's house, and, quite properly, the owner commissioned an oil painting of the sloop. In the fifties, suffering from a severe economic decline, Boston merchants sent out only about half a dozen ships; doubtless they either sensed surer gains elsewhere or lacked the capital to invest in vessels.

Private warfare held no appeal for Quaker merchants, and the few ships that sailed from Philadelphia usually had their backing from Anglicans and Presbyterians. Captain John Sibbald of the *George* on one cruise took two ships valued at £45,000 sterling, which with other captures worth £90,000, made some of the "greatest booty" of any colonial privateer in the war. On another occasion Sibbald came in with 34,000 pieces of eight for his owners. Small wonder that after such stories Frederick Smith, a hatter, proposed to command his own forty-gun ship, advertising for subscribers to fit her out at fifty pounds a share! By November 1744 Philadelphia had thirteen craft out cruising, but in May 1746 Davey & Carson advised London correspondents that "privateering here is Brought to a very low ebb" from too much competition. At this time over 113 private war vessels had been commissioned by the colonies, and pickings were no longer good.

Although few privateers sailed out of Philadelphia, perhaps the most spectacular commander of the French and Indian War was Captain John MacPherson of the *Britannia,* twenty guns, from the city on the Delaware. Already wounded nine times, this fighting Scot fell in with a French warship of thirty-six guns in May 1758. A cannon-shot carried away his right arm and he had seventy men killed and wounded before he struck his colors in a bloody encounter off Monte Cristi. By September, however, he was back on the Main taking prize after prize, a single one of them netting him £18,000 "in cash." At Martinique in May he impudently notified the French that if they did not yield an English prize to him, he would "come in and beat down the Town." The French naturally refused, and by noon his guns had so battered the fort that his crew landed and destroyed half the town and its shipping, with the loss of only two men. He arrived home in June, having taken eighteen vessels, "mostly small," on the way. In November he decided to beach himself and invest his large fortune in partnership with one Miranda at a store on Stamper's Wharf. Meanwhile the *Britannia* sailed again under Captain Taylor, but unsuccessfully. With his arm healed, MacPherson took over her quarterdeck in October 1760 and advertised a cruise, stressing that the decline of Britain's war forces permitted seven hundred Frenchmen on the seas, "which is a great Encouragement to Adventurers." He sailed on the 6th of the month for even greater triumphs in the Caribbean.

The merchants of Charles Town sent out a few privateers, but the gains for the city were pretty well restricted to the refitting business for Northern privateers and an increased activity in prize courts. Both of these naturally depended on the successes and failures of the venturers of the North.

Privateering made lasting gains for such a small percentage of merchants that they had to look elsewhere for profits. During Queen Anne's War resourceful Yankees had discovered possibilities in trading profitably outside the Empire, and, despite the obnoxious and celebrated Molasses Act of 1733, had continued to do so. In time of war, exchanging provisions and lumber for molasses and sugar with the French in the Caribbean was not only illegal, but treasonable. Weighty arguments can be advanced on either side of the question of the expediency of trade with the enemy. Some persons regarded it as a kind of warfare that enabled the colonists to earn the wherewithal to fight elsewhere; on the other hand, naval officers insisted it delayed the collapse of the enemy by nearly a year in each conflict. This much must be remembered, however, that *nationalism* and *patriotism* as understood today did not then exist. Many colonial gentlemen sincerely believed that the clandestine traffic they pursued entailed no stigma of treason or loss of respectability, and a large proportion of the citizens agreed with them.

Whatever the justification for trading with the enemy, it is certain that a large amount of it took place in King George's War. The traffic flowed in several channels. It went through neutral ports such as Surinam and St. Eustatius, where the Dutch reaped a nice middleman's profit by exchanging English provisions for French sugar and molasses. Another stratagem that grew in favor was sailing ostensibly as a "flag of truce" under a license to exchange prisoners with the enemy but actually with intent to trade. Illegal traffic could also take place by use of false ship's papers.

The Rhode Island port, with its location and surroundings almost designed by nature for smuggling, became the American center of clandestine commerce in both wars of this period. Newporters tried every device and, in addition, opened a forbidden intercourse in tea and European goods with Amsterdam and Rotterdam. Flags of truce were the preferred means, and one could acquire them from provincial officials without much difficulty. Shirley declared in 1748 that over sixty flags had sailed from Rhode Island to San Domingo and Martinique in the past eighteen months, and many had cleared without a single prisoner or prior inspection of their cargoes, which ordinarily contained lumber and provisions for the enemy. Joseph Whipple's brigantine, *Victory,* left without clearance papers in January 1747 for Cap François, where 300 quintals of refuse cod, 20 barrels of shad, and 200 bundles of onions were traded for 174 casks of molasses, and got safely back without paying any duties. A profitable voyage that! The following year crafty John Banister wrote to his Amsterdam correspondent that "the sweets of French Trade p[er] way of flags of Truce has put me upon turning my Navigation that way, which is the most profitable business I know of." He had a prospect of a flag, "which if I effect a Cargoe of Sugars will clear upwards of Twenty thousand pounds," but, my friend, of this you "must not lisp a word."

The other cities followed Newport's lead. Governor Shirley of Massachusetts wrote to the Board of Trade in 1743 about "the Illicit-Trade which appears to have been carried on in this Province and some of the neighboring colonies (within this past Year more especially,)" and Samuel Powel of Philadelphia refused to buy any legally imported tea, because he could not compete with the Boston men who "make no boggle at any clandestine trade they can get any thing by." French prisoners for flag-of-truce vessels were permitted to walk openly in the streets of New York in 1744. Four years later a "Fair Trader" warned that scarcely a week passed that illicit traders did not supply the enemy, going in and out of the port "under the specious Name of Flags of Truce." Philadelphians also quietly participated in such commerce, but the Charles Town Grand Jury came out courageously on April 15, 1745 with an indictment of the practice, through which the enemy received provisions, lumber, ammunition, arms, and vital intelligence. Nevertheless the *South Carolina Gazette* continued to report the coming and going of flags from Cap François and St. Augustine. At the very end of King George's War the arrival of ships from England drastically lowered the price of European goods, but a Boston newspaper complained that bread and flour were higher "than was ever known here, occasioned too visibly by the illicit Trade with the French Islands; a Trade which must undoubtedly in Time ruin many Fair Traders, however it may enrich those who are the Carriers of so pernicious and destructive a Practice."

Cessation of hostilities after the Treaty of Aix-la-Chapelle in 1748 did not end illicit commerce, which troubled both French and English officials. Reports had it that on conclusion of peace there were in the West Indies "near seventy Sail from North America, which hurried away with Provisions, &c. to the French Islands," but upon being refused entry, they had to return to English ports, "which has reduced the Price of every Thing produced in these Parts to almost nothing." In spite of stories that the French at Léogane had been "extremely severe and unjust in their treatment of our countrymen lately," the traffic continued. In 1750 James Birket discovered at Newport many "Transient French Merchants" concerned with the trade to Cape Breton (now returned to the French) and Cap François, besides a plentiful supply of Dutch goods, which had been paid for with Honduras logwood shipped to Holland, and had been "run [in] by the Connivance of good natured Officers who have a feeling Sense of their Neighbours Industry." Robert Robinson of the Customs, however, placed the blame on Deputy Governor Ellery, who would not back up the officers and allowed Newporters to unload French and Dutch vessels behind Conanicut Island. "By this management, Sir, you may see how the power of the King's officers is eclips't. . . . I am weary of complaining." Under oath in 1752, a sea captain testified "it was notorious" that William Allen & Company of Philadelphia, because of their large imports from Léogane, always undersold other dealers in "Sugar, Rum and Molasses" who had brought them in legitimately from the British islands, and also, because Abraham Taylor, the Collector of Customs, "was one of the Company," the "Trade must be entirely engrossed by them." It was indeed hard to beat the combination of collector and chief justice!

During the French and Indian War the only city not deeply committed to trade with the enemy was Charles Town; the others entered into it with greater vigor than ever, and Rhode Island again took the lead. In 1755 Newport and Boston traders carried provisions from the Middle colonies to Cape Breton, where they took on French sugars and molasses. The main stream of commerce, however, ran from New York and Philadelphia to the Caribbean. Fully apprised of these developments, royal authorities directed the colonial governors to proclaim embargoes on the export of foodstuffs and, as soon as war was declared, ordered the navy to break up such traffic in the West Indies. These measures proved inadequate, as wary skippers again resorted to flags of truce and trade through neutral ports. When the navy closed up St. Eustatius, trade shifted to Monte Cristi or the "Mount" in the Spanish portion of Hispaniola near the French frontier, where cargoes might be shipped to and from Cap François. To this Godforsaken hole, vessels of the four Northern ports resorted in ever greater numbers until by 1760 over one hundred rode in its harbor at one time—all employing this rather dubious subterfuge to screen a direct trade with the enemy. Governor Bull of South Carolina also pointed at the clandestine relations of Newport with Florida and New Orleans.

Alarmed at the "enormous extent" of Rhode Island's illicit commerce in 1757, James De Lancey ordered Captain Isaac Sears to cruise off Block Island in a New York province vessel and intercept it. Putting into Newport, he was jailed on a trumped-up charge for a few days. Before very long this shifty captain was himself deeply involved in the Monte Cristi business as master of a sloop belonging to Gerardus Beekman of Manhattan. As a matter of fact, although British officials blamed Newport for the major portion of this trade, there is ample evidence that ultimately the greatest number of vessels came from Philadelphia and New York, whose meats and cereals the French so desperately needed. When an embargo of 1759 prevented shipment of provisions, New Yorkers began buying molasses and paying for it with the city's limited supply of cash, which the French, in turn, used to purchase provisions from the neutral islands. Manhattan merchants also conducted a thriving business directly with Holland and Hamburg, whence ships unladed off Sandy Hook before proceeding to port in ballast, while their cargoes of tea, gunpowder, canvas, and other smuggled goods passed overland by wagon to New York and Philadelphia. According to William Smith, the customs officers winked at these proceedings.

The use of flags of truce aroused the British ire more than any other dodge employed by the colonials. If Newport deserves most of the obloquy for this "cartel Trade," it was New York that kept it going, though the greatest abuse was in Philadelphia, where Governor Denny openly sold blank flags for twenty pounds or less, as did Governor Francis Bernard of New Jersey. Prisoners were hard to get in the Middle colonies; so the merchants there paid high prices to Rhode Island privateers for them. Henry Collins of Newport got into trouble in 1758 for buying French prisoners at Boston to meet voracious demands from merchants at New York and Philadelphia. Philip Cuyler, withdrawing from unprofitable privateering the following year, began procuring flags-of-truce permits through his Newport connections, John and William Tweedy, Richards & Coddington, and Joseph Wanton. Can you get a flag, leaving the prisoner's name blank, "as I am unacquainted with the methods they have at your Place for to obtain a flag?" he inquired. But he soon learned: "Purchase me as many flags you can" even if they cost £500 each. This was a cash business, and Cuyler felt safe in asking several Newport connections to get him commissions for flags "on the best Terms" as well as a "Certificate to Carry a few Goods." He joined Richards & Coddington in a flag venture to "Misasipia" in 1759, and the following May he endeavored to shift all of his flags to the New Orleans route because the navy had throttled trade at the Mount. In December he sought assistance in clearing a sloop from New Haven to Jamaica without giving the required bond. The peak of this trade came in 1759, for another year saw the efforts of the Royal Navy to stamp it out meeting with marked success.

As the scene of the conflict was transferred to the West Indies after 1760, the sweets of trade with the French soon soured. James & Drinker of Philadelphia lamented that "the Capture of so many of our Ships that were in the Flag Trade loaded with Sugars is much felt by many merchants here." Colden believed that Manhattan traders had been "too generally concerned in this illegal trade and that the merchants of Philadelphia have been more so." From New York, David Jamison informed a Newport correspondent: "I am now about trying a Voyage to our own Islands, since Trading with the Enemy has turn'd out so very ill." This savors of desperation!

Privateering and trade with the enemy might have their ups and downs, might enrich some and impoverish more according to the vagaries of warfare, but then as now, government contracts seemed to entail little risk and to pay off handsomely. In the first war Christopher Kilby threw much of the business of supplying the British Army and Navy to Thomas Hancock and associates at Boston, and this lone good fortune served to alleviate the town's acute commercial distress. New York also came in for a goodly share. James Alexander's correspondence shows what war meant in opportunities for a politically favored merchant to furnish food, shoes, clothing, and all kinds of equipment to troops at Albany. De Lancey & Watts, principal government agents, and Peter Van Brugh Livingston were among those who grew rich in the King's service.

Upon the outbreak of the French and Indian War, fortune indeed favored Manhattan, even before the official declaration. Charles Ward Apthorp, John Watts, Robert Crommelin, and William Bayard, because of government contracts, built up large credit balances at London and Amsterdam, against which they issued the bills of exchange needed by fellow merchants for remittances to Europe. Moses Franks, of the London house of Colebrook, Nesbit, & Franks, conveniently arranged for his brother David Franks of Philadelphia, and Jacob Franks, Oliver De Lancey, and his brother-in-law, John Watts, all of New York, to be made government agents, while Thomlinson & Hanbury, who received the money contract, designated Charles Apthorp & Company and Colonel William Bayard as colonial representatives at Boston and Manhattan. In 1755 New York was made the "general Magazine of Arms and Military Stores" as well as the concentration point for the forces, a decision that permitted many merchants to amass fortunes as subcontractors if they enjoyed the proper family connections. Although Philadelphia and Boston participated somewhat in this profitable business of supply, their combined share was not as large. As Benjamin Franklin readily admitted in 1756: "This only I can plainly see, that New York is growing immensely rich, by Money brought into it from all Quarters for the Pay and Subsistance of the Troops." Every year Gotham grew richer. John Watts told Isaac Barré that during the war the provincial customs receipts doubled, amounting to £10,000 currency annually, "the military being exceedingly public Spirited in the consumption of strong Liquors." Privateering, illegal trade, government contracts, and a free-spending soldiery combined most fortuitously with a superb location and the efforts of an energetic people to start New York on its rise to eventual primacy among American cities at the same time that it put into the coffers of many of its merchants the wealth to consolidate an aristocracy.

The conditions of conflict did not everywhere produce the same effects. Philadelphia ran a close second to New York, which was the grand beneficiary, and Charles Town seems to have recovered from the severe depression of the mid-forties. Boston suffered severely from the military expeditions it mounted, even more than from losses at sea, and its decision to go on a specie basis in 1749 caused immediate strain. Newport—small, lacking a hinterland, and always put to it to remain in the urban race—lost between ninety and one hundred ships by 1758 (twice as many as New York and four times as many as Boston). In pleading the town's case against a tax increase in 1759, James Honeyman stated that her merchants alone had "lost, in the course of their trade, upwards of two millions of money" since the war began, and the indirect loss this meant to the remainder of the inhabitants can only be guessed at. When Andrew Burnaby visited Newport, he learned that the final toll of shipping approached 150 sail and that trade was in a "very declining state." The same held true for all five cities at the close of 1760. Each Northern port had needed illegal as well as regular trade to survive in peacetimes, but these parlous years when all commerce was radically dislocated, as an English historian has so cogently put it, "proved once more that the burdens of patriotism were imposed by England and the West Indies but borne by . . . North America, and that America might not always find it convenient to fight in England's wars."

III

The commercial life of the cities was wholly controlled by the energetic colonial merchants. As a class, in war or peace, they strove with imagination, daring, and notable success in international and intercolonial commerce to acquire the capital for expanding the economy of a new country. In so doing, some of them won large fortunes while others failed and dropped lower in the economic scale. The number of merchants doing business in each seaport, however, mounted annually, and the range of their fortunes, in contrast with the more modest estates of small traders, became wider than in earlier years, as the richest took their places with the Southern planters among the colonial bigwigs worthy of the brush of a Smibert, a Feke, a Blackburn, or a Theus. Collectively they embodied a ruling class that displayed more self-conscious unity of opinion than any other segment of the colonial population.

Who were these men and from what walks of life did they come? Most of those who acquired great wealth and rose to public prominence belonged to families of known affluence and influence in either town or country. Such for instance were the Hutchinsons and Lloyds of Boston, the Newport Redwoods and Banisters, the Beekmans of New York, the Powels and Allens of Philadelphia, and the Wraggs and Manigaults of Charles Town. At this time many urban businesses were being conducted by members of the second and third generation of such families as the Hancocks, Van Hornes, and Morrisses. Then there were those who came from the British Isles with sufficient capital—£2,000 sterling was the minimum—to establish themselves as merchants in the New World. Philadelphia attracted many of these: Charles Willing from Bristol, the Hamiltons and Cunninghams from Scotland and Ireland, and English-born Lynford Lardner, who got off to a flying start by marrying the daughter of William Branson, whose annual income from trade in 1743 was £4,000, supplemented by £400 in city house rents. Captain John MacPherson easily assumed a favored position among the Quaker City's merchants with a fortune won by privateering.

Not a few mercantile families had relatives or connections by marriage in two or more ports of the Empire. The Schermmerhorns could be found at New York and Charles Town, the Amorys at Boston, Salem, and Charles Town. The Lloyds of Queen's Village on Long Island placed sons in New York and Boston, and the presence of members of the House of Apthorp in these same cities proved unusually fortuitous when war contracts were let. Perhaps no colonial family better exemplifies these ramifications than the Quaker Redwoods, whose paterfamilias was Abraham of Newport, but whose sons and nephews prospered in Antigua, where the great plantation at Casada Gardens produced the sugar and molasses used by the family in trading with Rhode Island, Philadelphia, and Bristol in England. New York Crugers also had Bristol family connections. Birth, marriage, inheritance or good connections, and always the capital to start with virtually pointed the way of the wealthy to more wealth.

Few merchants were wholly self-made men. Occasionally an artisan forsook his trade and advanced to the countinghouse. Henry Laurens of Charles Town, son of a saddler, was one of these, as was the Newport silversmith Samuel Vernon. More often a man who began life as a retail shopkeeper, by dint of thrift and diligence, rose to considerable affluence. Perhaps the signal example was Thomas Hancock of Boston, who, as son of a country clergyman, started as a bookseller's apprentice, became a stationer in the twenties, and, at his death in 1764, bequeathed a great fortune of about £100,000 to his grateful nephew, John.

The lasting significance of the colonial merchant derived from the fact that he exercised his influence, not in a corporate capacity as in our own day, but in a highly individual manner. Personal integrity and ability enabled him to acquire and supervise most of the commercial and industrial life of his city and province, and this fact is constantly borne in upon anyone who reads the many fascinating letter books which have survived from that era, a sustained intercolonial correspondence of great import. By careful marriage alliances, common national or religious ties, as with the Scots, Jews, and Quakers, an intercolonial solidarity developed among the merchant gentry, who promoted intimate relationships along with trade. Nor were these merely paper bonds. As increase in travel by land as well as by sea took place, the families of colonial bigwigs came to know each other personally. They also drew together as they discovered common interests that transcended provincial, and often imperial, boundaries when war conditions forced them frequently to work in concert. To them, commerce was, in a very real sense, a way of life.

Like the businessman of today, the urban merchant's goal was the acquisition of wealth, but, despite the uncertainty of trade, he did not have to spend much time in his countinghouse. A few hours each day were enough; apprentices kept the accounts and copied out letters, and not a few merchants even retired early from the market place to live in ease at their country houses. Under such a dispensation these men, unlike their planter correspondents, came to be men of leisure—the only ones in all America. They had ample time for reading, conversation, fine dining, and contemplation, time in which to write long personal letters, keep diaries, and serve their communities in many ways. Moreover, the mercantile dynasties of the five cities and their growing satellites coalesced into the only recognized colonial social class. This group, which reached its apogee at the end of the French and Indian War, controlled the economic life of the colonies; through the assemblies and city governments it ruled with planter allies. The prestige of this gentry had never been so great before nor would it ever be again.

For the first time in colonial history some city merchants sought to invest accumulated capital in local enterprises other than shipping or commerce. In the Northern cities they were urged to this by the constant need to make returns for imports, and also because, during wartime, "prodigious profits" often seemed safer when invested in some form of industry than risked in a deranged trade. There had always been some manufactures conducted in each town, but after 1743 they became not only a permanent but an important feature of urban economic life as more capital was available.

The older maritime industries, those auxiliary to shipping, first felt the stimulus, and chief among them was shipbuilding, which flourished with the demand for new privateers and the replacement of ships lost in the wars. "We have from 10 to 15 Sail of large vessells now a building," Davey & Carson of Philadelphia advised a London merchant in 1747; we can "build a vessell from 10 to 15 percent cheaper" than you can, "and as good." By 1754 there were twelve yards along the Delaware where twenty large ships could be constructed at once, but Pennsylvanians did not build as good ships as those of Old and New England. "Our Ship Carpenters never season a Stick," Lewis Evans admitted, "whence you may know the short duration of Ships built here." Nevertheless the industry centering at Kensington prospered and provided employment for hundreds of artisans, not only at the ways themselves but in ropewalks, anchor forges, smithies, sail lofts, cooperages, and dozens of crafts whose products were needed in the building of a great ship.

The best and cheapest colonial vessels were produced at Newport. In soliciting orders from such important Londoners as John Thomlinson or Jacob & Clark, John Banister claimed he could build a vessel "near 20 p cent" under what it could be done at Boston. Although sloops were the Rhode Island specialty, ships as large as four hundred tons slid off the ways, and many a slaver for Joseph Manesty and other Guinea traders of Liverpool came from Narragansett Bay. Once, when nearby yards could not oblige him, Banister contracted with a Newbury shipwright, to the great disapproval of Manesty, who wrote: "I beg no Vessel may be built for me out of Rhode Island Government. I hate everything Eastward of Martha's Vineyard as my men may be imprest, the Ship froze up and many charges arise which I should otherwise avoid in Newport." The industry gave Newport merchants one of their most profitable returns, and they kept yards at Taunton, Bristol, and Providence, in addition to those in their own city, busy with orders for "Topsail Ships," sloops, and privateers of all sizes and rigs. Although much of the canvas, cordage, and ironwork needed on the larger vessels came from abroad, shipbuilding at Newport actually supported over twenty different arts and crafts, ranging from riggers and painters to tallow chandlers and instrument-makers like the famous Benjamin King.

The Boston Town Meeting of 1742 stated unequivocally that in the past the "greatest Advantage" it had reaped from an extensive London traffic "was by Ship Building which employed most of our Tradesmen." In 1746, however, the Meeting was bemoaning that this "ancient and almost only Manufacture the Town of Boston ever had" was gone to other places, especially Newbury. Where there had been forty-one keels laid down in 1738, there were only fifteen a decade later. Vessels constructed in other nearby towns were rated by John Custis of Virginia as "the worst ships in the world," and this reputation undoubtedly injured Boston's business even though the Bay Town's shipwrights were unexcelled. The decline of the industry contributed heavily to the city's economic plight, since the industry supported numerous trades.

Shipbuilding did not figure as prominently in the economic life of the other two cities. New York had three or four yards, and the Waltons took a great interest in the business, but despite the granting of thirty-one freedoms to shipwrights during King George's War and twenty-six in the next conflict, refitting and repairs rather than construction occupied their time. The same held true at Charles Town, where most merchants purchased what ships they needed from New England. Local shipyards, for the most part, turned out periaguas, large canoes, and small craft for the inland produce traffic. In 1749 Governor Glen sought to persuade the Assembly to encourage shipbuilders; the following year, a Scot, John Rose, opened an establishment that monopolized the refitting business of the Royal Navy, and so well did he fare that by 1761 he was able to retire with more than £65,749, being "reckon'd a Rich Man." This failure to develop shipbuilding on a large scale at Charles Town and New York explains in large measure the backwardness of those communities in the arts and crafts.

One of the manufactures growing out of urban maritime activities was the spermaceti-candle industry. Newporters had ventured into whaling in the thirties, but it was at Rehoboth in Massachusetts sometime after 1749 that an Englishman, Benjamin Crabb, exercised his "Sole Privilege" of making candles from spermaceti, or head-matter, taken from the sperm whale. When his works burned down late in 1752, he was engaged by Obadiah Brown to set up and operate a candle manufactory at Providence. Within four years Aaron Lopez, followed by Isaac Stelle & Company, and others had built a flourishing spermaceti-candle industry at Newport. Henry Lloyd of Boston carried Lopez's product, and at

Manhattan Philip Cuyler got his from William Tweedy. There were probably a dozen factories in New England by 1760 producing the most satisfactory candles yet devised, though it must be admitted that Governor Jonathan Belcher of New Jersey, who had tried some from Colonel Josiah Quincy's establishment, insisted that the so-called "odorless" candles had "as nausious a Stink as any other Whale oil."

Rum-distilling was second only to shipbuilding among urban industries. Here, too, Boston lost much of its former advantage, because not only did the British Caribbean islands distill much more of their molasses, but Watertown, Medford, and Charlestown (Mass.) entered into the manufacture. In 1743 Boston did not produce one third of the rum it made in 1735, and when war broke out, the molasses supply grew scarce. Nantucket rum won out in the Newfoundland trade, and in 1751 news of the erection at Halifax of "a large Distillery Works" by a former Bostonian aroused genuine fears that it would "deprive us of the Best Branch of our Trade to that Province."

Coastal trading, whaling, the fisheries, and the extensive Rhode Island slave traffic with the Guinea Coast took off the product of Newport's sixteen distilleries, an industry just twice the size of Boston's in 1760. Widow Ann Maylem and Madam Sarah Rumreil competed in the manufacture with James Rogers, Jabez Carpenter, Benoni Gardiner, Weeden & Bennett, and Benjamin Greene. New York customers preferred rum distilled from English molasses, but most of the "Kill Devil" shipped from Newport was, of course, made from the smuggled French variety. Samuel Freebody's "still House" catered principally to the slave trade: in January 1757, for example, Captain Walter Buffam purchased 1,023 gallons "in Guinea Cask" from him.

The capitals of the Middle colonies also manufactured large quantities of this fiery potation. In the forties the Beekmans, Verplancks, and others at New York had relied on Newport rum, but by 1753 they operated ten distilleries of their own. The leading "works," belonging to Livingston & Lefferts, was erected "at great expence" on ground behind Trinity Church leased from the Vestry. Philadelphia's investment in the rum manufacture was nearly as great. Peacock Bigger owned one still house in the city and another at Charlestown in Maryland, but the firm of Allen & Turner dominated the business; and Chief Justice Allen imagined that his stills produced a better article than the famed New England variety. Each community also had numbers of breweries that made beer for the export trade to such places as Charles Town, where no "Carolina Beer" was made until Nathaniel Scott opened his "Brew House" in 1752. Nor did the Southern port have a rum distillery before 1756, but, inspired by Bostonians, New Yorkers, and Philadelphians, whose sugar bakeries yielded steady profits, a group of Carolina proprietors had opened a "sugar House" to manufacture sugar, brown candy, treacle, and molasses in 1750. This venture, however, lasted only three years.

Because of its growing importance as a center for processing and shipping agricultural produce, Philadelphia assumed the lead in manufacturing, and, like their coreligionists in England, Quaker merchants were quick to see the advantage of investing in various industries. Anthony Morris, sometime Mayor of the city, had an interest in land, flour-milling, iron manufacture, and brewing. His brewery, begun in the 1680's by a forebear, still exists today as Perot & Sons, maltsters, the oldest business house in the United States. What might be termed the container industry—the making of all kinds of barrels, hogsheads, and casks for shipping flour, wheat, corn, ship's bread, biscuit, salted meats, beer, rum, and a dozen other products—brought into being a very large cooperage business that employed hundreds of artisans. Nehemiah Allen became one of the city's wealthy craftsmen through the profits of his cooperage. The hides of cattle butchered for export required a host of tanners and curriers to prepare leather for shoemakers, leather-breeches-makers, glovers, and sundry leatherworkers who made so many articles today demanding different materials. Indeed, more artisans were engaged in the leather trades than in the woodworking manufactories. Only a few miles from the city lay Germantown, already famed for woolen-stocking manufacture but actually more important for its leather goods. In the environs of Philadelphia, also, were flour mills, of which those along the Wissahickon Creek were the best known, as well as most of the colonial paper mills, which were coming under the control of Benjamin Franklin, printer. Somewhat farther distant flourished the celebrated iron furnaces of Pennsylvania, supplied chiefly with funds by Philadelphia merchants desiring pig and bar iron for export. Within the city's bounds, several linseed-oil mills and numerous smithies and foundries turned out nails, shovels, hoes, axes, hardware of several sorts, and bells.

Although no other city rivaled Philadelphia in the value and variety of its manufactures, Newport craftsmen concentrated on making several export items of high quality and originality of design, and in so doing earned a wide reputation. The Townsends, skilled cabinetmakers, who, with the Goddards, their kinsmen by marriage, evolved the impressive block or "Swell'd front" chests and desks, nevertheless expended most of their skills in fashioning cheap furniture for sea captains to take on consignment to the Southern or island colonies. Newport riding chairs sold well at New York. John Stevens and his fellow stonecutters earned renown for the beauty of the carved gravestones they sent everywhere. The Manhattan Beekmans purchased one of his handsome "Marble Hearth Stones," as well as one of William Claggett's superb clocks. Bostonians, New Yorkers, and Rhode Islanders paid no attention to the

Hat Act of 1732, and Newporters worked up a good "Counterband Trade" in beavers with the West Indies. Although New Yorkers prospered mightily in this war era, the city was slow to develop crafts, and when they were not importing from Europe, the citizens bought Newport furniture, "Boston Axes," and many Philadelphia items. Both at Manhattan and at Charles Town, tanning was the only industry of importance before 1760.

In 1743 Boston led all the cities in shipbuilding, the leather trades, meat-packing, hatmaking, the axe and hardware manufacture, cheap export furniture, and the fabrication of such horse-drawn vehicles as chaises, chairs, and chariots. One by one these industries suffered from the effects of the wars, high taxes, migration of workmen to nearby towns, and numerous contributory causes. Only the furniture and carriage business remained profitable when Quebec fell. Tradesmen suffered more than merchants in the economic decline of the forties, and the large number of unemployed poor embarrassed the city fathers.

Everywhere except Charles Town, especially after the mid-century, the cities were served by an increasing corps of craftsmen of all kinds. Philadelphia even exported them to New York, Maryland, and South Carolina. In skills and varieties of mysteries the colonial artisans emulated those of Europe, and under urban stimuli, familiar trades divided and subdivided—carpenters split up into joiners, housewrights, cabinetmakers, carvers, and chairmakers, and the blacksmiths into half a dozen specialized kinds of ironworkers. As a result they turned out better and more intricate articles. Craftsmen also tended more and more to make up goods for display in their shops for buyers who wandered in and to rely less upon "bespoke" or custom work, because their market steadily expanded and could be depended on. Artisans ordinarily belonged to the middle or lower classes, as in Europe, but they were coming to constitute a vertical rather than a horizontal segment of the urban population. Ascending from apprentice and journeyman to master, some of them grew rich and founded important families which ranked with the mercantile gentry. Among silversmiths, the Philadelphia Richardsons and Boston Hurds, and the Boston Bagnalls among watchmakers, are typical of these affluent and socially prominent families. Even at Charles Town it was not unusual for a successful craftsman to purchase land and slaves and set up for a planter. As the period ended it was clear that industrial activity would henceforth be an essential and permanent part of city life.

Although the wars curtailed importations of goods from Europe and slowed down ordinary business, these were years in which the volume and methods of retail marketing noticeably improved. Among importing merchants, the wholesaler and the one who sold by both wholesale and retail could be more readily distinguished, especially at Boston and Philadelphia. Often the wholesaler refrained from advertising in the newspapers, because he sold to "a regular sett of Customers" who came directly to his "store" for what they wanted. Allen & Turner, and the elder Samuel Powel of Philadelphia, and the Inmans and Quincys of Boston belonged to these "Old Traders," as did the New York Crugers, Gabriel Manigault of Charles Town, and Godfrey Malbone, the Guinea merchant and privateersman, who maintained a wharf and warehouse at Boston as well as at Newport. Their interest, according to the analysis of Henry Lloyd of Boston, lay principally in shipping and "Foreign Commerce" in contrast to "Town and Inland business."

The leading merchants numbered about one hundred in each of the three largest cities, and nearer forty at Newport and Charles Town. Most of them dealt by both wholesale and retail, with a growing preference everywhere for wholesale trading. Christopher Gadsden, chief among the native merchants of Charles Town, not only traded rice and large quantities of dry goods for slave clothing, but in 1756 took advantage of the war to turn an honest shilling or so in "Trooper's Belts, buff broad cloth, gold hat lace, carbines, fowling pieces, etc." Most of them sold "by large and small measure" at their warehouses, but some followed the custom of Jacob Richardson, who advertised to sell at wholesale from his store in Brenton's Row, or by retail at the shop in his Boston house.

Whether they dealt in great or small quantities, many merchants inclined to concentrate on a particular kind of European importation. Dry goods attracted most of them, but at Philadelphia William Logan carried wines, rum, sugar, and cocoa; William Bingham stocked saddlery and ship goods; James Wragg handled ironmongery and brassware. Near the Town Dock at Boston, Gilbert Deblois made a fortune in hardware and firearms "suitable for Privateers," but in November 1759 announced that henceforth he would sell "only by Wholesale (as he declines Retailing his Goods at the same low Rates they are sold by Wholesale to the great Disadvantage of these Persons that buy to sell again)." As he mounted the mercantile ladder, William Bowes continued to vend hardware in large and small amounts, engaging "to sell as cheap as can be bought in any Shop in Town."

With greatly enlarged populations and the presence of many privateersmen and soldiers who desired to make small purchases, those who bought to sell again gained in importance. Retailers, customarily referred to as "shopkeepers," acquired their stocks from merchants. Down at Newport a merchant, Sueton Grant, supplied the shop of Samuel Rhodes with dry goods. When the ship *Mercury* from London, Charles Hargrave master, docked at Philadelphia in December 1746, six firms advertised goods brought over in her, usually for cash or three months' credit. Soon the newspapers ran notices of shopkeepers like Alexander and John Forbes, whose offerings came from the shipment one of these merchants had received in the *Mercury*. The town of Boston earned a sizable income from renting shops near the Town Dock to retailers. In general the shopkeepers, like the merchants, restricted themselves to one or two items. At Boston, Israel Eaton carried good "English shoes, Women's Shoes of many Sizes," and Joseph Griggs sold "new and second hand wearing apparell." Daniel Fourtane's shop in Newport was stocked with china, sugar, indigo, and wax valued at £936 Rhode Island currency. Hadwen & Thurston kept the kind of grocery business one found in every town. Typical of city specialty establishments around Hanover Square in New York or any urban shopping center were those dispensing wines, notions (including "Hooks and Eyes"), tobacco, china, glassware, stationery, and teas. Perhaps no colonial emporium offered a richer and more expensive assortment of imported jewelry than the shops of John Paul Grimke and Joshua Lockwood of Charles Town. Nor were South Carolina shopkeepers, milliners, and tailors the only ones who prepared for a big business in mourning apparel on the death of George II in 1760.

Much urban retailing fell into the hands of women, for it was one of the few means for the sex to earn a living. Merchants' wives, like Elizabeth Schuyler of New York, frequently retailed for their husbands, and during long lonely periods the spouses of sea captains kept shop with silks, yarns, shoes, pins, ribbons, threads, buttons, and yard goods. As disasters at sea and in military campaigns created a disproportionate number of widows, the "relicts" turned to keeping store, often with considerable success. Mary Singleton Copley ran a tobacconist's shop and eventually moved it from Long Wharf to the fashionable upper end of King Street in Boston, where she continued to sell both wholesale and retail even after she married the musician Peter Pelham. Sarah Logan at Charles Town, Jane Blundell at New York, and Sarah Decoster, Susannah Newman, and Sarah Winser of Boston virtually monopolized the profitable trade with town and country in domestic and imported garden seeds. Although millinery, dry goods, and groceries were the favorite lines for women, they were to be found conducting a surprising variety of small retail enterprises, but only a few, such as the Franklins of Philadelphia and Boston, who sold their "genuine Crown Soap" at the post offices through family pull, ever got into the wholesale intercolonial trade.

Another popular method of disposing of goods was the auction. From the earliest times each community designated a public auctioneer, but most sales had been the kind familiar today—a house, the effects of a deceased person, or some sort of forced vendue. In this period, however, merchants who found themselves unable to move a consignment of goods through town shops and country stores, put such lots up at auction. Manhattan in particular took to this form of selling, and there the greatest number of auctioneers flourished. Captured enemy ships always went on the block too. A New York vendue master conducted so many auctions in 1755 that he felt safe in estimating the value of plate and furniture of "the First, Middling and Lower Classes of Householders" at £700, £200, and £40–20 respectively. Bostonians did not go in so much for auctions of goods in large quantities, but there was enough business to keep four establishments going. When "The New Auction Room" opened there in 1759, the proprietor, mindful of ungenteel scenes when bidding grew brisk, guaranteed to conduct sales "with Honor, Fidelity, Decency and Decorum—So that, even the Matron or the Damsel need not fear being offended, when they have a mind to come to buy a good Bargain."

In the other cities abuses in auctioneering aroused public resentment and brought complaints from shopkeepers against what they deemed unfair competition. In 1741 accredited vendue masters had to post bonds of £5,000 with the Town Treasurer of Newport, since experience had shown that many buyers "suffered considerable Loss by their Goods." On the other hand, a year later the auctioneers received permission to call special courts to try persons who failed or refused to pay for goods bid in. Their fees were limited to one and one half per cent of the value of the goods sold in 1747, and William Coddington, vendue master, grumbled in 1757 that allowing the marshal of the vice admiralty court as well as the sheriff to knock down vessels and cargoes deprived him of legitimate business. The appointment of South Carolina's sole vendue master was a prerogative of the Crown, and Charlestonians often deplored conditions that sprang up under his monopoly. In 1750, when a committee told the Commons House that "the retailing of Goods at Auction is attended with very pernicious Consequences to the Shopkeepers," that body limited auction sales to large amounts only and drastically curtailed their frequency. Philadelphians who complained in 1752 that unlicensed auctions were held in the Northern Liberties, and that "at present the Vendues being no other than Retail-shops" were "very injurious to all regular Dealers, whether Merchants or Shopkeepers," received no relief from the Assembly. There can be no doubt that the common people were often misled about the "bargains" at auctions.

Urban shopkeepers' resentment of peddlers and hawkers, who not only kept country people from coming to town but also competed as interlopers at fairs and on market days, set off a great debate in England during the late forties. Similar friction occurred at Charles Town, where peddlers, outfitted by merchants, drove their packhorses far into the interior; at least one petty chapman traded a piece of gaudy calico for a "Banquet of Love," thereby becoming the original of the yarn about the salesman and the farmer's wife, a news story much relished by the readers of the South Carolina, Maryland, and Pennsylvania press. A law of 1737 had required South Carolina peddlers to be licensed, but a multitude of violations impelled thirty-one city shopkeepers, including four women, to advertise that they would personally enforce it after April 1752. No other city went to the extent of organizing vigilantes of trade. New York and Newport denied entry to the markets of even licensed hawkers, though William Beekman and other merchants financed country chapmen. Bostonians lent some credence to the habitual suspicion of peddlers when Katherine Smith was detected and convicted of stealing goods from shops which her "fence," Dominick Caveny, hawked in the country. Nevertheless the peddler with his horse and mysterious pack did perform a valuable service in the distribution of notions and goods by retail throughout rural America.

Maintenance of a continuous and ample supply of perishable foods for the citizens to purchase at retail raised new problems, and everywhere the erection and regulation of markets concerned the authorities. A question perennially debated in the cities was whether one large central market or several smaller ones would best suit the needs of the people. Both methods were tried, but expanding boundaries eventually dictated in favor of the latter. If the Boston Selectmen thought that the thirty-year conflict over a centralized market was settled with the opening of Faneuil Hall in 1742, they were soon disillusioned, for year after year trouble arose in town meetings over the conduct of this market. This, as in former times, was aggravated by the countryfolk who opposed the building of Faneuil Hall and resented by those townsmen who wanted to assess them for trading in Boston. Perhaps the most acute situation, however, stemmed from the decline in the number of butchers from thirty to four or five by 1746, occasioned by high taxes and the removal of tanners to neighboring towns. Consequently many inhabitants resorted to Roxbury, where meats sold much cheaper. Gradually Bostonians became accustomed to their great market even if economic conditions continued to affect adversely the retailing of food throughout the war period.

The two smallest cities naturally had to provide new market facilities. Charles Town had two markets after 1739, one on the Bay and the other at Broad and Meeting streets. The latter, called the Upper Market, was reported to be "well regulated and plentifully supplied with provisions." With £3,500 provided in part by the Assembly, the Commissioners of the Markets began in 1760 the construction of a "neat building, supported by brick arches, and surmounted by a belfry." Newport's two markets proving inadequate in 1751, "sundry Gentlemen" were accorded permission by the Town Meeting to build an addition to the South Market. The next year the town voted to set aside a piece of land next to the school for a "West Market," which "shall always be used and improved for a Market for the accommodating the Country people and all others who have any provisions and other things to dispose of proper to be sold in the Market-House." Soon residents at the southernmost part of the city clamored for a meat and fish market, because the existing markets were too far away, and their petition was granted. Finally, in 1760, the Proprietors of the Long Wharf presented Newport with a lot adjoining the pier at Thames Street, on which "a handsome brick building," designed by Peter Harrison, was to be erected out of the proceeds of a lottery. The lower part, consisting of open arches, was to be used as a market "forever," and the floor above was to be divided into stores, the rents going to the Town Treasury for the support of a public granary. Work on the edifice commenced promptly, but many years passed before it opened.

Five markets furnished all sorts of country produce and butcher's meat to New Yorkers during this period, though only three attracted much business. James Birket believed that "if they were all Fixed in one place it would be much the best," but both the public and the Corporation preferred the existing arrangement. Indeed, William Smith declared that "no part of America is supplied with markets abounding with greater plenty and variety. We have beef, pork, mutton, poultry, butter, wild fowl, venison, fish, roots, and herbs, of all kinds in their seasons." One day in April 1759 "upwards of 75,000 Pidgeons" were brought to market, where they sold fifty for a shilling.

In spite of these New York claims, most observers agreed that for careful regulation and profusion of offerings, the markets of Philadelphia excelled all others, and that food was cheaper there than in Manhattan. The great market in High Street provisioned the entire city until 1745, when the Shippens persuaded many in "the South part, who live at a Great Distance," to petition for another market, which they would erect at their own expense if the Corporation would provide the land. Soon a new brick building with sixteen stalls rose in the middle of Second Street between Pine and Cedar, and in 1746, in answer to another petition from 145 property-owners in the Northern Liberties, Philadelphia County authorized the construction of a third structure, known as the Callowhill Market. On several occasions in the fifties new stalls to care for increased traffic were added to the High Street Market. There the "ordinary meat stalls, which are over 100 feet long," an amazed Palatine tells us, "hang on both sides full of all kinds of meat, which is always bought up and consumed by the numerous population. . . . I don't think there is any country in which more meat is eaten and consumed than in Pennsylvania." Peter Kalm marveled at the pageantry of Philadelphia markets in 1748: "On those days the country people in Pensylvania and New Jersey bring to town a quantity of victuals, and other productions of the country, and this is a great advantage to the town.

It is therefore to be wished that the like regulation might be made in our Swedish towns. You are sure to meet with every produce of the season, which the country affords. . . . Provisions are always to be got fresh here."

Everywhere officials found it difficult to enforce market regulations prohibiting countrymen from forestalling the market by selling before the opening bell rang, or the citizens from engrossing the market by buying up provisions in advance, with the intention of raising prices. "Many well dispos'd Poor white People" at Charles Town complained in 1746 of Negro slaves who, because they were not under regulation, forestalled the market and often vended commodities "by very indirect Methods," and the Assembly forbade slaves to huckster anything except fish, oysters, and "Herbage." For several years prior to 1748 "forestalling, engrossing and regrating of Butter, Cheese and Meat" going to the Newport markets greatly enhanced prices, which was particularly hard on the poor, and the Town Meeting decreed large fines for such unsocial practices. In 1759 an ordinance setting penalties for stealing the official weights and measures became necessary. A Philadelphia Grand Jury of 1754 presented the abuse of the markets by hucksters who bought up provisions and then raised prices to the injury of both townsfolk and the farmers.

In general such difficulties ended in the framing of regulations and proper enforcement, but at Boston the market problem remained critical. The *Evening Post* reported in 1748: "It has been computed, that there are above one thousand able bodied Men in the Towns not far from Boston who have wholly left off Labour, and are turn'd Butchers, and Forestallers, and their Practice is, to buy up, at any Rate, Cattle, Sheep, Calves, Fowles, etc., (dead or alive) to sell out at an exhorbitant Price in Boston. This is a most pernicious Practice, and a very growing Evil, which it is high time some effectual Methods were found to prevent. By this Means the Country loses the Labour of a great Number of Men, and the Inhabitants of this poor Town of Boston are grievously oppress'd; most of our Butchers quite broke up, and consequently unable to pay Taxes to the Publick." City dwellers believed themselves the innocent victims of rural cupidity as they paid "prodigious Prices" for provisions, especially when, after 1748, the cost of the salt, rum, sugar, molasses, and cotton the farmers took home had fallen over thirty per cent. Charges of hypocrisy were flung at those countrymen who, after having fasted and prayed for rain during a drought in 1749, made greater profits by an "abominable Extortion" than a full crop would have yielded. Nor was urban suspicion of rural Yankees' business methods allayed by numerous detections of dishonesty, such as the dodge of Amos Brown of Stowe, who attempted to sell twenty pounds of putrid butter covered by a thin layer of good butter; his attempt at fraud cost him six pounds and the posting of a bond before he could sell again at the market.

Philadelphia and New York alone enjoyed an unfailing grain supply because of their fruitful hinterlands. Elsewhere authorities had, on occasion, to take measures to ensure ample grain for the poor in the event of natural disasters or scarcity caused by war. After Boston had established a public granary in 1713, its citizens no longer experienced the terrors of bread riots; during the war years the Grain Committee made frequent purchases. The South Carolina Assembly in April 1753 sought to relieve an alarming corn shortage by designating seven prominent Charlestonians to import grain for those in want and to arrange for fair distribution. Prompt arrival of shipments from Virginia saved the day, but the city's dependence on other colonies for its food supply is evident from the fact that between November 12, 1752 and April 23, 1753 it had to import 24,120 bushels of corn from the Northern colonies. Threats of food shortages at Newport during the French and Indian War alarmed the inhabitants, and the *Mercury* in 1760 announced that both corn and pork would meet there with a fine market. At the same time the Proprietors of the Long Wharf agreed that all rents from their new market house should be used to support a public granary to aid the poor.

IV

In a mercantile age still largely swayed by medieval economic ideas and practices, there were few who questioned either the right or the propriety of government regulation of individuals or business groups. Concern about markets and granaries has just been mentioned. As in former years certain other activities were carefully, even rigidly, circumscribed by local ordinances, and certain new ones were brought under municipal control; in still other cases the influence of American conditions led to a negligence or eventual elimination of outworn or unnecessary regulations.

As the cities grew, opportunities for fraud in weights, measures, and quality of foods, firewood, and other "merchantable" commodities so increased that officials had constantly to be on the alert to detect and discipline those "chiselers" who sought profit at the expense and discomfort of their unsuspecting neighbors. In all Northern cities an "assize of Bread," specifying the size, weight, quality, and price of bread, was regularly published and, on the whole, well enforced. In 1744, complaints by the Grand Jury at Charles Town of the "want of a due Regulation in the Sale of Loaf Bread" finally produced an assize law by 1750.

At Boston and New York less success attended efforts to control quality and measures in such articles as butter and meat brought from the country to city markets. The press performed a true civic duty by exposing fraudulent cases, which, as might be expected, reached their height during wartime. "Surely we are very defective in our Morals, notwithstanding all our other Pretences," declared a self-searching Boston printer in 1748 as he described "Several horrid Frauds . . . discovered in the Eatables brought to Town for Sale, especially Butter. . . . To such a Pitch of Wickedness are some of our Farmers grown, that several Firkins sold here for good Butter, have been found to contain nothing but sorry, nasty Grease, except the upper layers; and two of our Neighbours who lately bought a Firkin of Butter between 'em . . . found in one Place seven Pounds Weight of Salt." At Manhattan thirty-seven barrels of "stinking Beef," rejected by the army at Albany, were "repacked by Town Packers" and resold. Short-weight butter and other deceptions frequently came to light, but when some "Hibernian Butchers" were caught cheating a country drover, the *New York Evening Post* called for "Justice" to "run down our Streets as a mighty stream" and flush them out.

Laxity in regulating measures and quality of wheat, flour, bread, butter, and meats shipped from New York and Charles Town awakened the merchants to the need for supervision when their shipments failed to compete in the West Indies with produce from other colonies. A baker and a bolter were convicted and fined sixty pounds by the New York Supreme Court for baking and selling unmerchantable bread of short weight in false cask. Frauds in meat at New York became so "notorious abroad" that Lieutenant Governor De Lancey requested the Assembly to curb them. This was after the *Independent Reflector* had pointed out with its customary directness the superiority of Burlington pork and Irish beef. Ten thousand firkins of butter annually came to this market, Livingston claimed, but since there were no quality or quantity requirements, the butter of other provinces always got the preference. Conditions did not improve much before 1760, however. Need to ensure honest weight in the rice, beef, and pork exported by South Carolina produced a law in 1746 to prevent frauds and deceits, which was rigidly enforced by the five elected packers of Charles Town.

Carters, draymen, and porters—the men who carried cargo, freights, and all manner of goods about the cities—composed the first important urban public utility. As city boundaries widened, their services grew in importance, and their numbers, charges, speed of travel, and such matters required perennial attention as the merchants kept the city fathers promptly advised of transportation problems. William Livingston showed in 1755 the advantage New York enjoyed over other towns because cartage from the waterfront to any place in the city never exceeded a quarter of a mile. There from forty to fifty carters were licensed every year at a cost of twelve shillings each and were required to paint their numbers on their carts. In 1743 Boston's Town Meeting received permission from the province to regulate the weight and size of trucks and carts and set prices for services, and Thomas Williston was chosen the first traffic officer to enforce the regulations. Because a "thorough reform in the Carrs and Carr-men" was needed by 1750 at Charles Town, a new street law required teamsters to register, wear badges, and list the "fares" set for them by the commissioners, and further provided that one white man on foot should walk alongside every cart. An annual license cost five pounds, and a twenty-pound fine faced any carter who overcharged, refused to carry a load, or defaced the number on his cart or dray. Porters, who were everywhere so much in demand for carrying small loads, were licensed at Boston, Philadelphia, and Charles Town and forced to abide by officially determined rates of hire. At the Southern city, where many slaveholders allowed Negroes to serve as porters, a law of 1755 stipulated that they must be licensed and wear badges.

In earlier times protection of business and trades had been afforded to town dwellers by the requirement that all newcomers desiring to open shop in a community take out a "freedom," which was granted upon payment of a certain sum of money. Boston suffered from an exodus of craftsmen in this period and therefore did not concern itself with this problem, and because it did not attract immigrants, Newport was in much the same position. With the inrush of Scotch-Irish and German immigrants after 1730, the Philadelphia Corporation allowed its privilege of granting freedoms to lapse, and its records are barren of any further interest in regulating the settlement of new craftsmen. A similar falling off in requests for freedoms took place at New York, where in 1753 at least fifty-four men, of whom twenty-two never became freemen, were advertising their crafts and trades in the *New York Mercury*. Those who did become free of the city appear to have done so principally to acquire the right to vote rather than for reasons of trade. Conditions in America, where men with skills or capital were always in great demand, had shorn this medieval survival of its value by the midcentury, and it became a decadent institution in the New World long before it expired in provincial English cities.

Through the inherited system of apprenticeship, municipal authorities exercised some control over labor, though in this instance, too, New World needs limited the effectiveness of the institution. The Elizabethan Statute of Artificers had as its object the maintenance of quality in workmanship and restriction of the number of craftsmen. The ravenous American cities demanded more and more artisans and tended to shorten the legal term of apprenticeship in order to get them. Nor did a large class of journeymen really develop in the colonies; nearly any ambitious young man free of his indentures could set up for himself as a master in his trade. It should be emphasized, however, that apprentice standards were always much higher in the cities than in rural regions. In 1753 a Jerseyman protested in the *New York Gazette* the failure of his province to make apprentices serve three years, whereby they became "rather Jobbers and Coblers than Workmen . . . it is almost incredible to think what a Number of such Insects infest this Country." Although few urban apprentices served the full seven years, standards in the cities remained high; the Rhode Island Assembly sought in 1750 to apply the English statutes in their entirety. More influential than anything else in preserving this urban superiority was the continual arrival from England of well-trained craftsmen, whose competition forced colonial workmen to maintain high standards, and the existence in the Northern cities of numerous families who had earned reputations for two or more generations in a particular mystery further strengthened the crafts. Attractive offers to sign on a privateer for nine pounds a month "unless he proves a coward or otherwise" had much to do with the disruption of the system in colonial seaports, especially at Newport, which also lured many a lad from Boston or Manhattan into trying a cruise.

The apprentice system not only served to train youths for trades but also relieved the strain on the rising poor rates. Orphans and bastards were everywhere bound out until they came of age. Especially active on this score was St. Philip's Vestry at Charles Town. South Carolina law stipulated that no boys so bound could be forced to serve beyond their majorities or girls beyond eighteen years, and in no case if they were not willing (though undue pressure must have often been used). In 1743 the Vestry bound out James Talbot to Samuel Stevens, but the following year shifted the indenture to Daniel Badger, painter. Thomas Miller, who in 1740 at the age of five was bound to John Laurens to learn saddlery, was turned over in 1745 to James Glenn, tailor, "for a Tryall, and if the Boy likes, he shall be Bound Apprentice" for seven years. He did not like Glenn, however, but did enjoy tailoring; so within a few months he became the apprentice of Robert Hamilton, another tailor, for eight years. Elizabeth Chandler, who was bound to Rebecca Tubbs for six years "to learn to be a Mantua Maker," was but one of the orphan apprentices who, in 1757 and thereafter, appeared before the Vestry in August to give testimony concerning the treatment accorded them. Likewise when Robert Fisher drank so heavily that his master reported he could not get any work out of him, the Vestry took him back and sent him to sea before the mast.

These pre-industrial seaports harbored no large resident working class that might be designated a proletariat. Even humble carters and porters occasionally turned out to be property-owners. Among "the lower sort," the men who followed the sea always constituted the most numerous laboring element. Statistics are scarce, but these "mariners"—local boat-men, watermen, fishermen, common sailors—always made up the largest segment of the urban working class, and in a very literal sense proved to be a floating population. Governor George Clinton told the Board of Trade in 1749 that New Yorkers owned 157 vessels that shipped "1228 men of Sea Employ." Yet Manhattan was much less of a maritime com-munity than the other Northern cities and often had to seek recruits elsewhere to fill the ranks of the 3,500 seamen needed for its ships in 1760. At little Newport, sooner or later, nearly every male above six-teen went to sea, and in 1760 Rhode Island's extensive merchant ma-rine required "at least" 2,200 sailors to navigate it. The fact that in 1742 Boston had over a thousand widows "in very low circumstances," because of losses from fishermen and commercial vessels, indicates that it probably had the largest seagoing population of any city. The scale of pay for able seamen was only slightly above that for ordinary laborers; New York merchants in 1758 offered the former five shillings a day and four shillings to the latter, "with the usual Allowance of provisions; and no other, or greater Wages whatsoever." Although they belonged to a depressed and often very badly treated class, which spent most of its time out of town, this group exerted a profound influence on the life of every city.

Indentured servants did not figure prominently among urban laborers, even at Philadelphia and Charles Town, which were their chief ports of entry. Most of the Palatine and Irish servants, whose time was for sale by masters of vessels or local merchants, were purchased by farmers who took "suitable . . . healthy persons" to the interior. Only in Eng-lish or Irish artisans with unusual skills or young girls fit for domestic service did townsmen show any great interest. These were the dear, dead days beyond recall when a Philadelphia gentleman could actually specify what manner of housemaid he would employ:

> Wanted Immediately, A Young German Girl, from 13 to 15; it is not insisted upon, that she should be a beauty; good teeth and eyes are absolutely necessary, delicate hands and tolerable legs, are very desireable articles, but a smooth skin is absolutely requisite; 5 feet 6 inches without shoes, altho under that size will answer; The least of masculine about her, will make her less acceptable, the colour of her hair is left to fortune.
>
> Any person having such to dispose of, may find a Purchaser, by applying at the London Coffee-House.

If this gentleman be thought either too frivolous or too fastidious, one must not forget the Reverend Henry Melchior Mühlenberg's lament over his countrymen in 1751: "so many rotten people are coming . . . and acting so wickedly that the name [of Palatine] has begun to stink."

Far more important than servants in urban economies were Negro slaves, who could be found in considerable numbers in all cities, except Philadelphia, where Quaker pressure and popular distaste for them had already appeared. "We do not like Negro Servants," Franklin wrote to his mother, and very few merchants ventured into the slave trade. Elsewhere slaves and free Negroes were a familiar sight in city streets and along the docks. According to censuses of 1755 and 1756 the black population of Newport totaled 1,234 and that of New York, 2,278, or sixteen per cent of the population of each town; Boston's colored inhabitants composed eight per cent of her population in 1760. Despite absence of exact figures, Charles Town's Negroes increased rapidly after the resumption of slave imports in 1750, and at the end of the decade probably forty per cent of its people were black. Newporters were the great traffickers in "Black Ivory," supplying slaves to most of the other cities, though they did not discover the profits awaiting them at Charles Town until 1754.

In two of the cities Negroes supplied the brawn needed for heavy labor. This was to be expected in the Southern metropolis, but a British naval officer expressed surprise at discovering in New York in 1756 that "the laborious people in general are Guinea negroes, who lie under particular restraints." In domestic service and as body servants they were to be found in every town. No defensive assertions of the black's innate incapacity to learn the most intricate trades as yet prevented the entry of the Negro into the crafts. Many worked as fishermen and oystermen, as coopers and barbers; Black Peter delivered the *Boston Evening Post* for Thomas Fleet, and at his death left a small property to his son. A slave offered for sale at Newport was "a Hatter by Trade and a compleat Workman for fine and course Hatts." Only at Charles Town, however, did the Negro artisan provide serious competition for white craftsmen, and there he actually dominated certain trades. Owners of slave workers allowed them to stand for hire daily, or rented them out for stated periods. Andrew Ruck petitioned the Commons House in 1744 on behalf of himself and other shipwrights for relief from the ruinous competition of Negro artisans in the mending and caulking of boats, declaring that they would otherwise have to give up their trades. In reply he was told there was business enough for all workers and that the white men were seeking "to engross the whole Trade within their own hands" and at their own prices. Agitation to protect "the lower Sort" continued, and finally in 1751 the authorities forbade slaves to hire out as porters, laborers, fishermen, "or otherwise," unless they belonged to orphans; and, to assist "the Middling Sort," owners could only allow two of their slaves to work as handicraftsmen, and those two at the stated wage of five shillings currency a day. All evidence indicates that the Charles Town slave frequently drove the white man from his trade, and that virtually all of the profits of the black workman went to the master who hired him out.

V

The expanding urban economy required more extensive business agencies and more complex methods than in former years, and also introduced new economic activities. Only Newport failed to acquire an exchange building where merchants might meet daily and "walk on 'change." This generation of Americans probably lived up to as high a code of commercial ethics as any of its successors. The merchants of New York grew famous for fair and punctual dealing, as did those of Philadelphia. Whether fairly merited or not, suspicions of the inhabitants of New England seaports were aroused to the southward, where the Yankees were branded as "cunning, and deceitful, and selfish." In most city newspapers in 1750 there appeared a sensible set of "Rules Proper to be Observed in Trade," copied from a London source. These admonitions, Daniel Defoe's *Complete English Tradesman,* and numerous didactic pamphlets, such as *A Present for an Apprentice* or *A Present for a Servant Maid,* met with a ready sale, indicating a concern with proper behavior and honest dealings, which no doubt had declined under the impact of war.

Intensified commercial activity and the siphoning off of nearly all coin in payments for English imports produced an acute money shortage. One way out of this dilemma, and one universally adopted, was by extending long-term credits; first by the English to the colonial merchants, then by city traders to local shopkeepers and individuals as well as to country stores. Typical of many advertisements was that of Levy & Franks of Philadelphia in 1753, which concluded: "N.B. All persons indebted above a *twelve month,* are desired to be speedy in their payment, or they may depend on being sued without further notice." One gathers the impression that very little money actually changed hands in the majority of colonial business transactions: book transfers took the place of cash, and three-way and four-cornered settlements were not uncommon. Not infrequently the shrewdest merchants misgauged their men and unwisely granted liberal credit. Arriving at the Quaker City from North Carolina in 1760, John White was able to command "near Four Thousand Pounds" credit, which built, equipped, and laded with valuable cargo "a fine single deck'd Brigantine." After announcing that he would locate in Philadelphia and that he had just sent his vessel to sea, Mr. White, Captain John Thornton, and their wives drove by coach down to New Castle, boarded the waiting *Raven,* and disappeared. Among the more than twenty defrauded creditors who advertised for the return of this dead beat were a shipwright, a sailmaker, several rope-makers, a ship chandler, and an anchor-maker, together with the powerful mercantile houses of Willing, Morris & Company, Sims & Cadwalader, and Samuel Purviance. Who could blame a New Yorker for exclaiming that colonial commerce floated "on an Ocean of Scepticism!"

A secondary but vital means of facilitating trade was by the issuance of paper money. The currency issues of the provinces of New York, Pennsylvania, and South Carolina, where the leading merchants and traders requested and promoted their use, were successfully and conservatively managed and gave important economic benefits to their towns, although "the want of small change" often hampered retail shopkeepers in both Philadelphia and New York. Printer Timothy fulminated in 1749 against "Petty traders" from the northward carrying off all of Charles Town's small coins, to the city's disadvantage; and again in 1753, merchants and planters combined, fruitlessly as it turned out, in measures to keep coin at home because the issues of small-denomination bills in 1745 had not met all needs. "Money comes in very slowly in Carolina, especially to me," Timothy explained in 1754 when he fell behind in payment for paper sent down by Benjamin Franklin.

The difficulties Rhode Island incurred when its currency depreciated and fell to shocking levels have overshadowed the indubitable advantage of a managed currency. Here also merchants had initiated the demand for paper money. Moreover, in Rhode Island alone, where unrestrained emissions of bills of credit did become a flagrant abuse, did the currency question create a clear-cut division between rural and urban populations. Seven "banks" or issues of paper took place by 1740, and the Newport mercantile community realized the harm a runaway inflation was doing to its commerce, especially after 1742, when Massachusetts forbade the circulation of Rhode Island bills. When the Assembly debated another issue in 1743, "almost all the Merchants in Newport appear'd in a Body" at the Colony House bearing a petition against any further emissions—"but it was not taken Notice of" despite the urging of Speaker Peter Bours! When the ninth "bank" came out in 1750, having been snubbed once, the city's leaders addressed a petition to the Crown, accompanied by another from Providence, and besought the support of British merchants, declaring that the recent printing of £50,000 would be "pernicious to the Trade of the Colony," which had already been losing its sugar and molasses trade to Massachusetts and was gaining an evil reputation with creditors everywhere. The answer was an act of Parliament restraining the New England governments from issuing paper money after September 29, 1751. This victory for the urban element (won principally by British mercantile pressure, however) did not come in time to save a merchant like Joseph Whipple from bankruptcy in

1753 or Newport from serious depreciation troubles. Nor did the scars of the conflict between town and country heal over rapidly.

Save for a few hard-money men, a large majority of Bostonians favored the use of paper money. Here the issue was not an urban-rural matter in spite of Dr. William Douglass's efforts to make it appear so. It would seem that the inflation of the early forties did benefit many substantial merchants and most of the community. Governor Pownall, commenting on the general question somewhat later, observed: "it was never yet objected that it injured them in trade. In truth, if it had, as they principally subsisted by commerce, they must have been ruined and undone long ago." But as more paper was printed to finance the war efforts, particularly the Louisburg expedition, Massachusetts money depreciated further. Charles Apthorp of Boston wrote in 1746: "our Currency is very bad and I think must be worse," and when Thomas Hutchinson's plan to use the bullion promised by Parliament in compensation for the colony's war expenditures to redeem paper currency was presented to the Assembly, it was enacted into law and approved by English mercantile circles. But no matter how sound this arrangement may have seemed in theory, a rapid and drastic deflation at the very moment military purchasing ended posited a genuine and serious threat to trade that many merchants and others foresaw at the time. When the first £175,000 was unloaded at Long Wharf in September 1749, and as ten trucks carried the one hundred casks of silver bullion through the streets to Mr. Treasurer Foy's, "Few Tokens of Joy were shown . . . but on the Contrary, an uncommon Gloominess appeared in most Countenances." That the populace expressed nothing more than gloom was due, no doubt, to the forehandedness of the redemptionists before the money arrived in rushing a bill through the Assembly against riots and unlawful assemblies, a strong-arm measure which, be it observed, many Bostonians never quite forgot.

As required by law, the provincial Treasurer redeemed paper in silver for one year from March 31, 1750, and all contracts thereafter had to be made in silver. So drastic was the deflation that, notwithstanding its eventual good results, the immediate effect on Boston's trade, as also for the next few years, was most unfortunate. "Our change of Currency at present Stagnates all business almost," conservative Henry Lloyd wrote to his father in May 1750. A month later the *Pennsylvania Journal* printed a letter from a Bay Town resident: "Trade is quite dead; the Town being dull and still as a Sunday; full of Goods but no Money to buy; less Paper than formerly, by £500,000 of our own Province Bills, besides all those of the other Governments that used to pass here, and not so much Silver stirring as we had before the Treasury was opened. Not a Dollar has come to my Share yet. . . . We curse one another, especially those are cursed, that were for the Act. . . . As soon as the Dollars come out, they are shipp'd for London, New York, Philadelphia, or Hispaniola, or are laid up to worship! What a deplorable picture here!"

Accompanying the collapse of trade were the genuine annoyances of having to learn how to translate "Old Tenor" sums into "Lawful Money," and two kinds of counterfeit money. These were not matters for lower-class resentment alone, as Hutchinson and his followers sought to imply; they extended to all ranks, for all felt the pinch equally. Henry Lloyd blamed too rapid redemption for "the constant complaints and discontented murmurs and almost threats of the people at the scarcity of money," mentioning that "great numbers of our labour people [are] daily removeing to Halifax either for want of Labour or want of money when their work is done to purchase provisions for their Familys." Less sympathetic with the whole scheme, Thomas Hancock growled: "This d—d Act has turn'd all Trade out of Doors and it's impossible to get Debts in, either in Dollars or Provincial Bills." Boston men, thoroughly alarmed, hastened in desperation to extricate themselves from this economic morass. One wrote despondently to a Philadelphia correspondent: "You can't possibly imagine, what an Alteration there is in our Affairs, for want of a Medium, there being scarce any Money of any sort to be seen except a few Coppers, and they seem to diminish; all Trade seems to be stagnated, and little else goes on but Drinking; There are frequent Meetings of many of the best Friends of the Place, in order to Consult Ways and Means to improve our Trade, or revive a Spirit of Industry and Frugality amongst us; but it seems probable that nothing but the greatest necessity will open our Eyes:—The worst of it is, no body knows how or where to begin . . . or where it will end, God Knows; but if something is not done soon, we shall be obliged to fall to making Old Tenor [currency] again; and that will certainly ruin us quite."

In writing his *History of the Colony of Massachusetts-Bay,* Thomas Hutchinson passed lightly over the immediate effect of his rigorous fiscal measures, but many of Boston's "substantial merchants" did not overlook their days of trouble. It seemed to them that they had been hit when they were down—when the entire city was down, for Boston's economic dilemma was real, and everyone except the rich, who lived on incomes, and the lawyers felt the blow. It is a matter worth reflection that twice, in 1750 and again in the 1780's, the hard-money men of Boston forced hard times upon their fellows by insisting upon putting into effect a sound policy too quickly and too ruthlessly, and that in each instance the entire commonwealth had to pay dearly for good intentions applied by socially astigmatic gentlemen. An excess of conservatism in each case proved as costly as an excess of radicalism, though it may be doubted if men like Thomas Hutchinson ever perceived or admitted the fact.

With the steady growth of shipping, each seaport needed large sums of money to insure vessels and cargoes. This form of investment, despite wartime risks, attracted much of the free capital of Northern merchants. More and more, American shippers underwrote each other's maritime insurance, and, save in the cases of Newport slavers, which Thomlinson, Trecothick, & Company of London often insured, and clandestine Rhode Island voyages to Holland protected by Amsterdam policies, a steady trend to writing colonial insurance took place. Ships were frequently insured by a group of merchants in one town for a correspondent in another. The Cuylers, the Beekmans, and other New Yorkers insured most of the shipping out of Newport, which had insufficient capital to do much of this kind of business. The great Philadelphia firm of James & Drinker took out insurance from Walter and Samuel Franklin, Quakers of New York; and Tench Francis secured underwriters for a slave venture of the Browns of Providence in 1759. Because Charles Town's commerce was almost wholly carried in English bottoms controlled by resident English factors, insurance was written in London. Likewise, policies for the many coasters calling at Charles Town had been underwritten in Northern ports. If any further evidence is needed to demonstrate the high degree of economic interdependence attained by colonial cities in this period, this widespread distribution of insurance risks provides it.

Some enterprising merchants began to make insurance their principal line, and others devoted themselves to it exclusively. Deacon Joseph Marion and Benjamin Pollard had opened insurance offices at Boston prior to 1743, and by 1760 four brokers competed for commission fees for procuring underwriters of marine policies. Samuel Philips Savage guaranteed that his "policies will be under-wrote by Gentlemen of undoubted Credit, and upon reasonable Terms." Manhattan early developed into an insurance town: "through the jealousy of the Different Offices, I have obtained the Insurance you ordered," Gerardus Beekman wrote to Evan and Thomas Malbone in 1762. Anthony Van Dam, clerk of the "New York Insurance Office," deemed it profitable to run an advertisement in the *Pennsylvania Gazette* informing Philadelphians in 1759 of the opening of his new business, hoping no doubt to win some commissions away from his local competitors, Keteltas & Sharpe, of the "Old Insurance Office." In Philadelphia, too, Joseph Saunders, Walter Shee, and Tench Francis dealt in marine insurance. One of the largest insurance businesses in the colonies was that of Thomas Wharton, whose office was on Carpenter's Wharf. These men, however, still continued to traffic in general merchandise, and one may be pardoned for wondering if Wharton wrote out his policies with one of those "enamelled fountain pens" he had for sale in 1753.

Many of the proprietors of insurance offices had risen from the ranks of public notaries or scriveners, whose services the public needed so often that in most communities they came under official regulation. They performed all kinds of clerical and notarial work, especially drawing up contracts, deeds, conveyances, bills of sale, indentures, "Privateers men's Shares," and translating French and Spanish commercial documents. Prominent among such paper-work experts were Richard Nicolls, who in 1756 completed thirty-four years of scrivening for New Yorkers; and the Philadelphians Lewis Evans, famous for his maps, prospects, and surveys, and Paul Isaac Voto, the linguist, were others.

In Philadelphia, where all sorts of commercial activities throve, two notaries branched out to offer services hitherto lacking in the colonies. William Meyer opened the Public General Register Office of Intelligence near the Indian King on Market Street in 1756 as an employment agency to supply town and country with journeymen artisans, apprentices, Negroes for hire, and common laborers, such as "a boy to go of errands, who can read and write High-Dutch, and knows the Town." Before long his custom warranted a branch office on Moyamensing Road in Southwark. Embarking as a buyer and seller of city real estate in 1753, Scrivener John Reilly next undertook to handle ground rents, to rent houses, borrow and lend money on good security, and deal in mortgages and "annuities" with "the greatest Care, Dispatch, and Secrecy" at his office on Chestnut Street, where henceforth James Humphreys performed the notary work. Within a few years Reilly was advertising sums from £150 to £1,000 "to be put out at Interest on Land Security in the City and County of Philadelphia."

Notwithstanding ventures by notaries (and also printers) into private banking, the merchants still controlled the money markets of the cities. Long Island money found its way to Boston for the purchase of six per cent provincial treasury notes. Some Newporters, like Ezra Stiles, put their funds into the Susquehanna Company's land offerings, but others placed sums as high as "several Thousand dollars to Let on good Security" through Joseph Fox. New York's mobile wealth, of which the war produced a large amount, outran the capacity of ordinary commerce to absorb it and flowed into real estate, bonds, mortgages, and British government loans; and newspapers frequently announced funds to be loaned on sound security. Nearly half of Hugh Wallace's estate of £20,000 was out at interest. A similar situation developed in Philadelphia. "The War hath occasioned . . . a plentiful Circulation of Cash in this and the neighbouring Provinces," observed James & Drinker in 1760. Philip Syng, silversmith, in true Renaissance style, made loans to many people.

As rice and indigo fortunes accumulated at Charles Town, neither shipping nor manufactures attracted investment, and the planters, once having sufficient land and slaves, had money to lend. The Timothys, proprietors of the *South Carolina Gazette,* acted as outlets for this capital, using their advertising columns. For one man who desired "3, 4, Or 500 pounds, for which he is willing to mortgage a Sufficient Number of valuable Negroes," Timothy could find half a dozen having "from 1000 to 6000 Pounds, to be let at Interest upon good personal Security." A striking feature of the South Carolina money market was the fact that many organizations like the South Carolina Society and the Vestry of St. Thomas, Berkeley, often advertised one or two thousand pounds to be let out, and in 1756 Peter Manigault announced his intention of loaning "several Thousand Pounds" belonging to the orphaned children of the late Daniel Huger. If one had good security, money could easily be "hired" at Charles Town.

The intricacies and growing magnitude of commercial transactions, settlement of large estates and inheritances, searching and transfer of land titles, maritime matters, and admiralty law called for the services and understanding of specialists in the law. Likewise the accumulation of a body of colonial statutes applicable to an urban commercial society made similar demands. Thus lawyers became indispensable in American cities, and in this period emerged slowly but surely as a distinct group ranging themselves as a profession alongside the clergy and physicians. Because they needed an extensive and costly education, members of the legal fraternity were drawn from the gentry. Under the ægis of John Read, the Massachusetts legal profession rose first to eminence. A pioneer in the use of technicalities, Read "reduced the jarring and contradictory forms of practice to a system, taught the courts the advantages of precedents, and practitioners the value of knowledge." In 1750 Henry Lloyd asserted that there was "a Dearth of Lawyers here," but at that time the Nestor of the Boston Bar, Jeremiah Gridley, was training in his office such great legal minds as those of Benjamin Pratt, James Otis, and John Adams. Whereas most Massachusetts lawyers were graduates of Harvard College, those of the other communities read their law at the Inns of Court in London. Charles Town's great colonial bar had just begun to take form in 1760; but everywhere the profession was still in its infancy. James Honeyman was probably the only well-trained barrister at Newport. In 1753 the *Independent Reflector* warned fellow New Yorkers about the "Abuses in the Practice of the Law"; even though he admitted that "the Gentlemen of the Long Robe" had somewhat restored their guild to repute, he believed that the Supreme Court alone ought to license lawyers. Two of the genuine contributions of these years came from Philadelphia barristers-at-law, Gilbert Buchanan, who in 1749 published an *Abridgement of the Acts of Assembly of the Province of Pennsylvania,* and from Abel Pooley, who gave legal advice to the poor gratis before he went south to settle in Charles Town. John Moland and Tench Francis, with his law library of more than three hundred volumes, stood at the head of the Philadelphia Bar, which in 1760 led all the cities in distinction.

A further agency promoting interurban exchange and communication was the colonial post office, which vastly improved the carrying and delivery of mails by 1760. Elliott Benger of Virginia served as Postmaster General until his death in 1753; then William Hunter and Benjamin Franklin, postmasters of Williamsburg and Philadelphia, received appointments as joint deputy postmasters general for the colonies at an annual salary of £600 each, to be paid from postal revenues. Franklin immediately made an inspection tour of all post offices except that at Charles Town, after which he operated a greatly improved system from Philadelphia, and for the first time the post produced a revenue. He promptly started a weekly service to New York, and in July 1753 instituted a delivery by "Penny Post" to "Persons living in Town of letters uncalled for a day after their arrival." After 1754 the mails left Philadephia on Mondays, Wednesdays, and Fridays, arriving at Manhattan thirty-three hours later. Better service improved the business of the post office all the way from New England to Virginia, though the rates continued too high for the poorer colonists. Following complaints of inconvenience by merchants in 1755, the postriders set out weekly the year round from Philadelphia for New England, instead of on the once-a-fortnight schedule formerly followed in the winter. About the same time the first inland postal route began with weekly stages leaving Philadelphia for Lancaster, York, the back parts of Virginia, the camp of the British Army, and Winchester in the Great Valley. After 1760 the Southern Post to Williamsburg and New Bern rode once a week in the summer and every fortnight in the winter. But the greatest single improvement was the initiation in February 1756 of monthly packet sailings from Falmouth, England, to New York. Under Deputy Alexander Colden, the New York office thereafter handled the largest volume of mail because all transoceanic letters were sent there.

Distant Charles Town had no overland postal connections with the northern cities until August 1756, when the "first post" arrived, and the postmaster, Printer Peter Timothy, announced that regular fortnightly posts to Boston would be henceforth dispatched "for the Benefit of Commerce, facilitating Correspondence, and more ready Conveyance of Public Intelligence." Timothy had long been provincial postmaster and had made arrangements with private carriers to deliver throughout South Carolina all letters that came by sea. Now, under an appointment from his former employer, he became an official of the colonial post.

Private postriders or "carriers" also supplemented the work of the colonial post office in the Northern provinces by carrying letters and parcels along routes not yet served officially. One private route, sustained by subscription, ran from Philadelphia to Bethlehem after

1742; and a post between the Quaker City and Northampton County, Virginia, via the Eastern Shore of Maryland had ample patronage. To Lancaster once a week rode Ludwick Bierly to deliver the Philadelphia newspapers, and New York had the benefit of a private "Albany Post" by 1744. Newport and Boston also enjoyed interurban carrier service in addition to the official post, which in this period ran via Rhode Island to New York. Between Boston and Hartford, Moses Holmes of Ashford rode weekly to "serve his good Customers with Newspapers, &c.," and Christopher Page served as "News Rider" from Boston to Springfield, calling at every inn and tavern along the way. With these private riders and the colonial post, communications between the cities and with their respective environs improved remarkably, and at the close of the era showed signs of great activity.

VI

In the course of two wars the five cities expanded into great entrepôts of international commerce and inland distribution. There can be no question of the contemporary importance of this extensive economic advance to the mother country. Quite as much as the American seaports, did Bristol, Liverpool, Glasgow, and other English and Scottish cities become the beneficiaries of the transatlantic traffic. In 1760, although fighting still raged in the Caribbean, to the colonial merchants the prospect for peace seemed very near. All of them, but especially those of Boston and Newport, had weathered the two conflicts only after long years of hazardous trading involving great profits and ruinous losses. Now, welcoming the third Hanoverian to the throne with all sincerity, they looked forward to the adjustment of the commerce that sustained them and their fellows with great hopes for the "normalcy," reasonable profits, security, and deep satisfaction that membership in the victorious Empire should bring them.

CHAPTER 3

Urban Problems in Wartime

NOTHING SO DIFFERENTIATED early American cities from the rural and wilderness areas as those problems arising out of the very fact of thousands of people dwelling together in close proximity. During these years the rapid expansion of the cities and the prevalence of aggravating war conditions made the facing and solving of normal problems of urban life both trying and difficult. Yet municipal authorities acted with commendable alacrity, often, it is true, as a result of prodding by an aroused citizenry; and when they fell short of accomplishment, private initiative exerted through voluntary associations frequently achieved better solutions. The momentum generated by more than a century of experience in civic matters enabled Boston to maintain its excellent record; New York underwent a satisfactory and normal development; and Philadelphians at last began to recognize and understand their civic responsibilities as their city became the colonial metropolis. Charles Town and Newport, but recently arrived at city status, succeeded in coping effectively with many public issues. Taken together in 1760, these American communities had attacked many of the problems of living in congested societies earlier and rather more successfully than contemporary provincial cities of the British Isles, and in one or two instances London itself.

II

Defense against fire, the dreaded and ever present threat to the security of town dwellers, concerned them even more than defense against the Spaniards or the "turbulent Gallicks." Much had been achieved before 1743 by Boston, New York, and Philadelphia, each in its own way; and now that there was constant communication between cities, ideas and innovations rapidly circulated, producing a considerable uniformity in fire protection as one borrowed from another.

Precautions against fire by means of municipal regulations and forced removal of hazards gained in popularity everywhere. Requirements that houses be built of brick or stone did not have to be made at New York and Philadelphia because of the customary wide use of these materials, but twice in 1749, alarmed by the fires of Charles Town and Boston, the *New York Gazette* printed letters from citizens calling for a law forbidding roofing houses with wooden shingles. No serious fire in frame-built Newport emphasized the need for similar ordinances, but the same could not be said for Boston; in the seven years before 1750 the Boston Selectmen granted only five permits for the erection of wooden buildings, and from 1749 to 1752 the province authorized the town to exact licenses for sailmakers' and riggers' lofts as a fire-prevention measure. When the burned-out districts were rebuilt after the disastrous fire of 1760, the officials ordered the widening of certain streets and directed that all new structures be of brick or stone and roofed with slate or tile under a penalty of fifty pounds.

Vividly recalling the heavy losses in the "Dreadful Fire" of 1740, the South Carolina Assembly sought to enforce its law for pulling down frame buildings between the "Curtain Line" and the Cooper River and for prohibiting frame construction or shingle roofs after December 20, 1745. Periodically the Fire Masters inspected for infractions, but adherence to the regulations was frustrated by the absence of cheap noninflammable building materials. Wooden structures went up steadily. Still the city had some protection for its buildings, for nowhere did Benjamin Franklin's lightning rods meet with readier acceptance, especially after Dr. John Lining repeated the famous kite experiment in May 1753. Within two years Peter Timothy's paper reported that fundamentalists were warning "Anti-Electricians" against this infernal "meddling with Heaven's Artillery."

Sooty chimneys probably caused most city fires. A Boston committee, set up to study the problem, recommended that, in addition to two official sweepers already authorized, anyone refusing to clean his chimney after forty-eight hours' notice or anyone whose chimney blazed be fined ten shillings. Each night at nine curfew rang in the Bay Town, but nevertheless at least forty-four chimney fires were reported between 1754 and 1762, and complaints about defective flues continued to pour in on the harassed Selectmen. One of the difficulties was the lack of "any Person or Persons inclined to undertake the Business of Chimney-Sweeping." Newport experienced similar troubles. Grand juries at Charles Town regularly presented chimneys as "of dangerous Consequence to the Neighbourhood," particularly those that did not extend more than three feet above the roofs. Elsewhere blazing chimneys posed no great problem.

Although Charlestonians, Philadelphians, and New Yorkers were anxious about the storing of hay and straw within city limits, gunpowder understandably aroused the greatest fears. Boston and New York had already grappled with the problem, but the first concern about powder storage at Newport came with the war. In 1741 the Rhode Island General Assembly ordered a magazine constructed; in 1750 it directed that all powder be stored therein, except that each householder might retain twenty-five pounds in a tin flask. Evidently this magazine was never erected, for after a long discussion in 1755, the town built "a good [brick] Powder House" of its own. Fear of an explosion induced by lightning impelled the South Carolina Assembly to order "proper points or Electrical Rods" for Charles Town's magazine and also for Fort Johnson. So many infractions of the Philadelphia powder ordinance occurred that the directors of the Philadelphia Contributionship for Insuring Houses from Loss by Fire announced in 1760 that henceforth they would prosecute all violators and pay five pounds for information leading to a conviction.

Not content with taking all known precautions against the outbreak of fire, the cities provided themselves with the most up-to-date fire-fighting equipment and organized the inhabitants into groups to combat conflagrations. In 1743 Boston had eight engine companies, each consisting of a captain and from eleven to eighteen men, who met regularly to "exercise" their engines; a new company formed in 1753. In lieu of pay for their work, the firemen were excused from all other civic duties, and the first company to arrive at the scene of a fire received a bounty of five pounds. In addition, each of the elected Firewards possessed authority to order ordinary citizens to assist at fires. The few men who balked received proper chastisement, but "the pernicious Practice of Women's attending Fires, especially those that happened in the Night, who, if they do nothing worse, are a great Interruption," worried the Firewards. The New Yorkers read of the solution to the predicament in a *Gazette* of March 1753: Boston's chief had cracked down with the decision that the "law makes no Discrimination of Person or Sex," and thenceforth "every such curious cloaked up Lady" would have to take her place at a pump. So well did the Boston fire officials perform their duties that the Fire Society, founded in 1717, restricted its activity to preserving the property of members and became more or less a select gentlemen's club.

Probably Boston suffered more fires, in spite of its precautionary measures, than all the other cities put together; not a year passed without serious and extensive damage to property, and the newspapers reported many of minor nature. A fire in a warehouse in November 1743 caused a loss of between five and six thousand pounds. A midnight fire on Copp's Hill during bitter weather late in 1744 consumed three houses "occupied by a great many Families." On another occasion a spark from a South End smithy flew to an adjoining shop where it exploded an open keg of gunpowder "in a terrible manner." Boston lost its "spacious and Beautiful" State House along with valuable records, paintings, and books on December 9, 1747; the General Court had to meet for a time at inconvenient places. The worst fire in "upwards of Twenty Years" destroyed thirty North End buildings and much expensive merchandise near Bronsdon's Wharf in 1753.

The year 1760 was fraught with disaster for the Bostonians, who considered that they had already had troubles enough. Chimneys had grown well-fouled and hearth fires still burned high as March came in; on the 17th occurred a bad blaze in the West End; on the 18th a fire on Griffin's Wharf reached the artillery stores, which exploded, injuring five persons; and on the 19th the cry of fire brought out the inhabitants five times. All this, however, was but a prelude to what happened at two o'clock in the morning of March 20. Flames accidentally blazed up in the dwelling of Mary Jackson at the Brazen Head in Cornhill and were carried eastward by a strong wind. Raging with "irresistable violence," the fire "carried all before it and, still widening in its progress, proceeded with such a rapid course to the water's edge, that . . . houses, and other buildings . . . were in a very little time reduced to ashes." Charlestown sent its fire engine over in a boat, and surrounding towns proffered aid quickly, but, said the *Post Boy,* "the haughty flames triumphed over our Engines, our Art, and our Numbers." Miraculously, despite a great explosion, falling walls, and tumbling chimneys, not one life was lost in the conflagration, whose light could be seen as far off as Portsmouth in New Hampshire.

As usual, accounts of the fire losses varied. The press estimated the four hundred structures destroyed to be worth £300,000 sterling; Governor Pownall, "by a moderate Computation," put it at £100,000 or more. But figures alone cannot convey any real sense of the blow to Boston, dealt, as some thought, in retribution by the Almighty to a wicked generation:

> Then can we clear ourselves, a'nt we to blame
> Who sin without Remorse, and cast off Shame,
> And pay no Rev'rence to his holy Name?
> This is the Cause He sent his Judgment down,
> This awful Desolation! on the Town.
> The North-west wind, and Flame he did employ,
> Our stately Habitations to destroy,
> What spacious Structures stood but th' other Day,
> And now they all in Heaps of Ashes lay.

It was a frightful experience for everyone. Hundreds lost not only their dwellings but most or all of their furnishings, quantities of which were stolen by looters. An inspiring sign of growing intercolonial sympathy for the welfare of all Americans, as well as a genuine comfort to the distressed, came with the generous contributions from individuals and public bodies throughout the colonies. Foremost among charitable Americans stood the officials, clergy, and inhabitants of the four other cities. Ultimately a town committee distributed among 439 "sufferers" the truly amazing sum of £13,317.11s.9d. dispatched to the Bay Town by friends and correspondents all over the Empire, benevolence rare for this age or any other.

Philadelphia owed its fine fire defenses to the energies of private citizens rather than to the excellence of public planning. The Corporation took good care of its four fire engines, hundreds of leather buckets, and other equipment, but it purchased very few new articles in this period. This lethargy was no doubt due in part to the earnestness with which groups of inhabitants associated in fire companies modeled after Franklin's Union, the Fellowship, and the Hand-in-Hand, all founded before 1742. These three organizations maintained four engines at their own expense, making a total of eight in the city. In January 1743, Franklin noted in his paper: "We hear there are several new Companies erecting in Town for mutual Assistance in Case of Fire." Within a month the Heart-in-Hand had formed, and by 1760 the Friendship, Britannia Hibernia, Cordwainers, Northern Liberty, and Vigilant fire companies were all active. Nearly every group bought an engine from "Richard Newsham of Cloth-Fair, London, Engineer," who distributed broadsides in the colonies describing his six different-sized engines, the amounts of water discharged by each, prices, with or without suctions.

The fire societies very well suited the Quaker City's "genius," which Franklin shrewdly assessed when he made the Union into what amounted to a lodge while at the same time stressing the private advantage and civic service. Such Friends as John Smith often "spent the Evening at our fire company meeting in more debate than was profitable," and Henry Drinker usually made a quick call on Elizabeth Sandwith before "going to meet the Fire Company." Convening regularly at a tavern or at the London Coffee House, the members dispatched the routine business of collecting dues and fines, checking over such equipment as bags, buckets, axes, hooks, ladders, and their engines, and then settled down to the sociable part of the evening—and not infrequently the political. As might be anticipated, the Union Fire Company always took the lead under Poor Richard's direction. When "evil minded, dissolute Persons" swiped the "nossels of most of the Pumps in Market Street" in 1744 and 1745, it was the Union that offered five pounds' reward for recovery of the fixtures. In 1749 the Union persuaded three other companies to share in a scheme to inspect the city's engines and ladders, and in 1752 joined with the Hand-in-Hand to import a fire bell to hang in the Academy belfry. When the Union's stock became ample enough in 1752, Benjamin Franklin prepared a plan to lend part of it out at interest, which was to be used for the relief of members who lost over one hundred pounds in goods by fire. In 1755 the company voted to place two buckets in each of the city's sentry boxes and six with the constable of the watch; two years after this they gave money to the Pennsylvania Hospital to buy an engine, buckets, and ladders, as well as a sum to the "distressed french Neutrals."

Although houses often caught fire, good fortune, brick and stone houses, slate roofs, and the alertness of the inhabitants preserved Philadelphia from any "great fire." In 1743 when six dwellings were consumed on the waterfront, it was the most serious blaze of the period. A member of a fire company collected nearly eight hundred pounds for the victims, which almost made up their losses. In 1757 Edward Shippen, Jr., wrote to his father, who had suggested that chimney sweepers were needed in Lancaster, that he had "spoken to two of the master chimney sweepers . . . but they are at present so busy in town that they can by no means stir as yet."

Perhaps it was the relative immunity of the Quaker City from fire that emboldened members of the Union Fire Company to found the first successful American fire-insurance company. Prior to this at Boston, in 1728 and again in 1748, Joseph Marion issued proposals for insuring "Houses and Household Goods from Loss and Damage by Fire in any part of the Province" at the "New-England Sun Fire Office." If the good deacon ever issued any policies, no record of them remains, and if he did, the Great Fire would have been the ruin of his undertaking. The way was left open in consequence for the members of the Union to take the first step under the ægis of Benjamin Franklin, Hugh Roberts, and Philip Syng, who agreed on February 26, 1750 to raise "a fund for an Insurance Office to make up the Damage that may arise by Fire to this Company." Nothing further happened for over a year, and then, at a meeting in the Widow Pratt's Tavern, the Union's committee explained its plan to the approving clerks of the other city companies. The articles closely followed those of the Amicable Contributionship of London, as did the company's device—a Hand-in-Hand.

Subscribers to the new insurance scheme met at the Court House in February 1752 to sign the articles, and on April 13 the Philadelphia Contributionship for the Insurance of Houses from Loss by Fire was formally launched with about seventy-five members, mostly Quakers, twelve directors headed by Benjamin Franklin, and a treasurer, John Smith. Insurance was limited to houses within ten miles of the city, and premiums varied with types of construction. In May, Joseph Saunders, clerk of the Contributionship, opened the office in his house on Water Street. When the first dwelling-house fire occurred in December 1753, the newspaper account of the blaze ended with a "plug" for the Contributionship: "the House being insur'd, the Damage will be immediately repaired, without Cost to the Owner." The company also proved its interest in preventive measures by successfully petitioning the Assembly for a more thorough law governing "imperfect work" by chimney sweepers. Conservatively operated under Quaker directors, and fortunate in having to pay off on but four fires before 1760, the Contributionship proved a going concern.

Just before this period opened, the Corporation of New York had taken steps to give its city adequate fire-fighting equipment by purchasing new engines and setting up public companies of seven firemen for each of the six wards. Like the enginemen of Boston, the Gothamites were unpaid but relieved of all other civic responsibilities, including jury service. They made an efficient force, for when a fire occurred, the press usually reported that with "the timely Assistance of the People, and Fire Ingines, it was soon extinguish'd." One spectacular incident that thrilled the onlookers was when Fireman Francis Dawson opened the roof of the City Hall directly over the fire on a cold day in January 1747, and the engines played water on him, coating him with ice; as a reward the Common Council presented him with five pounds and the freedom of the city. At another time the engines went out on the ice to quench a blaze aboard the ship *William,* icebound in the East River. Two additional Newsham engines arrived in February 1750, but they did not prevent the loss of Trinity Church Parish School a few weeks later. The *Independent Reflector,* in praising the skill of the enginemen in 1753, insisted on the need for an engine powerful enough to reach church spires; it also remonstrated that there was too much shouting at fires: let the directors do this. Livingston might also have suggested that one or two fire societies be formed to prevent the pilfering that took place only too often at Manhattan's fires. Yet comparing its record with those of other places, fire, like the economic troubles familiar elsewhere, passed New York by.

Newport also escaped any general fire in these years, but nevertheless continued to add to its fire-fighting equipment and to strengthen the organization of enginemen. In 1743 five young Negroes, diverting themselves in a loft, ignited some gunpowder and blew off the roof, but the fire was speedily brought under control. "Engine No. 1" always came through with "timely assistance" when a blaze broke out; in 1747 a second engine was acquired, and the Town Meeting chose a committee to see to the enforcement of all fire ordinances and punish violators. It required every citizen to possess a leather bucket with his name painted on it, and assigned three more men to each of the engines. Two years later there were three engines, each with a team of nine men. A special Town Meeting in 1750 dealt with fire precautions and defense; it ordered a size "No. 6" engine "with furniture" from Newsham's broadside, along with ladders, fire-hooks, and other equipment, and designated eight prominent merchants to direct at fires "with Trumpets." At the same time the Meeting proposed new fire laws to the Assembly, which responded by authorizing pulling down or blowing up buildings to prevent spreading of fire, "by Reason of the Contiguity and Adjoining of Houses and Dwellings" in Newport. The act also allowed compensation to owners, annual appointment of firewards, and penalties for thieving at fires. Four companies now had a total of forty-five enginemen, who exercised the apparatus once a month. A new suction engine required a fifth company of eight more men in 1755. The Heart-in-Hand Fire Company, modeled after that of Boston, with a silk-stocking membership of thirty-one, undoubtedly inspired much of this public activity to prevent fires in a congested town consisting almost entirely of frame buildings.

With the specter of the Great Fire of 1740 haunting them, Charlestonians made important advances in protecting their city and fortunately underwent no devastating conflagration before 1760; at a blaze along the Bay in 1744, Governor Glen, arriving early, "by his prudent Directions" prevented it from having "dreadful Consequences." The South Carolina Assembly procured three new engines from London in 1754, an event important enough to be reported in New York, and two years later authorities framed elaborate rules for managing, directing, and housing the city's five engines with "sucking pipes." Engine managers were empowered to "enroll" poor white men or slaves to serve the apparatus: white men were fined five pounds and Negroes were whipped with thirty-nine lashes for refusing to appear at the cry of fire, but every time an engine went out, the white pumpers received fifteen shillings, plus twenty shillings for every hour they worked the engine, while the Negroes received but ten shillings for turning out and ten shillings an hour for pumping. Once in three months the engine companies drilled at a "publick well." Charles Town thus took the first step toward a paid fire department. When "some hellish incendiary" set fire to some pitch on Colonel Beale's Wharf only a month after the passage of the new act, "the Town Engines were there in a short Time, and played with great Judgment," preventing a general fire even if they could not save the stores on the wharf.

III

Expanding boundaries, threats of fire, and household needs of the inhabitants joined to make provision of an adequate supply of water a matter for public action everywhere, except at Newport, which apparently had plenty of water. Since Boston did not grow during these years, its only concern about water came after the Great Fire with the General Court's order that if relocation plans placed any private pumps in the streets, the Selectmen were to see to it that the people living nearby kept them "in good order."

Few cities in the Western World enjoyed a better water supply than Philadelphia. "They are stocked with plenty of excellent water in this city," Dr. Hamilton recorded in 1744, "there being a pump att almost every 50 paces distance." Peter Kalm warranted it "good and clear," and added that it could usually be found at a depth of forty feet and that there was a well in nearly every house, besides good drinking water in the Delaware River. The Corporation took good care of the public pumps, proceeding promptly against vandals who broke the handles, put stones in them, or "other wise" altered the water supply. Not satisfied with official maintenance, however, the Union Fire Company's pump committee pulled a surprise inspection in 1752, reporting 127 pumps in good condition and 39 needing repairs. In 1756 the Assembly placed control of the pumps in the hands of wardens and authorized them to construct new wells and to buy up private pumps in the streets. The following year it empowered them to assess all householders who drew their water from the city supply.

The water at Charles Town was good for drinking, but various advertisements and comments indicate that the householders were far from adequately supplied. Joseph Shute maintained several pumps at his warehouse on Elliott Street to supply "Shipping and housekeepers," and Thomas Fox, after renting a brewhouse, issued tickets at forty shillings entitling holders to fetch water for a year. Of course many private houses had wells and pumps, and there were also some public pumps and wells in the streets, which after 1756 the managers of the fire engines kept clean and in repair. But the conclusion that many inhabitants lacked a ready supply is further borne out by a comment of the *Gazette* after a fire on King Street in 1760: "The want of publick wells and pumps in the streets of that part of town was felt."

New York's principal municipal deficiency was good drinking water; the contents of most private wells were so brackish and unpalatable that water for drinking and tea was carted from out of town by several people who made a living selling it "by the pale." A few streets contained municipal wells six or eight feet in diameter, but they could be sunk only by permission of the Common Council and at the cost of the users. Consequently few were built until after 1750, when a "Citizen" warned in the columns of the *Gazette* of the shortage of water in case of fire. He proposed laying a brick "Channel" underground from low water, and then connecting three pumps at stated distances along it to provide sea water for the engines. At the channel's end near City Hall, there would be a "well or Bason" from which he hoped water could be conveyed to other parts of Manhattan. The rich, who have property, declared Parker, could bear the costs and carry the "quotas" of the poor. But such a project did not appeal to the rich. In January 1753 the *Independent Reflector* again drew attention to the shortage of public wells and the fact that many of those which did exist were inaccessible for the engines. Finally in December the Assembly ordered the Corporation to nominate overseers of pumps and wells, who were to repair and maintain the existing water supply and construct new facilities with funds from a "Reasonable" annual tax, not exceeding 120 pounds. Thereafter New York's water supply improved, though conditions proved far from ideal.

IV

During these years of conflict, vastly complicated by wartime abnormalities, ordinary municipal peace officers found it difficult—indeed, often impossible—to ensure quiet and public safety. Large accretions of population, including substantial proportions of floaters—sailors, soldiers, runaways from the country, immigrants, and rougher elements —exerted more pressure on the feeble guarantors of law and order than they could withstand. The failure of colonial cities to solve the police problem in spite of serious efforts parallels similar frustrations in English cities. No colonial town's ineptitude in preserving order rivaled that of Bristol, where street riots, drunken brawls, and like disorders occurred daily without interruption. Farley's *Bristol Journal* of March 16, 1760 thus paid tribute to the city's guardians:

> *The watch burn Tobacco while Houses are burning,*
> *And the* Glass, *not the* Watch, *goes its rounds,*
> *A burning shame this and sad subject of mourning,*
> *That our Guard's such a mute Pack of Hounds.*

During daylight hours constables attempted to keep the peace in every city and performed necessary police duties of quelling disturbances, making arrests, and enforcing local ordinances, but so onerous did the job seem that authorities had difficulty in persuading men to serve as Dogberrys. Out of seventeen chosen at Boston in 1743, only five were sworn, ten gentlemen having refused and paid fines rather than assume the burden and two being excused. Attitudes were the same in 1745, 1748, and 1755; only in the last year of the period, when peace had come, did twelve of thirteen selected accept constabular duty. As a more bucolic community, Newport found it less difficult to get its six to eight constables to take responsibility. Even so, when Samuel Banister refused to give possession to a man who had bought his house at a public sale in satisfaction of a judgment, the attending constables must have reflected that the job was no sinecure, for Banister threatened to shoot Sheriff Peleg Brown, and actually did fire, killing a lad of eighteen. In a city the size of Philadelphia, one constable for each of the ten wards could scarcely have performed all the duties, though the hazards remained theirs.

Maintenance of nocturnal security was usually a matter for paid watchmen. Newport was a most peaceful city, for its maritime population was drawn almost entirely from local families; when the mariners came ashore they did not brawl about the town, they went home. Two watchmen were deemed sufficient to keep the city quiet at night until 1747, when the number was doubled for "preventing fire in the town, and to prevent disorders." There were times when the town committee could not keep good men on the job, and in 1749 the Meeting instructed them to hire four men "upon the best terms they can, and draw the money out of the Treasury to pay them." Specially appointed officials commenced walking about Newport at night to take up Negroes abroad after curfew sounded. Fear of attacks by Morpang and his French privateers resulted in the founding of the Newport Artillery Company at this Quaker stronghold in 1744, the setting of an armed military watch, and the posting of a lookout on the Neck from dawn to sunset whenever danger threatened.

Sixteen men distributed at four watchhouses tried to provide security for Bostonians. Thomas Fleet, of the *Boston Evening Post,* however, regarded them as a sorry lot and seldom missed a chance for a gibe at them. Some of "the Watch-Men who *hapened* to be awake" saw a comet in February 1742. The addition of a "Military Watch" in 1745 inspired Fleet to report gleefully that the "Standing Watchmen" were complaining "of the Rudeness of the Soldiers, who, they say, will not suffer them to take their *natural Rest, as usual.*" About the same time, a fire in a tailor's shop near the Town House "very much disturbed the poor Watchmen in their Lodgings in the Neighbourhood!" Such needling undoubtedly alerted as well as annoyed the peace officers, since official investigations substantiated the printer's allegations. Improvement came with the payment of higher salaries in 1747 and the fining of any watchman discovered asleep on duty. In addition to making the rounds to guard against fire and disorders, the watchmen cried the time and state of the weather "in a moderate tone," questioned all persons abroad in the streets, and took up all "rude and disorderly Negroes" after nine at night.

The paid watch established at New York after the so-called "Negro Conspiracy" of 1741 was abandoned late the next year for a citizens' watch, which was summoned from among the inhabitants each night by a constable. With the advent of war and disturbed conditions, the Corporation's mistaken parsimony elicited acid remarks from all quarters.

Need for an armed military watch in 1747 worked hardships on the poor, who could not afford to pay substitutes; some craftsmen complained that many people having three or four apprentices and servants, and as many sons, who must take their turns in the watch, got the onerous duty once in every four or five weeks at a cost of forty shillings or more to them. Pleas from the Common Council to the Governor brought a dubious form of relief in a company of fusileers from Albany sent to take over the military watch. During the war years, seven citizens and a constable watched in addition, but since respectable citizens paid fines to escape serving, the watch consisted largely of a "Parcel of idle, drinking, vigilant Snorers, who never quell'd any nocturnal Tumult in their Lives; (Nor as we can learn, were ever the Discoverers of a Fire breaking out,) but would, perhaps, be as ready to join in a Burglary as any Thief in Christendom. A happy Set indeed, to defend the rich and populous City against the Terrors of the Night." William Livingston, James Parker, and other "Judicious Persons" protested at paying a thousand pounds a year for such poor protection when five hundred pounds would support a good watch, like that of Philadelphia, where "scarce a Robbery is heard of now-a-Days."

At the end of the period Philadelphia did boast of an efficient police force, but it had taken much time and effort to get it. In 1743 the Grand Jury, presenting "the conduct of the Watch" as expensive, and "unequal and Grievous to the poorer part of Citizens," demanded a "Stated Watch" paid regularly out of taxes. Reluctantly the Corporation applied to the Assembly for a new watch law. Country Quakers in the legislature may have suspected that this watch bill was another of the city's martial measures, for at this time Franklin and his cronies were forming the "Association" to protect their homes against the enemy; at any rate the Assembly took no action. In 1749 Mayor Charles Willing prodded the Council about the "Weakness and Insufficiency" of the watch and the pressing need of a tax for its support, "as is done in London and the other great Towns in England." This time, perhaps because Franklin and his committee handled the members more adroitly and also because of "some pitiful Night Robberies" in the city, the Assembly acted, passing a bill creating wardens to supervise lighting the streets, public wells, and a night watch. The Wardens were to hire as many watchmen as they needed, pay them, and remove inefficient persons; the Corporation, on the other hand, drew up the watch regulations. Constables superintended the watchmen and inspected them nightly, while the guardians themselves received ample power to perform their duties properly. The Wardens and tax assessors together levied and collected the watch tax. So successfully did this extreme application of Montesquieu's famous maxim work out that the Philadelphia night watch soon became the colonial standard.

The presence of two races added to the normal complications of preserving peace in Charles Town. Negro discipline was maintained by the mounted patrol of St. Philip's Parish; it consisted of a captain and five men who rode on weekends and holidays to take up all blacks traveling about without passes from their masters. Little complaint ever arose about this body. Less happy was public experience with the "Standing Watch." Frequent burglaries and the fact that one officer kept a punch house where many did their watching incurred condemnation by the Grand Jury in 1744; and the next year's jury presented the "Supiness" of the watch in permitting the robbing of several warehouses. Not infrequently, though, the watch did perform hazardous duties, as in 1748 when Governor Glen ordered it to "take up all Idle and Deserted Seamen" from the two privateers in the harbor. The "usual Pay" did not attract the "Persons of Good Character" wanted, and in 1754 it was rumored that some public-spirited gentlemen would soon go about the city to take down the names of "such as will (with them) voluntarily undertake the Duty of a Watch." Times were indeed ripe for the South Carolina Assembly to set up an effective watch for its metropolis.

V

These years witnessed an alarming increase in robbery and violent crimes in the colonies, and although the situation never attained the proportions it did in contemporary urban England, the same forces seem to have been at work. Since there was now sufficient mobile wealth in or near the cities to make it pay, crime was made attractive in America for the first time. Among the immigrants of all nationalities who poured into these centers were some with European experience of the wrong sort; in fact many people of the Middle colonies attributed the major part of their troubles to imported felons, even though more native Americans actually participated in criminal activities. Urban congestion offered a welcome anonymity to hardened lawbreakers, while the great extent of the provinces made quick and permanent getaways possible. Above all, the ease with which dishonesty could be perpetrated on hitherto unwary folk explains such developments, which, of course, the tumultuous and demoralizing tendencies of war aggravated.

In previous periods the larger communities had experienced violence and theft, but the striking feature of the war years was the extension of crime on an intercolonial scale. This was the era of that great rascal Tom Bell, who between 1743 and 1752 was the most traveled, most notorious, and probably best-known of all the colonists either on the continent or in the West Indies. Capitalizing on the "practical" value

110

of his Latin and two years at Harvard, Tom Bell started his career by impersonating in one colony the son of an eminent person of another. His Latin, ready address, quick wit, and plausible stories marked him as a gentleman, and for years he operated in each of the cities. Though often detected, he usually managed to break out of jail or escape by some "cunning Stratagem." In 1749, "as an old Offender, who has been as great an Instrument of Fraud, Oppression and Injustice, as has been known, perhaps, in any Age of the World," Gentleman Tom received a death sentence in his native Charlestown, Massachusetts; he escaped, however, and continued to be the best copy the colonial press ever had —confidence man, impersonator, robber, petty thief, horse-thief, forger, counterfeiter, bully boy, stool pigeon, mariner, soldier, surveyor. By about the age of forty this "notorious Sharper" had transformed himself into legend and, having played the pedagogue "in almost every Government in America," he retired into Hanover County, Virginia, to teach school and go straight. The "famous American Traveller" emerged briefly in 1752 with proposals to write his memoirs as a warning to others to avoid his wicked ways, and we last hear of him taking subscriptions at Charles Town in 1754. What a priceless item of Americana these would have made! Yet the memory of "the notorious Tom Bell" lingered: in 1755 Daniel Dulany used him as the American standard for measuring impostors.

Less "romantick" than this fellow who "made a great noise in every American colony," yet far greater enemies to society, were the silent and unobtrusive men and women who counterfeited money. Privately manufactured provincial currencies turned up in every city and unwary shopkeepers frequently found their tills full of bad bills of credit. Because so few expert printers and engravers dwelt in America, counterfeiters seldom "uttered" really good imitations; Owen Sullivan and John Tyas of Roxbury owned a complete set of equipment when arrested in 1749 for manufacturing Massachusetts notes, which were, however, "done off very black, and may be easily distinguished from the true ones." Gangs of counterfeiters, including both those who made the money and those who passed it, located in Rhode Island, whence they issued New Jersey, New York, Connecticut, and Massachusetts currency. Many were caught and brought to justice. John Stevens swung from the gallows for the crime at New York in 1744. While awaiting trial at the same town after fourteen years of money-making, Jonathan Woodman of Narragansett committed suicide rather than face the court "and was found hanging dead in his Garters at the Grate of his Prison." Owen Sullivan, the money-boy of Boston, had both ears cropped and a C branded on his cheeks at Providence in 1752, but finally came to his end in the home town four years later after admitting printing £12,000 in Rhode Island bills, £1,600 of which he had passed in one day. Before he was "turn'd off," he told the assembled throng of Yankees: "I cannot help smiling as 'tis the Nature of the Beast." Nor would he divulge how many and what denominations of New York bills he had printed, saying to a chagrined official: *"You must find out that by your learning,* and so died obstinate." Tom Bell even squealed on a counterfeiter and his gang for passing bad money at New York in order to ingratiate himself with the law. First and last, tens of thousands of pounds' worth of bogus bills must have passed into circulation in the cities, not only harming the defrauded individuals who accepted them but also severely injuring provincial currency systems.

All the cities had their burglaries and homicides, but Boston, Newport, and Charles Town luckily escaped the waves of crime that plagued the other two cities. "The streets of Boston," observed Dr. Hamilton with surprise in 1744, "are very quiet and still a-nights, yet there is a constant watch kept." Even when the Louisburg troops were in town, life remained reasonably orderly; underprivileged servants and slaves caused what little violence there was. In 1751 the Grand Jury was discharged because there were no matters for presentment, and the Philadelphia papers, commenting on the news, said: "This Shews the Difference between Colonies that do not receive Convicts and those that do." Still what seems to have been America's first trunk murder excited Boston in 1760, when Mary Waite was committed on suspicion of being concerned in it. At Newport serious robberies and violent crimes occurred so seldom as to be noteworthy. Various thefts happened occasionally, such as times when Newporters learned that "divers Sorts of Linnen have been taken from the Lines whereon they were hanging and carried off." Punishment was meted out promptly when crime was detected: it took a jury twenty-four hours to declare Nathaniel Alcock guilty of murdering his wife in 1746, and several ruffians went to jail in 1749 for assaults and attempted burglaries. When numerous soldiers and outside mariners arrived, petty crime increased noticeably, but the hanging of Samuel Parkes and Benjamin Hawks for piracy in 1760 was such a rare event that it drew between five and six thousand spectators.

Charlestonians had the dubious advantage of witnessing many such ghoulish spectacles, because all trials and executions for the whole province of South Carolina took place there, but the number of local cases was surprisingly small—minor misdemeanors and petty thefts for the most part. Mary Stammers, for instance, received a whipping in 1752 for "assaulting a Constable in the Execution of his Office." During the French and Indian War, however, community order was disturbed by numerous highway robberies committed just outside of town by sailors and soldiers, and in 1759 frequent burglaries occurred while the Cherokee Expedition was being formed. Such a state of affairs fortunately proved only temporary.

Before the passage of the night-watch law of 1750 various kinds of crime flourished in Philadelphia. Courts had to deal with cases of petty larceny, robbery, rape, assault, felony, and homicide—an unusual number of which involved women. Many guilty persons went to jail because they were too poor to pay their fines. Two of three laborers convicted of burglary were hanged in 1747, and although Thomas Fielding and James Johnson, the Jack Sheppards of Pennsylvania, swung from the gallows following a daring attempt to escape from prison in 1749, the epidemic of thefts and holdups continued on into the next year. Three more, including a woman, were hanged for burglary in 1751. After the fashion of Captain Macheath, highwaymen often lurked in the city's environs. By 1752, however, the now thoroughly aroused and reformed constables and watch had brought crime to a halt, for a time at least. With the last French War, conditions again grew worse, and the country learned on February 15, 1758 that "Thefts and petty Robberies are now become so common in and about this City, that no less than eight Persons were last Saturday chastised at a Cart's tail, in the Market-Place, and carted about and whipt at the Public Corners of the Town, notwithstanding the rigidness of the Season."

Not until about 1749 did Manhattan consider crime as a major problem. Then one newspaper sadly commented: "It seems to be now become dangerous for the good People of this City, to be out late at Nights, without being sufficiently strong or well armed, as several Attacks and Disturbances have been lately made in our Streets." Thereafter rogues and thieves aplenty infested New York "with Pillages and Robberies," attracted no doubt by the city's war wealth; one "Gang of Fellows of no good Aspect, came in the Stage Waggon from Philadelphia." At the same time gentlemen suffered petty annoyances from "some low-liv'd People" who repeatedly stole the brass knockers from front doors, and pickpockets ranged the shopping district. While Mary Anderson, "a loose and profligate Wretch" from Philadelphia, was being whipped with "Forty Stripes save one" for theft in 1754, "she afforded some Diversion while at the Post to the Mob, as she was very obstinate and resisting, causing several to try the Sharpness of her Teeth, others to feel the Weight of her Hands, a third got kick'd by her, and poor Ned himself was oblig'd to call loudly for Assistance." Hugh Gaine complained in 1756 that one or more houses were robbed every night, and that no relief was in sight. Two years later James Parker asserted that recent crimes had been perpetrated by "knowing Villains" who had practiced in the city for many years. Things had come to a pretty pass indeed when a two-fisted, swashbuckling privateersman like Isaac Sears had his desk rifled of £2,500 in gold and currency; "but alas!" admitted Parker, "the Watch . . . is in Vain."

One of the most portentous manifestations of the spirit of this age was the mobbish temper of the masses. Whatever may have occasioned the rise of the mobs at London, Liverpool, Bristol, and Dublin, it is evident that in American cities those who constituted the mob, so called, were far from being a mere "rabble" seeking bread and an opportunity to release pent-up boorish boisterousness by despoiling the Egyptians. Of course hosts of sailors on shore leave, unemployed dock and shipyard workmen, and even "Gentleman Rakes" supplied an ever present element of social instability in communities lacking efficient police. Such men were responsible for disturbing the peace, but the contrast with the still medieval English mob is striking in that the colonial variety had in them always a majority of middle-class citizens and the approval of many more. All evidence points to the fact that the colonial mobs symbolized the first fumbling efforts of a people far advanced from the brute stage of their English contemporaries—they were groping, however haltingly, toward the expression of a new force in society, public opinion. Rumblings, followed by outbursts from below, came from a citizenry once prosperous but now economically depressed, despairing, and driven by an urge to right wrongs. In short, they were provoked into displaying, unwisely and crudely to be sure, those aspirations and feelings of "liberty" which we have more recently recognized as democratic; these were among the first outward and visible signs of the profound revolt of the Western World against aristocratic rule, and they convinced a few royal officers at least that England's American colonies would never remain docile.

At uneasy Boston, bowed down by commercial stagnation, almost unsupportable taxation, and large losses of life "beyond the seas," public order nevertheless prevailed to a greater degree than anywhere else in England or America. Very little window-breaking disturbed the inhabitants. Only on November 5, 1745, when servants, sailors, workmen, apprentices, and Negroes of the North and South ends paraded, each with their "Pope," and finally met for a free-for-all in which many were "sorely wounded and bruised, some left for dead," did the annual observance of the Gunpowder Plot degenerate into a "Protestant Mob." Thereafter warnings and eventually, in 1753, a prohibition of such "pageants and shews" in the streets brought Pope Day and like celebrations within reasonable bounds.

The first of the many ill-considered actions of the British government that led eventually to colonial revolt was the rigorous impressment of seamen into the Royal Navy in complete disregard of a law of Queen Anne's reign exempting the plantations from the practice. Beginning in 1740 with a brutal gang operation from the *Astrea* and a press by Captain Edward Hawke of the *Portland,* after saying he would refrain from it, Bostonian resentment festered. In November 1745 Governor Shirley issued a warrant for H.M.S. *Wager* to press fifteen men. Sheriff Hasey of

114

Suffolk County, "knowing he had some dirty Work to do," with several officers and sailors from the man-o'-war, went after mariners just in from the sea, and in so doing stirred up a great uproar in which two seamen were horribly hacked with cutlasses. On November 20 the Suffolk Court found Boatswain John Fowle and a boy, John Warren, of the press gang guilty of murder, but, "because of a flaw in the indictment," sentence was not pronounced. A Town Meeting of March 11, 1746 approved a petition to the House of Representatives drafted by Jeremiah Allen, John Jones, and Deacon Samuel Adams, all highly respected citizens, which deplored the "no less than three several Warrants for Impressing Seamen which (altho we apprehend 'em to be illegal) have been executed in an oppressive manner, before unknown to Englishmen, and attended with Tragical Consequences." Boston, they continued, had lost three thousand seamen, could not send out privateers, or even properly man its merchant vessels. The press gang had forcibly "entered the Houses of some of the Inhabitants in the night to their great Terror." Such conduct by a "lawless Rabble," concluded the petition, is a breach of Magna Charta, the province charter, the act of Parliament of the sixth Queen Anne, and a violation of the pledge of the government to "those brave men" who volunteered for the attack on Cape Breton. More timid counsels eventually forced a reconsideration of this petition because of its reflections on authority, but the weighty indictment and the standing of those who proposed it reflected the rising exasperation of the large majority of Bostonians. Had they known that within two months Parliament would bow to the pressure of the West India Lobby and specifically exempt the Sugar Colonies from impressment, their collective temper might then have snapped.

The breaking-point soon came, however. On the night of November 16, 1747 Commodore Charles Knowles, without seeking the customary official warrant from Governor Shirley, sent out a press gang from Nantasket, where his squadron had just anchored, to procure replacements for the many desertions he had suffered at Louisburg. The gang took men out of all the vessels in the harbor "in their General Sweep." They also covered the waterfront, seizing many landsmen, apprentices, craftsmen, and laborers who were found around the docks in the early hours of the next day, most of them inhabitants of Boston. By ten o'clock a "Tumult," or a "great Number of Seamen and other Lewd and Profligate Persons," or "an outragious Mob," or an incensed citizenry, depending on the point of view, had gathered, assaulted the sheriff and seized hostages for the release of the impressed Bostonians. When Governor Shirley went to the Council Chamber at four o'clock to issue a proclamation against the now several thousand rioters, some of them heaved brickbats through the windows of the State House and forced their way into the lower floor. A friendly councilor then sought to quiet the crowd, but they demanded to know why Warren had never been executed for killing the two sailors the previous autumn. On November 18 the Governor ordered out the militia, though none but officers appeared, the drummers having been interrupted by certain persons. Finally Governor Shirley fled to Castle William, where he sought to restrain Commodore Knowles from ordering a bombardment of the town and to secure the release of the impressed Bostonians in spite of Knowles's heated assertions that the proceedings savored of "arrant rebellion."

For some days government was at an end in the Bay Town; then the House of Representatives and a hastily called Town Meeting expressed horror "at the Destruction of all Government and Order," but the statements suggested far more fear of reprisals and concern for the town's reputation than genuine contrition and also attempted to place the blame for the riots on "Scotch foreigners," sailors, Negroes, wild boys, and low life in general. Truer by far was Shirley's admission to Secretary Willard that "the Insurrection was secretly Countenanc'd and encourag'd by some ill-minded Inhabitants and Persons of Influence in the Town." Bostonians, at least a large segment of them, had had enough. Threats of a fuel and provision shortage because coasters rightly feared the press gang added to an already volatile situation, and Commodore Knowles stupidly and illegally touched it off.

"The principal cause of the Mobbish turn in this Town," Shirley told the Lords of Trade, "is it's Constitution; by which the Management of it is devolv'd upon the populace assembled in their Town Meetings; where . . . the meanest Inhabitants who by their Constant attendance there are generally in the Majority and outvote the Gentlemen, Merchants, Substantial Traders and all the better part of the Inhabitants to whom it is Irksome to attend." He did not, however, fully grasp the situation. Here was the best-ordered community in the Empire, certainly in all America, best-policed at night, most willing to share its mite for imperial defense. Boston, noted for its sacrifices to take Louisburg, was revolting against the King's officers. It was too much, one spirited citizen insisted with understandable exaggeration, to "give us up a Prey to every Lawless Plunderer," and "too shocking to be born" by the people. "They must contentedly behold their Wives abus'd before their Faces, as had been heretofore practis'd, and their Brethren drag'd away or murder'd as formerly." When government fails, as it has so signally, to protect its own, the people have a lawful right to assemble; nay, it is "a Natural Right." Why, argued another correspondent of the *Independent Advertiser,* does government say the late disturbance reflects upon the character of the people? This is a mockery. Rather, let us inquire are the people "peculiarly disposed to Riots" or "is it because they are subjected to peculiar Temptations?" The truth is that the Bostonians angrily resented the press gang and the royal government, which showed itself too weak to restrain the crew of even one sixty-gun ship. What else could they do? Let us speak out, then, wrote another citizen, and criticize our governors, here and at home: "Perhaps there never was a Time when an honest Freedom of Speech was more necessary." Here was public opinion voicing the spirit of '76 in 1747.

These protests against the press gang and the fear of a mob rising when the currency was redeemed produced in 1751 an act for suppressing riots, which provided penalties of confiscation of all personal and real property, and a whipping of thirty-nine lashes every month for three months, for anyone engaging in an unlawful assembly or in destroying property. Even for the age this was a brutal law, and, though an immediate triumph for the reactionaries, it did not go down well with the bulk of Bostonians. Subsequently Governor Thomas Pownall handled cases of impressment from fishing boats and coasters during his administration so understandingly that on his departure in 1760 the people of Boston, addressing him almost tenderly, recalled that he had "with great prudence answered the demand for Seamen for his Majesty's Service, and yet preserved them from the burden of naval impressments; a burden which they had sometimes severely felt."

The mobs of other cities consisted principally of unruly or drunken mariners, privateersmen, or local rowdies. In all of them the "rabble" gathered to celebrate the taking of Louisburg in 1745, and at Philadelphia and New York they broke windows of houses they thought were not properly illuminated. When the news of the defeat of the Young Pretender arrived, the Quaker City's Mayor thought it wise to forbid bonfires lest property be destroyed by drunken crowds; and Gunpowder Treason Night always provided an excuse for a little rough work by Newport's boys. New York, having many transient soldiers and sailors, soon earned a reputation for disorderliness. Particularly obnoxious too were seamen from Newport privateers, who always managed to get into fights at Manhattan. Oliver De Lancey and a crowd of "young Gentlemen Rakes" with "their faces blacken'd and otherwise disguised" broke all the windows in the house of a genteel young Jewish couple recently arrived from Holland, entered the premises, and "tore everything to pieces; they swore they would lie with the woman, Oliver saying that because she was like Mrs. Clinton, and as he could not have her, he would have her likeness." The powerful influence of the De Lancey family kept the attorney general from prosecuting the perpetrators of this outrage. Actually New Yorkers evinced numerous evidences of anti-Semitism and anti-foreign feeling, as the Reverend Henry Mühlenberg discovered when he preached at the Lutheran Church. More comprehensible was the fact that when flour was scarce in 1748, Gerardus Beekman recorded that for "every Load that's Cartaged down to the Vessell, the Shipper [got] at Least Twenty Curses from the Common People, with many hard Wishes for sending of it." Over such incidents authorities could exercise little control, but few royal officers were as wise as General Jeffery Amherst, who refused to use troops to quell anti-military riots at Philadelphia in 1759 and 1760, insisting that such authority "belongs of right to none but the civil power."

Prevalence of widespread crime and disorder required penal arrangements in colonial cities just as in contemporary Great Britain. Although the prevailing theory called for quick corporal punishment in the spirit of the Levitical Code, jails and prisons were needed to confine poor debtors and persons awaiting trial; few colonists ever served long prison terms. Every Northern community had a prison before 1743. In that year Newport constructed an addition to its jail; New York repaired and strengthened the portions of the City Hall used for a prison until 1759, when an excellent "New Gaol" of solid brick with double floors was erected in the Fields. The Assembly of South Carolina was slow to provide adequate detention facilities for Charles Town. Both Governor Glen and successive grand juries agitated for "a good and Sufficient Prison to confine Malefactors," but as late as 1760 Charles Woodmason freely criticized the city's "close, stinking gaol," where sixteen persons were incarcerated in a room twelve feet square. This inadequate structure and the workhouse for the correction of slaves had to serve the Southern city throughout the period.

Conditions within prisons everywhere were deplorable. Confined in Boston's stone prison in 1754 for printing a pamphlet displeasing to the authorities, Daniel Fowle wrote: "If there is any such thing as a hell upon earth, I think this place is the nearest resemblance of any I can conceive of." New York's prisoners made a public appeal for relief in March 1751 because they had not "one Stick to burn" in freezing weather, and when charitable people aided them, the captives published a rhymed letter of thanks in the *Gazette*. Anne Gordon, jailed as a felon at Philadelphia, lay pregnant in the prison and was not permitted to procure her clothes, which the constable had retained. Small wonder that inmates, women included, went to any limits to escape, and nowhere, apparently, did any prison long confine the resourceful criminal. Accounts of jail breaks filled the columns of the urban press; "the notorious Tom Bell" was a past master at escaping, especially at Philadelphia and Boston. After three felons had cut through the wall of Charles Town's jail, which was only one brick thick, Timothy said in his paper that a strong prison would reduce robberies, because as things were, "few Criminals Stay 'till the Times appointed to make their Trials."

Imprisonment for debt was a procedure so illogical that, even at the mid-century, James Franklin of Newport published a pamphlet against it: *The Ill-Policy and Inhumanity of Imprisoning Insolvent Debtors,*

Fairly Stated and Discussed, which probably contributed to the passage of the Rhode Island and Massachusetts laws relieving many debtors when the misfortunes of the times led to their incarceration. Newport jailers had always been generous in construing "the Liberty of the Yard" to include the whole town if the prisoner could provide a bond. In spite of an "Essay on Insolvent Debtors" in a *New York Evening Post* of 1750 stressing the unfairness of this remedy for debt and demanding that all prosecutors appear publicly to swear out warrants, so many people went to jail for insolvency the next year that the New York Assembly passed laws providing some relief for them. In the Philadelphia prison in October 1751 there were thirty-two debtors to sixteen criminals. Although only a mere beginning had been made in the attack, colonial urban opinion was slowly mobilizing against this outmoded English practice.

A reputation for earthiness and lustiness has always attached to the eighteenth century, nor should this surprise us in the light of the well-known demoralizing effects of prolonged wars upon society. Even though the American cities were no exception, public and private morality remained on a much higher plane in the colonies than among either the lower or the aristocratic classes of the mother country. Neither the cynicism of the gentry nor the desperation of the denizens of Gin Lane ever challenged the middle-class attitude toward morality on this side of the Atlantic, but urban morals did decline in comparison with the almost bucolic virtue of most rural areas. In the cities vice could, and for the most part did, conceal itself; there the wars left permanent moral scars. In short, townsmen lived in the moral climate of most seaports of the day, and yet they appeared wholesome to those acquainted with London's Whitechapel and the tenderloins of the great outports.

Public manners, so carefully cultivated by the gentry and the aping bourgeois, declined as "the Great Law of Subordination" gradually gave way among the mass of inhabitants. Profanity and blasphemy plagued the cities over here as they did at Bristol, where, in 1746, persons hearing others curse went "privately" to report the offense and swear out a warrant under a new Parliamentary act providing a twenty-shilling fine and two hours in the stocks for such offenders. Found guilty of "the heinous Sin of blasphemy," Samuel Rhodes of Boston, after being whipped, had to sit in the stocks for only one hour and then give security for a year's good behavior. Profanity increased there in spite of the severity of the law, especially among soldiers. The *New York Evening Post* sadly admitted that the same held true at Manhattan. Even hitherto quiet Newport moved to regulate this "execrable Vice," as did Quaker Philadelphia, whose enlarged floating population and immigrants seemed particularly profane to older residents.

No surer sign of the decline in the old moral standards existed than the failure to maintain a strict observance of the Sabbath. Bristol, England's second city, worried much about violations of Sunday laws, and, in 1753, attempted to suppress the scandalous practice of shaving on the Lord's day at barbershops. After 1749 in Philadelphia the mayors periodically warned against transgressions. Boston kept a ward on Boston Neck every Sunday from seven in the morning until sunset to prevent "prophanation of the Sabbath, travelling, etc." Few taunts so exasperated Bostonians as those that several sanctimonious country people published in the newspapers from 1758 to 1760 blaming the town's economic plight on the decay of religion and morality in the metropolis, though they had to admit that Sabbath-breaking was "a growing evil," and "that the Breakers of those Laws are arrived to a greater Degree of Resolution, than hath been usual." In Newport in 1746 three "Special Constables" were elected to enforce observance of the Sabbath, and later three more were added. More rigorous was Charles Town's experiment with sentinels stationed at the "Town's Gate" every Sunday to prevent drovers, butchers, and servants from coming to market and also to guard against "all Loose and Idle Persons from going a Pleasuring during the Time of Divine Service." Stoutly voiced objections to this hated "military rule" from the press and grand jury did not force Calvinistic Governor Glen to relax his order.

With accumulating wealth and relaxed attitudes, gambling flourished in some places. A legally approved lottery gave most people an opportunity to indulge their instincts for chance, and at Newport this became a common diversion. When Joseph Fox, the scrivener, was put in jail for a debt of three thousand pounds, he received permission to run a private lottery for discharging his obligation. Rhode Island Quakers undertook through their meeting and the Assembly to restrict other forms of gaming in 1749. About the same time New York forbade private lotteries, and the *Evening Post* lashed out at dice games; the Corporation agreed upon a heavy fine "to prevent Rafling," and, responding to public sentiment, outlawed lotteries. South Carolina also forbade private lotteries but tolerated other forms of gambling. Sophia Hume exhorted the women of Charles Town in 1747 to cease trying to mix "Religion and Cards," desiring "her neighbour to hold her Cards till she steps up and says her Prayers." Gentlewomen at the gaming table, said the eloquent Quakeress, are bound to no good.

All classes drank heavily, and drunkenness increased in all the cities. The importation of liquors at Charles Town in 1743 staggers the imagination—1,500 dozen empty bottles, among other items, to be used for "six months' supply" of 1,219 hogsheads, 188 tierces, and 58 barrels of rum. "Hezekiah Broadbrim" of Philadelphia urged John Zenger, Jr., to employ his *New York Weekly Journal* in a crusade against the "carnal-minded . . . and ungodly Practice of adding Drunkenness unto

Thirst," which the *New York Gazette* was conducting. Sottishness bred quarrels, street fights, duels, and often deaths. Dr. Hamilton, himself a capable toper, discovered the nocturnal clubs of Manhattan were mere drinking societies, where he who could not "drink stoutly" with "bumper men" met with a poor reception.

Perhaps the most striking moral outcrop of the war years was the steady increase and openness of sexual laxity. Keeping a mistress was common enough to evoke nothing but the amusement of one's friends and acquaintances. Dr. Thomas Moffatt of Newport paid seventy pounds "to clear him from charges of the child" he begat with Mary Young; Robert Proud, watchmaker of Newport, acknowledged "his disorderly conduct" of marrying out of meeting and having a child born "before due time"; and numerous other well-known Rhode Island Friends confessed fornication or giving birth to bastards. Newport, however, was no worse in this respect than other seaports. Relations between Negroes and whites went on in every city, but miscegenation at Charles Town grew so notorious as to bring denunciation from the clergy of other cities as well as from local arbiters of public morals.

Commercialized vice was a concomitant of both a maritime and a wartime society. For years prostitutes had plied their trade individually in each community; at Manhattan in 1744 a friend told Dr. Hamilton that to walk out on the platform at the Battery after dusk "was a good way for a stranger to fit himself with a courtezan; for that place was the generall rendezvous of the fair sex of that profession after sunset. He told me there was a good choice of pretty lasses among them, both Dutch and English." Bolder prostitutes went aboard privateers, one receiving a ducking from the yardarm and a tarring and feathering from the skipper of the *Castor and Pollux*. At Boston the constables sent "the two noted Fire-Ships, Sarah Floyd and Nab Howard" to the Bridewell. Many widows of the Bay Town turned to selling themselves for lack of other employment, and town charges for the lyings-in of "lewd women" became so large that in 1759 the Selectmen received authority to bind out for five years each woman bearing a bastard. As might be expected, many "loose women" of New York were pickpockets; in 1751 one tart and her husband played the badger game by shaking down their victim for fifty pounds; when he recovered from his fright he had the couple arrested.

Patronage of "Ladies of Pleasure" encouraged the opening of bawdy-houses in all cities. Newport had the only establishment run by a Negress, Madam Juniper; elsewhere there is record only of white brothels. Dorcas Griffiths of Boston conducted a grocery shop with a retail liquor license as a blind; Hannah, wife of Thomas Dilley, let rooms at their dwelling in Cold Lane to whores and "procured for them," being a "notable Bawd," for years until the law caught up with her in 1753 at the age of sixty. It was for good reason, it appears, that the Reverend Andrew Eliot preached that year's fast sermon on the subject of the town's immorality. He sadly perceived that the change in population had raised "an evil and adulterous generation": things "did not use to be so in New England." Nor at Philadelphia, either, for the Quaker minority could no longer control the city's morals. Such women as Prudence Sherrald openly kept bawdyhouses, where British officers like Captain Charles Lee and local rakes plunged themselves into the "vortex of dissipation," until they were made "to smart severely for their violation, by the Mayor's Court."

Organized vice rooted itself at New York as soon as it became the depot for the British forces in the French and Indian War. A raid on "several Houses of Ill Repute" in July 1753 netted twenty-two "ladies of Pleasure," five of whom suffered fifteen lashes each at the workhouse before "a vast Number of Spectators" who came to view the spectacle. After this punishment was administered, they were ordered to leave the city within forty-eight hours or go to prison. But this example utterly failed to stop the traffic. In August 1755 a sharp fight took place when the watch entered a brothel. At least one house sprang up near the new King's College, and Thomas Pearson, mate of H.M.S. *Mercury,* killed a woman there who picked his pocket while vending her "Commodities." Cadwallader Colden sympathized with the condemned mariner, however, and wrote to William Pitt soliciting a King's pardon for him.

VI

For more than half a century before 1743, public care of the indigent had been a matter of major importance to local governments. American colonial cities may not have had the swarms of beggars so familiar to European communities, but they did have their poor. The arrival of large numbers of immigrants, plus the shifting of native population and losses of life incident to the wars, thrust upon authorities a relief problem of considerable proportions.

There was little that the cities could do to prevent strangers from coming in to live off the poor rates. Immigrant English, Scotch-Irish, and Germans arrived by the shipload at Philadelphia, Charles Town, and New York, where, though most of them passed through to the country-side, some became public charges. Very few immigrants sought out Newport, because regular shipping connections with England were non-existent, and, moreover, the Town Council succeeded in preventing strangers from going on the rates by its alertness in "warning out" all intruders. By 1752, "Mendicant Foreigners," particularly from the Palatinate, lacking skills and a knowledge of English, so burdened New York's charities that the Churchwardens had to borrow £150 against the next year's taxes to care for them. Philadelphia received the most immigrants, and although a careful registration system had been worked out in the thirties, the cost of looking after the sick and the paupers went up yearly. In January 1748 Friend John Smith wrote in his diary: "It is remarkable what an Increase of the number of Beggars there is about town in winter, many more than I have before observed, and I have not yet sent any away Empty handed."

Boston's difficulty with poor strangers arose not from immigrants, who seldom landed there, but from war refugees coming from the Eastern parts and Nova Scotia, or from nearby towns that did not provide so generously for the poor. With an actual drain of population going on, the Selectmen did not need to warn out so many strangers as in previous years, but they nevertheless retained John Savell to inquire into the business of every newcomer, especially "Poor, sick, and Lazy" sailors. They also prosecuted inhabitants who failed to report the presence of strangers at their houses. So many had poured in by 1756 that the Selectmen appointed two men to investigate each case and record its status on printed forms. Yet so difficult was it to discover these people that one may question whether the majority were ever detected. On the other hand, generous assistance for those in real distress was always proffered in money, provisions, or transportation homeward. At the province charge in 1744, groups of twenty-three from Canso and twenty more captured from a French privateer on a passage from Ireland to Pennsylvania received shelter at the Alms House.

Pauperized strangers undoubtedly caused more trouble at Charles Town than to the northward because it was the only city of the Southern colonies and offered the only adequate relief in the province of South Carolina. After 1747 the Vestry had the responsibility not only for alien immigrants and impoverished mariners but also for the wives and children left on the parish by soldiers; later discharged soldiers themselves returned, seeking charity. The same situation developed again in the next war, and the Vestry was overwhelmed by the number of wounded or destitute soldiers and the widows and orphans of military men for whom it had to make provision. There were, also, by 1749, many pensioners of the Chelsea Hospital, who had stayed so long that they had acquired residence rights, and the Vestry urged the Assembly to supply them with passages back to England. Then, in 1753, numbers of "poor, lame and Impotent persons" were sent down by wagon or cart from the Congarees, Waterees, and other upcountry settlements for city aid without any warrant or funds to provide for them. Accordingly they had to go "begging from Door to Door" or "perish in the Streets." In addition, not a few of the "miserable Acadians" earlier distributed through the Low Country returned to the city in want. At last, in 1757, the Assembly voted to relieve the churchwardens of the charges for invalid soldiers, their widows and orphans.

Each seaport, in providing charity for members of its own community, expended large sums in the form of out-relief, because it was both less embarrassing to the recipient and sometimes less expensive. Where families could partially support aged, infirm, or poor members, municipal authorities provided assistance. The more or less expected loss of life at sea created many widows in the Northern ports, whose numbers were greatly augmented by the heavy incidence of disease and battle in the several military expeditions. The assessors reported in August 1751 that there were 1,153 widows in Boston—more than seven per cent of the entire population—who, with their many children, were legitimately entitled to public largess. The same situation obtained at Newport, and to a lesser degree in other towns where assistance in the form of fuel, provisions, nursing, medical aid, and small money payments quietly dispensed enabled them to maintain an uncertain living with some semblance of independence. For example, the Town Council supplied one or two cords of wood to each of four Newport widows in 1747. The Charles Town vestry administered a large amount of out-relief, as when in 1750 it gave clothing and schooling for two children of Hannah Caesar, and in 1754 when it paid for a midwife to deliver the wives of two absent soldiers; in 1757 it spent three hundred pounds on clothes for Acadians.

Probably the cities had more orphans than widows to look after, but the majority of the children were bound out as apprentices as soon as they attained the age of eight or ten. New York's Churchwardens advertised in 1750 to notify persons in town or country that they had several children at the Alms House "from Ten Years and under, to be put out Apprentices." The Town Council of Newport bound out orphans for whom they were responsible. In fact few of them remained at poorhouses any longer than could be helped, and in Newport, too, the Town Meeting leased the unused workhouse to Jahleel Brenton, Edward Scott, and James Honeyman "for themselves and Company to carry on the Linen Manufactory for 3 years" to keep a number of poor children at work.

Boston's "Manufactory House," established by the Society for Encouraging Industry, and Commerce and the Employing the Poor in 1748, was the model for the Rhode Island undertaking. Genuine distress over the pauper problem, coupled with the advantage of cheap labor, induced many prominent merchants to subscribe £2,300 for the establishment of a linen manufactory for employing children over eight years old. A supporter of the scheme wrote in a promotion pamphlet: "I have often beheld with Concern, the Swarms of Children of both Sexes, that are continually strolling and playing about the Streets of our Metropolis, cloathed in Rags, and brought up in Idleness and Ignorance; and who must probably come, in a very short Time, from picking of Sticks to picking of Pockets." A large building, financed initially by Thomas Gunter, was erected at the charge of the province, to be paid back by a tax on carriages, which, however, yielded only £738 a year. For a time it operated as planned, with some children employed at spinning and weaving, and a school for "a Number of modest Maidens [thereby] furnish'd with the Means of gaining a Livelihood, who must otherwise, perhaps, have eat their Bread at the Expense of their Innocence." This abortive scheme, borrowed from England, ended its active phase shortly after 1753, but it is most significant, perhaps, for its open recognition that a New World city had a pauper problem of real proportions.

As more and more townsmen needed shelter, those charged with city charity were forced to rely increasingly on poorhouses, which could provide relief cheaper than the more costly though genteel out-relief method. In the thirties all towns save Newport had built almshouses; those of Boston, Philadelphia, and New York were substantial brick edifices, and to such institutions the authorities sent homeless paupers to board at public expense. The New York poorhouse was found to be too small, and in 1746 it was enlarged. The Boston Alms House always had ample room for the local poor, but by 1754 the refugees and sick soldiers sent at the province charge crowded it. The warden of "the Workhouse or Hospital" at Charles Town, who had to be "a Sober, Humane and Careful Person," issued "summer Cloathing and Oznabrig Sheets" during the hot humid weather and in winter lit warm wood fires. Medical care, usually at the hands of one or more leading practitioners, was made available to the poor of each city: St. Philip's Parish paid Doctors Alexander Garden and George Milligen for regular attendance on the sick; the Town Council of Newport hired Norbert Vigneron and Clarke Rodman to treat charity patients; and the Corporation at Manhattan often called in Mrs. Christian Scott as a midwife and nurse at the poorhouse.

The hard times and disasters of these years required the opening of additional facilities for the poor. By 1746 Newport had built a "Workhouse and Alms house," superintended by a "Master" and under a very complete set of rules to guarantee decency, comfort, cleanliness, and proper behavior. Inmates supported there had to perform useful tasks daily, and, like all recipients of town charity, wore "a distinguishing badge," which must have been a humiliating identification. The ten Overseers of the Poor and Workhouse reported in 1760 that the paupers were becoming a great expense and that they themselves were overworked. The Charles Town workhouse needed frequent repairs; in 1752 the Vestry added four more rooms to it so that all persons on "Out-Rents" might be moved there. So crowded did the Philadelphia Alms

House become that Anthony Benezet was forced to solicit private funds to erect a small building for the 454 Acadians the Overseers of the Poor had housed in an old dilapidated barrack in 1755.

Cases of insanity, which society had not yet recognized as primarily a medical problem, were handled as pauper cases; the relatives of a distracted person cared for him at home, often with the aid of public charity as at Boston and Newport, but when they were unable to do so, the patients were confined at the poorhouse. As early as 1746 the Overseers of the Poor asked the Boston Town Meeting to support a proper house for the insane. At Charles Town in 1754 the Vestry requested the opening of an apartment "distant" from the workhouse for insane persons, and the next year the Assembly began to consider a house, chiefly a hospital, "for confining of Persons disordered in their Senses, Fugitive Slaves, etc.," but they reached no decision. The Alms House at Philadelphia had separate apartments for the insane, but before 1749 these unfortunates had been transferred to the Workhouse. A petition of 1751 from humane citizens describing the deplorable plight of the city's lunatics and pointing to the cures effected upon half of those in London's Bedlam, pled for a small hospital for the insane. This plan came to fruition in the separate mental section of the new Pennsylvania Hospital, which opened in 1756.

There can be no doubt of the soaring costs of taxes for poor relief in towns. Beginning in 1743 with £900 currency, Charles Town's expenditures rose to £1,500 in 1750, £3,000 in 1754, £4,000 in 1758, and £6,000 by 1760. The Vestry had to use all of its persuasive powers to wring permission to raise the rates from an Assembly of planters. It is difficult to calculate Boston's outlays because of the inflation, but in 1760 the Alms House and Workhouse alone required £2,155. 11s. 11d. sterling, without any consideration of the out-relief and other expenses. New York's charity cost the inhabitants £1,200 in 1759; the elaborate arrangements in the Quaker City suggest that the Overseers of the Poor, who were incorporated in 1749, must have dispensed a much greater sum. They also received proceeds from certain fines: the sheriff in 1758 turned over £24. 5s. 0d. "paid by Laughlin MacLeane for kissing of Osborne's wife" (a costly buss, that!). No colonial city but was continually vexed with the permanent and costly burden of the poor.

Much private charity supplemented public support of the urban poor. Philadelphia and Newport Quakers assumed a large share of the obligation by relieving their own unfortunates through their meetings. Rhode Island Monthly Meeting laid out £20 for Lydia Norton in 1746; in 1751 it found a place for Hannah Smith to live and paid the rent of £30 a year. When the smallpox afflicted so many in 1752, the Overseers of the Poor asked for and received a general collection for benevolence in all Boston churches. During his several trips up and down the coast from Boston to Charles Town, the evangelist George Whitefield preached many sermons for charity; one in a Presbyterian church at New York attracted the greatest assemblage ever known there and a generous collection. This was an age of emerging humanitarianism in the Western World, and the prosperous citizens of the American cities led the middle classes of all countries in the extent of their generosity and their concern for their fellow men. Their almost lavish contributions to Boston's fire victims in 1760 bear witness to this truth.

The first half of the eighteenth century brought a great development of friendly societies in English cities, which colonial communities were quick to imitate. Boston had its Scot's Charitable Society 'way back in 1657. This body, combining conviviality and benevolence among men of Scottish birth or descent, cared for its own poor from a fund of nearly £1,000 and served as a model for other nationalities. Dr. Hamilton recorded that he attended a meeting with Dr. Douglass in 1744 and that "I contributed . . . 3 pounds New England Currency." The Episcopal Charitable Society (1724) and the Charitable Irish Society (1737) continued their good work of assisting the distressed. A new body, the Quarterly Charity-Meeting, gathered at Faneuil Hall on Sunday evenings in 1750, and four years later the Boston Marine Society, formed with the twin purposes of disseminating nautical information and aiding poor mariners' families, was incorporated by the province. The Scotch Society in Newport, with Sueton Grant as treasurer and the Reverend James Honeyman as president, made generous loans to needy people at Rhode Island. Nineteen sea captains of Newport and vicinity incorporated in 1754 as the Fellowship Club, "a loving and friendly society to promote the interest of each other and their families," with the same objectives as those of the Boston Marine Society. Philadelphia acquired its Scottish charity when the St. Andrew's Society was organized in 1749 at the Tun Tavern in Chestnut Street. Dr. Adam Thomson, a founder of the Philadelphia organization, was the prime mover in establishing another St. Andrew's Society at New York when he moved there in 1756. Another eleemosynary body, not restricted to the Quaker City, was the Corporation for the Relief of Poor and Distressed Presbyterian Ministers, Their Widows and Children established by the Synod of Philadelphia in 1755.

In every way a cosmopolitan city in which generous gifts for charitable uses were the mode, Charles Town became the seat of many private benevolent societies. The St. Andrew's Society, founded in 1729, was the oldest, but the Huguenot membership of the South Carolina Society (1739), which met every Tuesday evening at Poinsett's Tavern, was the wealthiest and most prominent. Incorporation by the Assembly in 1751 allowed it to "erect, endow, and support proper schools" and almshouses, and perform all other "Charitable and Generous Actions." Famous for elegant suppers at Robert Raper's Tavern, the St. George's Society bestowed its largess on needy Englishmen and their families. The three Masonic lodges completed the "Publick Societies." Supported by gifts, dues, and handsome bequests, these organizations played a very important part in the excellent record of the Southern metropolis in meeting the challenging problem of the poor.

VII

Ordinary everyday living in congested urban areas forced concern with public health, for illness and death were far more common occurrences in the experience of all citizens in the eighteenth century than in our own day. Separated by the Atlantic from the teeming centers of Europe, the five seaports providentially escaped many of the dreaded visitations that so often decimated Old World cities. By strenuous efforts to use every known theory and weapon against disease, the townsmen succeeded remarkably well for their times in combating all scourges except smallpox and yellow fever. This fact is patent when the state of health and the death rate in the colonial cities is compared with contemporary achievements in the British Isles in sanitation and medical reform.

Long familiarity with problems of health had caused the towns to take measures as soon as a threat of an epidemic arose, and since 1720 they had built up a series of regulations that guarded the public health as far as prevailing medical knowledge would permit. Boston agrees with English constitutions, "for which Reason the Gentlemen of West Indian Islands go thither," observed William Price in 1743. He might also have mentioned that careful regulation of funerals, burials of humans and animals, cemeteries, drainage, and payment of bounties on rats, together with strict enforcement of the quarantine laws and prompt isolation of infectious diseases, preserved the inhabitants from many ills. New York was equally healthy. During the years 1743 and 1744 Cadwallader Colden, an M.D. from Edinburgh, adroitly employed newspaper columns in a war on the nastiness of the docks and the necessity of draining stagnant pools and marshy ground as well as the regulating of skinners and tanners, who produced most of the city's "Noisom Smells." Officials at Newport, Philadelphia, and Charles Town took similar precautions in the name of health and to ensure the "purity of the Air." In 1744 the Grand Jury protested against allowing Charles Town's tallow chandlers to work in "the heart of the Town," and the *Gazette* emphasized the importance of "active scavengering" in a warm climate. Actually only newcomers could view these large cities through the eyes of a person like the Reverend Henry M. Mühlenberg, who complained at New York in May 1751 of being "confined to the oppressive, impure, and unaccustomed air of the city"; by July, even he had changed his tune, however, admitting readily that "the air in New York is very healthy, especially for me."

By the standards of the time, the inhabitants of all cities enjoyed better health than their European contemporaries. More people died from such common diseases as the bloody flux (dysentery), respiratory ailments (colds, influenza, pleurisy, pneumonia), heart troubles, and malaria than from more dramatic and virulent epidemics that struck suddenly, concentrating mortality within a short but terrifying period of time. Of these, smallpox was unquestionably the most feared.

Boston underwent a great epidemic of smallpox as a sort of conclusion to its other serious troubles. An isolation hospital at Rainsford's Island in the harbor had been opened in 1744 for victims of infectious diseases and the reception of sick passengers arriving by ship; numerous other measures had been taken to prevent the entry of disease by sea. Largely a result of this regulation, the city remained free from any visitation until 1752. In January the scourge appeared, and for a time the Selectmen tried to minimize it, but on March 23 the General Court moved out to Cambridge. In April the Suffolk County Court went to Dorchester, where it met for the country people and the Bostonians on separate days. About thirteen hundred of the frightened inhabitants fled to nearby towns. Realizing the gravity of the situation, the Selectmen now ordered all dead bodies wrapped in "a tarr'd sheet and bury'd in the Evening after their decease and without the usual solemnities of a Funeral." Deaths from smallpox increased steadily from about twenty-five a week in April to more than eighty in July, but by August 31 the epidemic had disappeared, and the relieved Selectmen could urge fuel boats and market people to come into town again. The Reverend Thomas Prince, writing in the *Newsletter* of July 12, emphasized the good work performed by local physicians, some of whom had been accused of gouging and monopoly in treating and inoculating. Doctors Nathaniel Perkins, William Rand, and William Clarke inoculated over seven hundred persons, black and white, and lost only four patients. According to the Selectmen's figures, between January 1 and July 24 a third of the population (5,544) contracted the disease, of whom 514 died; out of the total of 2,109 inoculated, only 31 succumbed, a ratio of 1 death in 70 for those who risked inoculation and 1 in 7 for those who contracted the disease in the natural way. The publication of these statistics made it abundantly evident, not only in Boston but at the other cities, that the action of giving the infection to prevent it from becoming virulent had more than proved its efficacy.

Disadvantage of climate and nearness to the tropics caused Charles Town to suffer more and severer epidemics than the Northern cities. That "great and Malignant Sickness, called the Yellow Fever, in which they die suddenly" invaded the city on four different occasions during this period. Comfort rather than scientific knowledge impelled citizens to purchase Kenting (netting), "the Inhabitants being almost devoured by the Mosquito's, for want thereof." Dr. John Moultrie's careful study of the severe epidemic of 1745, when published as his Edinburgh thesis in 1749, described scientifically for the first time what was commonly called the "Black Vomit." Angina maligna (diphtheria) carried off many children in 1746 and 1756. To prevent the importation of contagious diseases from the Caribbean or Africa, the South Carolina Assembly hired port physicians to inspect all incoming vessels, and maintained a pesthouse on Sullivan's Island. There was agitation in 1749 for "a public hospital," remote from the city, to which sick sailors could be taken from the overcrowded "rotten punch houses" they ordinarily lived in when ashore, and as a result, the Churchwardens and Vestry set up such an establishment for seamen and other "indigents."

Introduction of smallpox by Cherokee Indians who were brought to town by the Governor on February 2, 1760 set off the most fatal epidemic of the period. Business of all kinds came to a standstill and many citizens fled in terror to the Low Country. So alarmed were they, said Dr. Alexander Garden on March 13, that they were "driven precipitately to have many more inoculated than could be attended by the practitioners of physic. Not less than 2,400, and I believe not more than 2,800, were inoculated in the space of 10 or 12 days." One doctor had "upwards of 600 patients." Many Charlestonians also contracted the disease naturally, and the city fell into great confusion. By April, Dr. Garden had improved on his method of inoculating, partly by reading about Dr. Adam Thomson's use of mercury in the *Discourse on the Preparation of the Body for Small Pox,* published at Philadelphia in 1750.

Peter Timothy estimated that when the smallpox first broke out, 6,000 of the inhabitants of the city had never had it, but that the number had been reduced by inoculation or "the Natural Way" to 500 on March 22, and on April 26 he printed the piece on inoculation by Dr. William Heberden of London which Benjamin Franklin had circulated in the colonies the previous year. In all, about 300 white persons (including 115 Acadians) and 350 Negroes (an actual total of 730) succumbed to the scourge—more than in the Boston epidemic of 1752. During most of the year "the scarcity and Dearness of Provisions" caused by the unwillingness of country people to come to market bore heavily on the lower class. Although the worst of the epidemic was over in July, many merchants did not begin to move back into town with new stocks of goods purchased since the infection until December. Inasmuch as nearly all the Charlestonians had contracted the smallpox one way or another, they were now immune to the disease and were spared any further serious visitation for the remainder of the colonial period.

Other cities escaped long sieges with epidemic diseases. Philadelphia's principal difficulty came from Palatine or ship fever (typhus) brought in by immigrants, but isolation of all cases recognized by the port physicians at a hospital erected on Province Island in 1743 kept it from spreading. Angina maligna, or the "putrid sore throat" in local parlance, caused many deaths among children in 1746, and yellow fever threatened occasionally. Smallpox appeared with frequency, but never in epidemic proportions. Nevertheless inoculation gained in popularity with the middle and upper classes as a result of Franklin's advocacy of the treatment and the news from Boston and Charles Town. New York's experience was much the same, except that Palatine fever did not appear there.

The incidence of epidemic diseases was lightest at Newport, but the fear of them was exceedingly great. The Town Meeting, looking into every possible means of keeping disease out, laid down very strict rules about contagious ships in order to save the town from "the very great expense" incurred in the past. Whenever news arrived of an outbreak of smallpox at Boston or New York, Rhode Islanders became almost hysterical. Vessels arriving from Manhattan were searched and overland travelers from Boston were turned back at the ferries to wait five days on the province borders. During the great Boston epidemic of 1752, the Newport Town Meeting charged that "many wicked and indiscreet persons" slipped in from Boston in small boats, and fixed a fine of twenty pounds for any detected in the practice. Inoculation evoked little sympathy and less understanding among "mistaken, tho' otherwise good and well-meaning People" in this community, even when "Humanus" wrote in the *Mercury* of the fear that returning troops would bring the smallpox with them in 1759, and explained that "inoculation under due Restriction would certainly relieve the rising Generation from this Dread."

The one institution of lasting value bequeathed by this generation as a symbol of the awakening of urban opinion to the responsibility of society for the health and welfare of its members was the Pennsylvania Hospital. Filled with enthusiasm for the excellent work of the English hospital movement, Dr. Thomas Bond returned from London in 1748 determined to give better shelter and treatment to the sick and the demented of the Quaker City than that afforded by the Alms House. Immediately he proposed founding a hospital "for the reception and care of poor sick persons, whether inhabitants of the province or strangers." Indifference or distrust greeted his efforts until he enlisted the support of Benjamin Franklin, who won over the public with stories planted in the *Pennsylvania Gazette* and so shrewdly played the populace and the Assembly against each other as to gain both a large popular subscription and a general legislative grant. With £4,750, the Contributors to the Pennsylvania Hospital received a charter in 1751 creating a pri-

vate corporation, which inhabitants of all ranks and estates, all nationalities and faiths, supported so enthusiastically that in 1754 the
managers could state that "few of the Wealthy, or those of a middling
Rank, failed of contributing according to their circumstances."

While a handsome building was going up, the Pennsylvania Hospital
opened on February 6, 1752 in a house on Market Street. Admission
might be gained on a paying or a charity basis for either lunatics or sick
persons, excepting incurables and those having infectious diseases. Before the east wing of the great structure, designed by Samuel Rhoads,
was ready for occupancy, in December 1756, over two hundred patients
had been treated at the hospital. Planned with real understanding of its
needs, the new building contained a walking-gallery and special apartments for the insane, the best bathing, heating, and sanitary facilities
available, and ventilators for expelling foul air. No European infirmary
of the time surpassed this civic undertaking in providing humane treatment for the mentally ill, comfortable quarters for the sick, and competent medical attendance. Soon not only the Germans and Scotch-Irish
of the province, but families as far away as Rhode Island were sending
members to the Philadelphia institution for mental treatment. Well might
Benjamin Franklin share with his fellow citizens in "the real and lasting
Satisfaction to humane Minds . . . of having made such a social Use
of the Favours of Providence . . . to open a Door of Ease and Comfort
to such as are bowed down with Poverty and Sickness."

VIII

During the second quarter of the eighteenth century a striking new
phenomenon began to make its appearance in the Western World. Europe's population was rapidly growing; it was filling up old countries like
England and Germany, and creating in colonies in America the equivalent of whole new nations. Just as the cities of the mother country commenced to feel the pressure of their people, so did those across the
Atlantic. In the wake of such rapid expansion came a host of problems
that turned out to be urban, not rural, in their nature, requiring new or
novel solutions—or having none. The inhabitants of the five American
cities attacked these problems—fire, public safety, morals, poverty, public health—with considerable vigor, much ingenuity, and some success
in the midst of distracting complications incident to the wars. Their
achievements were uneven, varying from place to place, and with the
particular problem. But the interesting—perhaps unique—fact is that because these were relatively new communities, when compared with the
centuries-old towns of Europe, the citizens were less restricted in their

actions by the forces of tradition and inertia. Having no huge lower class and no privileged aristocracy to contend with, the prospering middle classes could propose and carry to fruition their own plans for civic betterment, and increasingly demonstrated a willingness to tax and be taxed for the common good. In the newspaper press they discovered, moreover, a powerful vehicle for exposing nuisances, criticizing authority, and instigating reforms. It is no accident that the first citizen of the age was a printer. As a consequence, the middle-class passion for neatness, decency, and safety of property, given free rein in American cities, made for impressive municipal advances.

CHAPTER 4

City People

O F EVEN GREATER IMPORTANCE than either the environment or the economy in the determination of the nature of urban society are the men and women who compose it, for, as a character in *Coriolanus* inquires, "what is the city but the people?" Five large aggregates of human beings now lived prosperously amid artificial surroundings in relatively congested areas. Heavy immigration and the absence of the rigid social order of the Old World hastened a mingling of nationalities and classes that was producing a distinct American urban society. This people—optimistic, secure, ambitious—tended to devote some of its new wealth to various forms of comfort, luxury, and diversion. According to their lights, new or old, the citizens worshipped fervently or walked on untrodden paths; but all of them participated unwittingly in the subtle, but relentless, trend away from the religious to the secular outlook on life, an attitude that this period clearly reveals for the first time in American history.

II

Natives of the cities shared in the high colonial birth-rate, to which Benjamin Franklin called attention in 1755 in his remarkable *Observations Concerning the Increase of Mankind, Peopling of Countries etc.* Families were often very large, but because marriage came later and many people remained single all their lives, urban population did not double every twenty-five years with that of the country as a whole. Accidental deaths and losses at sea further served to check growth; the great accessions resulted from the steady arrival of "forreigners."

Immigrants of many nationalities went to Philadelphia because it was the best publicized of colonial cities. Every year English artisans migrated, attracted by such advertisements as that in the *Bristol Journal* of April 5, 1755, which promised, among other inducements, a new suit of clothes for any handicraftsman who would "go over to the most flourishing city of Philadelphia." Irish and Welsh tradesmen also located there; in 1753 one vessel from Milford, Wales, landed two hundred passengers. Scotch-Irish immigrants who settled in the Quaker City swelled the Presbyterian element and merged with comparative ease into the English-speaking population. Most of them landed at New Castle, but in 1750 over a thousand came up the Delaware to the metropolis. Nor should the self-induced migration of a small number of well-to-do men, who soon rose to prominence, be overlooked. Not all of the newcomers from the British Isles made good inhabitants, however; in 1751 Franklin wrote for his *Gazette* the famous proposal to exchange American rattle-snakes for the felons that English authorities had sent over, persons who contributed measurably to the growth of immorality and crime.

Differences in language, religious affiliations, appearance, and customs set the Germans from the Rhenish Palatinate apart from all other immigrants. Making profitable cargoes, they were brought over in droves during the several peaceful years. Of 600 Palatines indentured to servitude in return for their passage before Mayor Hamilton during 1745 and 1746, 360 remained in the city or in Philadelphia County. The flow slackened during King George's War but then increased again in 1749, when more than 7,000 arrived, "many of whom stayed in . . . town." Every autumn twenty to twenty-four ships discharged so many at the wharves that by the time the French and Indian War broke out, Gottlieb Mittelberger recognized that Palatines had become "very unwelcome, especially in the city of Philadelphia."

Wartime interruption of the German influx was probably fortunate in that it permitted some absorption of the strange people to take place. The Palatines took over the section of the city along the Delaware north of Race Street and adjacent parts of the Northern Liberties, and here, in what became the first foreign-language area of any American city, they opened Reformed and Lutheran churches and set up German schools. One of their few gentlemen discovered that "in this country there exists (what we do not find in Old England), among the English settlers, a supreme contempt for the Germans. This may be owing to the fact, that the former see members of lowly and poor German immigrants, in comparison with whom they entertain an exalted opinion of themselves." By 1753 the usually serene Franklin, fearful of French Catholic influence among the Palatines, had commenced to worry about the difficulties, potential and actual, that the language barrier created between the two nationalities: "Advertisements, intended to be general, are now printed in Dutch and English. The signs in our streets have inscriptions in both languages, and in some places only German. . . . In short, unless the stream of their importation could be turned . . . they will soon outnumber us." He did not advocate any narrow nationalistic policy of exclusion; rather did he propose distributing them among the English and teaching them our language. As for the newcomers, homesickness, misery, and concern for their future in the strange city must have been deeply felt by many, but were seldom given public expression.

Many immigrants also found their way to Charles Town. There in 1742 came the great Lutheran leader, the Reverend Henry Melchior Mühlenberg, who lodged at the house of the painter Jeremiah Theus, brother of the German Reformed minister. Encouraged by the provincial government, shipmasters began to bring in loads of from three hundred to four hundred Palatines "willing to serve anyone who will buy their time," and by 1749 Peter Timothy was advertising in German to sell a German calendar printed at Philadelphia. Simultaneously shiploads of Dublin "Tradesmen" came in, and in 1756 three hundred Acadians arrived in custody. These nationalities, plus a handful of Sephardic Jews, lent to the Southern metropolis a definitely cosmopolitan air by 1760.

Few Germans settled in New York until after 1750, but thereafter many of them, some of whom were artisans, came there to add to a population already compounded of English, Dutch, and miscellaneous nationalities. In 1753 one master was responsible for bringing in two thousand Palatines. To them and the many Scotch-Irish and English immigrants, New Yorkers, perhaps unfairly, ascribed the rise in crime at Manhattan, and in 1754, the Corporation ordered all masters of vessels to notify the Mayor within two hours of landing any strangers at the docks.

The New England seaports did not attract immigrants; shipmasters and merchants in the servant traffic found readier sales from New York southward. The Society for Encouraging the Importation of Foreigners met at Wethered's Tavern, but accomplished little. Occasionally ships brought in a few foreigners: two hundred Irish passengers reached Boston in September 1750, "among whom, 'tis said, are Persons of Considerable Substance," who would be welcomed inasmuch as they threatened no strain on the poor rates; and the arrival of three hundred Germans to settle at Braintree and make glass created a stir in 1752, chiefly because forty children had been born on the passage. Except for a sprinkling of French, Genoese, and Spanish merchants, who were naturalized, and an especially active group of Jewish traders, headed by Aaron Lopez and Napthali Hart, there were few foreigners migrating to Newport. The island city's population increased almost wholly by the natural birth-rate, and by 1760 some of it had actually been drained off by emigration to Nova Scotia and New Brunswick. Newport remained the most English of all the cities.

III

Widespread prosperity and wartime tensions inevitably affected the social order, which, for more than a century, leaders had been endeavoring to fashion after the English pattern. An exact copy they could never make, because a counterpart of the British nobility was lacking, and another element, the middle class, was present in overwhelming proportions. What resulted was a realignment of the two European lower ranks into three classes. Contemporaries, recognizing the new American distinctions, carefully labeled their upper class "the better Sort," whose role in society always transcended those of "the middling Sort," and the "inferior Sort." Under the impetus of the new wealth, society attained a stratification that bore a strong surface resemblance to that of the mother country, albeit governed by bourgeois ideals and standards. Yet the impulse to emulate the British aristocracy triumphed, and, as in all ages and places, out of the transplanted middle class emerged an urban colonial gentry with pretensions paralleling and in some respects outshining those of the rural tobacco and rice planters of Virginia and the Carolinas.

Few witnesses to this significant transformation better understood what was happening than Arthur Browne, who, as an Anglican clergyman, lived in Newport, Boston, and Portsmouth: "Yet even there (without nobility, or orders of gentry) you might see a proof how necessarily some difference of rank, some inequality must and ought to grow up in every society, and how Eutopian and ridiculous the contrary idea and attempt is. The inhabitants of the town by more information, better polish and greater intercourse with strangers, insensibly acquired an ascendancy over the farmer of the country; the richer merchants of these towns, together with the clergy, lawyers, physicians and officers of the English navy who had occasionally settled there, were considered as gentry; even being a member of the church of England gave a kind of distinctive fashion. A superior order thus formed by better property and more information existed even to a degree sufficient to excite jealousy in the agricultural system, and to be a gentleman was sufficient in some parts of the country to expose the bearer of that name to mockery and rudeness, a specie of inconvenience which a liberal mind pardoned as compensated by the comfort and independence which produced it."

Both by word and by deed the men of this era displayed a consuming interest in status. Preaching a sermon on *The Fall of the Mighty* to a mixed auditory of the gentle and the vulgar at Boston, the Reverend Samuel Mather pronounced a benediction upon inequality: "It appears very evident, that the supreme Governor of the World has been pleas'd to constitute a Difference in Families: For, while most of the Sons of Men are Brethren of low Degree or of common Derivation; Some are Sons and Daughters of the Mighty: They are more honorably descended, and have greater Relations than others: These therefore may well wear the Character of the Mighty. . . . Some are Mighty by Means of the Wealth, which the Providence of a bountiful God has given them."

Few, if any, townsmen seriously questioned this ancient rubric. What did deeply concern them was the individual's place in the social hierarchy. Whereas in the British Isles and on the Continent most people expected to remain permanently in the rank into which they had been born, in the New World of the English the "Great Law of Subordination" had never been re-enacted. In the colonial cities the ambition to better their condition possessed all classes alike, and they doggedly insisted that not only the way to wealth but the road to place be kept open. This was the promise of America.

Admission to the urban gentry was open to all who possessed wealth acquired by inheritance, by marriage, or in trade. Prestige also weighed heavily, whether derived from birth into an old established family, professional or college education, religious affiliation, office-holding, or proper introductions for those recently come from abroad. The gentry welcomed the possessors of power. In cases other than the clergy, whose social position remained impressive, power customarily equated with property. And in these years, whatever the failures of many, more and larger individual fortunes than had been known before ushered their owners into the ranks of "the better Sort." In 1756 Thomas Chesebrough confided to Ezra Stiles of Newport his secret plan for winning the way to affluence and influence: (1) Never divide or alienate any land or other estate, said he, for it is bound to increase in value, and " 'tis not good to be upon a Level, or under the Foot of every Schoundrel." (2) If you have more than one child, leave your property to the eldest son, and, for the rest, "give them Trades, Merchandizg., Physic, &c.," taking care that they learn to write and cipher well. "Such come often to Live as well as the Heirs." (3) Keep your scheme quiet, "but encourage others to divide their Estate." (4) "When you have a Landed Estate, have no Concern with the Sea. With Diligence and Frugality, your Estate will encrease fast eno' without exposing it to Hazard— Festina lente."

The most powerful and solidly entrenched city families were those of Boston and Philadelphia. The Hutchinsons, Bromfields, Clarkes, Quincys, and Phillipses, descended from the early Puritans, had behind them several generations of wealth and position, and members of the local Congregational clergy like the Mathers and Chauncys were esteemed by virtue of their cloth, a Harvard education, and wise marriages. With the advent of royal government after 1691, a "court circle," composed of crown officials and Anglican merchants, began to form. Vassalls, Royalls, and Olivers from Jamaica and Antigua, Wendells from Albany, Ervings from the Orkneys, and the Huguenot families of Faneuil, Bowdoin, Johannot, and Deblois, attracted by commercial opportunities and the climate, were eligible because of superior fortunes and a gracious manner of living. In 1746 when Father Lloyd despaired of marrying off his daughter "Betsie," his worldly son Henry advised that you "might Consider the matter in a proper Light and that if you sell the Neck [estate] and Goe either to York or Boston, that under your then Circumstances she stands as Good a Chance to make her Fortune by Matching Well as any Young Lady allmost without Exception." Not until 1754, when she was thirty-two, did Betsie espouse Samuel Fitch, a Boston lawyer. Nathaniel Lloyd, a brother, fared even better when he won the hand of Elizabeth Davenport and thereby came into a share of the Faneuil fortune—"Twenty-five hundred pounds sterling in the Stocks in England at 4 per cent," Henry calculated, "is £100 per annum, her present income."

Under the ægis of these newcomers, provincialism dissolved and so did New England restraint and thrift. Boston's quality grew accustomed to a gay and expensive existence and took on the cosmopolitan outlook, hauteur, insistence on privilege, and elaborate ritualism of a free-spending, pleasure-loving, Anglican coterie. No longer could such a gentleman as frugal Byfield Lyde support a wife, six children, and five servants, "which is a large family," on £200 sterling out of an income of "near 1000£ a year." These large fortunes, of course, belonged only to the few; Boston had many merchants of middling estate, as Birket learned on his visit, and some had "Acquired Opulent fortunes and with great Reputation."

Prosperous Quakers from London and Bristol had established themselves at Philadelphia in its early days, and others came over in the eighteenth century to join with them as the Front Street aristocracy and rulers of the province. But, as at Boston, the Logans, Mifflins, Norrises, Pembertons, Powels, and Whartons soon discovered that they must share power and prestige with successful merchants of Church of England and Presbyterian connections, whose families eventually became arbiters of Philadelphia society, as the election of Anglican James Hamilton as Mayor in 1745 and his appointment as Lieutenant Governor in 1748 strikingly indicate. Henceforth Presbyterian Allens and Shippens, and such communicants of Christ Church and St. Paul's as the Willings, Francises, McCalls, and Hopkinsons, set the pace for the gentry by their dress, hospitality, taste, and patronage of the arts at the same time that they rivaled the Friends in public service and charity. So alluring, in fact, did the latitudinarian discipline and Anglican ritual seem to many a Quaker that he followed the example of William Plumstead by passing over from the meeting to Christ Church, though few matched his service as a vestryman and churchwarden. Ideas of grandeur and pride of position captured the minds of Friends who clung to the meeting house. Elizabeth Sandwith tells us that on September 26, 1759 eight Quakeresses dined at Ann Warner's with some other ladies, "which made it 14 of the best Sort, ourselves included." A smaller proportion of the members of this gentry came of English descent than at Boston, for the

Scots, Scotch-Irish, and Irish in the persons of the Thomas Graemes, George Bryans, Redmond Connynghams, and more, provided they otherwise met the admission requirements, found a ready welcome. So too did Philadelphia's aristocracy openly embrace wealthy Jews, two of whom it included on the beadroll of sixty subscribers to the Dancing Assembly of 1749.

Newport's first families presented the unique spectacle of what might be termed a sea-bred or maritime gentry. Nearly every family fortune had its origin on the quarterdeck if not before the mast; thence its possessor stepped ashore to set up as a merchant and eventually to retire as a country gentleman. This was as true of the Almys, Browns, Freebodys, Coggeshalls, Sanfords, and Wantons stemming from the seventeenth century as it was of the more recent Ayraults, Collinses, Malbones, Channings, and Grants. The little city's most aristocratic family in 1753 consisted of the three beautiful daughters of the late Edward Pelham, gentleman of leisure and ample fortune. By winning the affections of Elizabeth Pelham in 1746, Peter Harrison from York, England, catapulted himself into the colonial aristocracy only seven years after he arrived at Newport as a cabin boy in his brother's vessel. John George, a sea captain who spent some time on Rhode Island in 1748, thus cynically assessed its gentry: "A Man who has Money here, no matter how he came by it, he is Every thing, and wanting that he's a meer Nothing, let his Conduct be ever so ereproachable. Money is here the true Fuller's Earth for Reputation, there is not a Spot or Stain but it will take out."

New York and Charles Town had their old families, of course, but conditions peculiar to each had hindered the development of a ruling urban class until this time. Dutch and English families, among whom the Beekmans, Bayards, Phillipses, Van Dams, Morrises, and Livingstons figured prominently, dated from the days of the West India Company's rule, but theirs remained more a landed than a commercial interest until the great spurt in Manhattan's trade came with King George's War. Then these landowners and such mercantile families as the Cuylers, Waltons, Crugers, Crommelins, Rutgers, Watts, and Ludlows, by intermarriage and increasing wealth, merged into a true urban gentry, albeit with strong rural leanings. Chiefly, however, they continued to be a coterie whose prestige arose more from riches than from birth, education, or cultural eminence. Even though America had no family with more aristocratic pretensions than the hosts of Morrisania, William Smith recorded in his diary after entertaining Lewis and Staats Morris that "Staats by his late marriage with the Duchess of Gordon thinks of Business and serving himself." During the period, twenty-five persons took out the freedom of the city as "Gentlemen," probably because they did not have to work for a living. The coming of British officers in each of the wars lent further tone to an incipient gentility. Some of the new gentry claimed

more privileges than were their due: James Livingston was forced to tell
William Alexander, a kinsman, that the law required him to pay for a
substitute on the night watch: "I cannot Excuse you altho I did it the
Last Time." The De Lanceys' place at the top of the province, as we
have seen, saved Oliver in 1749 from prosecution for outraging the
Jewish couple.

Coming to live in South Carolina in 1741, Elizabeth Lucas found the
leading families of the capital hospitable, polite, and gentle in behavior
but far from the rank of the planters of Antigua, where her father was
Governor. The new gentry of this Southern colony was still concerned
primarily with getting and spending and was composed chiefly of rice
and indigo planters who lived in town only during the hot summer
months. In these two decades many of them made the city their permanent residence, joining with rising native merchants, factors representing
English houses, and Scottish physicians in the building of an urban
group of "the better sort." Wealth wrung from trade, rice, indigo, or
lumber gave them a passport to this society. Perhaps with less reticence
than Northern newspapers showed, Timothy's *South Carolina Gazette*
bared its pride in the merging of fortunes by carefully arranged marriages. Captain Thomas Frankland, R.N., brother of Boston's Sir Harry,
made a brilliant match with Sarah Rhett, "a beautiful and accomplish'd
young Lady, with a large Fortune," which he consolidated with the one
he had acquired from the capture of Spanish treasure ships when he
commanded H.M.S. *Rose*. Abraham Bosomworth, royal Indian agent,
won in Susannah Seabrook "a young Lady endowed with all agreeable
Accomplishments, and a fortune of £15,000," but John Ainslie, with
true Caledonian calculation, won in Mary Child "an Heiress—reputed
the richest in this Province." In each account of "considerable Matches"
—Charles Pinckney and Eliza Lucas, Christopher Gadsden and Jane
Godfrey, John Drayton and Governor Glen's sister, George Roupell and
Elizabeth Prioleau—the *Gazette* assured its readers that the lady was
beautiful and possessed of "a handsome fortune and other amiable Accomplishments."

The aristocratic tradition as handed down in eighteenth-century England dictated certain ways for the conspicuous spending of money and
set forth approved canons of taste and behavior for its votaries. Aspiring
ladies and gentlemen of the colonial cities unquestioningly accepted
these standards, conforming to them with the same literalness with which
they obeyed injunctions found in the etiquette books. The result was a
species of family display conducted by almost classic rules of formal
living, with town and country mansions as backdrops.

Fine town houses reminiscent of Old World bourgeois magnificence,
though on a smaller scale, made their appearance after 1750 as the
gentry in each seaport amassed sufficient wealth to build and maintain

them. "The modern taste in building" and the number of new mansions led to a competition for elegance that ensured the adaptation of the various elements of the contemporary urban architecture of Georgian England. Such ideas derived mainly from the manuals of William Halfpenny, Batty Langley, and the London builders, though George Harrison crossed to Philadelphia, Dudley Inman to Charles Town, and Theophilous Hardenbrook to New York in search of commissions as architects and building surveyors, and advertised that London training equipped them to undertake "buildings of all kinds, with more convenience, strength, and beauty, than those commonly erected." City taste, however, found its best expression in the interiors rather than the outsides of town houses. Spacious rooms, paneled or "hung" with the new Chinese wallpapers, finely carved furniture of mahogany and walnut or of imported lacquer, upholstered with imported English fabrics—these seemed, as indeed they were, expressly designed for an open hospitality symbolic of prosperity and station.

As the residence of the royal governors, Boston's famous old baroque Province House had set the style for expensive building in the north or "court" end of town. Many gentlemen were erecting detached mansions, but probably no town house anywhere excelled the Clarke house for richness of interior decoration and furnishings. Sir Henry Frankland purchased it in 1756 for £1,200 sterling when he returned from abroad with Agnes Surriage, now Lady Frankland, determined to launch her in such magnificence that Boston quality would be forced to accept her. The handsome Faneuil, Bromfield, and Hancock mansions, with their celebrated formal gardens, are but the best-known of those built by men who indulged in luxury notwithstanding war and commercial tribulations.

War fortunes built a number of sightly town houses at New York. The first of these, No. 1 Broadway, belonged to Admiral Sir Peter Warren, husband of the former Elizabeth De Lancey and captor of Louisburg, who had won a very large fortune in prize money and invested it in Manhattan real estate. Also on Broadway the merchant John Watts, another De Lancey connection, and Captain Archibald Kennedy erected impressive residences. The detailed Palladian treatment of the latter, with its cupola, made it one of the great town houses on the continent. Scarcely less attractive was the Ludlow House, but more usual were severe structures like the one William Walton built near his shipyard in 1750. With the seal of aristocratic approval, current English styles of architecture for private as well as public buildings now began to submerge the older Dutch mode, which had so long given the city of New York its unique appearance.

Newport was not renowned for great town houses in this period. Mostly of frame construction, residences were much smaller than in

By J. F. W. Des Barres for the *Atlantic Neptune*. Courtesy of the Huntington Library

PLATE 5 · *Shirley Place, Roxbury, Massachusetts*

One of the finest colonial show places, charmingly situated not far from Boston. Because it is enlarged from a contemporary engraving this view does not show the elaborate architectural detail of the mansion.

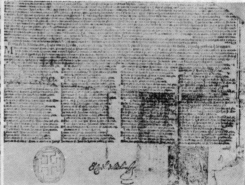

The great Honour of a valiant

London Prentice,

Being an Account of his matchless Manhood and brave
Adventures done in *Turkey*, and how he came to marry
the King's Daughter, &c.

To the Tune of, *All you that love good Fellows*, &c.

Of a worthy London Prentice
 my purpose is to speak,
And tell his brave Adventures,
 done for his Country sake,
Seek all the World about,
 And you will hardly find
A man in valour to exceed
 a Prentice gallant mind:
For he was born in Cheshire
 the chief of men was he,
From thence brought up to London
 a Prentice for to be,
A Merchant on the Bridge,
 did like his service so,
That for three Years his Factor
 to Turkey he should go.
And in that famous Country,
 one Year he had not been,
Ere he by tilt maintained
 the Honour of his Queen:
Elizabeth his Princess,
 he nobly did make known,
To be the Phoenix of the World,
 and none but she alone.
In armour richly gilded,
 well mounted on a steed,
One score of knights most hardy;
 one day he made to bleed;
And brought them to the ground,
 who proudly did deny,
Elizabeth to be the Pearl,
 of Princely Majesty.
The King of that same Country,
 thereat began to frown,
And will'd his Son, there present,
 to pull this Youngster down;
Who at his Father's words,
 these boasting speeches said,
Thou art a Traytor, English Boy,
 and hast the Traytor plaid.
I am no Boy, nor Traytor,
 thy speeches I defie,
For which I'll be revenged
 upon thee by and by:
A London Prentice still
 shall prove as good a Man,
As any of your Turkish Knights,
 do all the best you can.

And therewithal ... him
 a box upon the ear,
Which brake his neck asunder,
 as plainly doth appear:
Now, know proud Turk, quoth he
 I am no English Boy
That can with one small box o'th'ear
 the Prince of Turks destroy.
When as the King perceived
 his Son so strangely slain,
His Soul was sore afflicted
 with more than mortal pain;
And in revenge thereof,
 he said that he should dye,
The cruel'st death that ever Man
 beheld with mortal eye.
Two Lions were prepared
 this Prentice to devour,
Near famish'd up with hunger
 ten days within the tower.
To make them far more fierce
 and eager of their prey,
To glut themselves with human gore
 upon this dreadful day.
The appointed time of torment
 at length grew near at hand,
Where all the noble Ladies
 and barons of the Land,
Attended on the King,
 to see this Prentice
And buried in the hur...
 of those fierce lyons
Then in his shirt of
 with silks most rich
This worthy London ...
 was from the Prison
And to the lyons giv...
 to stanch their hun...
Which had not eat in ...
 not one small bit o...
But God, that knows a...
 the matter so cont...
That by this young l...
 they were of Life
For being faint for fo...
 they scarcely could ...
The noble force, and ...
 and courage of his

For when the hungry lyons,
 had cast on him their eyes,
The elements did thunder
 with the eccho of their cries;
And running all amain
 his body to devour,
Into their throats he thrust his arms,
 with all his might and power;
From thence by manly valour
 their hearts he tore in sunder,
And at the King he threw them,
 to all the Peoples wonder:
This I have done, quoth he,
 for lovely Englands sake,
And for my Country's Maiden Queen
 much more will undertake.
But when the King perceived
 his wrathful lyons hearts,
Afflicted with great terrour,
 his rigour soon reverts,
And turned all his hate
 into kindness and love,
And said, it is some Angel
 sent down from Heaven above.
No, no, I am no Angel
 the courteous young Man said,
But born in famous England,
 where Gods Word is obey'd
Assisted by the Heavens,

Printed and sold at the Heart ...

Courtesy of the New-York Historical Society

PLATE 6 · The Great Honour of a Valiant London Prentice, *printed by
Thomas Fleet on the back of a Spanish Indulgence*

*This broadside of 1748 is typical of the kind of ballad that was so popular in
the cities.*

other cities, doubtless because fewer of the very rich lived there and possibly because of a tendency in the owners toward shipboard compactness. But the taste in building that caused Newporters to applaud the superb architecture of Richard Munday and Peter Harrison reflected itself in their private dwellings. For proportion, pure detail, and beauty of line, they had few American equals. Landsmen like Abraham Redwood, Jahleel Brenton, and Dr. William Hunter had the first large houses. Toward the close of this era several imposing ones went up, among them those of Collector Charles Dudley, Metcalf Bowler, Francis Malbone, John Banister, and John Maudsley. In 1760 Metcalf Bowler enlarged his mansion in the modern mode, replacing the old clapboards with a new sheathing of rusticated wood as Peter Harrison had done at the Redwood Library. Built to show off from the street front, nearly all Newport houses had small-scale gardens in the rear where the families could enjoy a certain amount of privacy.

Philadelphians similarly did not erect many large town mansions prior to 1760. Solid, substantial comfort without distinction of design or aristocratic pretension characterized the homes of its merchants, who were willing to occupy comparatively modest quarters in the city until they could afford a country seat, for this gentry was rural in its inclinations. Urban elegance had its start in 1750 with the construction at Fourth and Locust streets of a fine brick house for Dr. William Shippen the elder, but not until a decade later did other Philadelphians begin to emulate him.

Charlestonians did not come to think of great town houses until they rebuilt after the hurricane of 1752, though Governor Glen did state just prior to that catastrophe that there were "many Houses that have cost a thousand and twelve hundred pounds sterling. The furniture in those Houses must be very considerable and Plate begins to shine upon their side Boards, and in proportion as they thrive they delight to have good things from England." But as yet, generally speaking, planters had not remained long enough in town to warrant maintenance of elaborate city residences. To this period belong the Eveleigh House at 39 Church Street, the Huger residence on Meeting, and Captain Thomas Frankland's mansion. Dudley Inman had told the gentry in 1751 that "a structure, tho' ever so beautiful, cannot yet be perfect, unless supplied with all the conveniences necessary to remove the disadvantages proceeding from great heat and cold, or, the country wherein it is built: Of such there are but few in or near this town, tho' put up and finished at a greater charge than if they had all the conveniences and beautiful proportions of architecture." Perhaps he was referring to Chief Justice Pinckney's house at Colleton Square, erected in 1745 at a cost of £6,688, as the detailed accounts show. Not until the close of the period, under the tutelage of Samuel Cardy and Inman, were the gentlemen who lived permanently in the city ready to house themselves in a becoming style.

In the Northern colonial cities, as in England, the newly enriched gentry sought as soon as possible to root themselves on the land, for the greatest distinction of the day was a country estate. There the merchant prince might build a great house, lay out a formal garden, dig a canal or fishpond, plant an orchard, and, if he had money and land enough, even enclose a deer park. There, surrounded by his family and with all the appurtenances of country life, he could have the satisfaction of extending lavish hospitality to his friends and prominent visitors.

The merchants of each city began the movement to the nearby country as soon as their means permitted them to assume the responsibilities of a second household. Sir Henry Frankland lived twenty miles out of Boston in a spacious rambling house on a five-hundred-acre estate, where he indulged his Anglican friends in hunting, feasting, and musical treats. Nearer the city, rural villages attracted other wealthy families who wished to alternate the town and country existence by traveling to and fro in their carriages. The second Isaac Royall kept a residence in the city and an extensive estate at Medford, whose outstanding feature was a summerhouse standing on an artificial, terraced mount, underneath which was an icehouse. About 1746 Governor William Shirley began the construction of a formal house, complete with flankers, outbuildings, gardens, and a maze, which turned out to be one of the most palatial and academic of eighteenth-century colonial mansions. Like many great houses of England, "Shirley Place" was especially designed for sumptuous entertaining, having a great decorated hall with a balcony for musicians at one end. By 1760 the country encircling Boston from Danvers to Medford to Middleborough was dotted with gentlemen's seats laid out and built to display the elegance of a rising aristocracy.

Fewer country estates could be found in the neighborhood of Newport, but some of them rivaled Boston's in pretentiousness. In 1744 Dr. Alexander Hamilton visited the estate of Godfrey Malbone, about half a mile from town: "It is the largest and most magnificent dwelling house I have seen in America. It is built entirely of hewn stone of a reddish colour; the sides of the windows and cornerstones [quoins] of the house being painted like white marble. It is three stories high, and the rooms are spacious and magnificent. . . . The whole stair case, which is very spacious and large, is done with mahogany wood. This house makes a grand show at a distance. . . . Round it are pritty gardens and terraces with canals and basons for water, from whence you have a delightful view of the town and harbour of Newport with the shipping lying there . . . and behind the house . . . a pleasant mount gradually ascending to a great height from which we can have a view of almost the whole island." Although neither Dr. Hamilton nor James

Birket approved the architecture of "Malbone," General Jeffery Amherst spoke of it in 1758 as "an extremely good House, much the best of any I have seen in America."

From Kingsbridge to New York City, the island of Manhattan was "butified with many handsome Seats belonging to the Gentlemen." Perhaps the show place was "Greenwich," built by Sir Peter Warren within sight of the Hudson River. Oliver De Lancey's "Bloomingdale" was "a handsome house built in good taste of stone, whited"; the country seats of James De Lancey, the Bayards, and the Murrays won Hannah Callender's enthusiastic approval in 1759, even if she did note with Quaker directness that "they have no gardens in or about New York which come up to ours of Philadelphia." Some city people already preferred locations on Long Island, while others built across the Hudson in New Jersey. Colonel Peter Schuyler's stately mansion, park, and gardens near Passaic Falls always attracted travelers. "In the gardens," wrote Burnaby, "is a very large collection of citrons, oranges, limes, lemons, balsams of Peru, aloes, pomegranates, and other tropical plants, and in the park I saw several American and English deer, and three or four elks."

Nicholas Scull and George Heap issued a *Map of Philadelphia and Parts Adjacent* in 1750 showing about one hundred and fifty of the principal country places situated within a twelve-mile radius of the metropolis. Wealthy Quakers had led the van of this move in which Anglicans and Presbyterians joined in the forties. As a rule the earliest buildings were not large but rather small "Plantation Houses" with cool "Piazzas" but no bedrooms, since at most they served as week-end lodges or retreats during hot spells or smallpox visitations. Soon, however, larger country houses began to appear: James Logan's "Stenton," Samuel Morris's lovely "Hope Lodge" at Whitemarsh, and Chief Justice Allen's great house, "Mt. Airy," gave a real impetus to the rage for elaborate country estates, each of them demanding one or more "complete Gardeners" to care for the superb plantings that had evoked the local pride of Miss Callender. From the Proprietor's place at "Springettsbury," James Alexander annually sent cases of oranges and lemons to Thomas Penn at London. Joseph "Duke" Wharton's estate, "Walnut Grove," lying south of the city along the Delaware, had an imposing house with dependencies as well as famous gardens, and "Bush Hill," seat of the Hamiltons, with its "fine house and gardens with statues," was in every way superior, but for classic proportions and architectural distinction William Coleman's "Woodford" (1742) was the finest country house erected near Philadelphia before 1760.

While citizens of the North sought to escape from the city to the country, South Carolina planters fled from the miasmic Low Country to the city. They had no need for the rural; they had their plantations.

When Robert Pringle ordered "Statues for Gardens of Lead, Pots, and Vases" from London in 1747, he wanted them for Richard Lake's farm or plantation, but in spite of this, the vogue was definitely urban, and it was in the city, not in the Low Country, that Carolinians indulged their tastes for conspicuous consumption.

The vastly extended scale of living on which the gentry embarked in this period created work for all kinds of artisans. Construction of town and country houses employed hundreds of carpenters, bricklayers, and masons; decorating and furnishing required the services of paperhangers, upholsterers, tinsmiths, silversmiths, pewterers, and men of a dozen other skills, all of whom prospered when a great house went up. In newspaper columns, advertisements for the so-called luxuries of the rich appeared with ever greater frequency, and shopkeepers of all sorts avidly bid for genteel custom.

The rage for country life rendered possible and guaranteed the survival of the coach industry. Wheeled carriages—chairs, chaises, chariots, coaches—were used by the well-to-do in going to and from their estates and about town as well. The middle class imitated them by hiring vehicles. In 1749 Benjamin Franklin sent his mother a moidore for "chaise-hire that you may ride warm to meetings" in Boston that winter. Coaches were still scarce in the colonies; Massachusetts had only 20 in 1753–7 as compared with 1,200 chaises and chairs; but 37 Philadelphians drove the next best equipage, a four-wheeled chaise, in 1759. "There is scarce a tolerable House in Charles Town," said Governor Glen, "which has not a Chaise or Chair belonging to it." Friend Abraham Redwood impressed all and sundry by riding about Rhode Island in his great coach driven by a liveried English coachman, and Jonathan Belcher, ardent New Light Governor of New Jersey, flew over the new road from Burlington to Cooper's Ferry across from Philadelphia in two hours, attended always by a London footman, who, we are relieved to learn, was "not bred to the Church of England."

By far the largest proportion of urban population was that known in Europe as the lower middle class, which in American cities strode forward and was invariably called "the middling Sort." Composed of tradesmen, craftsmen, and retail shopkeepers, these people of middle rank traded for a living and lived for trade. Most of them resided and worked in the same house, where every member of the family old enough to perform a task did so. As a result, their daily social activities were much less spectacular than those of the quality.

The "middling sort" prospered with the expansion of their communities. By both necessity and training, they worked long and hard at making a living. Incomes varied considerably within the group, but, with the exception of Boston's lean years, most of them lived comfortably and many succeeded in accumulating property. Perhaps a majority hired at least one servant, owned the time of an indentured servant at Philadelphia, New York, and Charles Town, or, in all towns save the Quaker City, possessed a Negro slave. John Bassett of New York, pewterer, owned a house and ground, and when he died in 1760, left £110 currency, two Negroes, and his tools. His fellow townsman William Eagles, saddler, possessed two houses, one of which he rented to the Reverend Mr. Auchmuty of Trinity Church. Over at Philadelphia, Plunket Fleeson, who began as an ordinary upholsterer, moved steadily ahead in fortune and became well enough known to be chosen an ensign in an Association company in 1748.

Fortune did not mark them all for her own, however. Rising prices, caused partly by the wars, partly by inflated currencies, meant distress for many a tradesman and artisan. A Boston blacksmith took in £600 in currency for work in 1747, but his iron and coal cost him £588, leaving only £12 "to keep the Pot boiling." By working up his materials he made barely enough to maintain his family, but new prices for 1748 would buy only two thirds of the iron and coal, leaving him behind. Blaming the war for his troubles, "T. A." declared he must turn either soldier or pauper. In some respects, the case of "John Clericus," a minister, was even more touching. In 1717 his Boston congregation allowed him £3 a week, on which he was able to feed a wife, five children, and a maid, with sixteen shillings left for clothing and incidentals. Thirty years later, in 1747, his salary was the same, but he had to pay out £11. 6s. 9d. a week merely for necessary food, omitting such small luxuries as tea, chocolate, cider, and wine.

Sensible, shrewd, frugal, ostentatiously moral, generally honest, and gossipy, these hard-working citizens were also public-spirited, anxious to serve as minor officials and militia officers. Above all, an insatiable desire to get ahead in the world drove them onward. Industry, thrift, and education, they believed, showed the way to wealth, and they eagerly scanned Poor Richard and a dozen similar publications for further clues. Gawen Brown came to Boston in 1749 from London to try clock- and watch-making, joined the Hollis Street Church, and within a year made the first of three marriages that would take him far socially and professionally. Anthony Lamb, reprieved at Tyburn gallows in 1724, served out his transportation time in Virginia, became an instrument-maker at New York, then Philadelphia, devised an octant, taught mathematics and navigation, and set up his son John (the Revolutionary general) as a sugar and wine merchant at Manhattan in 1758. From the middle ranks emerged Benjamin Franklin, not only the leading townsman but the foremost colonial of the age, a man who aspired to the comforts and opportunities of prosperity but who deliberately never attempted to leave his station. Like him, also, was his good friend John Bartram, who informed Peter Collinson of London in 1755: "My son William is just turned sixteen. It is now time to propose some way for him to get his living by. I don't want him to be what is commonly called a gentleman. I want to put him to some business by which he may, with care and industry, get a temperate reasonable living."

Few day laborers and journeymen were to be found in any city, and such as there were did not belong on the same base level as the lower classes of Europe. "Common people are not incapable of discerning the motives and springs of words and actions," was a discovery John Adams made when he practiced in the courts of law at the age of twenty-three. Immigrants from all countries soon acquired that "conviction of freedom" which a German gentleman thought so astonishing and "inexplicable" in the lower orders of the colonies. In spite of long hours and much toil, and frequently amid bad working conditions, these people did not feel that the colonial class structure had rigidly fixed their status. They commanded very high wages for the day—at Charles Town, journeymen received a bonus of twenty shillings a week above wages in 1758 —and not a few actually acquired small estates. James Bell, a carter of Newport, had personal property valued at sixty-two pounds, and Daniel Saneman, a Manhattan teamster, left two houses to grateful heirs. They could also, on occasion, better themselves, or their children could: a Hebridean, Ronald McDougall, arrived at New York and worked as a milkman for the remainder of his life, but his son, Alexander, strode the quarterdeck of a privateer and later attained fame as a merchant, general, banker, and legislator. There was, indeed, in the cities little evidence, save among the Negroes, to controvert William Allen's assertion: "You may depend upon it that this is one of the best poor Man's Countrys in the World."

Manners as well as places of habitation and scales of living set the three classes apart. Dress supplied the most obvious distinction, as the epithets "laced Coat," "silk-stockinged," "big-wig," "leather-aprons," immediately suggest. The leather breeches and plain shirts of the artisan and tradesman contrasted sharply with the cloth knee breeches and small wig of the merchant in his countinghouse, though in many instances prosperous shopkeepers and working people donned Sabbath finery in emulation of, and to the disgust of, their betters. Yet it would be a mistake to assume that there existed any serious class cleavage. All were, in reality, attuned to bourgeois ideals and standards. Cadwallader Colden, Edinburgh graduate and member of the New York Council, could in 1747 "observe that Riches are not always acquired by the honestest Means, nor are they always accompanied with the greatest Integrity of Mind, with the most Knowledge, or with the most generous Sentiments and publick Spirit"; and conclude that "the middling Rank of Mankind, in all Countries and in all Ages, have justly obtain'd the Character, to be generally the most honest. . . . And I am likewise fully

148

perswaded that we may much more safely trust our Liberty and Property with our neighbours of a middling Rank than with those of the greatest riches who are thereby tempted to Lord it over their neighbours."

Whatever its station, the family served as the center of social, economic, and religious life for all city people. Woman's place was in the home, caring for "swarms" of children or assisting in conducting a shop or craft. Upper-class mothers, imitating the current London fashion, often turned their babies over to hired wet nurses. They availed themselves of more comforts and luxuries than their less fortunate sisters, but otherwise few striking differences in modes of existence stood out. Trade was no bar to gentility either. Elizabeth Murray conducted a retail dry-goods shop at Boston, and though she married Thomas Campbell in 1755, continued in her business until 1760, when, widowed again, she married a rich sugar baker, James Smith, who was a "£30,000 man, ten thousand Ster. of which he has settled on Betsy, besides her own Fortune" and the "Life Rent of a valuable Farm" at "Brush Hill" in Milton.

Many middle-class wives spurred their spouses into getting ahead by demanding a higher scale of living than they either desired or could provide. The women arrayed themselves and their daughters in costly clothes, gadded about town, spent money on stays or such unheard-of luxuries as tooth powder and "The Princely Beautifying Lotion" that Garrat Noel of New York sold "by Appointment." City dames won the admiration of British visitors, who reported the fair sex to be "comely and dress well, and scarce any of them have distorted shapes." When a Boston tradesman's wife wanted to send her adolescent daughter to dancing school to acquire poise, the father laid stress on the cultivation of modesty and avoidance of heavy expense, hoping that she would read her Bible and learn to speak well, never reading "Cunstable for Constantinople":

> *I tell thee Wife; once more, I'll have her bred*
> *To Book'ry, Cook'ry, Thimble, Needle, Thread,*
> *First teach her these, and then the pritty Fool,*
> *Shall jigg her Crupper at the dancing School.*

Conscious as the middle and lower classes were of the distinctions between their ways of life and those of the aristocrats, the country people were more sensitive to the city's attitude of exclusiveness, and they openly recorded their resentment and hostility, particularly against the snobbery of language. "Write with the learned, pronounce with the vulgar," Poor Richard advised in the realization that even more than dress, which is distinctive enough, speech and manners separate social groups. As the use of the Dutch tongue at Manhattan declined, citizens made fun of unlettered country Dutchmen, looking upon them as "Brutes, of course." "De Dam Barbare of de Town," was the retort from up the Hudson. Likewise in Pennsylvania, the Palatines came in for much condescension and ribbing about their uncouth tongue or broken English. Already, too, the Boston accent offended the feeling of the rural Yankee. One convinced New Light declared in 1759 that he read the Bible and other books and could hold his own in any village conversation, but could scarcely understand the highfalutin speech of "several polite Gentlemen" who had come to live in his community. "I think by endeavouring to embellish our Language, they spoil it by their new-fangled Words, and by altering the Pronounciation of other Words," which, alas, his minister hastened to imitate, saying "Naishur" for "Nature," "Susetem" for "System"; and substituting "Virtue" for "Holiness," "Misfortune" for "Affliction," and turning downright Arminian! Worst of all, the Bostonians laughed at this Yankee for reading "De Quesne" and "aid-de-camp" as an Englishman, telling him to mouth "Du Cain" and "aide-cong."

Many countrymen did resemble those people of the Hudson Valley and Rhode Island whom Dr. Hamilton found "in general . . . very unpolished and rude." Curiosity won them the reputation of being forward, and most of them would admit that they lacked the politeness of the gentry, but fully aware that they were dominated by the first American class of patricians, whose rich group life they deeply envied, they nevertheless took great pride in being producers and freeholders and resented the practical jokes ill-bred apprentices or roistering sailors played on innocent bumpkins when they came to town.

IV

Considering the great numbers of immigrants of various nationalities, the disrupting influence of war, the relaxation of moral standards, and the social ferment of these years, it is not surprising that the colonies also experienced a profound transformation in religious life. Sects multiplied, destroying any hope of religious unity; denominations split under the pressure of revivalism; Rome maintained its toehold in one city; war and irreligion played havoc with orthodoxy and worship; churches assumed unchristian and undesirable class distinctions and political complexions. Each year more and more city people remained outside of church fellowships, and the prevalence of conflict hastened a dereliction among immigrants and natives alike, the younger citizens in particular. In short, the old established religious habits and customs were crumbling under the impact of changing social conditions, and secularism slowly, almost imperceptibly, was filtering into the minds and actions of city dwellers everywhere, transforming their communities long before rural regions felt its corrosive effects.

In 1738 George Whitefield, fiery English evangelist, made the first of seven visits to America; before 1760 he made important tours of the Northern cities in 1744, 1747, and 1754 and preached at Charles Town in 1752. Contending for souls, not creeds, he attracted hundreds of these spiritual wanderers, who were drawn by his reputation and the promise of a great and unusual spectacle; and, in or out of the pulpit, he lived up to his billings. He excited more intercolonial interest than any other individual and furnished more themes for religious discussion and pyrotechnics in pulpit and press than anyone who had ever been in America. Whitefield undeniably brought solace to many listeners and aroused a compassion for the unfortunate that expressed itself in generous collections for charity, but he and his followers also kept alive the evangelical movement and "the pernicious spirit of controversy," which shattered the peace and solidarity of the towns. Dr. Hamilton spoke truly when he said that "the people are generally more captivated with speculative than with practical religion."

Urban Protestantism itself opened the door to secularism by its serious internal divisions over the Great Awakening, which in New England was essentially a theological movement, but also involved matters of church polity and clerical protocol. The ministry of Boston divided over the revival, and the town became "the Seat of the Paper War"; accounts that the Reverend Thomas Prince published serially in the *Christian History* found readers in faraway South Carolina. But whenever Whitefield preached, he attracted enormous crowds; when attendance seemed only "moderate," three or four thousand were meant. "I am sorry to see you here," said Anglican Timothy Cutler coldly upon encountering him on a Boston street. "So is the Devil," was Whitefield's retort courteous. His farewell service in 1747 on a hill by the North Burying Ground was attended by about twenty thousand from Boston and surrounding towns. In 1754 ten Boston churches offered their pulpits; he chose the Old South and the New North as being "the most capacious at each end of the Town, holding near six Thousand People when fill'd as they continually were, near 30 crowding into some single pews." His audience consisted of "all Sorts and Denominations, both Low, Middle, and High, both less and most Polite" on the occasion of a timely sermon against Rome (he had viewed with Protestant satisfaction the earthquake that an angry God had visited on Catholic Lisbon), the imminent Gallic menace, and for their souls.

The same scenes were re-enacted everywhere; "the Pious were greatly enlivened," and the impious both moved and entertained. Whereas on his earlier journeys Congregationalists and Presbyterians were his principal auditory and their meeting houses the only ones open to him, by 1745 members of nearly all bodies except the Quakers and Anglicans welcomed him. At Charles Town even Commissary Alexander Garden ceased to attack Whitefield's defection from the established church, and the *Gazette* reported "persons of all Denominations constantly attending his Discourses." Eschewing theology and sectarianism, the evangelist "recommended the pure Religion of Christ to every Company," and his preaching proved the greatest solvent to denominationalism on this side of the Atlantic, gradually forcing clergymen of every stripe to adopt certain features of his "new method."

The Great Awakening and, perhaps even more, the heavy immigration of Scotch-Irish and Scots accounted for the spectacular growth of Presbyterianism in the Middle and Southern colonies. A schism over the revival occurred in 1745 when the "New Side" Presbyterians established the Synod of New York, leaving that of Philadelphia in the hands of the Scottish-trained "Old Side" ministers. The New York group actively conducted "home mission" work in Virginia and the Carolinas, and also backed the establishing of the College of New Jersey at Princeton. Finally tiring of internecine strife and alarmed in the presence of war and a fierce enemy, the "divided state of these colonies," and the "abounding of profanity, luxury, infidelity, error, and ignorance," which were speeding "the evident suspension of spiritual influences," the two synods came together in 1758 as the Synod of New York and Philadelphia and began to remodel their presbyteries. Thereafter, from Philadelphia, a united Presbyterian Church with "New Side" leaders in the ascendant worked effectively in spreading the Gospel and forming presbyteries from New York to Georgia. By 1760 this denomination outnumbered any other religious group at Philadelphia, and in New York showed a great accession of strength.

The spread of Anglicanism in the Northern colonies was one of the most significant religious and social developments of the period, and it is noteworthy that the Church of England made its greatest inroads in the cities. The opening of King's Chapel for worship in 1754 symbolized the social triumph of Anglicanism at Boston, for although the Congregationalists added a thirteenth society and the Baptists founded another, the distinction of the clergy, the beauty of its edifices, and the wealth and prestige of the parishioners of King's Chapel, Christ Church, and Trinity Church produced what John Adams was shortly to brand "sacerdotal impudence and ecclesiastical pride." At Newport, Trinity Church's membership increased conspicuously, and in 1759 Ezra Stiles, now at the Second Congregational Church, became alarmed at the "spirit of Episcopal intrigue already working with great Cunning." Newport's 170 Anglican families were assessed £4,323 out of the total of £15,000 for the entire community.

Political preference at New York aided the Anglicans to wax strong enough to contend with the Reformed Dutch and the Presbyterians for pre-eminence. William Smith admitted that many young people of Dutch descent accepted the established faith; and St. George's Chapel opened to relieve the pressure on Trinity in 1752. The victory of "the most fashionable religion" in gaining control of King's College in 1754 assured it the place of honor among all denominations at Manhattan. Philadelphia went through much the same kind of religious shift, as many wealthy Quakers swung over from simplicity to ritualism in worship. Christ Church could no longer accommodate all its parishioners, and in 1754 plans were laid to erect another edifice in the southern part of the city on ground donated by the Proprietors. Church of England influence on higher education came with the selection of the Reverend William Smith as provost of the Academy and College of Philadelphia in 1754. Always comparatively strong in numbers and influence at Charles Town, the Anglicans formed St. Michael's Parish in 1751 to care for inhabitants as new people arrived and Huguenots changed over to the modish liturgy.

The rapid advance of Anglicanism to prestige and power did not escape attention. Leaders of the Congregationalists, the Presbyterians, and the Society of Friends noted it with mixed emotions of jealousy and dismay, which soon turned to fear, over not only the number of new churches and communicants but the overtures to the Lutherans for a union with the Church of England and the rumors that soon a bishop would be sent to the colonies. Wealth, social ascendancy, political influence, and the prospect of more—these were a combination no other communion could command. Never permitted a charter because of Episcopal intrigue, New York Presbyterians deeply resented the establishment; in 1753 the *Independent Reflector* expressly denied that the Church of England was legally established in New York province, and Livingston also fulminated against a union of church and state, which prevented local printers from treating the bitter debate over ecclesiastical control of the proposed college with fairness and giving both sides a hearing. There was no doubt that religious issues thereafter had political overtones at Manhattan.

At Boston in February 1750 the Reverend Jonathan Mayhew preached a celebrated *Discourse Concerning Unlimited Submission and Non-Resistance to the Higher Powers,* which gave the answer of a convinced dissenter to the Tory-Anglican effort to raise Charles I to "saintship and martyrdom" and enjoined his hearers and readers to resist tyranny whatever form it might assume. For some time this issue reached the general public in the newspaper exchanges between those who attacked and those who defended Dr. Mayhew's stand. Down at Newport, Ezra Stiles, mulling over the threat of Episcopacy, concluded that the best defense was a good offense, and in a *Discourse on Christian Union,* preached to a Congregational convention in 1760, drew attention to the fact that the increase of their denomination in the maritime towns was not equal to that of the inland ones. Emphasizing Anglican militancy and proselyting gains, he reasoned that nevertheless the Church of England might easily be defeated in its designs by a union of dissenting churches, no longer differing widely in doctrine or polity, on a basis of Christian harmony that would preserve a "universal protestant liberty." That the march of Episcopacy should lead at least one divine openly to seek accommodations between Arminianism and Calvinism so soon after the Great Awakening was indeed a sign that the central issue for the so-called dissenters was religious liberty.

Several new sects appeared in the urban scene. The Unitas Fratrum, or Moravians, led by Count Zinzendorf and Bishop Spangenberg braved the unchristian denunciations of ministers like Gilbert Tennent and established congregations at New York in 1751 and at Newport in 1758. In the latter year the German Reformed Church separated amicably from the Reformed Dutch at Manhattan. At Charles Town in 1742 the Reverend Henry Melchior Mühlenberg gathered a Lutheran congregation, which, however, had no minister before 1755 nor a church edifice until 1759. There, also, in 1749 a few Sephardic Jews organized Congregation Beth Elohim Enveh Shallom on Union Street. A handful of Seventh-Day Baptists, led by the town hay-weigher, Nathaniel Wardell, began to worship at Boston in 1743.

Concurrent with the founding of these new sects came a decline of denominations formerly of great importance in the cities. At the close of the period the once dominant Quakers, whose Rhode Island Yearly Meeting had been the largest in the world, found their numbers fewer than either the Congregationalists or the Anglicans. At Philadelphia, too, Quakerism lost ground despite outward appearances of vigor and spirituality. Attendance at first-day meetings held up, but the strength of the Society lay in the rural meetings. Increasingly city Quakers cast their lot with Christ Church, and although the German sects offered great opportunities for proselyting, the Friends never made any efforts in so doing. A directory of Friends by streets, 1757–60, clearly indicates that not over a quarter of the inhabitants of the city of Philadelphia belonged to the meeting. The Reformed Dutch Churches of Manhattan underwent the same decline, although there it was complicated by the refusal of the oldsters to give up the use of the Dutch tongue in services. Few new members joined the church even when the Consistory took the radical step in 1747 of urging the ministers not to preach more than fifty minutes or an hour, "so as to remove the complaints about long sermons, to increase the audiences, and to hold the people together." Still the young people flocked to the fashionable Trinity Church, where sermons were not only short but in English.

All churchmen conceded the decline of religiosity, of morals, and of standards of conduct after 1745, and usually regarded it as the accompaniment of conflict. What was worse, many British officers appeared to propagate "Infidelity and Gratification of the Senses" among innocent colonials "in a genteel and in sensible Manner," and ridiculed "the notion of . . . rewards and punishments in another life." Few ministers of the time were more tolerant than Ezra Stiles, but the religious consequences of the last French War filled even him with foreboding: "I look upon it that our Officers are in danger of being corrupted with vicious principles, and many of them I doubt not will in the End of the War come home minute philosophers initiated in the polite Mysteries and vitiated Morals of Deism. And this will have an unhappy Effect," spreading "Deism or at least Skepticism thro' these Colonies."

Infidelity in the form of deism did have many adherents among the upper class in each city. Commissary Garden of Charles Town thought deism almost as dangerous to the established church as enthusiasm. In 1752 the New York faithful got after James Parker for printing an allegory, which had appeared years before in Philadelphia, wherein Indians professed deistic principles. Most stray lambs, however, were those whom Mr. Stiles called "Nothingarians." What astonished Gottlieb Mittelberger at Philadelphia was the multitude who did not believe in "a true God," devil, heaven, or hell, and had no knowledge of the sacraments or the Holy Bible. A sacrilegious New York "Rabble" consisting of "nigers, apprentices and the like" gathered outside of the Lutheran, Reformed Dutch, and Presbyterian churches on certain occasions to make "a great uproar," according to Mr. Mühlenberg, "and there was not much that could be done about it." The same kind of "loose unthinking people" desecrated the Jewish burying grounds of New York and Philadelphia.

Materialism, commercialism, and rationalism were certainly more potent in the seaports than in any "corner of the country," as Jonathan Edwards said of Boston, but they likewise made for a greater degree of tolerance than existed in the Old World or in the rural and frontier districts of America. As the fires of the Great Awakening died down in the cities, worship and let worship became the motto of most townsmen. Philadelphians were already famed in England for "a laudable and religious charity towards one another," and considered that though they differed from one another in form, they were "all in motion towards the same point." Such sweet reasonableness also pervaded Newport, which by old standards had always been "privately whimsical in religion." Charles Town earned similar plaudits from Gerard de Brahm. During the Spanish and French wars, the normal and not irrational fear of the Church of Rome found vent in most places in newspaper attacks on the "Whore of Babylon." Nevertheless, in actual practice the townsmen showed themselves to be Christians, treating prisoners decently and permitting Roman Catholics to worship privately in their own way. "This city," wrote Anglican Robert Jenney of Philadelphia in 1745, "is very much infested with Popery and systematical divisions among the Protestant inhabitants; and its influence spreads into the country." But nobody thought of interfering with the conduct of St. Joseph's Chapel, and Father Robert Harding, though a Jesuit, was highly regarded in the community. What city in a Roman Catholic country could show such a record for tolerance? The best indication of the distance urban America had come from persecution for the cause of conscience occurred at Boston when the Selectmen allowed the city's few Quakers to fill Faneuil Hall with "a crowded and polite Auditory" for the talk by the great Samuel Fothergill.

Such religious laxity, or indifference, or genuine unbelief as the cities uncovered should not obscure the fact that the generality worshipped regularly and that many people were truly devout. Moreover, the five cities acted as the religious centers of colonial America. Congregationalism's capital was Boston, where ministerial conventions frequently convened. The Friends held their New England Yearly Meeting at Newport, which was second only to that of Philadelphia in size in 1760. Charles Town was the Southern stronghold not merely of the Church of England but also for Baptists, Presbyterians, and Lutherans. The Coetus of the Reformed Dutch Church had its seat in New York, as did colonial Jewry. Just as Philadelphia in these years rose to commercial leadership and surpassed the other cities in population, so too did it become the religious capital of the Presbyterians, Baptists, Lutherans, and German Reformed throughout the colonies, and, of course, the Society of Friends. Christopher Saur in nearby Germantown, through his press and his role as Bishop of the Baptist Brethren, became the spokesman of the German sects, or "plain people." With such far-flung intercolonial religious connections and numerous meetings of the clergy of every faith, it is really an inaccuracy to call the Mecca of colonial Protestantism the Quaker City.

V

The tavern was the most flourishing of all urban institutions. The colorful signboards carrying such intriguing names as the Bunch of Grapes, Old Fortune of War, the Harp and Crown, and Ship-A-Ground were probably better known to the mobile colonials than the town halls and public buildings. Expanding its activities at all levels to meet the heavy demands of a growing population, the public house assumed new specialized functions. It served the cities chiefly as a place for male sociability, but it also provided hotel, restaurant, and political facilities, and, as a consequence of its prime importance in urban life and of the abuses not infrequently attending the sale of liquors, the need to regulate it always existed.

New taverns and retail establishments that sold beverages in small quantities like the modern "package store" opened to get the wartime business, for soldiers had to be billeted, fed, and, of course, supplied with rum and brewed drinks. As the British military and naval depot, New York supported more public houses than any other city. In 1744 the Corporation licensed 166; the number rose to 334 in 1752 and fell back to 232 by 1760. Considerably fewer were the taverns and groggeries of Philadelphia. In 1744 a Grand Jury reported upwards of one hundred licensed houses, which, with the retailers, made "near a Tenth Part of the City." Although the proportion had been reduced to one seventeenth by 1752, the Governor sold licenses to 120 taverns, and 118 more people dispensed liquors by the quart; in 1756, without counting the suburbs, the city had 117 public houses. Boston granted fewer licenses, having in 1752 but 36 innholders and 126 retailers; yet within a few years Governor Pownall would report "every other house a tavern"! Statistics do not exist for Charles Town, whose many taverns certainly exceeded the thirteen in Newport in 1744 or the thirty-four in 1748.

In 1753 Pastor Israel Acrelius listed forty-eight tavern beverages served in the colonies. Teneriffe, Vidonia, and Madeira wines as well as all sorts of cordials could be called for at the better inns, such as the Sign of Pitt's Head at Newport opened by James Brooks in 1759; but cider, beer, applejack, peach brandy, and, above all, rum were the favorite drinks. Some idea of the consumption of rum is given by Pennsylvania's importation of 526,700 gallons in 1752 in addition to 80,000 distilled there, and most of this was consumed in or near the city. Rum punch was the specialty of many a public house, and each host had his own special secret recipe. Limes were an essential ingredient, and the popularity of the drink may be gauged by Andrew Elliott's request to a Bahama correspondent to "ship 30/40 bbls limes by every vessell as they have for a year Past sold high and have been much Wanted for the Army makes a great demand for Frute Jam."

Tavern life varied widely with the time of day, the type and location of the establishment, and the class of patrons. By day and by night the inhabitants and strangers frequented public houses for entertainment—conversational and bibulous—supplemented by backgammon, shuffleboard, and cards, not to mention games of chance. Billiards became the rage everywhere, particularly at Charles Town. Exhibitions drew in many people. And all the time, it seemed, as moralists carefully pointed out, "every publick Corner, Tavern and even Dram shop is now full of pretended Politicians."

In any city a traveler could find taverns, like the people, of the better, middling, and inferior sort. One of the first-class establishments of Philadelphia, which the Reverend Francis Alison recommended to Ezra Stiles as the city's best in 1754, was Friend John Biddle's Indian King. Daniel Fisher was sufficiently impressed to comment upon it at length in his diary: "For tho' this house is one of the greatest business in its way in the whole city, yet everything is transacted with the utmost regularity and decorum. There is a regular ordinary every Day, of the very best provisions and well dressed, at 12d a head, that is 8 pence sterling, the best of liquors proportionately moderate; and the very best use taken of horses. Yet there is one, old custom attends this house, which tho' agreeable to me, may not perhaps be so to all People. For whom remains here after Eleven of the Clock in the Evening is very civilly acquainted with the time by a servant, and that after that hour, it is the invariable custom of the House to serve no more liquor that night to any Body, and this Custom I am told never is infringed. And this I think is a true specimen of what every House of entertainment should be."

First-class public houses took pride in the quality and variety of their food and wines. Samuel Francis of the Mason's Arms won fame for his culinary offerings, and the steady patronage of Todd's, also of New York, is proof that it was one of the better sort. Luke Vardy's Royal Exchange surpassed all Boston inns. At his tavern in Charles Town, John Gordon, after 1753, offered what must have been an incitement to the gout: an ordinary at ten shillings currency daily, "finding Madeira Wine, Punch, Toddy, and Sanger," and he soon outbid his rival Charles Shepheard for large affairs. But it was not just extraordinary occasions that drew the gentry out for meals; some single gentlemen dined nightly at their favorite houses. Dinners were customarily cooked to order, but some taverns served an "ordinary"—that is, a public meal at a fixed price and ready at a specified time each day. Thomas Lepper from London announced in the New York papers in 1750 that he had heard many persons express the wish for "a Regular Ordinary" and that at the Duke of Cumberland he would have one daily at one o'clock. Shortly thereafter Anne Stockton, also recently arrived in New York from England, started an ordinary in a house on Dock Street, with dinners and suppers at from "one to Two Shillings."

Then as now certain places were known for their specialties, or else their locations and surroundings attracted those who wanted more than just food and drink. Being a Quakeress did not seem to restrain Hannah Callender from visiting many public houses on her trip to New York in 1759: one day it was a visit to "a row of neat little wooden houses within the palisadoes called the Mead houses, where it is customary to drink this liquor and eat cakes"; on another it was breakfast at the Glass House in Greenwich; on still another it was a jaunt to a public bower along the North River to drink sangaree. Like James Birket before her, Hannah praised Friend James Stephenson's tavern at Kingsbridge for its beautiful location and delicious food. In her own city of Philadelphia, ladies as well as gentlemen drove to Germantown, where there were three houses of entertainment on the main street that served tea and dainties. The Centre Square Tavern offered bowling and billiards; at another on Society Hill, the summerhouses in the gardens were added attractions. For Charlestonians who wanted to make an occasion of dining out, Ann Shepheard opened an inn about a mile away from the city where, she said, "I am determined to deal for ready Money only," and there were others such as the Orange Garden "up the Path" and the Old Quarter House near the racetrack for those seeking diversion, and there were many such. Few men were as considerate as William Ellery, who, as a bachelor, had spent every night at his chosen Newport tavern before marrying Ann Remington in 1750, but abandoned the practice when he found an entry in her almanac diary indicating her delight when he stayed home on a single evening.

The line between upper- and middle-class establishments was often blurred, and many that were patronized by gentlemen were slack in some measure. Jonathan Nichols, at the Sign of the White Horse, kept the principal place at Newport, but Dr. Hamilton stayed there one night and recorded that he "was almost eat up alive with buggs." The Maryland doctor saw a good cross-section of the country's inns during his travels and usually managed to find some incident or scene to arouse his sense of the ridiculous: "I observed severall comicall, grotesque phizzes in the inn where I put up which would have afforded variety of hints for a painter of Hogarth's turn. They talk'd there upon a variety of subjects—politicks, religion, and trade—some tollerably well, but most of them ignorantly."

Middle-class public houses predominated. Many of these catered to special groups, or at least were patronized by them. Countrymen coming to town often elected to put up near the ferries at such places as Scotch Johnny's Crown and Thistle in New York or at Caleb Carr's Union Flag at Newport. Pennsylvania drovers and wagoners stopped at the Conestogoe Waggon in Market Street when they reached Philadelphia, and there, also, Henry Keppele made a small fortune out of entertaining German customers. The place of most frequent resort for New Englanders in New York was George Edmonds's Horse and Cart. Boston tanners met at the Three Horse Shoes when they convened to prevent a further rise in the price of hides. All in all, these and their competitors fed and housed a substantial portion of the urban population.

Less respectable groggeries with lower charges could be found near the waterfront and in such sections as Philadelphia's Hell-Town, where many tippling houses were "little better than Nurseries of Vice and Debauchery," and tended "very much to encrease the Number of our Poor." Here servants, apprentices, and Negro slaves often got drinks in violation of the law. Once the Charles Town Grand Jury presented the names of twelve taverners, including three women, who retailed liquor to Negroes. Not infrequently the owners used their establishments as blinds for "disorderly houses" and places of call for lewd women. Brawls and fights were common occurrences; an argumentative sailor at one of New York's dockside taverns received "6 or 7 cutts in the Head" from an irate proprietress and nearly died. Probably most of the disturbances of the peace that the night watch had to deal with had their origins in such dives.

Irrespective of the merits of any of the inns, and of course even the lower-class ones aimed at respectability, few gentlemen cared to take rooms in a city tavern for any length of time, because the hustle and noise lasted until late at night and the places afforded little privacy. As soon as Dr. Hamilton arrived in a new city, he arranged to take lodgings in a private house near an inn that served good food and provided well for horses. Good and inexpensive quarters in abundance might be had at Charles Town, such as those of John Smith, Jr., who kept "a private house of entertainment" for country gentlemen and ladies in Church Street. Margaret Keighly on Fort Hill at Boston had a "very pleasant chamber and, (if desired,) a lower Room fit for one or two gentlemen." Dr. Hamilton, his friend La Moinnerie, and a Mr. Hughes from Maryland lodged comfortably with Madam Guneau near Beacon Hill, "a very pleasant part of town situated high and well aired." At Newport the Misses Cole, and at Manhattan Joseph Forten, near the Spring Garden, rented "genteel Apartments for the Accommodation of Gentlemen."

Beneficial and necessary as the tavern and kindred institutions might be, their very nature led to abuses that called for strict public control. The deviations of the tavern from its original design shocked the sensibilities of John Adams: "Here the time, the money, the health, and the modesty, of most that are young and of many old, are wasted; here diseases, vicious habits, bastards, and legislators, are frequently begotten." Severe as these strictures were, others agreed with the youthful attorney in demanding, not abolition, but a reduction in the number of houses licensed. In New York, where altercations with soldiers and privateersmen so often arose, either taverns were well regulated or the authorities were indifferent to the problem. When complaints reached the Pennsylvania Assembly about Philadelphia's Hell-Town in 1750, the members "inspected" the laws and concluded that they covered all exigencies, but that the Governor ought not to license so many houses and none without prior consultation with the justices who recommended them to him. Artisans and tradesmen of Charles Town often found that they could make out better by retailing liquor than at their chosen vocations, and, to prevent an exodus from the crafts, a law of 1741 denied them this privilege. Another act made it a misdemeanor to trust any seaman for drink or lodgings. Newport's problems revolved around disorders in public houses rather than their number. Entertainment of Indians, Negroes, or mulattoes without the consent of their owners or employers was prohibited in 1750 by a law that also authorized a local excise of two pennies on each gallon of wine and liquor retailed. Three years afterwards the Town Council received permission to require sureties from neighbors of probity that no gaming, unlawful drinking, or encouragement of common tipplers, children, apprentices, or servants would be allowed before issuing a new tavern license. Considering the unprecedented numbers of inns, taverns, and tippling houses, the cities succeeded very well in bringing them under reasonable control, even if the liquor problem had come to stay.

The business activities formerly carried on in the taverns declined, though tickets could still be purchased, passages arranged, and the like, but for the most part business engagements and commercial activities passed into the hands of the keepers of coffeehouses. In them arbitrations, auctions, posting of ships' mailbags, sales, and reading of news took place. They still savored of the inn, however, for their specialty remained refreshment. This was particularly true of the Crown and North End coffeehouses of Boston, and the one kept by Jacob Hassey, "a comicall old whimsical fellow," at Newport. James Cahoone "reopened" another for Rhode Islanders in 1760. New York had two coffeehouses in 1744, and another, "the Gentleman's Coffee House and Tavern," was added in 1751; it seems probable, also, that when Kean and Lightfoot opened a "Coffee Room" on the second floor of the New Exchange in 1754, it served the same general purpose. William Monat started a coffeehouse at Charles Town in 1743, but he soon lost out to Charles Shepheard, because the well-known taverner drew all the trade to his "British Coffee Room" when he was made deputy postmaster. Alexander Chisholm announced in 1753 that he would run the Exchange Coffee House on the Bay in the same manner as those abroad, but he also rented out lodgings.

Prior to 1750 three coffeehouses catered to Philadelphians: the Widow Robert's, the Widow Jones's, and John and Thomas James's. Many real-estate sales, ship and merchandise auctions, and like commercial transactions took place at Robert's until the retirement of the widow in 1754. Perceiving the need for just such an establishment, William Bradford, printer, solicited subscriptions from 234 merchants and traders amounting to £350, and on July 8, 1754 he opened the London

Coffee House on the southwest corner of Front and Market streets. Centrally located in the mart town of the colonies, this differed from previous coffeehouses through Bradford's determination to make it exclusively a center for business, public affairs, and the news. The traditional coffee urn was set up on the ground floor, and upstairs were rooms for committees and a large hall, with the King's portrait on the wall, for public meetings. There the merchants assembled daily at noon on "high Change" to listen to reports from captains of ships, the latest commodity prices, and news of maritime and political happenings, to transact business and make appointments. Strangers of note preferred to call there for letters rather than at the post office. All colonial and many English newspapers, magazines, and public notices might be consulted at Bradford's, where writing materials were always to be had. Busy tradesmen had no reason to appear on change every day, but not a few attended promptly on "Post Days" to hear the reading of the "latest Advices, both Foreign and Domestick."

VI

The secular trend of urban life manifested itself in a growing sophistication made possible by the new wealth and the ability of all classes to spend money on something more than mere existence. The Great Awakening only temporarily arrested the trend; the coming of the wars accelerated it. Always gregarious, city people now evinced a gaiety far more like that of their European brethren than of their own country cousins. Poor Richard might teach the honest apprentice that time is money and that a penny saved is a penny earned, but as never before in American life, people having time and money to spare sought recreation and diversion, and their communities began to supply it.

A zest for social activity and amusement seized the aristocrats because it was a recognized accompaniment of gentility, and they devoted generous portions of their leisure and fortunes to the embellishments of existence. Above all, the eighteenth century was a man's century, and in the cities he exploited his advantage to the full through the agency of informal and formal clubs. The American has seldom displayed his impulse to be a joiner to a greater degree than did the mercantile aristocracy of colonial days. "New York," said the *American Gazeteer,* "is one of the most social places on the continent. The men collect themselves into weekly evening clubs." Other communities, however, yielded no precedence to Manhattan in this respect. At Philadelphia in 1744 William Black of Virginia was introduced to "the Governor's Clubb, which is a Select Number of Gentlemen that meet every Night at a certain Tavern, where they pass away a few Hours in the Pleasures of Conversation and a Chearful Glass," and also to the Saturday-night meetings of the "Beef-Stake Clubb," which were devoted to beef and twenty other gourmet's dishes.

Formal associations for convivial and good causes spawned amazingly in this period as each city encouraged organization of those spontaneous and responsible groups so necessary to a free society. The numerous national societies that have already been mentioned for their charitable work also had their lighter side. Even more intercolonial in scope were the Freemasons, who observed St. John's Day with impressive processions of members (wearing aprons, white gloves, jewels, and badges, and headed by a band of music), special church services, and Lucullan feasts. In 1760 from one to four lodges were active in each seaport; Philadelphia had a spacious hall in Lodge Alley, and Masons of both Newport and Charles Town made plans to erect buildings.

Good fellows got together in many a fraternal order or club. The "right worthy and amicable order of Ubiquarians," an English society to emulate "the Virtue and Morality of the Ancient Romans," established a chapter at Charles Town in the forties, while at the same time "the ancient loyal, and hospitable Society of Callicoes" met regularly at the Bunch of Grapes in Boston under a London charter to "behave like Callicoes," and "there to do no Business at all." The levity and goodfellowship of Dr. Hamilton's celebrated Tuesday Club at Annapolis so captivated the fancy of a guest, Thomas Cummings, that on his return to New York he organized the Monday Club, but the exclusive Marylanders could never be brought to recognize its fealty to their body. No clubs anywhere equaled the fishing clubs of Philadelphia, the Colony in Schuylkill and the Fishing Company of Fort St. David's, for culinary activity and genuine exclusiveness. "When Clubs (consisting of Knots of men rightly sorted) meet together," declared a joiner of the day, life is really worth living, and the avidity with which the colonial gentry scrambled for membership bore him out.

One of the accomplishments associated with quality in the eighteenth century was the ability to dance with grace and tirelessness. Consequently dancing masters flourished everywhere under the patronage from all persons with social ambitions. It was the upper class, however, who gave public balls whenever an occasion presented—a military victory, a birthday in the royal family, a charity, or very nearly any other reason. When the St. Andrew's Society held an anniversary meeting at New York in 1757, the press had this to say: "The Ladies in particular made a most brilliant Appearance, and it is thought there scarcely was before, so great a Number of elegantly dress'd fine Women seen together at one Place in North America. As there were a great many of his Majesty's officers present, several too of the first Rank, who had never before seen a public Company of Ladies in this Part of the World, they were most agreeably surprized and struck with the Charming Sight." Yet balls were far less frequent at New York than at Charles Town, where the Queen Street Theatre and Mr. Gordon's "Long Room" were the scenes of many brilliant dances attended by such grand dames as Madam Gabriel Manigault, whose diary is punctuated with accounts of balls, horse races, and preachings by Mr. Whitefield. Even though staid Philadelphia, under Whitefield's pall, eschewed dancing in public for a few years, its gentry turned out for the grand ball at the State House for one hundred ladies and even more gentlemen on the King's birthday in 1752, which was followed by Governor James Hamilton's supper treat in "the Long Gallery."

One certain indication of arrival in the urban gentry was membership in a dancing assembly. There is a certain delicious irony in the fact that in the two cities where the Society of Friends have been reputed to dictate manners and morals, the Episcopalian gentry would dance and called the tunes. A committee of thirteen bachelors of Newport in 1747 sent a general invitation to thirty-two single ladies to attend assembly cotillions for the season. Other persons were invited only on specific occasions. Each gentleman subscribing four pounds on entrance and paying forty shillings to the "Master of Ceremony" every other Saturday evening, or a fine of three pounds if he was absent "though in Town and in Health," ensured a large stag line. The assembly met at six in the evening and dismissed at midnight after the guests had partaken of chaste refreshments—chocolate, milk, tea, biscuits, and ordinarily four quarts of Madeira for the ladies and some rum for the men. This association closely followed the plan and rules of the assemblies held at Bristol and other English cities at the time.

The Philadelphia assembly of 1740 did not survive the Great Awakening, as Dr. Hamilton learned in 1744, for the Virginia commissioners to the Indian Treaty tried to get up a ball, "but could find none of the female sex in a humor for it." Sternness had disappeared four years later when, envious of the success of Terpsichore at Rhode Island, eighty gentlemen subscribers and as many ladies formed the now famous Philadelphia Assembly; half of them met every Thursday night from January to May. Admission of ladies and gentlemen was by playing-card tickets only, and the company either sat at cards or danced from six until midnight according to a set of rules which wisely called for minuets before the country dances, and always ended with an elaborate repast. The high point of the organization occurred in 1759 when a British general gave a breakfast in the Assembly Room (at Andrew Hamilton's store) and the guests danced until two in the afternoon before breaking up for several parties on the Schuylkill's banks. And this was the Quaker City!

The other towns had their assemblies, but none attained the brilliance, exclusiveness, and longevity of that in Philadelphia (which still goes on). Some kind of subscription assembly met at Blythe's Tavern in Charles Town in 1746, but little is known about it. New York's dancing assembly was not formed until early in 1758; in November the directors advertised for subscribers, stating that "no Non-subscriber will, for the future, be admitted." Under Anglican auspices gay Boston seemed less and less a puritan town. Captain Francis Goelet dined in state one evening in October 1746 at Edmund Quincy's, and then at six thirty accompanied his host to the Assembly, "he being Steward or Master of Ceremonies, a Worthy Polite Genteele Gentleman. The Assembly consisted of 50 Gentn and Ladies, and those of the Best Fashion in town; broke up abt 12 and went home." Until 1753 these dances took place at "the late Assembly-Room in King Street," and thereafter in the new Concert Hall.

In pleasant weather aristocrats of both sexes delighted in rural parties; one of the choicest of these was a turtle frolic. Merchants had standing orders with correspondents for live West India turtles, which were towed astern from the Caribbean, and their arrival gave the signal for a feast. On Christmas Day 1752, Samuel Freebody was host at a famous turtle party for the Newport gentry on Goat Island. Prepared by the slave Cuffy Cockroach, it was a more than worthy predecessor of the clambake. The company sailed over and dined at two, drank tea at five; thereafter the musicians played "Pea Straw," "Faithful Shepherd," and "Arcadian Nuptials" for the country dances. New Yorkers held turtle barbecues twice a week in 1759. Another popular outing was driving in Italian chaises to the banks of a stream for a picnic, fishing, tea, and a return by moonlight. As many as forty New Yorkers of both sexes made such excursions, while a mixed fishing company of Philadelphians went fortnightly to the Schuylkill to angle, drink tea, stroll, and go boating, for sailing naturally found favor with many of this maritime gentry.

It is evident that after 1743 the aristocrats of America had begun to play, and that diversions and recreations aplenty existed in or about every city. This surprised the English officers of the two wars, who hastened to make the most of it and also to introduce new and exciting entertainment bearing the London label. At once puritan Boston, Captain Francis Goelet of New York arrived in 1746 to purchase a ship and sample the "Amuzements." His first large evening began with a turtle dinner for forty gentlemen, with many toasts and more songs by the company, who were "Exceeding Merry untill 3 a Clock in the morning, from whence Went upon the Rake, Going past the Commons in our way Home, Surprised a Compy Country Young Men and Women with a Violin, at a Tavern Dancing and making Mery. Upon Our Ent'g the House the Young Women Fled, We took Possession of the Room, hav'g the Fidler and the Young Man with us with the Keg of Sugar'd Dram, we were very merry, from thence went to Mr. Jacob Wendell's where we were obliged to drink Punch and Wine and abt 5 in the morning made our Exit and to Bed." Within a few days the New Yorker took in a turtle frolic at Cambridge with Miss Betty Wendell, "who was my partner," and about twenty couples of the "Best Fashion in Boston." Next it was several stag punch parties at the Bunch of Grapes, a Masonic meeting that broke up at three in the morning, then a whole round of dinners and card parties, followed by attendance at a concert with Collector Thomas Lechmere. Best of all were the excursions by carriage into the country with ladies and gentlemen, such as the time they fished for silver eels in the Quincy's "Beautifull Cannal" at Milton, "caught a fine Parcell and Carried them Home and had them drest for Supper." If, as Goelet recorded, the Sabbath was strictly kept at Boston, it would appear in his case to have been a much-needed day of rest. Even New York could not match the good times one had at Boston, "the Petite Londre of English America."

Ownership of country houses made peripatetics of the wealthy citizens. They drove about to visit one another and see the sights, as eagerly and almost as often as their descendants now do in motors. What is more, those of one city began to take extended trips to other cities merely for pleasure. A daughter of James Alexander of New York went over to Philadelphia for a stay; and Hannah Callender, with a party of twenty youthful Friends, went to see Manhattan in April 1759. They rose at four in the morning and took the stage wagon, and en route observed with curiosity the country people along the King's Highway, "all strangers in their manners to us young travellers." New York itself was full of interesting sights and pleasures, all of which the Quakers took in before their return. At this time, too, Newport's wonderful climate began to attract West Indians and South Carolinians during the summer months, when they fled from the oppressive heat and dreaded malaria. Daniel Dulany went up from Annapolis for his health in 1760. At the Quaker City, the taking of water at a mineral spring grew to be as fashionable an indulgence as in the mother country. When such respected physicians as Thomas and Phineas Bond informed the public that "the Author of our Being has contrived waters to restore Health," the rush was on. Soon sensible John Bartram could write to Dr. John Fothergill in London: "We have several springs in our province, on which people have bestowed a large income." Of these, the most frequented was the Yellow Springs thirty miles out in Chester County.

Two amusements that gained favor in those years and which the gentry shared with members of other classes were horse-racing and the theater. An occasional race meet was held at Newport and Philadelphia, but at Charles Town and New York the sport of kings became an organ-

CITY PEOPLE

ized recreation. At the York Course, about a mile outside the Southern city, in 1743 John Hanbury held monthly races for costly prizes, and at nearby Goose Creek a Newmarket Track opened. In 1754 Thomas Nightingale from Yorkshire inaugurated the famous "Charlestown Races" over a new course on the Neck. Four years later the founding of the Carolina Jockey Club brought the sport to a peak with the running of the Colt's Plate and the Sweepstakes for purses as high as a thousand pounds. Throughout the period annual horse races took place at Trinity Church Farm in New York. There in 1744 Peter De Lancey ran his mare Ragged Kate against the Honorable William Montagu's horse Monk for two hundred pounds, and at the mid-century the "New-York Subscription Plate" brought out a fast field. Races were also held near the Warren mansion at "Greenwich Farm." Over on Long Island in 1750 the Newmarket Track at Hempstead Plains came into fashion: the day before the meeting that year more than seventy chairs and chaises crossed Brooklyn Ferry, and over a thousand horsemen crowded the plain during the races. As one might expect, the betting was heavy. Another course opened at Beaver Pond in Jamaica in 1755, as the presence of sporting gentlemen from the armed forces provided additional patronage.

Favorites with all classes were a variety of tavern entertainments somewhat resembling circus sideshows of our day. An African leopard was on view in Boston, New York, and Philadelphia in 1743–4; Charlestonians were paying to see another kind of an African, "A White Negro Girl," having gray eyes and white woolly hair. David Lockwood's Musical Clock and Camera Obscura, a microscope, a set of perspective views of leading European cities, Punch and Judy shows, waxworks, and the celebrated Philosophical-Optical Machine all toured Northern cities before 1750. Occasionally Ann Manigault and her friends at distant Charles Town got an opportunity to pay thirty shillings in currency to marvel at a slackwire act by someone like "Mr. Sturges from London," but it could not have compared with the Broadway tightwire performance of Anthony Joseph Duggee and his wife, "the Female Sampson," who brought down the house in an afterpiece by lying "with her Body extended between two Chairs," bearing "an Anvil of 300 lb. on her Breast," and suffering "two Men to strike on it with Sledge Hammers." The most successful of all tavern shows of this era was that "Elaborate and Matchless Pile of Art, called the Microcosm, or the World in Miniature." Built in the form of a Greek temple and showing celestial phenomena, it played music and portrayed landscapes, and was exhibited by James Bridges from Virginia to Massachusetts during the winter of 1755–6 before large crowds of awed colonials. The sight even inspired "Amicus" to write half a column on its educational value and

167

another to publish verses of tribute in the *Pennsylvania Gazette*. Bridges used the press with an almost modern skill to win advance publicity prior to his arrival in New York.

The prestige of the theater appealed greatly to the gentry, and in this period playgoing rooted itself in three of the cities. Quaker middle-class morality condemned attending plays as an unnecessary expense and "Encouraging to Idleness." John Smith of Philadelphia learned with sorrow on August 22, 1749, at Peacock Bigger's, of "His daughter being one of the Company who were going to hear the tragedy of Cato," even though the youthful Friends would listen to such a virtuous apostrophe to liberty as:

> But what is life?
> 'Tis not to stalk about and draw fresh air
> From time to time, or gaze upon the sun!
> 'Tis to be free. When liberty is gone,
> Life grows insipid and has lost its relish.

The Murray-Kean Company of Comedians from London put on plays, afterpieces, and singing entertainments at Penn's city in William Plumstead's warehouse on Water Street for a time before leaving for a more receptive New York. There, in a building owned by Rip Van Dam on Nassau Street, they played during 1750 and 1751, offering such current London favorites as *The Beggar's Opera, Richard III* (in Cibber's version), *The Recruiting Officer,* and *George Barnwell* to full houses, which proved, said James Parker, "that the Taste of this Place is not so much vitiated" as many have thought. Boston, agreeing that theatrical entertainment was an unnecessary luxury, prohibited further performances after a number of Englishmen and citizens played Otway's *The Orphan* at the Royal Exchange Tavern in 1750.

The American stage came into its own in 1753 when the "London Company of Comedians," headed by Lewis Hallam, an English actor of good repute, arrived at New York from Virginia after carefully preparing the public mind to accept its offerings, erecting a building, and securing permission to perform "by Authority." Philip Schuyler, aged twenty and just down from Albany, thought the performance of Steele's *The Conscious Lovers* only mediocre, but New Yorkers of rank generously patronized the Nassau Street Theatre, keeping the company there until March 25, 1754. Moving their London-made scenery and fancy costumes over to Philadelphia in April, Hallam's company gave thirty performances at Plumstead's, now refitted with a new gallery, pit, and stage. They had come at the request of a number of gentlemen including Governor James Hamilton, who granted permission for them to put on plays. Their rendition of *The Fair Penitent* on April 15 was, said Franklin's *Gazette,* received by a large audience "with universal applause." Religious opposition could not down the Thespians this time, for in the person of the Reverend William Smith they found an ecclesiastical champion. From Philadelphia, Hallam took his troupe to Charles Town, where a second "New theatre" in Queen Street awaited the giving of the first professionally acted plays since 1736. Whitefield's damper on the theater having been removed, the company played regularly from October to December before departing for the Caribbean.

Returning to New York in 1759 with David Douglass, who had married the Widow Hallam, the London Company opened with *Jane Shore* in a theater on Cruger's Wharf, playing with "great applause, to a most crowded audience," many of whom were British officers. So admired was the prologue spoken by Lewis Hallam, Jr., that the *Mercury* immediately printed it. After an unsuccessful run of little over a month, however, Douglass took his comedians to Philadelphia, where a theater had been going up on Society Hill. A local limner, William Williams, painted the scenery. There, "by Authority," the London Company performed three times a week in the face of great opposition by Presbyterians, Quakers, and Lutherans; but the Philadelphians enjoyed a fine repertory of well-acted plays from June to December that year. This long stay was made possible because Governor William Denny had kindly altered the date of a law passed to exclude the actors, so that it did not go into effect until January 1, 1760.

Members of the middle and lower classes had their own diversions in addition to sharing cockfights, horse races, mineral springs, bowling, billiards, tavern shows, and the theater with the gentry. Many tradesmen, like Benjamin Franklin, belonged to fire companies, which always had their sociable side, as did serious clubs like the Junto. Because the colonial city was a sort of *rus in urbe,* lovers of nature not only could get into the country quickly but could swim, skate, and slide in the winter or go fowling or fishing any time they desired. A favorite recreation of humble New Yorkers was oystering, and as many as seventy or eighty small craft could be found at the banks at one time. Small boys played street games and marbles, and little girls learned to dance, while older boys and men tried "Wicket" on Boston Common or rowed in whaleboat races in the harbors. Sullivan's Island in Charles Town harbor was a great resort for pleasure parties, as were the islands of Boston Bay. Ordinary people enjoyed all spectacles, and the celebrations of the victories at Louisburg and Quebec, with free liquor for all, drew great crowds. On such occasions the roughness of the mob often ended in vandalism, but in general it may be said that the lower orders in the colonial cities, being better off than those of England, were able to enjoy themselves in many simple and a few sophisticated ways, and that with the passage of the years such opportunities measurably increased.

VII

As any community attains age and traditions, its inhabitants begin to display distinctive traits. So it was with the five cities. At the opening and again at the end of this period, two travelers of British background analyzed the people of the four Northern towns and in so doing pointed out certain local differences among them. As he rode along the coast from Maryland to New England and back, Dr. Hamilton found the colonists were "much alike except in the great towns, where the inhabitants are more civilized, especially att Boston," for, notwithstanding the persistent Yankee inquisitiveness of the common people, their metropolis excelled in the urbanity of its upper classes. If the merchants and shopkeepers of Newport seemed cunning and grasping, one fondly remembered it for the beauty of its women—"This town is as remarkable for pritty women as Albany is for ugly ones." The good company and conversation always on tap at Manhattan's tavern clubs early in the evening usually descended to bawdy talk with excessive toping, in which Governor George Clinton shone and, for that reason, was "esteemed among these dons." By way of contrast, Philadelphia was a sober town, devoted to getting rather than spending; gay John Swift, fresh from London in the mercantile way, confessed himself "prodigiously afraid of getting an ill name, and am therefore much upon my guard." Upon visiting Charles Town in 1745, William Logan and James Pemberton, two young Pennsylvania Quakers, were delighted to find that the commuting Carolina gentry "live in the Genteelest manner and are Exceedingly civil and kind to strangers."

Of far greater significance than these minor variations, however, was the evidence of common characteristics in the colonial urban society. Five cities waxing rich under the broadening influence of overseas commerce, stimulated by the quickening effects of war, and guided by numerous British officers, sought to emulate the sophistication of Old World cities. Visitors inevitably discovered the citizens to be more open, civil, and approachable than the countryfolk, who had had very little contact with the outside world. The very processes of urban growth generated that secularism which henceforth so irrevocably set the city apart from the country. *Stadt luft macht frei* ran the German proverb; and that this freedom had already begun to turn the citizens into "great republicans," Andrew Burnaby suddenly realized in 1759, when he described the denizens of each town as having "fallen into the same errors in their ideas of independency." The tone set by the urban gentry was decidedly bourgeois, and all classes of this plastic social order exhibited the most praiseworthy of the virtues of the Enlightenment—concern for their fellow men. "I would rather give up my interest in a future state, than be divested of humanity," exclaimed David Rittenhouse. "I mean that good will I have to the species, although one half of them are said to be fools, and almost the other half knaves."

CHAPTER 5

Spacious Minds

I N THE MIDST of a lusty young colonial society bent upon conquering a continent and building an economy, the five cities were little oases of culture and taste. The British acts of trade and navigation did not prevent a traffic in new ideas from outside as well as from within the Empire, for they crossed the Atlantic with each ship; ocean-borne commerce fed the minds as well as clothed the bodies of townspeople. Prominent citizens of both the upper classes succeeded in importing the Enlightenment to these shores and domesticating it under difficult conditions. Nor did they act merely as passive agents in the transfer of civilization from the Old World to the New; they themselves contributed something and, at the end of the period, had even excelled their European contemporaries in certain instances.

Increasing demands of trade, available wealth, and bourgeois hopes for advancement in a society in flux encouraged at the same time that they forced a remarkable extension of education, the opening of libraries, and the development of a powerful press. These in turn led to an improved taste in literature and the fine arts. Also, from the ranks of the physicians and printers appeared a number of gifted cultural leaders to guide the formulation and expression of a public opinion on intellectual and political questions, and to initiate the spirit of inquiry so essential in the pursuit of the new science.

II

An abiding faith in the value of widespread education possessed all townsmen, though much confusion and debate arose over the nature, methods, extent, and goals of schooling. Among many of the aristocrats, the Renaissance ideal of classical training as a sure mark of a gentleman and scholar still prevailed; whereas the rising middle and lower orders, by force of circumstances as well as by the structure of the New World society, felt a need for a vernacular education with a certain amount of emphasis upon vocational, mechanical, and commercial subjects. Familiarity with the pedagogical theories of Milton, Locke, and Fénelon induced a healthy ferment, inclining some citizens to embark upon new schemes at the same time that others clung determinedly to the traditional, with the result that all types of schooling then current could be found in these cities—religious and genteel, classical and vernacular, theoretical and vocational. And in keeping with the spirit of the times, the secular goal of education to prepare one for one's place in society gradually won ascendancy over the ideal of training gentlemen and ladies exclusively.

The city of Boston provided the best education for boys available in the colonies. Its two grammar and three writing schools were free as well as public institutions and were attended by from six hundred to eight hundred boys annually during the period. About four fifths of these scholars enrolled in the writing schools to learn penmanship and arithmetic. Youths entered the North and South grammar schools at seven and left at fourteen able to converse in Latin and as well grounded in Greek syntax and literature as if they had attended any of the English grammar schools. Competent and well-paid masters, many of them Harvard graduates, taught with thoroughness and dedication in the five institutions and, like pedagogues of other ages, also wrestled with the perennial problem of trying to keep their lads from using bad language or behaving "unmannerly and Indecently in the Streets." Every year a large committee of officials, ministers, and prominent men inspected the schools, and between these visits the Selectmen acted in the capacity of a school board. The Town Meeting always appropriated generous sums for education, even during hard times. When a committee on the growing charges of the local government reported in 1751 that the schools absorbed more than a third of the town's entire income, but refrained from recommending a cut because "the Education of Children is of the greatest Importance to the Community," the inhabitants not only accepted the report but also refused to endorse the committee's proposal to require those able to pay for their children "to ease the Town of the Charge."

Newport also maintained "a publick school" which numbered several Harvard men among the masters it chose every June. This was not a free school, but after 1754 the master was ordered to accept as "many poor children gratis as the overseers of the Poor shall think proper to send to school." Despite the excellence of this institution, such public-spirited and cultivated men as William Ellery and Josiah Lyndon, deploring the "great deficiency in this Colony of Schools for the Education of youth," formed a plan in 1760 for a "literary institution" with two masters to provide instruction in the ancient languages, history, mathematics, geography, and other branches of useful knowledge, which they hoped to incorporate publicly like the Redwood Library.

Sectarian interests continued to provide and control the education of children at Philadelphia, where the European tradition of church schools and the classical curriculum were deeply rooted. At several places in the city the Friends opened primary schools, whence young boys proceeded to the "Public School," known today as the William Penn Charter School. This institution had an English department headed by the able Anthony Benezet from 1742 to 1745, but by 1750 the Latin department had begun to overshadow it as urban Quakers endeavored to assume the hallmarks of gentility and wealthy Presbyterians like William Allen sent their sons there. The same urge possessed German immigrants; when the Reformed and Lutheran denominations, which had jointly supported a primary school since 1735, established separate institutions in 1742, each taught a classical curriculum. A Moravian elementary school opened about 1745, and a decade later the Baptists astounded the community by founding a Latin grammar school "for the promotion of learning among us."

The Provincial Free School at Charles Town represented a fusion of sectarian and public education since, under Anglican auspices, it was supported by the colony. Actually the religious influence dominated, and few of the poor dissenters willingly enrolled their sons among the twelve scholars accepted free of tuition. Nevertheless, before 1750 this school virtually alone offered instruction in the classics, and the School Commissioners could report, after a visitation in 1754, the satisfactory progress of the scholars under William Henderson and George Sheed, master and writing teacher, and confidence in the quality of the education provided.

New York lagged behind the other cities, perhaps because of the prevalence of two languages, but more particularly because of a general indifference to culture. "The want of Education is not only seen in Men in Office, and the most eminent Stations among us," complained a correspondent of Zenger's *Journal* in 1749, but "Ignorance, horrid Ignorance! Reigns in every Act, Trade, Business and Character." William Livingston attributed this sad state of learning to the absence of grammar schools: "We have scarce ever had a good One in the Province." Even sectarian schools were few. A second Dutch institution had been opened by the Reformed Church to care for children living too far from the old one in 1743, but in 1754 Livingston asserted that though it had been "well regulated" and "richly supported," the Dutch had found it almost impossible to transmit their tongue to their children. Three years later the Consistory closed the second school for lack of patronage. In that same year, 1757, William Smith uttered the severest judgment: "Our schools, both in town and country, are in the lowest order—the instructors want instruction; and through a long shameful neglect of all arts and sciences our common speech is extremely corrupt, and the evidence of a bad taste, both as to thought and language, are visible in all our proceedings, public and private."

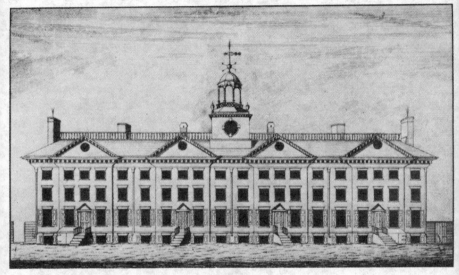

From the *New York Magazine*

PLATE 7 · *King's College in New York City*

Designed by Robert Crommelin and opened in 1760.

PLATE 8 · *King's Chapel, Boston, 1754*

*Designed by Peter Harrison of Newport; the handsome spire was never erected,
but is here reconstructed from original data by A. Lawrence Kocher. It was
meant to be as elegant as a London church by Wren or Gibbs.*

For the sons of the poor some of the cities provided excellent charity schools, but attendance, of course, carried a definite social stigma. The Society for the Propagation of the Gospel in Foreign Parts (S.P.G.) maintained such establishments in Newport, Philadelphia, Charles Town, and New York; Manhattan's flourished under Joseph Hildreth, who taught over fifty students regularly in Trinity Church School. Considerable success attended the efforts of the S.P.G. to teach city Negroes to read the Bible and Catechism to members of their own race. Commissary Garden of Charles Town, upon the founding of the first school in 1743, asserted that "this good work must not be attempted in the gross or inclusive of the whole Body of Slaves of so many various Ages, Nations and Languages," but should commence with the "Homeborn" under ten years of age and under the tutelage of Negro masters. Throughout the period about sixty black children a year learned to read the Scriptures from "Harry, the Negro Schoolmaster," whose only pay was the clothing the Vestry supplied to him. The Bray Associates of London opened a Negro school at Philadelphia in 1758, which immediately had thirty-six boys and girls studying to read and sew under a white mistress, who had previously kept a private school for blacks; and in 1760, under similar auspices, a free school for Negro children began at New York.

Whether the principal schools were sectarian or public, they were alike in their tendencies to adopt the emphasis placed by English schools on Latin and Greek to the exclusion of the English language and subjects suitable for those who would grow up in a commercial and middle-class society. Into the vacuum thus created, hundreds of private schoolmasters poured their energies and talents, giving instruction in any subject called for by subscribers and the times—double-entry bookkeeping, mensuration, mathematics, drawing, architecture, navigation, astronomy, gunnery, modern languages, geography, history, ethics, metaphysics, and even shorthand.

New York, Philadelphia, and Charles Town had more private schools than the two New England cities where a good public education was available. Doubtless the many masters who advertised in the newspapers turned out to be frauds or ill-equipped, or mere birds of passage; New York had twenty-two writing masters in 1751, but only six of these "pretending teachers" were thought to be "tolerably qualified." Others, however, made genuine contributions to the learning processes of city students. Such a teacher was George Brownell, Franklin's old mentor, "a then famous man" who rounded out a long career of teaching at Charles Town. "Persons of both Sexes from 12 Years of age to 50 who never wrote before" learned to write legibly in five weeks "at one Hour per Day" under William Elphinstone, who came from England to New York in 1753 and then taught at Philadelphia and Boston before settling down for the balance of his career at Manhattan in 1758. Franklin insisted that Master Elphinstone actually could improve "a veteran scrawler" in thirty hours. Other teachers stayed in one place, often becoming local celebrities like David James Dove of Philadelphia, who, teaching in the Academy and then in his own school, trained several able masters before he became the first headmaster of the Germantown Academy in 1761.

Ordinarily private masters taught day classes. Many of them took as boarders children from country districts whose parents desired them to acquire a city polish with their schooling. Boston schools attracted students from all over New England, and until 1755 not a few Newport youngsters were sent there. Philadelphia's private schoolmasters drew scholars not only from rural Pennsylvania but also from New Jersey, the Lower Counties, and Maryland. Because so many pupils came in from the plantation country, Charles Town probably had more children in boarding schools than any other city.

In every community there were increasing numbers of boys and young men who could not attend school at the regular hours because they worked as apprentices; likewise many adults—servants, journeymen, artisans, clerks—desired to study with a view toward self-improvement or for further vocational training. Originally started to instruct apprentices whose indentures stipulated a certain amount of reading, writing, and ciphering, the private evening schools expanded their offerings to suit the tastes and needs of all who were "confin'd in Business in the Day-Time." Too, occasional gentlemen entered the evening classes, and numerous advertisements were directed to them. Although the greatest demand was for practical courses, more than a few offered instruction in Latin and many more taught French. The tongue of the fashionable enemy became so popular that at New York in 1758 "Antigallicanus" refused to permit his son to study French, voicing a familiar form of war hysteria: "Let us banish from among us all French Doctors, School-Masters, Dancing Masters, Fencing-Masters, Musick-Masters, Hair-Cutters, Valets, and French Cooks; may the Ladies that encourage them be forced to marry them, or live single all their lives."

Until city children reached the ages of five or seven, girls and boys learned their letters and elementary reading together, either at home with their parents or from a schoolmistress, often the wife of a craftsman. They spelled and read out of the New England or New York primers or from an Anglican or Presbyterian catechism. Beyond this level boys proceeded to the public, church, or charity school, whereas little further attention was thought necessary for small girls. Nevertheless some ambitious daughters of artisans desired to learn how to support themselves by the needle, cooking, or weaving, and it was not uncommon for female shopkeepers to attend night school to learn merchant's accounts. The so-called female embellishments, such as drawing, embroidery in all its branches, painting on glass, making artificial flowers, music, and especially the French tongue, must have had numerous students judging from the number of teachers who announced their willingness to give instruction in these arts and crafts. Without doubt the best girls' school in the colonies was that opened by David James Dove at Philadelphia in 1751. The ladies, he announced, "excited by the laudable example are solicitous that their Daughters too might be instructed in some parts of Learning, as they are taught in the Academy," and had prevailed on him to teach spelling, pronunciation, arithmetic, writing, and accounts, for which he would charge ten shillings on entrance and twenty shillings' tuition each quarter.

Country families sent more of their girls than boys to board in the city. Jane Day of Boston thought it worth while to advertise her Cornhill Street School in the *Newport Mercury* after Sarah Osborn set up as a competitor there. After 1750 little Miss Huntington went up from Norwich to a Boston boarding school at the age of twelve. She took twelve dresses, but her mistress wrote that she needed another "of a recently imported rich fabric suitable for her rank and station," and her indulgent parents gave in. Commenting on the progress of his daughter Dolly, who attended his sister Elizabeth's boarding school in Boston, James Murray wrote to Scottish relatives: "the other Branches of her Education have not been neglected, but you would not be pleased to see the indolent way in which she and the young Ladies of this place generally live. They do not get up even in this fine Season till 8 or 9 o'clock. Breakfast is over at ten, a little reading or work until 12, dress for dinner till 2, after noon in making or receiving Visits or going about the Shops. Tea, Supper, and that closes the Day and their Eyes about 11. I do believe I do them great Justice in allowing that they employ to some good purpose two hours of the twenty-four." Like many of their modern college-bred descendants, fashionable young ladies in the colonial towns, beyond acquiring the rudiments of "genteel behaviour," were content to put in time until marriage gave them full employment.

For more than a century Boston had enjoyed a marked educational advantage over the other cities because of the presence in its environs of Harvard College. Almost coeval with the province, Harvard, through its graduates, had become integrated with the community and earned its respect. In a very real sense the two grammar schools and several private masters aimed at preparing boys for study across the Charles in Cambridge, where commencement was always the most important public event of the year for Bostonians. With the founding of the fourth colonial college at Prince Town in New Jersey in 1746, New Light Presbyterians of Philadelphia and New York won the means for advanced education for their young men. Its success and, even more, the example of the Presbyterian Latin grammar school at New London, Pennsylvania, which was established by the Reverend Francis Alison in 1743, attracted the attention of cultivated Philadelphians and encouraged Benjamin Franklin to issue in 1749 some *Proposals relating to the Education of Youth in Pennsylvania,* ideas he had been mulling over since 1743 but had withheld because of the distractions of war.

Since "Art is long, and their Time is short," Franklin thought that the youth of the city would benefit more from useful than ornamental studies; the better sort wanted to buttress distinction with the classical, with what the printer so felicitously called "the chapeau bras of modern literature." In 1751 Franklin further elucidated his theories in *The Idea of the English School,* but to win the support of the gentry, the Academy and Charitable School in the Province of Pennsylvania, which opened in Philadelphia on January 7, 1751, included both an English and a Latin school. Within a few months the trustees also started a charity department in order to gain title to the "New Building" erected with funds collected by George Whitefield. Under Francis Alison, who came up from New London in 1752, the Academy immediately flourished. From its very beginning Franklin and Richard Peters had it in mind that the Academy should become a "regular college," and in 1755 the Proprietaries granted a supplementary charter to "The College, Academy, and Charitable School of Philadelphia." Provost William Smith and Rector Francis Alison installed a liberal collegiate curriculum, emphasizing not only the classics but the English language, geography, and the sciences. They assembled a capable and dedicated faculty, and the college, now the University of Pennsylvania, soon became the center of the cultural life of the city and appeared destined to achieve a brilliant and useful future.

The success of the College of New Jersey served to arouse New Yorkers to the need for advanced education in their city. After several abortive starts, the Assembly authorized a lottery, the proceeds of which were to lay a foundation "for the Advancement of Learning . . . and towards the Founding of a College." Immediately, however, the projected college fell afoul of the torrid ecclesiastical politics of New York province and of urban-rural animosities. Not only were the Presbyterian and country interests fearful of the temptations youth would face in the wicked city, but they were apprehensive lest the Anglican Manhattan gentry dominate the institution. After nearly seven years of bitter, unseemly debate, of charges and countercharges in which the *Independent Reflector* championed a non-sectarian institution like the one in Philadelphia, the Anglicans won out; in 1754 King's College opened with the Reverend Samuel Johnson as president. One disgusted country gentleman had this to say about his son's education: "I indeed was something fond of sending him to the City, in Hopes of his increasing there in human Urbanity, and genteel Civility; but having for some Time past, perceived so much Vexation, superceeding Hucksters, Rangles, Cartman's Dotage, and Mariner's Shrewdness, emitted from your City; and as I must suppose from the more polite Sort, which being communicated, cannot fail of corrupting good Manners, and the Contagion infecting the Evil may become insanable"—he would keep him at home. Although some concessions were made to other faiths, King's embarked on its course as "a Party College," conceived in a denominationalism that ran counter to the contemporary drift toward religious freedom.

III

A remarkable expansion of the book trade attested to the development of a constantly widening reading public in town and country. During the period, fifty booksellers opened shops at Philadelphia; Boston, with a much smaller population, had at least forty-two; New York had sixteen; Charles Town had eleven; while Newport, well supplied from Boston, had but two. This total of 121 for the five cities compares more than favorably with the 116 booksellers (including printers) of the ten leading English provincial cities.[1] Citizens who ventured into colonial bookshops either to browse or to buy generally found a choice of reading matter currently popular in the mother country besides editions of the classics, school texts, religious works, sermons, pamphlets, magazines, and treatises on sundry topics. Of course one could not always buy the particular book desired, as Edward Shippen, Jr., discovered in 1760 when he searched Philadelphia in vain for Garth's *Metamorphoses* and Trap's *Vergil;* and merchants with London accounts often imported books directly: "I have a little Boy, who teazes me to send for the Books undermentioned," Judge Allen wrote to David Barclay & Sons when ordering copies of *Clarissa Harlowe* and *Sir Charles Grandison* for himself.

Upon the arrival of new shipments, booksellers ran long advertisements in the newspapers, and the more substantial ones frequently issued printed catalogues also. Garrat Noel, whose Dock Street shop in New York was one of the best-stocked in the colonies, not only advertised in the *Pennsylvania Gazette* but sent a supply of catalogues to the Indian King Tavern at Philadelphia for free distribution. Broadsides, single sheets having woodcuts and ballads or other popular printed matter such as lists of books for sale printed on one side, were cried on the streets by hawkers, who succeeded in disposing of large quantities of such ephemera.

---

[1] The Yorkshire or Welsh gentleman who went up to London once a year built up a major library more easily, perhaps, than the colonial who ordered directly from the same great center. Of 566 known English booksellers from 1743 to 1760, 244 were in London, 18 in Bristol, 14 in Newcastle, 13 each in Cambridge and York, 12 in Oxford, and 11 in Bath.

A favorite device for attracting customers and promoting sales in the three largest cities was the book auction. For many years Thomas Cox, a London bookseller, sent an agent over to Boston to conduct auctions in taverns, but it was a Scot from Glasgow, Alexander Carlile, whose artful sales technique so diverted Dr. Hamilton in 1744: "After dinner I went with Mr. Vans to an auction of Books in King's Street where the Auctioneer, a young fellow, was very witty in his way. 'This book,' says he, 'gentlemen, must be valuable. Here you have every thing concerning popes, cardinals, anti-Christ, and the devil. Here, gentlemen, you have Tacitus, that elegant historian. He gives you an account of that good and pious person, Nero, who loved his mother and kindred so well that he sucked their very blood.' The books that sold best at this auction while I was there were Pamela, Anti-Pamela, The Fortunate Maid, Ovid's Art of Love, and the Marrow of Modern Divinity." The physician confessed that "the books sold so dear I could not procure such as I wanted."

The larger book dealers, such as Noel and Rivington of New York, Franklin & Hall and William Bradford of Philadelphia, Wells of Charles Town, and Church of Boston, sought more than a local retail trade by selling books and pamphlets in wholesale lots to schools, country stores, or country chapmen. In this expanding and lucrative line, "Bibles, Testaments, Psalters, Primmers, Psalm-Books, and Spelling-Books" sold steadily and well, but "entertaining histories," priced at a shilling and known in the trade as "Chapmen Books," outsold everything else in rural as well as urban districts. Among the best-selling titles, which serve incidentally as an index to popular taste, were the *Interpretation of Dreams, Wit's Cabinet, Pleasures of Matrimony, Quaker's Art of Courtship, French Convert,* and *Scotch Rogue.* Prevented from traveling by Sabbath regulations, Dr. Hamilton diverted himself at Case's Tavern in the Narragansett country by reading the *History of the Nine Worthies,* one of the popular chapbooks at that time.

With books so readily at hand, it is not surprising that many persons built up private libraries. Ministers and physicians naturally specialized in their purchases, but merchants usually acquired a balanced collection. In the late forties Peter Harrison of Newport began to assemble what eventually became a notable library. Prosperous and ambitious craftsmen also took to buying books: when Postmaster John Franklin died at Boston in 1756, an auction of his "large and Valuable Collection of Books" was held at the British Coffee House; and at faraway Charles Town, John Laurens, saddler, purchased many books, which he generously loaned to his friends. Book-borrowers were no different in that day, judging from public announcements asking for the return of books. "Jedediah Bookworm" of Boston, who claimed to have had over seventy volumes of such famous authors as Rabelais, Cervantes, Butler, Addison, Newton, and Locke out on loan for four years, advised posterity to insist upon receipts for all books and petitioned all "Borrowers and Retainers of Books" to return them promptly without dog-ears and with their indexes intact.

Imbued with "a taste for learning," Franklin's Junto and a number of gentlemen made books available on a divided-cost basis in 1731 by founding the Library Company of Philadelphia. In 1746 the Union Library was established by a group of artisans and professional men, soon to be followed in 1757 by the Association Library, a Quaker company, and the Amicable Library, composed of "humble" craftsmen. By 1760 six villages and towns in the neighborhood of this metropolis, including backwoods Lancaster, had established subscription libraries. During a visit to the city of Philadelphia, Abraham Redwood was so impressed with the Library Company that upon his return to Newport he promptly emulated the example of a forebear who had given the English city of Bristol a library in the previous century. His donation of five hundred pounds for books and Henry Collins's gift of a piece of land led to the founding of the Company of the Redwood Library in 1747. When the library opened in 1750, it was the first and long remained the finest colonial monument to letters.

Interest in "social" or subscription libraries now spread rapidly. In 1748 a group of Charles Town merchants, lawyers, craftsmen, and a few planters organized to raise a fund for purchasing pamphlets and magazines from England. Two years later, with a membership of 128, the Library Society, as they called themselves, had sufficient funds to branch out and add books to their collection and make plans for a course on experimental philosophy. Incorporated by the Assembly in 1754, the Library Society provided the stimulus needed to awaken Charlestonians to the joys and satisfactions of literary culture.

The Corporation Library established at New York in 1730 was eventually opened to the public in 1746 when the librarian, Printer James Parker, issued free catalogues, but after 1750 so many volumes of this predominantly theological collection had been lent out and lost that few "Lovers of Reading" came to consult the remainder. Responding to the desires of the public, William Smith, the Livingstons, William Alexander, and John Morin Scott instituted a subscription "for the Erection of a publick Library for the Benefit of the Subscribers," raising nearly six hundred pounds in a few days. When trustees were being considered, John Chambers, "a jealous envious Bigot," insisted that choosing Presbyterians to the board would injure the Church of England. William Smith tells us that his coreligionists, aware of the prejudice against them, "ran thro' the Town" with their subscription lists before the Anglicans could cabal against them. Thus politics assisted at the birth of the New York Society Library as it had at that of King's College. In announcing the housing of the books at the City Hall in October 1754, Hugh Gaine's *Mercury* expressed the hope "that New York, now she has an Opportunity, will show that she comes not short of the other Provinces, in Men of excellent Genius, who . . . will take off that Reflection cast on us by the neighbouring Colonies, of being an ignorant People."

Boston's public library, dating from 1656, was wiped out when the Town House burned for the second time, in 1747. Most of the books were destroyed and no effort was ever made to replace them. Urged on by his friend Benjamin Franklin, Dr. William Clarke tried to start a subscription for a social library, but in November 1748 he had to confess that "the spirit of subscribing is very much flagged." The magnificent collection of books and manuscripts willed by the Reverend Thomas Prince, who died in 1758, to be housed in the steeple of the Old South Church were on the history of New England, and, in spite of stipulations in the bequest, many items were borrowed. Probably Boston's citizenry, laboring under heavy taxes and other war burdens, felt that a new library was beyond their competence at the time; moreover they had proved themselves the most avid readers of all the cities.

The reading interests of the urban public were also served by collections of books other than those in subscription libraries. Many Bostonians enjoyed access to the five thousand volumes in the Harvard College Library, the largest in the colonies; and with the founding of the College of Philadelphia and King's, both Philadelphia and New York acquired important libraries. Collections of religious works for the use of the clergy were brought together in each of the Anglican churches, those of King's Chapel at Boston and Christ Church, Philadelphia, being the largest. In the latter city, the Friends established a parochial library for their school and country use, and the Presbyterians maintained a similar one. The Carpenters Company of Philadelphia continued to purchase books on building and architecture, and in 1745 a useful legal collection was started at the State House. That same year James Logan erected a one-story brick building on Sixth Street for his fine library of nearly three thousand volumes, which, after his death, passed to the city "for the use of the Public," to whom it became available in 1760 under the librarianship of Lewis Weiss. By this time Penn's city possessed as many and as complete literary facilities for earnest readers, of whom there were many, as could be found in most of the towns of Europe, and a good beginning had been made in other cities.

IV

By means of the written word, in books, sermons, pamphlets, almanacs, magazines, and broadsides, the seminal ideas of the Enlightenment circulated in America with astonishing rapidity, facilitated largely by the printers of the colonial cities, for more than any other group they controlled the movement of ideas. Newport had but one printing house, as did Charles Town until late in the period, but in the other towns from four to six printers made a living by their mystery, for it was organized as a craft and recruited its personnel from the middle class. Printers like Benjamin Franklin and William Bradford of Philadelphia, James Parker and Hugh Gaine of New York, Thomas Fleet of Boston, Peter Timothy of Charles Town, and Widow Ann Franklin of Newport were good business people as well as artisans, grew up with the cities, and shared in their prosperity. What was said of Thomas Fleet in 1758 may stand as the obituary for all: "He was for many years a considerable Printer in this Town: and was remarkable for his Understanding and Industry in the Business of his own Profession; Besides which, he had a general knowledge of the World."

Printing was above all a profitable trade; so much so that in 1748 Benjamin Franklin could retire at the early age of forty-two. The work that paid consistently and best was what is known as job printing: blank forms, such as contracts, deeds, insurance policies, bonds, bills of exchange, indentures, and broadside advertisements. And for those fortunate enough to win government patronage, the printing of proclamations, proceedings of the provincial assemblies, laws, and paper money proved a most lucrative business. In addition nearly every printing house contained a bookshop in which stationery, paper, ink, lottery and other tickets, Crown soap, and a variety of imported patent medicines were sold; and a sort of information and general brokerage service was provided for newspaper advertisers. Franklin, Parker, and Timothy also used their establishments as post offices.

Although the profits from publishing never matched those from job printing and bookselling, the leading printers acquired both reputation and influence thereby. A ready sale could generally be counted on for almanacs, sermons, broadsides, and many pamphlets. Charles Evans's *American Bibliography* lists 3,666 titles published between 1743 and 1760, of which 2,747, or seventy-five per cent, issued from presses in the five cities.

City	English	Foreign Language
Boston	1,321	0
Philadelphia	765	45
New York	495	32
Newport	77	0
Charles Town	12	0
	2,670	77

These figures represent only surviving imprints, but they do indicate the importance of the urban printer and that the present-day pre-eminence of Boston, Philadelphia, and New York as publishing centers began in colonial days.

Book-publishing expanded appreciably in these years as more titles came from the presses in larger editions than formerly. Schoolbooks naturally sold well: James Parker's *New-York Primmer* entered the market of the *New-England Primmer* in 1746; the latter was reprinted twice at Boston and New York and once in Germantown and Philadelphia before 1760. The reissuing at Boston in 1749 of James Burgh's *Thoughts on Education* indicated some popular interest in current Scottish views on that subject. Garrat Noel's *Short Introduction to the Spanish Language* (1751) and Peter Papin de Préfontaine's *Direct Guide to the French Language* (1757) were other popular native texts. A large audience existed for religious books, for the Great Awakening and the spread of Anglicanism fed the presses with polemics despite the decided secular trend of colonial reading. Books on daily affairs and manuals of instruction found increasing favor, and such works as *The Dealer's Pocket Companion, The Country-Man's Help, and Trader's Friend, The Servant's Directory or Housekeeper's Companion,* or *Observations upon Beauty, Coquetry, Jilting, Jealousy, &c. With Reflections on a Married State* were reprinted from English editions. Nor was English literature neglected, for American editions of *The Beggar's Opera,* Addison's *Cato,* Swift's *Journal of a Gaming Lady of Quality,* and the poems of John Pomfret appeared before 1760, and in 1744, only four years after its first publication, the colonials hailed the birth of the new middle-class novel with editions of *Pamela* at Philadelphia, followed shortly by New York and Boston printings.

The popularity of the *Gentlemen's, London,* and other English magazines, for which most bookshops placed subscriptions, suggested the possibility of American ventures in the medium. Of eleven periodicals started, all had ceased publication by 1760 for lack of support, which in most cases can be attributed to their inability to match English magazines in interest or to compete with colonial newspapers in vitality. At Boston the Reverend Thomas Prince's *Christian History* had the longest life—three years—because it chronicled New Light activities during the great religious upheaval. The *Independent Reflector,* a weekly published by James Parker at New York in 1752-3, gave a new direction to colonial journalism as its principal writer, William Livingston, made it a vehicle for reform until it was suppressed. The nearest approach to English literary periodicals in originality and subject matter was Bradford's *American Magazine, or Monthly Chronicle for the British Colonies,* edited by Provost William Smith of the College of Philadelphia. Beginning with a subscription list of over 850 in 1757, it lasted two years. The fact that Bradford had sixty-three agents in fifty-two communities scattered from Halifax to Barbados, as well as all the booksellers in those places and additional agents in the British Isles, affords some evidence of the ramifications that intercolonial and interimperial intellectual communications had attained by the end of this period.

The greatest service rendered to the public by the printers was the publication of newspapers. In 1743 the five cities issued twelve of these little four-page weekly journals, of which all but one were printed in English; in 1760 the number remained the same, though no non-English paper existed. Between these dates four newspapers surviving from an earlier day went out of business, four new ones succeeded, and nine others started, ran for a time, and then ceased publication. In 1758 Rhode Island acquired in the *Newport Mercury* its first newspaper in nearly thirty years; prior to this time the Newporters subscribed principally to the *Boston Evening Post* and the New York journals. Postriders and carriers circulated the newspapers throughout the colonial hinterland, while coastwise shipping carried them from port to port. In addition to having a few subscribers everywhere, most newspapers found their way to taverns, coffeehouses, and country ordinaries, where persons might consult them or hear them read. Only Christopher Saur of Germantown, who virtually monopolized the German audience, could boast, as he did in 1753, that he circulated 4,000 copies of his *Pensylvanische Berichte.*

Colonial newspapers owed much of their distinction to Benjamin Franklin of Philadelphia. Not only did he train many of the best printers at his Market Street printing house, but he also financed the setting up of presses and founding of newspapers from Connecticut to New York to South Carolina and Antigua. Acting as a silent partner, he ordinarily withdrew when he recovered his initial investment. His paper mills supplied stock to many printing establishments, to which he also sold books and almanacs in wholesale quantities. He attempted to promote the assimilation of the Germans of Pennsylvania by publishing during 1751–2 the *Hoch Teutsche und Englische Zeitung,* a bilingual newspaper, and in conjunction with Anthon Armbrüster, a former apprentice, the *Philadelphische Zeitung.* He also quietly backed the *Philadelphische Teutsche Fama,* 1749–51, and Miller and Holland's *Lancastersche Zeitung,* but Christopher Saur's grip on German readers never relaxed. In his own *Pennsylvania Gazette,* Franklin introduced illustrations (or cuts) into advertising before his English contemporaries used them, and, by use of leads and spacing, gave more emphasis to his notices. In 1754 he produced the first American newspaper cartoon, the famous snake device, "Join or Die," which other journals quickly copied. Only in his typography did Franklin's presswork suffer by comparison with that of Parker and other printers.

The events of the period, both foreign and domestic as the press would have put it, broadened and enlivened the contents of colonial newspapers. European news continued to make up much of the reading matter, but items of more interest to the general public were selected for reprinting. The *Pennsylvania Gazette* catered to public taste for sensation by printing a long account of the confession of Elizabeth Jeffries in 1752, and the *New York Gazette* got out a supplement on July 2, 1753 containing the story of the abduction of Elizabeth Canning, which so enthralled contemporary London. With the establishing of regular monthly mail packets in 1756, foreign news thereafter reached the cities more regularly and promptly. Even so, the doings of provincial legislatures, the speeches of governors, other political happenings, and especially news of the two wars narrowed down the amount of material culled from English journals. Such enterprising printers as Franklin, Parker, Timothy, and Fleet spoke out in their columns against public abuses and heartily lent support to worthy civic causes. Some even eschewed nonpartisanship and threw their weight, albeit gingerly, into political scales. Culturally, too, these little sheets contributed not only by disseminating news about the services of schoolmasters and painters but by providing an outlet for most of the scientific news of the time and publishing many a literary essay on manners and morals.

Within limitations, the English-speaking world enjoyed the only free press of the age, but the victory in the Zenger case of 1735 did not prevent authorities from bringing pressure to bear on offending colonial printers. In 1753 the New York Assembly censured Hugh Gaine for printing materials in his *Mercury* that allegedly impugned the honor of that body. Three years later, political and religious discussions in the New York press grew so warm that James Parker and William Weyman had to crave pardon for publishing remarks derogative to the people of Ulster and Orange counties. About this time Governor Sir Charles Hardy came out against a free press, and Governor William Denny of Penn's province agreed with him. Thomas Fleet's *Boston Evening Post* so frequently carried terse and often sarcastic or oblique comments on the social scene which irritated the conservatives that ministers denounced Fleet from the pulpit, recommending that he be muzzled. But it was another printer, Daniel Fowle, who was briefly imprisoned in 1754 for publication of *The Monster of Monsters,* a witty though harmless satire on the debates of the House of Representatives over an excise bill, which hawkers said had "dropped from the Moon." Although confined only two days, Fowle started a countersuit against the government and, the next year, took revenge by describing his treatment in *A Total Eclipse of Liberty.*

For a number of years in the fifties, tension existed between the authorities and the press at Boston. In January 1755 the Assembly passed an act levying a tax, which was to last for two years, on vellum, parchment, and paper, and requiring that a halfpenny stamp be affixed to every printed newspaper. Thomas Fleet animadverted frequently upon the act, which severely affected the Boston press: according to a letter from Boston in the *Pennsylvania Gazette,* of the Bay City's four printers, one went out of business, another temporarily ceased publication, and the loss of customers by the other two exceeded the revenue collected by the stamp master. The *Boston Gazette* worked for repeal by printing the London advices against such duties, one of which argued that freedom of the press was essential to the cherished liberty of the subject and "coeval with all free government." Governor Shirley increased the strain by procuring the passage in September 1755 of an act prohibiting publication of any news about the Crown Point expedition without permission from the General Court. Finally, perceiving that the stamp tax yielded only a meager sum, the House allowed it to lapse on May 1, 1757. The printers, being but a handful of people, had not succeeded in arousing popular resentment about the issue, but there can be no question that bitter memories of that measure were still fresh in the minds of Edes & Gill and their colleagues of the press when Parliament levied stamp duties on their craft and its activities in 1765. And they were not then caught napping.

This friction between the authorities and the printers served to strengthen public conviction of the need for a free press. The Anglo-French conflict had revealed to the Americans the nature of "Absolute Power" in Bourbon France, about which the press had rung every change. In a series of letters to the *Pennsylvania Journal* in 1758, the "Watchman" upheld the freedom of speech and celebrated the virtues of "British Liberty"; and a South Carolinian living in the country far from Charles Town sent a letter to Timothy's *Gazette* praising it as the only source of news about the doings of government. By 1760 the newspaper press had definitely swung over to the popular side, in part because of the curbing of its activities, an interference it would not brook for long. It had developed into a great organ for expressing colonial opinion, and the printers well knew its strength.

This accomplishment arose from the fact that the leading city printers had proved themselves to be more than mere successful men of affairs; with Thomas Fleet they all evinced "a general knowledge of the World." Not only had they worked out an intercolonial correspondence with each other like that of the merchant princes, but their craft brought them into contact with all classes in the colonies—high and low, religious and political—and in every public project they participated prominently. As the middlemen in the movement of ideas from Europe to America, as the principal arbiters of colonial taste, and as successors to the clergy, as molders of public opinion, these middle-class urban craftsmen rose to a position of power, later not unhistorically denominated the fourth estate, and produced from their ranks the leading colonial—the first American of international renown.

V

In this period of rapid growth and change, uncertainty and instability rather than calm and security were the norms; men commenced to subject ancient religious and social standards to searching analysis, to evolve new political doctrines, and to apply deductions from the new science to their lives and problems. Eighteenth-century America was a society in rapid transition, and the transformation proved quickest and most convulsive in the cities. Furthermore, as a society rapidly growing up, it desired to express itself and thus signalize its approaching maturity.

To prosperous and educated citizens accustomed to reading and enjoying a measure of leisure, the urge to write came readily. The presence of a vehicle of publication in the press as well as an interested and ever widening reading public provided the necessary elements for the creation of a native literature. Being English colonists, the townsmen naturally regarded Swift, Pope, Fielding, and Richardson as their own countrymen. They thought of a sort of imperial division of labor by which cultivation of the embellishments of existence fell to the mother country, in consequence of which one should not expect to find in provincial cities much evidence of imaginative literature. The vital writings of colonial America therefore constituted a literature of action and controversy expressing the religious, economic, social, and political aspects of contemporary life. By its very nature this literature took the form of prose, appearing for the most part, as we have seen, in the columns of newspapers, in magazines, in pamphlets, and only occasionally in book form.

Printer, publisher, and author, Benjamin Franklin towered above his fellows and best exemplifies the secularization colonial literature had achieved by 1750; he also exhibits the high level to which native prose could aspire. In his *Pennsylvania Gazette* he permitted his wit to sparkle anonymously, while in Poor Richard's almanacs he preached a homely philosophy representing more what his audience wanted to read than his own convictions. *Father Abraham's Speech* (1758), later titled *The Way to Wealth,* presented a distillation of Poor Richard's sayings about *economy* and soon became a colonial best seller. For persuasiveness and clarity, few writings of any age surpass his utilitarian pieces advocating the use of the Pennsylvanian Fire-Place or the establishing of an academy and hospital. In *Observations on the Increase of Mankind, Peopling of Countries, etc.,* he not only adumbrated the theory of the influence of the frontier on American development but made a fundamental contribution to demography; and his electrical and other scientific papers were immediately accepted and are still recognized as models of writing in that difficult genre.

The writings of three able men contributed to raising the city of New York from its low cultural rating. First in point of time was Cadwallader Colden, whose *History of the Five Indian Nations* (1727) continued to stand as the best work on the aborigines and went through several reprintings. Publication in 1745 of *An Explication of the First Causes of Action in Matter, And of the Cause of Gravitation* marked him as the first materialist of the New World; in this work he endeavored to demonstrate that matter and mind are phenomenal modifications of the same common substance. A second edition came out at London in 1746 and others in 1748 at Leipzig and Hamburg; three years later he issued it as a revision under the title *The Principles of Action in Matter.* One of the most vigorous of the chronicles written in this period was William Smith's *History of the Province of New York,* published at London in 1757. This work, though largely a political narrative, contained a long appendix on the economic and social conditions of the colony, which, despite its occasional devastating condemnation of the low state of education and learning, on the whole gave an accurate and impartial estimate of New York. As a facile writer of both poetry and prose, William Livingston proved more versatile than his friend Smith. The fashionable yearning of the city-bred for the contemplative pleasures of rural scenes found vent in his long poem *Philosophic Solitude* (1747), which echoes the *Georgics,* but Livingston made his most effective contribution by championing public welfare and "the inestimable value of Liberty," together with his determination "to oppose superstition, priestcraft, bigotry, tyranny, public mismanagement and dishonesty in office," in the *Independent Reflector* and the "Watch Tower" essays attacking aggressive Anglicanism in the *Mercury.* Lively, caustic, informed, these controversial pieces reached a wide audience, and they suited the mood of the times.

Boston presses still turned out quantities of sermons and religious tracts. In addition to the normal predilection of New England clergymen of every denomination to rush into print, the disputations engendered by the Great Awakening, followed by the spreading of Episcopacy, released a flood of ecclesiastical polemics. This literature reached its peak in the works of a Boston Congregationalist of Arminian tendencies, Jonathan Mayhew. The substance of his sermon on *Unlimited Submission* has already been mentioned, but he published numerous discourses which, surcharged with pathos, wit, fervor, and power, were no mere essays to be read in the pulpit. In the sermons of John Cotton, Cotton Mather, and Mayhew, we can trace the distance the Boston clergy had traveled in a single century.

From early Puritan times the good people of New England had always laughed and enjoyed themselves; their ways merely differed from our ways, though not a few moderns fail to realize the fact. At any rate, this Boston generation produced in Joseph Green, wealthy distiller and local wit, a man whose raillery and satirical propensities represented a distinct secular advance over the forced ecclesiastical humor and studied puns of his rival, the Reverend Mather Byles. John Singleton Copley's portrait preserves the puckish quality of pudgy "Stiller Josey." Known throughout New England for his bawdy verse and letters, Green delighted people with his lines on his Anglican friend John Checkley's portrait, which he thought too ugly to burn in hell. Without stint, contemporaries applauded such appropriate occasional broadsides as *A Mournful Lamentation for the Sad and Deplorable Death of Mr. Old Tenor* (1750), but valued highest his rollicking burlesque of the pomp and ceremony of the Freemasons: *Entertainment for a Winter's Evening: Being a Full and True Account of a Very Strange and Wonderful Sight Seen in Boston* (1750). "The great Satyrist" received the supreme compliment of imitation from John Maylem, Newport's sole literary aspirant of the period, but by comparison the islander's flame was feeble, for *The Birdiad* bore many evidences of having been "wrote extempore." Service against the French evoked in 1758 from this "poet of small talent and . . . warrior of little distinction" *The Conquest of Beauséjour, Gallic Perfidy,* and *The Conquest of Louisburg,* efforts that make up in robust nascent Americanism for their poetic deficiency.

The cities uncovered no lack of poetasters and uninspired essayists who sought consciously, as Addison had, to influence manners and taste or to rival Pope. These writers stemmed usually from the upper class and stood for the ultimate in colonialism, with the result that the imitations they produced were pallid and lifeless because they had not been called out by the teeming new world about them. Foremost among such literary aspirants stood William Smith, provost of the College of Philadelphia, and his "Society of Gentlemen," composed of undergraduates and bright young men—Francis Hopkinson, John Beveridge, Joseph Shippen, William Hicks, and Thomas Godfrey. For two years, through the *American Magazine,* they tried to improve the culture of their neighbors and stimulate an interest in the arts, but this was only the dream of a few aristocrats and scarcely suited to the genius of a rising democracy. One immediately senses the self-consciousness and artificiality of Francis Hopkinson's "Ode on Music":

> *Hark! Hark! the sweet vibrating Lyre*
> *Sets my attentive soul on fire.*

At Charles Town, also, reverence for things English and the cultural passiveness of the town's leaders frustrated any hope of native literature, and the poetic effusions in Timothy's newspaper must have cloyed discriminating tastes. One J. Dumbleton, alone, displayed a sense of humor and had the satisfaction of seeing his "Rhapsody on Rum" reprinted in the *London Magazine* from the *South Carolina Gazette* and copied by Annapolis, Williamsburg, and Philadelphia journals:

We owe, great DRAM! *the trembling hand to thee;*
The headstrong purpose; and the feeble knee;
The loss of honour; and the cause of wrong;
The brain enchanted; and the fault'ring tongue.

. . . .

O grand deluder! such thy charming art,
'Twere good we ne'er should meet, or ne'er should part;
Ever abscond, or ever tend our call:
Leave us our sense entire, or none at all.

While gentlemen tried to sing in exalted strain and the Reverend Samuel Cooper of Boston gave up "the songs profane" for "a nobler Theme" by penning thirty-three stanzas in imitation of "Mr. Pope's *Messiah*," ordinary people everywhere, but in New England cities particularly, came out strongly in favor of the songs profane. Each new broadside ballad offered by hawkers met with a brisk sale on city streets just as in English towns. Many London ballads were reprinted in the colonies; *Fair Rosamond,* which goes back into the mists of ancient balladry, was reissued at Newport in 1746. Two years later at the sale of a Spanish prize cargo, Thomas Fleet bought a large quantity of the bulls and indulgences of Pope Urban VIII, which he quaintly advertised to sell "by single Bull, Quire, or Ream." Finding that Protestant Yankees had no need of Romish paper, Fleet resourcefully used the backs for reprinting *Black Eyed Susan, Handsome Harry,* and what seems suspiciously like a prototype of *Yankee Doodle—Teague's Ramble to the Camp.* At twopence such broadsides, with the indulgences thrown in, were real bargains. Entertaining no respect or affection for pettifoggers, colonials, in 1755, lustily sang *The Lawyers's Pedigree* to the tune of "Our Polly's a sad Slut." Among Manhattan's best sellers stood Parker's *Songs of Robin Hood.*

Not only did the inhabitants of the cities treasure the great tradition of English popular balladry, but they kept it growing with contributions of their own. By making a few changes, they acclimated old ballads to the new land, retaining, however, the English tunes. One, *The Yorkshire Maiden,* emerged from the *New York Gazette* as "Dumb Betty: A New York Song," relating plaintively in ten verses the tale of one of a vanishing race of servants: pretty, demure, and industrious at her drudgery, she never gossips or tells tales about her mistress. When the contributor who sent in this piece asked for a collection of all the Indian songs then being sung around Manhattan, Parker proudly announced that he had anticipated the request and that such a collection would be ready for sale the following day for one shilling.

Such native themes as controversial public issues brought out rashes of verse in New England. Newport's native ballads focused on the French War and the bitter political rivalry of Hopkins and Ward over the governorship. Paper money inspired many a doggerel song at Boston, as did the visits of George Whitefield, executions of criminals, and the romantic death of General Wolfe. Two songs of 1745 to the tune of "Chevy Chase" celebrated "New England Bravery" at Louisburg, and the earthquake of 1755 provided excellent materials for broadside verses. In the merry month of May 1752 the Reverend Henry Mühlenberg journeyed with a company of "all sorts of nationalities" on the stage from Borden's Town to New York. In the coach there was "continuous shouting and singing on the part of the company," including a Quaker youth, until two in the morning, despite its being Ascension Day. "Satan's Servants," the German cleric thought them all: "The English people have a kind of songs which are set to melodic music and describe all sorts of heroes and feats of arms on land and sea. Respectable people sing them as a pastime, and regard it as a serious invasion of their liberties if one protests against these songs, etc. Now, if one rebukes them on account of their amorous songs, they believe they can justify themselves by referring to these songs about heroes. The musical settings and melodies of these songs of heroic deeds are very similar to those which our Germans use for Church music."

VI

"A man that has a taste of musick, painting or architecture, is like one that has another sense, when compared with such as have no relish of those arts," said Addison; and many colonial readers of the *Spectator* agreed with the dictum. Those who lived in the cities frequently devoted substantial portions of their new wealth and leisure to seeking an acquaintance with the arts. In this quest, cultivated British officers and Edinburgh-trained Scottish physicians, who frequented the towns during the war years, supplied both examples and guides, as did also the mounting number of citizens who had lived or traveled in the Old World. As he prepared to move from the country village of Amboy to the city of Boston in 1760, Governor Francis Bernard explained to Lord Barrington the contrast between the two places: "This Town struck me Very much at first for the pleasantness of its situation; and I think still that I never saw a more delightful place for a country seat. But when I found myself wholly secluded from refined conversation and the amusements that arise from letters, arts, and sciences, I learned that there might be too much of retirement. On the other hand Boston is perhaps the most polished and scientific Town in America. I shall find there a good public library [sic], many very considerable men, tolerable musick and other amusements to which I had bid adieu not without regret."

The secular trend of the era affected musical tastes as it did literature. In communities where the works of Corelli, Alberoni, and Handel were well known, young people of the better sort and a few of middle station now began to study with music masters like Charles Love of New York, who offered to teach the violin, viola, hautboy, bassoon, French horn, and flute. For the last instrument, Robert Coe of Philadelphia invented a mouthpiece to ease the playing of short-winded gentlemen. Young ladies preferred the harpsichord, spinet, dulcimer, and guitar, and some became accomplished performers under the instruction of Peter Pelham at Boston or his son, Peter ("a very Genteel Clever young man"), who taught the Fenwick sisters at Charles Town. Headed by Charles Theodore Pachelbell of the noted German family of musicians and composers, a series of skilled organists played at St. Philip's Church in Charles Town. That they could earn from 100 to 150 guineas annually by giving instruction on the organ and harpsichord is proof of the popularity of those instruments in South Carolina.

A sure sign of interest in music was the presence of music dealers in several cities. Chief among them was Michael Hillegas (later first Treasurer of the United States), whose stock in 1759 included "a large Assortment of Music of the best Masters," books of instruction, a harpsichord, English and Italian violins, Italian flutes, strings, and reeds. The next year he wrote to "Baron" Stiegel, the glass-manufacturer at Manheim, that he would sell an Italian violin for nineteen pounds "as well Loud as Bold," and offered him several of "this Country make" at seven pounds each. Four organ-makers made fine spinets, virginals, and organs at Philadelphia, and one of them, John Klem, built organs for Trinity Church at New York and St. Philip's, Charles Town, as well as for local bodies. Toward the close of the period at Manhattan, John Mimum from London advertised that he would construct "the new invented Organ," and one of Gilbert Ash's was used in a concert at City Hall. Chamber organs for private use came into fashion, and down at Charles Town in 1754 Jonathan Badger, joiner, announced that he had one of his own make for sale.

Music in the churches underwent a vast improvement. Most denominations, save the Congregationalists and Quakers, used organs in their service; and at Philadelphia the Moravians introduced horns and stringed instruments, producing, as William Black reported, "some very agreeable Church musick." Everywhere but Newport voice teachers contributed measurably to improving congregational singing by instruction in psalmody. In 1750 David Wheeler, Caleb Eddy, and seven other young Boston tradesmen formed a society, with dues and officers, to meet once a week for instruction in psalmody from Samuel Holbrook. Pastor Mühlenberg marveled in 1751 at the proficiency of New York Lutherans: "the whole congregation sang very pleasingly and inspiringly, for the English Church people here in New York know how to sing very beautifully and acceptably because they have a very fine organ in their church and have been taught how to sing." The Anglicans went even further in 1754 when William Tuckey, formerly of Bristol Cathedral, arrived "to encourage and amend the singing in publick congregations." Jonathan Badger contributed to Charles Town's musical life by publishing in 1752 *A Collection of the Best Psalm and Hymn Tunes,* engraved on copper plates "for Lovers of Vocal Musick." This work preceded by eight years the proposals of James Lyon at Philadelphia for subscriptions to "the first Attempt of the Kind to spread the Art of Psalmody, in its Perfection, thro' our American Colonies." Badger also conducted a school for "plain Psalmody" in 1755. At Boston, Thomas Walter's *Grounds and Rules of Musick Explained, or, An Introduction to the Art of Singing by Note. Fitted to the meanest Capacities,* and recommended by several ministers, reached its fifth edition by 1760. The writing master William Dawson brought out the *Youth's entertaining Amusement, or a Plain Guide to Psalmody,* based upon tunes used by Philadelphia churches.

With so many people learning to sing or play, townsfolk turned to organizing musical groups. At a New York tavern one evening in 1744 a visitor "heard a tollerable concerto of musick performed by one violin and two German flutes. The violin was by far the best I had heard played since I came to America." Before long, James Parker published *The American Mock-Bird. A Collection of the most familiar Songs now in Vogue* (1760). About 1740, "the Musick Club" had gathered at Philadelphia. William Black, the Virginian who both fiddled and played the flute, enjoyed their concerts in 1744, while Dr. Hamilton thought them only fair: "one Levy there played a very good violine, one Quin bore another pritty good part; Tench Francis played a very indifferent finger upon an excellent violin." The most ambitious and successful amateur effort of the time demonstrated the advance of choral and instrumental music in the colonial metropolis. Several performances of Dr. Thomas Arne's *Masque of Alfred* were given at the College in December 1757; the students recited the "oratorical Exercises," and, assisted by the Misses Lawrence and Hopkinson, sang the hymns as gentlemen played the instrumental parts. To raise money for instructing the charity students in psalmody in 1759, Hallam's comedians played *George Barnwell* at the College as a benefit, and between the acts "several celebrated Pieces of Concert Music" were performed by some "Gentlemen of this City." Orpheus had met with greater response in the so-called Quaker City than elsewhere in America.

Further indications of the secular drift and growing sophistication of urban musical entertainment came with fairly frequent performances of concerts after 1750. Apart from an early beginning, Charles Town had no concerts from 1735 to 1751, and then only three before 1760. In April of the last year of the period, Newporters attended their first "Vocal Concert," a benefit for Benjamin Reynolds. The annual subscription concerts held in Philadelphia, like the dancing assembly, ceased under Whitefield's denunciation, not to be resurrected until the coming of Lewis Hallam and his London Company in 1754 from New York to introduce ballad opera to the city. Then the inhabitants heard the scores of Pepusch, Arne, and other favorite English composers played by local musicians. George Washington took in John Palma's concert as he passed through the city in March 1757, without knowing that it was the first public professional concert in Pennsylvania—and the last of the period. Probably the dearth of such entertainment gave some impetus to the greater development of amateur music in Penn's city.[1]

The giving of public concerts, usually for the benefit of some professional musician, proceeded without hindrance at New York and Boston during these years. Manhattan enjoyed only a few in spite of the fact that one by John Rice at Todd's tavern in 1745 was "thought by all competent Judges, to exceed any Thing of the Kind ever done here before." In 1755 William Cobham and William Tuckey played an "Ode to Masonry," composed by the latter, at the New Exchange; and Alexander Dienval and W. C. Hulett, formerly with Hallam, started a subscription series for the winter of 1760. At Boston in 1744 the Selectmen granted permission to William Sheaffe, Stephen Deblois, and a group of gentlemen to celebrate the King's birthday with a concert in Faneuil Hall. It cleared about two hundred pounds, which was donated to the poor. Commodore Charles Knowles sponsored them in another concert at Faneuil Hall in 1747, and in 1750 these or some other amateurs still played together, for they invited Captain Goelet to a concert: "I went accordingly, the Performance was as well as Could be Expected, it Consisted of One Indiferent, Small Organ, One Base Violin, One German Flute, and Four Small Violins." Stephen Deblois built and opened the "Concert Hall" on Queen Street and inaugurated an annual series of concerts of "Vocal and Instrumental Musick" on January 9, 1755. John Rice played that year, but Thomas Dipper assumed charge thereafter. His programs always consisted of "Select Pieces by the Best Masters," and in March 1758 he gave, so far as is now known, the colonial première of vocal music from "Mr. Handel's Sacred Oratorios."

[1] The earliest known public subscription concert in England had been held at London in 1672 by John Banister; not until 1749 did the famous "Gentlemen's Concerts" commence at Manchester.

VII

When citizens of the better sort decided to adopt and carry out canons of taste borrowed bodily from Georgian England, they speedily patronized the limner, or face-painter. For a full-length or kit-cat of the master and mistress of the family was as necessary to the complete furnishing of a town or country mansion as heavy plate, Chinese wallpapers, or a piece in the manner of Chippendale. Since craftsmen essayed only such canvasses as members of the gentry commissioned, portraiture dominated colonial painting, and in confining themselves chiefly to this branch they continued in the mode of Britain, where historical scenes alone challenged face painting.

Boston had no rival as the center of colonial painting until midcentury. Up to the time of his death in 1751, Scottish John Smibert, the only colonial familiar with European art, who "lived always handsomely and with great reputation," was the dean of limners. Beginners in the craft always sought out the collection of copies of Italian masters displayed in his King Street studio and print shop. He executed few commissions after 1745 because of failing eyesight. A few portraits by his son, Nathaniel Smibert, suggest real promise, but an early death deprived the colonies of his talents. The 1748 visit to Boston of Robert Feke, the best native painter of that time, resulted in some of his finest portraits, including the charming likeness of Mrs. Barlow Trecothick. John Greenwood served as painter-in-ordinary to Boston's rich, whose faces he limned ruthlessly, from about 1745 until he went down to Surinam in 1752. For a brief period another local painter, Joseph Badger, contested with Joseph Blackburn, limner from England, for commissions. That indefinable something already attached to the imported article, and, regardless of his probable use of headless ready-made figures to which he merely gave faces, Blackburn succeeded in getting Apthorps, Bethunes, Bowdoins, Ervings, Faneuils, Phillipses, and Winslows to sit for him. With the exception of Robert Feke, none of these craftsmen, for such society considered them, developed into an artist of distinction, though to their credit they did portray their subjects with a provincial candor rather than a metropolitan flattery.

The versatile Peter Pelham, music and dancing master, occasional portrait-painter, successful mezzotint scraper, and intimate of John Smibert, took as his third wife Mary Singleton Copley, the tobacconist, in 1748. Her son, John Singleton Copley, commenced at the age of fifteen to paint portraits reminiscent of Greenwood, Feke, and Blackburn. His superior talent appeared early, however, and it was not long before

William Brattle, the Royall sisters, Benjamin Pickman, President Holyoke, and the elder James Otis sat for him. By 1760 he had painted more than forty of the first gentlemen and ladies of New England in all their dignity and finery more successfully than any of his predecessors. More significantly, in his characterizations of James Tilley, Mrs. Moses Gill, and Epes Sargent, there appeared those qualities that would set him apart as one of the great portrait-painters of the English-speaking world.

Prior to 1750, a brief visit by Feke and a few portraits by John Hesselius had to satisfy the aristocratic demands of Philadelphians. After the founding of the Academy, painting was encouraged by William Smith and his circle, who sponsored native efforts in oil by John Green and John Meng, and the water colors of Francis Hopkinson and William Bartram, and hired a German named Creamer (Kremer) to teach "some kinds of painting." In all, fourteen daubers of varying degrees of skill lived in or visited the Quaker City before 1760. Of the English itinerants, John Wollaston and William Williams fared well, but it was the local face-painter, Matthew Pratt, who earned the largest sums by his brush. Although portraiture brought the commissions, the decade of the fifties saw the emergence of two Philadelphians who would distinguish themselves in other branches. Benjamin West tried likenesses until his departure in 1760 for Italy, after which he won fame as a historical painter and president of the Royal Academy of Arts, and young William Bartram, on a trip with his father beginning in 1756, drew in ink and water colors specimens of native American flora and fauna, dramatically (even romantically) posed, thereby founding the genre that Audubon and Wilson made famous over half a century later.

At Charles Town, Jeremiah Theus conducted a perennial one-man show, for none of the English itinerants or the native Northern limners ventured down to South Carolina in this period. Alexander Gordon of the Governor's Council, scholar, musician, and professional artist, painted his friends Hector Béranger de Beaufain and the Reverend Henry Heywood ("One of the greatest scholars in America"); and George Roupell of the Royal Customs made useful scientific drawings and caricatured the gentry with their wigs off, but beyond this, the stiff but competent likenesses of Mr. Theus had to satisfy Charlestonians unless they, as many eventually did, had their portraits taken during voyages to England.

Manhattan painting lapsed into the doldrums in the forties, and today not a single surviving painting can be dated from that decade. Gerardus Duyckinck advertised himself in 1746 as a limner, but most of his work was ordinary painting and gilding. Even though for a time, including 1749, John Wollaston was in New York, it was not until 1754 that the arrival of Lawrence Kilburn, a Danish limner, augured a revival of portraiture there. Kilburn offered Knickerbockers the same "Choice of attitudes suitable to each Person's Age and Sex," and "agreeable Satisfaction," he had given in London. On September 30 he exhibited his pictures, asserting that no other painter was then available in town. In 1757 Valentine Haidt, a painter of religious scenes, ministered to the Moravian congregation, but there is no evidence that he executed any Biblical paintings before he moved to Bethlehem. Sensing a market, painters came in from elsewhere; by 1757 Philip Cuyler was among the New Yorkers who had sat for Copley, and the following year Benjamin West came over for a round of commissions. In the meantime Thomas McIlworth apparently advertised in vain for custom. Anxious as New Yorkers were to expend some of their new wealth on paintings, at no time did Manhattan produce a competent craftsman.

Only the very wealthy could afford portraits with which to adorn the walls of their houses, and art collecting was in its infancy. Inventories of Newport patricians indicate that most of them possessed from one to four portraits of members of their families. Henry Collins commissioned the pictures of Thomas Hiscox and John Callender from Feke and assembled other paintings, which gained him the somewhat grandiloquent title of the Lorenzo de' Medici of Rhode Island. Hector Béranger de Beaufain of Charles Town acquired some valuable works of art, but Philadelphians led the colonies in systematic collecting. Judge William Allen made a good beginning, and James Hamilton assembled some fine pictures at Bush Hill, which, with the statuary on his grounds, even attracted Quakers. Not by accident did the Rawles, Allens, and Shippens start in the fifties to send their sons on the grand tour, or Chief Justice Allen and Mr. Hamilton finance Benjamin West's trip to Rome.

The graphic arts appealed to all groups, and both upper and middle classes now had the means to indulge their tastes. Bostonians purchased all sorts of prints, many of which they framed and hung on the walls of their houses. John Smibert imported large numbers from Pond of London, reporting that the taste of the town did not run to "Landskips," but that the "few virtuosi here" bought prints of Roman ruins. Views of cities and scenes from estates in England also sold readily at William Price's Picture Shop in Cornhill Street. Newporters purchased their prints and maps from Boston dealers, and few of their inventories fail to mention "Pictures" or "pictures in Frames." A large business in graphic materials was carried on at New York by Gerardus Duyckinck, and Garrat Noel, the bookseller, in 1753 offered plain, polished, and gold burnished "bustoes" of Shakespeare, Milton, Homer, Virgil, Cicero, Congreve, Addison, Pope, Locke, Dryden, and Newton on black pedestals, along with the "newest and genteelest" pictures, for display in gentlemen's houses. Over at Philadelphia, Matthew Clarkson's stock included neatly framed mezzotints or glass paintings of the four seasons, the Countess of Coventry, the Duchess of Hamilton, Monamie's sea

pieces, and Manieschi's views of Venice, together with scenes of Vaux-
hall and Ranelagh Gardens, of London, and of Amsterdam. Residents
of Charles Town imported their prints and engravings directly from
London.

VIII

The philosophy of the Enlightenment, with its optimistic faith in reason
and knowledge, its intellectualism, and its practical and utilitarian spirit,
crossed the Atlantic Ocean in this period and proceeded to acclimate itself with astonishing ease in the American cities. There could be found
little groups of men, long resident or but recently arrived, who, by means
of travel, education in the Old World, experience, and the books in their
libraries, had kept themselves well abreast of their times, and to whom
the study of science proved especially congenial. If any evidence is
needed to demonstrate the intellectual alertness of the men of the colonial cities, it is quickly perceived in their avid interest in natural science.

The practice of medicine had attained the dignity of a profession in
urban centers early in the eighteenth century. After 1742 each town
boasted a number of skilled physicians who had received their education
at the leading schools of Edinburgh and Leyden, and often a course in
the London hospitals. Among the additions to this group were a considerable number of Scots who, lacking opportunities in their homeland,
emigrated to the colonies and promptly rose to positions of intellectual
eminence as devotees of learning as well as superior practitioners of
physic.

Amid the distractions of large and profitable practices, some city doctors found time to publish medical papers based on diseases or ailments
peculiar to their communities and of which they had made studies based
on clinical knowledge. The empirical quality of these essays attracted attention at Edinburgh, London, and Leyden, where not a few were first
published or reprinted, for the colonial approach to the healing art came
nearer to being "scientific" than most contemporary analyses in Europe.
Absorption with the annual visitations of yellow fever produced the first
literature on this important subject. In 1743, *Observations on the Fever
which Prevailed in the City of New York in 1741 and 1742,* a theoretical piece, was written by Dr. Cadwallader Colden, and in the next ten
years he sent another study of the disease and one on throat distemper
in a letter to Dr. John Fothergill, the great Quaker physician of London.
At Charles Town, where the yellow fever caused many deaths every
year, Dr. John Lining wrote a very accurate description of the plague of

1748, which Timothy published for him in 1753 and which shortly appeared in the *Edinburgh Medical Journal* (1753). This reprinting probably occurred at the instance of Dr. John Moultrie of Charles Town, whose *Dissertatio medica inauguralis, de Febre maligna bilosa Americanæ* (Edinburgh, 1749) had been based upon data collected during the South Carolina epidemic of 1745.

The several outbreaks of smallpox gave rise to a considerable literature on the fever. At Philadelphia on November 21, 1750 Dr. Adam Thomson, an Edinburgh graduate, read in the Academy before the trustees and a large audience what was possibly the first public medical lecture in this country, and it was promptly published as *A Discourse on the Preparation of the Body for the Small-Pox, and the Manner of Receiving the Infection* in both Philadelphia and New York. Dr. Thomson advocated a light, bland diet, small doses of mercury and antimony, and moderate bleeding and purging; he also stated his conviction that inoculating in the leg was safest because that member was farthest from the brain and vital organs in event of a serious reaction. Dr. John Kearsley at once attacked Thomson with his well-known sarcasm and thereby started a violent medical controversy of the European type, which, however, concluded with his having to regret publicly that he had injured the Scot's feelings. The clans gathered quickly as leading practitioners gave Thomson their aid, the most effective being Dr. Alexander Hamilton's able *Defense of Dr. Thomson's Method*. It is significant that the newspapers carried most of these medical exchanges before they reached the public in pamphlet form. Thomson's Method proved of great utility during the Boston epidemic of 1752, and, adopted widely in Europe after M. de La Condamine's praise of it before the Royal Academy of Science at Paris, it became known as "the American Method." Other persuasive advocates of inoculation at Philadelphia were Dr. Lachlin Macleane, who in 1756 wrote *An Essay on the Expediency of Inoculation and the Seasons most proper for it,* and Dr. John Redman, the city's most popular medic, who published a tract in 1759. At this juncture Benjamin Franklin performed one of his most useful public services by arranging for free distribution in nearly every town of a pamphlet on inoculation by Dr. William Heberden of London. Samuel Kneeland printed in 1752 *The Method of Practice in the Small-Pox, with Observations on the Way of Inoculation, by Dr. Nathaniel Williams*—the sole medical work produced at Boston in the period.

Urban physicians published more than twenty-three studies on medical subjects between 1743 and 1760 and in other ways advanced the dignity and standards of their profession. That many Philadelphia gentlemen were suffering from lead poisoning contracted by drinking punch concocted with rum distilled through lead pipes, Dr. Thomas Cadwalader proved in *An Essay on the West-India Dry Gripes* (1745). At the request of "a Weekly Society of Gentlemen" in New York, an address by Dr. John Bard was printed as *An Essay on the Nature of Malignant Pleurisy in 1749*. The London *Medical Observations and Enquiries* for 1753 contained valuable contributions by Cadwallader Evans of Philadelphia on the use of electricity in therapy and one by Dr. Thomas Bond on the case of a worm in the human liver. Frequently, too, newspapers served as outlets for medical knowledge and reported on delicate and unfamiliar surgery, as in the case of two successful operations for gallstones performed by Dr. Sylvester Gardiner of Boston in 1759. Newport was the scene of a major innovation, which was announced in the Boston press, when Dr. William Hunter, another Edinburgh graduate, gave courses of anatomical lectures with anatomical demonstrations at the Colony House in 1754 and the two succeeding years.

Natural philosophy won many votaries who, besides making some contributions in several branches, succeeded in bringing some understanding of the new science to a large colonial audience. In this work the physicians found allies in a few educated, curious gentlemen, a number of printers, and other alert artisans in each city. In fashioning precision instruments needed for experiments, the skills of such craftsmen as William Claggett and Benjamin King of Newport, Thomas Godfrey of Philadelphia, and Anthony Lamb, who also worked for a time in New York, were particularly helpful. The practical needs of a young society and the wonders of a new continent more or less dictated the direction that colonial investigations of nature would take. One indication of the quality and extent of urban activity in science is the fact that these men contributed twenty-eight papers to the *Philosophical Transactions* of the Royal Society of London in the same period that their contemporaries in nine English provincial cities contributed forty-nine.

By the time colonial population pressed inland and claims against French intrusions had to be urged, a good start had been made toward a scientific mapping of the country. Maps could be produced in the colonies as well as at London because of the presence of such skilled engravers as Lawrence Hebert, James Turner, and Peter Pelham at Philadelphia and Boston. If maps were sufficiently "embellished" they sold as often for display in mansions as for more utilitarian purposes. In Lewis Evans, Philadelphia had a first-class surveyor and geographer, who, making use of information supplied by many acquaintances, published between 1749 and 1756 a series of excellent maps depicting the Middle colonies and first delineating the contested Ohio Valley. In 1759 Nicholas Scull and James Turner combined talents in *A Map of the Improved Part of the Province of Pennsylvania,* and Turner engraved one of *Nova Scotia,* about which so many colonials wanted information. In the North, Dr. William Douglass issued a map of New England, "Compos'd from actual Surveys," in 1756. As befitted a maritime society, attention was given to charting the Atlantic coast to aid navigation. Daniel Dunbibbin undertook to survey "a great part" of the North and South Carolina shoreline in 1756, but he appealed in vain for enough South Carolina subscriptions to support his men and vessel, let alone to publish his map. The sea may have seemed no concern of rice and indigo planters, but it was ever in the minds of Philadelphia's "Merchants and Insurers." They gladly encouraged Friend Joshua Fisher to make a pioneer effort in hydrographic surveys, which he published in 1756 as a *Chart of Delaware Bay,* showing the tortuous channel from the Capes to Reedy Island. Engraved by James Turner, it was a beautiful as well as unusually serviceable piece of cartography.

With the revival of English voyages of exploration in the eighteenth century, hopes of discovering the fabled Northwest Passage soared anew, and colonial merchants joined in the rush to locate it first, hoping to vex the Arctic Sea with their fisheries and trafficking. In 1748, or earlier, a New York privateer had sailed along the Labrador coast and roused the enmity of the natives. An English expedition touched there in 1752; and the year after, Captain Taylor embarked in a sloop of thirty-five tons, outfitted at Newport, "to go in Pursuit of a North West Passage," and "if not successful to come down on the coast of Labrador" for a try at whaling. A few years prior to this, Chief Justice Allen, Benjamin Franklin, Archibald McCall, and other Philadelphians joined by several Boston, New York, and Maryland merchants with "no View of any Monopoly," subscribed £1,100 to finance a voyage, but severe winter weather prevented the dispatching of their vessel in 1751. Not until 1753 did the *Argo,* Captain Charles Swaine, sail in search of the strait, failing which, he too had instructions to explore the Labrador coast, establish trade with the Eskimos, and investigate the whale fishery. Becoming icebound, Swaine returned to Philadelphia in November. He took the *Argo* north again in the following May and came back in October because of trouble with the Labrador Indians. Although he cruised as far as latitude 56° and explored Davis's Inlet, Captain Swaine failed to establish a whale fishery at Labrador. He did, however, prepare a good chart of the coast and bring back some curious Eskimo artifacts for the Library Company's "Cabinet"—one of the earliest museums in the colonies.

Most thinking townsmen by the end of this period had come to accept rational or scientific elucidations of natural phenomena for which superstitious or theological explanations had previously been given. "The Comet: A Poem," widely circulated in newspapers and magazines in 1744, conventionally interpreted the appearance of one as an awful portent of divine anger:

> *Now at the sun it glows, now steers its flight*
> *Thro' the cold desarts of eternal night,*

Warns every creature thro' its trackless road
The fate of sinners, and the wrath of God.

Concurrently, however, such a powerful cleric as President Clap of Yale offered a more rational interpretation, and by 1759 Professor John Winthrop could give two public lectures in the chapel of Harvard College explaining the latest astronomical theories and have them fully reported in a New York newspaper before he got them out in pamphlet form. An earthquake of middling intensity threw a fright into Bostonians on June 3, 1744, causing much wild speculation over its origin, but when another occurred in 1755 starting similar speculation, Winthrop delivered a *Lecture on Earthquakes,* the rational calmness of which brought relief to many an agitated Yankee sinner even if the professor's printed pamphlet did not fall into the hands of that credulous purveyor of news and ancient lore to the Pennsylvania Germans, Christopher Saur.

Rationalism of course did not yet eliminate age-old superstitions of the sea, even among otherwise sophisticated gentlemen. Few vessels were dispatched from Newport without the aid of horoscopes, an added insurance, over and above the regular policy, which even Quaker merchants thought efficacious. In 1745 John George found the Rhode Islanders to be "Naturally credulous withall," and reported that nearly everyone consulted "those Gentry called Conjurers of which here are many who make a gainfull Trade of their Credulity, Though they'l Dispose of Fortune's favours at an Easy rate." For twenty shillings one would promise at least two thousand pounds of good fortune, "if he finds the Stars to favour his Design and he has made no Blunder in the Calculation." One "Gentleman Conjurer" had been in practice for twenty years. As long as the merchants employed astrologers to frame horoscopes before sending out ships or closing business deals, Captain George believed that "Tradesmen as well as Merchants" will "Trust their fortune to the Sea," and if they succeed will themselves "commence Merchants." When Captain Shearman's vessel was taken by the French in 1759, the *Mercury* said: "How unfortunate it is for the Owners that she did not sail on the lucky minute; for if the Stars were consulted for a successful Voyage, as probably they were, there must be some great Mistake in the Governing Planet. Such egregious Blunders clearly demonstrate that the Art of Conjury is not infallible."

In the cities both the great and small manifestations of nature appealed to investigators. So many amateur astronomers purchased telescopes and set them up during eclipses that at Philadelphia both newspapers devoted space to these events. In 1748 Thomas Godfrey sent information about a forthcoming eclipse to Bradford's *Journal,* and in 1751 Professor Theophilus Grew used the *Gazette* to request all gentlemen observers to communicate their findings to him at the Academy.

Two years later, when the Royal Society and "Foreign Professors of Astronomy" sent out a call to "the Curious in North America" to observe the transit of Mercury across the sun, Franklin printed detailed instructions along with some careful "precalculations" for the latitude of Philadelphia prepared by "T. Fox, Carpenter." Clouds obscured the transit on this continent, but the lone observation at Antigua was reported by the New York and Philadelphia press, and Benjamin Franklin sent William Sherrington's data to the Royal Society for publication. Ezra Stiles of Newport frequently corresponded with John Winthrop about the aberration of fixed stars and its philosophical implications.

Other gentlemen, like Dr. Thomas Moffatt, first librarian of the Redwood, preferred to study "the order, elegance, and uniformity of Nature in the texture of all bodies" through the microscope and doubtless read with enjoyment and profit in the *American Magazine and Historical Chronicle* a précis of Mr. Baker's popular London manual, *The Microscope Made Easy,* and took pardonable pride in the Reverend Thomas Prince's account of the discoveries with the instrument made by Edward Bromfield, a Bostonian of "a most accurate mechanick Genius and penetration," who unfortunately died in 1746 at the early age of twenty-three. For several years Governor James Glen tried keeping a diary of Charles Town weather until he heard about Dr. John Lining's far more complete journal containing complete meteorological tables for use in conjunction with studies in human metabolism. In this important subject Lining was the world pioneer, but when he published his findings in the *Philosophical Transactions,* contemporaries seemed to place greater value on the meteorological data.

Strange and beautiful new species of plants and animals discovered in the New World served more than any other natural wonder to draw the attention of *cognoscenti* to America. This was because the sciences of botany and zoology were then in the stage of description and classification, the systems that the Swedish botanist Linnæus, had just devised. Familiarity with Linnæan classifications, coupled with tirelessness, boundless enthusiasm, and keen perception, had made of untutored John Bartram, sometime Philadelphia Quaker, a field investigator without a peer—one whom the learned Swede is said to have called "the greatest natural botanist in the world." Aided by his friends Colden and Franklin, he became acquainted with all American botanists and entered into a "brisk, lively and free correspondence" with such eminent Europeans as Peter Collinson, J. F. Gronovius, Bernard de Jussieu, Queen Ulrica of Sweden, and Linnæus himself; Collinson arranged for the publication of five of Bartram's descriptions in the *Philosophical Transactions.* Colden introduced him to Dr. Alexander Garden, who presided over natural philosophy at Charles Town and who assisted the Pennsylvanian during his several Southern tours in search of new species. To

Garden and Colden, in 1756, Bartram broached a fully reasoned scheme for a geological survey of each colony, by which "we may compose a curious subterranean map." His own son, Billy, and the Colden children, David and Jane, took after their parents and had made remarkable progress in botany by 1760. To Bartram some of Jane Colden's "Botanical curious observations" appeared so excellent that he sent "several sheets of plants" to Gronovius in Holland.

Commencing in 1752 Dr. Garden labored long and valiantly, though with small success, to stimulate scientific interest among his fellow Charlestonians. This virtuoso from Edinburgh had a wide range of acquaintances with whom he corresponded, among them Linnæus and the English philosophers Ellis, Hales, Baker, Huxham, Shipley, and Collinson. Locally he worked with William Bull, George Saxby, Thomas Lamboll, and his own brother-in-law Alexander Peronneau, botanizing and collecting specimens of fish, reptiles, and insects for Linnæus, to whom he wrote of his keen sense of isolation from the learned world. Dr. Garden, upon his return from a Northern journey for his health in 1755, during which he met Franklin, Bartram, and Dr. John Clayton of Virginia, Cadwallader Colden and "his lovely daughter" (who named the gardenia after him), dispatched to George Ellis of London a box containing more than one hundred and twenty curious seeds in return for scientific books that "I value more than gold." He frequently mentions in his letters an "avaricious desire after new correspondents" because "some such thing is absolutely necessary to one, living under our broiling sun; else *ce feu, cette divine flame,* as Perrault calls it, would be evaporated in a few years." Probably Charles Town's cultural isolation, more than the heat, brought on this burst of *Weltschmerz.* His friend Ellis proposed membership in the Royal Society as a means to this end, but the Scot replied that he would not pay a fee to join: "It is what I would not do to any society under the sun." He hoped that he might be taken in as a foreign member. The Royal Society of Arts printed Garden's "hints" on vegetable colorings in 1757, and Charles Witworth, one of its fellows, suggested trying out different vegetables. The Garden circle made an effort to get planters interested by running an advertisement in the *South Carolina Gazette,* but nobody answered the appeal. When Dr. Ellis proposed that they establish a "provincial botannical garden" at Charles Town, the physician thought one might be started if the Englishman approached the Assembly directly. *Vox clamantis in deserto* might well have been the good doctor's motto, for as he wrote to Ellis: "Ever since I have been in Carolina I have never been able to set my eye upon one who had barely a regard for Botany."

The activities just described represent only the planting and spreading of an interest in the various branches of science, only a diversion for amateurs; save for the identification and description of hitherto unknown

American flora and fauna, no discovery or even significant colonial contribution had been made to natural philosophy. One would not expect any from a new and dependent society; such accomplishments, according to the theory of imperial division of labor, were the responsibility of the mother country. Still, at Philadelphia, assisted by his friends and neighbors, Benjamin Franklin made a most important contribution to pure science, one that caused him to be hailed by European philosophers and academies as one of the principal theoretical scientists of the century.

It was Dr. Adam Spencer, another Edinburgh acquaintance of Adam Thomson, Thomas Moffatt, and Alexander Hamilton, who first introduced new and exciting Old World discoveries in electricity to the colonial cities. His "Course of Experimental Philosophy" attracted many auditors, who followed the experiments in his printed syllabus. During a tour of 1743–4, Spencer's demonstration inspired James Bowdoin of Boston, William Claggett of Newport, Cadwallader Colden of New York, and several others to undertake electrical studies. But his principal convert was Benjamin Franklin, who learned about electrical fire, "a subject quite new to me," during one of Spencer's Boston lectures in 1743. The Scot repeated his course at the Library Room in Philadelphia the next year, and probably after his return from Virginia in 1746, Franklin purchased Spencer's apparatus with a view to discovering what he and his cronies could do on their own.

Starting far behind the European experimenters, in 1747, the Philadelphia group overtook and then passed them in the short space of two years. Here, as in so many ventures, is where Benjamin Franklin's genius displayed itself. Superintending Thomas Hopkinson, Philip Syng, and Ebenezer Kinnersley in their investigations with glass tubes, which he had persuaded Caspar Wistar to have blown for them, he initiated experiments that enabled him to work out generalizations that are still fundamental to electrical theory. Every bit of electronic equipment now in use rests on the principle of the condenser which he elucidated in 1748. Completely absorbed in the study of "pure science," he enthusiastically described his findings in letters to Colden, Bowdoin, Claggett, and Dr. Lining, urging them to similar experimenting. When he informed Peter Collinson of "the Philadelphia experiments," that generous patron of arts and sciences communicated the information to the Royal Society and procured its publication at London in 1751 as *Experiments and Observations on Electricity, made at Philadelphia in America,* by Mr. Benjamin Franklin. Immediate international acclaim, the award of the Copley medal, membership in the Royal Society, and later, in 1756, honorary degrees from Harvard, Yale, and William and Mary, and a long tribute in verse to his lightning rod in the *South Carolina Gazette* attested the acknowledgment of the entire Western World that the colonies had produced a great natural philosopher.

The new science received a hearty welcome in the five cities from all classes of people, and its exponents intelligently made use of every device to propagandize it throughout the colonies. By means of long and detailed letters, philosophers communicated with one another, and newspapers and magazines not only opened their columns to extracts from these epistles but served as the first and principal vehicles for publication of scientific writings. When Jeremy Gridley of Boston printed "An historical account of the wonderful discoveries, made in Germany, etc. concerning Electricity" in his *American Magazine and Historical Chronicle* for December 1745, the piece "raised the curiosity of several Gentlemen" at Newport, and within a month the watchmaker William Claggett had "fixed a Machine, by which a great Variety of these Experiments have been repeated." Some months afterwards he succeeded in setting fire to "spirits of Wine" by electricity. Thus Claggett must have constructed a Leyden jar, which the *Boston Evening Post* had told its readers all about before Franklin began his experiments. A regular department of Provost Smith's *American Magazine* was a "Philosophical Miscellany," wherein priority of Thomas Godfrey's invention of "the Quadrant commonly called Hadley's" received its first public defense. In submitting accounts of two new experiments in 1758, David Colden of New York expressed the hope that "American Electricians" would use this magazine to report their discoveries, and when it ceased publication, he turned to James Parker's *New American Magazine* for an outlet.

Other agencies facilitated the dissemination of scientific knowledge. Printing shops and bookshops sold quantities of pamphlets, and the colleges introduced natural philosophy among their courses of study and procured sets of philosophical apparatus. A more popular means was the public lecture, inaugurated by Dr. Spencer's courses on the nature of the eye and on electrical fire in 1743. In August 1747 William Claggett repeated his Newport lectures before Boston audiences, and after his departure Captain John Williams continued them. By October, Daniel King was imitating them at nearby Salem, and the following year Richard Brickell was entertaining curious ladies and gentlemen with divers electrical experiments at New York, as was Samuel Dömjen at Charles Town. Two Philadelphians soon achieved intercolonial prominence as lecturers on science. Ebenezer Kinnersley of the Academy, encouraged by Franklin, who wrote and published his first syllabus, toured the four Northern cities for many years, stopping occasionally at smaller towns. His lectures contained the most up-to-date account of the developments in electricity; at Boston and Newport in

1751 he tried out some experiments of his own that his patron reported to the Royal Society. More ambitious in scope were thirteen lectures comprising a complete survey of natural philosophy and mechanics, "illustrated by Experiments," given by Lewis Evans in New York, Charles Town, and the West Indies in 1751–2. That these performances were well patronized by people of fashion, in spite of the relatively high cost of tickets, is an indication of an awakening interest in the wonders of science that swept over the upper classes of Europe at the same time.

When the new colonial vogue for science is considered against the background of two disturbing wars, it appears all the more remarkable. In 1739 John Bartram had proposed the formation of a learned society at Philadelphia, but Peter Collinson warned that times were not yet propitious. Four years later Franklin believed such an undertaking could succeed, and, as later with Dr. Bond's hospital scheme, he set about promoting it. His *Proposal For Promoting Useful Knowledge Among the British Colonies in America* had the blessings of Collinson and met with approval from such devotees of science as Colden and Dr. John Mitchell of Virginia. Established in 1744, the new learned body never really got off to a proper start. In later years its founder thought "the French War . . . took off our Thoughts from . . . promoting Useful Knowledge in America." At the time, however, John Bartram placed the blame for the failure of "our proposals" on "the laying up of large estates," indulgence in luxury by the wealthy, and the need of the less affluent to labor, concluding that "most of our members in Philadelphia embraces other amusements that bears a greater sway in their minds." The society was dead on Peter Kalm's arrival in 1748. It took the accomplishments of this era, the international renown of Bartram and Franklin, and more popular knowledge about this great secularizing force to prepare the minds of the colonial citizenry for an organization on an intercolonial scale such as these two Philadelphians dreamed of and in which, ironically, neither would take a prominent part.

IX

In 1760 the five intellectual centers of the English colonies had shown an awareness of most of the leading ideas of the Enlightenment. Moreover, on the basis of this provincial cultural development, a few contemporaries with prophetic insight already predicted a great future for America. A rapid extension of private and public schools, the opening of numerous bookstores, and the establishing of subscription libraries had made this possible. Aided by a vigorous printer's craft, which was evincing cultural as well as acquisitive traits, much of the best English literature reached the colonies through reprints, and whatever the people themselves had to say reached the public in book, pamphlet, or newspaper form. To ensure that a now emerging public opinion was properly informed on all issues, this same craft stood foursquare against attempts by authorities to restrict a free press. "The first drudgery of settling new colonies" being "pretty well over," as Benjamin Franklin remarked, there were in the cities many persons with "leisure to cultivate the finer arts." The outcome was a steady improvement in colonial taste as practitioners and patrons of prose literature, painting, architecture, and music provided more of the embellishments of existence and endeavored to bring urban culture abreast of the age, just as the virtuosi were doing in natural philosophy. All this accomplishment took place on the urban scene, from which it spread in some measure to rural areas. Susanna Wright, living on the banks of the Susquehanna, longed for "the elegant converse" of Philadelphia and possibly did not relish Mr. Franklin's half-serious reply: "You Would not regret the want of City Conversation, if you considered that $9/10$ of its Impertinence." But it was this very impertinence, this alertness, that gave the colonies five vital centers of culture.

War, Expansion, and Prosperity:
Conclusion

O<small>NE DAY</small> at William Allen's the conversation turned "on the un-common Event of such a town as Philadelphia arising, amidst a wilderness, in so short a time, and becoming so fine and populous a City as we all saw it" in 1755. Thomas Pownall addressed himself to the Chief Justice's mother, and the old lady told him that she had lived to see this great city with "near Thirty thousand [*sic*] inhabitants in it, en-joying every comfort and elegance and even luxury that the first town in Europe could offerr." She had also seen the beginning of it, and, what was more, remembered when Pennsylvania was a wilderness. "That any Person should live to see any Object brought forward from speculation and realized in so extraordinary a manner" is a "singular Anecdote in the History of Man." And what was true of the youngest city was true also of the oldest; Boston, ever a community on the hill, never hesitated to compare itself with London, Paris, and Rome in urban matters.

With well-nigh incredible speed, as Europeans measured it, the colo-nists reared their cities, and in this building they worked eagerly and hard, sustained in their efforts by a sublime belief in progress. Theirs was no theoretical conviction; they were a secure people, and their cities represented to them, as to those who had preceded them for more than a century, the carrying out of part of the promise of America. As they looked about them, progress was a demonstrated fact.

It must have been clear to an impartial observer of 1760, if he was familiar with the European scene, that the five colonial communities matched English and Continental provincial cities and, in more ways than one, bettered their models. Far more than the still half-wild to-bacco and rice plantations of the colonial South, the American cities and their immediate environs bore a strong physical resemblance to those of the mother country. Suffolk and Middlesex, Newport and New York, Philadelphia and Chester counties were cleared, fenced, and cultivated, with here and there groves of oak and hickory, and rolling fields dotted with orchards strongly reminiscent of the English countryside.

210

The five cities, in turn, served as models for what their denizens may have thought of as American provincial towns, aggregates of from three to five thousand people in settlements up and down the Atlantic coast. All of them, except Lancaster and Bethlehem, were seaports and owed their prosperity to commerce; all of them were maturing and putting on the familiar urban trappings; with the completion of a "Colony House" in 1760, Providence symbolized its determination to challenge the over-lording of Newport; Bethlehem's Moravians enjoyed running water from the first municipal system, and they listened to the best music in all America; in 1751 Portsmouth had acquired both a fire engine and a social library. The inhabitants of Salem, Providence, Germantown, and Lancaster had access to subscription libraries; while citizens of Portsmouth, New London, New Haven, and Lancaster read local newspapers, at least for a time. Amateur theatricals introduced by British officers to Dutch Albany in 1758 led to official permission for a month of plays by Hallam's Company of Comedians in 1760. These and similar evidences of growth in other secondary towns indicated that an important expansion of colonial urban life had taken place.

In general well-being, the average colonial townsman was better off than the English city dweller, whose sense of insecurity continually clouded his existence. The American found his community superior in provision for education for all classes and in opportunities for employment and getting ahead in the world. No impassable class barriers held him down. He saw more of his neighbors participating in governing the city and rejoiced in the power of a well-articulated public opinion, which already swayed causes and got some results. And if he thought beyond these matters, he took pride in the leaders the city produced—Benjamin Franklin, Thomas Bond, Ezra Stiles, William Livingston, Dr. Alexander Garden, Peter Timothy, Thomas Fleet.

These years of strife had seen individuals from the five cities accepted as members of the international urban community—the source from which the Enlightenment emanated. Colonials had earned this recognition. Men with spacious minds did not permit wars to interrupt the study of nature; science was, above all, cosmopolitan. During King George's War, Peter Collinson instructed John Bartram to address all shipments of plants for him to M. de Jussieu of the Jardin du Roi at Versailles, knowing that if they were captured, the French scientist would not allow the existence of hostilities to prevent them from reaching their destination. The warfare of this era, moreover, was to some degree civilizing. In their letters home, British officers made Europe aware of American cities at the same time that they introduced some of the graces and arts of the Old World to the New.

The growth, prosperity, and what might be termed the Europeanizing of the urban centers were noted by the farmers of rural and frontier

America quite as much as by foreign travelers. A widening gulf in outlook, interests, and manner of living between country and town was apparent to all, especially the contrasts between agriculture and commerce, between dispersion and congestion of population, in architecture and housing, and most notably in wealth and luxury. Political and economic control by the metropolises tightened with the advance of commercial capitalism, which yielded a disproportionate share of the gains to the merchant, which in turn aroused increased resentment in the rustic. The countryside held on longer to the old and familiar ways of Christianity as secular influences made headway in the cities, and rural parsons hurled many a charge of godlessness at the strongholds of Mammon. The rivalry of the city slicker and the hayseed, so persistent a theme in American life, had made a lasting appearance; and it may be remarked, parenthetically, that more significance attaches to the fact of this urban-rural tension than to the geographical accident of east-west antagonism.

Having brought their communities safely through adolescence in the midst of unsettling conditions generated by war, city leaders looked ahead to a prompt conclusion of hostilities after the fall of Quebec and the transfer of the fighting to the Caribbean. Forming a ruling class and having reached the summit of their power and prestige, the gentry faced the future with buoyant optimism, anticipating that it would bring them profits and greater freedom of action in commerce, and guarantee development of the hinterland and the western wilderness. Their eager expectancy blinded them to the fact that their days were numbered, and that they and their fellows of the lower classes had already unleashed the revolutionary forces that would consume them. They did not perceive the lesson of history that "normalcy" and prosperity after wars are but chimeras.

Part Two

DEPRESSION, TENSION, AND REVOLT, 1760–1776

CHAPTER 6

Urban Elegance

FROM THE BUSTLING TOWN of Baltimore a gentleman wrote to an Annapolis friend in 1773 about some measures that were pending in the Maryland Assembly. Cogently expressing the widely held European view that, historically, law and subordination took their rise in the cities of the late Middle Ages, he went on to say: "Liberty, science, and commerce, the great friends of man, are sister adventurers. They are intimately, indeed inseparably connected together, and always take up their chief residence in the cities. Thither the greatest geniuses of the age generally resort, and incited by emulation or fired by ambition, they stimulate each other to successful exertions of native talents; which might have otherwise lain dormant, and forever deprived mankind of much useful instruction. To them repair the patriots, the men of letters, and the merchants, who become the guardians of the people's rights, the protectors of learning, the supporters of their countries trade. Thus free cities, considered in this light are the repositories, preservatives, and nurseries of commerce, liberty, and knowledge." This is true not only of Rome, London, Paris, and the great centers of the Old World, but "even in this new, and as yet uninformed American world, a Boston, a New-York, and a Philadelphia add lustre and dignity to the colonies to which they belong, and are advancing with rapidity towards perfection in arts and sciences, commerce and mechanics." If Maryland but had a "commercial capital" to spur her people, she would no longer lag so far behind her sisters.

The forces that brought the five cities to this high point of development by the end of the colonial era were the same ones that had governed their destinies between 1743 and 1760, with this exception: they operated under conditions of peace instead of international conflict. The scene of the French and Indian War shifted from continental North America to the Caribbean as England warred on Spain, and in 1763 peace was officially concluded at Paris; but it did not bring the piping times so fondly anticipated by civic leaders. Times did indeed change, but not necessarily for the better, for from the beginning of this period through the early seventies the colonies experienced a depression, whose incidence fell largely on the cities. Readjustment of commerce and trade to postwar deflation is always a difficult and delicate operation, but in this instance the decision of the British government to reform its commercial system in the midst of hard times gave rise to an acute situation that seriously hampered, and probably postponed, economic recovery. Thus an age that began auspiciously with the accession of George III soon became one of tension and, ultimately, ended in revolt.

Under such a dispensation, life in the cities did not attain normality, if by that is meant times as they had been before 1740, but it did expand. Urban growth continued, stepping up its pace each year as population multiplied, boundaries widened, houses increased, and, in spite of violent fluctuations, trade and industry assumed ever larger proportions. An already mobile people moved about more than ever. Now free from enemy marauders, commercial shipping once more crowded the Atlantic sea lanes, bringing the inhabitants of the British Isles and the colonies face to face more than ever before and permitting, for the first time, direct cultural as well as commercial relations with countries on the continent of Europe. Time had much to do with the maturing of the urban society of America; the year of Lexington and Concord could also have been the year for New York to celebrate its sesquicentennial; Boston had existed for 145 years, Newport for 136; Charles Town and Philadelphia had nearly reached the century mark.

II

The ending of the great Anglo-French conflict permitted a renewal of immigration, and the Scotch-Irish and Germans poured into the colonies adding large numbers to communities already growing very rapidly from their normal birth-rate and accretions from the countryside. The combined population of the five cities rose from 72,881 in 1760 to 104,000 by 1775—an increase of thirty-three per cent in fifteen years. This rate of growth approximately paralleled that of the provincial centers of England, whose unprecedented spurt did not begin until about 1770.

POPULATION OF COLONIAL CITIES, 1760–1776			
	1760	1775	1776
1. Philadelphia	23,750	40,000	21,767
2. New York	18,000	25,000	5,000
3. Boston	15,631	16,000	3,500
4. Charles Town	8,000	12,000	12,000
5. Newport	7,500	11,000	5,299
Total	72,881	104,000	47,566

On the eve of the American Revolution, Philadelphia with its forty thousand inhabitants was larger than any city in England except London itself and had taken its place not only with the largest provincial cities of the British Empire but with those of western Europe.[1] New York, Charles Town, and Newport enjoyed considerable growth, but Boston's population remained around sixteen thousand until 1775 when the country Tories flocked in to raise it to about twenty thousand. The eventful year of 1776 saw a 45 per cent drain of people from all cities save Charles Town, occasioned by occupation or threatened approach of British forces. The significant growth of the five largest colonial cities was accompanied by an even more notable one in fifteen other communities, each of which numbered over three thousand inhabitants.

ESTIMATED POPULATION OF SECONDARY COLONIAL CITIES, 1760–1776

6. New Haven (1771) *	8,295	13. Hartford (1774)		4,881
7. Norwich (1774) *	7,032	14. Middletown (1775)		4,680
8. Norfolk (1775)	ca. 6,250	15. Portsmouth (1775)		4,590
9. Baltimore (1775)	5,934	16. Marblehead (1776)		4,386
10. New London (1774) *	5,366	17. Providence (1774)		4,361
11. Salem, Mass. (1776)	5,337	18. Albany (1776)	ca.	4,000
12. Lancaster,		19. Annapolis (1775)		3,700
Pa. (1776)	ca. 5/6,000	20. Savannah (1775)	ca.	3,200

* Actual census

As the population of these secondary communities mounted, they passed through the same stages of urban growth experienced earlier by the five metropolises—a recital that awaits another chronicler.

III

In the last two decades of the colonial period, municipal government underwent very little fundamental change. Newport's Town Meeting kept adding more local officials to the roster each year until, in 1772, it had to elect 188, which rivaled Boston's 212, inasmuch as the Selectmen of the Rhode Island port doubled as Overseers of the Poor and Work-

[1] I am no longer as certain as I was in 1942, when I stated that Philadelphia exceeded Edinburgh and Dublin in population, and was, "as nearly as we can deduce from the imperfect statistics of the eighteenth century . . . the second largest city of the British Empire" (*Rebels and Gentlemen*). Whether it was second or fourth makes very little difference; it was a very large city for its day. Adam Anderson declared that "Bristol is universally allowed to be the second largest city in Great Britain." In 1775 its population was 35,440; Liverpool's was about 34,407, Birmingham's 30,804, and Manchester's 27,246 (1773).

house. Since the New York Assembly passed the necessary legislation for raising taxes, Manhattan's Mayor and Common Council succeeded remarkably well in keeping pace with the rapid expansion of New York.

The Philadelphia story remained the same. The sphere of action of its exclusive and lethargic Corporation was further limited: in 1762 the Pennsylvania Assembly created a board of six commissioners, like the Wardens of the watch and pumps, to oversee the construction, cleaning, and maintenance of streets and watercourses in the city; to this distribution of responsibility, which at least had the merit of giving popularly elected officials a decisive voice in vital matters, an additional scattering of authority took place, leaving the Corporation little more than its judicial duties, supervision of the markets, and management of its own property by 1775. Control of the Almshouse had passed to a board named by the private contributors in 1766, and another law set up Wardens of the Port.

The Quaker City's problem was complicated still more by a suburban expansion that produced the first congested metropolitan area in this country with its attendant complexities. The Assembly erected the District of Southwark in 1762 and provided it with popularly chosen highway officials; in 1771 it allowed the Northern Liberties a similar privilege, though the County Commissioners made all appointments and the Court of Quarter Sessions confirmed them. In caring for the poor, contributors from the Northern Liberties, Southwark, Moyamensing, and Passyunk were incorporated with those of the city in 1766. This miscellany of municipal bodies mirrored similar developments in England, where suspicion of the capacity and public spirit of closed corporations forced the creation of *ad hoc* bodies. It is not surprising that with the revolt in Philadelphia in 1775 the Mayor and Common Council quietly went out of existence.

The planters' Assembly of South Carolina never responded to the pressing needs of its metropolis with the readiness of that of Pennsylvania, where public pressure induced action. The Grand Jury of 1762 initiated the demand for the incorporation of Charles Town as a city so that it might adequately cope with municipal problems. Although the Commons House ordered a bill brought in, the measure never became a law. Agitation continued without letup, as successive grand juries, like that of 1770, presented "as a very GREAT GRIEVANCE, the want of many wise and wholesome regulations, for the benefit of the community in general, from Charles-Town NOT BEING MADE A CORPORATE CITY." Peter Timothy was but one of many thoughtful citizens who realized that the careless distribution of authority among the many nonresident commissioners designated in provincial laws, together with some elected parish officers and the justices of the peace (upon whom enforcement of the law depended), was responsible for their lax government. In not a few matters the Assembly failed to fix responsibility on anyone. In 1771 the Grand Jury asked for "a Number of Sitting Justices" to meet in Charles Town weekly to hear grievances; the next year its successor complained that the character of those appointed as justices had not been sufficiently looked into; many justices are "nominal," desiring merely the title of "Esq." in the newspapers, said the Grand Jury of 1773 as it condemned the purchase of commissions and forcefully demanded that the legislators incorporate the city "as the only Means that will effectually remove many Enormities, and redress many Grievances, and otherwise tend to introduce many wise and salutary Regulations." Notwithstanding the tireless efforts of the leading Charlestonian, Christopher Gadsden, the members of the Assembly displayed either callous indifference or stubborn resistance to the legitimate requests of the city. Josiah Quincy of Boston penetrated to the core of their policy in 1773: "Who do they represent? The laborer, the mechanic, the tradesman, the farmer, the husbandman or yeoman? No. The representatives are almost if not wholly rich planters. The Planting interest is therefore represented, but I conceive nothing else (*as it ought to be*)."

The most pressing postwar problem everywhere was the raising of sums adequate to provide municipal services. The three largest cities enjoyed an income from rentals of property, licenses, and fines. New York's revenues from such sources rose in the decade following 1760 from £2,287 to £3,034; the others took in smaller amounts. To produce the large sums expended on highways, bridges, street paving and cleaning, taxes were essential; and throughout this period they went up and up. Containing no more than a fifth of the population of New York province, the city paid one third of all the taxes in the colony in 1773 because of "a confederacy of all the country members against the citizens." Said "Aristides": "The city has been stung by a serpent," but "her citizens, too, even below the order of Mechanicks know their rights." The inhabitants generally showed themselves willing to pay for urban improvements, but found it impossible to do so because of the heavy provincial exactions, which continued to be from one third to one half of the total. Charlestonians paid out about £3,600 annually for local administration, and their share of the general provincial levy, which had amounted to one fifth of the total prior to 1759, thereafter went up to one quarter. A petition fruitlessly presented by Mr. Gadsden in 1770 demonstrated that a merchant with £7,000 in real estate, slaves, and stock in trade had to pay a tax of £35; whereas a planter with the same amount invested in 350 acres of land and twelve slaves paid only £7. Philadelphia also bore a disproportionate share, twenty-three per cent, of the taxes voted by the unpopular Quaker government.

The inhabitants of the New England cities twice went all out in a war effort, devoting their energies and funds to raising troops, fitting out ships, and willingly submitting to as heavy taxation to further the cause as any of their descendants ever have. From peace they hoped for much, and they expected tax relief, but it became necessary to continue high rates until provincial debts were paid off. Moreover, rather than allow municipal services to deteriorate, both cities voted increases of local rates. As each community contained many poor people who simply could not meet their obligations, tax delinquency spread alarmingly.

The Newport Town Meeting memorialized the Rhode Island Assembly in 1761 urging relief for its citizens, who were "grieved by the heavy Taxes laid on them"—one fifth of the entire colony levy plus £10,000 in town taxes (which rose to £21,000 Old Tenor by 1766). The inability of many Newporters to pay their assessments brought Collector John Read to grief in 1768; the General Assembly threw him into debtors' prison for deficiency in payments to the Treasury. The Town Meeting had the privilege of the prison yard extended to the town's limits to enable him to make collections on the missing £1,753 lawful money and £5,479 Old Tenor owed the colony. He was also behind in town taxes: £4,440 for 1766 and £1,168 for 1767, plus "considerable deficiencies in rates from the year 1756 to the present," though he had paid in more than he ever collected. The citizens knew that poor John had tried his best and came to his rescue by borrowing money enough to save him from further prosecution by the colony, but the Town Council finally had to sue him. When Newport's Treasurer, Edmond Townsend, also had to go to jail in 1770 for failing to make payments to the province, a sympathetic town voted "to hyre" the amount needed to discharge his account. Again in 1774 Jacob Richardson fell behind £1,355 in collections and was given six months to make good the deficiency. There can be no question that the tax burden of the average Newporter was almost unbearable, nor that this condition aggravated the already rising temper of the people on Rhode Island.

Massachusetts made the greatest sacrifice of lives during the French Wars, incurred the largest debt, and levied the heaviest taxes; and Boston paid more than its proportion of all three. It is worth recalling that in 1760 the citizens paid 13*s*. 6*d*. in the pound on personal property and real estate. No relief accompanied the postwar depression, and, as at Newport, numbers of taxpayers became delinquent. Of the four tax collectors, three—John Ruddock, Jonathan Payson, and John Grant—had been serving in this capacity for years, and Samuel Adams after 1761. An investigating committee for cutting expenses informed the Town Meeting on May 10, 1763 that a total of £17,321. 4*s*. 8*d*. remained uncollected for 1761–2; and again in 1767 that £17,891. 19*s*. 2*d*. had not come in for the period 1762–6. The largest sum due was from Samuel Adams, though all collectors were deficient in getting in both province and town taxes. At no time did any persons rise to blame the collectors, and they were re-elected to office. Even the most zealous detractors of the great revolutionist cannot impute to him anything more than injudicious leniency with his fellow townsmen; he paid all that was due the province, town, and county for 1761–3, and received the premium due for his work. In 1774 the Town Meeting voted to wipe out "what Mr. Samuel Adams, a late Collector, erroneously stands Debtor for on Town Treasury Books." The widespread tax delinquency at Boston and Newport stemmed directly from the wars, and when further burdens from without the city and province were proposed, the road to revolt led straight ahead. Taxation was one cause of the uprising.

Sectional differences arising from the success of rural interests in the assemblies in shifting the incidence of taxation onto the cities, which were underrepresented, combined with other grievances to give shape to the urban-rural conflict in these years. Boston's strong leadership in the House of Representatives saved it from any such discrimination, whereas the issue between New York City and the Hudson Valley was clear-cut. At both Philadelphia and Charles Town the point was often obscured by the fact that when the leaders from the interior inveighed against the seaboard, they seemed to include the city elements in their charges, whereas they actually were aiming their resentment at the ruling gentry of the east, in whose interest the government was conducted. The Reverend Charles Woodmason drew up a blistering indictment of the South Carolina planters for their criminal neglect of the back parts in refusing to ensure law and order to them, but, as a former Charles Town official, he knew that the same sort of complaint could as readily come from the neglected city. His friend Christopher Gadsden also realized that thousands of decent people, white and black, suffered from an absence of properly constituted authority and much needed municipal arrangements, because they, too, were underrepresented. The extra-legal Provincial Congress of January 11, 1775 provided "the most complete Representation of all good People throughout this Colony that ever was," and for once Calhouns, Caldwells, Chestnuts, and Kershaws attended as delegates of the upcountry along with several Charles Town gentlemen. Likewise, Philadelphians, with only two seats in the Pennsylvania Assembly, felt a kinship with the people of the western counties, who could never outvote the Quaker-German members of Philadelphia, Chester, and Bucks counties.

In those cities where the populace could express its desires by voting, politics reflected economic distress and involved more than local issues. The large number of freemen at Boston enabled skilled manipulators to introduce modern methods of democratic control, which took the Town Meeting out of the hands of the gentry before 1760. Three years later, John Adams discovered how "a clique of intriguers" managed things: "This day learned that the Caucus Club meets, at certain times, in the garret of Tom Dawes, the Adjutant of the Boston Regiment. He has a large house, and he has a movable partition in his garret which he takes down, and the whole club meets in one room. There they smoke tobacco, till you cannot see from one end of the garret to the other. There they drink flip, I suppose, and there they choose a moderator, who puts questions to the vote regularly; and selectmen, assessors, collectors, wardens, fire-wards, and representatives, are regularly chosen before they are chosen in the town. . . . They send committees to wait on the merchant's club, and to propose and join in the choice of men and measures." The smoke-filled room has a long history.

The tickets agreed upon circulated as broadsides and occasionally appeared in the newspapers. Elections took all morning, and presumably the inhabitants were to spend the afternoon framing instructions to their representatives to the General Court. There were so many freemen who went home because they were either tired of the proceedings or unable to stay away from their business so long, that the vital work was left to the henchmen of the Caucus. An analysis of the principal offices of Boston, 1760–75, shows that the Caucus and the Merchant's Club so managed elections that their men won out regularly. This was upper-class rule as before, but now control rested with only that segment of the gentry whom Bernard and Hutchinson branded "The Faction," a group whose members entertained definite opinions about political and economic issues that had strong popular support. At town meetings, so the Commissioners of the Customs lamented in 1768, "the lowest mechanics discuss upon the most important parts of governments with the utmost freedom; which being guided by a few hot and designing men, become the constant source of sedition." Gentlemen of character avoided these meetings, fearing insult and resentment should they oppose any popular measure, and thereby permitted Samuel Adams and his shrewd cronies to transform what had been a convocation for prudential matters into a revolutionary forum, though without in any way seriously deranging its efficiency in coping with the problems of urban life. The conservative gentry were never able to fathom the gradual but inexorable democratic drift of the century, and they could never resolve the "Paradox" of political control of the many by a few of "the better sort," who appeared to one side as tribunes of the people and to the others as traitors to their class.

Newport's citizenry was nearly as well organized as that of Boston, and in much the same manner, by the Vernons, Townsends, and other mercantile leaders; but their efforts had to be directed toward defeating, if possible, the forward thrust of the men of Providence to commercial and political leadership in Rhode Island. Party violence, including election bribery, during the Ward-Hopkins contest for governor has been regarded as more of a struggle among men than over issues, but the scramble for power between the two communities was basic to the dispute. Unable to fight Providence after 1770, the liberal element in Newport's gentry thereafter skillfully piloted their Town Meeting over a course laid down by their Boston correspondents as trouble with the mother country came to a head.

In December 1765 John Watts wrote to Governor Monckton of New York that he was fortunate in having left the province. "The ill-boding aspect of things, cramping of trade, suppression of paper money, duties, courts of admiralty, appeals, internal taxes, etc., have rendered people so poor, cross, and desperate that they don't seem to care who are their masters or indeed for any masters." One fifth of the men of military age in the province had taken to the field in the late war, and the load of debt that the inhabitants labored under in the sixties impelled many a merchant and artisan to take out the freedom of the city in order to express his opinion at the polls. But the expanded electorate did not bring improved politics. The word flew around the West Ward one evening in 1768 of a certain dram shop where "every Freeholder or Freeman, who was willing to part with his vote, might there meet with a purchaser." A bill to substitute the secret for the open ballot failed in 1770, but in the next session the Assembly did make an initial move to improve elections and define voting qualifications.

Where the voters were few, as at Philadelphia and Charles Town, popular desires found little expression through lawful agencies. Chief Justice Allen, a strong Proprietary man, feared the coming of the "younger folks" under the influence of "that Disturber of the Peace, Franklin and his creatures." In 1764 this "grand Incendiary's" power proved insufficient to sway the German vote, which put Henry Keppele into the Assembly on the Quaker side, or to prevent the uneasy Corporation from opposing the abolition of the Proprietary. In fact, Franklin lost his seat. But the ill-concealed sympathy of many with the grievances of the Paxton Boys augured the day when the disfranchised people of Philadelphia would make their voices heard through Charles Thomson, David Rittenhouse, William Bradford, James Cannon, and Dr. Thomas Young. Annual parish elections seldom brought out a large vote from the Charles Town oligarchy eligible to participate in them. In 1771 the Grand Jury censured this neglect "by which Persons interested in serving those offices, although often ignorant of the duties incumbent upon them, find means to get themselves elected, to the great Prejudice of the Public." When "Mechanicks and others" met at Liberty Point on the call of Christopher Gadsden in 1768 to consult about representatives for the next Assembly, they "occasioned a great stir" by their nominations. This hitherto unheard-of procedure, so distasteful and shocking to gentlemen, won the election and gave the ordinary Charlestonians their first intimation of latent power.

With the single exception of Charles Town, where a laggard and jealous legislature persisted in ignoring the capital's needs, these cities had arrived at forms of government able to deal with problems of urban growth rather more promptly and adequately than contemporary English communities. Continued improvement in public services was evident in all of them; but at Boston, Newport, and New York shrewd manipulators transformed public forums into smoothly operating political engines, which ultimately drew the colonies away from the mother country. Governor William Bull of South Carolina, a native-born Tory, clearly perceived, as early as 1769, the direction that city politics were taking under leaders and followers "inclined more to the democratical than regal Scale."

IV

The physical expansion of the cities proceeded under the most favorable conditions of any period in colonial urban history; no major catastrophe occurred in any community. With the close of the Old French War, fortifications were allowed to crumble, but notwithstanding the discouraging state of economic affairs for at least a decade, a substantial amount of new construction went on steadily, and in the seventies a decided building boom started in city and suburb alike. By acquiring more public buildings and a number of stately new churches, as well as by replacing old structures with new and often impressive town houses, each city further accentuated its individual appearance.

To provide adequate housing for more than sixteen thousand new inhabitants Philadelphians put forth a major effort; until about 1770 they erected about two hundred houses annually, and thereafter they more than doubled that number. Solomon Drowne wrote home in 1774 that "there have been *only* four hundred and seventy three Houses built in Philadelphia this year." Such activity doubtless kept David Rittenhouse, Robert Smith, and the three other "Regulators of Party Walls, Buildings and Partition Fences" very busy inspecting work at new premises. The 2,969 dwellings standing in the city and immediately adjacent suburbs in 1760 had doubled by the end of the period when an enumeration disclosed 3,861 houses in the city proper, 1,207 in the Northern Liberties, and 889 in Southwark—a total of 5,957.

Philadelphia still contained many wooden houses in 1760, but brick structures, roofed with shingles, and the majority having three stories "besides garrets and cellars," predominated in "the interior parts of town." There was "scarce one that could be called grand," but in succeeding years many of the "old and shabby" dwellings were replaced.

Averaging about fifteen to twenty feet on the front and seventy-five in depth, they ranged the streets in rows. Some observers considered them "very uniform, plain, and neat" as befitted a "Regular" city, but more sophisticated critics thought there was "no particular plan of building observed in the houses," and their eyes "were not delighted with that variety here, which sometimes is observable in smaller places." Let a Quaker girl tell of her mother's house: "Below are the shop and count-inghouse in front; one large and one small parlor back, a delightful entry from the street to the yard. Up stairs is a good drawing room and three large chambers, with the same size cool passage." Probably a small structure in the back of the lot contained the kitchen and laundry. Comfort, not elegance, was the prevailing note.

The members of the Carpenters Company were giving serious thought to improved designs and safer construction. To Samuel Rhoads in 1770 Benjamin Franklin sent a suggestion once made to him by Michael Hillegas about the possibility of covering roofs with copper as a fire-prevention measure, but an English engineer had said it would be very costly. Rhoads himself experimented with a paint and sand roofing, and, together with Robert Smith and other builders, began substituting the new and fashionable stuccowork for the old and more combustible wainscoting. Demand for wallpaper and "Paper Mache" moldings in place of carving had risen to the point in 1769 where Plunket Fleeson, the upholsterer, advertised that these articles were now manufactured in the city. Another decorative touch was the brass knocker found on practically every front door, which was often wrenched off during "the wanton Frolicks of sundry intoxicated Bucks and Blades of the City." Daniel King, brass founder, "invented" one, "the Construction of which is peculiarly singular, and which will stand Proof against the United Attacks of those nocturnal Sons of Violence."

The unprecedented demand for housing forced real-estate values to dizzy heights, enriching those fortunate enough to own lots and encouraging speculative enterprises. After renting a house for a number of years, Henry and Elizabeth Drinker not only built one for themselves on Front Street but rented several properties to Friends. Joseph Wharton advertised in 1767 to sell or lease on perpetual ground rents five well-located lots, and John Parrock, a successful merchant, built two houses for £300 each on land worth £500 and then rented them for £35 a year apiece; he and his wife possessed other town properties worth £4,600. In 1768 Caleb and Joshua Cresson sold off some valuable lots on Sassafras Street between Fifth and Sixth, which were large enough to have stables on the alleys behind them. The assessors reported in 1773 that the annual rents of tenanted dwellings amounted to £63,753 and the value of rents in the hands of owners came to £28,-865.

Like its Pennsylvania neighbor, New York grew rapidly, adding probably a thousand houses to the 2,600 of 1760. Comparisons were inevitable: Lord Adam Gordon declared in 1765 that this city "has long been held at home, the first in America, tho' it neither comes up to Philadelphia in Beauty, regularity, Size, or the Number of its Inhabitants, and houses." Those who preferred regularity continued to favor the Quaker City, but Robert Honyman and others admired the mingling of Dutch and English styles of architecture, Manhattan's irregular but impressive skyline, and the numerous handsome mansions of the gentry. Although John Singleton Copley, always loyal, thought "it is not Boston in my opinion yet," he did concede that New York had more "Grand Buildings" than his own native town. For the most part, the houses were built of brick, with tiled roofs, and balconies where the occupants sat on summer evenings to enjoy the open air and view the prospect of the opposite shores and the harbor.

The housing shortage created by British troops and their families encouraged Knickerbocker merchants to acquire income property as avidly as Philadelphians. When business declined, however, more homes became available as hard-pressed owners put them up for sale: a single newspaper of 1763 carried notices of fourteen auctions of houses and lots at the Merchant's Coffee House, and in February of the next year the press stated: "we hear that there are more Houses now to be let, in this City, than have been at any Time for 7 Years past." Despite letters to the newspapers berating landlords for gouging "so as to ruin their Tenants and Customers, or drive them from the City," rents continued to be very high. John Cox paid £500 for a house renting at £80. Heads of families desperately looked for smaller ones at a "yearly Rent of Ten or Fifteen Pounds"; two or more families of the poor often occupied one tenement. Premises suitable for business yielded from £30 to £60, and some brought £100 a year. Yet "the sales of household goods for house rents almost every day," the *Gazette* pointed out, prove the distress of the people; "landlords ought to lower their rents"—in particular, those who ride in carriages. After 1770 the situation eased somewhat, but at no time were housing conditions favorable for the poor of Manhattan.

Some people thought that Newport made "a mean appearance," because it contained very few houses not of frame construction; Admiral Lord Howe's secretary sneeringly said: "the Style of the Town perfectly suits the Genius of the People." To the modern eye, Newport, where more colonial buildings survive today than anywhere else, the conclusion of J. F. D. Smyth, who found it "a large and beautiful town," seems more acceptable. True, most of the dwellings were small, but they were well built and unusually tasteful in proportion and detail as a result of care in design and execution by such able master builders and joiners as Wing Spooner, Henry Peckham, and John Townsend, who put up a number of small houses on the Point costing around £1,000 Rhode Island currency. Arthur Browne relates that ordinarily the neighbors assisted a tradesman in building his house, receiving in return "a whole hog barbecu'd" at a feast celebrating the completion. Approximately two hundred new dwellings for the middling and better sorts went up before the British occupation.

Even in this, the smallest of the towns, local merchants imitated those of other cities by investing in real estate. In 1763 the town leased eleven acres of school land in small lots "to build on or for gardens"; speculators such as John Chapman and Judge Martin Howard made money from the sale of house and shop lots. Several Providence gentlemen used new wealth to purchase property at Newport. Whereas in former times few places changed hands, the *Newport Mercury* now began to run advertisements of houses for sale and of many more for rent at reasonable rates. This does not mean that there were enough to go around, but that under duress many people had to get cash by such sales and that others found themselves forced to double up in what must have been cramped quarters. Renting brought greatest returns from May to October, when summer visitors came from Carolina and the West Indies and took either apartments or whole houses according to their purses and the size of their families.

Both Charles Town and Boston faced the necessity of rebuilding after the hurricane and fire disasters of the fifties. Speaker Benjamin Smith told Ezra Stiles that an enumeration of 1761 showed only about four hundred houses at Charles Town, and he judged it "not half so big as Newport," but at the close of the colonial period the Southern city had about fifteen hundred houses of wood or brick; "many of them," said a native, "have a genteel Appearance, though generally incumbered with Balconies or Piazzas. . . . the Apartments are contriv'd for Coolness, a very necessary Consideration." Judge Egerton Leigh, Charles Pinckney, Richard Beresford, and the Harlestons became heavily involved in urban properties, though Christopher Gadsden was probably the largest operator of any city with his large development at the North End along the Cooper River. City rents, varying from £80 to £800 (£927 in currency) a year in 1767, exceeded those of any other town; landlords reaped fruitful harvests indeed. During the next five years, three hundred new houses went up, and the ruined area of White Point again shone with many summer mansions of the planting gentry. Small wonder that the *Pennsylvania Magazine* said of Charles Town in 1776 that it was inhabited by a people both "shewy and expensive in . . . their way of life," and that it was "large and well-built, and rent is extremely high."

In no city did the dissimilarity between the dwellings of the very rich and the rest of the population stand out so obviously as in the Southern capital. In congested districts there was much jerry-building, which "Benevolence" described in the *Gazette:* "I passed through Meeting-Street, and in a low Set of Wood Tenements, with Walls little thicker than a Sheet of Brown Paper, pent up on all Sides by Wooden Structures." Such buildings were fire hazards and existed in spite of the law forbidding them. Into these abodes crowded the tradesmen, the largest segment of the population next to the Negroes. Claudius Guillard gave up his bakery and moved from King Street in 1773, announcing that "the House Rent was too high for him, and his Profits would not allow him to pay 250 £ per annum." Nor could members of the lesser ranks afford £100–200 a year in 1774 for one of the seven tenements that the real-estate broker Jacob Valk had for sale, let alone purchase any of them at prices of £700 to £1,100.

Recovery from the disastrous fire of 1760 had scarcely begun at Boston when harder times than that stricken city had ever known descended. Very rarely did the Selectmen need to enforce the law requiring brick and slate construction in new buildings inasmuch as brick buildings could be erected at one fifth the cost of wooden ones now that lumber had to come from distant Maine. Not until 1765 did the town permit small frame outhouses. John Joy of Boston and John Nutting of Cambridge were among the master builders who employed as many as fifty artisans in the erection of new houses in the Bay Town. New dwellings commonly had gardens in the rear, and a private pump. Although single houses predominated, not a few multi-family tenements went up; four families occupied the house of Zachary Morton, baker.

Unlike real estate elsewhere, few Boston properties were ordinarily advertised for rent. As the depression deepened, however, many people had to sell theirs to satisfy debts. The following is but one of the notices indicating their plight: "To be Sold for the Sake of Cash, Two Dwelling-Houses for £80 each, at the North End, in Middle Street . . . which are occupied by two punctual Tenants at Will, at £6 per Annum; each will want no Repair for ten Years." As many of the poorer people were moving to Salem, Lynn, and other nearby towns, tenants were hard to find. "There are now seventy houses in town empty and like to continue so and the number even to increase," Ezekiel Goldthwait informed James Murray in 1770 after he had "in vain offered . . . for less rent than they used to let at" two of the latter's houses; and very little improvement in Boston real estate took place. In 1775, when the siege began, Timothy Newell noted in his diary in October that Gage's troops "began taking down houses at the South end, to build a new line of works"; after November 16, "Houses, fences, trees, &c pulled down" by order of General Robinson.

The fine beginning that the cities had made in the eighteenth-century vogue for expensive public buildings was continued in this period despite hard times. At Philadelphia a burgeoning civic enthusiasm enabled two exceptionally gifted carpenter-architects to produce a number of distinguished edifices. Robert Smith, a Quaker master builder from Glasgow, first attracted attention as a designer in 1753 with his plans for Nassau Hall, which became a model for the most satisfactory style of college architecture; his "New College" (1765) at Fourth and Arch streets, in the mode of Nassau Hall, provided city students with "a collegiate way of living," and his success with these two academic buildings resulted in a request to aid in planning the "College Edifice" at Providence. Friend Robert also applied his talent to church architecture: he drew the plans of St. Peter's Church for the Episcopalians (1758), of Old Pine Street Church for the Presbyterians (1766), of Zion Church, perhaps the finest in the colonies, for the Lutherans (1767), besides working on these buildings and designing the steeple for Christ Church. And since he had the carpenter's contract for St. Paul's Church (Anglican) in 1761, he doubtless shared in its designing too. As master carpenter for the Bettering House (1766–7), and in view of his record, it is most probable that he assisted Samuel Rhoads in the planning of this, the largest and most imposing structure in English America. A tribute from his own craft came with the commission to design and erect a hall for the Carpenters Company (1768–74). His final contribution to Philadelphia's public architecture was the great Walnut Street Prison, a fireproof structure with floors supported by groined arches and antedating Robert Mills's famous building at Charles Town by nearly half a century. His fame had spread beyond the city, for, in addition to the Rhode Island request, came one to prepare "a Description of the Plan and Elevation of a Hospital . . . for the Reception of mad People" at Williamsburg in Virginia.

As if impressed by all this civic magnificence and dissatisfied with the medieval cast of their old Court House in Market Street, the Mayor and Common Council acquired title to the northeast corner of the State House Square in 1775, had the walks paved and posted, and looked over plans for "a City Hall and Court House" in which Mayor Samuel Rhoads certainly had a hand. Only the collapse of the Proprietary government prevented the beginning of construction. Even without it, the city on the Delaware evoked praise from visiting Europeans: "the publick buildings are spacious, and convenient, and some even elegant, especially the churches, the [Bettering] work-house, court-house, jail and hospital, which are all fine buildings." In fact, these edifices would have adorned any city of the age.

Charlestonians energetically pursued the beautification of their city started in the fifties. Construction of St. Michael's Church proceeded slowly, but with the building of the steeple and the installation of a set of chimes in 1764, it was complete, and Samuel Cardy, its builder, could take pride in the achievement, which emboldened him to embark on plans of his own and eventually earn local repute as "the ingenious Architect." On Queen Street in 1763 the American Company of Comedians erected what the *Gazette* hailed as "an elegant Theatre"—the city's third—"upon the very Spot where an established Church formerly stood." Across Meeting Street from St. Michael's, a new watchhouse went up five years later. Ingeniously combining the need for a merchant's exchange and gentility's yearning for an assembly room for elaborate balls, the parliament of planters voted a large sum for such a building. A plan was drawn by William Rigby Naylor, and the contract was let to John and Peter Horlbeck, German master builders, who agreed to undertake the construction, which included pilasters of imported Portland stone and a roof of "Welsh Carnarvon Slate." When it first opened, in 1771, this "New Exchange" was thought to be one of the sights of America; about the same time Charles Town acquired a new jail. The spaciousness of the city, with its beautiful churches and civic buildings, caused Crèvecœur to call it "the Lima of the North."

Several new buildings lent dignity to New York. The finishing of Robert Crommelin's stone hall for King's College in 1761 was followed shortly by a thorough refurbishing of the City Hall, one of Manhattan's structures judged worthy of inclusion in Pierre du Simitière's sketchbook. A Scot, named McBean, prepared plans for St. Paul's Church in 1766, and a year later the Lutherans dedicated a new church, while the Reformed Dutch erected a new edifice from designs by "Andrew Breested, jr., Carpenter and Projector." When it was about ready for use in 1775, the New York Hospital, a stone structure "upon the plan of the Royal Infirmary at Edinburgh" produced by an intercolonial architects' competition, was destroyed by fire, but a large gray stone Bridewell did open that year as well as the New Gaol and Alms House in the Fields. When Ambrose Serle went ashore to view the city in 1776, he admitted that it could boast several structures "not by any means contemptible."

Finishing public buildings under construction or replacing those lost by fire occupied the two New England cities, whose already existing structures were serviceable if not imposing in appearance. Peter Harrison's synagogue for Congregation Jeshuat Israel had its first service on December 2, 1763, and its exquisitely proportioned interior has never failed to delight visitors. Delay upon delay attended the work on his Brick Market, which, though started in 1760, did not open for public use as a market and granary until December 1772. At Boston a fire burned out Faneuil Hall in 1761, but, in the face of stiff opposition, it was rebuilt, and opened again in 1763 in time to become "the cradle of liberty." The only other new structure added for public use was a Court House on Queen Street, dedicated in 1769, but Arthur Browne, who knew both communities, expressed the opinion in the seventies that Boston's "numerous spires gave it at a distance a much more spacious appearance than the great city of Dublin has."

Suburban development went on apace at Philadelphia as congestion, high rents, and noise drove members of all classes to seek refuge beyond city limits. Edward Shippen, Jr., advised his father in 1760 about a petition to the Assembly to erect the lands immediately south of the city into a borough, "which, it is said, will be the means of drawing a great number of people there, and of course will improve the value of the lands." Who could have thought, he went on to say, that your property, "so remote" from the center of town, would be built on by "any but the lower sort of people," but now the case was altered, for "good houses are daily building. . . . Lots are grown very scarce," and business people would not move westward on Market Street "while they can get lots near the water"; the Shippens, Whartons, and associates made a good thing out of their development. The District of Southwark contained 603 houses by 1769, whereas the Northern Liberties had only 553; but by 1776 the latter was larger, in part as a result of the promotion of such men as Michael Hillegas, the music dealer, who let "sundry Lots" at "Campington" between Second and Fourth streets at Charlotte to his Palatine countrymen on perpetual ground rents in 1767. Beyond this settled suburb, houses and gentlemen's estates lined Old York, Germantown, and the Ridge highroads. The borough of Germantown, though eight miles from Market Street, was virtually becoming a suburb; many people spent their summers there and others passed to and fro daily on affairs of trade; in the seventies Moyamensing and Passyunk townships, lying below Southwark, received the city's overflow, Isaac Snowden and Andrew Yorke breaking up farm lands for building lots.

The rise of these suburbs had immediate effects on the city. The area below Cedar (South) Street built up so rapidly that, as noted earlier, the Assembly made it a district in 1762, "for making the Streets and Roads laid out therein Public Roads," and for regulation of party walls and drains. So many Germans had moved into the Northern Liberties by 1764 that Mr. Mühlenberg had to make frequent pastoral calls to Spring Garden. "Residential lots in the city are from day to day becoming scarcer and more expensive," he complained. In 1769 fifty-two residents petitioned the Assembly that since for "some years past [a] very Considerable Number of Buildings have been Erected, and further Improvements are continually making," some authority over prudential matters be granted, and, after some delay, the Northern Liberties was awarded district status on March 9, 1771. Its officials were empowered, among other things, to regulate party walls. Thus did the expansion of Philadelphia clearly reveal while it was still under the dominion of Great Britain, many of the problems of later American metropolitan development.

Suburban growth also affected the municipal development of Charles Town. In the sixties the community overleapt its walls, and a petition to the Assembly recited the fact that the city's confines had been greatly extended; new houses were being erected on the tract "commonly called Rhetsbury" and Coming's Point, while Ansonborough was already built up. The residents of these sections, now paying city instead of county taxes, asked for new streets, especially in Ansonborough, arguing that they would be both "useful and ornamental to this large and growing Town." The request met with prompt compliance.

New houses rose on the outskirts of the other cities too, but there was no question of extension of boundaries. Having ample space for growth, Newport spread northward from the Point, and so much construction occurred on the school lots north of Tanner Street that people called this section "New-town." As William Gregory from Ayrshire came down the bay from Providence in 1771, he quickly admitted that "it far surpasses the idea I had formed of it . . . the principal street one and one half miles long and the houses very compact, being called Thames Street—the whole town making a very agreeable prospect from the water, being situated on an easy rising hill." Expansion up Manhattan Island was gradual and normal since the Corporation owned the land and put it up for leases when it needed funds. The King's Farm, between Broadway and the Hudson, which had been surveyed into lots before 1760, filled up quickly; in 1762 the Corporation had its surveyor lay out lots east of the road in portions of the Out Ward lying between the East River and the Boston Road and offered them on twenty-one-year leases at four pounds annually, and the following year leased thirty-one lots of five acres each at Murray Hill for farms or gentlemen's seats. Opportunities for work and a lower cost of living drew some of Boston's artisans to the surrounding villages. Because of ferry connections, Charlestown became more urban in every way, even more than Brookline; and Cambridge continued its growth as a unique suburban center for the gentry. To Lord Adam Gordon, who saw all the cities in 1765, Boston seemed "more like an English Old Town than any in America . . . and all the neighboring Lands and Villages carry with them the same idea."

The procurement of sufficient fuel at a price the poor could afford grew more and more difficult each year, despite the cessation of wartime interference with the supply. As early as 1763 John Bartram, remarking about the clearing of Pennsylvania lands "quite to the mountains," warned: "What our people will do for fencing and firewood fifty years hence, I can't imagine."

All trees on Rhode Island suitable for firewood had been cut by 1738, but a convenient supply brought by water from upper Narragansett Bay had sufficed during the wars and after 1760 boats brought cordwood in from Block and Long islands to Caleb Godfrey's Wharf. Nevertheless the price of fuel mounted, and Newporters bent on economy anxiously searched for a substitute. Samuel Duval at the falls of the James River advertised his Virginia coal in the *Newport Mercury* in 1763 for twelve shillings a bushel, and Nathaniel Coggeshall, at least, imported a quantity of it. Within a year a vein of coal "emitting an intense Heat, and more durable than any . . . imported" was discovered on Benjamin Almy's land on Quaker Hill. The *Mercury,* clipped by the Boston and Charles Town press, held forth excitedly about "the vast Sums which the Town will annually save, as the Price of Firing must be greatly reduced, and the Cash . . . be Continued among us." The Town Meeting proved more circumspect and did not adopt Captain Almy's suggestion that it "carry on a part of the Coal Mine." Discovery of more "Sea or Pit Coal" at Providence further elated Printer Southwick, and the Town Meeting saw fit to elect four measurers of coal in 1768, increasing the number to six four years later.

There is no doubt that the discovery of coal deposits came as a boon to Rhode Islanders. Coal had to be burned in grates, however, and many of the middle class as well as all of the poor, having no money to buy them, had to rely on wood as formerly. In 1767 "A Friend to the Poor" announced that he intended to ask the Town Meeting to appropriate money to purchase firewood at a "just Price." A year later one signing himself "A Peasant" proposed cutting a one-mile channel through "an easy Bog" from Narragansett Bay to Point Judith Pond to open up a new supply of wood for the city. All that was accomplished was passage of a new set of regulations authorizing the sealers of wood to appoint or remove measurers, who were to examine all cordwood brought in for sale. Upon the blockading of the entrance to Narragansett Bay by British ships in 1776, the town's troubles commenced in earnest; the supply of fuel ran so low that the desperate poor started to dismantle the wharf at Goat Island. Many of "the rich and poor, in one common Distress," joined with Ezra Stiles in leaving town, but there was worse to come. During the occupation of Newport, the redcoats denuded all of Rhode Island, Prudence, and the lower shores of the bay of trees by December 1777, and, before their departure, had burned all of the town's fences and torn down many frame houses for fuel.

Cadwallader Colden estimated in 1761 that the fireplaces and stoves in New York's houses and shops consumed above twenty thousand cords of wood annually, and when it is considered that all of it had to come by water, principally from the Shrewsbury region of New Jersey or the distant Queen's Village section of Long Island, its high cost is not surprising. The price fell from fifty shillings for nut wood and forty for oak in 1761 to twenty-five and sixteen in 1766, a price the poor could pay; then it rose again to fifty shillings for oak in 1772, a situation one paper called "alarming": "Times are so bad only the most wealthy can keep abreast of them—Wood grows scarcer and dearer every Year, whilst the Demand increases with the Growth of the City." The writer thought a paper-money issue would help somewhat, but "Our patriots should attempt the discovery of coal mines before our wood is entirely consumed," and avowed that even coal from England was now regarded as cheaper than wood.

Boston procured most of its firewood in boats from Penobscot in Maine, though enough arrived overland by cart and sled to warrant measurement regulations in 1762. Country wood-peddlers fleeced the poorer inhabitants unmercifully, forcing the town to add three more measurers of cordwood in 1765 to handle the traffic when "good Sledding" brought large amounts to town; but the proclivity of inland Yankees for selling short sticks persisted, bringing down stringent orders in 1772 against frauds. Smiths, distillers, braziers, and countinghouses consumed large quantities of Newcastle coal, and other establishments bought shipments of charcoal from the vicinity of the ironworks in the Old Colony. In 1765 Joseph Harrison, brother of the Newport architect, prepared some "Observations relating to the Consumption of Sea Coal in New England" for the Commissioners of the Customs, in which he observed that at Boston, when Newcastle coal sold at twenty shillings a chaldron and oak wood at ten shillings a cord, a coal fire cost about one third more than one of wood; but if the British authorities encouraged the shipping of more Cape Breton sea coal at the usual price of fifteen shillings a chaldron, householders could afford to burn it and Nova Scotia would prosper from the traffic. Nothing came of this sensible mercantilist proposal, nor did the price of wood come down, for in 1768 Michael Malcom, one of the leading importers, continued to advertise firewood at sixteen shillings a cord. No feature of the Boston Port Act caused more distress or so contributed to the implacable hatred of the Bostonians toward the mother country than the requirement that all wood boats bound for their port unload and load again at Marblehead, for it at once increased the already high price and decreased the supply of fuel. When the patriots laid siege to their great town, they took a sweet revenge by cutting off the wood supply of the Tories and troops, forcing the latter to destroy fences, trees, and houses in order to warm themselves. The pen of Samuel Adams was never needed to labor this grievance—it was too obvious and too real.

Navigable waterways from the thick woods of the Carolina Low Country converged at Charles Town, ensuring a plentiful supply of fuel at all times. Yet firewood brought higher prices there than anywhere else; in the fifties it averaged thirty-five shillings a cord in the summer and between forty and forty-five in the winter. With an eye for profits, John Marley, having acquired a few carts, arranged with the boatmen to take their loads at the wharves, which allowed them to return home promptly. He thereby came to engross the supply, for which he charged two and a half per cent as a factor, and by 1761 the price of wood had gone up to seventy shillings, "besides cartage." Naturally others hastened to get in on such a good thing, and the poor suffered grievously from the greed of three or four engrossers, who, it was charged, often created "an artificial dearth" to raise prices. Nothing came of the Grand Jury's de-mand for regulation of the fuel traffic by the Assembly. The press carried numerous communications denouncing the "Forestaller, who is a Wretch that, Tyger-like, preys . . . on the Vitals of the Small and Great," and the "Ingrosser," who was "less respectable than a Highwayman." A tradesman, who paid out nearly all of his small income for rent, food, and clothing for his family, had very little left with which to buy wood at £5 a cord. At last, in 1768, the Assembly did order the selection of five "Wood and Coal Measurers" at the annual parish elections, but it continued to ignore the engrossers, who forced the price of fuel up to £7 in 1771. Few matters so clearly demonstrate the callous attitude of the planter-legislators to the needs of the ordinary people of Charles Town; so long as the New Exchange contained a ballroom for the qual-ity, they considered that they had done enough for the city.

Philadelphia never suffered any shortage of firewood, because small craft constantly brought it to the wharves in large amounts from sources of supply up the many navigable creeks that flow into the Delaware. As the distance the boats had to come lengthened each year and the demand increased with the population, prices, of course, went up. Public-spirited men toured the city's wards in the winter of 1762 to collect funds to provide the poor with fuel. The city's craftsmen burned large amounts of imported coal or locally-made charcoal. In 1767, when the Townshend Acts were stimulating Americans to restrict importations and develop their own industries, it was thought a source of coal had been found to relieve the situation, but unfortunately the vein of coal at Pennsbury did not prove productive. The inexhaustible needs of the great Pennsylvania iron industry for charcoal forced up the price of that article as well as of cordwood, but it never went as high as in other cities. Even in the midst of the War for Independence, in 1778, a Hessian officer could say: "There is plenty of wood here; I burn seven kinds of firs, besides the varieties of sassafras, cedar, and walnut in my chimney place and in the watch fires."

V

Patterns for city expansion that had been worked out before 1760 largely accommodated the towns for the remainder of the colonial period. Newport and New York did not need any new streets, and although the Assembly authorized the Corporation of New York in 1764 to appoint commissioners to lay out new "High Roads" for the whole of Manhattan Island, they confined their activity to the rural parts. At Philadelphia, where future highway extensions westward toward the Schuylkill had long since been planned, the inhabitants, as previously noted, spread north and south beyond the city's limits, preferring to be near the Delaware for reasons of trade and comfort in the hot summers. It was the demand for new streets in the area from the Delaware along Cedar or South streets to Passyunk Road, then south to Greenwich Road and east to the river, that brought about the establishment of district status for the Southwark section. A cumbersome arrangement was set up: three surveyors and three regulators built streets and laid down gutters and conduits for drains, while three assessors and three other regulators controlled repairing and cleaning; all of them, together, enjoyed the power to tax for all highway improvements. When the Northern Liberties became a district in 1771, assessors and regulators taxed the residents for construction and maintenance of streets and conduits. The districts faithfully adhered to Thomas Holme's original plan by carrying city streets into their precincts. James Whitelaw, a Scot, and Josiah Quincy of Boston agreed in 1773 that the city "perhaps is the best laid out in the world, the streets are all broad and straight, and all cross at right angles, extending itself upon the banks of the Delaware between .two and three miles"—all the way from Ball's Town to Moyamensing Township.

For many years Boston had virtually filled up its peninsula, and no room remained for expansion, but the Selectmen and Overseers of Highways were involved with the rebuilding after the fire of 1760 and in complicated negotiations over straightening and resurfacing the streets as well as problems of eminent domain. In 1766 when Pudding Lane was enlarged to the width of a street and renamed Devonshire to honor a gentlemen of Bristol for his gift of one hundred pounds to the fire sufferers, the work of reconstruction ended, and after that the occasional broadening of a narrow way to make a street, as in the case of Paddy's Alley in the North End, was all that was called for.

The capital of South Carolina, like that of Pennsylvania, had a gridiron plan—in fact, it had it first. The lack of a municipal government competent to regulate highways and the fact that expansion had been blocked by the 11,000-foot moat before the wall running from the Ashley to the Cooper imposed a serious highway problem upon the citizens. Indifference on the part of the Assembly further postponed action. After hearing a strongly worded petition in 1767, it passed a law providing for the extension of Church Street to intersect George Street in Ansonborough to allow "Travellers" and residents of Charles Town

Neck to go to town, and authorized the condemning of property needed for the thoroughfare. Thereafter several additional acts created public streets, usually after the people of the neighborhood agreed to give land for the projects. New streets were badly needed in such a suburban area as Coming's Point "to enlarge communications between that and other parts of" Charles Town; dwellers in Ansonborough rejoiced in the laying out of Boundary Street in 1769, and other streets were laid out in the next few years. Grand Jury action was responsible for most of the new construction, but as late as 1773 these tireless guardians of the public's interest were forced to report that the moat still needed filling though the city had built on both sides of it.

Subsurface drainage in newly built districts required more sewers or conduits under the streets. Colonial citizens would have been properly scandalized if they had read a complaint in the *Liverpool Chronicle* of February 11, 1768 that privies emptied into the streets of that great commercial city during the busy hours to the great abuse of cleanliness and decency. In the straightening of Boston's streets following the fire, it became necessary to move and rebuild the "Common Shores" and grant more than sixty permits for connecting private drains. These operations so damaged street paving that in 1767 the Selectmen refused to grant any more permits unless they themselves designated in advance who should perform the work. Throughout this period they issued one hundred and eight permits, and probably no city anywhere had better subsurface drainage.

Very satisfactory systems for disposal of waste water were worked out at both New York and Philadelphia. Commencing in 1769 Manhattan authorities provided the Out, Montgomerie, and North wards with trunk drains. About the same time, replacement of the old and inadequate sewer under High Street began at Philadelphia, and, as new thoroughfares were constructed in the liberties as well as in the city, provisions were made for sinking conduits. In addition, the Street Commissioners, now very much on the alert to improve public sanitation, secured added powers from the Assembly to regulate the digging of wells or privies, or Temples of Cloacina as one Commissioner's wife called them.

A law of 1764 placed supervision of all of Charles Town's drains and sewers under the Street Commissioners and provided that the moat be filled immediately (which, as noted above, never took place), and all common sewers emptying into it be "continued through" to the Cooper River. Soon their clerk, Charles Woodmason, was advertising for bids on sinking a sewer in Church Street, though a little more than a year later one who lived there claimed that his cellars had always been dry, "even before the drain was made in the street." In 1772 Peter Bonnetheau gave the specifications for one of these conveniences in Old Church Street: "a Drain, to be Two and a Half Feet wide, and Three and a Half

Feet high in the Clear, and to be floored with good Two Inch Cypress Plank, and deep enough to admit of Cellars Six Feet Deep." Even though Dr. Lionel Chalmers, pioneer student of public health, asserted that the sandy soil and many new common sewers did much to preserve the health of the inhabitants by carrying off all surface water during the rainy season, the Grand Jury persisted in presenting the need for more "publick drains."

For cities throughout the English-speaking world, this was an era of great activity in street paving. Discovering in the previous period that well-paved streets, besides being easier to clean, expedited traffic and promoted public health, Americans now insisted that all new thoroughfares be surfaced, and large sums were spent on them. Boston contracted in 1764 with Messrs. Fosdick, Thornton, and Putnam to work on the streets by the year at twelvepence a yard, but by 1774 the price had fallen to eightpence. When the Boston Port Bill threw many persons out of work, the Selectmen employed them by the day to repair the streets at 3*s*. 4*d*., "but some few of them grumble that they are oblig'd to work hard for that which they esteem as their right without work." The natural rights of Bostonians notwithstanding, the city's streets were paved, but there were no sidewalks, only posts to protect the pedestrian from passing traffic. The Corporation of New York also embarked upon a program of paving, with the injunction that the work be completed "with all convenient Speed," and the pavements, like those of Boston, were made "descending towards the centre," where a gutter carried off the water. The Mayor and Common Council also set up "16 mile Stones" for the use of travelers, and in 1774 Holt's *Journal* praised the board for the "affixing the names of streets at every corner," even though the painters had not done the job very carefully.

After a slow start the other towns made commendable progress in paving. Philadelphia acquired a new and responsible agency in 1762 when the Assembly passed an act for "Regulating, Pitching, Paving, and Cleansing the Highways," which set up a board of six street commissioners to contract for and supervise paving and receiving the moneys raised by lottery as well as to assess and collect taxes for such purposes; seven years later they were authorized to levy an annual street rate and to borrow in anticipation of such taxes. Hugh Roberts and his associates proceeded with vigor, which incidentally created an excellent market for stone and gravel. In 1764, drawing on forty years' experience, Roberts worked out a suitable plan for paving High Street, which had market sheds running down the middle for several blocks, and for determining the proper width of footways so that the "Benefits of a regular City" might be distributed "to a general advantage." Inevitably charges of being unjust were hurled at the commissioners, but their records indicate a studied determination to treat all alike and improve their city; and the

PLATE 9 · *Some Leading Citizens*

Reverend Thomas Hiscox of Newport by Robert Feke;
Nathaniel Hurd of Boston, Engraver, by John Singleton Copley.

PLATE 10 · *Plan of Newport by Charles Blaskowitz, 1776*

The finest map of any colonial city.

fact that within a few years Philadelphia possessed the best streets in America gave them an unanswerable reply. Moreover, this controversy, thoroughly aired in the newspapers, turned out to be a healthy one in that it focused public attention on street problems and kept the commissioners hard at their jobs. By 1769 they had paved 120,582 square yards, and as more funds came in, the work speeded up measurably. The city undertook the surfacing of the middle of the streets, requiring the abutters and possessors of vacant lots as far west as Twelfth Street to pave and repair "with good well burnt Bricks, or good square flat Stones, the Footways and Gutters," the latter not more than four inches deep and twenty-two inches wide. For some years prior to 1761 Philadelphia streets had been given a slightly convex surface so that they drained toward the side gutters, a procedure that the Parliamentary acts for Westminster and London made so popular in England after 1762.

Funds raised by lottery were expended on convex gravel surfaces for the streets of Newport. Over a seven-year period, it took £20,000 in Rhode Island currency to repave the mile and a quarter of Thames Street, and "John Bazin, the Paver," no doubt prospered on the job. Mill, King, and Pelham streets were repaved by 1772, at which time the town was divided into highway districts, whose inhabitants had to perform or provide a stipulated amount of labor on the streets each year. Although some of the smaller lanes and alleys remained unpaved, Newport had no reason to be ashamed of its main thoroughfares.

With the act of 1764, which for the first time conferred ample authority upon the Street Commissioners, Charles Town began to have some properly paved sidewalks. Clerk Woodmason contracted with workmen to pave a regular footway of "bricks laid flat in mortar" and erect cedar posts along the principal streets, but it was not always possible to hire skilled "paviours," and householders objected to bearing the cost. Although the commissioners doggedly kept at their task, the streets were never paved in the colonial period. Sandy soil prevented mire in rainy weather, and brick sidewalks six feet wide afforded satisfactory passage for pedestrians. Had the Southern city ever been accorded the self-government it wanted so much, in all probability its streets would have approached those of the Northern towns.

"I did go to Bristol, the dirtiest great shop I ever saw, with so foul a river [the Avon] that, had I seen the least appearance of cleanliness, I should have concluded they washed all their linen it it, as they do in Paris." Horace Walpole may have found England's second city very dirty in 1766, but Manchester "excelled in filthiness" and a citizen exclaimed: "Our streets are no better than a common dunghill." During dry spells the side lanes of Newport filled up with filth that gave off noxious fumes. Although some citizens thought the situation bad in 1770, the Town Meeting seems not to have considered it critical enough to warrant public action and placed its reliance on frequent rains. Charlestonians may have failed to do as well with public sanitation and street cleaning as other colonial communities, but it had no cause to fear comparison with towns in the old country, even if its principal scavengers were the turkey buzzards which, Dr. Schoepf tells us, consumed "what sloth has not removed out of the way, and so have a great part in maintaining cleanliness and keeping off unwholesome vapors from dead beasts and filth." Goats and swine also acted as scavengers. In 1761 the Grand Jury agitated for commissioners to stop the inhabitants from "throwing tubs and filth near the lower Market into the Moat" and to govern all street cleaning, because the Negro scavengers were inefficient. Fear of infectious distempers spurred the Assembly, which enacted a comprehensive measure for cleaning and repairing streets and fixed large penalties for casting rubbish, garbage, or filth into them, save at points designated by the Commissioners, from which scavengers removed it at the charge of the individual householders who placed it there. The ten commissioners, led by Isaac Mazyck, Gabriel Manigault, and Thomas Smith, Jr., hired the scavengers with the £1,400 currency raised by an annual tax. This made a vast improvement for a time, but the Grand Jury felt it necessary to report again in 1771 that "all kinds of Filth are thrown into the Streets," and that many Negroes refused to work for the commissioners. The latter complained in 1773 that the citizens "pay no Regard" to the cleaning regulations, but that henceforth they would enforce them strictly.

Elizabeth Sandwith stayed home from the Friends' evening meeting on January 20, 1760, "it being very dark and the streets dirty," but in a few years this situation was to be remedied. Street Commissioners of Philadelphia, created by the act of 1762, employed scavengers to remove once a week all rubbish and filth swept from the pavements into the cartways. And householders had to keep shavings and ashes until the collectors took them off at fixed rates, or pay a twenty-shilling fine. The scavengers also removed dirt, dung, and tradesmen's rubbish weekly after 1765. About this time the commissioners divided the city into three divisions, assigning two men with a horse and cart to each. These measures met with criticism from common folk like "Tom Trudge," who thought the rich paid less proportionately for such services than the poor. He wrote to the *Pennsylvania Chronicle* that he resented having to help pay for "the opulent merchants, and gentry, whose luxurious boards and floors furnish the scavengers with weekly loads of clam and oyster shells, soiled sand, etc.," when "such poor fellows as I . . . whose lean kitchens rarely produce any refuse . . . whose wives must, at many seasons of the year, wade to the knees in carrying a loaf of bread to bake," seldom or never see the cart nor hear the sound of the paver. If taxes for cleaning and paving gave such offense to many of the lower orders, the fact remained that their city had streets so clean that visitors marveled.

Comments on the other communities varied, but they succeeded in keeping their thoroughfares in a presentable state. Lord Adam Gordon ascribed the "clean and wholesome" streets of New York to their "standing on a descent" and the frequent rains that washed them down, but much of the dung and ordure of Manhattan were taken by barge to fertilize farms bordering on the East River. A correspondent of Holt's *Journal* was not satisfied with the city, however, for he wrote that strangers often censured its slovenly lack of cleanliness and "every Inhabitant must join with them." Two years later this paper needled the Mayor and Common Council again, but they apparently did not regard any additional ordinances as necessary. Critical John Adams, arriving about this time, had nothing but praise for the condition of New York streets, which is noteworthy, for the Boston Selectmen had given street cleaning much attention. Removal of most of the rubbish from the great fire had been accomplished within two years, and in 1765 Robert Love and John Sweetser were appointed inspectors to report all violations of the law and superintend the scavengers, who tended to loaf on the job. As in former times the town still showed a profit from the disposal of street dirt. Newport seems to have trusted to swine and rain to do the cleaning, and with some success, for the Town Meeting ruled only on the leaving of building materials, firewood, and carts in the highways in 1770. Still, "A Friend to the Town" at this time urged clearing the narrow streets of the filth, "with which they too often abound," in the interests of health and to please the summer visitors.

Colonial communities responded to the increasing need for lighting their streets at night by following the example of Philadelphia. There, in 1767, the Lamp Wardens reported setting up 320 oil lamps since the law went into effect in 1752, and in 1771 they purchased a large number of new ones for Third Street and all streets to the westward. The severe fine of £20 for breaking a light was rigidly enforced, and when three men were convicted and fined a total of £150, the Mayor's Court turned the sum over to the Wardens for purchasing new lamps. The New York authorities procured from the Assembly in 1761 permission to tax for street lights, oil, and the hiring of lamplighters. John Balthus Dasch, John Ellis, and John and William Landson made more than a hundred lamps that were erected by the Corporation at strategic spots in the city. These were not enough, for Weyman's *New York Gazette* attributed the success of a gang of burglars in the winter of 1762 to the cover of darkness, and on the occasion of the robbery of the Albany postrider in the Bowery in 1763, Parker's newspaper insisted that on dark and stormy nights, when the lamps were most useful, they often went unlighted. This became the problem of Isaac Stoutenburgh, overseer of the watch, who supervised the lamplighters, and he improved the service. Using the London system of having lamps ten feet high placed at intervals of fifty feet along the streets, New York received a handsome return for the £760 it paid out annually for lamplighting, whale oil, and repairs. Fifty lamps were added in 1764 "in some of the most publick Streets." Two years afterwards more than half were broken when four drunken British officers issued from a tavern at midnight, smashed thirty-four of the city's lights along the Broad Way, and wounded four watchmen.

The next community to light its highways was Charles Town. About 1762 Joseph Wilson, a loyal citizen, formed a plan for lighting the streets, which some leading gentlemen encouraged. He laid out £300 currency on six lamps for the State House, three at the Guard House, and three at the Vendue House, and maintained them at his own expense for three months. Although he petitioned the Assembly for some reward, he complained in 1763 that he could not even get a liquor license when he opened the Orange Gardens. In 1767 and 1768 two grand juries presented in strong terms the "want of Lamps." Action came in 1770, when the Assembly directed the erection of more than twenty lights "at the Public Expence" in front of all public buildings in the city, soon followed by "upwards of 100" more that civic-minded residents hung out before their houses and the expression of a "general wish that a Law may pass for lighting the Town throughout." Timothy believed that but for the Townshend duty on glass four or five hundred lamps would have been imported from England and urged the Assembly to procure globes from the Wistar works at Philadelphia. All the planters would vote was a twenty-pound fine or thirty-nine lashes for any white or black who wantonly broke a lamp. Repeatedly the grand juries called attention "to the want of Public Lamps in many of the Streets," but the close of the colonial era came before Charles Town saw further improvement in street lighting. Newport, by contrast, clung to its earlier system of private lighting, and, since no mention of the matter occurs in the records, the inhabitants seem to have been content with the situation.

Provisions for tax-supported street lights came late at Boston, but once entering upon the project, the Selectmen proceeded with characteristic thoroughness. In February 1772 a writer in the *Newsletter* proposed a system of "public Lamps," because people nowadays go out so frequently at night on "calls of friendship, humanity, business, or pleasure" and need protection from insult, abuse, and robbery as well as "scenes of lewdness and debauchery which are so frequently committed with impunity at present." Since Boston supplies the whale oil for the lamps of Europe, and since most American cities have them, he makes a plea for the erection of private lamps if the town fails to act. Within a month the Town Meeting chose John Hancock to head a committee to consider whether Boston could legally tax to support lamps. The Meeting approved a favorable report in March 1773 and voted a tax for the lamps and their upkeep. Local blacksmiths forged most of the ironwork, and Captain Loring of one of the tea ships brought the lamps from London; had he not landed his detested cargo, the town would have had another dark winter. On March 2, 1774, Boston streets were lighted for the first time by 310 lamps tended by Edward Smith and his seven lamplighters—and that incorrigible purveyor of puns, Mather Byles, could frighten a credulous woman of evangelical bent by telling her that "this morning three hundred new lights have . . . arrived from London, and the selectmen have wisely ordered them put in irons." [1]

Save in a few instances, no new traffic laws were demanded in this period. Lacking sidewalks, Boston would be no place for foot passengers if fast driving were permitted, for trucks, drays, and carts jammed its crooked and narrow streets, often causing true traffic snarls on weekdays, and the crowding of coaches and chaises near the churches on the Sabbath resulted in frequent accidents. In 1765, for the benefit of both town and country readers, four newspapers printed rules for riding and driving in the city, "which is strictly adhered to by all well regulated Cities in Europe, especially in London. . . . Namely, *Always to keep on the Right-Hand Side of the Way.*" (One cannot refrain from speculating about when the mother country first swung to the left.)[2] In 1775 the Selectmen instructed the watch to put an end to the "driving of Slays thro' the Town, with beating of Drums and other noises, at unseasonable Times of the Night." Fewer traffic accidents took place in other cities. New Yorkers protested in 1766 about the insolence of British officers who, on going the rounds, took up so much room in narrow ways that it was "difficult for People to pass, especially with Horses and Carriages."

Philadelphia was as noisy as Boston. Heavier traffic meant more confusion and uproar, especially north of Market Street. When the botanist James Young rode in from Horsham one July day in 1763, he remarked that he gave the city no thought "till we found ourselves in Second Street, Entangled amongst Waggons, Dreys, Market Folks and Dust." Solomon Drowne, a medical student at the College, wrote home that through his window on Second Street "the thundering of Coaches, Chariots, Chaises, Waggons, Drays, and the whole Fraternity of Noise almost continuously assail our Ears." Very little could be done to deaden the clatter of hoofs and rumble of wheels, but the authorities took every precaution to protect the surfaces of their newly paved streets from being cut up by the iron tires of heavy vehicles. A province law specified

[1] In 1776 Liverpool did not have as many street lights as Charles Town; Birmingham first lighted its thoroughfares in 1769; Manchester received permissive legislation in 1791, Norwich in 1806.

[2] Peter Timothy advised Charlestonians in 1763 that in most countries vehicles keep to the *left* and suggested that they follow suit. *South Carolina Gazette*, April 16, 1763.

that the tires of carts and wagons should be seven inches wide, and to the protest of the wheelwrights of the city and Northern Liberties that they could not get proper lumber of this width for fellies, the commissioners turned a deaf ear. In 1767, however, the law was repealed for private carts with loads under half a ton. Further restrictions on sizes, number of horses and oxen, weight of loads, speed, and even rates for hauling placed the carters under careful governance by the commissioners, who were regarded as interfering with private enterprise with as intense a bitterness as are the regulators of modern transportation. Still, such regulations guaranteed real benefits by protecting both the lives of the public and the city's investment in pavements.

Charlestonians believed that their traffic difficulties arose principally from the irresponsibility of Negro slaves with carts, drays, and wagons to hire. The street law of 1764 required the licensing and numbering of all such vehicles and forbade drivers to ride on their carts unless another person on foot guided the horses or oxen. It also fixed heavy penalties for galloping. Within a year the inhabitants petitioned the Assembly that all carts for rent be driven by competent white men in order to protect the carriages and pedestrians from unskilled Negroes. The new sidewalks were protected by rules denying their use to horses, handcarts, and wheelbarrows, and porters were told not to roll rice barrels or drag lumber along them, nor were they to "interrupt" pedestrians, but the commissioners' efforts at control seemed futile. By 1772, carters and draymen rode on their carts with impunity, encumbered sidewalks with lumber and stones overnight, fed their horses on them by day, and drove all beasts too fast.

Civic pride induced colonial townsmen, in both their corporate and their individual capacities, to take steps toward beautifying their communities. No park matched Boston Common, which was a constant joy to all of the people, especially its 1,400-foot walk called the Mall. The Selectmen proceeded against inconsiderate citizens who drove their horses and carriages over the Common in 1764 and levied fines for breaking down the posts separating it from Common (Tremont) Street. To protect it further, the Town Meeting ordered the Common fenced and "kept inclosed" in 1771. Residents planted elms and a few lime trees before their houses in some of the wider thoroughfares, and Boston Neck was improved by rows of stately elms. Adino Paddock, militia officer and coachmaker, in 1762 set out a row of English elms bordering the Common; nine years later he offered a reward for the detection of the persons who "hacked" one of them down. Two such vandals went to jail in 1773 for destroying trees on the Common.

Elsewhere town authorities sought to adorn public squares as in London. The Swiss artist Pierre du Simitière praised New York's four squares during a visit in 1767: Bowling Green, "a beautiful ellipsis railed in with solid iron," Hanover Square, St. George's Square, and the "commons or Fields before the New Gaol." At Philadelphia in 1763 the Assembly ordered the superintendent of the State House to "prepare a Plan for laying out the Square behind the State House in proper Walks, to be planted with suitable Trees for Shade," and Newport acquired elms along the Parade in front of the Colony House.

An obelisk dedicated to the memory of General James Wolfe was set up on De Lancey property in 1761, giving New York priority in public monuments, but to Charles Town fell the honor of erecting the first statue. England itself possessed only three outdoor statues in 1766 when the South Carolina Assembly appropriated £7,000 in currency to purchase a likeness of the great William Pitt. The Royal Governor refused to sign the bill, declaring the expenditure unwarranted, but the planters defied him and made their own arrangements. Joseph Wilton of London, sculptor of the Wolfe memorial in Westminster Abbey, executed the statue, and when it arrived at Charles Town and was set up in the center of Broad and Meeting streets, nearly everybody admired it; Josiah Quincy referred to it as "a large colossal statue" and thought the drapery "exquisitely well done: but to me the attitude, air, and expression of the piece was bad." The same Wilton's equestrian statue of George III, "very large, of solid lead gilded with gold, standing on a pedestal, very high," was placed in the Bowling Green at New York, and a gilded lead copy of Charles Town's Pitt was put up in Wall Street. When Manhattan tempers neared the breaking-point after the Tea Act, the Assembly had to threaten patriotic vandals with a fine of £500 or a year in prison for defacing either statue. Not until hostilities opened did the likenesses of King George and the Earl of Chatham go into the crucible to make rebel bullets.

VI

Maintenance of waterways and aids to shipping was the constant concern of all five seaports. Because they had constructed or acquired most of the basic facilities before 1760, in the latter part of the period, colonial merchants directed the attention of municipal and provincial assemblies to making improvements or to adding useful refinements.

Existing ferries at Boston and Newport easily handled the increased traffic and, because of better management, had fewer accidents than before. Elsewhere only a few new ones had to be established. The most important of these was the "long-wished Ferry" across the North River from Meisier's Dock at New York to Paulus Hook on the Jersey shore, operated by Cornelius van Voorst of Bergen County. By 1765 two new ferries plied the Delaware to Philadelphia from Cooper's and Kaighn's points to accommodate Jersey farmers going to market, and in 1775 another ran across from Callowhill Street for the benefit of the Northern Liberties. To assist "passengers, horses, chairs, and chaises" from the plantation country east of the Cooper River in getting over to Charles Town, the Assembly authorized a ferry from the north side of the city to Clement Lampriere's, and another from the Neck operated by J. Scott, who advertised in 1765 that he kept "Convenient Canows for passengers." Andrew Hibben started a ferry over the Cooper to Hobcaw in 1769; with a great flourish he opened his front room to passengers waiting "While the Boat is getting ready." Apparently he gave good service when others failed to do so, for in 1770 the Assembly awarded him the franchises of Lampriere's and Scott's for a term of fourteen years. Josiah Quincy took the Hobcaw Ferry on March 20, 1773: "we were rowed by six negroes, four of whom had *nothing on* but their kind of breeches, scarce sufficient for a covering."

Led by Christopher Gadsden, the merchants of Charles Town undertook some remarkable projects along the Cooper waterfront, and constructed wharves out into the Ashley for the first time. The activity began after a severe hurricane on May 4, 1761 had caused damage to shipping and piers estimated at £20,000 sterling. Beresford's new wharf provided berths for four ships to unload at once, fifteen dry stores with cellars and eight lofts, a scale house, kitchen, and "negro house." On his Cooper River frontage between what are now Laurens and Calhoun streets, Gadsden commenced in 1767 a far more extensive operation than any colonial merchant had yet attempted when he framed a very long wharf that reached 840 feet into the water, with space for ten or twelve ships at a time. Completing it in two years, he next began construction of a dock twenty feet wide, with six feet of water contiguous to the wharf, so that purchasers of his house lots in his new development, which was the leading urban real-estate venture, might have firewood landed free of charge, as well as lime, lumber, bricks, and building materials.

Christopher Gadsden's "Stupendous Work" inspired other merchants to similar though less ambitious ventures after another storm in 1770 did great damage to most of the wharves save his—sufficient "proof of its Firmness." A substantial wharf, "equal to the best on the Eastern Bay," with stores and an adjoining dock was built by Samuel Prioleau, Jr., and another by John Gaillard; while three now appeared on the South Bay along the Ashley where there had never been a pier for large ships: William Gibbes's eight-hundred-foot wharf, and those of Captains Edward Blake and Robert Mackenzie. Gibbes also turned a penny by selling fifteen lots adjacent to his wharf, with the same free landing privi-

leges offered by Gadsden. All this construction called for regulation of
wharfage and storage charges, which, according to grand-jury findings,
soared beyond reason and bore heavily on both "trading and planting
interests" until finally, in 1768, the Assembly set legal rates.

Northern cities also did much to improve their waterfronts. Boston's
Long Wharf was widened in 1763, and in order to finance additional
warehouses and make extensive repairs, the Proprietors incorporated in
1772. Such piers as Rome's, Lopez's, Redwood's, and Overing's gave
Newport harbor splendid docking facilities, which, taken with the many
smaller wharves, totaled sixty-six spread along nearly a mile and a half
of shore. The convenience of this superb and spacious roadstead led
Governor Robert Melville of Grenada to propose Newport as the central
supply station in Northern waters for the British Navy in 1763, and
soon the Champlins were furnishing beef to "the menawars Men." Beyond the erection of a two-hundred-foot pier at the cost of £1,000 by
a number of merchants in 1766, the East River front of Manhattan underwent no marked change, but a larger volume of traffic on the North
River resulted from the completion on this less-sheltered shore of several
new quays and wharves, of which the "Corporation Dock" was perhaps
the largest. Floating ice damaged piers in the Delaware every winter,
costing Philadelphians heavily for repairs. With new wharves, which
served Southwark and the Northern Liberties, particularly those north
of the city's limits as far as Ball's Town, Philadelphia could boast the
largest port in the New World; along its three-mile waterfront nearly
ninety wharves jutted so far into the river that by 1773 topsail vessels
worked between them and Windmill Island only with difficulty.

To guide ships in and out and to reduce risk of their running aground
on shoals and bars, additional aids to navigation were introduced. The
Pennsylvania Assembly established the Wardens of the Port of Philadelphia, a nine-man board composed of such distinguished merchants
and mariners as Robert Morris and Captain Oswell Eve, to examine and
license pilots and regulate pilotage on the Delaware from Cape Henlopen
up to the city. In 1774 David Rittenhouse surveyed "the Courses and
Distances" of the river for the authorities. Peter Harrison supervised the
installation of a new "lanthorn" like that at Boston in Beaver-Tail Light
in 1761, and on June 20, 1764 Sandy Hook Light, an octagonal tower
with forty-eight oil blazes built by Isaac Conro, entered on its long career of marking the entrance to New York harbor. Another light, whose
original structure is still in use, was constructed at Cape Henlopen to
guide vessels into Delaware Bay in 1765. Two years later, on Middle-Bay
Island in the harbor of Charles Town, the Commissioners of Pilotage
laid the cornerstone of a lighthouse designed by Samuel Cardy, now
called an architect, and Thomas You, "engineer." The opening of two

more lighthouses on Thatcher's Island in Boston Bay on December 24, 1770 completed the measures taken by colonial seaports "for the Benefit and Safety of Navigation."

VII

As the five cities approached the time when they could celebrate centennial and sesquicentennial anniversaries, the prospect, singly and collectively, that they offered to the visitor from overseas was one of mellow maturity and physical modernity. To the Briton and the Scot, the environs of the Northern cities seemed unusually attractive, reminding them of the fair English countryside. The view of Boston and vicinity from Beacon Hill charmed Dr. Honyman: "the country on the other side of the Bay and Harbour to a considerable distance . . . being entirely cleared and open; consisting of gently rising hills and vallies, thick planted with Churches and country seats." No wonder William Gregory declared it to be "as delightful country as I ever saw." The pastoral loveliness of Rhode Island won similar compliments; even sour Ambrose Serle had to admit its beauty. To Patrick M'Robert the neat and cultivated aspect of Manhattan Island farms and estates, as well as that of adjacent parts of Long Island and Westchester County, were a real surprise: "Where nature has done so much, art has had very little share in making them." However, along the Delaware from Bristol to Wilmington and westward beyond the rolling Schuylkill Hills almost to Devon lay the garden spot of the American colonies, "finely interspersed with genteel country seats, fields . . . orchards," and great barns of field stone—a fitting background for the metropolis of Philadelphia, which always stirred the imagination of readers of Young, Gray, and Cowper. To those who shared the emerging romantic feeling for grandeur and the exotic, the dense moss-festooned growth along the banks of the Ashley and the Cooper in the "neighbourhood of Charles Town" appeared "beautiful beyond description."

Upon closer view, each city had further developed its individual appearance, together with a degree of urban elegance. Charles Town's broad, airy streets, lined with more costly mansions than those of any other city, provided a striking contrast to Boston's North End. New York still looked half-Dutch, and the undistinguished, though comfortable houses with party walls in Penn's city suggested a well-being for the many probably unequaled anywhere in the world.

The five communities had welcomed thousands of newcomers in these years, and had succeeded signally in housing them and in providing well-drained, well-lighted, and clean streets, often adorned with sightly shade trees. In varying degree, an air of neatness pervaded them all. The physical improvement of the colonial towns had been carried out by municipal authorities made increasingly responsive to public opinion, and it was the tragedy of the city on the Ashley and Cooper that its permanent inhabitants—persons of the middle and lower classes—were never accorded the kind of official care they so richly deserved.

CHAPTER 7

Merchants and Craftsmen
at Bay

O PTIMISTICALLY AND ENTHUSIASTICALLY the colonials welcomed the prospects of peace and the new monarch in 1760 as portents of happier days to come. Disillusionment followed quickly as barriers of every sort together with new and undreamed-of trading conditions loomed up before them, dashing their hopes and adversely affecting not alone their commerce but the entire economic structure of the cities and, sooner or later, that of the agricultural countryside. High taxes, governmental shackling of trade, with consequent political and social unrest, and a severe postwar depression—the stimulus of a remarkable growth of rural and urban population notwithstanding—kept the towns in a constant state of tension, during which readjustment and recovery came but slowly and with uncertainty. Urban merchants, though understanding the speculative nature of commercial ventures of the eighteenth century and accepting the primary role of chance in their affairs, found it ever more difficult to win a fortune. Nevertheless the leaders, merchants and craftsmen alike, adopted heroic measures to eliminate one obstacle after another and, except for banking, introduced all known agencies and methods for conducting business; and when the separation came in 1776, their cities had reached a stage of maturity that defied paternal treatment and enabled them to survive eight years of war.

II

After the fall of Montreal in 1760, the continental phase of the Old French War ended, and the Caribbean became the theater of hostilities. The English, with Spain an added enemy, dispatched successful expeditions to capture Havana and Martinique. With this shift, the invigorating flow of specie into the ports of New York and Philadelphia to pay the forces and contractors slowed down to a trickle and, by 1762, virtually dried up; moreover, no resumption of the vitally necessary traffic in molasses and sugars with the foreign West Indies could be undertaken. The Royal Navy saw to that. Newporters unwisely stayed in ruinous privateering while at the same time they pursued certain profitable lines, but soon they and their neighbors at Boston experienced the onset of hard times. Rice exports fell off a third at Charles Town in 1761–2. Thus, very early, the cities felt the effects of what is now understood as a normal contraction during a changeover from a wartime to a peace-time economy, and by 1762 the recession was settling down on all of them.

High taxes for payment of war debts and the ordinary processes of re-adjustment would have been sufficient to produce the depression, which was general in 1763, but the design of the Grenville Ministry at London to reorganize the British Empire and to bring the colonies back into a more subordinate status at the very time when socially, culturally, and politically, as well as economically, they were coming of age, substan-tially prolonged it. Parliament's decision to enforce the long-dormant Molasses Act of 1733, and the legislation of 1764 intended to confine colonial commerce to the Empire exclusively and at the same time to produce revenue, dismayed urban trading interests. In framing instruc-tions for its representatives to the General Court, the Boston Town Meeting pointed out with much truth that "our Trade has for a long Time laboured under great discouragements, and it is with the deepest concern that we see such further Difficultys coming upon it, as will re-duce it to the lowest Ebb, if not totally obstruct and ruin it." The Stamp Act of 1765, falling as it did upon a much broader group, provoked such a disturbance everywhere in the colonies as to bring about its re-peal the next year and the reduction of the duty from threepence to a penny a gallon on all molasses, whether English or foreign. Northern merchants could have made a profit in rum under this new arrangement, but the levying of additional revenue duties by the Townshend Acts on the importation of necessities—paper, painter's colors, lead, glass, tea— and the reorganization of the customs service in 1767 further postponed recovery. From the autumn of 1760 to 1770, possibly later, the colonies found out how a postwar period of contraction could be greatly ag-gravated by ministerial policies and the political events consequent upon them.

The year 1770 ushered in an illusive calm for imperial relations, per-mitting the citizens to prosper, but late in 1772 commerce again slack-ened. Ezra Collins of Boston lamented that "Trade [is] in a most miserable situation, carried on with almost no profit," and shortly after-wards Levinius Clarkson reported to New York that business was so dull in Charles Town that many persons were selling their lands. Peace had still not spelled material well-being to the cities, which for fifteen years had known very little of it, especially Boston and Newport, whose inhabitants found it difficult to recall when times had not been bad. Recovery had come, but not prosperity; and when in 1774 the specter of monopoly arose from the East India Company's tea, many conservative merchants were ready to join with more venturesome elements to do something about it.

The depression of the sixties deranged the entire credit structure, which reached from England to the distant frontier in America. The London merchant usually allowed one year for payment when he shipped goods to a colonial city; after that he charged interest. In disposing of merchandise to shopkeepers in town or country stores, the colonial merchant also granted credit for a year to fifteen months; while the retailers in turn allowed a similar time for the ultimate urban or rural consumers to pay for their purchases. As hard times set in and money for remittances disappeared from the towns, the city merchants tried valiantly to get in their debts, and, failing to do so, fell behind in payments to London and Bristol. The experience of Stephen Collins, a Philadelphia Quaker merchant of good credit and high repute, nicely illustrates the dilemma of a colonial trader. Most of his transactions appear to have been with country storekeepers of Pennsylvania, New Jersey, Delaware, and Maryland. From 1763 to 1765 he spent much of his countinghouse time dunning these rural traders "in the strickest manner" for payments, because he himself was being sorely pressed by London correspondents. The laboriously penned replies he received make tragic reading; their persistent and despairing theme is that the country storekeepers, most of them Quakers, desire to pay up, but are unable to do so because of poor crops and an almost total absence of cash.

The perennial shortage of a circulating medium made the postwar slump more serious than it might otherwise have been. War contracts ended and hard money to pay the troops no longer relieved the situation. Hastening to discharge their war debts, provincial governments raised large sums by taxation to retire paper issues, and then in 1764 the Currency Act prohibited any further printing of paper money in any of the colonies, a statute that worked havoc with business, for as the amount of money shrank, barter seemed the only means of making transactions, and neither debts nor taxes could be collected.

New York was particularly hard hit. As early as 1762 John Watts wrote that "Gold is very scarce here and I believe at Philadelphia too"; some years later the situation had become desperate: "notwithstanding I have many thousands owing to me by Persons of undoubted Estates," James Beekman explained, "yet they are unable to pay by reason of the Scarcity of Cash amongst us." In 1770, speaking of foreclosures, he put it very plainly: "For my part I could ruin many [an] honest and able family should I take such steps at present, whereas a circulating Currency would have enabled them to pay these Debts without having their houses and Lands taken from them." Nor were conditions much more favorable for him and many of his associates in 1772. Boston, Newport, and Philadelphia also lacked sufficient cash to conduct normal business affairs.

The plight of Charles Town seemed unusually grave to its people. All the Spanish milled dollars its merchants gained in the provision trade to Havana were shipped away, "either for England or North-America by way of Remittances," and bills of exchange went by the same routes. In 1763 Henry Laurens repeated the old refrain: "Money is an article that grows scarcer with me than I could have expected from the large Sums that are due to me." Even small change disappeared, leaving little to effect "common marketting," and by 1767 cleverly counterfeited bills occasioned no great surprise. Two years later, Peter Timothy declared that in recent years importations of British superfluities alone had taken "upwards of £1,000,000 sterling," while the anticipated cost of slaves in 1769 would amount to £270,000 more. But what vexed South Carolinians of modest estate most of all, it seems, was the fact that Northern merchants "drain us from our Specie and mostly for mere Trash" (except bar iron, sheep, and oil), and had it not been concerned for the virtuous farmers and artisans to the northward, the province would have voted for commercial nonintercourse with its rivals. Right down to the War for Independence the Southern city never had the benefit of a suitable circulating medium.

With money scarce and trade in the doldrums, it is no wonder that John Watts declared that "Every thing is tumbling down, even the Traders." About a year and a half later, in 1765, he wrote to London that "Business is here very languid, the weak must go to the Wall, frequent Bankruptcys, and growing more frequent." Nor was the depression peculiar to New York. As Ezra Collins of Boston put it, many "failed thousands worse than nothing." The failure in 1769 of William Richardson of Newport, a most influential and respected merchant, fractured the town's economy; his fifteen missing ships were valued at £132,168, and his "bad debts" totaled £37,000. Another bankrupt was Napthali Hart, Jr.; he stated in his petition that his difficulties came "thro' inevitable and unforseen cross Events, and a long Series of Missfortunes." At Philadelphia, John Gualdo could not make a go of the wine business and had to give it up; in 1769 he opened a music store. And in the Carolina capital, George Flagg ran a notice in 1770 which probably reflected the sentiments of many tradesmen: he thanked his customers for supporting his oil business, but requested them to pay up back accounts "as there is no possibility of carrying it on without money."

The career of George Rome affords an insight into the desperate state of affairs at Newport in these times. The loss of more than a hundred vessels and two millions of pounds in the last war nearly ruined the city.

When John Channing and numerous other merchants failed to make prompt remittances to England, the creditors sent George Rome over in 1761 with a power of attorney to collect from the Rhode Islanders. By 1767 this Scot could brag to Dr. Thomas Moffatt, a Stamp Act victim, that "With great industry, caution, and circumspection, I have not only reduced our demands, and regulated our connections, in some measure, but kept my head out of a HALTER, which you have had the honor to grace." It had been difficult as well as onerous to force men into bankruptcy, seize their vessels for debts, and dance attendance upon the courts, which always favored the natives. If, as he insisted, he collected little, Mr. Rome did exceedingly well by himself, managing in the midst of his duties to sell £1,500 worth of spermaceti candles a year and to improve opportunities to acquire much land, a wharf, a town house, and "my country villa" at Narragansett. In so doing he first embittered, then enraged the Newporters with his arrogance, ruthlessness, and cupidity as well as by loose talk about the need for a royal government in Rhode Island to promote "the cause of integrity" and curb "the dark purposes of independence," but when independence came, the islanders had their innings.

Less noted individually, because of smaller estate, but collectively of ominous future significance, were the large numbers of tradesmen and artisans who fell into financial troubles through no particular fault of their own. Although failures among the middle class occurred throughout the entire period, the most critical time came in 1767–8 with the "alarming scarcity of money and consequent stagnation of trade, and the almost universally increasing complaints of debt and poverty." The sums owed them may seem trifling, but a writer in the *Boston Gazette* told the gentry that it would be a tremendous service if they would pay their tradesmen's bills and ease their burdens. Two issues of the *Boston News-letter* contained twenty-one notices about insolvent debtors—a glazier, a hatter, a leatherworker, a tin-plate maker, and other craftsmen, as well as several merchants. At Newport, John Collins averred that "Their is but few Purses in Newport that hold fifty Pounds Lawfull Money in Cash." Responding to demands for payment of a debt, Tabitha Crispin of "Little Crick" assured Stephen Collins of Philadelphia that, given more time, she could pay the principal, but needed the interest to feed her large family of children, and Anne Batten prayed that since he had been "Very good to waite so Long, I Beg you not to Sew me." But good old Quaker stiffness rather than meekness comes out in a letter from Sam Thomas of Susquehanna in 1771:

Friend Collins,
    I assure you that I have Honner, and am punctual when I have any Person to deal with that has Honner, but when I have such

fellows as thou art to deal with, I treat them as they Deserve, as I shall the, and so if Ever the getts thy Money the shall come on or send for it, I want neither thy Money to lay in my Hands nor any favour from the, &c.

Explanations and pleas for leniency did not suffice to save many of these afflicted debtors from imprisonment. Edward Thurston of Newport, admitting that "almost everybody is complaining of hard times," reported that "MacGee, the baker, has failed and gone to goal. Silas Downer of Providence ran away and gone to Georgia" to avoid debtors' prison. In 1769 the Rhode Island Assembly went to the rescue by passing an act for the relief of insolvent debtors. New York's prison bulged with debtors, whose sorry plight caused Whitefield to take up a collection for them, and other generous inhabitants to contribute firewood, blankets, and provisions. In reasoned prose from "Reading Gaol," Michael Hester pled for release, "for Confined as I am You'l be the longer out of your Money and the more Time I shall lose. . . . Pray set me at Liberty that I may be doing something towards paying you and others honestly." The *Pennsylvania Chronicle* gave space to a moving article on the suffering of helpless debtors, and shortly thereafter the same newspaper came out for a change in the laws for incarcerating those who could not pay what they owed. If no legislative action, beyond the relief granted in bankruptcy laws so relentlessly opposed by British merchants, passed in this period, members of the middle class grimly nursed as a grievance the personal experiences they and their friends had in debtors' prison. In 1776, middle-class Philadelphians procured the inclusion of relief for debtors in the new fundamental law, thereby initiating the movement that in the next century brought about the abolition of this obsolete form of action.

III

Faced with harsh realities, the mercantile leaders of the cities displayed commendable resourcefulness in their efforts to find every legitimate way out of the economic morass. Each of the Northern towns, in varying degrees and according to its capacity, increased its shipping to ports in the British Isles, to Lisbon, the Mediterranean, and the Wine Islands. Because Charles Town had no fleet of ships, its sister cities shared in the re-exportation of the rice and indigo crops, and Boston and Newport masters also carried portions of the grain, meat, and lumber shipments from the Middle colonies to West Indian and European markets. Malbones and Vernons, Riveras and Lopezes, and Christopher Champlin of Rhode Island kept about twenty vessels in the slave trade from Africa to South Carolina and Virginia, surpassing New York in the Guinea trade. Using rum as currency on the Coast, they sold their slaves at Charles Town and in the Chesapeake country for much-needed specie and bills of exchange; in 1763 an investment of 200 gallons of "neat rum" would purchase a slave who would sell for £24–29 in America. Some merchants also succeeded to a marked degree in promoting new articles in old markets.

The preference of the colonial gentry for Madeira wines furnished the incentive for a considerable traffic to those islands, to Fayall and Teneriffe, and occasionally to Lisbon and Oporto. Boston importations of Madeira were exceeded only by those of New York, whose three-bottle men developed such an astounding capacity that one merchant thought they would consume the whole vintage of the Portuguese islands. Theophylact and Richard Bache of Manhattan maintained a branch office on Water Street, Philadelphia, for selling their "choice genuine Madeira wine, in New York pipes"; in fact, New York supplied both Philadelphia and Newport with a large part of their wine.

The more common use of whale-oil lamps in houses and on city streets brought this illuminant into great demand and encouraged the pursuit of leviathan that so thrilled Edmund Burke. In 1764 more than a hundred sloops and schooners from New England hunted whales in the Gulf of St. Lawrence and the Strait of Belle Isle, and one of the Boston Gridleys procured a monopoly of the sea-cow fishery at the Magdalen Islands from Governor Murray of Nova Scotia. Newport pursued whaling "with Spirit." "By way of experiment" in 1767, the sloop *Lydia* joined others in trying the south latitudes; most captains still sailed for hunting grounds north of Davis Strait. Three years later, in May, the little city sent out sixteen whalers in one week. This was a hazardous adventure from which many a vessel never returned, but when the *King George,* John Greenwood master, came back in 1775 from the Falklands (51°50″ So. Lat.) with 170 barrels of oil, 1,000 weight of bone, and 500 sealskins, the enterprise seemed worth the risk. In that year Newport sent nearly forty whaling ships to sea, being surpassed only by Nantucket and Bedford-in-Dartmouth. Boston and Newport vessels also engaged extensively in the cod fishery off the Grand Banks and in the Gulf of St. Lawrence.

Boston retained its position as the leading entrepôt for British manufactures down to the outbreak of the war, but for tonnage of shipping and for exports Philadelphia was the grand mart. Indeed, in 1767 "Publicola" assured readers of the *Pennsylvania Chronicle* that "in the scale of exportations" from ports in His Majesty's dominions, their city shipped annually "a greater number of tons of merchandize, though perhaps not of greater value, than from any other British port, save that of London." Traffic in the Delaware increased from that time until 1773 because of the unprecedented expansion of agriculture in the Philadelphia hinterland. Flour became the great export item, which, together with other commodities, totaled £720,135 sterling in 1774, giving the city a balance of exports over imports of more than £100,000. Such commerce, vast for its day, required 350 ships and employed 7,500 seamen.

Every seaport stepped up its coastwise carrying trade. In this traffic Boston led all other communities, sending its vessels everywhere, from Canso to St. Augustine and the Mississippi with cargoes of European goods, especially drugs, sailcloth, cordage, and tea, and Yankee products such as rum, fish, lumber, cabinetwork, carriages, New England axes, and candles. The customs figures, 1768–73, show that 557 coasters (topsail vessels, sloops, schooners) entered at Boston, while 588 cleared outward; but counting smaller craft that did not go through customs, the total entering came nearer 1,500. Shipping from north of Boston predominated, with 579 entering in 1773. Captain Patterson had a "coasting Business" carrying passengers and freight in his sloop between Boston and the Kennebeck for many years, and the *Nova Scotia Packet* made regular trips to Halifax. Newport pressed the Bay Town, with 488 entries and 493 clearances. Local traffic south of Cape Cod and along the shores of Long Island Sound accounted for much of its coasting trade, and several Rhode Island vessels ran regularly as packets to New York; Captain Joseph Anthony operated his sloop *Peace and Plenty* on a schedule to Philadelphia, delivering such shipments as two boxes of spermaceti candles from Thomas Vernon to Benjamin Franklin, and bringing other items back with him. Joseph Durfee traded in rum, cordials, cider, codfish, potatoes, cheese, candles, and whale oil at Beale's Wharf on his scheduled trips to Charles Town, but in the spring and fall he refurbished the sloop *Charlestown* in order to transport in modest comfort numbers of Carolinians and West Indians to Newport for their annual stay at the island resort. After the Last French War, also, Rhode Island sloops sailed regularly into Chesapeake Bay, where they had struck up a lively trade, especially in slaves, with Virginia and Maryland planters. Carter Braxton thought the Guinea business so attractive that he proposed himself as Virginia agent of the Browns of Providence.

Philadelphia and New York had far fewer vessels in the coastal trade, but their traffic was nevertheless of prime importance. New York continued to supply Newport with most of its foreign manufactured goods and some provisions, and the Van Hornes and others kept up a profitable commerce with Charles Town through the Schermmerhorns, whose sloop *Sally* plied between the two cities. Philadelphia dispatched cargo after cargo of foodstuffs to all of the colonies, but particularly to New England and the Carolinas. From the latter they imported rice, indigo, and sole leather. What might be termed a Quaker network was operated by

Stephen Collins and his brother, Ezra, of Lynn with the Redwoods of Newport and the Barrells of Boston and Portsmouth. Inasmuch as New England coasters took off large quantities of Pennsylvania produce, the tendency toward protectionism, noticed earlier, cropped up again. In 1767, when proposals to levy export duties on Yankee vessels were voiced in the Assembly, "Mercator" exposed the fallacy of such reasoning by pointing out that by selling flour and iron to New Englanders, who, having no staple, paid one third in merchandise, another in bills of exchange, and another in cash, Philadelphians enabled their city to earn an annual balance of £52,000 "in our favour." New York ran between fifty and sixty per cent behind Philadelphia in the tonnage of this important and lucrative coastal commerce, and Charles Town slightly below that, but most of the profits in freight went to Boston and Newport skippers.

Every Northern port strove to win a place in the newly opened trade with Canada and sent agents to Quebec and Montreal. Boston and Philadelphia merchants seem to have met with success at Quebec, and those of New York at Montreal. Newporters went after the commerce of West Florida and the Mississippi at the same time the Charlestonians brought East Florida within their trading orbit.

When traffic along legitimate highways of commerce failed to bring in enough specie and bills to pay for goods imported from the British Isles, some merchants, recalling profitable enterprises during the recent wars, did not hesitate to venture down forbidden lanes of trade. Under the Molasses Act of 1733, smuggling had been necessary for survival, and the Sugar Act of 1764 "made an important part of the trade of the . . . colonies virtually impossible if the provisions . . . were obeyed, or illicit if they were disregarded." Disregard them they did, though the vulgar thought of running molasses as merely "cheating the Devil." How much smuggling actually went on can never be known, but it is safe to say that even if the customs officers did succeed in framing John Hancock and making illicit trade unprofitable by many seizures at Boston in 1771, elsewhere they were not so efficient. New York merchants carried on a large trade in forbidden goods and tea, particularly with Holland and Hamburg. This European traffic was condoned by many who regarded smuggling of West Indies produce as reprehensible, especially after the lowering of the molasses duty to one penny in 1766. Wines, sugar, and molasses came in via the Caribbean and could be smuggled because the environs of Manhattan lent themselves to it and because cordial relations between importers and officials obtained. The many small creeks and inlets tributary to the Delaware offered ideal avenues for running goods destined for Philadelphia—after being landed, cargoes went to the city either in shallops or overland in wagons; Wilmington became "a notorious Place for Smugling." Comptroller Weare of Lisbon reported that "the German Transports" with immigrants for Pennsylvania ordinarily carried prohibited duck, linens, gunpowder, tea, and cordage from Holland. In 1767 Inspector George Mills of the Southern Customs District discovered evidence at Charles Town of "much Smugling from Holland, France and the West Indies," and that the traders "publicly advertised the Goods of Manufactures of those Countrys to be sold. The Smugling is carried on in the Coasting Vessels. No country better calculated for Running Goods than this."

The fine art of evading revenue officers at Newport virtually attained the perfection reached at the Isle of Man, Bideford, Liverpool, and more out-of-the-way harbors in Scotland, where in sixteen years such tremendous quantities of tobacco and European goods clandestinely got in that the King lost a million pounds in duties. Displaying unusual ingenuity, Rhode Islanders managed to outwit or bribe the officers; Aaron Lopez had his captains secrete the chests of tea and bolts of duck shipped to Surinam for him between hogsheads of molasses, a dodge he got away with until 1763. The Vernons sent their ships in ballast to Gothenburg to take on hemp, textiles, and East India goods, which passed as herring cargoes bound for the West Indies. Wines from Madeira and Barcelona silks and handkerchiefs, with a cover of legitimate Lisbon salt, found their way to Newport warehouses, but the consumption of 14,000 hogsheads of molasses by Newport distilleries when only 2,500 of them came from the British islands demands some tall explaining. The assignment of H.M.S. *Squirrel* to Narragansett Bay in the winter of 1763–4 "for the encouragement of fair trade and the prevention of smuggling" augured trouble for many traders. The word got around, however, that one could arrange matters with the new collector, John Robinson. William Vernon, who should have known, insisted that "he well knows the Collector makes Six Thousand [Spanish] Dollars a year," though his salary amounted to a mere £100, "and that the Merchants would gladly compound for Seventy Thousand O.T. per Ann. with the Custom House." Customs receipts revealed the state of affairs somewhat when those for Newport proved less than for the smaller port of New London. In retaliation, officials began charging excessive fees and purposely prolonging entries and clearances. Numerous nasty brushes with the several naval vessels stationed in Narragansett Bay to detect contraband traders, who had taken to landing their cargoes at night in coves on the Sakonnet River side of Rhode Island, aroused an anger that culminated in the burning of the *Gaspee* on June 10, 1773. This ended the practice, but it had by that time achieved the purpose of enabling Newport to make a more rapid comeback than her more carefully policed Massachusetts neighbor.

With reduction of the duty on molasses in 1766, much of the smuggling of that item ceased, since it could be imported legally and a profit made on it. An analysis of the Customs figures, 1768–72, shows that of the molasses imported by the Northern cities, at least half was marketed as sweetening in the coastwise trade, and the other half was distilled into rum, of which four fifths was used on this side of the Atlantic and only one fifth in the pursuit of the slave trade. Thus the molasses duties affected the entire population, the common people in particular, to whom a doubling of the price in 1764 had proved a real hardship; and not merely a few local rum-distillers. When John Adams spoke of molasses as "an essential ingredient in American independence," he had even less cause to blush than has usually been assumed; it was more of a food than a beverage and, above all, it was the prime staple of colonial commerce.

IV

"It is a fact indisputably certain, that what port soever on this continent can acquire the greatest share of its inland commerce, must proportionably advance in riches and importance," contended "Philadelphus," one of the first Americans to glimpse the commercial possibilities in westward expansion. In order to counter the effects of depression and unfavorable British regulations, each city energetically sought to control a large trading region by means of a more intensive exploitation of its hinterland trade and an extension of the areas it served as a collecting and distributing center.

Dominance of the well-settled country behind it that cried for urban services and an outlet for produce raised Philadelphia to pre-eminence among colonial capitals and provided it with an actual and potential trading domain such as few European cities possessed. With the eastern counties of Pennsylvania, the Delaware Valley, West New Jersey, and northern Maryland, the city's merchants measurably increased their traffic, and such towns and villages as Germantown, Bristol, Trenton, Burlington, Salem, Wilmington, and New Castle served as depots for collecting and forwarding by water to the city agricultural produce for export to foreign markets. Urban wholesalers also distributed local and imported merchandise to rural storekeepers and kept open communications between city and country: James & Drinker supplied Christopher Hoagland of inland New Jersey with rum and took off his pork via the Burlington stage boat. Cheese from Greenwich, beer from Deer Creek, flour from Chester Mills, flaxseed from Amwell and Woodstown—these were some items of "country produce" that Stephen Collins accepted from nearly a hundred storekeepers whom he supplied with dry goods, laces, shoes, hats, saddles, lime, metal buttons, and sundry other articles. Trade like this had to be conducted on the barter basis during the years of currency shortage, for the farmers had no other means of payment, and even so, payments in kind often came in slowly. Delayed payments notwithstanding, this trade provided the city with profitable staples for export.

The merchant was not slow to follow the immigrants westward; in fact, indirectly through retailers, he furnished them with the goods and tools needed for the journey and the first year of house-raising and land-clearing. The Scotch-Irish and Palatines poured into the five western counties east of the Kittatinny Range, filling the Great Valley of Pennsylvania from Delaware Water Gap to Mason and Dixon's new line with farmers, whose trade the metropolis expected to monopolize. These people were not so self-sufficient as might appear at first, and to stores in Easton, Bethlehem, Reading, Lancaster, York, Carlisle, and Shippensburg they sent produce by wagon to exchange for much-needed articles. As the starting-point of the southward migration and the entrepôt for the Indian trade, Lancaster enjoyed boom times, and several Philadelphia houses either moved out there or established branches from which they dealt with country stores. Stephen Collins maintained correspondents at Reading, Bethlehem, and Carlisle, but stayed out of Lancaster because the Shippens, the Frankses, and a few others had a grip on its trade. The failure of Stewart Rowan's country store in Cumberland County in 1773 meant a loss of £900 to John Wilkins, Collins's Carlisle agent.

The Peace of Paris gave the Philadelphians their long-awaited opportunity to assume the lead in opening a rich inland fur trade by which they aspired to offset the declining profits of ordinary commerce. The Quaker firm of Baynton, Wharton & Morgan and their Jewish rivals, David Franks & Company, who were associated with Simon & Levy of Lancaster and Moses Franks, the London war contractor, made bids for fortunes in the Illinois peltry trade. In 1766 the Quaker partners dispatched six hundred pack horses and many wagons with goods worth £50,000 to Pittsburgh, where George Croghan sent them down the Ohio in new batteaux manned by three hundred boatmen. Big business had reached the West! Although this enterprise failed to divert the Illinois trade from New Orleans, Philadelphia merchants now found an outlet in land speculation and joined with the westward-pushing settlers to bring about the creation of Northumberland, Bedford, and Westmoreland counties by 1773.

No colonial area expanded with the rapidity of the back parts of Carolina after the defeat of the Cherokee in 1761; when the colonial period closed, the population of the Southern upcountry numbered close to 150,000, and that of Piedmont South Carolina alone accounted for seventy-nine per cent of the whites in the province. Charlestonians had already set up stores throughout the Low Country at such places as Georgetown, Beaufort, Dorchester, Monck's Corner, Combahee Bridge, and Beaver Bluff, tying the rice and indigo districts closer to the capital's economy. Now, in answer to the need of the German and Scotch-Irish farmers of the South Carolina back country, who raised quantities of grain, corn in particular, and meats, hides, tobacco, and hemp, the hustling merchants of Charles Town hastened to provide outlets for these staples. Joseph Kershaw's store at Pine Tree Hill (Camden after 1768) on the Wateree flourished after 1763, and he took in his brother Eli and John Chestnut as partners. Eli opened a branch at Cheraw Hill (later Chatham) on the Pedee, while at Granby, the head of navigation on the Congaree, Chestnut tried another. When Ancrum, Lance & Loocock retired from this partnership in 1774, the three stores were worth £15,000, £9,628, and £8,100 respectively. At these provincial points and others, like Augusta on the Savannah and Wilmington on the Cape Fear, merchants assembled produce for shipping to Charles Town and dispensed supplies brought up from the Low Country. Although located more than three hundred miles away, the Moravians of Bethabara and Salem in North Carolina dealt with Henry Laurens, who looked after their smallest commissions, even to procuring a pair of glasses from Philadelphia for Dr. August Shubart and sending them up by "your spring Waggons" in 1764. North Carolina butter made by the Scotch-Irish at Rock River sold in fifty- and one-hundred-pound kegs at Atkins & Weston's warehouse on the Cooper. Altogether North Carolina's trade with Charles Town came to £20,000 a year. Although the formerly lucrative trade in deerskins declined markedly as a result of Virginia's competition, by 1770 the farmers of the back settlements were supplying 4,000 barrels of flour annually to fill home-consumption needs and allow a little for export, besides quantities of Indian corn. This approach to self-sufficiency in foodstuffs aided South Carolina in recovering from the effects of the depression.

The development of Savannah as a satellite of Charles Town and the economic control of Georgia achieved by the Carolinians through the purchase of lands continued. Governor Wright told the Lords of Trade in 1766 that because Savannah owned no large ships, all European goods arrived at Charles Town and were transshipped in return for Georgia's produce. After the erection of East Florida in 1763, "Many Gentlemen of worth and Substance, from Carolina and Georgia" took up lands for indigo and rice planting. The boom ended by 1768, however, when Henry Laurens remarked that "a damp upon East Florida credit was not unknown to the people of Charles Town." On the Gulf of Mexico, Pensacola came under the ægis of the Carolina merchants; the *Hillsborough Packet* carried cargoes of indigo, cochineal, logwood, deerskins, and specie won in trade with the Spaniards and the Indians to Charles Town, and occasionally a drove of black cattle made the six-hundred-mile trip overland by way of the Creek villages to Pensacola.

For the most part the Northern cities were restricted to a more intense cultivation of economic domains staked out before 1760. Boston merchants built up a very large inland business of supplying European articles to their rising competitors at Salem, Marblehead, Newbury, New London, Norwich, Hartford, and even Providence and Newport. Every New England town had its store, and Boston merchants always cultivated country traders, whom they promised to supply "by the Quantity, at the lowest Advance." The brothers Deblois maintained their headquarters at the Bay Town under Louis; George ran a warehouse at Salem, and Gilbert one in Newport; while Stephen, Jr., kept a retail shop at Dr. Nathaniel Ames's in Dedham, as outlets for their large hardware importations. The *Essex Gazette, New Hampshire Gazette,* and Rhode Island and Connecticut newspapers carried advertisements by Boston importers. Thomas Whalley announced in the *New London Summary* that his wholesale and retail business was located in Dock Square, "very handy to the Place where the Vessels from Connecticut lay, and any Gentlemen may depend upon being as well used by a Letter, as if present themselves." In truth Boston traders and craftsmen made a big thing of mail orders, particularly with customers in western Massachusetts and Connecticut.

A nobleman passing through Connecticut in the early sixties compared it "to a cask of good liquor tapped at both ends, at one of which Boston draws, and New York at the other, till little is left but lees and settlings." This was certainly true, but as the colonial era ended, Manhattan had whittled down Boston's traffic with this province, especially in the Connecticut and Thames valleys. Pig iron from the Livingstons' Ancram Furnace and the Forest of Dean went to Norwich through the agency of Printer Samuel Loudon in 1763, and at the same time a direct road from New York to Litchfield drew the products of the upper Housatonic country to the Hudson Valley. By 1770 Yankee annoyance at the hegemony of the Yorkers inspired a "Connecticut Farmer" of New London to dream of the day when "the plumes of that domineering city may yet feather the nests of those whom they have so long plucked." And there were those in New Jersey who agreed with the *New American Magazine*'s proposal for an export duty on all Jersey produce shipped from either New York or Philadelphia and a bounty on exports from Perth Amboy and Burlington. Up the Hudson at Albany most mercantile establishments were little more than branch agencies for city traders, though an occasional Dutchman advertised articles "as cheap as can be bought in New York." Throughout these country districts dozens of storekeepers dealt with urban wholesalers.

Situated between New York and Boston and relying heavily on each for European goods, Newport had no hinterland to develop. In 1761 Ezra Stiles computed that each year the town sold about £80,000 worth of shop goods, of which the inhabitants consumed one third and the remainder sold in places trading with Newport—"Middletown, Portsmouth, Tiverton, Little Compton, Dartmouth, Freetown, Taunton, Swanzey, Kingston, Narragansett, Volentown, Canterbury"—in other words, the bay, and adjacent Massachusetts and Connecticut communities, to which might be added Block Island, Martha's Vineyard, Nantucket, New London, Saybrook, and Sag Harbor. But the whole region produced little more than small quantities of onions, red clover seed, the well-known Rhode Island cheese, Narragansett horses, sheep, and fish, which never made up full cargoes for one of Newport's coasters, and their skippers had to take on local manufactures or seek freights at other ports of call.

Always accustomed to pulling themselves up by their own bootstraps, the Newporters would have made an excellent comeback after the war if they had not been forced to share their gains with the traders of Providence. That port, which was but a short sail up the bay from the capital, had direct access to the hinterland of Rhode Island, Connecticut, and southern Massachusetts via the Blackstone Valley and therefore possessed real advantages for future growth. The men of Providence were not content to wait; in 1758 they had begun to agitate for an admiralty office of their own and, headed by the Browns and Hopkinses, they drove ahead in trade with the West Indies and inland towns and also established colonial and European connections independent of Newport. Obadiah Brown & Company, the largest candle manufactory in America, sold quantities of spermaceti candles to the Newport Malbones, John Coddington, Samuel Goldthwait, Thomas Robinson, and their friends, thereby meeting Newport manufacturers on their home grounds. The Rhode Islanders felt this competition keenly; such prominent merchants as Christopher Champlin, John Channing, and Napthali Hart deemed it necessary to advertise that they could sell goods as cheaply "as they are sold in Providence, having regulated the Prices at the same Rates as they are sold in that Place." One who knew conditions intimately at the end of the period said of Newport: "It had been one of the most commercial places in America, but was then falling into decay. Its fortunes were waning before the superior activity of its rival, Providence." Newport's fate had been sealed by 1775; the War for Independence dealt it the final blow.

City goods reached the more remote and thinly settled rural districts that were not supplied by country stores through the services of the peddler, whose pack of notions few countryfolk could resist. Always welcome for what he had to sell, he was nevertheless a trifle suspect too. Some of the hawkers forged orders on merchants for their stock, others failed to repay when credit was given, and many were suspected of dealing in stolen goods. All colonies regulated the peddling traffic, and in January 1767 New York forbade it entirely under a penalty of five pounds. Later, however, recognizing that it served a real need, not only to the countryfolk but to merchants, New York reversed its position and permitted the chapmen to operate under a very strict licensing system, which imposed a fee of eight pounds for a horse and five pounds for wagons and sledges. Pennsylvania's system of regulation worked fairly well, and the number licensed by Joseph Shippen rose from nineteen in 1766 to forty-nine in 1770.

Inland trade rested on the improvement of transport facilities as settlement moved westward and southward. Lancaster County craftsmen living along Conestoga Creek had, by 1760, completed their transformation of a dumpy covered English vehicle into the great Dutch wagon, which was drawn by sturdy Conestoga-bred horses with bells and driven by a teamster seated on an outboard or astride the off horse; these "ships of inland commerce" were one of the sights of America. Upon inquiry in 1765, Lord Adam Gordon learned that the farmers of Penn's province possessed "not less than Twenty Thousand Waggons" and four times as many horses. When Crèvecœur's Andrew, the Hebridean, saw his first Conestoga team at Philadelphia market in 1770, he asked in amazement "what was the use of those great moving houses, and where those big horses came from," for "these huge animals would eat all the grass in our island." As trade from Lancaster to Philadelphia mounted in volume, Conestoga wagons crowded the highway going to the city, "sometimes . . . there being above one hundred in a company, carrying down the produce of the country, and returning with all kinds of stores and merchandize." The amount of "Dutch Wagon flour" transported to the metropolis eventually equaled that delivered in shallops.

Conestoga wagons made the long journey south on the Great Philadelphia Wagon Road to the Carolina back country, but the Piedmont farmers must have procured many vehicles from other sources as yet unknown. At any rate, traffic to Charles Town grew steadily until, in 1770, Governor Bull stated that "as many as three thousand wagons per year" came into town. One December day in 1771 a citizen counted 113 of these teams on the way into the city, whereas 30 was the most he had ever seen before in one day. Merchants constructed spacious wagon yards behind their warehouses, and some even opened stores outside the city gates to attract incoming produce. James Riddle's livery stable, at the Horse and Groom, specialized in caring for horses and "country Wagons." Despite the very high cost of freight, increasing quantities of flour, flaxseed, tobacco, and other bulk loads reached Charles Town by wagon from places two and three hundred miles inland. The Grand Jury of 1770 presented the public roads as "too narrow for the great and increasing inland trade, now carried on throughout this province by waggons," and also requested the appointment of tobacco and flour inspectors for those "staple commodities."

Having no important staples requiring large-scale overland transport to seaboard markets, the other cities did not develop as large a wagon trade nor need as heavy vehicles. John Hughes, former stamp master and Philadelphia merchant, was astonished to find on a trip to New Hampshire in 1769 that "these People from Rhode Island Eastward work Oxen chiefly, and it is Rare to Meet a Team with a horse in it; and I am told that many of these Ox Teams Come 80 and 100 miles to Boston Market and it is much the same here." Much of the overland trade that was carried on by these communities consisted of smuggled items. Christopher Champlin sent chests of bohea and Dutch linens by wagon to John Powell of Boston, and a considerable amount of contraband moved from near Sandy Hook to Philadelphia by the same means. Worcester County produce went in carts to Boston or Providence; the latter town, lying strategically athwart the lower post road to New York, became the starting-point of the "great North Road . . . through Plainfield into the internal Parts" of Connecticut, another means by which it managed in time to divert much of Newport's country business. In one week of March 1772, "upwards of Three Hundred Sleds" arrived in Providence with "various Kinds of Country Produce."

Good connecting highways were essential to the further development of inland trade. Extensive road-building and improvements along old highways not only stimulated inland communication but encouraged more travel along the Atlantic seaboard. The engineer De Brahm's description of South Carolina roads provides the reason for Charles Town's growth as a shipping center. "The Province is conveniently traversed with public roads, thirty-three foot wide, well coswayed in low and boggy places, and the rivers are made passable with well-constructed wooden bridges, as well for the conveniency of Travellers from North Carolina to Georgia as also from Charlestown to the interior settlements for the benefit of carriages and coming to market." This genuinely remarkable, though already overcrowded, highway network can be traced with ease on Henry Mouzon's *Accurate Map of North and South Carolina* published in 1775.

The other colonies were not remiss in improving their highway systems. Sometimes it was accomplished by private initiative, as when the Philadelphia Contributionship erected milestones on the two highways from their city to New York and the one to Maryland. In the same year, 1767, the *Pennsylvania Chronicle* called for similar aids to interior travel; the press announced that "they write from New York, that the roads at the Back of that Province, New England and Virginia have been so greatly improved that they have established public caravans and stage coaches, for the convenience of passengers." Communication must have been in the minds of many that year, for an up-and-coming man visited several cities selling *A New pocket Map of Virginia and Maryland, with part of the Jerseys, Pennsylvania, and North Carolina, on 8 sheets, with the Waggon Roads up to Pittsburgh, and the Cross Roads.*

Concern over inland trade impelled the townsmen to pay attention to several projects which, though abortive, marked the beginning of agitation for those "internal improvements" that bulked so large in the next century. Basing his plea on the success of the French, Russians, Dutch, and English in enlarging the spheres of urban merchants by cheap transportation, a New Yorker proposed in 1771 the practicability of making the Mohawk navigable and connecting it with Lakes Oneida and Ontario (the Erie Canal!) and also the construction of a route from the Hudson to Lake Champlain with the view to extending the interior communications of his city. At this time, too, James Cook advocated "opening a communication from Santee to Cooper river, by a navigable cut" twelve miles long to ease the transportation of lumber from the 112 mill seats on the Santee to Charles Town; in 1773 Henry Mouzon published a map of the project, which in 1792 became the Santee Canal. The citizens were fully informed about the Duke of Bridgewater's great system of canals between Manchester and Liverpool; they lacked only the capital to undertake them in America.

It took the successful competition of another community to bring the necessity for internal improvements home to Philadelphia leaders. The rise of Baltimore from the mere village of 200 people pictured in John Moale's painting of 1752 to 5,934 in 1776, when it ranked ninth among colonial cities, set an American record for urban growth. Quaker City merchants had petitioned for improved inland navigation in 1762, but not until 1768 did they seem to apprehend fully the inroads that Baltimore traders had made in their western trade by diverting it down the Susquehanna to their Chesapeake port. Once thoroughly alarmed, the Pennsylvania mercantile gentry added their voices to those of the western inhabitants, who for a decade had been asking in vain for better transportation. Proposals were made to join the Susquehanna and the Schuylkill by a canal, or to dig one between Delaware and Chesapeake bays to tap the back-country traffic before it reached Baltimore. "We expect shortly to be canal mad," Samuel Rhoads wrote to Franklin in 1771; but before any actual work could be started, hostilities broke out, and when peace came again, Baltimore was too well entrenched to be ousted from the interior trade.

V

"With regard to American manufactures," James Bowdoin advised a member of Parliament in 1769, "tho' the progress of them has not been so rapid as the warm sons of liberty has represented on the one hand, nor so small and diminutive as ministerial sycophants have represented on the other, I can assure you it is considerable and growing, and all you can do on your side of the water, except the restoring things to their old course, will but increase it."

To many thoughtful citizens the only solution to the problems of depression, currency shortage, and imperial restrictions seemed to be the cutting down of consumption of imported goods, accomplishable by promoting frugality among all classes and resorting to manufacture of those articles needed for a simple living. In December 1764 a group of New Yorkers founded a Society for the Promotion of Arts, Agriculture, and Œconomy, in imitation of the London Society of Arts. The plan was that this nonpartisan body should award premiums, disseminate useful knowledge by pamphlets, and encourage the formation of like bodies throughout the colonies. At Boston the old Manufactory House took a new lease on life and opened its spinning school again, and the best pupils received premiums. With the repeal of the Stamp Act, however, the province closed the school and put the building up for sale for £1,500. Philadelphia tried a "Linen Manufactory" in 1764, and eleven years later formed a joint-stock "co-partnership" known as the United Company of Philadelphia for Promoting American Manufactures, with Benjamin Rush as president. The Reverend Ezra Stiles and Printer Solomon Southwick pushed the spinning of Rhode Island wool and silk culture with more eagerness than success. Like efforts were made in 1771 when the Society for Encouraging Manufactures set a subscription on foot to bring industries to Charles Town. The role of these undertakings and the press was to provide a stimulus and popularize a movement already well rooted and hardy, and though none of them succeeded financially and interest lagged as soon as ministerial pressure on colonial trade relaxed with the repeal of the Stamp Act and the Townshend duties, there can be no doubt that industries established before 1760 grew more rapidly and by 1775 had become much stronger as a result of the non-importation agitation.

Philadelphia was a prime example of a city that had large enterprises requiring substantial outlays of invested capital, which was what Englishmen meant by manufactures rather than the small handicrafts that produced articles used in daily living. Flour-milling, now thoroughly commercialized, concentrated at places where water power existed, such as along the Wissahickon near Roxborough and the Brandywine near Wilmington. Thomas Gilpin, George Clymer, Thomas Fitzsimons, and the Whartons had interests in these "merchant mills," superintended coopers, bolters, and bakers who prepared flour and bread for shipping, assembled cargoes at their wharves, and dispatched them to distant markets. Also important, though nowhere nearly as large, was the colonial iron industry, which in 1775 produced 30,000 tons, or about one seventh of the world's iron. The valleys of the Schuylkill and Delaware were the heart of the manufacture, for which the Zanes, Allens, Turners, Mc-Calls, Plumsteads, Cliffords, and Colemans of the metropolis furnished much of the capital. Whitehead Humphreys erected a "Steel Furnace" on Seventh Street in 1767, the first in the province, at which he made good edged tools. Two years later Jonathan Zane joined him in the production of "This Country Steel," and in 1771 Humphreys advertised a screw-cutting machine. At Philadelphia yards many a ship was framed, sheathed, launched, and rigged, and twenty vessels of all sizes could be seen on the stocks at one time; Joshua Humphreys, David Thomson, and fellow shipwrights at Kensington and Southwark built more "great ships" than any other city, the number in 1774 being 25 out of 119 of all tonnages.

Industries of moderate size attracted less attention, but they employed many workmen and contributed decisively to the Quaker City's welfare. Robert Proud noted the opening of "many new sugar houses" in the sixties: "large quantities of loaf sugar are made to great perfection; which before was all imported." The city kept fourteen rum distilleries running in 1772, and these and the breweries produced beverages for export as well as for home consumption. Prior to 1774 a successful glassworks, John Elliott & Company, a "China Works," a potter turning out "Philadelphia Earthenware," and two establishments making "paper Hangings" had opened. And of course such industries as papermaking, coopering, and tanning, which supplied hundreds of leatherworkers, flourished and gave work to many men. All this industrial activity escaped most observers, who, like "Anglus Americanus," thought that "Philadelphia is by no means the most proper place for such purpose; our hands are sufficiently busied in maritime and other employments, wood and provisions are dear, rents high, and the methods of living, if not luxurious, are at least elegant." Manufactures prosper, he contended, in small rural towns where labor is cheap.

Governor Francis Bernard of Massachusetts told Lord Shelburne in 1768 that Pennsylvania, "which advances much faster in arts than other Colonies," might compete with England, but any threat from New England "is the idlest bully that ever was attempted to be imposed upon sensible people." Insisting that they had neither the materials nor the "inclination for such works," he was right in the main; yet he overlooked certain important industrial developments. From the Boston shipyards of Benjamin Hallowell, Thomas Gray, and others, many a ship slid into the water, and a number of whaleboat-builders managed to keep busy; collectively they employed a large number of hands, even though their city was losing out to other Massachusetts towns "where they build cheaper" because of lower wages. Rum-distilling was another large industry, at least until the Sugar Act was passed in 1764; in that year the distilleries had imported £100,000 sterling worth of molasses. Although some distillers failed, others, like Thomas Amory, Apthorp & Scollay, Thomas Brinley, Joseph Green, and Arnold Wells, managed to survive and make a profit when the molasses duty was reduced to a penny a gallon; and Peter Johonnot, who became a Tory, had one distillery that paid him nearly £600 a year and a partnership in another bringing in between £700 and £800 annually. In 1771 the city had thirty-six of these establishments. The new revenue laws, according to James Murray, spelled "the ruin of the Sugar Refiners," and have "in course shut up the sugar houses, and ours among the rest." Three or four spermaceti-candle works, an earthenware pottery, using clay from Martha's Vineyard, a "Button Manufactory," whose owner "keeps a Pattern Card," and a paper mill at Milton, all testified to Boston's effort to compete with the nascent industries of the nearby towns of Suffolk, Middlesex, and Essex counties.

The men of Newport displayed great energy and no little courage in their attempt to foster local manufactures. The town had sixteen distilleries in 1761; the Malbones were the leaders, closely followed by the Cranstons, Freebodys, Brentons, Thurstons, and Cookes. Hogsheads of molasses landed at the wharves legally or illegally went in two-wheeled drays to the distilleries to be converted into rum, put up in new casks, and delivered back to the owner for a processing charge of from seven to ten shillings a gallon. The demands of the Newfoundland fisheries, the Massachusetts Bay fishing fleet, the African slave trade, but especially of the colonies to the southward gave the town a profitable industry after 1766, and toward the close of the colonial period it is said that thirty distilleries were operating. Rum placed an "engine in the hands of the merchant" to pay for British imports, as did the construction of 179 topsail vessels between 1769 and 1771, an industry in which the town led all other ports.

In 1769 Hays & Pollock began to manufacture spermaceti candles; "it is a Business that Numbers in this Country have thereby Inhanced, Great Riches." Prospects of large profits had lured many new manufacturers into this industry, thence creating a price problem for head matter, which was always in limited supply. In September 1760 the Browns of Providence and three Newport firms joined to serve notice on Joseph Rotch, who controlled all head matter from Nantucket, the top price that they would pay. On November 5, 1761 the Browns, Richard Cranch & Company, and Edward Langdon & Son of Boston, and the five Newport firms of Napthali Hart, Isaac Stelle, Thomas Robinson, Aaron Lopez, and Collins & Rivera formed the United Company of Spermaceti Chandlers to fix ceiling prices for head matter. Philadelphia manufacturers were later admitted. The agreement of 1763 specified the persons from whom the subscribers would purchase their supplies and allocated

PLATE 11 · *A View of Charles Town, 1771. By Thomas Leitch*

The Cooper River Waterfront from White Point to Gadsden's new development. In the detail (above) several town houses, St. Michael's spire and the Exchange appear.

The Jail Philada.

Malcom del. A f.

PLATE 12 · *Walnut Street Prison, Philadelphia. Robert Smith, architect*

quotas to each company, the Browns receiving twenty per cent as the largest company. Faced with a limited supply of raw material, over the years the chandlers tried to avert a too rapid increase in price and to protect their interests by price-fixing and quota agreements, which, as the leading authority has said, provides "a prime example of colonial interdependence in the economic sphere." In spite of charges of bad faith and mutual suspicion, this attempted monopoly never wholly accomplished its purpose, though the members believed that it saved the candle business from disaster.

"The people of New York seem, to me, to be too infatuated with a foreign trade, ever to make any great progress in manufactures," a Londoner advised the Society for Promoting Arts, Agriculture and Œconomy when it revived at the time of the Townshend Acts. A few of the Knickerbockers, however, did make some progress with local industries. In defiance of the law, hatmaking became a "very considerable" industry, frightening British manufacturers into procuring orders in 1767 for the customs officers in the West Indies "to observe and detect" illegal imports of hats from Manhattan, Newport, Philadelphia, and Boston, because of the "great Quantities being sent from those colonies of the fine Beaver Kind, to the great Prejudice of the Beaver Hat Trade at Home." Several new shipyards opened, from one of which in 1775 was launched the *Maria Wilhelmina,* eight hundred tons, the largest ever to enter Charles Town harbor. Beginnings were also made in the manufacture of wallpaper, ordinary paper, spermaceti candles, and pottery. Capitalizing on large-scale smuggling, twelve of the city's seventeen distilleries operated "constantly" to produce around 540,000 gallons of rum in 1768. Manhattan also brewed quantities of beer for home consumption and for export, and its numerous large sugarhouses became famous. The foundry craft took its start with the excellent ironware—stoves, boilers, iron plate, kettles, pots, pans—turned out at the "New York Air Furnace" under the direction of Peter T. Curtenius and his partners, Sharpe & Lyle. When the fight for freedom started in 1775, Colonel Alexander McDougall and Curtenius contracted for the making of bayonets and muskets.

Reporting to Lord Hillsborough in 1768, Governor Bull listed only three ropewalks and two sugarhouses as the industries of Charles Town, discreetly omitting the tanning business that produced the famous Carolina "Sole leather" and a tremendous number of "Negro shoes" each year. Two years later John Bartlam & Company brought over English workers, "proper Hands" for a china and pottery manufacture on Old Church Street. They requested clay samples from the country, probably because they knew Josiah Wedgwood had sent Thomas Griffith to investigate the possibilities of "Cherokee Clay" in North Carolina in 1767. They fired good queen's ware, "equal to any imported," but the enterprise soon failed. When Peter Manigault and associates backed Egan's Brewery, it proved a success and in 1774, according to Timothy, it was able to "retain in this Province near 20,000 pounds a year" that formerly went to Philadelphia and New York. Efforts to foster ship-building failed because of the difficulty of procuring good white work-men, but Rose's Yard still refitted navy and rice ships, while smaller establishments like Emery's, Wright's, and Black's built most of the 130 small craft and schooners of ten to fifteen tons that freighted rice and country produce to town. In the seventies several large ships came off the Charles Town ways, and about twelve Carolina-built vessels plied with the rice fleet. Late in the period, also, two distilleries produced enough rum for Levinius Clarkson to discourage David Van Horne from seeking an outlet there for his Manhattan product. Upon the whole, it must be admitted that the Society for Encouraging Manufactures met with scant success in establishing new industries in the Southern city, where crafts had never prospered.

In Great Britain and on the continent of Europe nearly all manufac-turing was carried on by handicraft methods, and the same held true for the colonies. There was a noteworthy increase in the number of master artisans, journeymen, and apprentices who worked in the es-sential mysteries—trained natives, English workers who crossed to the cities after the peace to try their luck, and the Scots, Irish, and Ger-mans—all of whom added many skills, so that almost every trade fa-miliar in the Old World was introduced to the New; and the succeeding fifteen years saw the start of many additional crafts and a striking proliferation of trades. Philadelphia was the center of the crafts; its tax list for 1774, including Southwark and the Northern Liberties, indicates that of 3,432 property-owners, 934, or thirty per cent, were artisans. This figure represents only heads of families, possessing real estate, servants, slaves, and domestic animals, and does not even indicate the total num-ber of master craftsmen, let alone journeymen and apprentices. It is clear that in the four commercial cities of the North between one third and one half of the gainfully employed—thousands of citizens—were ar-tisans; while down at Charles Town the percentage of white mechanics was considerably less.

As the cities attained economic maturity and more wealth accumu-lated, crafts divided and subdivided even more, permitting a high degree of specialization. No longer did the carpenter perform all the operations in woodworking; in each city he had the assistance of joiners, turners, cabinetmakers, chairmakers, carvers, upholsterers, coachmakers, and half a dozen more artisans. In the busy building trades, housewrights, bricklayers, and stonemasons were joined by roofers, slate roofers, glaziers, "plummers," painters, plasterers, and paperhangers. Likewise in the metal trades the labor of the village blacksmith split into a dozen or more skills—those of the anchor-forger, ornamental ironworker, coppersmith, tinplate worker, whitesmith, brazier, or the brass-turner, like Isaac Fowls of Boston, who could make true billiard balls of brass, silver, iron, ivory, or wood. A German tinman, John Balthus Dasch of Manhattan, produced "the best French Horns, Philadelphia [brass] Buttons and Shoe Buckles." The leather industry in all its branches— tanning, currying, saddlery, harnessmaking, and the fabrication of many leather containers and other items—perhaps came nearer to rivaling the woodworking craft in size. With the non-importation movements, the clothing industry grew and subdivided; local tailors and makers of trimmings acquired more custom. Peter Rushton, Manhattan furrier, made muffs and tippets of the latest mode and "drest" them to keep moths away, as did John Fromberger over at Philadelphia. Caspar Wistar's "Philadelphia Brass Buttons," famous since the twenties and the first continentally advertised product in our history, held their own against New York imitations, and Germantown stockings earned an intercolonial reputation for excellence and durability. The *South Carolina Gazette*'s endorsement of the stockings, gloves, and breeches woven by Peter Giroud of Charles Town indicates the development of clothing trades in the Southern city.

Many artisans practiced mysteries representing extreme types of specialization. Henry Christian Geyer of Boston and John Ballard and John Stevens, Jr., of Newport monopolized stonecutting in New England. Geyer's versatility led him to cut and carve tombstones; Ezra Stiles admired one of "the Composit Order with twisted Pillars." He also fashioned stone jars with covers and cast plaster of Paris busts of Homer, Milton, Prior, and the reigning monarchs of Europe. At Philadelphia, Bartholomew and Lucas Florin made "all sorts of Plaster of Paris figures in full Stature, and Busts; likewise Birds, and many other Sorts of Ornaments fit for ornamenting Garden Walks, Mantle-Pieces, Book-Cases, Beausets, and Chests of Drawers." John Smith manufactured brushes of all sorts, Robert Hewes sold "Glue and Horn-Button moulds" of his own make, Edward Winter drew "electrical wires" for lightning rods, and Abraham Cornish turned out "Cornish's New-England Cod-Fish Hooks" at Boston, where many such esoteric mysteries were practiced. Some New Yorkers hammered out the first American pins. Charles Robertson carved stucco either "in modern or Gothick Taste," and hung doorbells for Charlestonians when business was slack. For Pennsylvania farmers Richard Truman fashioned "Dutch Fans and Screens," and his neighbor Thomas Morgan would make an "Alarm clock" on order.

Although male staymakers, who artfully made "Crooked Women appear strate," usually had the call, female craftsmen were found in the occupation of milliners, mantua-makers, dyers, menders, and scourers. Jane Mecom, Benjamin Franklin's sister, was a Boston milliner in 1768. At Philadelphia and Charles Town the last dressing, laying out of the dead, and attendance at funerals were largely a woman's business. Blanch White, New York upholsterer, seems to have worked out a familiar combination of furniture-making and undertaking: "Funerals furnished with all Things necessary and proper Attendance as in England." Gentlemen and ladies alike preferred male hairdressers and peruke-makers, particularly if they paraded foreign training, as did Peter Lyons, who advertised in the *South Carolina Gazette* as "Hair Cutter and Peruke-Maker" from Paris.

According to Peletiah Webster of Philadelphia, who made a visit to Charles Town in 1767, it was far behind the Northern cities in craft development: "They have very few mechanic arts of any sort, and [a] very great quantity of mechanic utensils are imported from England and the Northern Colonies." Because of the ruinous competition from Negroes and the rage for things imported, artisans found it most difficult to support themselves by their crafts alone. When an occasional Northern artisan tried to establish himself in the Southern city, he more often than not returned to his earlier location: John Bull, stonecutter, and Benjamin King, instrument-maker, practiced their crafts there for a brief period before returning to Newport; and many who came from England, finding the atmosphere of Charles Town uncongenial, moved to Savannah, Maryland, or Philadelphia. Furthermore, when a master craftsman like Thomas Elfe managed to make a small fortune at cabinetmaking, he quickly turned planter and moneylender, or retired, like John Rose the shipbuilder.

In contrast to the Southern city stood the Northern ports, which steadily developed into manufacturing as well as commercial centers, offering a hearty welcome to the skilled craftsman. Moreover, these cities contributed much of the capital and some of the management for inland industries, which blossomed concurrently in answer to the demands of a market not more than half supplied by imported goods. General Thomas Gage showed that he understood what was taking place in America when he warned Lord Barrington in 1772 that it would "be for our interest to Keep the Settlers within reach of the Sea Coast as long as we can; and to cramp their Trade as far as it can be done prudentially. Cities flourish and increase by extensive Trade, Artisans and Mechanicks of all sorts are drawn thither, who Teach all sorts of Handicraft work before unknown in the Country, and they soon come to make for themselves what they used to import. I have seen this Increase."

In every city the citizens and countrymen thronged the streets making purchases in the shops, some of which were large and impressive places, and others just a room in the dwelling house of the shopkeeper. Nearly every street had its retail establishments, for more and more the merchants dealt less and less by "small measure," with a consequent increase in emporiums maintained by artisans who sold imported articles in their line in addition to goods they had made up and bespoke items. The largest and richest variety of offerings naturally could be found in the centers of the towns—Hanover Square at New York, Market Street at Philadelphia, Cornhill or King streets in Boston, along Thames in Newport, or on the Bay in Charles Town. But then there were some shops on the outskirts, like the one John Greaton opened on Boston Neck because it was "properly situated and provided for a Trade with the Country people."

When a New York Grand Jury condemned "divers Incroachments" of shop windows on the streets, an annoyed citizen explained that "It is necessary the Public should be informed that the several Windows mentioned . . . are Glass Windows, such as are commonly used in large Towns and Cities by Milleners, Stationers, Watch-Makers, &c in order to expose their Merchandise for Sale, to the View of Passengers, passing and repassing the Streets." As a matter of fact, he continued, New York had more than two hundred of these and it was also covered with sign-posts descriptive of the proprietor's employment. Elizabeth Drinker's diary reveals that shopping was a favorite pastime of Philadelphia Quakeresses, and on a trip to New York she and her husband spent many mornings in what might be called comparative shopping. Old Edward Shippen of Lancaster kept lists of things for Ned Burd or his granddaughter, Peggy Shippen, to buy for him when they found them on their shopping tours; in 1774 his son wrote from Philadelphia: "Peggy has searched every Shop in town for a Blue and white China Coffee Pot, but no such thing is to be had, or indeed any other sort that can be called handsome." Sometimes the customers shopped for gossip as much as for service or merchandise. "A Barber's Shop is the Fountain Head of Politics," a cynical Newporter insisted, "for the most grand Disputations upon the Conduct of our Superiors are most judiciously held, and the most learned Arguments most nobly supported, whilst the Towles, Napkins, Basons, Soap, Combs, Powder, Razors, Razor-Strops, and Blocks are busily employed in the respective Duties of their Office."

Merchandise, other than the articles produced and sold by artisans in their own establishments, was procured by shopkeepers from the merchants, ordinarily on a year's credit, for few retailers had ready cash and it took them some time to move their stocks; and they too had to sell on credit. Dorcas Earle, a Newport Quakeress, told Christopher Champlin that she sold only for cash and never wanted to ask for credit herself, but goods were selling slowly and she needed a little time to pay. Actually the shopkeepers suffered more than the larger traders during the depression, and even as late as 1773 William Barrell wrote of the many "daily accounts of heavy failures among the Shopkeepers" of Philadelphia, mentioning that a committee of "seventy principal Importers" had formed to work out some scheme to revive retail trade. The situation was still more acute in the less prosperous communities; retailers found themselves being squeezed between delinquent customers and demanding merchants with the debtors' prison just around the corner.

During this period the number of shops with a general stock like country stores declined, and retailers limited themselves to a few specialized lines. At Boston, hardware dealers carried little else; the stock of Harbottle Dorr, for example, ranged from nails to elaborate tools; and Thomas Crafts, Jr., narrowed his goods to paints, oils and varnishes, brushes, and glass, as did Benjamin Hawes of Charles Town; at New York Richard Sause went in exclusively for cutlery. More shops carried dry goods and clothes than anything else, and even within this category some of them specialized: John Milligan had a "Woman's Shoe Store" on Beaver Street, New York; Nathaniel Abraham of Boston carried women and children's clothes only; and Charles Town had one selling Germantown stockings. There were exceptions, of course, such as "the Universal Store" in Hanover Square, New York, where Gerardus Duyckinck, commencing with drugs and medicines, added item after item until he approached the assortment of a present-day drugstore; and Joshua Blanchard's Dock Square establishment at Boston initiated a trend anticipating the modern cut-rate department store.

The variety of the specialty shops testified to the sophisticated buying habits of the townfolk. Richard Carpenter opened "the Perfume Shop" for Boston gentlemen and ladies, and James McCall did the same at Charles Town, with a side line of "Teeth brushes with spunges, tooth picks with cases, scented pomatum, plain, violet, musk, civet, and superfine Poland hair powder." Boston had its "Irish Linnen" shop; Philadelphia had Peter Thompson's china emporium on Race Street, and Bernard & Jugiez's "Looking Glass Store" on Walnut Street, which had the largest display of glasses, sconces, girandoles, and plaster busts in America and ran advertisements in Charles Town papers. At Richard Wistar's button shop, window glass and "electerising globes and tubes," made in the family's New Jersey glassworks, went on sale in 1769. A year later Henry William "Baron" Stiegel of Manheim arranged for Brooks & Sharpe to be his Philadelphia agents and in 1771 opened a factory sales branch in New York for his American flint glass.

The public auction, where many shopkeepers frequently acquired their stocks, continued as a method of distributing goods, and auctioneers spawned at such a rate and "the Multiplicity of publick Sales" became so "injurious to the regular Trader" that many of the latter had to adopt the practice. Fifteen or more mercantile houses at Manhattan conducted auctions on the side: John Watts marketed three hundred chests of sugar in that fashion in 1763, and in 1765 wrote that wines "were never a greater Drug than at present" and were selling almost every day at auctions for low prices. No one denied the propriety of the vendue as a means of disposing of an estate or giving the straitened trader relief: a gentlewoman of Philadelphia reported from New York in 1772 that "many failures are expected here; the city is overstocked with goods that in many shops you may buy cheaper than in London, and the needy Trader is constantly obliged for the sake of ready cash to send his goods (often with the bales unopened) to vendue, where they sometimes sell under the prime cost, which is productive of universal bad consequences." But the merchants and retailers who were being undersold were both irate and despairing. This state of affairs was not confined to Philadelphia; a New York merchant claimed that the "merchants here can neither sell at private sale or get in Money as 'tis a great temptation to the Country to lay out the Money due at these Auctions." And Samuel Eliot tried to console William Barrell by pointing out that Boston offered no improvement over Philadelphia.

The abuses attendant upon auction sales gave rise to regulation: English manufacturers sometimes made up goods of second quality that looked like first grade; vendue masters liked to hold sales at night, when candlelight made close inspection of goods difficult; and primarily because a few rather unscrupulous vendue masters resorted to tactics that worked great hardship on hundreds of fair traders. Conditions at Boston did not reach an acute stage until 1772. One disadvantage to the town was that seven auctioneers sold goods for New Hampshire and southern New England people, who took the cash home with them. In January 1773 the General Court limited the number of vendue masters to four, but a protest went up from those rejected and the court allowed the Selectmen to license six more until June. Royal disallowance of this law, because licensing was the prerogative of the Governor, gave the merchants another cause for resentment. The New York Assembly forbade auction sales after sunset. Newspaper agitation at Philadelphia encouraged the merchants and traders to concert to overthrow the auction system by an agreement of 1770 not to buy any merchandise at vendue for less than five pounds, woolen goods not in the bolt, or ironware in packages of less than a dozen articles, and to boycott auctioneers who did not conform. The poor, regarding this as a monopoly, clamored against the agreement until the outbreak of the war. Charles Town and Newport each had an official vendue master, the position in the latter town becoming a political plum after 1768, but neither community seems to have suffered greatly from the system.

Vending food in its various forms to the inhabitants was a leading activity in the five cities. The marketing facilities for the sale of meats, vegetables, and other perishable goods brought in from the country had been provided by urban authorities and put under reasonably satisfactory regulation long before this period. In Boston, Faneuil Hall burned down in 1761, but by March 14, 1763 had been rebuilt. Newport's Brick Market was ready late in 1772, and the Town Meeting also erected a fish market next door to it and a new Ferry Market in 1774, providing the community with four market buildings and probably the finest facilities in the colonies. To accommodate the large fish trade at Manhattan, the authorities enlarged the Fly Market at the foot of Maiden Lane in 1771 about the time that the Broad Way Market was torn down. The city acquired four new market houses between 1763 and 1771: one of brick at Peck's Slip, the Oswego Market on the east side of Broadway, a large structure on the site of the present Washington Market, and a final one, the Crown. Altogether New York had six markets, well located for the convenience of the inhabitants. Charles Town built a new market adjoining Motte's Wharf on the Bay in 1764 for grain, vegetables, and melons, and, in response to several presentments by the Grand Jury, opened the Fish Market at the foot of Queen Street in 1770.

By common consent the great High Street Market of Philadelphia excelled all others in the profusion of its offerings, but it could not accommodate the increased business; so in 1763 additional covered stalls were erected from Second Street eastward to Front. The next year the Corporation confined the sale of fish to a new structure near Dock Street drawbridge, and, as we have seen, the people of the Northern Liberties got the Callowhill Market House in 1771. In 1773 a westward extension of the High Street Market was ordered, which provided, together with the old stalls, 1,300 feet of sheltered accommodations for people bringing produce to sell. The latest addition so angered the abutters between Third and Fourth streets, who considered it a violation of the charter rights of the people, that they slowed down construction by carrying off lumber and other building materials gathered there for the work.

The grocery stores, of which there were many, supplied the sugar, tea, spices, coffee, flour, rice, and all the dozens of food products called for by the citizens other than the green groceries and perishables found at the market houses. Molasses was used by the common folk for sweetening and was commonly stocked, and tea, though coffee became popular, was sold by more than 212 persons at Boston in 1770, which explains why the tea tax was anathema to all classes everywhere and why some dealers advertised: "No Tea till Duty Free." Small shops, often run by women, served the hand-to-mouth trade of the lower classes; whereas large or well-to-do families, desiring to purchase such articles as meal, chocolate, butter, and cheese in bulk, could do so from merchant

278

grocers like Fletcher of Boston or Brenton of Newport, who could also supply choicer items.

Numerous food service shops existed to assist the cooks of many houses lacking ovens, for only the better dwellings boasted this luxury. To Mathew Potvin's "Cook Shop" New Yorkers took their "prepared victuals" to be roasted or baked just as Newporters did to John Jent, who heated his oven twice a day. At Charles Town, William Patterson had his oven ready at ten in the morning "to bake for dinner whatever may be sent to him," at the "reasonable price of one shilling and three pence per dish." Many bakers made bread and "Hot Roles," and Sarah Sells of New York baked muffins and crumpets twice daily. Those Charlestonians who savored "rich plumb cake iced . . . jellies, sylla-bubs and white custards in glasses . . . tarts and cheese cakes," patronized Eleanor Bolton or Margaret Creswell, both trained in London. Thomas Selby of Boston shipped his "Bride and Christening Cakes" anywhere in New England on receipt of mail orders and did catering of all sorts in town. To judge from the number of tradesmen in the business, Boston and Newport made away daily with huge quantities of gingerbread, and in the late sixties confectioners opened shops in all communities to dispense conserves, nuts, drops, "rock candy," sugar images, sweetmeats, and "Figures suitable for Desart tables, Fountains, Landscapes, Sculpture, and Ovidic Pieces in the Italian Manner," as Frederick Kreitner notified Charlestonians, and what amounted to a delicatessen shop was started in Philadelphia in 1772 by Anthony Vitalli, "late from Italy."

Wines and fancy groceries were easily available to the epicure. The newspapers of all five towns carried innumerable advertisements of wine importers with lists of imported varieties: Paul Gallaudet of New York claimed to have twenty different kinds in stock, and James Purcell of Charles Town had all sorts but especially port and Madeira. The consumption of untold gallons of punch each day necessitated the importation of lemons and limes, and to supply these, shopkeepers known as "Lemmon-Traders" set up and sold them by the dozen, or the hundred. John Crosby of Boston also dispensed orange juice "that some of the best Punch Tasters prefer to any lemmons, at One Dollar per Gallon," and Jacob Abrahams at New York even had "Pine Apples" on occasion. Large quantities of oysters were eaten in the Northern ports; blue points were most highly regarded at New York, where the oyster trade amounted to £12,000 a year. Philadelphians bought quantities of Man-hattan lobsters in kegs. A syndicate fitted out the sloop *Amherst* and another vessel with fore-and-aft watertight bulkheads to carry live fish to the New York markets in 1763, and four years later a Philadelphian with a "Smack" similarly equipped sold live fish daily at Wragg's Wharf in Charles Town—an ingenious solution for the days before refrigeration.

One significant aspect of the depression and the money shortage of the sixties was a concurrent rise in the cost of food, especially meal and meats. Whatever the real causes, such as drought and epidemics, city dwellers put the blame for the high cost of living or the dearth of food on the "infamous practice" of forestalling the market by certain traders, and the willingness of countrymen to deal directly with them rather than to bring their produce promptly to market. Throughout the period Boston newspapers condemned the practice; and forestalling hucksters seemed to New Yorkers to create a bad situation, just as they did at Newport, where "Doll Stew Pan" insisted that if forestalling must continue, it should be confined to "poor helpless Women and devastated Widows" instead of "lively able-bodied Men" who have estates. At Charles Town charges of forestalling the market fell on Negro hucksters.

Political or external considerations also figured largely in popular explanations of high food prices. Unemployment among seamen because of the anticipated stagnation of trade before the Stamp Act went into effect, and the consequent scarcity of food after November 1, 1765, aroused great concern at Boston. The following year heavy shipments of provisions to Europe led many New Yorkers to predict a sharp rise in prices, "already too high for the poor of this city." The boatmen who supplied Newport with fish stayed away while H.M.S. *Squirrel* rode at anchor, causing Captain Smith to publish a guarantee that he would not impress them.

The civic authorities of the eighteenth century were well aware of the sufferings of the poor during times of food shortages and high prices and instituted measures to alleviate their distress. Boston's Granary Committee always kept a supply of grain on hand, and from 1769 to 1774 it dispensed 5,060 bushels at around six shillings a bushel. When the Port Act went into effect in 1775 and contributions of food poured in from the other four cities and many country areas, the city had an institution and a grain-keeper available to handle the largest relief problem of the colonial period. With the completion of the Brick Market at Newport in 1772, Newport used space there for a public granary, as had been planned, and its services were soon needed. No grain or flour shortage bothered the cities in the Middle colonies, but Charles Town's poor often went hungry because of the high price of imported Indian corn. In 1766 they had to be aided by emergency importations, and again in 1772. When 25,446 bushels of maize came in during the first quarter of 1774, Peter Timothy hailed the break in price that it brought, for the poor had been paying thirty shillings a bushel "to those whose avarice has no Bounds." In the high cost of food and scarcity of provisions, whatever the economic reasons, popular leaders found a genuine grievance upon which to capitalize.

VI

The merchant class of each colonial town had attained its peak by 1760, though the members did not then suspect the fact. For years they had piloted the colonial economy with skill and daring, in normal trading and war enterprises, to the point where their surplus capital, if wisely handled, would win them handsome returns. A valuation of estates made at Newport in 1761 indicated that the merchants possessed a trading stock of £3,091,636, factorage of £192,668, sums at interest totaling £709,527, and annual rents of £299,189. Since theirs was the least affluent of the five, the other cities must have had much larger amounts in these categories, and it was ardently expected that the readjustment to the old ways of commerce would be a rapid one.

Bright prospects faded quickly as the depression, new revenue laws, lack of circulating medium, and trade restrictions stretched the merchant's credit lines until they broke. Immediately after the peace, they set about devising ways out of the dilemma. At first all of them manfully explored, as we have seen, every legitimate method of procuring returns for their English creditors, and some of the more venturesome resorted to dangerous but lucrative illicit transactions. When conditions grew worse, not a few either wisely or somewhat hysterically withdrew from trade altogether: William Allen, Pennsylvania's richest citizen, sold his commercial and industrial enterprises and placed thousands of pounds in British government annuities and stocks. On a more modest scale Henry Lloyd of Boston took the same precautions, investing in securities and land, though he did not succeed in getting out of business entirely. The Newport Malbones, Evan and Thomas, heavily hit by privateering losses and failing to recover after the war, withdrew to a rural life at Pomfret, Connecticut. Henry Laurens gradually pulled out of the commission business in favor of planting and land speculation. But it was Joseph Barrell of Boston, in 1765, utterly discouraged and admitting that he was "heart sick," who determined upon "flying from this Dying Town to an agreeable Retreat" in Sudbury, to install himself as a mere country storekeeper.

Service under the Crown at a stated salary, payable in sterling, plus the expectation of a far larger income from fees, wooed some of the conservative merchants away from trade. Moreover, for many in this age, a place in the King's employ meant a step upward in status, because the chosen places in society frequently fell to royal officials. For these reasons the English-bred Harrisons closed out their Newport business, availed themselves of influence at home, and became port collectors in the American revenue service, Joseph at Boston (to his ultimate sorrow) and Peter at New Haven. Many scions of the mercantile gentry found legal and medical careers more to their liking than those offered at the countinghouse as they witnessed the failure of merchant after merchant.

Having for thirty or more years gradually built up among its members a feeling of intercolonial solidarity through trade, partnerships, constant correspondence, much social intercourse, and frequent intermarriage, the more spirited merchants naturally turned their talents for voluntary association to planning unified action. A Merchant's Club met in Boston at Cordis's Tavern in the fifties, and by April, 1760, the members had organized the Society for Encouraging Trade and Commerce within the Province of Massachusetts Bay. Within a short time their confreres of the other four ports began to concert and form committees to consider matters of common interest. These bodies initiated the well-known non-importation movements by which the Americans hoped to force repeal of legislation deleterious to colonial interests at the time of the Stamp Act and the Townshend duties, and in the long run a continent-wide plan for economic coercion in the Association of 1774. To counterbalance the shortage of imported goods and scarcity of cash, they simultaneously started a campaign for home manufactures and promoted frugality by counsel and example. Up and down the coast in 1770 the newspapers reported the trip of Henry Lloyd from Boston to the Southern colonies: "And it was observed that the Gentleman's whole Apparel and Horse Furniture were of American Manufacture. His Clothes, Linnen, Shoes, Stockings, Boots, Gloves, Hatt, Wigg, and even Wigg Call, were all manufactured and made-up in New-England."

In 1765 the merchants had been of one mind about the kind of protests to be made and the action to be taken; but, after having called the lower orders to their aid in the Stamp Act demonstrations, many shrank from further use of force, especially as the rioting ominously portended a threat to them from below. Timid men and convinced conservatives feared the loss of the hegemony over colonial life their class had so long exercised. Thereafter the merchant class split on the issue of political action and over joining forces with the ambitious middle class. At Boston and Newport, where the Town Meeting provided a forum, this division ran along the same lines that had been drawn in the forties and fifties over the impressment and currency issues.

Actually the mercantile gentry did retain the control—economic, social, political—of their cities and provinces down to 1776, but the composition of the group changed after 1760, and its numbers grew inordinately. Although some of the older well-established gentlemen, whose fortunes had been won in commerce, increasingly invested in personal loans, urban rents, and British securities with a view to living off their incomes, and a few, paying no heed to Parliamentary laws, put money into manufacturing, the sums of surplus capital not put into trade or urban activities were never large nor widely held; the majority of the able and energetic merchants still made the market place their chief concern. Furthermore, shopkeepers moved up into the rank of merchant, at times without sufficient funds to hold on. Captains of successful privateers like John MacPherson and Alexander McDougall and several contractors from England also entered upon merchandising. In consequence wide gaps existed between the old established gentry and the new men with war fortunes, between the great and small traders. In spite of the differences, it was a dynamic class, which, when the fateful decision had to be made, supplied leaders to both sides, though only at New York and to a lesser extent Philadelphia did anywhere near a majority of the merchants side with the King. By 1776, as a group, the merchant aristocracy had passed through a transformation that irrevocably augured the end of its class.

In the meantime the very events and conditions that were causing mutations among the mercantile gentry were also elevating the middle class to a prominence and influence which ultimately led to a thrust for political power, the most portentous development in the urban life of this era. The largest segment of city populations, artisans, shopkeepers, and tradesmen and their families, composed perhaps two thirds of the inhabitants of each Northern community and a little less than half of Charles Town. They were somewhat contemptuously branded "Mechanicks" and "Tradesmen" by the upper class, as though they were somehow really of "the inferior sort"; their best label, considering numbers and influence, is *citizens*.

Upon these citizens of middle rank, the small-business men of the day, the incidence of the depression and dearth of money fell with more weight than upon the merchants, who usually had greater resources to tide them over the crisis. All of the twenty or more trades connected with shipbuilding were periodically idle, and tailors experienced "Cucumber times" because their customers boycotted imported cloth. Many felt the pinch and, like the Philadelphia upholsterer, had to agree to work for a much lower rate than previously because "Times are hard and Money Scarce." Not a few went into debt to pull their trades through: Thomas Elfe, wealthy Charles Town cabinetmaker, held bonds or notes from Samuel Cardy, housewright, Edward Weyman, upholsterer, Teunis Tiebout, a craftsman, and Benjamin Backhouse, innkeeper. Others, unable to meet their obligations, went into bankruptcy or to debtors' prison. One concludes that a depressed state of affairs was almost endemic for these people from 1760 to 1775, and that it sustained a state of tension and discontent, which, combined with their inability to seek redress politically, made them willing listeners to the men who preached about liberty. In 1772 Ezra Stiles assured Mrs. Catharine Macaulay that "American liberty" was not asleep, "except in a few Gazette ebullitions." Few observers "mingle with the common people," or they would realize that those beneath them would soon "draw forth a burst of the public spirit into achievements and revolutions astonishing to the world itself."

Imitating the methods of the merchants when the new trade restrictions injured them, the middle class turned to political activity and used their several craft organizations to canalize their collective feelings. The *Boston Gazette* reported in 1764 that "a very great Number of the respectable Tradesmen of this Town, have come to a Resolution to wear Nothing but Leather for their Working Habits, for the future, and that to be only of the Manufacture of this Government"; shortly thereafter Adam Colson advertised moose-skin jackets "fit for Apprentices," warranted to outwear "at least seven Jackets made of broad Cloth, and will wear handsome to the end." At the time of the Stamp Act, craftsmen worked out an intercolonial correspondence through such peripatetic artisans as Teunis Tiebout from New York, who participated actively in the work of the Sons of Liberty at Charles Town, and through mariners, who had acquaintances up and down the coast. The Carpenters' and Tailors' companies of Philadelphia helped to mobilize sentiment, and of course the printers, being the most influential of the class, not only furthered organization but incited overt action by the pieces they published. The middle class formed their principal audience. In each successive stage of the revolutionary movement, the craftsmen and tradesmen actively joined, producing leaders to voice the wants and aspirations of a class that was daily growing stronger numerically and economically in spite of the parlous state of trade and the many failures of individuals.

In these turbulent days, members of the gentry seldom went to the trouble of distinguishing between the middle and lower classes, but lumping them together in one broad category made little sense. The seamen, the largest segment of the lower class, together with the journeymen, male and female house servants, carters, porters, boatmen, common laborers, and a few free Negroes constituted the free elements; while apprentices, servants under indenture, and slaves composed those of unfree status. Nor did all members of this class necessarily live on a subsistence or even a depressed level. Under normal conditions, when wages were high and labor scarce, a hard-working man could support his wife and family and even lay by a little money for the future. At New York in 1760 Theune Van Dalson, a boatman, left more than £140, and Thomas Montanie, carter, bequeathed three houses and a lot in Pearl Street to his family of thirteen.

Times were never normal in this period, however; unemployment was

the lot of many in the lower class during the postwar depression, just as
it was for the dockside workers and journeymen in trades auxiliary to
shipbuilding. "Our tradesmen begin to grow clamourous for want of
employment," Benjamin Rush advised a New Yorker in 1765. "Our city
is full of sailors who cannot procure berths, and who knows what the
united resentments of these Two numerous people may accomplish."
Complaints in 1769 about out-of-town carpenters, who paid no taxes,
underbidding New Yorkers in construction work evoked no response
from authorities. A reduction of wages for journeymen tailors at Manhattan in 1768 led twenty of them to strike and set up their own "House
of call" at the Fox and Hounds Tavern. And over at Philadelphia, in
1776, a temporary organization of journeymen printers struck and won
an increase in wages. Ordinarily, however, this inferior group could not
accomplish very much; the workman was at the mercy of his employer,
with no recourse and no guarantee against wage cuts or unemployment,
and repeatedly, from every city, came disturbing reports about "the
poor People, many of whom are almost starving for want of Employment." One of the shrewdest and most effective of Samuel Adams's
tactics was to persuade John Hancock to build ships, a wharf, and some
warehouses to provide work for Boston's needy poor; John Adams asserted that one thousand New England families shared in this bounty.

Where the free laborer concerned himself over threats to the standard
of living that set him above his European brothers, the white bond
servant and the Negro slave could do nothing except run away. The
servant's status was temporary, and his well-being depended upon the
kind of master he had. Authorities still bound out bastards and orphans,
particularly at Boston, but most apprentices served under voluntary indentures, the principal feature of these years being a shortening of the
time to be served. This also held true for the indentured servants who
continued to arrive at Philadelphia and Charles Town in large numbers.
As domestics they seldom gave satisfaction: "You can have no idea of
the plague we have with servants on this side of the water," complained
Alexander Macraby from Philadelphia to Sir Philip Francis in 1769.
"If you bring over a good one he is spoilt in a month. Those born in the
country are indolent and extravagant. The imported Dutch are to the
last degree ignorant and awkward. The Irish . . . are generally thieves,
and particularly drunkards; and the negroes stupid and sulky, and stink
damnably." The fact was that persons in bondage loathed their status
as they watched freemen moving upward in society; and yet far fewer
ran away from their city masters than in the countryside.

Slaves, who performed much of the heavy and menial labor, made up
half of the population at Charles Town, twenty per cent at Newport, and
at New York about fourteen per cent. Many served as domestics or as
gentlemen's waiting men in all towns except Philadelphia, and not a few

worked at crafts. Newport had Negro sailors, coopers, barbers, painters, and gardeners who performed excellently in their trades. The skilled slave artisans of Charles Town not only worked in their masters' shops, but also hired out by the day, week, or job, offering a crippling competition to white craftsmen, who frequently complained that they faced ruin. Huckstering, hawking, carting, porterage, fishing, and a host of activities conducted by white men in other cities belonged exclusively to the Negroes. Their labor, being forced, not unnaturally often fell short of that of free men and goes far to explain why Charles Town lacked the civic drive so evident in Northern seaports. The Grand Jury recognized this in 1773 when it presented the slaves as "a great Means of preventing Industry amongst the white Inhabitants."

VII

"The chief object here is commerce, which, you know, when pursued closely, sinks the man into a machine," remarked Dr. Benjamin Rush as he surveyed the colonial scene. The very existence of trade barriers and administrative regulations, plus hard times that cut down profits and curtailed credit, drove the merchants to greater efforts and gave impetus to services that would help to eliminate risks and speed up business transactions. The mere size of the cities made it difficult for sellers to find buyers; the extension of trading areas to foreign lands as well as the hinterlands of the towns increased the complexity of the economy. The trader had truly become a cog in commercial transactions; he could not go it alone.

Many of these aids to commerce had appeared earlier, as we have seen, but they now became commonplace. Great merchants took on from one to four apprentices each to copy their letters; translators handled their Dutch, French, Spanish, and Portuguese correspondence; while both smaller traders and retailers resorted frequently to professional bookkeepers and notaries, who, like Azariah Vaun of Philadelphia, advertised "Posting of Books and all Kinds of Instruments of Writing." The broker, too, became a fixture in merchandising: an enterprising agent informed Boston merchants "inclining to send Goods out of Town for Sale" that he would "Vend largely into good Hands, and for good Pay." At his "Information Office," Benjamin Leigh of Boston undertook, for a commission, to arrange for the buying and selling of goods, ships, and real estate, renting of houses, writing of insurance, or lending of money. John Turner of Newport had for sale at one time a house, consignments of rice, indigo, rum, and tea, a Guinea slaver for sale or exchange, two Negro women, and was seeking freights for

Kingston, Jamaica. "The Philadelphia Office of Intelligence" and several brokers filled all needs of the Quaker City; and at Manhattan the functions of auctioneer and broker were combined until 1774 when "Messrs. Pulman & Co." opened the "Universal Register and Intelligence Office" to supply "Servants of every denomination and with unexceptionable Characters without the least trouble," and William Tongue started a "Merchant Broker's Office." The presence at Charles Town of so many factors who executed most of the commissions planters might have given to brokers forestalled the development of this urban service until about 1772, when three such offices opened.

The marine-insurance business, which spread with the promise of high premiums during the war, blossomed after 1763 with the formation of many new firms. The six insurance brokers of Philadelphia sold marine protection, making their profits from commissions for securing underwriters among the one hundred merchants willing to risk funds in this business. John Kidd and William Bradford opened an office in the latter's London Coffee House in 1762, in which year they insured 204 vessels besides cargoes and parcels of freight. Quaker City brokers wrote policies for merchants from Massachusetts to Maryland, often competing with New York offices, whose underwriters appear to have been less conservative in taking risks, for in 1766 they entered into an agreement about the terms and rates for underwriting at Philadelphia. Ezekiel Price, Nathaniel Barber, and Joseph Turrell wrote policies at their offices for Boston and the smaller New England cities. Although Newporters had Thomas Wickham in their own town, Price of Boston advertised in the *Newport Mercury* and two New York firms also solicited business. Most vessels in the rice fleet were insured from London, but in 1768 John Benfield opened a marine-insurance office at Charles Town.

Another device for gathering commercial information, promoting trade, ensuring the quality of local products, and shoring up sagging business ethics was the trade organization. The Society for Encouraging Trade and Commerce founded at Boston in 1760 led the way, closely followed by the New York Society for the Promotion of Arts in 1764. But not until the formation of a Chamber of Commerce by twenty Manhattan merchants in 1768 did this kind of institution attain maturity. This body arranged arbitration of trade disputes, determined the rates at which various colonial currencies would pass, broke up a "Combination" of millers, bolters, bakers, and flour merchants by importing Philadelphia flour to force down the price, endeavored to raise the standard of local flour to that of Pennsylvania, and set fair commission fees for most business transactions. The Chamber received its charter of incorporation in 1770. In Charles Town, at a meeting held on December 11, 1773, a group of merchants founded the second Chamber of Commerce. Some who did not approve of the scheme suggested establishing a "Chamber (or House) of Counterpoise." The new organization, consisting chiefly of native merchants, proceeded to follow the New York pattern, and in *Wells' Register and Almanack* for 1775 published its list of acceptable charges on protested bills of exchange.

The availability of reasonably large sums of capital in some quarters and the steady demand for funds to invest in new enterprises suggested the need for banking. Robert Morris and a group of Philadelphians laid plans for a bank in 1763 and began negotiations for European financial assistance, but their scheme met with opposition from influential conservatives fearful of inflation from an issue of bank notes. Only the outbreak of hostilities prevented the enterprise from succeeding, however. Gentlemen or merchants with money to lend continued to put much of it out personally or through the brokers who made the handling of money a central feature of their activities. Jacob Valk of Charles Town promised to execute all loans with due "Caution, Secrecy, and Punctuality." The valuation of Boston's estates in 1771 reveals that money at interest amounted to £103,975, while "Factorage, or the Value of Commissions on Merchandize" totaled but £14,859. John Erving had £15,000 out, John Hancock £11,000, Madam Hancock £10,000, James Bowdoin £5,000, William Philips £3,630, and James Pitts, James Otis, and Thomas Amory, £2,000 each. Some of the town's leading physicians also had sufficient practice to enable them to lend at interest between two and three thousand pounds. To some extent this condition prevailed in other cities after 1770, and none of them organized banking facilities either, depending on the brokers to handle such matters if the merchants themselves had no means of placing the loans.

All this business activity gave patronage to the legal profession, and its members, nearly all belonging to good families with some claims to wealth, rose to positions of distinction and political influence. The New York Bar set high standards in an agreement of 1764, designed to prevent "the unrestrained Admission of clerks for the future," and the thirty or more lawyers of the city waxed wealthy at their work and improved themselves with debates on fine legal points at the Moot Club they founded in 1770. Scarcely less eminent and perhaps more able, the Bay Town's lawyers insisted upon high standards also. In 1765 Benjamin Gridley, Samuel Fitch, and John Adams organized the Sodalitas club to study law and oratory, and in 1770 the Suffolk Bar met to form a monthly club, of which Adams was the secretary and drew up rules of the admission of young lawyers to practice. The next year they sought successfully to extend their influence to the entire province by the familiar device of a committee for correspondence. Philadelphia numbered thirty residents of the Inns of Court among its men of law, and thirty of Charles Town's thirty-four practitioners were Templars. Few lawyers anywhere outshone Martin Howard and James Honeyman, Jr., of Newport in learning and courtroom address.

Fortune, prestige, and perhaps political preferment were the goals of the successful city lawyer. Thomas Phepoe crossed from Ireland to Charles Town in 1771, earned at least £900 a year from his practice, and sat in the Assembly for Prince Frederick Parish. When Josiah Quincy, perhaps the ablest young colonial lawyer, discovered that the *Practical Justice of the Peace* was the sole collection of laws available to Carolinians, he exclaimed: "No wonder their lawyers made from £2000 to £3000 sterling a year! The rule of action [is] altogether unknown to the people." Cadwallader Colden was of the opinion that New York lawyers greatly augmented their power by taking the popular side and deprecating that of the Crown. At Philadelphia, where the practice was carefully conducted, Speaker Joseph Galloway made over £2,000 a year and others became as affluent through their practices. The phrase "Philadelphia lawyer" had not yet been coined, but many ordinary people looked with suspicion upon the lawyer with his green bag full of technicalities. Upon refusing a legal training in 1767, James Willing said "he would rather be brought up to a Profession in which there was a Possibility of being honest," and six years later James Allen, Esq., bared his doubt in his diary: "The further I engage in law matters, I find it necessary to put a guard on my Virtue." But as the period ended the urban lawyers, articulate and politically alert, ranked at the very top of the colonial gentry with the most affluent merchants and planters.

VIII

Among the significant developments of the late colonial period, none deserves more attention for its bearing on colonial union than the remarkable extension and improvement of communications; and in this the five cities were the vital focal points. No one familiar with the really startling network of roads, postal services, packet lines, and stages could fail to realize not only that the colonists were aware of what was going on in the Western World through the medium of the printed word, but that many, many citizens had traveled far beyond their local habitats and were actually acquainted with people and places outside their own provinces. The union of the colonies, when they determined to free themselves of British rule, was not a combination of insulated, particularistic settlements joined by nothing but a common hatred of King George. They were people bound together by economic and social experiences that had been made possible by communication.

Water transportation increased tremendously after the introduction of the first packet boats. Newport, particularly because of its location, had regular scheduled sailings for New York, Providence, North Kingston, Swanzey, and Bedford. All of the other cities, too, had passage boats; John Griffith, master, of the "Pensacola Packet," advertised in the *New York Journal* of 1767 that he had "extreme good accommodations for passengers, as well as for carrying slaves" and that he "intended for that trade only" and took good care of both. Numerous boats plied between Charles Town and more southerly ports in Florida, Georgia, and the Islands. Certainly colonial commercial life profited and broadened with the multiplication of such facilities, and with it social and personal relationships.

The postal service had been greatly expanded during these years, for hundreds of pieces of mail and quantities of freight moved overland between one city and another. Not only were there more authorized postal routes and riders, but a great many private services, paid for by subscribers, supplemented the official post, carrying not only letters, newspapers, and parcels but freight and passengers as well. Silent Wilde, the rider from Deerfield to Boston, often traded for his customers and was considered a safe chaperon for young girls traveling to the capital and back. Schedules were adjusted to coincide with the departure of packet boats, and the time taken to carry the mail from one city to another was reduced: letters from Manhattan reached Boston in six days after 1764, whereas formerly they took three weeks. Only in the South was the postal service poor by the standards of the day. In 1770 postriders set off from Charles Town every week, but it took ten weeks to deliver mail to the Northern cities. More success attended the delivery from Charles Town to St. Augustine, but even with private postriders the Southern city did not have as good communications as the other towns.

The colonials were well aware of the usefulness of the postal service. The Newport office, probably the smallest of the five, received annually between 3,000 and 3,350 pieces of mail from 1772 to 1774. This may seem picayunish to a modern, but for that day it was a considerable volume and consisted almost entirely of correspondence from a distance. Perhaps even more mail came in via private individuals and ship captains. When crown agents began opening mail, increasing postal rates, and other "petty tyrannies," the Americans countered by establishing by subscription the "Constitutional Post." Instituted by William Goddard, Baltimore printer, with the strong backing of the New York Sons of Liberty and the colonial committees of correspondence, it was in operation from Portsmouth to Williamsburg by August 11, 1774. The new post put the old one out of business less than a month after the first bloodshed at Lexington. Thus occurred the first institutional change of the American Revolution, one which the Continental Congress completed shortly by assuming control of the Constitutional Post. Indeed, the Colonial Post Office had played a vital role in bringing about American independence; the committees of correspondence could not have succeeded had not communication lanes been so readily available.

IX

Chance and the imperatives of trade contributed to the revolutionary economic and political changes of this period that emanated from the five cities and the secondary communities along the seaboard. During the French Wars seeds of economic change had been planted which germinated and commenced to grow rapidly after 1760; the five cities and their satellites were maturing and were too far advanced to regress to the inferior status to which English rulers might wish to confine them. A capitalistic economy developed continuously in the cities; and when the leaders found their commercial existence threatened by the new policies of the British government, they had to face up to the situation. The merchants, hitherto famous for their solidarity, divided into conservatives and liberals, the timid as opposed to the bold and optimistic. This split came at the very moment that the middle class, now great in numbers, confidence, and collective prosperity, met their first setback in a depression that hurt them severely and stirred up an ominous restlessness, not only concerning the mother country's restrictive attitudes but even more about the gentry who held them in credit bondage and enjoyed all of the privileges in society. It was this great, energetic middle class that listened to the siren call of a liberty it thought by right it ought to possess. Considering thirty-five years of hard times and the frustration caused by what the townsmen regarded as unnatural external and internal restraints on their commercial efforts, it would have been surprising if revolt had not come first in the cities.

CHAPTER 8

Civic Improvements

Ⓘ N WAR OR PEACE, prosperity or depression, each of the five cities always faced a series of formidable urban problems, and the expense and magnitude of the solutions grew as the communities became larger. Long experience resulted in many improvements in preventing and fighting fires, in providing new and better supplies of water, in protecting citizens against criminals, in safeguarding their morals and the public's health, and in ministering to the poor and unfortunate. Conversely, the turbulent state of political and economic affairs throughout the period definitely aggravated certain of these problems: it increased the number of the poor, it fostered a demand for larger and stronger prisons, it condoned slack moral standards, and it encouraged mob violence on an unprecedented scale.

II

Fully aware of the disastrous consequences of a general conflagration, municipal authorities worked persistently on their existing fire defenses, enjoying a large measure of success as they inclined to place more stress on fire prevention than previously, while at the same time acquiring the most efficient fire-fighting equipment the age provided. No "great fire" broke out in these years, but many serious blazes kept the citizens constantly apprehensive. Realizing that the use of combustible materials in building construction created the principal fire hazard, each city government attempted to prevent their use. In 1761 New York ruled that after 1766 only brick or stone buildings could be erected, and required all structures, new and old, to be roofed with slate or tile. Protests pleading the shortage of materials, hardships on workers in the building trades, and the obstructing of the growth of the city held up strict enforcement of this ordinance until after 1774, but it produced a salutary effect on the whole. At Boston a series of bad fires in Bray's bakehouse at the North End led to the licensing of such premises in 1762. Philadelphia and Newport made no additions to their building codes, but the Grand Jury of Charles Town periodically presented non-enforcement of the law of 1740 requiring that buildings be of brick, stone, tile, and slate. "Miso

Pyros" complained in Timothy's *Gazette* that the people "seem quite insensible of the danger they constantly are exposed to from FIRE, else surely more care would be taken to prevent it." A dreadful fire of 1771 next to the Exchange with losses amounting to £7,000 sterling would have swept the whole town had not the wind providentially shifted.

Numerous other fire precautions were taken, not only in the cities but in smaller communities. The people of Waltham placed lightning rods on their church steeple in 1770 after reading Professor John Winthrop's piece in a Boston newspaper about their value, and the author informed the inventor that "they are now becoming pretty common among us." Dr. Milligen bragged in 1775 that many of Charles Town's public buildings and some private houses were so equipped. The Southern city was the only community, however, where prohibitions against storing powder, hemp, and any inflammable materials were not carefully enforced. As in the previous period, chimney blazes caused many fires. Some flues were so small that the sweeps could not get in to clean them; usually, however, plain neglect was the fault, as the overworked Fire Masters of Charles Town stated when they recommended replacing Negro slaves with white chimney-sweeps. The act of 1772 gave Philadelphia the best chimney regulations; all sweeps were licensed and then penalized if a fire occurred in a chimney within one month of its cleaning. Dissatisfied with the results of private attempts to solve this problem, the Boston Town Meeting considered a proposal of 1771 to levy a tax for the support of a public master and six sweepers, directed by the Selectmen, who would clean 21,600 "funnels" a year at a saving to the people of £800. At New York Hermann Zedwitz, "a Musician," opened a Chimney Office for subscribers, whose flues would be cleaned once every six weeks. Estimating that a master and fifteen sweeps could clean the city's chimneys ten times a year for £1,050, Zedwitz aimed to make a profit of £1,250, out of which £250 would pay for repair of the fire engines, and the remainder would go to a new hospital.

City governments expended almost lavish sums for ladders, buckets, and fire engines; when the movement for home manufactures reached its height, equipment made in the larger cities took precedence over the costly Newsham & Ragg or Nuttal engines from London. David Wheeler and John Green presented one of their own make to Boston in 1766, and soon after contracted to construct one like the Charlestown, Massachusetts, engine, which some thought the finest in the colonies. Jotham Horton and Adino Paddock also ventured into fire-engine manufacture, and David Hunt of New York claimed that the ones he made were "as cheap and as good as any imported from England." This capable artisan repaired fire-fighting equipment, and sold the Corporation an excellent full-size engine in 1772. Five fire companies presented the Bettering House with a fire engine constructed by Richard Mason, a carpenter of

Philadelphia's Northern Liberties, in 1768. Mason improved on London designs by placing the pumping lever at the end instead of the sides of his machine, gaining twice as much room for the bucket brigade to pour in water; he also made small engines fitted with a fan "to sprinkle water like rain" on gentlemen's gardens. During a fire in 1771, Mason's engines "worked far better, and with greater effect, than any of those imported from London." The town of Newport purchased "a Machine to stand on to put out fires in Chambers" invented by Samuel Greene about this time.

When it came to putting out fires, those cities having regular engine companies got the best results. Boston increased its Firewards from twelve to sixteen in 1763, and maintained ten engines, each manned by a captain and a company of thirteen to twenty men. This department earned an excellent record for prompt arrival and competent work at the city's numerous fires. Following the Boston model, Newport supported five engine companies and fifty-six firemen. Each of the six wards at Manhattan had an engine and seven firemen assigned to it in 1761, but within a little more than a year thirty more freeholders were added by the Assembly, and by 1769 the New York force totaled one hundred. In addition, nineteen men exercised the new engine located at St. George's Square in 1772. The system for handling Charles Town's engines instituted before 1760 proved satisfactory to the critical press, but nevertheless many Carolinians worried about the weakness of their capital's fire defenses and called frequently upon the Assembly to invest the Fire Masters with more authority.

The Philadelphia Corporation kept up its four engines throughout the period, but, as before, the citizens trusted more to private organizations to protect them against fire. The ten fire companies of 1760 nearly doubled by 1765 with the founding of the Star, King George III, Neptune, Fame, Queen Charlotte, Sun, Crown and Beaver, and Amicable societies. Other cities also formed private fire companies with the express view of protecting property during fires. The old Fire Society of Boston was joined by the Anti-Stamp Fire Society in 1765, the Free-American in 1767, and possibly one or two more "Fire Clubs" in addition to the one across the river at Charlestown. Newport's Fire Society continued to flourish, as did the Hand-in-Hand established at New York about 1752; this last became unusually active in the late sixties. Pilfering at fires, the Charlestonians thought, would be eliminated only by setting up by law a fire company "with a handsome gratuity for their services." When the South Carolina Assembly neglected to act, a group of citizens formed a private society in 1766; yet the Grand Jury and the press hammered away fruitlessly on the need for a paid public organization to mount guard at fires.

An interesting development occurred in 1764 when the Hand-in-

Hand, Neptune, Fame, and Queen Charlotte companies of Philadelphia joined to elect a common president and board of managers, though each retained its identity as an independent organization; in keeping with the drift of politics, further integration of the activities of the city's fire companies continued down to 1776. Composed of both gentlemen and prominent craftsmen, they performed yeoman service in putting out blazes, and their organizations also served as potent political engines for stirring up fires of resentment and promoting action against British policy. When the Stamp Act went into effect, the Heart and Hand Fire Company expelled John Hughes, the Philadelphia stamp agent. "Under the deepest Impressions of Concern for their injured Country, and of righteous Indignation at its Oppressors," the Anti-Stamp Fire Society at Boston voted that in case the Stamp Office took fire, and if no other buildings were in danger, "they would not assist in extinguishing it." The Fellowship, Hibernia, Crown and Beaver, and Sun took a stand against eating lamb in order to encourage the growth of wool for home manufactures until the Stamp Act was repealed, and in 1769–70 the latter two again took such action against the Townshend Acts. The Tory printer and "Informer" John Mein was expelled by the Free-American Fire Company of Boston in 1768. The fire societies turned out to be ideal "cells" of sedition as well as useful civic bodies. And "where is New York?" demanded William Weyman's newspaper as it printed this news.

Mindful of possible fire losses and of the ancient Friendly Society of 1735, and further motivated by the success of the Philadelphia Contributionship, certain Charlestonians attempted to set up a mutual fire-insurance company when they called a meeting at Dillon's Tavern on October 16, 1765 of "all former subscribers to the Friendly Society" and others interested. It is not known whether this project succeeded or not. At Philadelphia in 1768 the Proprietaries granted a charter to the Contributionship, and at Boston, Ezekiel Price, the marine-insurance broker, announced that he would underwrite "Policies for assuring houses and other buildings from loss or damage by Fire."

The building up of each city necessitated provisions for a good supply of water for the inhabitants of new districts. For Newport and Boston this was not a serious matter, except in zero weather when pumps froze; the press suggested that householders pump a tub full of water before retiring, in order to raise warmer water into the exposed part of the pump. Many houses, of course, had pumps in the cellars. The water in Charles Town's city wells was thought to be brackish and unwholesome by Dr. Lionel Chalmers, who also observed that it was primarily the women who drank water; the men consumed punch. Egan & Calvert framed in the Workhouse well in 1766 and allowed people to pump all of its fine water they needed for ten shillings a quarter, and later Egan's Brewery maintained a well sufficient to supply excellent drinking water to the whole city "at the usual price." Additional wells for fire purposes were requested by the Grand Jury regularly, with the usual negative response from the Assembly. During a drought in 1773, there was much discussion about the shortage of wells and public pumps in the streets in event of fire, but the most the Assembly would do was to pay Bernard Beckman for repairing existing pumps and John Stevenson, limner, for painting them.

Philadelphia luxuriated in an ample and satisfactory supply of water. The Wardens sought to keep up with the expansion of the city, sinking new pumps every year, but there were those who objected to all citizens being taxed for this purpose when "not half receive any benefits," over-looking, of course, the fire protection thus afforded. A controversy arose in 1771 over the cost of the pumps set up by the Wardens, and the respective merits of public and private installations. From this rather heated exchange it appears that on sixty-three "well built on" blocks north and south, forty-three east and west, and twenty-eight lanes and alleys, there were three or four pumps to a block, or 498 in all, of which 120 were publicly owned. Many Philadelphians felt that about 378 new pumps ought to be erected, and the Assembly, responding to public opinion, ordered them and enabled the city to buy up private ones or to repair such pumps at the charge of the owners who failed to maintain them properly after due notice.

The Mayor and Common Council made every effort to improve the water supply of New York. They placed the "Tea-Water Men" who sold water carted from outside of town under regulation in 1761; from time to time they ordered new wells sunk and kept public pumps in good re-pair. In 1774 Christopher Colles, an English engineer recently come from Philadelphia, persuaded the Corporation to accept his plans for a public waterworks. "According to this Design, the Water will be con-veyed through every Street and Lane in this City, with a perpendicular Conduit Pipe at every Hundred yards, at which Water may be drawn at any Time of the Day or Night, and in case of Fire, each Conduit Pipe will be so contrived as to communicate with the extinguishing Fire-En-gines." East of Broadway between Pearl and White streets Colles built a walled and covered reservoir holding 20,000 hogsheads of water from which a steam engine, whose cylinder was cast in town by Sharpe & Curtenius, pumped two hundred gallons of water fifty-two feet a minute. The water was to be conveyed from the reservoir in hollow log pipes joined with cast-iron fittings, for which 72,730 feet or thirteen miles of pine logs had been floated down from Albany. This praiseworthy enter-prise, costing the city £3,600, lacked only the pipes when the onset of revolution deprived it of the first great waterworks, though the residents of both Bethlehem and Providence had had running water in 1755 and 1772.

III

Urban methods of ensuring the security of persons and property failed to keep abreast of city growth, for the seaports were rapidly filling up with men and women of all classes and conditions, and the medieval institution of the night watch was unable to cope with tough, hardened characters and the gangs that henceforth infested city streets at night. The watchmen did accomplish what their title implied—they looked for signs of fire or disturbance while the citizens slept, but they were not a police force; and neither did the constables, who superintended the watches, succeed as custodians of the peace in a society as restive as this. With all the authority of the county and province behind him, Stephen Greenleaf, Tory sheriff of Suffolk County, Massachusetts, shook with fear every time he had to deal with one of the darlings of the Boston mob. Apart from the distasteful use of the military for constabulary duty, no colonial official broached a feasible plan for keeping the peace, nor, it may be noted, did anyone in London, Paris, or Rome, either. There is no doubt of the conspicuous failure of the eighteenth-century municipalities to solve the police problem.

Save when invasion threatened, Newport never made elaborate provisions for a watch. As late as 1764 only sixteen inhabitants attended a Town Meeting warned to vote money for the watch, and they declared that unless more came to the next one, "there will be no Watch for the Town the ensuing Winter." Within a year this peaceful community had been so disturbed by "riotous proceedings" that it voted for a military watch for several nights before and after Gunpowder Treason Day, and by 1770 so many disorderly servants and Negroes roamed around at night that additions to the watch became necessary. It was perceived that Newport would never have an adequate watch as long as Collector Jacob Richardson selected poor men for duty in order to give them an opportunity to work out their colony and watch taxes instead of giving them regular pay.

Closely supervised by the Wardens, Philadelphia's paid watch carried out relatively well their orders to apprehend "all night-walkers, malefactors, rogues, vagabonds, and disorderly persons whom they shall find disturbing the public peace." During daylight hours in 1770 twenty-seven constables kept the peace. New York replaced the military guard of the war years with a paid watch in 1762, and on occasions when trouble loomed, Overseer Isaac Stoutenburgh doubled the watch. In 1773 the Corporation placed "Centinal Boxes" around the city for the use of its twenty-four watchmen and the next year provided them with uniforms, "including Bearskins for the two captains." This panoply of the law proved all too ephemeral, for an ominous decision of the Corporation on May 8, 1776 symbolized the end of an era: "Ordered that the present number of Watchmen be reduced to a Capt. and three men after the fifteenth Instant: and that the several publick Lamps be taken down and put in some secure Place."

The inability of the Boston watch to preserve the famed nocturnal security of former times frightened many substantial citizens and put some of the Tory persuasion in the frame of mind to welcome the arrival of British troops in October 1768. The General Court increased the wages of the watch from twenty-four to thirty shillings a month in 1761, authorized the addition of more men to the force, and, because "considerable numbers of dissolute persons have sometimes riotously met and opposed the watch," fixed penalties from forty shillings to five pounds for such offenses. The Selectmen immediately drew up a model set of instructions and added sixteen men to the watch. During the Stamp Act troubles, the difficulty of keeping the peace at night led them to provide ten more for "enabling the Town Watch to make greater Exertions." After the soldiers arrived, tipsy officers often tangled with the watchmen and treated them ill, nor could the watch control the actions of the enlisted men at the guardhouse in the South End. Getting no satisfaction from the soldiers' superiors, the Selectmen set up a new watch house and special watch near the fortifications on the Neck to try to check the nuisance, but things grew worse instead of better. In 1770 the Selectmen requested Governor Thomas Hutchinson to provide a military watch to protect the citizens, who "are still apprehensive of danger from the Soldiers in the Night Season," but the Governor failed to act "as it would be Reported on the other side of the Water that he had raised the Militia to drive the Soldiers out of the Town," and passed the buck by saying that Colonel Jackson of the Boston militia regiment possessed the necessary authority. Whether he was right or wrong in his contention, Hutchinson's action antagonized many people. One wintry night "about twenty regular officers attacked the Watch," nearly inciting a riot, and the Town Meeting had to order twelve more men on night duty. The added pressure of an irresponsible soldiery in an already difficult and costly police situation did much to aggravate popular feeling in all cities against British policy, and as citizens in other colonies read in their newspapers of the troubles at Boston, they feared similar threats to the peace in their own communities.

Charles Town members pushed a bill establishing a civilian watch through the Commons House in 1761, only to have the Council reject it, but when it passed again, the Council acquiesced and the city got its watch. Seven years later the finest guardhouse of any community rose at Broad and Meeting streets at a cost of £5,500. With added population, the Grand Jury commenced presenting the "insufficiency of the

Watch" to protect the town, always calling for an increase in its numbers and "the procuring of men of property and repute" for service. Although John Bremar, captain of the watch, often disguised himself as a sailor and circulated around, checking on sleeping watchmen, whose arms he always quietly took away, he and his lieutenant and ensign were discharged in August 1770 for allowing an effigy to be burned in the city. At this time thirty-six men mounted guard nightly "to prevent disturbances among disorderly negroes, and more disorderly sailors," but the Grand Jury insisted that the watch was ill managed: its members "defeat the good end intended" by "beating and abusing negroes sent on errands by their masters with tickets, and letting others escape that have none, by which irregularities the negroes in general so disregard them, and . . . are not afraid of being out all night." City constables were charged with being men of "mean and low character," easily and frequently bribed; the Governor had most unwisely appointed Richard Barnet, his dog-keeper, to be captain of the watch. Conditions grew worse before they improved: the watchmen neglected Sunday patrols, half of them working at other jobs; constables and watchmen received permits to sell liquor; and the number of men hired seldom proved sufficient. Then early in 1775 Charles Crouch's newspaper began to praise the sudden and remarkable improvement of the watch; robberies ceased and noisy meetings of Negroes in the streets at night no longer troubled the citizens.

Whatever the derelictions of the watchmen, the dangers incident to their work cannot be passed over. One night when Constable John Syms of the Boston South Watch tried to protect a Negro from "a number of young Fellows" who were breaking into his house, they menaced him with drawn swords. In 1768 some villains cut the frame of the guardhouse "so as to Render it useless." In Philadelphia, when Constable Arthur Campbell tried to break up a fight near a bawdyhouse at one o'clock in the morning, several sailors bludgeoned him to death and badly beat several of his watch. On another occasion Michael Hess was stabbed to death by a third person as he wrestled with an unruly drunkard, and Constable Graham of New York also died from wounds received in a fight after having many "hair breadth escapes."

IV

In the wake of the French and Indian War came not a diminution but an increase in crimes of all sorts: counterfeiting, petty thievery, housebreaking, burglaries of every description, highway robbery, rape, assaults, and murder. Worse still, the cities had no police to curb them.

It seemed to many law-abiding persons that the age of violence had arrived when they assessed the grave effects of the postwar period and realized what a large number of unemployed seafarers and women of the lower class had turned criminals, and it was small comfort to them that the situation resembled on a provincial scale that of the great cities of contemporary Britain.

Professional criminals now operated on an intercolonial scale, cleaning out one neighborhood and then moving along to another. The most vicious and far-flung of these undertakings was carried on by a gang with headquarters in the Carolina back country which specialized in stealing horses. "The Villains had their Confederates in ev'ry Colony," reported the Reverend Charles Woodmason. "What Negroes, Horses, and Goods was stollen Southwardly, was carried Northerly, and the Now'd Southward. The Southward shipp'd off at New York and Rhode Island, for the French and Dutch Islands, the Now'd carried to Georgia and Florida, where smuggling Sloops would bargain with the Rogues and buy great Bargains." There is some reason to believe that the "Den of Thieves," consisting of four men and two women, discovered at Boston with quantities of plate and goods in 1769 may have had some connection with this earliest American crime syndicate, which had operated "for a Year or two past, and very extensively." At least, the Massachusetts authorities said that "as their Correspondence is pretty extensive on this Continent, 'tis thought they must bring out their Accomplices. 'Tis reported that when those concern'd with them at Providence, Newport, New York, Philadelphia, etc had got any Booty, they convey'd it to their Correspondents this Way, and likewise these to them, in order to prevent being detected." When the heat was on, the members in New York and Pennsylvania moved up to Boston, where penalities were lighter. Charles Town fortunately escaped this visitation, but its entire population turned out in August 1767 to see the public hanging of two horse-thieves captured in the back country. In this year, too, Newport had its first real passage with a confidence man since the days of the notorious Tom Bell; passing through the Rhode Island city on his way to Boston from a successful tour of New York and Philadelphia, Robert Jamieson deftly fleeced Robert Lillibridge, Jr., while posing as a commissioner sent by Parliament to investigate American conditions.

As a matter of fact, the hitherto Arcadian little city on Rhode Island came in for a series of rude shocks after crime signalized its coming of age with the execution of John Shearman for burglary in 1764; thereafter Newport had no long surcease from criminal activities. Reports of housebreaking and robbing of shops, warehouses, and ships crowded the columns of the *Mercury*. Sacred honor more than lives or fortunes was involved when some "evil minded person or persons" stole the copperplate commemorating the repeal of the Stamp Act from the Newport

Liberty Tree. One of the earliest cases of pleading insanity in extenuation of a crime got John Moore free of charges of highway robbery before the Superior Court in 1767. Southwick of the *Mercury,* knowing that times would not get better, warned his readers in October 1767: "The Public would do well to keep a Look-out at their Shops, Houses &c, as there are at present a Number of loitering Persons, of the Infamous Sort, lurking about Town—some Thieves narrowly made their escape in their Attempt one Morning last Week, being discovered in their Attempt to rob a Store belonging to Mr. Bird." When Henry Sparker, Newport shoemaker, and Philip Dexter from Providence were stabbed and killed in a quarrel with the mate and two midshipmen of H.M.S. *Senegal* in May 1768, the public regarded the affair as more than a mere waterfront brawl and cried out for justice.

Boston likewise lost forever its reputation as a town where property and persons were unusually secure. The period opened with the trial of Dr. Seth Hudson and Joshua How in the Superior Court for counterfeiting. So many burglaries occurred that the newspapers advised the populace to lock all doors and windows securely at night. Gangs of thieves looted shops and warehouses with impunity, and footpads held up people in the streets at night in defiance of the watch and the provincial law of 1761 making highway robbery a felony punishable by death. Bostonians were startled in 1768 by the discovery of a bunch of keys that would open any house, which they were sure belonged to "the Light Fingered Night Gentry, which of late seem to encrease fast upon us." Notwithstanding the many thieves picked up and jailed, said the *Newsletter,* "many little pilfering Fellows nightly patrol the Streets," and some were audacious enough to enter houses in broad daylight. Never had thefts and robberies been so frequent as in August 1772, when this newspaper charged that peddlers were selling stolen goods in the country. Early in September 1773 Levi Ames and Joseph Atwood confessed to membership in a gang of robbers, and after trial they were ordered hanged on October 21. Such speedy justice seized the public's imagination, producing at least nine lachrymose broadsides with lurid woodcuts describing the life, crimes, "the Last Words and Dying Speech of Levi Ames," and his "Exhortation to young and old to be cautious of small crimes, lest they become habitual":

> *Beware Young People, and look at me,*
> *Before it is too late.*

No wonder "many Thousand Spectators attended the Execution," including that elegant merchant John Rowe.

Even more disturbing to serious observers was the rise of violence at Boston. Cases of infanticide and rape occurred with some frequency, and persons no longer felt safe on the streets at night. Several men "dressed like navy officers" assaulted Samuel Mumford, the Newport postrider, on Boston Neck in 1769, knocking him out with a sword hilt; when he recovered and said he was on His Majesty's service, "they immediately went off," but poor Mumford died several months later from the ill effects of the attack. When two "tayloresses," coming "pretty late" across King Street on November 18, 1772, were set upon by a "man of war's man," the press commented: "We should be much obliged to the author of the late Journal of Occurrences for the resumption of his pen on these occasions, which for some months past have been but too frequent among us."

The province of Pennsylvania had a harsher criminal code than any other colony, but crime still flourished. Some truth attached to charges that better enforcement would deter violations of the law, but few persons seemed to have grasped the connection between criminality and poverty. The grim reality faced by many unfortunates following the Last French War created conditions favorable to misdemeanors and violence at Philadelphia: sailors without berths, discharged soldiers, and transported convicts easily purloined the wealth of unsuspecting citizens. In the winter of 1761–2 several women were "wounded in a very barbarous and unheard of manner, as they were going about their Lawfull Occasions along the Streets of the City in the Evenings." Harrowing accounts of holdups on the highways and stories of seaport gangs roaming the streets, along with tales of housebreaking and pilfering, filled the newspapers. Many offenders were detected and brought to justice, and not a few received the death penalty. One point came out clearly: the Mayor's Court, embarrassed by the inadequacy of the Philadelphia prison and the expense of confining malefactors, compounded with them by forgiving them fines they could not pay and shipping them off to other provinces; convicted of larceny in 1765, Elizabeth Griffin agreed to inflict herself on distant Pensacola. The great city of Philadelphia had by this time lost permanently its famed peacefulness and security.

True crime waves also broke over New York, and John Holt, printer, wrote in 1762 that "such various attempts to rob, and so many Robberies actually committed, having of late been very frequent within the Circuits of this City, both Day and Night; it is become hazardous for any Person to walk in the latter." And it continued thus until the end of the colonial era. Taking up goods at shops in the name of other persons grew to such proportions that the Assembly decreed corporal punishment for the crime. Some footpads evidently worked at their profession alternately in New York and Philadelphia with much success, extending their art to highway robbery when they were changing cities; sixteen such criminals were caught and transported from Manhattan in 1765: four footpads, three burglars, one horse-thief, and eight guilty of grand larceny. Pickpockets, many of them women, circulated on market days relieving people of their watches and purses, and in 1771 Mary Daily and Margaret Siggins were hanged for such offenses. Properly suspecting vagrants as prospective criminals, the authorities bestirred themselves in 1773, when a series of shopbreakings reached its height, and allowed constables two shillings for every vagrant apprehended "wandering in and about this City." In 1774 an attack by two footpads on New York's leading politician and turfman, James De Lancey, demonstrated that Manhattan's reputation as the least safe city in the colonies for both property and persons was well deserved.

Charles Town was spared much of the theft and violence that plagued the Northern seaports, in part because it had a smaller seafaring element and because it strictly supervised the slave inhabitants. For a time in 1765 Timothy reported a robbery "almost every night" and the flooding of the city with counterfeit money, but relatively little violence took place. In August 1769, however, a Negro man and woman were burned alive on the Workhouse Green for poisoning three white people; two years later when Anne O'Hara killed "Anne alias Agnes Spalding" on King Street and was convicted of manslaughter, she got off with branding in the hand. No colonial duel excelled in excitement or the celebrity of its principals that in which Dr. John Haly shot and killed Peter De Lancey, deputy postmaster and New York grandee. Dr. Haly later surrendered himself, and Governor Bull granted him an executive pardon. Another wave of burglaries and shoplifting perpetrated by "an infamous and dangerous Set of Villains" broke out in 1773 and 1774, prompting Timothy to instruct his readers "to be as guarded against these Pests of Society—as against the Ravages of Fire."

The moral and economic collapse after the French wars filled urban prisons with debtors, light offenders, and hardened criminals, male and female alike. Overcrowding and hideous conditions resulted, and unless an inmate could fee the jailer, he or she had to go without even firewood or blankets; their suffering in winter was most pitiable. The Reverend Charles Woodmason graphically described Charles Town's prison in 1767: "A Person would be in better Situation in the French Kings Gallies, or the Prisons of Turkey or Barbary, than in this dismal Place—Which is a small House hir'd by the Provost Marshall containing 5 or 6 Rooms, about 12 feet square each and in one of these Rooms have 16 Debtors been crowded. . . . They often have not Room to lye at length, but succeed each other to lye down—One was suffocated by the Heat of the Weather of this Summer—and when a Coffin was sent for the Corps, there was no room to admit it, till some Wretches lay down, and made their wretched Carcasses, a Table to lay the Coffin on. Men and Women are crowded promiscuously—No Necessary Houses to retire too." At Philadelphia in January 1770 thirty-two men and twelve women lay in jail, most of them already sentenced and awaiting punishment. They had no bedding and only one blanket for two people (these having been sent through charity), and, said the report, "Many of them are almost Naked and without Shirts." For petty larceny Peter Kearns had been incarcerated for four years and John Harrison for three; although their fines had long since been forgiven, the sheriff would not release them until they gave security for good behavior. All this the Assembly learned plus the horrible fact that another prisoner had died of starvation.

Real concern arose everywhere about the sad plight of the debtors. They were not criminals; they were unfortunate neighbors of the townsmen, and persons accustomed to living orderly lives amid decent surroundings. Building on the theory enunciated in the fifties, "A Friend to the Distressed" wrote with eloquence and irony in the *Newport Mercury* against "the cruelty of punishing insolvency with imprisonment," which not only denied the debtor a chance to pay obligations but subjected him to the corruption and vice prevalent in all prisons. "An unfortunate Prisoner" had his say on the same subject. Leaders among the gentry and the middle class petitioned the Rhode Island Assembly in 1769 to enlarge the prison's bounds for debtors so that they might walk the streets to get fresh air, and a second petition pointed out that the imprisoned debtors faced a loss of health, "particularly in the summer season." On September 18, 1769 the Fellowship Club of Newport gave "their Friends who are under the Misfortune of being confined for Debt" an elaborate dinner at the prison, following which "a Number of Patriotic Toasts were drank." About fifty debtors languished in the Philadelphia prison in 1771, "the most of whom are Strangers destitute of any provision made for their Releasement." A large subscription taken to celebrate the repeal of the Stamp Act had made a general jail delivery of debtors possible at Boston, but others soon took their places. The Charles Town Grand Jury took notice that the city's jail was unable "to contain the numbers of debtors and criminals frequently put therein, whereby their healths are greatly endangered."

Fixing public attention upon the deficiency of city prisons, the average citizens who knew them from the inside goaded municipal authorities into action. Suffolk County began the dismantling of its old prison in 1766 as a safer and more commodious stone one neared completion. Resourceful inmates, however, twice broke out of the new jail before its first anniversary, and, hoping to get a hole to slip through, some more frenzied ones set fire to it in February 1769, and the county had to spend £3,000 sterling to rebuild it. Three more times this desperate expedient was tried by 1774. Thrifty Newport built a new cage twelve feet square for its criminals in 1761, but the debt situation forced the erection of a brick building on Marlborough Street in 1772. Responding to the Grand Jury's plea for a prison, the South Carolina Assembly appropriated funds in 1770 for a substantial brick "Goal" on the Green next to the Workhouse in 1771. The Corporation of New York reached the conclusion in 1767 that a Bridewell was needed for the confinement of debtors and minor offenders. While a building, designed by the "Surveyor" Theophilous Hardenbrook, went up in the Fields, the policy of segregating inmates was introduced at the new prison with good results. When the Bridewell, built in line with the prison and Alms House, opened for occupancy in 1775, it made an imposing appearance with its three-story central portion, two-story wings, and heavy stone quoins.

A petition from Philadelphia insisting that the city's prison was too poorly built to prevent escapes, that it was too small for the health of prisoners, and that better handling was essential stimulated the Assembly in 1773 to authorize the construction of a new prison at a cost of £25,000 on the ground near the hospital west of the thickly settled part of the city. With the avowed purpose of providing better accommodations and some rudimentary comforts for prisoners, this stone edifice, designed by Robert Smith, was unrivaled in its day. A European visitor declared it to be "the largest building for that purpose I ever saw." On the south side of the prison grounds a smaller structure facing Prune Street near Sixth, enclosed by a stone wall twelve feet high, had been built solely for the confinement of insolvent debtors. Richard Wistar and other Friends formed, on February 7, 1776, the Philadelphia Society for the Relief of Distressed Prisoners, whose members trundled wheelbarrows marked "Victuals for the Prisoners" from house to house gathering food and clothing, thereby institutionalizing private prison welfare efforts of the previous decade.

V

For three quarters of a century the inhabitants of colonial cities had, upon one occasion or another, risen in protest against abuses. As emphasized earlier in this work, such gatherings were almost the sole means the people had for expressing their opinions; they struck out not blindly but with a pretty certain understanding of what the issues were, but unfortunately violence and destruction of property often resulted. When these outbreaks occurred, those who took the conservative position usually inclined to speak of the people as "the mob," "the mobility," "the rabble," assuming, because the middle and lower orders used strongarm tactics and, like any other aroused groups, succumbed to mass hysteria, that they acted without thought and that their grievances had no legitimate basis. It might be said that it was the frightened and sometimes guilty upper class that failed to do the thinking, for a few of its more astute leaders knew that the demagogue always has to have some concrete dissatisfaction to exploit. Any conclusion about city mobs and the rioting of the Revolutionary era must take into consideration the existence of many deeply rooted, popular grievances, and these were widely shared by the two lower classes and also by a substantial proportion of the gentry; they were periodically exacerbated by the callousness or obtuseness of American conservative and British official actions and were frequently goaded into direct action—action at first spontaneous, then later controlled. However fumbling this action appears, it presaged an ultimate threat to the power of those who were trying to confine the benefits of the New World existence to their own class—benefits that the lower orders determined no opponents should permanently deny them.

For the lower class, the end of the war and the ensuing depression, which so agitated the mercantile group, bred a host of additional and exceedingly serious problems. Former privateersmen, common seamen, and recently discharged soldiers, unable to find work or pay for food and shelter, lived idly in the seaports. The new British regulations stifled trade, postponed recovery, and raised the prices of the necessities of life. Where troops were stationed, many soldiers eked out meager pay by underbidding the citizens at wage labor at the same time that their officers treated the middle class with an aristocratic disdain to which they were not accustomed. Impressment did not end with the Peace of Paris. Especially rankling was the arrival from England of a host of placemen, who took away from many of the upper and middle classes the new and profitable jobs and elbowed them aside as they moved into the favored social circles of the cities. Signs of a nativist resentment against "Forreigners" appeared on all sides.

On the rank and file of the citizenry—the ultimate consumers—fell the full force of hard times, high prices, and scarcity of money. If few starved, still many suffered hardship and misery, and the sight of aristocratic display embittered many as they watched certain elements of their own gentry fraternizing with hated royal officials, playing the sycophant, and being accorded favors (they knew or supposed) denied to others. Many of them at the same time were being pressed for payments of moneys due to this very gentry. In several cities the long suppressed indignation against the ruling class welled up into an ominous hatred surpassing in intensity popular feeling against rulers across the sea. Incipient democratic aspirations burst their bonds when from press, pulpit, and platform an intelligent and literate people began to read and hear its grievances persistently rehearsed and learned of the threat to its liberties by the alliance of part of the colonial aristocracy with British officialdom in much the same manner as the press reported was currently going on in England itself.

The whistle of the mob and some occasional rioting were no new feature of Boston life. Sheriff Stephen Greenleaf had had no end of trouble with spontaneous and unruly assemblages long before the showdown of 1765, and suspicion of Thomas Hutchinson and the oligarchy of gentlemen at the top of the province traced directly back to the days of the currency crisis of the forties. Nor was the raising and managing of the mobility by members of the upper class any innovation. What was new after the Stamp Act Riots was the systematic and highly effective translation of mass anger over wrongs into overt action participated in by members of all classes by means of secret caucuses, the press, and town meetings.

What Governor Francis Bernard branded an "Ochlocracy, or government by a mob," commenced on August 14, 1765, when the cordwainer Ebenezer Mackintosh, "First Captain General of the Liberty Tree," supervised his South End bully boys in the hanging in effigy of Andrew Oliver, the stamp agent, and the Earl of Bute. The stuffed images had been prepared by Benjamin Edes of the *Boston Gazette* and his compeers of the North End Caucus Club, who succeeded in uniting the two former Pope Day gangs for popular and patriotic ends. At dusk twelve days later a great crowd gathered at a bonfire in front of the Town House shouting "Liberty and Property"; it then proceeded to loot the houses of William Story of the Admiralty Court and Benjamin Hallowell of the Customs—both Massachusetts born and bred. Filled with the latter's good Madeira, the rioters followed Mackintosh on to the Hutchinson mansion in Garden Street, forced its way in as the owner fled, and for two hours vented its spleen upon the first gentleman of New England by carrying off or destroying everything within and without this beautiful establishment—furniture, plate, books, manuscripts, and a large sum of money. "Such ruins were never seen in America," wrote the Lieutenant Governor, who estimated his entire losses at £25,000 sterling. Exceeded only by the Knowles Riots of 1748 in its flouting of authority, the incident demonstrated that in addition to opposition to the stamp taxes, "the Democratick Thermometer" had again risen "some Degrees above the Boiling Heat" in what Peter Oliver dubbed "the Metropolis of Sedition." Writing to England in November, James Murray said: "the multitude, among which are many men of figure and fortune, imagine that such proceedings will surely procure a Repeal of the Act." But the fury displayed by the mob dismayed law-abiding men of property, even some of those who had been behind it. However, the peaceful and open reconciliation of the North and South End leaders, Swift and Mackintosh, on Gunpowder Day 1765, meant that henceforth nearly all popular demonstrations would give evidence of careful prior planning.

From this time until the "Bloody Work in King Street," the "trained mob," as Bernard called it, more often than not had a special but sometimes unvoiced grievance underlying the obvious cause of its outbreak.

This was true in the notorious case of the riots following the seizure of John Hancock's sloop *Liberty* by Collector Joseph Harrison and Comptroller Benjamin Hallowell on June 10, 1768, when the Collector was manhandled, his pleasure yacht burned on the Common, his windows stoned, and both his son and the Comptroller severely roughed up. It is doubtful if sympathy for the generous Mr. Hancock, who was being framed by the revenue officers, incited their action. Rather the impressment just shortly before of "only eighteen men" by H.M.S. *Romney,* under whose guns the *Liberty* had been moored for safety, had whipped up a frenzy. Realizing this, Thomas Hutchinson admitted that although no men with families had been taken up, "yet the fear of it prevents Coasters as well as other Vessels coming in freely and it adds more fewel to the great stock among us before. It is a pity that in peaceable times any Pressing of Seamen should be allowed in the Colonies." When Captain Comer called the Bostonians "damned villains" and swore "by the eternal God he would make their hearts ache before he left," he did not endear himself to either the owners of ships or the denizens of the waterfront. In 1769 and 1770 Commodore Hood pressed men from coasters, but the presence of the troops in Boston checked any uprising, and in September Hood promised not to seize any more mariners.

Interference with the collection of customs duties, threats and actual bodily harm to revenue officers, and the alarm of citizens who took the government's side had led the Commissioners of the Customs to request military aid. Two British regiments arrived in the city on October 1, 1768. During their stay, friction between the citizenry and the hated troops intensified daily; and dozens of minor episodes, sometimes fomented and always magnified by colonial newspapers in a column known as a "Journal of Occurrences," did not help matters. On the night of March 5, 1770 a mob provoked some soldiers into firing on them, and five of the rioters were killed. The "Boston Massacre"—so called—had three prime consequences: it secured the withdrawal of both regiments; frightened conservative people everywhere in the colonies; and heartened the "lawless Banditti" of the despised middle and lower classes headed by "Joyce Jr." to use ever rougher and less defensible methods with unpopular members of the gentry. The culminating episode at "mobbish Boston" was the Tea Party given by a band of Mohawks on December 16, 1773, the theatrical quality of which must have reminded oldsters of "a Number of Persons unknown" who, garbed as clergymen, gave the town its first masquerade by cutting down the pillars of the market house in 1737, and of the occasion of the stealing of the *Swanzey Packet* in 1772 from under the guns of a man-o'-war's tender at Martha's Vineyard by a gang disguised like the aborigines of Gay Head. Many of Boston's rioters felt a great kinship with the Wilkesites of London, whose doings the press reported fully; Mackintosh, a reader of poetry, named his first-born Pasquale Paoli. They must have smiled grimly, however, at the saying the press attributed to the Duke of Newcastle: "I love a mob (said he), I headed a mob once myself. We owe the Hanoverian succession to a mob."

Two fundamental grievances actuated the generality at Newport. Rumors were rife after 1761 that a faction of foreign-born residents, headed by Dr. Thomas Moffatt, Martin Howard, George Rome, the Harrisons, and their Anglican associates, and supported by Governor Bernard of Massachusetts, who urged the creation of "a Nobility appointed by the King for life," planned an assault on the Rhode Island Charter. Said Bernard, without proper knowledge, to Lord Barrington: "In Rhode Island the sensible people neither expect nor desire their charter should be continued."

Irrepressible anger among all classes at such high-handed interference with their government coupled with resentment over the use of the Royal Navy to prevent molasses smuggling in Narragansett Bay. Liberty and trade were the stakes; and "the Imprudence and Insolence" of both officers and men "greatly incensed the People of the Town." When Lieutenant Hill of the schooner *St. John* seized the cargo of a brig running in goods near Howland's Ferry and took the vessel to Newport as a prize in June 1764, only H.M.S. *Squirrel* prevented an armed local ship from recapturing it. Of seeming minor import but nevertheless infuriating was the stealing of some hogs and chickens in town by British tars; the sheriff was refused permission to board the *St. John* to serve warrants on the accused, but just at this time a landing boat pulled up to Malbone's Wharf, where a waiting crowd seized its officer and stoned the crew. Peleg Thurston and Gideon Cornell of the Council thereupon ordered the gunner at Fort George not to allow the naval vessel to leave port until Hill turned the culprits over to justice. Gunner Vaughan hailed the *St. John* as she got under way and fired several shots, but she managed to get out of range and under the protection of the *Squirrel*. In May 1765, H.M.S. *Maidstone* pressed more seamen from vessels in the harbor and boatmen bringing in fuel, causing fearful coasters to avoid the port. As a brig from Africa stood into the deserted harbor on June 4, a gang from the *Maidstone* boarded her and pressed the entire crew. At nine that night a mob of about five hundred "sailors, Boys, and Negroes" seized the ship's boat as it landed at a wharf, dragged it to the Parade, and burned it. The captain of the *Maidstone* had promised the sheriff not to impress any Newporters, and kept his promise, but in taking almost everyone else, he forced seamen's wages up a dollar and a half a month; and, just as bad or worse, nobody brought any wood, fish, or market produce to market for fear of the "hottest press ever known in this Town." A letter to the *Mercury* stated: "if a speedy Stop does not take Place, the lamentable Condition of the poorer Part of the Inhabitants, the approaching Winter, will be truly affecting, as in May, June, July, and August, the Town is mostly supplied with Wood." This writer deplored all rioting, but insisted that something must be done. Governor Samuel Ward pointedly told Captain Antrobus of the *Squirrel* that the press was "an Arbitrary Action, contrary to Law, inconsistent with Liberty, and to be justified only by urgent necessity," as he placed the blame for the riot squarely on the Royal Navy.

Such was the state of affairs when the Stamp Act passed. As early as August 1765 Dr. Thomas Moffatt, Martin Howard, the "Halifax Gentleman," and Augustus Johnston, the stamp agent, knew that they were to be burnt in effigy on the 27th, Town Meeting Day. On the appointed date, drink and Cheshire cheese awaited the people, along with "other incitements to intemperance and riot," before the Colony House; but nothing happened. The following evening, however, the mob sacked Howard's mansion in much the same thorough way that Mackintosh's boys had used at Hutchinson's house, suggesting collusion, for the news of the Boston riots had arrived only that morning; then, headed by John Webber, the crowd moved on to Moffatt's residence, which they despoiled of its fine furniture, paintings, and books. Proceeding to Johnston's, they were diverted by the promise of his friends that he would resign as stamp agent, though the Reverend Ezra Stiles harangued the crowd, questioning his sincerity. So menacing did the people seem that Johnston, despite his reprieve, departed the town, but returned the next morning to resign publicly. It is most significant that Collector John Robinson believed that the Boston riots stimulated Newporters "to imitate their Example"; and that the principal objects of the mob's animosity were the "Forreigners," opponents of the charter, more than Johnston, who was otherwise a popular Rhode Island attorney. "It is for liberty, that liberty for which our fathers fought, that liberty which is dearer to a generous mind than life itself, that we now contend," the Town Meeting had resolved when instructing its deputies to oppose the Stamp Act, and it was for liberty, as they understood it, that the people rioted under the direction of Samuel Vernon, William Ellery, and other respectable members of the local gentry.

The "Spirit of uneasiness and discontent, attended with innumerable surmises, jealousies, and fears hath been propagated and blown up among the lower and middling ranks of the people by a few crafty seditious and popular malignants . . . that the Colonies were now actually subjugated and enslaved by the rigorous injustice of parliament," Dr. Moffatt explained to Joseph Harrison when he found refuge at London in October. This was indeed a widely held view, and many incidents served to fortify rather than dissipate the belief. On November 2 some twenty or thirty cronies tried to spring John Webber, in prison for his part in the riots, but were dispersed, two of the leaders being "forced to take up their abode in the same place." The Newporters made life miserable for the revenue officers; they continually blocked the seizure of suspected vessels, beat informers, and clashed with naval personnel. A placard posted on the door of the Colony House in December 1767 summoned a meeting of the inhabitants "to seize the money in the Customs House" in reprisal for the Crown's refusal to pay Rhode Island its share of the French and Indian War subsidies because of the treatment given Howard and Dr. Moffatt. The Town Meeting repudiated this design lest the city acquire a bad name. Upper- and middle-class leaders never managed to bring turbulent Newport under the discipline achieved at Boston; and in 1770 a group of eighteen of the most conservative merchants, alarmed at the posting of a paper intended to "stir up the well designing tho' unthinking part of the Community" over the non-importation agreement, concerted to support the authorities in maintaining law and order. When the Providence radicals burned the revenue schooner *Gaspee* in 1772, and the Royal Navy made "a formidable Parade" in Newport harbor as the investigation of the outrage began, the city's mob activity virtually ended. But the populace had not accepted the leadership of those guilty of "the tame submission of fawning politicians" and "Ministerial Tools," as one Yankee labeled them: Augustus Johnston, Dr. Moffatt, and Martin Howard. They continued to hold lucrative and distinguished crown appointments, but not in Newport; they had departed never to return.

Certain happenings during the last years of the Old French War got under the skin of ordinary people at Manhattan. The merchants were angry, too, because the Duke of Albemarle forced them to sell bread to the army at Havana for half the price it commanded. "The people of this Colony are stark mad about it," John Watts testified. The province furnished Albemarle with more than five hundred men at a most critical time and then he excluded all but his own creatures from the trade. Worse still, "your Hyde Park Generals" treated the provincial troops "with great contempt because they were not high dressed," yet they really made the conquest a success. Now "the poor remains of our Provincials are dropping in from Havanna, 'tis melancholy to behold the Effects of that ill conducted, destructive expedition, that has been an advantage to no body but a few of the Leaders."

These disgruntled men, disbanded soldiers, and discharged privateersmen were such stuff as mobs were made of, and before long some of them demonstrated their prowess by attempting a jail delivery of the famous Major Robert Rogers, imprisoned debtor, and in the course of it freed most of the inmates. The same year, 1764, a naval vessel from Halifax impressed four fishermen; when the captain came ashore in a barge, a mob suddenly assembled, seized the boat, and dragged it to the Fields for burning. Although James McEvers resigned as stamp agent in

August 1765, when the stamped paper arrived the fury of the people fixed upon Cadwallader Colden, who, as Lieutenant Governor, was responsible for its disposition. On the evening of the day the law went into effect, the mob, with "grossest ribaldry," set up a scaffold in front of Fort George and hanged Colden in effigy. Then they broke into his carriage house nearby, took out his chariot, and carried the image around town in it, after which they burned it, a chair, and two sleighs. Colden claimed that the lawyers "are the Authors, Promoters and Leaders" and that many gentlemen "stood round to observe the outrage." According to Robert R. Livingston, the populace had been "already too much inflamed by a number of Publications in the Newspaper, which the Government did not dare to punish." Soldiers and citizens clashed frequently, and much ill will was fomented on both sides. In 1770 about eighty artisans and tradesmen led by Isaac Sears circulated a broadside against the troops who had cut down the Liberty Pole, thereby proving themselves enemies of both peace and freedom. The next day the well-known Golden Hill Riot took place, and before long the *New York Gazette* was urging the inhabitants not to hire any soldier: "Is it not enough that you pay Taxes for Billeting Money to support the Soldiers, and a Poor Tax, to maintain many of their Whores and Bastards in the Work House, without giving them the Employment of the Poor?" Manhattan's mobility found effective leaders in the former privateer captains "King" Sears and Alexander McDougall, as well as in John Morin Scott and the lawyers: men who told the people what their liberties were—freedom from impressment and freedom to work they already understood from bitter experience.

The middle and lower orders of Charles Town really had more reason to resent the gentry than their Northern brethren, but, being inferior in numbers, wealth, and influence in the city, they exploded over their lot much less frequently. By constant communication with Philadelphia, New York, and Newport they knew about happenings as soon as the ships brought the news. Early in February 1765 they were reading Stephen Hopkins's *The Rights of the British Colonies Examined,* and when the stamps arrived on October 20, they rioted for nine days and nights, during which a fundamental cleavage developed among the gentry, with Christopher Gadsden emerging as a tribune of the people and the even wealthier Henry Laurens, habitually suspicious of popular issues, as the leader of the conservatives. The latter faced the mob at his front door at midnight on October 23 and coolly and skillfully handled them, penetrating their disguises and addressing them by name. Lieutenant Governor William Bull believed that the people were disposed to pay the stamp taxes and were satisfied to protest respectfully, "but by the artifices of some busy Spirits the Minds of Men here were so universally poisoned with the Principles which were imbibed and propagated from Boston and Rhode Island (from which towns at this Time of the Year, Vessels very frequently arrive) that after their example the People of this Town resolved to seize and destroy the Stamp Papers."

In January, however, many hotheads cooled when a general disturbance broke out among the Negro slaves of the Low Country and the "Patriots were riding day and night for 10 or 14 days in most bitter weather and here in Town all were soldiers in Arms for more than a Week" on what proved to be a false alarm; Henry Laurens sardonically reported that "some Negroes had mimicked their betters in crying *Liberty*." Fear of a servile insurrection always transcended other fears, and the citizens thereafter acted with circumspection that resembled the Boston discipline, as exemplified on the occasion when the "Principle Mechanicks" gathered under some trees in a field near the ropewalks in 1768 to nominate "six gentlemen" to represent the city in the Commons House and dedicated the Liberty Tree, following which they paraded on Broad Street. Press rumors about the creation of a nobility in America doubtless caused democratic alarm, but not until the final crisis stemming from the Boston Port Act did Charles Town's middle and lower classes rise again and threaten such outspoken Tories as Dr. George Milligen and indulge themselves by tarring and feathering those who offended them.

The march of the Paxton Boys on Philadelphia in 1764 starkly revealed the growing divergence of the gentry of the east and the citizenry when the latter openly sympathized with the grievances if not the aims of the back settlers. Both groups were underrepresented in provincial councils. Many townsmen resented the newly passed riot act, and they ruthlessly made sport of the use of force intended by many Quakers who suddenly abandoned nonresistance when the countinghouse seemed threatened: "Look here! a Quaker with a Musket on his shoulder!" Samuel Foulke noted in his diary that the Paxton Boys were "invited and Encouraged by many Considerable persons in Philadelphia," who promised them "that they Shou'd meet with no opposition in the Execution of their Design." Although the immediate threat to the city passed when Benjamin Franklin's diplomacy turned the marchers back at Germantown, the furious pamphlet battle continued, and the peace-loving Quaker gentry with their allies had seen enough of democracy in the rough. Thereafter they moved with great caution and patriot leaders took every possible action to forestall the forming of mobs and rioting. But the curtain had been drawn aside briefly, affording a glimpse of what the future might bring, and class antagonism was an accepted fact in colonial Philadelphia after 1764.

The Stamp Act produced violence in other cities, but at Philadelphia the resignation of John Hughes as agent and the passage of non-importation resolutions by the "traders" and "retailers" proved acceptable to the populace, which as yet lacked a dynamic leader; everyone rejoiced, however, when the Heart-in-Hand Fire Company expelled poor Hughes in 1766. The revenue officers did not escape the crowd, however; one Saturday in 1769 Collector William Sheppard, aided by a few of the militia, tried in vain to prevent a large mob from recovering confiscated wine and smashing his windows; understandably he left town after being attacked and having his nose slit with a knife. The mobility everywhere detested informers, and Philadelphians always kept the tar bucket and pillow ready for them.

The self-respecting though unfranchised middle class had additional grievances. Alexander Graydon, himself a gentleman, tells us that among British officers in town a "studied contempt of the *mohairs* . . . was manifest on all occasions," and was without doubt one source of revolutionary discontent, as was also the ill-concealed social exclusiveness of some of the ruling class who were as yet not sufficiently sure of themselves to display a true sense of *gentility*. Mercantile pressures on urban debtors and small shopkeepers was another. Perhaps in no other city was the antagonism of the generality of the inhabitants against both their local and provincial rulers so pronounced, but as William Bradford wrote to James Madison in 1775, Philadelphia "seems as if it had expended all its vigor, in the time of the Stamp Act," while Joseph Galloway expressed his delight "that Moderation is taking place of the violence in this Province."

Thus in all the cities, the middle class ardently desired a redress of grievances and the accordance of privileges that they had come to consider rights, but which were usually denied them by the aristocrats, both colonial and British. Always present, class consciousness now opposed fear with hatred and jealousy. As many of the ordinary citizens looked at it, a long train of abuses revealed a design by their rulers to confine them within their former status. The bonds at which they strained had to snap sooner or later. No wonder a Charles Town congregation dismissed a "Reverend Divine" for "impudently saying [in the pulpit] that *Mechanics* and country *clowns* had no right to dispute about politics, or what king, lords, and commons had done! All such divines should be taught to know that mechanics and country clowns (infamously socalled) are the real and absolute masters of king, lords, commons, and priests though (with shame be it spoken) they too often suffer their servants to get upon their backs and ride them most barbarously." The spirit of Oliver was once more abroad in the land.

VI

Urban morals did not improve after the period of relaxation that unavoidably follows war. Most obvious, even to a casual observer, was

the spectacular decline of Sabbath deportment. New Yorkers and Philadelphians accepted the fact that Sabbaths would be "boldly profaned by
the most open and flagitious enormities." At Newport only the Quakers
put in a complaint about "vain and disorderly Persons, Negroes, Tawnies
and others" for gathering on Friends' meeting days to sell beer and
cakes, run horses, play with quoits, and induce Quaker lads to withdraw
from worship to play; the Assembly responded by prohibiting any such
shenanigans within four miles of the meeting house in 1769. In Boston
the inhabitants always betrayed great concern for the religious reputation of their city. In February 1761 the *Post Boy* gave over its front page
and part of the second to printing the new Sabbath observance law
passed by the General Court, which prohibited work, sports, travel, entertainment in public houses, unnecessary walking, loitering, or assembling in the streets on the Lord's Day and forbade shopkeepers to be
open, hawkers to peddle, or any public diversion after sunset on Saturday. Wardens enforced these regulations with as much success in the
Bay City as any urban center would permit. A letter to the *Gazette* in
1764 reveals the horror of a countryman upon learning that card-playing
"reigns in the great metropolis" every Sabbath, a sin he feared would
soon infect the simple countryfolk. A reply in the *Newsletter* said it was
but just to "inform the Country that we are not so abandoned." The
writer knew of no family that practiced gaming in any form on the Sabbath. Ignore this letter, the citizen went on, "he makes Puritanism and
Superstition one and the same thing." Rather more concern and less success attended the efforts of the Charlestonians to keep the Sabbath; they
could not keep it holy when barbers shaved customers, Negroes cried
fish through the streets, and godless men raced horses, "by which Means
a great Number of People are drawn there, and the Sabbath profaned."
Nevertheless most of the inhabitants turned out to be as strict Sab-
batarians as any city afforded.

The compulsion for heavy gambling did not disappear with the vanishing of easy war money and the coming of peace. The lottery, an old and
socially approved device, did, however, pass into disfavor at Philadelphia
in 1762, when the Protestant ministers joined to procure the passage of
a law declaring all lotteries public nuisances and forbidding them along
with all popular games of chance—dice, lots, cards—under a penalty of
five hundred pounds. This attempt at reformation arose from the indis-
cretion of an entrepreneur who conducted a lottery "for erecting public
Gardens, with Baths and Bagnios," in the Northern Liberties, where,
declared the clergy, the people might indulge their "immoderate and
growing Fondness for Pleasure, Luxury, Gaming, Dissipation and their
concomittant Vices." The Town Meeting of Newport requested a law
stopping white boys and Negroes from gaming in the streets in 1770.
Alarmed by the participation of common people in "deceitful" games of
chance, the South Carolina Assembly in 1762 voided all gambling debts,

made provision for the recovery of money or goods lost by playing cards, dice, bowls, "tennis," betting, shuffleboard, billiards, skittles, and nine-pins. Publicans permitting gaming were to be fined forty shillings, and any apprentice, overseer, journeyman, laborer, or servant found playing at a place with liquor for sale incurred a penalty of twenty shillings. What success was achieved by this measure is not known. The Grand Jury uncovered a disorderly gaming house in 1768, but the law was not renewed after its seven-year period. "Marjory Distaff" flayed the gentry of Charles Town in 1769, when coin was so scarce and patriotism demanded frugality, for their heavy betting at taverns, horse races, and especially cockfights.

The besetting vice of men and women of all classes was drink; townsmen joined with the "Tipling soldiery" in consuming tremendous quantities of the rum produced by colonial distilleries, and alcoholism claimed hundreds of victims. Samuel Hall tried to stir up his readers by printing "The Drunkard's Looking Glass: Or, a short View of their Present Shame and Future Misery" on the front page of his *Mercury,* a piece with all the lurid details of a temperance tract. Substitution of wine and brewed drinks for strong liquor was the text of Dr. Benjamin Rush's *Sermons to Gentlemen Upon Temperance and Exercise* published at Philadelphia in 1772. Most distressing to any thinking person was the succession of accounts of horrible deaths of children and women, as well as men, from excessive drinking. In 1771, for instance, a four-year-old girl drank from a pitcher of rum in a Boston tenement until she became stupefied and eventually died; and in 1764 at Manhattan Margaret Jones "drank too freely of spirituous liquors, fell from the Main Deck into the hold of the Coventry man of war . . . and was killed." Notices of deaths of journeymen and apprentices from overindulgence appeared frequently in the newspapers.

Commercialized vice spread as the population rose in each city, but New York particularly achieved an unenviable reputation in this respect. Bawdyhouses and prostitutes existed on the patronage of the floating class of soldiers and mariners, and some of the wealthy gentry, it might be added. It was middle-class morality that was expressed when mobs of artisans and tradesmen attacked the oldest profession: in 1761 they permitted one of the wooden forts on the Common to burn to the ground for this reason. By 1766 several "infamous houses" in the Fields openly catered to the soldiers of the King, and the *New York Gazette* admonished the civil power for not wiping out "receptacles, or nests of villainy" to ensure for "virtuous women" the "pleasure of their husbands' company at home." In 1767 at the house of Caty Crow two sailors killed a shopkeeper "in a riot," and the Supreme Court fined the madam one hundred pounds and sentenced her to a year's imprisonment for keeping the establishment. The next March, when she departed for Grenada, "to the great Mortification of many persons," one of them wrote a ballad about her. Other notorious Manhattan bawds were "Quaker Fan" Bambridge, who died from drink, and Hannah Bradshaw, alias "Man of War Nance," who burned in the most horrible death in colonial annals. Prostitution could not be permanently driven out of New York. The entrance to King's College was reached by one of the streets where the most noted whores lived, and Patrick M'Robert considered this a great temptation to youth. "Above 500 ladies of Pleasure keep lodgings contiguous within the consecrated liberties of St. Paul's," he continued. "This part of the city belongs to the church, and has thence obtained the name of the *Holy Ground*. Here all the prostitutes reside, among whom are many fine well dressed women, and it is remarkable that they live in much greater cordiality with one another than any nests of that kind in Britain or Ireland."

To many a soldier and sailor who saw little of the Massachusetts capital except the eighteenth-century equivalent of Scollay Square, it must have seemed like a bawdy Boston. One had a choice of houses of ill fame, plus the "several hundred" camp followers who sailed in from Halifax in the wake of the troops in 1768. Although the propagandistic "Journal of Occurrences" made much of the abuse of chaste young women by the "Lobster Backs," the military countered with statements that seduction was never necessary, so accommodating were the women of Boston. Such a state of affairs further angered the aroused citizenry, however, and in 1771 a mob "Routed the Whores" at a place called Whitehall; and the year after, the Selectmen took measures to stop "Strange Women" from soliciting men on King Street. In the district called New Boston the Misses Erskine, noted for "admitting all Comers to their b—d and board," impudently got away with indecent exhibitions at their windows in the company of British officers. We have the reliable testimony under oath of Thomas Flucker, formerly of the Governor's Council, that Sarah Hinson, daughter of the Dorcas Griffiths who kept a shop on Hancock's Wharf to cover up her other "Business of a common prostitute," was bred by her mother to the profession; and that "she was kept by the famous Handcock, and when he turned her off, she lived with Capt. Johnson" of the Royal Marines, and became a deserving Loyalist. The treachery of Dr. Benjamin Church, the Boston patriot leader, was exposed when his mistress was detected at Newport by "her former Enamorato" Godfrey Wainwood with a telltale letter from Church to the British in her possession.

Philadelphia had its bawdyhouses, too, but they did not attract so much public attention as at New York and Boston. In attempting to close up one of these places in 1769, Constable Campbell lost his life at the hands of a mariner, and the Mayor's Court tried many cases of bastardy and adultery; so the citizens could not have been unaware that fornication was common. Nor were the sons of the rich guiltless, for in 1770 Samuel Coates wrote to William Logan, then in England, detailing the exploits of twelve scions of leading Quaker families—drunkenness, gambling, and whoring. One of them was in debt more than £7,000, another kept gamecocks, and "he is said to give a Girl £50 to strip Stark naked before him." When Philip Hines brutally murdered an old woman in 1772 because he was "angry at a woman of ill Fame" and declared he would kill the first person he saw, David Hall of the *Gazette* hoped that this tragedy would jar the constables into "suppressing the many Houses of ill fame which dishonour this City."

Although many gentlemen and others sought the favors of Negro slaves, a Jamaican in 1773 was surprised that "in Charlestown he met only one man who acknowledged keeping a mulatto mistress and he was 'pointed at.'" The open miscegenation of former years now met with public disapproval, and as a consequence, perhaps, and also for the transient and seafaring population, white women competed with the slaves. Charles Woodmason got the Grand Jury in 1764 to present "Mary M'Dowell in Pinckney's street . . . for keeping a most notorious brothel and receptacle for lewd women, to the great annoyance of the inhabitants." They also lamented the want of "a proper House of Correction" for disciplining "notorious bawds, strumpets, vagrants, drunkards and idle persons." Conditions such as these prevailed throughout the period, for the authorities seemed powerless to stamp them out.

In verse frank even for that age, the *Newport Mercury* conjured Rhode Island's "Smarts and Beaus" to spurn all harlots, lest lechery end in disease and sorrow, but in such a maritime community houses of prostitution and individual harlots drove a thriving trade. The townsfolk were a very moral lot for the most part, thoroughly disapproving of conjugal infidelity; in one case they promptly chastised a married man detected visiting a paramour in disguise and paraded him through the streets on an old horse "as a Warning to all bad husbands." In discussing the high poor rates in 1771, a correspondent of the *Mercury* maintained that "Drunkenness and wh—ing is the cause of two thirds of the whole expense. Much money is also spent in riding out, with the lasses, by many who are scarce able to provide for themselves the necessary comforts of life." The moralists of '76 found ample cause for countless homilies about the prevalence of sin in the five cities.

The low state of morals and manners worried many city people, whose principal fear, as in all ages, was the corruption of the young. To John Watts, New York seemed "the worst School for Youth of any of his Majesty's Dominions. Ignorance, Vanity, Dress, and Dissipation, being the reigning Characteristics of their insipid Lives." Bostonians nominated their town, too; the *Gazette* condemned the blasphemy of Harvard commencements: "They have a strange Proverb at College, viz. *That 'tis no*

Sin to tell Lies in Latin." At Philadelphia, Pastor Mühlenberg agonized over the custom of boys "stripping naked on the banks, and bathing in the river" Delaware on Sundays. A further sign of the leniency that sealed the doom of Gomorrah he discovered when the sons of good Lutherans "poured out English curses" upon the deacons seeking to curb disorders during *Kinderlehre*. "Our City wants no Decoration but private Virtue," sighed another Philadelphian. Under the clerkship of John Young, the London agencies of the early eighteenth century were resurrected in 1769 with the founding of the Society for Reformation of Manners and the Suppression of Vice, in the City of New York, to maintain a watch and ward, raise funds, and prosecute offenders. At the same time the Boston Town Meeting appointed a committee to recommend methods for exterminating immorality and idleness, "the Parent of all Vices." White laborers at Charles Town complained that Negroes cursed and swore without punishment, whereas they themselves had to pay a shilling for every oath. Wicked and barbarous as the older inhabitants thought their cities, in comparison with more primitive times, these communities still wore an aspect of innocence in contrast to the openly condoned vice and immorality of contemporary London, Edinburgh, and most of England's provincial cities.

VII

The men of the Enlightenment devoutly believed that humanity could be made over by thinking and brought to new levels of perfection by the exercise of reason. This being true, then it became the duty of any right-thinking society to protect its individual members from the indignities of poverty, sickness, social injustice, and misfortune. Thousands of Europeans had sought a better life in the New World, where human misery would be alleviated, and in the colonial cities the very existence of social ills challenged the prophets of progress. Believing with Pope that the proper study of mankind is man, the urban press and pulpit kept the citizens informed about the state of the poor and through them forced municipal authorities to take action for the aid of the unfortunate. The new concern for suffering humanity was broadly secular in its impulses but coincided nicely with contemporary humanitarianism, as well as the scientific and religious (especially Quaker) temper of the age.

Basing its policy upon more than a century of successful experience, Boston continued to lead in public benevolence down to the close of the period. Since the province boarded its poor in the Boston Alms House, this institution was usually well filled, but the town was spared responsibility for poor immigrants, for the city officials carefully investigated all strangers to prevent their becoming a charge on the rates, returning all able-bodied countrymen to their native villages while at the same time evincing solicitude for the sick or incapacitated. To ensure the proper expenditure of the poor funds and the comfort of town dependents, the Selectmen, Suffolk County justices, and the Overseers of the Poor made an annual inspection of the Alms House and the out-relief cases in each of the city's twelve wards, after which they submitted a report to the Town Meeting. In 1769 a special committee to employ the poor, "whose Numbers and distresses are dayly increasing by the loss of its Trade and Commerce," reported 230 in the Alms House and 40 in the Workhouse, as well as many on out-relief, who could be put to work; with funds borrowed from the town, the Manufactory House was reopened under William Molineux. Annual charitable charges raised by taxes rose from £2,110 in 1762 to £3,506 in 1771. In addition so many private donations and bequests came in that in 1772 the General Court incorporated the Overseers, giving them the authority to supervise such sums to a total of £60,000 in lawful money. Thomas Hancock's bequest of £600 in 1764 toward the building of a house for the insane, which the inhabitants voted to call "Hancock's Hospital," proved insufficient; despite all efforts this "Bedlam" never opened, and the Selectmen kept on boarding out the mentally ill.

The burden of the poor so efficiently and humanely assumed by the Bostonians was materially augmented by generous group philanthropy. The several charitable organizations founded in earlier decades increased their benefactions to the members of their denominations or national groups; in 1772 the Massachusetts Society joined in this work. The several churches unostentatiously cared for many needy members, widows in particular, with moneys raised by collections or bequests; Widow Mary Ireland left a thousand pounds to her church in 1763, and the Honorable Thomas Hubbard and other gentlemen willed sizable sums to "the Poor of this Metropolis."

Having succeeded famously in caring for all of their poor during the trying years of depression, with resulting higher taxes, the people of Boston suddenly faced the greatest relief problem in colonial history when Parliament closed the port in punishment for the destruction of the tea. At a meeting on June 17, 1774 they voted that a town committee and the Overseers of the Poor should concert to handle all donations and work out means for employing the poor. The Overseers begged off from the latter duty, which was then entrusted to a special Committee on Ways and Means. Unanimously the Town Meeting voted to follow the committee's recommendations to erect a wharf and some houses, build some ships, repair and pave the streets, and undertake "any other public Work" possible with the funds "at this time of general Calamity." Many of the unemployed soon found work in a brickyard opened on Boston

Neck, and digging wells for use at fires. Meanwhile, sympathetic communities, urban and rural, from one end of the colonies to the other, sent contributions of money, grain, livestock, and clothing to aid the stricken city—a spectacle of relief in the grand manner and one inspired quite as much by humanitarianism as by patriotic feeling. Without this largess Boston's poor would have truly suffered.

In a famous passage of his diary John Adams compared the Boston and Philadelphia of 1774, finding, always, in favor of his city except in markets "and in charitable public foundations." The overcrowding of the Philadelphia Alms House resulting from many destitute people from the frontier districts flocking into the city during the French and Indian War grew worse during Pontiac's rebellion. In 1764 the number asking for charity was so great that five and six beds were placed in rooms ten feet by eleven, and the overflow was cared for in a church. Quaker influence in the Assembly produced an act for the better relief of the poor in 1766 which incorporated all of the contributors of ten pounds from Philadelphia and the suburbs of Southwark, Moyamensing, Passyunk, and the Northern Liberties. First giving them power to hold lands and erect a new poorhouse, the Assembly later authorized the managers to borrow money, and in October 1767 the Bettering House, designed by Samuel Rhoads and built by Robert Smith, took in its first 284 poor people. Silas Deane was not the only visitor impressed by this great institution, which cost above fifteen thousand pounds to build, but what surprised him most was the fact that it had been erected entirely by the donations of the citizens, most of them Quakers, who looked after their own poor in "a neat house" with a pretty garden.

The sole obstacle to complete satisfaction with the Bettering House, which was located in the fields between Spruce and Pine west of Tenth Street, was the dissatisfaction of the suburbs over what they considered the high proportions of their shares of the annual charges. The poor rates did increase, and the fact that one municipal authority did not govern the entire metropolitan area also complicated administration. The managers insisted that more poor people settled in the suburbs to get lower rents, and that actually the city paid a higher tax rate than the districts and that Moyamensing did not bear its true share. In 1768 the suburbs requested the Assembly to make them independent jurisdictions, but the managers persuaded the members to vote against a separation. Passyunk continued to voice objections, arguing that it contributed to the support of other suburbs. The nub of the problem was the rising number of persons to be cared for; about four hundred people were sheltered regularly, given suitable employment, or a comfortable living if they could not work.

The charitable work of private citizens and friendly societies was most praiseworthy. Anthony Benezet took it upon himself to procure help for the Acadians. To assist the "distressed Black Inhabitants" in 1763, collections in the churches supplemented a door-to-door canvass for funds; in the winter of 1765, when many white people had no work, a public meeting designated two gentlemen for each square to collect relief money, also sending solicitors into Southwark and the Northern Liberties. The sums thus raised exceeded all expectations. "Hardly a week passes that collections from Pennsylvania, New York, etc, etc, etc, are going around here in Philadelphia, but alas! *pauper ubique est,"* exclaimed Mr. Mühlenberg. Especially noteworthy, in the light of current conditions, was the concern shown by many persons for the plight of poor debtors in jail. George Whitefield took up several collections for them, as did other clergymen, and the press publicized their situation and the irrationality of confining them.

A cosmopolitan city like Philadelphia naturally developed a number of charitable bodies organized on national lines like the Scots of the St. Andrew's Society. In 1764 a group of the principal German immigrants, mindful of recent discomforts, crowded quarters, and bad treatment on the voyage to America, founded the *Deutschen Gesellschaft von Pennsylvanien* to look after needy Palatines when they arrived; within one year of its founding it persuaded the Assembly to regulate immigrant vessels. Another active body established in 1765 was the Sea Captain's Club, more properly known as the Society for the Relief of Poor and Distressed Masters of Ships, their Widows, and Children; by 1774 it numbered 217 members, and had a stock of £2,500. For benevolence as well as conviviality, twenty-four natives of Ireland formed the Friendly Sons of St. Patrick in 1771, and the Society of the Sons of St. George organized the next year. When a "Number of Americans" established the Sons of King Tammany on May 1, 1772, they expressed the hope that "from this small Beginning, a Society may be formed of great Utility to the Distressed; as this Meeting was more for the Purpose of promoting Charity and Benevolence than for Mirth and Frivolity," and a year later a "Considerable Number of the most indigent of the confined Debtors" at the prison published their thanks to this body for a gift of victuals and beer. About this time the *Journal* printed Matthew Clarkson's explanation of the Articles of the Philadelphia Society for Annuities, for the Benefit of Widows, Children and Aged Persons, whereby one received an annuity of three times the yearly premium.

The Charles Town Vestry cared for its poor both generously and decently; it administered out-relief where possible, and regularly bound out all orphans and bastards until they attained their majorities. In 1766 and 1774 the community raised by taxes the large sum of £11,000 for public charity, but in other years did not appear to need so much. The end of the struggle with the French and Spanish brought no decrease in the number of supplicants for relief; and the *Gazette* regretted that the citizens should have to support the indigents who crowded into the city from rural regions of South Carolina and the neighboring provinces. The "Workhouse and Hospital for the Poor" became so overcrowded that the Vestry asked permission of the Governor to use the army barracks outside the town; both the Vestry and the Grand Jury deplored having to house decent poor folk in the Workhouse with vagrants, criminals, and slaves under correction. After listening to a detailed report of conditions in April 1767, the Commons House appointed commissioners to select a site and erect a new brick almshouse, but there is no record that it was ever built. Had the city been able to stop vagrants from burdening the rates, its poor problem might have been solved, but it was faced with such burdens as the numerous Scotch-Irish immigrants who often landed in such condition they needed succor; it relieved them occasionally, as in 1772, by hiring wagons to carry some 173 of them to the back settlements. The Vestry also showed its generosity in the case of David Duncan, "an industrious man," who suffered severe injury by a trunk thrown from a window during a fire, by giving him twenty guineas for a passage to Edinburgh "to get into the Infirmary there."

"Charity is carried rather to excess in Charleston," Dr. David Ramsay declared, "for the bounty of the public is so freely bestowed and so easily obtained as to weaken the incitements to industry and sometimes to furnish facilities for indulging habits of vice." The year 1762 saw three new charitable organizations at work: the Fellowship Society, the Charitable Society, probably composed of Baptists, and the Society for the Relief of Widows and Orphans of the Clergy of the Established Church. The German Friendly Society, organized at the house of Michael Kalteisen on January 15, 1766, grew rapidly, sent its rules to Philadelphia to be printed, and by 1775 possessed a stock of £3,174. Aiming at the erection of a hospital for the sick poor and the insane, the Fellowship Society, with a membership of tradesmen and artisans, did not amass sufficient money to purchase ground until 1773. Private benefactions dispensed also exceeded those of any other city. The bequest by the Honorable Benjamin Smith of £1,000 in currency to the South Carolina Society was but one of many, which increased its stock to £70,000 by 1776, for charity sermons always inspired grandees to compete in conspicuous benevolence. It would have been surprising if all Charles Town had not joined in a generous collection in March 1775 for the relief of their fellow Americans at Boston.

The six Overseers of the Poor at Newport and four Overseers of the Workhouse, chosen annually, had their hands full in providing for charity cases. Inasmuch as the laws against strangers were strictly enforced, particularly that denying entrance to foreigners from anywhere except the British Isles, the poor were mainly of local origin, but needy cases piled up during the depression. The majority were cared for by out-relief; the Quakers used this method exclusively. A small Alms and Work House served as the only shelter for dependents whom the city supported directly, and in 1762 "Cabbins" for them to sleep in were built within the fence around the house. Perhaps to discourage idleness and permanent malingering, the Town Council regularly advertised to bind out able-bodied men, women, and children "who are poor Persons, that have no Employ, and who are likely to be a Town Charge." No other community thrust adults into this state of quasi-bondage, which might last as long as four years. Unemployment bred a serious situation requiring the grant of broad powers to the Overseers in 1765. Private benevolence and church collections in some measure aided distressed inhabitants, as did efforts to procure cheap fuel and the maintenance of a public granary.

When hostilities broke out in 1775, British war vessels immediately stopped traffic in and out of Narragansett Bay. Ferry, market, and fish boats never reached the wharves because the Royal Navy commandeered all fresh foods in them, and negotiations with Captain Wallace for an accommodation fell through. Many citizens abandoned Rhode Island for the mainland that summer, but the poor, who had to remain, faced starvation. In May the town purchased supplies of corn and in October prohibited the sale of any of the firewood on hand until December 1, fixing a reasonable price for each. The Assembly attempted to work out relief plans, and Providence County generously agreed to waive all regulations about strangers and accept "four Hundred of Such Poor of this Town, as might be willing to remove." A large donation from Philadelphia got through to the town in March 1776, but the plight of the island city was critical, even after more than half of its inhabitants fled.

Considering the size and wealth of New York, public poor relief there did not measure up to that dispensed by other cities, and private charity failed to make up the deficiency. Save for the purchase of "an Iron Cast Stove," "a set of Rasers," and some coal for the Alms House in 1767, the Corporation seldom busied itself with the destitute, leaving the administration of that institution to the city vestry. That the burden was heavy is clear from a report of February 1771 listing 339 paupers in the Alms House, "besides a considerable number of poor Persons and Families supported or assisted at their own Places of residence in this City." On March 1 the number had risen to 360, and during the ensuing year 372 more entered, while 307 were discharged or died, leaving 425 on March 1, 1772. Another aspect of poverty that forced itself into the public ken was that of the imprisoned debtors. A benefit performance of *George Barnwell* was given for them in 1765 by the American Company, moved also by the thought of removing middle-class opposition to the theater. Even so, a few years later the *Journal* berated those who lavished money for such entertainment which might better have been spent on fuel and food for their unfortunate neighbors, emphasizing that the fifty pounds paid for a box for the season would purchase many necessaries. Fairly regular gifts of food from sympathetic New Yorkers brought some measure of comfort, especially after 1769. Bowing to public demands, the Corporation sent food to the debtors during the bitter January weather of 1772. In order to increase the funds available for charity, the Assembly resorted to a tax of one shilling on each dog in 1774.

Most of the private relief dispensed in Manhattan was intermittent and casual, except that of the friendly societies. In 1761 the St. Andrew's Society employed needy Scottish women. Because the Society for the Promotion of Arts, etc., had died out in December 1767, after the repeal of the Stamp Act, a "Tradesman" called for its revival, as he told a dismal story of the gloomy prospects for all artisans throughout a long cold winter with no work, no firewood, no money, and soaring house rents. "Our Neighbours daily breaking, their Furniture at Vendue in every Corner. Surely it is high Time for the middling People to abstain from every Superfluity in Dress, Furniture, and Living. . . . Some former able Housekeepers starving, yet ashamed to beg; some families starving for Want of Work; some dragged to Gaol, whose miseries are heightened by leaving a tender Wife and helpless Family to starve." The Society was reinvigorated and for a time gave employ to three hundred people. The Marine Society, organized in 1769, provided relief for the families of sea captains and promoted maritime knowledge. Unquestionably undeserved poverty, coupled with ineffectual and insufficient public relief in the midst of great displays of wealth, contributed to the radicalism of the middle and lower classes at New York.

VIII

Concern for their physical well-being absorbed much of the time of all city families, as the diary of Elizabeth Drinker of Philadelphia so eloquently shows. Physicians advised Charlestonians and Philadelphians to carry umbrellas on hot summer days for protection from the sun, and in the Southern capital John Bartram discovered that nearly everyone had "what they call muschata curtains or pavilions; some is silk, some linen grass or Gaws," and "are wove on purpose for that use and make very comfortable lodging amongst thousands of those hungry vermin." What wouldn't Alexander Macraby have given for such a pavilion while he was being "mauled by mosquitoes" at Manhattan in the summer of 1768!

Municipal authorities assiduously followed out such theories of sanitation and public cleanliness as the age understood; in fact, they were ahead of their European contemporaries in this respect. Every city went to considerable expense to provide medical care for the poor. St. Philip's Vestry paid Doctors James Clitherall and John Farquharson each £600 a year in 1770, and later gave Dr. Tucker Harris a salary of £700 to attend and prescribe for the city's sick dependents. One of Newport's ablest physicians, Dr. Thomas Rodman, took care of smallpox cases in the isolation hospital at Coaster's Harbor, while Trinity Church employed Dr. Thomas Eyres to visit sick Negroes. Similarly Dr. Beekman Van Buren received £30. 5s. in 1768 from the Corporation of New York "for administering Sundry Medicines to Several persons Objects of Charity."

The contemporary craze for taking mineral waters to restore jaded health or prevent illness spread quickly in the American cities when springs with chalybeate properties were discovered. Dr. John Kearsley in 1764 built a house at a spring in Philadelphia's Northern Liberties at what came to be known as Bath-Town; the middle class were its patrons. Joseph Dawson's Cold Bath on Cambridge Street had long been popular with both hardy and valetudinarian Bostonians; in 1767 Jackson's Mineral Bath at New Boston competed with a rural spring at Newton by providing a hot bath and water in bottles to take away. Knickerbockers desiring fashionable therapy had to cross the bay to Perth Amboy, where in 1773 John Hampton kept a mineral spring "similar to the German Spaw," in addition to a conveniently enclosed sea-water bathing establishment he had operated the previous year. For the wealthier citizenry, trips and voyages to distant and more exclusive springs or to more moderate climes to escape the diseases common in the summer did much to preserve their health as well as to bolster their spirits.

Periodic visitations of infectious diseases remained a scourge to all citizens. Dysentery affected people everywhere, but especially those of Philadelphia, New York, and Charles Town, where it arrived with the spring. Scarlet fever caused the death of many children, and yellow fever carried off adults in alarming numbers at Philadelphia and Charles Town. Although Benjamin Franklin expostulated to George Whitefield in 1764 that he should not be persuaded from coming to Pennsylvania "by the bugbear Boston account of the unhealthiness of Philadelphia," the city had a good health record. "I think it is as healthy a place as any on the Continent," Silas Deane wrote to an anxious Connecticut wife in 1774. Charles Town, on the authority of Doctors Alexander Garden and Lionel Chalmers, was actually a bad place to live in during the summer; indeed, common opinion had it that "Carolina is in the spring a paradise, in the summer a hell, and in the autumn a hospital." If Newport suffered acute economic distress, fortune favored the health of its citizens by giving it the best climate along the Atlantic seaboard.

When the most dreaded of all diseases, smallpox, struck at the cities, it not only took the lives of many citizens but necessitated large expenditures at the very time it usually brought trade to a standstill. Communities then split asunder over the issue of inoculation, notably at Boston. When Dr. Sylvester Gardiner proposed that the town build an inoculation hospital in a remote place during the epidemic of 1761, offering incontrovertible statistics anticipating eventual immunity for all, the people voted him down. In January 1764, when the disease appeared again with great violence, the Selectmen agreed with Dr. Myles Whitworth to care for those afflicted in the Province Hospital at New Boston, but some other inhabitants declared it unsatisfactory, and Paul Revere refused to allow his daughter to be sent there. The General Court at that time prohibited inoculation until thirty families should have contracted the disease, for fear of spreading the contagion, and the great controversy began. Finally the wise and scientific reasoning of the Boston physicians won them permission to open inoculation hospitals at Point Shirley and Castle William, but many still feared "the spreading of that Distemper, so detrimental to their Trade and Business," which was already very dull. On March 12, Doctors Thomas and Turner received permission to open a hospital in the South End, but every precaution was taken to keep country people from entering any of the establishments. During the distemper twenty-one doctors had inoculated 1,025 of the city's poor, more than half of them free of charge.

The epidemic seemed to have run its course by April 19, when the Selectmen persuaded twenty-six of Boston's thirty-one physicians to cease inoculating. Then they summoned Richard Draper of the *Newsletter* and instructed him not to publish any information about the epidemic unless released by them and required him to inform the other printers of their wishes. Censorship was on, though to their credit the Selectmen did give the newspapers regular handouts. In June the official figures were released, stating that of 699 who had the smallpox the natural way, 124 died; while out of 5,247 (including 400 outsiders) inoculated, only 46 succumbed. They also reported that 1,537 persons "removed into the Country."

The blow to Boston's prosperity was of course incalculable. Shopkeepers and merchants fled and set up at places as far apart as Roxbury and Newport; many subscribers canceled delivery of the *Boston Post Boy* lest it carry infection; and terror settled on the city. It cost thousands of pounds for inoculation, bed, board, and nursing, apart from the damage to business. Hundreds of Bostonians, however, became convinced of the efficacy of inoculation, and in succeeding years those who could afford it took the precaution of going through the operation at one of the many hospitals operated by New York physicians who advertised in the newspapers, or at Dr. Gelston's on Martha's Vineyard.

It is a fact well worth attention that the death rate at Boston from

1743 to 1773 remained relatively constant in proportion to a constant population, except during the measles year, 1747, and the smallpox years, 1752 and 1764. Thus it cannot be said that this dread disease was a major factor in stabilizing the city's population. Child and child-bed mortality, many losses at sea, the numerous accidental deaths of the time, war casualties, and such perennial ailments as dysentery, tuberculosis, and influenza seem to have been the principal reasons for death at Boston. Moreover, after the general inoculation of 1752 and 1764, and again in the scare years of 1769, 1771, and 1774, many uninoculated citizens rushed to the physicians for treatment. The overwhelming majority of Bostonians were immune to the scourge by 1776, when it broke out in September, but nobody opposed the inoculation of 2,873 inhabitants, 786 soldiers, and 1,329 country people; the death rate was only one in 192.

Inoculation made remarkable headway during the sixties as physicians and civic leaders strongly advocated it and the press threw its weight behind the movement for immunization. Manhattan doctors, following the lead of Dr. George Muirson, who had introduced the use of mercury in inoculation, opened hospitals easily accessible to wealthy citizens from the Northern ports. By 1772, hospitals had opened at New York itself, Livingston Manor, Claverack, and Kinderhook on the Hudson, New Brunswick and Elizabeth Town in New Jersey, and, with a view to the Newport and Boston trade, at Sag Harbor, Shelter Island, Fisher's Island, Plum Island, Norwalk, Saybrook, New London, and Stonington. Dr. John Cochran, one of Manhattan's ablest physicians, advertised his New Brunswick establishment in the *Newport Mercury,* pointing out that a coasting schooner made a direct and easy connection between the two places. He also emphasized that "his method produces very small abcesses," lessening thereby the danger of disfigurement. Surgeon Latham of the King's Eighth Regiment had learned a special method of inoculation from the celebrated Dr. Daniel Sutton at London and was the only one at New York authorized to use it when he set up his "Inoculation Apartments" on Broad Street in 1770. Three years later he operated a chain of hospitals—five in New York province, one in Connecticut, and one at Worcester, Massachusetts—and he announced that any practitioner of character might become a principal for the Suttonian method in his county by applying to Latham. Parties were made up at Newport and other cities to go to one of these establishments and pass through the treatment in a "class." The Reverend Ezra Stiles and a group of his Congregationalists traveled to Stonington for the operation, taking their own Dr. Bartlett with them. The many hospitals set up indicate the profitableness of the treatment, and when New Yorkers learned in 1763 that Rhode Island might allow a hospital within its boundaries, they feared that "it will stop one Source of Profit to this City and East Jersey, whereto Numbers are constantly resorting from the above mentioned Colony," yet the project might lead to greater profits by lifting restraints on commerce caused by dread of that distemper.

The inhabitants of Charles Town and Philadelphia, having been won to inoculation in the previous period, raised few objections to the practice if suitable precautions were taken. In the Southern city the chief problem was provision for slaves, and in 1763 Dr. William Loocock, the principal drug importer, opened a hospital in his Broad Street house for both city and country Negroes, "providing Nurse, Medicines, and every necessary, and insuring (if required) at 5 per cent." In this profitable practice he inoculated 463 within three months, losing only 4, one of whom was insured for £300. Wholesale immunization of slaves took place thereafter, as masters insured their chattels with one of the thirteen practitioners who performed the operation for the fee and the customary five per cent. Peletiah Webster went out to Sullivan's Island in 1765 to observe between two and three hundred slaves "performing quarantine with the smallpox," which suggests how susceptible Negroes were to the disease. Virtually all of the white residents of the city were inoculated locally, though Daniel Sutton thought it worth while to run an advertisement in a Charles Town newspaper in 1772, for those who crossed to London to be inoculated à la mode for "10 guineas more or less according to the Apartments required."

Philadelphians went to Dr. Glentworth's private hospital, which had a "tender, skillful matron to superintend it." Although most of the upper and middle classes enjoyed immunity by 1774, still three hundred people died of the smallpox. Inasmuch as "the chief of them were the children of poor People," twelve gentlemen formed the Society for Inoculating the Poor, with a fund for that purpose. Eight leading physicians donated their services at a room in the State House at specified hours.

At Newport alone did the fear and superstition of the lower classes hold up progress in immunization. The Town Meeting rejected a proposal of Robert Harris to open an inoculation hospital in 1761 when the distemper threatened. In 1763, upper-class leaders, including Augustus Johnston, Martin Howard, Thomas Vernon, Silas Cook, Dr. Thomas Rodman, Ezra Stiles, and Gideon Cornell, joined with Providence gentlemen in a petition to the Assembly to permit "a fitt Publick and well accommodated Hospital" for inoculation, by which there would be "Large Sums of Gold and Silver Money Saved and Kept within the Colony." But fear transcended cupidity, and the measure failed to pass. During the great scare at Boston in 1764, the Town Meeting again turned down inoculation on June 5, placing reliance on a rigid quarantine. Tempers flared in August 1772 after Dr. Jonathan Easton, a recent graduate of the Medical School in Philadelphia, inoculated three Quakers—the first time in the colony's history. Immediately permissive legislation was sought from the Assembly, but for four days the Town Meeting seesawed back and forth, and finally the opponents, who feared spreading of the contagion by inoculation, barely defeated endorsement of the measure. The bill never passed, and much of Newport's hard-earned specie continued to flow out to other colonies for inoculation charges. Stiles estimated the mortality from smallpox in 1772 for those who acquired it naturally was one in eight; by simple inoculation, one in seventy or eighty; and by mercurial inoculation one in seven or eight hundred! But in keeping with its tradition, Rhode Island once more thought otherwise.

Among the great achievements of the colonial cities the establishing of the Pennsylvania Hospital ranks very high. Dr. Thomas Bond and the Staff steadfastly kept the hope that the hospital might become "a means of increasing the Number of People, and preserving many useful Members to the Public from Ruin and Distress." Out of 8,831 admissions to its medical and surgical departments from the opening to 1773, the managers reported 4,440 complete cures and only 852 deaths. The mortality rate was a mere fraction of that at the hospitals of London and Paris, where the number of patients lost in the same period was staggering. Dr. Benjamin Rush, who knew the hospitals of Europe intimately, asserted in 1774 that "the Pennsylvania Hospital is as perfect as the wisdom and benevolence of man can make it." Not the least of the institution's services was the opportunity it offered the medical profession and the medical students at the College to make careful studies of the many cases available and to listen to clinical lectures in which Dr. Bond and his associates supplemented their theoretical studies. The unique care given to mental cases attracted patients from other colonies; it was the cost of sending Virginians all the way to Philadelphia that led to the building of the first provincial mental hospital at Williamsburg in 1773.

"With great Pathos and Strength of Argument," Dr. Samuel Bard in an oration at the commencement at King's College in 1769 urged the necessity of establishing a regular hospital for the sick poor. Such a plan had been broached "for a long time past," Bard said, and a group of physicians known as the "Society for promoting the Knowledge and extending the Usefulness of their Profession" had made plans for a hospital, which had been delayed by the dispute with the mother country. Governor Sir Henry Moore now led the subscribers to what became the Society of the Hospital in the City of New York in America. In January 1770 the Corporation turned over a small house to the doctors, and in 1772 the Assembly issued a charter for the hospital, voting it eight hundred pounds a year for twenty years on the condition that the sick poor from any part of the province without regard to sect be admitted. Funds accumulated rapidly, and "a grand building" went up on a five-acre plot west of Broadway between Duane and Worth streets; but tragically it burned in 1775. Rebuilt a year later, it never was put to its intended use because of the outbreak of the War for Independence, during which time Hessian troops turned it into a barracks.

IX

Throughout the course of a century and a half, the people of the five cities had made a series of concentrated attacks on the numerous and pressing problems of urban living. By 1776 they had the prevention and fighting of fire, as well as the ensuring of an adequate supply of water, pretty well under control. Save at Newport, where opposition to inoculation persisted, the cities had marched well along the road to immunization against smallpox, and the hospital movement had made an auspicious beginning. In the understanding and counteracting of such other plagues as measles, scarlet fever, and dysentery they would remain helpless until the elucidation of the germ theory of disease made further advance possible. Had this period been one of normality, urban police and prison arrangements might not have appeared to be such conspicuous failures, but these were times of turmoil and uncertainty. All that can be said is that the great European cities failed to evolve police systems that might have served the colonists for models. That public and private morality patently declined as a consequence of the advent of secularism and, more immediately, the French wars, no citizen ever denied. In fact, immorality, crime, mob violence, and extreme poverty proved to be permanent accompaniments of urban growth and deepened in these years of economic, social, and political disturbances. Given a restless, ambitious population, distressed much of the time and resentful of unredressed grievances both by its local superiors and by the British government, it is a matter for commendation that ordinary urban problems were handled as promptly and skillfully as they were.

CHAPTER 9

The Twilight of Aristocracy

BETWEEN THE CLOSE of the French and Indian War and the meeting at Philadelphia of the Continental Congress, urban society, without its members being aware of it, underwent a profound and permanent transformation. If 1760 marked the high noon of colonial aristocracy, 1775 signalized the approach of its twilight. The first segment of the American people to become aware of its power and to achieve an inter-colonial unity, the gentry seemed to have won for themselves an enviable position of potency and prestige. Like any class of patricians, they expended their wealth upon the accompaniments of gentility—town houses, landed estates, elaborate equipages, costly attire—and they devoted their leisure to approved pursuits of culture—gardening, wining and dining, the art of conversation, the acquisition of paintings, listening to music, and travel. In all this the force most consistently urging them along was the desire to exhibit their wealth to an admiring world. Such a self-evident feeling of class was not for a moment lost upon another and larger section of the urban population, which in these years discovered its capacities and began to suspect that athwart its future course to power stood the gentry. Change and unrest permeated American life as the democratic yearnings of the middle class, and of not a few of the aristocracy too, were translated into demands and occasionally into action. Long-festering class antagonisms could now be detected in daily social interchanges, religious activities, the pursuit of diversions, and even in taverns and round and about the towns.

II

Resumption of immigration after the Peace of Paris augmented the non-English elements in the populations of Philadelphia, Charles Town, and New York. Only two ships brought Palatines to the Delaware port between 1756 and 1762, but from that time until 1775 at least eighty-six vessels arrived with human cargoes of two or three hundred each. Pastor Mühlenberg tells us that the majority of the Germans located "in the eastern and northern sections of the city, and farther out in the suburbs of Kensington, Pool's Bridge, Frankfurt, New Germantown Street," and the Northern Liberties in general. In such localities one heard little English spoken. "I am about to learn the Dutch language," Dr. Rush remarked in 1765, "inasmuch as so great a part of our city consists of that nation." Conversely, Henry Miller's *Philadelphische Staatsbote* published elementary English lessons in order to assist his countrymen in their commercial dealings, and he urged the advantages of naturalization upon them. There is no doubt that the language barrier kept the two nationalities apart. Mr. Mühlenberg ascribed the failure of Henry W. Stiegel's glass to sell widely to the fact that "he is only a German, not an Englishman or a Frenchman. The 'superior' nations look upon the Germans as nothing but wig-blocks, which are thick and hard to be sure, but wanting brains." Elizabeth Sandwith, a Quakeress, wrote in her diary in the same condescending vein about being assisted when her cart broke down by "2 or 3 honest dutchmen (for aught I know)." By this time, of course, many second- and a few third-generation Germans had come to live in Philadelphia, and some of them, such as the Wistars, were accepted in the circle of the local gentry. In 1764 Henry Keppele was elected to the Assembly with Quaker support, and such a music-lover as Michael Hillegas, and the fox-hunting enthusiast Jacob Hiltzheimer, were hobnobbing with gentlemen.

Philadelphia's population was also interlarded with numerous arrivals from Ireland, especially after the late sixties. Most of them were Protestants from Ulster, though a few came from the Roman Catholic southern counties. In his diary from May 21, 1774 to June 7, 1775 Christopher Marshall recorded the arrival of nine ships from Belfast, Waterford, Newry, and Londonderry with a total of 3,280 passengers to be sold as indentured servants. The condescension of the natives toward these people rankled in the heart of at least one Celt, for he published a poem in honor of Erin in the *Pennsylvania Chronicle* in 1767, hoping thus to teach "weak, saucy foreigners . . . to admire rather than despise, all the generous Sons of Hibernia." In the seventies, also, numbers of men and women emigrated from Liverpool and London to Philadelphia in search of better opportunities for employment.

The composition of Charles Town's population differed radically from that of the Northern cities in that more than half of the inhabitants were Negro slaves. According to Governor William Bull in 1770, the city contained 5,030 whites, 5,833 blacks, "Domestic Servants and Mechanics," and a mere 24 free Negroes or mulattoes. Many immigrants from Germany, Ireland, and Scotland joined the English elements during the last colonial decade: one January about 170 passengers landed from Belfast and remained in the city because of the unsettled state of Indian affairs in the interior; more than 1,000 farmers and artisans were expected from the same place in 1772, and those who stayed at Charles Town soon came to outnumber the German element. In time the *South Carolina Gazette* ran a piece on "the character of the Irish, Scotch, and English," finding the first gay, fickle, generous, indolent, and pleasure-seeking, the Caledonians frugal, strong in adversity, moderate in prosperity, and jealous of Scottish honor, while the English shone in superior reasoning, love of liberty, and excess in eating and drinking. Gentlemen like Arthur Middleton spoke sneeringly of "the Mynheers and their Frows" and the "Crackers" from the upcountry. Certain artisans from Scotland, reacting to such sweeping statements and the accusation that they had followed commerce instead of agriculture, protested that their fellows were by no means "in toto inimical to the Liberties of America."

"Many Scots and Irish are come here," John Watts reported from New York in 1774, and the names of artisans advertising in the newspapers confirm this. Native craftsmen and tradesmen resented competition from foreigners when business was so dull: a "Mechanick in Philadelphia" wrote to his New York friend in 1772 complaining that when one entered a Quaker City shop he only too often had to deal with a "vintner from London, a shoemaker from Bristol, or a schoolmaster from France," and by such means "our natives are reduced to want, and at last become burdens to their country." This was also true at Manhattan, commented "a Constant Customer," who had inserted this letter in the *New York Gazette:* "Without swerving from the truth, it is deplorable, that foreigners, of whatever occupation, are encouraged here rather than natives. If this be true, as it undeniably is, are we not too diffident of the abilities of our natives? as appears plainly by deifying almost to a degree of enthusiasm, [those] who in all probability could scarcely earn even their daily bread in the land of their nativity." It is time to stop all this! Apparently American labor's argument against the immigrants was born in the revolutionary movement.

III

Throughout the period urban aristocracy seemingly grew in prestige as well as in numbers and wealth. Scions of distinguished and long-established families acquired more power and influence by way of the law, politics, or medicine; and far from avoiding mercantile pursuits, they continued to pile cent per cent in the countinghouse. By the standards of the time, there were the rich and the very rich. Joseph Galloway had amassed £70,000 sterling by 1776, and if this was not the largest Philadelphia fortune, it still set him above and apart from lesser gentlemen like Samuel Rhoads, who was on his way up. Upon the death in 1769 of

PLATE 13 · *Music in Boston, 1770*

As conceived in Paul Revere's engraving for William Billings's The New England Psalm-Singer, *or* Chorister.

PLATE 14 · *A Dancing Assembly*

  Ladies and gentlemen painfully and dutifully danced the "stately minuet" at each assembly, but entered with unfeigned enthusiasm into the "country dances" shown here from Thompson's popular English manual of instructions.

his Uncle Edward, John Scott of Newport inherited a large fortune, which he succeeded in squandering in four years before he died "after a Bacchanalian Life," and at the same time Captain Simon Pease was salting away 18,000 Spanish dollars in the six per cent Massachusetts Treasury notes. So large did the Alexander fortune become that when one of the daughters married a British officer at New York, her share ran to £20,000 sterling, "there being a very great Estate in Lands and a considerable personal one." Bostonians rated John Hancock as one of the most opulent merchants and James Bowdoin as possibly the wealthiest man in New England, for in addition to his own estate, he received a very large dowry when he married Councilor Erving's daughter, Elizabeth.

Many new faces appeared at genteel balls, around festive boards, and at meetings of fashionable clubs and fire societies, for since wealth was the measure of all things, no possessor of it remained long outside of charmed circles. War fortunes elevated small merchants or sea captains to high status, at New York in particular, though John MacPherson of Philadelphia, who reinvested his large fortune of prize money in peaceful commerce, was pre-eminent in this group. His great wealth enabled this prince of privateers to buy thirty-one acres of land in the Northern Liberties from Benjamin Mifflin in 1761 and undertake the erection of what was to be the most imposing seat in the Middle colonies on an eminence on the east bank of the Schuylkill. His son "Jack" attended the College of New Jersey at Prince Town, after which he joined the gay blades of the younger Philadelphia gentry, and as if to seal with finality his social position, the elder MacPherson crossed to Scotland to take as his second wife Marianne McNeal, a connection of the Countess of Dugdale. Then there was the case of John Singleton Copley, whose painter's craft earned him an acquaintance with most of the aristocratic Boston families. When, in 1769, he married Susannah Farnam Clarke, daughter of Richard and great-niece of Governor Hutchinson, he entered one of the great Massachusetts Tory families. This brilliant marriage naturally brought the artist more business, but it also required a grander style of living and kept him from making his long-anticipated trip to Europe while he built on Beacon Hill a handsome house with the first "Peaza" in Boston.

Perhaps the principal effect of the new imperial policy upon the urban aristocrats arose from the presence of large numbers of officials required to implement it. To attain a royal appointment meant a step upward to Englishmen, and in the colonies the chosen places of society went, almost without exception, to such functionaries. Political henchmen from the mother country arrived in dozens to occupy the most lucrative posts in the reorganized customs service and admiralty courts. Joseph and Peter Harrison secured appointments in the revenue service through the influence of the Marquess of Rockingham, and although they had earned the respect of many New Englanders and had won admission to the American Philosophical Society, still they were regarded as foreigners at Newport. The office of vendue master at Charles Town was another example of a profitable royal appointment. These recently arrived gentlemen moved with familiarity among the best families, courted and won their daughters, infected not a few with highly aristocratic notions, and initiated them into "the superficial acts of intrigue" with an air that had never before been noticed in the cities: Duncan Stewart, collector at New London and Governor George Scott of Dominica each married a daughter of Councilor John Erving of Boston. The press took to speaking of "the better sort of folks, the friends of Government." The Crown did not win many colonial friends by rewarding the stamp agents with the best jobs, for not only did native Americans fail to win these secure positions, but many a merchant found himself paying new and fat fees to the placemen almost daily.

Religious affiliations weighed heavily in the determination of social position. Everywhere Church of England members assumed an air of gentility. At Charles Town and New York they had always enjoyed a preferred station, but henceforth at Newport and Philadelphia they challenged the ancient precedence of the Quakers and Congregationalists; the majority of the newly rich and placemen, moreover, gravitated to the Anglican communion.

Possession of great wealth guaranteed to a substantial number of the aristocrats of each city a life of leisure, and of semi-leisure to others, such as no recent upper-class group in America has ever enjoyed. It was also a leisure denied by the exigencies of rural life to all but a very few of the bigwigs of the Southern colonies. Unlike the planters, the urban gentry as a class were highly solvent, and their capital, not being tied up in land and slaves, was more mobile, and they could thus indulge more freely in all the forms of conspicuous display.

Central in the scheme of genteel ostentation was the grandee's residence, which meant both a town house and a country mansion. Wealthy absentee planters and citizens grown rich in trade erected the most impressive urban mansions of the age at Charles Town. "Near the rivers," observed a German officer, "one sees beautiful buildings of brick, behind which there are usually very fine gardens. . . . If one can judge from appearances, these people show better taste and live in greater luxury than those of the northern provinces." Certainly in the mansion Miles Brewton began to erect about 1767, with its charming interiors done by Ezra Waite, "Civil Architect and Carver, from London," the city could boast the finest town house and garden in the colonies. Not far behind it in magnificence were the houses of William Gibbes, Robert Pringle, William Branford, and Colonel John Stuart. To an English visitor of 1774 it seemed that both Broad and Meeting streets "contain many large handsome modern Built Brick Houses, also some of Brick inside and Plaistered over on the Outside so as to imitate Stone very well."

The town houses of the Northern cities, while not so spacious, were notable for good proportions, beautiful paneling, and architectural details. Perhaps the most imposing new residence at New York after 1760 was Walter Franklin's on Cherry Street. At Newport, Metcalf Bowler in 1760 put up a house with a rusticated exterior and unique frescoes of Chinese subjects in its northwest parlor. The small lots of Philadelphia forced even the well-to-do to build with party walls, but if the outsides left something to be desired, they made up for it by superb trim and ornate interiors, for the city had the skilled craftsmen needed for any such commission. Even critical John Adams found such residences as those of Thomas Mifflin and John Cadwalader "splendid," "grand, spacious, and elegant." The entire house and especially the music room of the Samuel Powel residence on Third Street were furnished with the articles collected by the owner on his grand tour of Europe; Quaker George Roberts had written admiringly of it to his friend: "it looks like the habitation of a Turkish Bashaw" and the garden is "the parade of a Seraglio—'tis the noblest spot in the City." Boston acquired few new residences during these troubled years, but as the revolt broke out, John Vassall completed what was "supposed to be the best House in Town" at a cost of £3,156 sterling on a lot with large stables and an acre of garden.

The country seats of the aristocracy were famous enough to warrant the sale of prints and scenes of the mansions just as formerly pictures of English country houses were purchased to adorn the walls. In 1762 Rivington & Miller advertised "Large and splendid views of some of the most remarkable Places in North-America and of the most magnificent Palaces and Gardens in England"; six years later Kennedy's Print Shop of Philadelphia offered "American Views of elegant gardens and Landscapes"; and a decade after visiting Rivington & Miller's and examining their views, Charles Willson Peale made a set of views of the estates of gentlemen in the neighborhood of Philadelphia. Unfortunately not one of these mementoes of the colonial aristocracy has ever turned up, but they must have stimulated emulation among its newer members.

Out from Boston in the village of Cambridge, many Anglican aristocrats built mansions displaying excellent taste and surrounded by attractive gardens. "I was agreably surprized to Find a pleasant Country, well inhabited by a Sensible, Welbred, Learned people, not Inferior to most parts of our Mother Country," Christ Church's new incumbent wrote to the Bishop of London in 1766. Some fifteen houses of the Vassall family and its connections, the Olivers, Lees, Borlands, and Lechmeres, all set on plots of five or ten acres along the road to Watertown, came to be known as Tory Row. East of the village lay the large estate where Ralph Inman dwelt in a roomy three-story structure that was surrounded by outbuildings, stables, servants' quarters, green fields, and fragrant pine woods, and here the retired merchant spent more time than at his Boston town house, lavishly entertaining on a scale unequaled in the colonies.

Many other country estates lay in the environs of Boston. The younger Sir William Pepperell, Isaac Winslow, Judge Eliakim Hutchinson, Judge Robert Auchmuty, Comptroller Benjamin Hallowell, and Commodore Loring all had seats in Roxbury, while at Braintree in 1770 the Josiah Quincy mansion rose from the ashes of an earlier structure. Dorchester was the locale of several fine houses, and Thomas Hutchinson's country house at Milton was justly famous for its formal gardens. But it was Brush Hill, the three-hundred-acre Smith estate, with its view of Boston Light, that was rated by some as "one of the pleasantest and most convenient seats . . . in the Country." There Madam Smith, the former schoolmarm and "she-merchant" Elizabeth Murray, gave famous entertainments to gentlemen and ladies. She kept a Scottish gardener with a black assistant busy maintaining the planting until she turned the place over to her brother when she married Ralph Inman and moved over to Cambridge and even larger parties. Boston's mercantile families had indeed assumed the manner of life of the English country gentry.

All well-to-do Philadelphians aspired, like Isaac Norris, to "live downright in the country way," and they spared no expense to make villas, gardens, orchards, and grounds more attractive and luxurious. Stuccoworkers like James Clow, "an Artist in the Craft," made over the interior of Belmont for Judge William Peters in a style that elicited compliments from the Marquis de Chastellux. Edward Stiles's Port Royal (1762) at Frankford, and John MacPherson's Mt. Pleasant (1762) ranked with the great houses of tidewater Virginia or the Carolina Low Country in both magnificence and architectural excellence. Exhibiting nearly every device of late Georgian design on its two façades, Mt. Pleasant suggests something of the vulgar splendor of the parvenu, but it is doubtful if any Southern plantation, Monticello included, had a superior location: a wide, easy, level approach from the nearby city on the east and its scenic westward vista across the curving Schuylkill, flowing gently sixty feet below the limits of the garden, to the opposite shore, where stretched the rolling fields and woods of Pennsylvania. This stone and stucco great house with its two dependencies made a fitting "palace" for Lieutenant Governor John and Ann Allen Penn in 1770, when they rented it after the death of Mrs. MacPherson. Upon Penn's return to England the next year, the hundred-acre estate into which John MacPherson had poured £14,000 sterling was "knocked off to one of his bidders for £4,900" when he and his sons suddenly determined on an extended trip to Scotland in 1771. More "in the modern Mode" than the frame construction of Shirley Place, this most distinguished of the great colonial mansions north of the Chesapeake met with no challenge until the completion of Chalkley Hall at Frankford in 1776, which marked the culmination of the Pennsylvania spirit in brick and stone.

New Yorkers spent hundreds of thousands of pounds of their new fortunes in constructing mansions and laying out gardens after 1760. Those visitors who drove out from the city along the Greenwich Road on the west side of Manhattan to Kingsbridge and then returned by the Boston Road would have found themselves passing the entrances of villa after villa along the entire distance—James Beekman's Mt. Pleasant, Abraham Mortier's Richmond Hill, Friend Robert Murray's Murray Hill, and literally dozens of lovely seats. At Turtle Bay (Fiftieth Street) on the East River lay the Le Roy, Van Zandt, Lawrence, Marston, Schermmerhorn, and Rhinelander estates, while two Livingstons had theirs across the Hudson in Bergen County. James Duane purchased land in the Outward, two and a half miles from the city, for his Grammercy place next to John Watts's Rose Hill in 1761. Among the master workmen who profited from all this building was John Edward Pryor, who performed the carpentry work on the villas of James Rivington, Elias Desbrosses, Evarts Bancker, Captain Kennedy, General Gage, and Charles Ward Apthorp, and whose commissions took him as far afield as New Rochelle and Perth Amboy, where at the latter he took a large crew to work on the estate of the Earl of Stirling. Roger Morris's country place (1765) had one of the very few grand entrance porticoes in America, and shortly after, Charles Ward Apthorp's Elmwood (c. 1767) was built with cut-stone ashlar, said to have come from Manchester in England, and its entire composition as well as the use of decorative detail has been judged by a leading authority to have more nearly approached the classical ideal than any pre-revolutionary structure. Lord Adam Gordon, fresh from an overland journey from South Carolina through Virginia and Pennsylvania, considered Morrisania's two thousand acres, valued at £22,000 sterling, "the prittiest and best conditioned Farm in America," though it had "a bad House on it."

Modest country estates dotted the island of Rhode Island, and some summer gentry even located on New Shoreham (Block Island); George Rome built his "little country villa" called Bachelor's Hall on a seven-hundred-acre tract in the Narragansett country; Malbone House, the only mansion equal to those of other communities in the neighborhood of Newport, burned down in 1766. The almost perfect Rhode Island climate, however, lured gentlemen into expensive gardening, especially the raising of exotics, in which they achieved a perfection seldom equaled. A variety of ornamental trees shaded the island's roads, and nearly every farm had its orchard of grafted trees. Charles Blaskowitz noted that "in the vicinity of the town are several fine gardens belonging to gentlemen of fortune and taste, having fish ponds of perch, trout, etc. and their greenhouses and hothouses producing the fruits and plants of every clime." Chief among these were the Malbone and Jahleel Brenton gardens near the city, and at Portsmouth, those of Abraham Redwood, Samuel Elam, and Gideon Cornell, the last, purchased by Metcalf Bowler in 1764. "We saw Mr. Redwood's Garden, one of the finest I . . . ever saw in my life," Solomon Drowne declared in 1767. "It grows all sorts of West India Fruit, viz: Oranges, Lemmons, Limes, Pine-Apples, Tamarinds, and other sorts. It has also West India Flowers—very pretty ones—and a fine Summer House. It was told my Father by a credible person, that the Garden was worth 40,000 Pounds, and that the man who took care of the Garden has above One Hundred Dollars per annum. It has Hot Houses, where things that are tender are put in the winter, and Hot Beds for the West India Fruit."

"There are but few country seats near the town," the Philadelphians Peletiah Webster and John Bartram were surprised to learn when they visited Charles Town in 1765. As in previous years, the Low Country gentry came in from their plantations in the spring and stayed until a killing frost ended the danger of fevers. Consequently suburban seats held little appeal for them. In 1763 James Reid advertised a fourteen-acre estate only a mile from the city with a thirteen-room brick mansion, a stable, and a carriage house, and although the premises were somewhat in decay, Reid opined that they were "exceeding well adapted to display the taste or genius of the purchaser." William Dillwyn toured the Goose Creek plantations in 1773, but seems not to have thought them superior to the Pennsylvania country seats he knew so well: Thomas Smith's Broom Hall made "a neat outside appearance, but a better inward" one, and the once fabulous Crowfields he found "now much in decay." Thomas Lamboll and Henry Laurens, with extensive properties, were distinguished for the formal gardens they created within the city itself, employing professional gardeners and seedsmen. Together, Mr. Lamboll, Dr. Garden, and Bartram did much to awaken an appreciation of horticulture in the local gentry.

Ownership of one or more horses and carriages was another of the immense satisfactions of a rich gentleman. To carry him to and from his country seat and his town residence or countinghouse, he needed an outfit which, together with the arms emblazoned on the equipage, assured him immediate attention as he drove about to visit his friends or make extended journeys not only in his own but to neighboring provinces. Few ladies and gentlemen drove around so much in their chaises as Henry and Elizabeth Drinker of Philadelphia; one day it is a visit to Frankford, tomorrow to Germantown, or Chester. "I have lately mett with so many frights," Elizabeth remarked after her chair overset with

340

herself and baby in November 1767, "that I can not bear to think of riding with any satisfaction." She continued to do so, nevertheless. In New York in 1769 James Beekman told Captain John Pell about his horses: "They are fast Trotters, I generally drive them to my Seat which is 4½ miles in 28 minutes," and the sole reason for selling them is that they are "too spirited" for the children. Madam Elizabeth Smith, formerly Campbell, née Murray, became a widow again in 1769, but her brother James kept the family in Scotland posted about doings at Brush Hill: "She roals in her chariot, for you know she's mistress of one, and makes visits to all the great folks."

The increase in the number of wheeled vehicles in each city was an accurate gauge of its families of wealth and distinction, for to ride in one's own equipage was indeed the hallmark of the upper gentry. Pierre Du Simitière, whose passion for statistics has given us much information on many subjects, made a count of them in some of the cities, and from him we learn that Philadelphia's thirty-eight carriages, including three coaches, of 1761 became ninety-one by 1772: nine coaches, thirty coach wagons, and fifty-two chariots or post chaises. In their great coaches rode William Allen, James Hamilton, Benjamin Chew, Thomas Willing, Edward Stiles, Tench Francis, Samuel Pleasants, Joseph Pemberton, the Widow Masters, and Henry Keppele. As Du Simitière made up this list, one *arriviste,* sure that it was Pennsylvania's Battle Abbey Roll, put his family down for two vehicles instead of one—in which act the Swiss detected him and ribbed him most unmercifully. Edward Shippen, Jr., exulted in a letter to his father announcing the birth of the ill-fated Peggy and the steady growth of his fortune that "it is but staying a few years before I ride in my Coach." In New York in 1770, the compiler calculated that Gothamites luxuriated in twenty-six coaches, forty-one post chaises or chariots, and eighteen phaetons—a total of eighty-five. Charles Ward Apthorp, Judge Daniel Horsmanden, and Jacob Le Roy possessed one of each! So many carriages crowded into narrow John Street on theater nights that a playbill of December 1767 stated: "To prevent Accidents by carriages meeting, it is requested that those coming to the House may enter John Street from the Broad Way, and returning drive from thence down John Street into Nassau Street, or forward to that known as Cart and Horse [William] Street, as may be most convenient." When four coaches arrived from London in October 1767, "notwithstanding the great Complaints of the distressing Times we have here," the New York press focused public attention upon such extravagances.

In the three other cities gentlemen also rode in their carriages. At Charles Town in 1774 an English traveler marveled that "Most People of Property keep single Horse Chairs which are very numerous indeed in the Town, but many of the genteeler sort keep handsome Four Wheel'd

Carriages, and several Carry this luxury so far as to have Carriages, Horses, Coachmen, and all imported from England." "Boston-made Chaises with Leather Tops" also sold fairly well. Du Simitière's lists have only twenty-two Bostonians with carriages in 1768, but he must have had in mind just coaches and coach wagons, for he was in the city the year before and in 1766 John Rowe had listed sixteen coaches and chariots among the fifty-seven vehicles in Dr. Jonathan Mayhew's funeral procession, and in 1768 Thomas Hutchinson counted "two or three Chariots and fifty or sixty chaises" at the anniversary celebration of Andrew Oliver's resignation as stamp distributor. Adino Paddock, leading carriage-maker of the colonies, kept the gentlemen of Boston supplied with any kind of vehicle needed, and on occasion built one to order for Newporters like Henry Marchant.

Lavish hospitality was the natural outgrowth of accumulating wealth and the leisurely life enjoyed by the very rich. The setting at town house or country mansion called for certain properties—drawing-rooms, parlors, and dining-rooms with flowered or Chinese wallpapers in the "modern taste," exquisitely fashioned and carved Philadelphia Chippendale furniture by Affleck, Folwell, Gostelowe, Randolph, or Tuffts, or the distinctively American product put out by the Townsends and Goddards of Newport, and finely wrought silver from the shops of Richardson, Myers, or Revere. Portraits by Copley, Theus, and Peale of the richly garbed master and mistress looked down gravely upon the scene as equally expensively attired owners and their guests moved about amidst the elegance that befitted their high place in society. John Adams had an unusual opportunity to compare the hospitality of several cities during his journey to the First Continental Congress in 1774. Bostonians and Newporters did not indulge in such luxurious display as the New Yorkers and Philadelphians. Dinners at the metropolis exhausted even this resourceful diarist's powers of description. To Abigail he confided: "I shall be killed with the kindness in this place." He met with the Congress daily from nine until three, then "go to dine with some of the nobles of Pennsylvania at four, and feast upon ten thousand delicacies, and sit drinking Madeira, claret, and Burgundy till six or seven." Every day brought "a most sinful feast again." Myers Fisher gave "a most costly entertainment: ducks, hams, chickens, beef, pig, tarts, creams, custards, jellies, fools, trifles, floating islands, beer, porter, punch, wine—and a long &c." New York excelled in wines, but table conversation turned out to be far from agreeable or elevating to a Bostonian. Dinners at Charles Town closely resembled those of Northern communities, as Josiah Quincy discovered—"profuse, excellent wines, no politicks." Roger Smith, who married Mary Rutledge, served "the best provisions I have seen in this town."

Of course there were many scions of the old and established mercantile families who accepted their status gracefully and in many instances avoided conspicuous consumption: Hannah Fayerweather Winthrop, consort of a member of one of America's really distinguished families, wrote from Cambridge to Mercy Otis Warren in 1773: "I have not been to the Capitol for more than three months. I suppose when I make my appearance I shall look not unlike one of the last Century, at least like one unacquainted with Polite Life, the encreasing dissipation, the round of Elegant amusements which are become the work of every Evening have not those Attractive Charms for you and myself." In spite of the fact that John Adams was wide-eyed at the splendor he participated in as a delegate to Congress, he did observe that "there is no conversation that is agreeable, there is no modesty, no attention to one another."

In recounting instances of such sumptuous entertainments, the colonial newspapers stirred up the resentment of the generality in the towns about the "Extravagances" of many of the gentry in eating and drinking at the very time that the public was being urged to exercise frugality. "In a few Years we shall all become Turtle Eaters, and a number of Vessels may be employed in that Branch of Fishing," was the beginning of a long sarcastic piece in the *Boston Gazette*. Perhaps the dignity of Harvard College cloaked the commencement blowouts at Cambridge, but from John Rowe, who never missed a party, we learn that after he attended the exercises on July 15, 1772, he dined elegantly with a distinguished company of gentlemen, "too many to enumerate," in "Col. Murray's son's Room." On the following day: "I went early to Mr. Inman's who made the Genteelest entertainment I ever saw on account of his son George taking his Degree yesterday. He had Three hundred forty-seven Gentlemen and Ladies dined. Two hundred and ten at one Table. Amongst the Company The Governour and Family, The Lieutenant Governour and Family, The Admirall and Family, and all the Remainder, Gentlemen and Ladies of Character and Reputation. The whole was conducted with much Ease and Pleasure and all Joyned in making each other Happy. Such an Entertainment had not been made in New England before on any Occasion. I came to . . . Cambridge and went to the Ball at the Town House, where most of the Company went to Dance. They were all very happy and Cheerful and the whole was conducted to the General Satisfaction of all present." To this account, Edes & Gill of the *Boston Gazette* added that "the Side Board Range would have put a new Smile upon the Cheeks of Bacchus and his jovial trains." In truth no entertainment like this had ever been given in any of the American colonies; not even "the almost Asiatic luxury" of Charles Town approached it.

Participation in such extravagant parties was limited to one's class, but visitors of approved status were welcomed, and foreigners seldom omitted mention of the good breeding and courtesy accorded them. Governor Robert Melville of Grenada described the Newport gentry as "celebrated for their hospitality to strangers, and extremely genteel and courtly in their manners." When Ned Burd met Madam Staats Long Morris, quondam Duchess of Gordon, at the Philadelphia Assembly in 1768, he informed his Uncle Edward Shippen at Lancaster that "she is well esteemed as she is pretty sociable and don't seem to require that Pre-Eminence over other Ladies which the [New] York ladies are so ambitious of." Carolina society, being the newest and in many ways the most leisured of all, on occasion gave evidence of the arrogance that goes with the *nouveaux riches*. A Low Country gentleman temporarily living in the back country at Pine Tree Hill reminded John Rutledge of a few things in 1771: "You call us a Pack of Beggars, Pray Sir look back to Your own Origins? . . . Step back only to the beginning of this Century. What then was Carolina? What then Charlestown?" The Quaker urbanity of William Dillwyn of Philadelphia met a test at a dinner when the Reverend Robert Smith of St. Philip's, great slave-owner of British birth and later first Bishop of South Carolina, "took occasion to observe that Persons coming from the Northward and England received a Polish at Charles Town which they all wanted at first coming there. By that Rule I concluded he had not been long there himself or he would have been too polite to make the observation in Company with four people just landed from Philadelphia."

But such arrogance turned to genuflection and often to fawning whenever someone of noble birth or station arrived from across the water. A title caused as great a furore then as it now does at Newport or Southampton. Lord Adam Gordon, one of the few members of Parliament ever to visit the colonies, made a progress from Charles Town to Boston in 1765, the Right Honorable Lord Hope did the same the next year, and four years later Sir William Draper, Knight of the Bath, took the same kind of trip, except that at New York he capitulated by espousing Susannah De Lancey. When Miss Margaret Cheer, "a Lady much admired for her Theatrical Performances," married the Right Honorable Lord Rosehill in Maryland in 1768, the American Company of Comedians profited so much by the new respectability that David Douglass engaged her to appear that season in Philadelphia and New York at what was then a fabulous salary. Great was the excitement in social circles in 1775 when "the Hon. Mrs. Abigail Grant, lady of Sir Alexander Grant," arrived at Newport from London to visit with her brother David Chesebrough on Mary Street; and, in spite of all snide comments about the validity of his title, William Alexander, Earl of Stirling, cut a great figure in the provinces of New York and New Jersey, and his sister Susannah met with no difficulty in winning a

British colonel with her brother's prestige backed by her "many aimiable accomplishments and . . . large fortune."

Catering to self-esteem and the need for family connections, many a New Yorker and Philadelphian sent to Boston to have John Gore or one of the other craftsmen paint their coats of arms. When Friend Stephen Collins was about this business in 1765, his artisan brother asked him to "let me know whether thou will choose the Family arms done in the best manner; the cost will be from 40/ to 70/£ ster," done by "a person Reputed to be the Best Workman at that Business in this town." Soon, however, the Quaker City uncovered in James Poupard one who cut heraldic devices in stone for seals, and a newspaper carried burlesque proposals to print the *American Genealogist,* containing accounts of the "origin, progress, and intermarriage &c. of most of the Considerable families in America."

"The evil itch of overvaluing foreign parts," especially where nobility was involved, got some Americans into trouble then as now. On July 7, 1772 the ladies and gentlemen of Charles Town thrilled with the news of the arrival of Sophia Carolina Mathilda, Marchioness de Waldegrave, and own sister to the Queen, who came overland from Cape Fear and Philadelphia. After a whirlwind conquest of the city and province, she departed in November when she found she was "engrossing a good Deal of public Conversation." Everywhere she turned up clad in fine apparel and bedecked with jewels, displaying the Queen's picture and promising commissions and offices with regal generosity to her wide-eyed hosts as she blandly borrowed sums of money from them. Some of the less ambitious suspected this gentlewoman, but, as Peter Timothy gleefully noted in his *Gazette,* "THE KNOWING ONES are sometimes taken in." At length Michael Dalton received a letter from William Devall of Bush Creek, Frederick County, Maryland, describing a runaway convict servant, Sarah Wilson, who, while attending Miss Vernon, a sister of Lady Grosvenor, maid of honor to the Queen, had stolen some jewels and was sentenced to be transported to Maryland in 1771; Mr. Devall had bought her time from a ship's captain. After escaping to Virginia, Sarah Wilson assumed her title and proceeded to fool the bigwigs of the South. In the spring of 1773 the Marchioness was exposed in the newspapers of nearly every city when her owner offered a reward for her return. Nevertheless she intrepidly arrived at New York from Philadelphia in September, went on by water to Newport in November, ultimately reaching Boston in January 1774, and set out for Portsmouth. In April, reports had her in residence at Newcastle in New Hampshire, and a Boston printer exclaimed with much reason that "she is the most surprizing genius of the female sex that was ever obliged to visit America." What an improvement on Moll Flanders! What a job she and the notorious Tom Bell together could have done on the colonial aristocracy!

The last report of the Marchioness de Waldegrave was the *Newport Mercury*'s notice of her arrival from the eastward and sailing for New York in July 1775. She bowed out with colonial history.

One of the striking features of urban aristocracy during these years was the highly developed sense of solidarity among the members. Socially and spiritually, as well as in trade and politics, the gentlefolk of all five cities came to know one another better, to exchange amenities, and to sense their common bonds in the leadership of an American society. By means of brilliant marriages certain great families became truly intercolonial in influence and importance. The Allens, Shippens, and Francises of Philadelphia, the New York De Lanceys, the Ervings of Boston, the Redwoods of Newport, and the Izards of Charles Town built up family connections in three or more provinces. Chief Justice William Allen's wife was a sister of Governor James Hamilton of Pennsylvania; and of his children, James married Elizabeth, daughter of Mayor John Lawrence of Philadelphia; Andrew wedded the "beautiful Sally Coxe" of New Jersey, whose mother was a Francis; and John espoused Mary Johnston of the prominent New York family. Ann Allen became the second wife of Lieutenant Governor John Penn, and Margaret espoused the leader of New York's aristocracy, James De Lancey. The Shippens enjoyed great prestige and distinction, and the scions of that family were officials, merchants, physicians, and lawyers. When Dr. William Shippen married Alice Lee, her family, hitherto known only in the Old Dominion, began to acquire the outside connections that would give it more than provincial prominence after 1775. The Izards of Charles Town, titled Warrens and Drapers from England, the Allens and Franks of Philadelphia—these were some of the alliances of the De Lanceys, whose wealth and political power paralleled their social position. The marriages of John Erving's daughters to James Bowdoin, Governor George Scott of Dominica, and Duncan Stewart of the British customs service gave this Boston family an interimperial position, whereas the Hutchinsons and Olivers married and intermarried for the most part with distinguished Massachusetts families, venturing on only two occasions to include two Sanford ladies from Newport.

Within each community the wealthy consolidated and augmented their fortunes by shrewdly arranged marriages. The winter of 1768 at Philadelphia saw at least five such matches. When Joseph Potts and Sally Powel joined hands in the presence of the city's leading Friends at the great Meeting House, the *Chronicle* emphasized that virtue, modesty, and good sense reflected far more luster on her character than "the Fortune of 20,000 £ which she actually possesses," but when her Anglican brother Samuel, with his new "London tricks and St. James customs," married Elizabeth Willing in Christ Church the next year, the city witnessed one of its most brilliant dynastic unions. Of prime future import was a similar set of entangling alliances concluded at Newport in 1773 by the nuptials of the attorney William Channing and Lucy Ellery, "a young lady adorned with a great deal of understanding and every accomplishment"; a year later John Channing married Miss Nabby Hazard. Some aura must have attached to a successful bookseller, even though he was of the middle class, for James Rivington, gay Manhattan spendthrift, won Elizabeth Van Horne, rich relict of Cornelius, in 1769, and young Henry Knox married into the highest Boston circles. Miss Lucy Flucker, a niece of the Inmans, who was "very much of a reader," went daily with other Tories to Cornhill to browse in the fashionable bookshop where, it is said, Knox's fine bearing and good looks so attracted her that, in defiance of her father, the last royal secretary of Massachusetts Bay, she married him and, of course, eventually became one of the first ladies of a new nation.

The amount of jaunting about and the hardihood of the gentry in undertaking it so frequently and avidly are truly astounding. The urban aristocrats not only traipsed around within their own and neighboring provinces but often managed, either by land or by sea, to visit in the more remote ones. Visitors at John Rowe's Boston residence in the autumn of 1764 included two Philadelphians, three Newporters, and one from Plymouth, and in between the pleasure-loving merchant embarked on several short trips himself. Mr. and Mrs. John Izard and Mr. and Mrs. Alexander Wright of Charles Town and Savannah went up to Boston for a visit during their Newport stay of 1772. In fact the Izards seemed to be always on the move. Ralph and Susannah De Lancey Izard sailed back and forth between New York and Charles Town, and Copley painted his well-known portrait of them at Rome in 1775. The tours of John Hancock, Thomas Brattle, and Henry Lloyd overland as far south as Philadelphia in 1770, and the journey of Josiah Quincy by water to Charles Town and then back over the coastal road in 1773 had profound political implications; likewise that year the Northern visit of Mr. and Mrs. Thomas Mifflin, during which they sat for Copley at Boston, had its political overtones. Henry and Elizabeth Drinker often drove between Philadelphia and East Jersey points; for a consumptive, Henry essayed very long drives on Quaker business to New Bern or westward "beyond the Blew Mountains." From Philadelphia John Hughes rode to Portsmouth in 1769, bearing letters of introduction from Benjamin Franklin that opened every door to him. "I must say that I never met with better Usage in my life than I have met with this Journey in Every place I passed through." When Hughes visited Charles Town two years later, he was delighted with the "Respect shewn me by all Ranks of People from the Governor down to the planter." From August 12–26, 1773, the Lawrences led a party in chairs on "a Summer Jaunt" from Philadelphia to Abington, Bethlehem, Easton, Nazareth, Allen's Town,

Reading, Lancaster, and back—210 miles—stopping at inns along the way. The ironmaster Daniel Leonard and his bride made a wedding journey about New England in their chaise in 1767, dazzling Yankee farmers with their elegance; but when Ned Burd rode into Lancaster County wearing a small sword in 1770, the yokels met him with gaping mouths: "A country Booby could not resist expressing his surprise at the sight of my destructive Weapon. 'I vaw, a Sword,' said he. It's well he was not a Feme covert enseint, else I could not answer for the consequences."

In addition to voyaging from city to city along the coast and occasionally to the West Indies, gentlemen, their sons, and often their wives and daughters made the formidable crossing to London or Bristol. And as many went from each Northern city, except Newport, as sailed from Charles Town. In 1764 Thomas Whately said of the former Lieutenant Governor of Pennsylvania that "Hamilton has always had one nephew or another in England, who corresponded with him. His brother [William] Allen too has been here the last twelvemonth." Some New Englanders crossed on the mast ships out of Portsmouth or New London because they were larger than ordinary merchant vessels, and Philadelphians traveled in Myers Fisher's *Pennsylvania Packet* after 1767.

A grand tour was not beyond the competence of some rich young Americans. When his son John had "an Inclination to see a little of the World," William Allen sent him and Joseph Shippen to Italy; and in 1765 Thomas Mifflin, like many other Quakers, made the grand tour before settling down to work in the countinghouse. Upon Dr. John Morgan's graduation from Edinburgh in 1764, he was joined at London by Samuel Powel and they set off for the Continent, visiting Voltaire at Ferney, taking courses in antiquities at Rome with James Byers (like Gibbon), and climaxing it all by an audience with the Pope. Quaker Samuel returned to Philadelphia an Anglican. From Newport in 1771 Henry Marchant set out on travels that took him to Berlin, Venice, Rome, Paris, and London, while Councilor Bowdoin's son James and Ward Nicholas Boylston commenced their sightseeing trip at Naples in 1773. It is probable that no contemporary European aristocracy was any more traveled than that of the English colonies.

In the same years that the members of the urban upper class were merging their special interests on an intercolonial and even an imperial scale, a rift appeared within the ranks which, by 1774, resulted in a fatal division. One of the unnoticed legacies of the mid-century wars was the strengthening of the hitherto small groups in the ruling class of each city that were ultra-colonial in outlook. War-born riches, the addition of many new members of British birth with aristocratic ambitions, dynastic marriages, an often shameless and usually ill-concealed pursuit of place and pelf, and the fortuitous support from the new imperial policy

—all these combined to bring this faction to the forefront. These people wanted above all else to amass by trade and lucrative officeholding riches sufficient to enable them to retire to their estates and live like English country gentlemen, setting the social and political tone for colonial society. This attempt at dwelling above and apart in conspicuous haughtiness was their way of drawing the line—a very sharp line it was to be—between their own cliques in the gentry and the inferior orders. Governor Francis Bernard called in print for the creation of an American nobility, and many a hopeful patrician at each city conducted himself with all the airs that he imagined went with such an exalted rank. Most of these people were members of the Church of England, or became so for social advantage rather than for reasons of piety; and they wanted more, not less, control from Whitehall because it would be exercised in the colonies through them and create additional high offices. The realities and ethos of America entirely escaped some gentlemen, who unfortunately dreamed of this other Eden, this demiparadise—the never-never land— in which they and only they, the *best of the better sort,* would rule.

Such sentiments as these did not, however, appeal to anything like a majority of the gentry in any city, nor, for that matter, to the great planters of the Southern provinces. Most of them knew that an exact replica of English life could not be reproduced on this continent, and, moreover, it did not captivate them. They already enjoyed wealth, luxury, prestige, and political power, and they were determined to maintain them against the enemy within quite as much as against the enemy without. When they realized that some of their neighbors actively sought to implement the new policy that would circumscribe the "liberties" they had recently won and now exercised through their Assemblies, they grew ever more antimonarchical in their sentiments as aristocracies of history have always done. Talk of a colonial nobility for life and the visible beginnings of a colonial civil list, from which they of course would be excluded, nepotism or the filling of new places with small men who not infrequently pieced out their authority with arrogance and lined their pockets by means that made smuggling look genteel, Episcopalian intrigue against a dissenting majority, unwarranted display in the midst of public distress—all these confirmed the majority of the aristocrats in the belief that the drift of affairs was not expressing what the age would have called the genius of America. Joseph Harrison, one of the Crown's best informants, wrote in 1768 to endorse Mather Byles, who was going to England, saying of him that he was the only Bostonian Harrison had heard of who opposed the Stamp Act Riots and disorders—"Mr. Byles has given such remarkable Proof of his Loyalty and Attachment to Great Britain (and I can assure Your Lordship, such Men are very scarce in this Country at Present)."

An irreconcilable difference in social and political philosophy, based not upon abstractions but upon the actualities of American life, drove these two groups into conflict with each other. The majority, who rebelled against the mother country, dimly, perhaps, but nevertheless accurately, perceived that unarticulated democratic forces, of which they had been the principal beneficiaries, were stirring in their cities, and somehow they understood that things had to be different over here. They were the more venturesome and farsighted members of the upper class, the less timid and less fearful. Late in 1776 Ambrose Serle recorded with dismay that Admiral Lord Howe "observed to me this morning, that almost all of the People of Parts and Spirit were in the Rebellion."

The very conditions that made possible the rise of a bourgeois aristocracy in the cities concurrently lifted up the middle class, who by 1760 had become numerous and prosperous as a class and stood ready to demand a voice in the determining of affairs affecting them in the society to which they had contributed so much. Although this was but a phase of the movement agitating the entire Western World in the eighteenth century, the absence of an all-powerful aristocracy and burdensome tradition of subordination in America gave the middle class a unique opportunity. The American tradesmen and artisans were rapidly acquiring a feeling of self-confidence issuing from a self-respect not yet evident in their European counterparts. More of the great intellects of the cities came from this group than from any other; now it was Benjamin Franklin and Peter Timothy, rather than Cotton Mather or James Logan, who set the tone of urban culture and provided leadership for the citizens.

To say that the urban middle class were antiaristocratic is not to conclude that they were levelers, notwithstanding upper-class charges. Far from it. But they insisted that no economic, political, or hereditary obstacles be thrown in the path of a man making his way to eminence and fortune by talent and hard work. At Boston, Adino Paddock began as an apprentice to a chaisemaker; soon he had his own shop and eventually became the principal coachmaker in the colonies. Entering public life, he served Boston in a succession of offices and rose to such dignity as to have the titles of "Major" and "Esq." affixed to his name in the town records, sufficient indication of his progress to the threshold of the aristocracy, which his son would enter upon graduation from Harvard. Tragically this lad, "the prettiest and likeliest of his class," drowned while swimming in the Charles in the summer of 1773. Crowds of Bostonians—better, middling, inferior—lined the streets to view the funeral procession, headed by the freshman class in caps and gowns; bells tolled even in the Latin School, and mourners gazed at his picture hanging in the schoolroom at the Manufactory House. Here was the tribute of the citizens to a craftsman who had attained the status of an entrepreneur, demonstrating, along with his fellow townsman Copley and many others, that the "Mechanicks" had come to compose a vertical, not merely a horizontal, segment of the city populations and were accordingly entitled to respect.

The middle class exhibited a wide range of wealth, education, and cultivation. Occasional members rivaled the gentry in their scale of living; not a few kept one or more servants and lived in great comfort, even sampling upper-class luxuries on occasion. Among the Charlestonians who summered at Newport were the printing families of Crouch and Wells, the bookseller Nicholas Langford, and Madam Jonathan Sarrazin, whose husband kept a fashionable jewelry shop. More impressive was the entry of Polly Weyman into the aristocracy by her marriage to John Brewton, for her father, an upholsterer, was a Son of Liberty and leader of the city's "Mechanicks."

Doubtless some of the well-to-do and cultivated members of the middle class joined with the gentry in denouncing "the universal affectation of dress which prevails among the sons and daughters of inferior mechanics" at New York as an "Evil," and even smiled in condescension at the "Thoughts on Conversation and Social Intercourse," which discussed such topics as "How not to be a Blockhead," that Solomon Southwick ran in the *Newport Mercury* to improve the manners of unsophisticated readers. At both Newport and Boston in 1769 John Hughes observed that notwithstanding "the Common people here have some Oddities in their behaviour and Speech," they treated him decently. Lord Adam Gordon remarked that "the Men here, resemble so much the people of Old England, from whence most of them are Sprung. I was rather surprized to find here, and not amongst the Richest, the respectable Names of Howard, Wentworth, Pelham, Pierpont, Dudley, Carey, Russel, Temple and many others of less note and Ambiguity; but the levelling principle here, every where Operates strongly, and takes the lead, and every body has property, and every body knows it."

The biggest mistake of the Tories was their inability to estimate the character and capacity of the middle class, and their arrogant condescension was a real cause of antagonism between the two segments of society. Alexander Graydon frankly tells us that his set decided to become merchants, "as to be mechanics was too humiliating," and among the New England gentry "Boston Yankyes" had already become a term of opprobrium. In 1773 a middle-class citizen of Philadelphia warned his fellows that the aristocrats were saying "it is time the Tradesmen were checked. They take too much upon themselves. They ought not to intermeddle in State affairs. They ought to be kept low. They will become too powerful." His communication reads as if they recalled Joseph Galloway's frightened vision of 1765 that "Democratic notions in America may lead to the independence of the Colonies from England." Especially obnoxious to the tradesmen was the bland assumption on the part of some of the gentry that middle-class people lacked the fitness to express political sentiments or to vote intelligently; that they did not think. Their leaders were indulging in some very profound thinking, and they themselves were aware that most of their cherished grievances touched on fundamentals.

The Spirit of '76 revealed itself in this clash of rebels against the self-designated best of the better sort who were supported by a small minority of the middle and lower orders and the prestige of British authority. Resistance to domination by the self-seeking gentry and to imperial rule first broke out in the cities, where these two sets of grievances fatefully coincided and where the mobility gradually realized their strength; thence it fanned out to the rest of the English colonies.

Since 1760 the tempers of the shopkeepers and craftsmen had been rising, as well as their pride, and they wanted political rights commensurate with their dignity and contributions to society. To achieve them they were willing to risk a showdown. "In regard to War and Peace," Peter Timothy pointed out to William Henry Drayton in August 1775, "I can only tell you that the Plebians are still for War—but the noblesse perfectly pacific." The rebels readily accepted the leadership of the majority of the gentry, who, like themselves, resented and condemned the privileges, costly show, and aristocratic pretensions of the Tory minority. Issues are seldom sharply and clearly defined, but this is certain, that no group entered the American Revolution with a surer comprehension of the issues over which it fought than the alerted middle class. And when the momentous decision was made in 1776, the tradesmen and artisans of the new United States stood to win by independence.

IV

Outwardly the citizens of the five communities appeared to be a very religious people, if the building of new churches and the attendance at Sabbath worship be taken as indexes; but many people lived beyond the confines of any creed, and even at Boston, in 1761, the Reverend Andrew Eliot calculated that 420 of the city's 2,000 families belonged to no denomination. And, to Ezra Stiles's regret, "in Newport there are many of no Religion," and some "persons that are Unbelievers," but "as for the West Indies," he continued on another occasion, "they will die in their iniquities. . . . I account . . . both priests and people most amazingly debauched." Benjamin Rush of Philadelphia asserted in 1764 that "Religion is at a low ebb among us. Sinners are secure indeed, and even the love of saints waxes cold. . . . Our young men in general (who should be the prop of sinking Religion) are wholly devoted to pleasure and sensuality, and very few are solicitous about the one thing needful." What held true at Philadelphia, where the sober Quakers now made up but a seventh of the population, obtained in rather greater degree elsewhere.

Religious emotions could still be appealed to by effective preachers; the influence of that "great and mighty Man of God," George Whitefield, still persisted in the land. At Philadelphia in 1763 when St. Paul's opened its doors to him, the Reverend Richard Peters deemed it necessary to invite him to Christ Church to avoid losing members, thereby arousing the ire of rural Anglicans who openly disapproved of the evangelist. During Whitefield's tour of 1764 he preached for seven weeks at New York with "more general Acceptance than ever," being received "with great Respect by many of the Gentlemen and Merchants." Another successful exhorter was a Scot, Robert Sandeman, who won adherents to his version of Christianity by preaching in playhouses and taverns from New York to Portsmouth, and who established a congregation at Boston. Large auditories of all denominations assembled in the five cities to listen to the "nervous, pertinent, and solemn" as well as "singularly penetrating" discourses of Rachel Wilson, one of the several "Foreign Friends." Likewise Sophia Hume, returning from England to preach to former neighbors in her native city of Charles Town in 1767, succeeded in bringing out old Gabriel Manigault to his first Quaker meeting in half a century. Dr. Rush testified to the strong convictions evoked by John Murray, who preached in Philadelphia, New York, Newport, and Boston; it was after his speaking at the Boston Manufactory House that the first Universalist society in this country gradually formed. Still more successful was the itineracy of Joseph Pilmore, who not only ministered at Manhattan to the first Methodist Chapel (1767), but won support for the Methodist faith at Philadelphia and Charles Town.

The outstanding Christian acts of the period took place at Philadelphia and Newport, cities famous for tolerance of diverse religious opinions. In the City of Brotherly Love, Anthony Benezet had begun his long and fruitful war on slavery about 1750 with a series of important publications condemning not only the slave trade but the institution itself. Stressing the moral and natural rights of Negroes in addition to the economic arguments advanced by Benjamin Franklin and others, he called in 1762 for outright ending of importations of slaves. The Society of Friends threw its whole weight behind him and John Woolman of New Jersey, and by 1773 Dr. Rush could say that three fourths of the people of the city and province "cry out against" slavery. Two years later Benezet established the Society for the Relief of Free Negroes Unlawfully Held in Bondage. In 1776 the Friends decided to censure and disown all members who persisted in holding slaves. A petition from the Rhode Island Yearly Meeting to the Assembly in 1774 to prohibit the importation of Negroes from Africa resulted in a law, and in this center of the Guinea traffic Samuel Hopkins had begun to raise funds in 1773 to send two colored members of his congregation as missionaries to Africa; only the outbreak of the revolt prevented their departure. Upon the declaring of independence, this true servant of Christ urged, in a tract dedicated to the Continental Congress, that all slaves be freed because the maintenance of slavery was inconsistent with a war for liberty. The Quakers, Presbyterians, and Congregationalists had made in the cities an effective frontal attack on America's greatest problem.

As religious centers of the colonies, the five seaports kept the scattered churches of each denomination in touch with one another and supplied assistance and guidance. The work of the synods and ministerial conferences offered another avenue along which certain portions of the American people drew together for some common purpose. "It was supposed there were 2000 people" at the Rhode Island Yearly Meeting in 1765; and while no meeting of other sects attracted so large a number of the laity, clerical conventions of Anglicans and Congregationalists at Boston, of Presbyterians and Anglicans at New York, and of Baptists and Anglicans at Charles Town were regular events. The Philadelphia Baptist Association, led by Morgan Edwards, corresponded with the London Board of Ministers, supervised the thirty-one churches under its jurisdiction, assisted struggling congregations in the Valley of Virginia, raised funds for Rhode Island College, consulted regularly with the Congaree and Kehokee Associations in the two Carolinas, contributed toward sending the Reverend Hezekiah Smith to England in 1770 to seek political relief for New England Baptists, and in 1774 appointed a committee on grievances to lay the New England case before the Continental Congress. By 1776, through these religious agencies, a substantial and significant unity crossing colonial boundaries had been worked out along denominational lines.

An Anglican clergyman of Rhode Island requested his British superiors to send over books "for the Suppressing of Deism, Infidelity and Quakerism"—an uneasy trinity! Among intellectuals of the upper and middle classes infidelity in the form of skepticism made little headway; for every young Godfrey Malbone, "a Gentleman of Politeness and great Honor," who came back from Oxford to Newport and said that he "dispised all religion," there were hundreds of orthodox believers. English deism, however, definitely appealed to some: John Adams, Dr. Benjamin Rush, Benjamin Franklin, and many of their associates were religious liberals if not confessed deists. In estimating this situation at Philadelphia in 1773, Josiah Quincy concluded that public men stayed away from church out of policy, "and they who call themselves Christians much sooner encourage and vote for a deist or an infidel, than one who appears under a religious persuasion different from their own."

During the fifteen years preceding independence, the social and political aspects of organized religion in all the cities predominated over the spiritual. Central in this respect was the increasing militancy of the Church of England. In each community the Anglican became the fashionable communion as hundreds of people forsook Congregationalism, Presbyterianism, the Huguenot Church, Quakerism, and Lutheranism. That the moving service prescribed by the Book of Common Prayer, with all its dignity and fine music, conducted in such beautiful edifices as St. Philip's, Christ Church, the two Trinitys, and King's Chapel satisfied æsthetic needs cannot be denied. To many citizens, however, the social prestige of the Church of England and its direct relation with the Crown was the great attraction; Anglican ministers had been ordained by the Bishop of London and had sworn allegiance to King George, Defender of the Faith. The sacerdotal elegance that proved irresistible to the new officeholders and local gentry seemed out of place if not actually objectionable to many humble people nurtured in the plain dissenting tradition. What must Manhattan Presbyterians and the Reformed Dutch have thought in 1766 as they read in the *New York Gazette* that rich parishioners of Trinity Church were busily subscribing for ten bells to go in the steeple because "Philadelphia vaunts in theirs of a Ring of Eight"? Inevitably in the popular mind, the Church of England was associated with aristocracy and government control of religion, and not only did the American priesthood fail to allay such suspicions, but by Episcopal intrigue for American bishoprics they brought eventual ruin to their church.

Any hope of success for an American episcopate died with the repeal of the Stamp Act. Few people realized this at the time, and colonial mistrust of the motives of the Anglican clergy from Philadelphia northward found vent in a violent paper war. The controversy had commenced in 1763 with an exchange of pamphlets by the Reverend East Apthorp of Christ Church, Cambridge, and Boston's great Jonathan Mayhew, who censured the S.P.G. for sending missionaries to New England and denounced the proposal for an American bishop. A reply by the Reverend Henry Caner of King's Chapel, substituting "pugnacity for piety," readily admitted that the S.P.G. desired a bishop, and "if presbyterianism, as he [Mayhew] calls the prevailing religion of the country, be disposed to go off, and make room for its betters, let it go." Another answer from Thomas Secker, Archbishop of Canterbury, elicited from Mayhew the most telling point of the anti-Episcopal position: granted the purity of the present Anglican motives, who can answer for the future? The upshot of this exchange was to link inseparably the scheme for a bishop with all its sinister implications and George Grenville's program for imperial reform.

Sound ecclesiastical reasons existed for establishing an American bishopric, but unfortunately for the Church of England in the colonies, the proposals implied ecclesiastical courts and political supervision of religion, which led other denominations to fear for their hard-won liberties. Nor were these wholly hysterical or partisan bogies. The parliamentary group seeking to reorganize the British Empire had the backing of certain of the higher clergy who wanted to carry "fire and sword to America" through Episcopal control, which would at the same time create new preferments for young curates. Many of the higher prelates in England believed that extension of the episcopal system would ensure a loyal colonial clergy who would teach the Americans the errors of their political opinions. Despite denials of any such intentions or any desire to limit dissent or to encroach on the freedom and privileges of any other Protestant group, it was known in America that many Churchmen dreamed, like the Reverend Charles Inglis of New York, that an episcopate would provide a powerful "Means of securing the Affections and Dependence of the Colonies."

Spurred on by the determination of colonial Anglicans to secure special privileges denied them in the Northern colonies, the Church continued to agitate for an episcopate in defiance of the rising tide of colonial anger. Dr. Charles Chauncy donned the mantle of the late Mr. Mayhew in 1767 to answer advocacy of the cause of Episcopacy by the Bishop of Llandaff, and was soon joined by New York's able pamphleteer William Livingston. Theirs proved only the preliminary bouts before the main match, in which the Anglicans, represented by the Reverend Thomas Chandler of Elizabeth Town, New Jersey, aided by Provost William Smith of Philadelphia, turned out to be inadequate opponents for Mr. Chauncy of Boston and Vice-Provost Francis Alison of Philadelphia. Though this began as a pamphlet controversy, the newspapers quickly took it up, with the result that the public heard both sides. It is abundantly clear that whatever the merits of the Episcopal case, and there undeniably were some, its champions admitted enough to confirm those dissenters who augured danger and loss of liberty in establishing bishops, not to mention the possibility of tithes, at the time the colonies were passing through a severe depression. The Anglicans, to their own detriment, succeeded in equating Congregationalism, Presbyterianism, and other forms of dissent (itself an ugly word to many) with republicanism and liberty, a formula promptly accepted by their opponents as American Whiggism or patriotism, while they in turn fastened on Churchmen the label of Toryism.

A natural outcome of this fierce politico-religious debate was the consolidation of the dissenting opposition. The New York Presbyterians took the first step, because the successful blocking of their charter by the Board of Trade had alerted them to the menace of Episcopacy if the earlier struggles over the Society Library and King's College had not already done so. While the Anglicans were convening at Manhattan in 1766, the Presbyterian Synod of New York and Philadelphia, meeting in the same place, endorsed a plan to set up committees of correspondence with the churches of Holland, Geneva, the Scottish General Assembly, the dissenting synods at London, the General Synod of Ireland, and the churches of New England and South Carolina. Overtures made to the Consociated Churches of Connecticut (Congregational) led to a convention of ministers at Elizabeth Town, the heart of the enemy's camp, on November 5, 1766—the anniversary of the Popish Plot! A year later a plan for joint action went into operation when the convention met at New Haven, another Anglican stronghold. Among the leaders of this movement were the Presbyterians Francis Alison of Philadelphia and John Rodgers of New York, and Congregationalist Ezra Stiles of Newport. Although Massachusetts Congregationalists did not affiliate, they maintained a very friendly interest in the common cause, as did the English dissenters, who corresponded regularly with the convention. This united front did much to embolden the resistance to Episcopacy, and after 1770 the controversy died down, when the Anglicans gave up "with grief" any hope of having American bishops, although conventions met annually until 1776.

At New York repeated proposals for legislation relieving dissenters from payment of taxes to the Church of England were overridden by the Council's vetoes. Supported by William Livingston, John Morin Scott, and Alexander McDougall, the Presbyterian clergy organized the Society of Dissenters in 1769, composed of Presbyterians and Baptists, to protect and enlarge their rights and prestige. This "new Solemn League and Covenant . . . against the Established Church," as the Reverend Samuel Auchmuty of Trinity branded it, was designed to be the parent of a federation of similar bodies bound together by committees of correspondence. In a circular letter, the Society described the steady encroachment of Anglican power at New York and proposed an exchange of information with England and Holland as well as the rest of America. In publishing this letter, the *Pennsylvania Chronicle* denied any intention of offensive action against the Churchmen, "but barely to counteract them," though Printer Goddard did ask all colonial, Scottish, Irish, and English papers to copy it. Realizing that many nothingarians might be left in ignorance of those religious liberties which were among the natural rights currently being defended against parliamentary power, President John Rodgers of the Society of Dissenters founded the American Society for Promoting Religious Knowledge among the Poor in the British Colonies in July 1773. This first home-missionary body followed a Scottish model in raising a fund to purchase Bibles and had agents in every city, who, being known Whigs as well as dissenters, could be counted upon to foster the good work. Thus some years before the politicians did the most numerous religious bodies of the cities, representing "the dissidence of dissent," close ranks and evolve efficient committees of correspondence—those "eggs of sedition." Ezra Stiles's vision of a "Christian Union" of the dissenting denominations of America and Europe had almost come about.

V

With all the hubbub going on in these years, it is no wonder that the tavern as a place of resort for all classes exceeded any other urban institution in importance. There town life came to a focus. At such establishments as the Green Dragon Tavern, next door to Edes & Gill's printing office at Boston, Samuel Francis's at Manhattan, the sign of the Bacchus in Charles Town, and Philadelphia's great City Tavern, gentlemen, Sons of Liberty, and other patriots met on countless occasions to "work the political engine." If the American Revolution was "cradled" in any place, it was in the urban public houses.

The number of public houses in each city except Boston soon outnumbered those necessitated by wartime conditions and the armed forces. Perhaps because of the presence of the British troops and the bellicose mood of the citizens, the Bay Town actually reduced the number of retailers of liquor from 32 in 1769 to 23 by 1774. Newport taverns gradually dropped off and then climbed back to 34 in 1774. The great concourse of strangers at Philadelphia created a demand for more public houses; by 1771, Second Street, with 26 to care for wagoners and farmers on market days, had passed High Street, which had only 17, most of them of the highest class. Suburban development in the Northern Liberties and Southwark accounted for 66 of the 171 licenses issued in the city and county in 1772. Year after year at Charles Town the Grand Jury protested the superabundance of tippling houses, but the justices insisted upon licensing between 102 and 117 of them. Ordinarily more permits went to women than to men, lending some credence to the charge that nearly every watchman's wife retailed liquors. The fact that the annual income from tavern licenses netted the Corporation between £418 and £593 may explain the existence of so many pubs at New York. The city lived up to its ancient reputation, for the 282 innholders of 1766 had become 396 within seven years, setting a new American record. Moreover, well-founded rumors had it that many other persons dispensed the good creature without having either a license or paying the provincial tax.

Tradition must have counted for something in the ratings of hostelries, for those of established reputation in the earlier period still seemed to warrant the best patronage, even when the management changed hands. The best-operated colonial public house in 1760 was probably that of John Gordon on Broad Street in Charles Town. When he died, two years later, Robert Dillon ran it for nine years and then William Holliday took it over. Always supplied with choice liquors and a "good Larder in Season," it attracted the city's quality, even attaining dubious fame when the De Lancey-Haly duel took place there. In 1762 Samuel Francis gave up his Mason's Arms on the Broad Way in New York and put up his new sign of Queen Charlotte, or the Queen's Head, near the Exchange in the former Stephen De Lancey town house, where he kept a popular ordinary. After a fling at other enterprises from 1765 to 1770, he returned to the Queen's Head, which he made into the city's most famous tavern (now known as Fraunces Tavern). John Biddle's Indian King at Philadelphia maintained its position until 1774, but lost out to Daniel Smith, who furnished the City Tavern on Second Street in the style of a London hostelry and announced in newspapers as far away as Boston that "in order the better to accommodate Strangers, he has fitted up several elegant bed rooms, detached from noise, and as private as a lodging house." Good food, wines, and a "Genteel Coffee-Room . . . properly supplied with English and American papers and Magazines," as well as a convenient livery stable, were featured. A few months after its opening, the Massachusetts delegates to the Continental Congress arrived, and John Adams relates that "dirty, dusty, and fatigued as we were, we could not resist the importunity to go to the tavern, the most genteel one in America. . . . After some time spent in conversation, a curtain was drawn and in the other half of the chamber a supper appeared as elegant as ever was laid upon a table."

As in former years, traveling gentlemen preferred rooms in some quiet house located near a favorite hostelry in order to be sure of privacy. Lodging and boarding houses were so well patronized that at Charles Town, even with the aid of Levinius Clarkson, Josiah Quincy had difficulty in finding suitable quarters. So much rent gouging took place that in 1772, the "Keepers of the Principal Lodging Houses" agreed on rates of twenty-five shillings a day for "every Constant Boarder" and thirty for "a Transient Person" or a "Country Gentleman." What was doubtless the most genteel establishment of this type was that kept by the Widow Graydon at the famous old Slate Roof House in Philadelphia. Outstanding among her lodgers were Baron De Kalb, Sir William Draper, Colonel George Washington, John Hancock, James Rivington, Lady Moore and daughter, and the comedian O'Brien and his wife, Lady Susan, from London. Each summer Newporters made money renting rooms or apartments to the West Indians and Carolinians who came north to Rhode Island for the season.

The vogue among the gentry for driving about the environs of their cities encouraged a number of publicans to set up suburban places of entertainment. Near Charles Town in 1761 Joseph Wilson took over the Orange Gardens, where he fitted up a large assembly room which he hoped to operate as a sort of club for subscribers, though he did have "Publick breakfasting" and afternoon tea. Several proprietors tried in vain to make the Orange Gardens pay, but Charles Town was not ready for such a place. Henry Bohrer & Company started New Vauxhall in 1767, giving concerts three times a week, but soon cut down to one, and the following season a stagecoach ran out to the place, but Vauxhall soon went the way of the Orange Gardens. Enterprising Philadelphians counted on summer heat and humidity to entice the public to spots such as John Dudley's Mead House on Society Hill, Daniel Duchemine's Lebanon near the Hospital, and Thomas Mullen's "Vaux-hall, on the agreeable Banks of Schuylkill." In 1769 Edward Bardin moved from New York to Boston for a time to run the King's Arms on the Neck, where he catered to parties of all sorts, even arranging for a hackney coach to bring ladies out from Captain Paddock's for a shilling. But in spite of the attraction of fireworks "in six Parts," his place went for rent in January 1770; in March it reopened for "select company" under the management of Thomas Brackett.

The idea behind these enterprises was to produce colonial versions of the famous London pleasure gardens of Ranelagh and Vauxhall, but only those of the same name at Manhattan ever remotely resembled the gay originals. In 1765 John Jones opened Ranelagh Gardens in the old Rutgers homestead with a concert; fireworks were scheduled for every Thursday night. Although the second performance "was interrupted by a Number of disorderly Persons (in a riotous Manner) breaking into the Garden," the place grew very popular and warranted additional scheduled concerts on Mondays. About the same time Samuel Francis started his "New Vaux-hall . . . being one of the Pleasantest rural Retreats in the City," with upper and lower gardens, an extensive prospect up and down the North River, good liquors, and entertainments. Two of his attractions in 1768 were an exhibition of "elegant waxwork figures," including Scipio, and a newfangled grotto; the next year Mr. Hulet and Miss Hallam of the American Company made personal appearances in a series of concerts. Francis moved his waxworks into town to the Queen's Head in 1773, selling Vaux-hall to Erasmus Williams for a lodging house called Mt. Pleasant.

Newport had its Vaux-hall too, as we learn from the career of Abigail Stoneman, publican of the late colonial period, a tale of storybook nature. Commencing as a "feme sole trader" in 1766, this young and attractive widow was set back almost immediately with a loss by theft of one hundred Spanish dollars and some china from her Marlborough Street house. In 1767 she opened the Merchant's Coffee House at the

Sign of the King's Arms, where she also sold West Indian goods for cash, but in 1769 she took over Bishop Berkeley's Whitehall at Middletown, renaming it Vaux-hall, and conducted a tea house with a menu of cakes, mead, tea, tarts, syllabub, lemon and orange cheesecakes and also offered "Genteel Lodgings" for some of the summer colony. Prospering, Mrs. Stoneman next ventured to Boston, where, in 1770, she managed the Royal Exchange Tavern on King Street as a coffeehouse with lodgings, but by 1772 she was back at Vaux-hall preparing to handle large entertainments that season. During the winter seasons she kept a coffeehouse or tavern at different locations in town, always specializing in large entertainments, and in 1773 the Dancing Assembly met at her King's Arms on Thames Street. An auction of her goods in August 1774 was followed shortly by the announcement that at Hampton, Connecticut, she had married "the Honourable Sir John Treville, Knight of Malta, Captain of cavalry in the service of his most Christian majesty." The *Mercury* could not bestow rank on her, but it did describe the bride as "a lady descended from a respectable family, of a good genius, a very polite and genteel address, and extremely well accomplished in every branch of family economy." This first Newport beauty to marry a title deserved a better fate than that in store for her. Her husband, a Tory, abandoned her at New York in 1777, and so once again she went into business, and next door to Francis's Queen's Head on lower Broad Street she operated the London Coffee House, where she served an ordinary breakfast and dinner every day.

VI

In searching for relief of unemployment and of economic difficulties, contemporaries universally pointed to the unwonted luxury and growing sophistication of the citizens, particularly in the three largest cities. The open and costly display of gentry, British officers, and recently arrived officials accentuated the social gulf between the rich and the poor, and town and country. Frugality and retrenchment were constantly urged on the people; Samuel Adams of Boston severely condemned the waste, immorality, and dissipation incident to the new modes and longed for a return to simpler and more virtuous times. But in spite of all this, and perhaps because of the very insecurity of these years, the desire for diversion and recreation possessed all classes, and in the cities many Americans were determined to play and play hard.

Tavern shows continued to attract the idle and the curious. High and low, they flocked to see any kind of exhibition, from a Punch and Judy show to joining hands and receiving a shock from the Caribbean electrical fishes. A model of the city of Jerusalem, seventeen feet by nine, which took Anthony Sulzer and Michael Kraft of Germantown seven years to complete, showed up in every city between 1764 and 1767, even though John Rowe judged it "a great imposition on the Publick" and persuaded the Boston Selectmen to close it up. "The two Italian Brothers from Turin" made a profitable tour in 1768 with their fireworks show with accompanying music, and in the same year Mesdames Rachel Wells and Patience Wright exhibited their waxworks at Philadelphia and New York. After a fire at New York in 1771, Mrs. Wright went on to London and a career as the forerunner of Madame Tussaud and as an American spy; her sister remained in America, capitalizing on White-field's death with a fine representation; also ones of the Pennsylvania Farmer, the murder of Abel by Cain, and the betrayal of Samson by Delilah. John Adams thought there was genius and taste in these wax figures, but decided that Mrs. Wells's art would "make but little progress in the world."

Celebrations of royal anniversaries had been one of the earliest forms of public entertainment, and after 1760 they took on a greater splendor with illuminations of houses, fireworks, and grand public dinners, as on Restoration Day at Boston in 1770, when ordinary townsmen partici-pated in an ox roast on the Common and "a Large Company" of the elite feasted at Faneuil Hall. New York had twenty-four such legal holi-days every year. Such demonstrations of loyalty yielded or succumbed to the rising American patriotism after the Stamp Act; and more en-thusiasm could be generated for a celebration of its repeal. The first ob-servation of the occasion, put on by the Sons of Liberty in the Rhode Island capital, set a high standard: a trumpet sounded and a cannon went off after each of twenty-eight toasts at the daytime gathering be-fore the Colony House; that evening, with the city illuminated and the Colony House brilliantly decorated, a parade with painted transparencies impressed all observers, and a burst of fireworks closed the great cele-bration. The *Mercury,* reporting on the occasion, declared: "Gentlemen and Ladies, who were in the Streets the whole Evening, viewing with the highest Pleasure, the Illuminations and Fireworks, met with no kind of indecent Treatment from the Populace; indeed the People seemed to be ambitious to out vie each other in Civility and Politeness." At Bos-ton, James Otis and Samuel Adams promoted numerous festivals to "tinge the minds of the people" and to "impregnate them with senti-ments of liberty" as well as to inculcate affection for their leaders. Paul Revere made a handsome silver bowl in 1768 for the gentlemen of Nathaniel Barber's Insurance Office in memory of the ninety-two mem-bers of the House of Representatives who had refused to rescind a reso-lution on Lord Hillsborough's demand; it was exhibited at a large dinner during which forty-five toasts were drunk and a new song was heard:

"In Freedom we're born, and in Freedom we'll live." This shrewd combination of entertaining spectacles and purposeful manipulation of patriotic or loyal symbols gave the people both a diverting evening and a patriotic emotional outlet.

There was a club for every kind of urban activity, and dozens of them, embracing more and more of the two lower orders than ever before, met nightly or weekly in the taverns. It has been said that Freemasonry, which stood at the front of urban associations, tended more toward middle-class membership, but if so, it supplied the occasions for members of the upper class to meet and come to know outstanding representatives of the middle orders. John Rowe, who moved in the most select Boston circles, faithfully attended lodge meetings with his many genteel cronies; in 1768 he succeeded Jeremiah Gridley as Grand Master for North America amidst great pomp and ceremony, and a year later Joseph Warren assumed the post. At New York, Sir William Johnson participated prominently in Masonic work, and at Charles Town Sir Egerton Leigh served as Provincial Grand Master. The fraternity rated high and its members knew this; in 1774, when a merchant in St. Eustatius enjoined secrecy on William Barrell and Paul Fooks of Philadelphia concerning business arrangements, Barrell replied: "As to secrecy, I need only remind you that both Fooks and myself are Free Masons."

The exclusiveness and reputation of the venerable Colony in Schuylkill and Society of Fort St. David tempted Philadelphia gentlemen to organize three new clubs for the city's expanding social set. The Mt. Regale Fishing Company, established in 1762, drew its membership of fifty-eight from Anglican and Presbyterian vassals of the "Penn Dynasty": Allens, Colonel Henry Bouquet, John and Richard Penn. Its clubhouse was situated between the upper and lower falls of the Schuylkill, and on every other Thursday from June to September the jolly company sipped Madeira as they were rowed up the river in their barge with its gaily painted awning. Sixty persons ordinarily sat down to a delicious dinner, and on occasion ladies could be admitted by ticket. In 1767 the White Oak Barges, under Captain Charles Lawrence, inaugurated an annual fishery and other gatherings across the Delaware in New Jersey, and the same year Jacob Hiltzheimer and associates patriotically formed the Liberty Fishing Company. As their fishing season began in April, they enjoyed more barge rides than the other companies located up the Schuylkill. The gastronomic activities of all these clubs produced in the *Pennsylvania Chronicle* of 1773 an account of a meeting at "Glutton Hall," burlesquing the feasts of the fishing clubs, whose members did not descend to breaking lamps or bullying strangers like the St. Tammany or the Patriotic, but more urbanely and leisurely passed the time after dinner by stabbing characters of those whom the members disliked.

When politics began to usurp the thoughts and attention of all and sundry, social clubs, like the fire companies, acquired a definite political complexion, for such tightly knit little groups proved ideal means for propagandizing and promoting either seditious or loyal action. To honor John Dickinson for writing the *Farmer's Letters,* in 1768 the Society of Fort St. David presented him with an address done up in a casket made of "Heart of Oak," and at this same time a writer in the *Pennsylvania Gazette* was urging Philadelphia's "many small societies, companies, and clubs . . . each to unite in sundry public spirited measures" such as home manufactures, frugality, and non-importation. For, he went on, "Is it not the many that spread and suggest a fashion?" Now fully conscious of their New World heritage, native Americans inaugurated the May Day observance of the memory of the local saint, Tammany, by wearing a piece of bucktail "in some conspicuous situation." The Sons of St. Tammany at Philadelphia really outdid themselves at a splendid public banquet on April 30, 1773 by providing a seven-piece orchestra. Philadelphia artisans founded the Patriotic Society to protect "our just Rights and Privileges to us and our Posterity against every attempt to violate or infringe the same, either here or on the other side of the Atlantic." At New York the Knights of the Order of Corsica, founded in 1770, combined entertainment with support to the cause of liberty, in which Pasquale Paoli was currently playing so prominent a part. The diary of John Adams graphically describes the adroit channeling of political propaganda through existing social organizations at Boston by his cousin, and the efforts of the Tories to do likewise. What had begun in the cities as "knots of men rightly sorted" for pleasure and recreation ended by being transformed into unusually potent revolutionary agencies.

It would be difficult to decide whether New Yorkers or Charlestonians won the wreath for being the greatest followers of horse-racing. While the turf fascinated all classes everywhere, racing at the other towns was a desultory pursuit. At a track on Boston Neck, races took place occasionally after 1765, and at Newport some gentlemen matched horses on Easton's Beach in 1763 and thereafter; but in contrast to this sporadic interest, racing meets in the three other cities were the most popular outdoor sport. Under the auspices of the Carolina Jockey Club, the Charles Town races were run for high stakes, and the large bets placed on the horses entered by the Draytons, Middletons, Gadsdens, Lynches, and Ravenels encouraged the *South Carolina Gazette* to print the betting odds after 1763 and to carry detailed accounts of the races. Races for handsome purses were run at Philadelphia's Center Square "for the encouragement of the Breed of Fine Horses," not to mention the pleasure of the spectators; for they came from miles around. In 1764 Peter Spence handled the betting according to His Majesty's rules. Two years later, entries were numerous enough to warrant the forming of the Jockey

Club, with a membership of seventy-one subscribers, who paid three pounds a year for its support, including Virginians, Marylanders, Jersey-men, and Yorkers as well as Pennsylvanians. The *New York Gazette* commented acidly in its report of the October 1767 meeting: "Great Numbers of Bye Betts were laid upon those Races, *Money being plenty with some yet.*" New Yorkers had tracks near Manhattan too; some citizens claimed it was the "Highway to most Vices," and the new courses across the Hudson at Elizabeth Town, Perth Amboy, and Paulus Hook all flourished on New York entries. By 1773 the principal sportsmen of the first rank—De Lancey, Fitzhugh, Hamilton, Galloway, Ogle—were running their horses at Leeds Town in Virginia, Annapolis, Philadelphia, West Jersey, and New York, a veritable circuit for colonial ponies.

Although American fox-hunting had originated at Charles Town with the St. Andrew's Hunt in 1757, this sport, so undeniably the most English in many ways, was pursued at Philadelphia in an unorganized fashion before the founding of the Gloucester Hunt Club on October 9, 1766. The twenty-seven members rendezvoused at William Hugg's inn in Gloucester, New Jersey, from which they rode out on Tuesdays and Fridays with sixteen pairs of hounds; they must have made a splendid sight when they first appeared in uniform in 1774—a dark brown coatee, buff waistcoat and breeches, and black velvet cap. At this time, also, parties of thirty, including Jacob Hiltzheimer, who had been secretary of the Jockey Club and chief factotum of the Center Course, wound their horns on the Schuylkill's banks near Darby. Slim evidence suggests that the Morrises and De Lanceys may have ridden to hounds on imported hunters at Westchester and on Long Island after 1768, and an advertisement of August 1770 for a pair of foxes further suggests that some summer visitor from Philadelphia attempted to introduce the pleasures of the chase on Rhode Island.

Sports regarded today as excessively cruel fascinated colonial big-wigs and many of the lesser sort. Baiting of bulls and bears by fierce dogs was a popular pastime at New York and Philadelphia, but cock-fighting had most devoted followers everywhere. Aaron Lopez received five year-old fowls in 1766 from Henry Cruger, Jr., of Bristol, who advised breeding the cocks first because they fought better at two years. Thomas Nightingale, manager of the Newmarket racecourse at Charles Town often scheduled cockfights between races. In 1768 the "Mechanicks of Charlestown" challenged any gentleman to show fifteen cocks for nine battles under English rules. The most famous main of the period was that put on by James De Lancey of New York and Timothy Matlack of Philadelphia at Richardson's on the Germantown Road in March 1770. It gave rise to some of Francis Hopkinson's ironical verse:

> *See from New York comes in state,*
> *And twenty fighting cocks around him wait*

All arm'd with steel and ready for the War.

. . . .

   . . . Chickens yet unhatch'd shall curse D[e Lancey]'s name.

Many wealthier gentlemen gambled heavily in the manner of English aristocrats, a tendency that had been encouraged during the wars by association with the military. According to Alexander Graydon, billiards and cards ranked highest with the men in the "seductive arcana of city dissipation," and the women also enjoyed playing cards for stakes. During the non-importation movement, patriotic Bostonians hoped this method of gambling would die out, but a merchant, whose name appeared on "the detestable list" of importers, got in a large shipment of cards. And by the seventies, the Bay Town had its scheduled Thursday evening "Card Assembly" just as Charles Town had its "Whisk Club."

In other ways too, both sexes of the upper class passed their time at diversions that set them apart from the rest of the population. Driving about ostentatiously in parties with several handsome equipages to picnics, or what they called frolics, engaged their leisure hours in the summer, or gay skating and sleighing parties relieved the ennui of the winter days. At the Quaker City in January 1769 Alexander Macraby accompanied a party in "seven sleighs with two ladies and two men in each, preceded by fiddlers on horseback," which "set out together upon a snow of about a foot deep on the roads, to a public house a few miles from town, where we danced, sung, and romped and eat and drank, and kicked away care from morning till night, and finished our frolic in two or three side boxes at the play." In March 1768 he and his companions, escorted by a band of ten musicians, paraded the streets late at night, stopping to serenade the ladies of their choice—and incidentally inspiring a letter to the press from an annoyed citizen protesting against such nocturnal revelry. Pleasure boating on the Hudson and Narragansett Bay appealed to the gentry of New York and Newport. At Rhode Island some three to four hundred Negro slaves annually participated in a mock election, assuming the relative ranks of their masters and mimicking gentility with dancing, games, and various sports, while from a distance the whites looked on with amusement tinged with misgivings.

The merchants and the graybeards may have been doleful, but depression had not cut down on the balls or dancing assemblies; in fact, life grew more hectic than ever. "What a terrible life do I lead," youthful Gouverneur Morris wrote to Ann Allen Penn from New York in January 1774. "Worse than at Philadelphia. There I was up all night it is true, but it was in company making merry. Here up all night writing [as an attorney]. . . . Pity it is you are not here—balls, concerts, assemblies—all of us mad in the pursuit of pleasure. Not a pause. Grave phizzes are grinned out of countenance, prudence kicked out of doors,

PLATE 15 · *Mrs. James Smith by John Singleton Copley, 1769*

Elizabeth Murray from Scotland (Mrs. Thomas Campbell, Mrs. James Smith, Mrs. Ralph Inman) was successively a plantation housekeeper in North Carolina, schoolteacher, shopkeeper, "she-merchant" of Boston, and ultimately one of the grande dames of urban America.

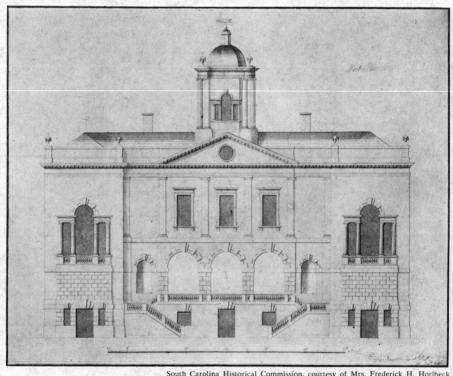

South Carolina Historical Commission, courtesy of Mrs. Frederick H. Horlbeck

PLATE 16 · *West elevation of the Exchange and Assembly-room, Charles Town, 1766*

Designed by William Rigby Naylor, erected by John and Peter Horlbeck. The lines of the original drawing are faint as the reproduction shows, but it is interesting as one of a very few remaining colonial building plans.

and your sober sedate friend (myself meaning) is becoming the butt of unfledged witlings." The Philadelphia Dancing Assembly still reigned supreme for sophisticated blades like the Londoner Macraby, who found it to their taste, and the ladies beautiful as well as good partners notwithstanding Jemmy Willing's boredom "because the Girls are so little." When the Duchess of Gordon appeared in December 1768, "richly deckt with Diamonds and other Jewels and dressed most splendidly in Silver Silks," all of Philadelphia took notice. Everything went well with the New York Subscription Assembly until 1768; then the consorts of General Thomas Gage and Governor Sir Henry Moore could not agree who should stand first couple in a country dance. That year no assemblies were held, but at the first of two private balls "there were high words, and Lady Moore retired in a rage," leaving the former Margaret Kemble the victor. The second produced a formal challenge from the general, to which the Governor "made the reply gracious, instead of the retort valiant." After this dismal season, society got on an even keel again, as Gouverneur Morris indicated. Politics split the aristocracy at Boston when in 1768 the Assembly held a ball that included too many of the official court clique to suit more American tastes—the Governor and Madam Bernard, the Commissioner of Customs, Commodore Hood, General Pomeroy, and most of the officers of the detested regiments policing the city. Some of the more determined proponents of "liberty" boycotted the assemblies (or were not invited), but genial John Rowe and Mrs. Rowe never missed a meeting. After the withdrawal of the troops, a South Carolina newspaper reported that "a large number of the principal gentlemen of both parties" in the recent disputes at Boston had subscribed when the "assembly was proposed in order to restore peace, harmony, and the blessings of social life."

When the quest for health first drove the aristocrats to mineral springs, it was for the supposed curative benefits, but soon a course of waters or baths became the mode just as at Spa, Bath, or Tunbridge Wells. Discovery of the therapeutic properties of a spring at Stafford in Connecticut and of another at nearby Mansfield in 1765 soon made them the resort of Bostonians. When a Dr. Tudor from London took up residence as a balneologist at Stafford, John Wood inaugurated a stagecoach and freight-wagon service to carry people and their effects there. John Adams visited this New England spa in 1771, sampled the "noctious" water, and plunged into the bath twice: "it is very cold indeed." A spring at Warwick, Rhode Island, enjoyed a brief popularity in 1766–7, as did another at Kinderhook on the Hudson, for which Dr. Thomas Young, the patriot, wrote a treatise extolling its value in curing the gravel, kidney, scorbutic, and rheumatic complaints. Salt-water bathing also came into vogue along with the rise of Scarborough in England. New Yorkers and Philadelphians in numbers flocked to Black Point at Shrewsbury, New

Jersey, to take advantage of protected seaside bathing. Here the Drinkers, Allens, Penns, Shippens, and Mifflins bathed, feasted on fish, crabs, and lobster, and visited the great Schuyler estate in the adjacent Passaic Valley. Some Charlestonians subscribed to build a "Bathing-Room" on Roper's Wharf about 1769, but it is doubtful if the usual condition of a colonial waterfront offered much of an inducement for the newfangled practice of cold-water bathing.

The nearest approach to the surroundings of European mineral springs was at the sophisticated spas of the Philadelphia area. Yellow Springs in Chester County, long a resort of the carriage trade, began to receive "vast Concourses of People," arriving "daily from Philadelphia and all parts of the Country as well as from the West Indies and other foren Parts." In 1763 John Cobble drove a stage out three times a week, and Jonathan Durell advertised accommodations at the reasonable price of twenty-two shillings a week. In the summer between one hundred and three hundred people a day frequented the resort, where two of the three baths were enclosed and had pump rooms and other "modern embellishments," besides shady walks through meadows and woods. A bit more exclusive was Bristol Spring, which stood supreme among colonial spas, luring "strangers of distinction" from places as distant as Jamaica and Santa Cruz. Dr. John De Normandie's clinical observations, published by the American Philosophical Society in 1769, and Dr. Benjamin Rush's *Experiments and Observations on the Mineral Waters of Philadelphia, Abington and Bristol* (1773) gave this spring a standing no other possessed. Here Verplancks from New York and Messrs. Hallam and Douglass of the American Company boarded along with leaders of Philadelphia society—Anglican, Presbyterian, Quaker—in the hot month of July at the Widow Merriott's and mingled daily at the pump room, as the diary of Elizabeth Drinker charmingly reveals. These two watering places and the lesser springs of Abington and Gloucester became important intercolonial resorts where representatives of the gentry from many colonies met in person, as did the members of the middle class. Such acquaintanceships acted as a powerful solvent of provincialism at a time when it was very much needed.

Rhode Island did not need chalybeate springs to become the vacationland of eighteenth-century America. The climate and gardenlike beauty of Newport impelled Crèvecœur to call it the Montpellier of America. In the eight years prior to the opening battles of the Revolution, Newport came into its own, and the social seasons were the most brilliant the city had ever known. The names of more than 500 summer residents are still known, 101 of whom went to Newport in the peak season of 1772. The *Newport Mercury* reported the arrival of distinguished guests by printing their names in small capitals, whereas those of ordinary visitors like the printer Isaiah Thomas and his wife appeared in ordinary type. The stay-at-home citizens of the Southern capital viewed this annual exodus in terms of the money taken out of the province, "3500 Guineas in Specie" in 1769, and Timothy rated the loss of cash by this route as third only to the payment of customs duties in silver, and payments for Northern goods. Some who came from the hot lowlands arrived as early as May and stayed into late October or November. So many Charlestonians summered there that the island was whimsically known as the Carolina Hospital; and the tombstones of West Indians and Carolinians in Trinity Churchyard show that all summer visitors did not find the health for which they journeyed so far. Before the War of Independence, Dr. Benjamin Waterhouse told Thomas Jefferson: "Rhode Island was in one view the Bath of the American world, and the lumber room of the colonial faculty. What they could not cure they threw in a heap here. This and the Redwood Library gave it both a literary and a genteel air; and rendered it the best bred society in New England." This idyllic life came to an abrupt end on June 12, 1775, when the *Mercury* printed its last social item:

> June 12, arrived here the Sloop *Friendship*, Captain Munro, in 14 days from Charles-town, with whom came Passengers, Mr. ISAAC MCPHERSON, Mr. JONATHAN CLARKE, Mrs. CLARKE, and Mr. NATHAN CHILD, all of South-Carolina. The vessel was taken under the *protection* of the men of war.

VII

The theater, besides being the most sophisticated form of public amusement, touched colonial life at all levels, winning popular approval and enthusiastic support in some quarters and, as in former times, arousing bitter opposition in others. To many in the audiences, it provided instruction in manners and human nature as well as diversion, and its ups and downs reflected the capriciousness of contemporary life in the cities.

The story of David Douglass and his company of comedians is virtually the history of the American stage in this period. Fresh from a successful tour of the Chesapeake colonies, Douglass and his troupe undertook their first invasion of New England in 1761, arriving at Newport in spite of an adverse vote of the Town Meeting against the opening of a theater. In a hastily built structure on Easton's Point, the Thespians gave about twenty performances from September 2 to November 3, two of which yielded £1,030 in currency for the purchase of corn for the city's poor. Opponents of the theater regarded such beneficence as merely a ruse to placate the inhabitants, for Douglass had procured the permission of the Assembly by giving passes to all of the members. The same critics also denounced the expenditure of from £3,000 to £4,000 in currency weekly on a playhouse during such difficult times, ridiculing the benefits to the poor as no equivalents for the loss of £30,000 to Newport. Since devotees of the stage had come from Boston and Providence, the next year, after putting on several plays at the King's Arms Tavern, the players moved up to Providence with the hope of drawing both Newport and Boston patronage there. The inhabitants of Providence succeeded in prevailing on the Assembly to pass a law aimed at the theater. The next Rhode Island visit of the comedians ended in tragedy in 1767 when the Malbone brig *Dolphin* from Jamaica burned off Point Judith with the loss of Mrs. Henry, Madam Storer, and Miss Sarah and two daughters of John Henry, the actor. In time Newport came to realize that the theater was an added asset to its summer business and the Town Meeting voted permission in 1771 "to act plays," but David Douglass chose to try the West Indies instead.

Douglass and his players focused their attention after 1761 principally on New York, Charles Town, and Philadelphia, making occasional excursions to Maryland, Virginia, and Jamaica. Theaters were erected at Manhattan in 1761, 1766, and 1767, the last being the famous John Street Theatre. The new scenery that Douglass brought back from London in 1765 was installed in the third "New Theatre" on Queen Street in Charles Town, where in 1773 he also built the fourth "New" playhouse. Philadelphia's theater, the "Synagogue of Satan," rose just across Cedar Street from the city limits in Southwark in 1766, a procedure reminiscent of the means by which players escaped municipal censure at London in an earlier day.

Significantly emphasizing their intercolonial character by calling themselves the American Company of Comedians after 1763, the actors used these theaters to give colonial audiences very good performances of the best plays then available to London audiences, and maintained a better stage than the English provincial cities. Performance at Manhattan on May 29, 1769, of Bickerstaffe's *The Padlock,* with Charles Dibdin's popular new score, after it had first been put on at London on October 3, 1768, indicates how up-to-date the American theater was; and the playing of Thomas Godfrey's *Prince of Parthia* at Southwark on April 20, 1767 after the forced withdrawal of Thomas Forrest's *The Disappointment* had demonstrated Douglass's willingness to encourage the best colonial efforts in comedy and tragedy. During the three seasons of 1772–4, regular playgoers in each city could have seen more than seventy plays, farces, and ballad operas, including many of Shakespeare's dramas in the several eighteenth-century versions. In fact, even in the present century New York has not offered a better repertoire.

Opposition to the theater on moral and religious grounds gradually gave way before secular pressures in the cities, but concurrently hostility arose over what many of the middle class and some of the more sober-minded gentry considered needless extravagance in the face of colonial adversity and the debauching of many of the lower orders, who developed an inordinate taste for playgoing. Douglass learned about such gallery ruffians at New York in 1762, when one threw eggs at the stage, missing the actors but spattering the gentry in the front seats (perhaps from design), an interlude in which "the Performance was in some Measure interrupted." Many craftsmen resented the attendance of their apprentices, wives, and daughters at plays, not only because they picked up ideas of elegance far beyond their stations, but also because it took hard-earned money. In New York in 1766, rumors that the new theater would be mobbed because of "public distress" and unemployment proved true; a "multitude" broke in, wrecked the interior beyond repair, and drove the comedians from the city. No such damage occurred with the opening of the Southwark theater, but the same arguments were raised against the stage, especially its tendency to inculcate "a false Taste of Pleasure." The press of both cities made much in 1767 of the refusal of the Corporation at Bristol, England, to admit the players until recently, where in fifteen weeks they took away about £4,000, "an amazing expence." Thinking that Charlestonians would offer less resistance, Douglass sent John Henry there to erect a theater in 1769, but the actor judged that the colony was too involved in difficulties over the Townshend duties for the citizens to devote themselves to viewing plays; so the American Company went to Philadelphia instead. Had times been normal, all would probably have gone well, but the drama was now caught in the meshes of imperial politics.

As the currency crisis eased in the seventies, more and more people grew fond of playgoing, and because the American Company behaved with admirable circumspection, opposition to the theater made little headway. Not even the strictures of Mr. Whitefield could close it any more. In all towns, however, it became integrated with the life of the upper-class citizens, and as the final crisis arrived, the American Company again had to protest against "repeated Insults" from "mischievious Persons in the Gallery." After the decision of the Continental Association ruling out all forms of public entertainment, the American Company sailed off to the West Indies, where it remained until 1785.

VIII

A London newspaper of 1767 sneeringly observed that the colonials, while publicly pleading poverty, showed in their private letters to English merchants "that the number of carriages kept in New-York has, in about four years, increased from five to seventy. Some houses are there let for 200 £ per annum. At Philadelphia a play-house is built, and as much frequented by Quakers, as by those who have fewer external marks of religion. Cock-fighting, fox-hunting, horse-racing, and every other expensive diversion, are in vogue in the colonies, yet the colonists pretend they are not able to pay towards the support of their government." All this was true, but it was not the whole truth, for the description applied primarily to some of the gentry and the well-to-do middle class.

These years had seen the American aristocracy reach its peak, a prosperous class surrounded by the trophies of wealth and devoted to the pursuit of pleasure. The Carolina planters and their wives, the most recently arrived in this exalted group, carried this cult of "the unbought graces of life" perhaps further because they possessed more leisure, but all of them indulged in a splendid display signifying status. Had it evolved gradually and always in good taste, it might have proved acceptable, but along with the sensible and cultured members of the upper class appeared those with war fortunes or political influence whose lavish existence and flamboyance as well as arrogance and ultra-colonialism not only served to divide the upper class but bred resentment among the middle and lower classes.

For decades the tradesmen and artisans had been beneficiaries of urban prosperity, and concurrently with the flowering of the gentry the middle class had stirred and asserted itself. By no means social levelers, they cherished ambitions of rising to the position where they too could ride in their chaises or take their families to the spas. But ominous threats to their hitherto steady upward progress confronted them; the postwar business slump stunned and confused them. Memories of past grievances taken with the depressed state of trade generated anger against a free-spending aristocracy that preached frugality to them or tried to relieve poor debtors by putting on a big banquet for the inmates of a prison. This ambitious middle class did not, however, lose faith in the ultimate promise of America, and sensing a tendency on the part of the gentry to seal off the approach to membership in "the better sort," the democratic elements understandingly listened to Whig criticisms and their own leaders.

That social stability so long regarded as the salient feature of the slow-moving eighteenth century now seems to have been an illusion; certainly it was totally lacking on the urban scene, where there was very little security at all. Underneath the apparent calm routine of daily life, which went on with only an occasional interruption, society itself was passing through a fundamental change. In numbers the tradesmen and artisans held an increasing advantage over those above and below them, and they were aware of their strength. The time had come when those who looked upon themselves as the best of the better sort were about to be regarded, in the words of the Pennsylvania Constitution of 1776, as "an inconvenient aristocracy" that ought to be "effectually prevented."

CHAPTER 10

The Minds and Hearts
of the Citizens

T HE INSECURITY AND POLITICAL DISSENSION that suffused urban life
during this decade and a half inevitably induced a similar confusion in the minds and hearts of the citizens. Rapid growth and improved
overseas and inland communications introduced new ideas, which served
to complicate existence further, forcing the inhabitants to examine their
attitudes toward every department of life and stimulating an interest in
the arts and sciences beyond that of all previous periods. Of course this
cultural ferment was in large measure the normal accompaniment of
passing years and the mellowing effect of social interchange. For more
than a century the cities had been filling with people, fostering a de-
sirable cosmopolitanism, and, in spite of the setback of a depression,
piling up more wealth; they were, in short, coming of age. The matura-
tion can be discerned in the education of youth, through the efforts of
adults to acquire additional knowledge from books, newspapers, pamphlets, and lectures, in the expression of the ideals and aspirations of the
citizens in writing, music, painting, and science. And all this time, in the
course of these pursuits, the colonists, or at least the majority of them,
were discovering that the love of locality was being transcended by a
love of country. American nationalism, though new and not yet fully
articulated, stirred in many a heart, and by 1776 had become a force to
conjure with.

II

Collectively the five cities could take some pride in their inhabitants
being as literate and intellectually alert as any society of the contemporary world, but the leaders of all classes were well aware that, considering the size of the towns and the temper of the age, their educational facilities were inadequate. In most of the schools, except in the

New England towns, instruction was strongly influenced by denominational supervision, and in all of them the emphasis on classical training was such that the curriculum was totally unrelated to the workaday world and consequently did not attract lads destined for menial or practical occupations. As a result, in Charles Town, at least, the charity classes did not even have capacity enrollment; while at the same time private and vocational schools flourished to meet the demands unheeded by public and religious bodies.

Perhaps it was the presence of colleges in three of the seaports that encouraged boys of studious bent to seek higher education or the educational training requisite for entrance into the growing professional classes, but whatever it was, teachers and schools attempted to step up their programs and raise the standard of instruction that their students might progress to institutions of higher learning. Charles Town and Newport both initiated movements to found colleges in their respective towns, but war and politics prevented either of them from completing the plans that would have given them some educational facilities on the same plane as the other communities.

The Charles Town school system, if it can be called that, suffered from the fact that many of the leading citizens were only part-time residents and consequently took no responsibility and offered no guidance or assistance to those who would better the schools. Poor children attended the Free School or the charity schools of the South Carolina Society, the Fellowship Society, and the German Friendly Society. The Negro school, which had started out so promisingly in the earlier period, was hit by the smallpox in 1761 and then abandoned in 1764 when the Negro teachers were no longer available. Henry Laurens, one of the few prominent men to give some thought to education, declared in 1763 that the schools of the province were a disgrace and that it was outrageous that her children had to go abroad even "for A B C and a little Latin." Fundamentally he was right, but the Province Free School tried out a plan that very year giving the classics more emphasis, and the parish schools certainly taught the A B C's, but of course the planters did not want to educate their children on charity. Timothy's *Gazette* asserted in 1765 that Carolinians spent £2,000 sterling a year in England on schooling for their sons, who ought to be trained in the province; in the seventies this was pared down somewhat by sending many lads to Philadelphia. There were many private boarding schools in Charles Town also for those planters who could not afford to send their children out of the province. The "British Academy on the Green," started by the veteran writing-master Osborn Straton, in 1769 made a unique experiment in coeducation, which was soon followed at William Walton's Academy in Queen Street and thereafter became an accepted procedure. The school opened by Messrs. Macaulay and Gordon in 1774 "under the

Patronage of several respectable Gentlemen" claimed to offer as good instruction as any of the Northern academies. Some people, at least, were aware that culturally their community was not abreast of the American standard.

In Philadelphia various religious denominations pretty much controlled elementary and secondary education, but enrollments were high. From eighty to a hundred boys and from thirty to fifty girls attended the Charity School administered by the College of Philadelphia, and the Lutheran, Reformed, and Moravian communions, fearing lest their children lose the cultural heritage of the German homeland, established their own elementary schools. The Quaker City had two Negro schools: one sponsored by the Bray Associates kept classes until the War for Independence ended its existence, and the Quakers supported another attended by both slaves and free blacks. The pride of the Quakers was the Friends (Penn Charter) School, one of the best college preparatory schools in the country in spite of Anthony Benezet's regret that only a few prominent Quakers showed any real concern about education beyond the elementary. Their neglect of the English School, however, drove John Wilson to submit his resignation, in which he incisively set forth the case of the majority of the pupils, who, intended by their parents for "Mercantile or Mechanick Employments," had little need to learn dead languages. Two graduates of Halle and Leipzig opened a German Seminary in Philadelphia to prepare youths for college by offering a curriculum even more traditional than that of the Quakers or the nonsectarian Academy. It had been the plan of the founders of the Academy that the English School would teach practical subjects. In 1761, ten years after its founding, the enrollment went over the three-hundred mark, but as the trustees followed their own preferences and gave short shrift to the English School, the succeeding year saw a decline in the number and quality of teachers, and students, despairing of finding the instruction they had sought for there, went to any one of a number of private schools. It is no wonder that South Carolinians sent their boys to Philadelphia when they could not send them to England.

Neither the province nor the religious bodies of New York did very much to elevate the instruction given to the children of Gotham. The personal industry and ability of Joseph Hildreth made a continuing success of the Anglican charity school, where about twenty-five girls and twice as many boys received elementary instruction, and then about half of these students were bound out as apprentices to various trades. Because the Reformed Dutch, Moravian, and Anglican schools of Manhattan failed to prepare students for entrance to King's College, that institution opened a grammar school of its own in 1762 under the direction of Mathew Cushing from Massachusetts. About thirty students attended for a time, but the number declined to a mere fifteen by 1769. Thomas

Jackson also kept a school, beginning in 1762, to prepare New York boys in Latin and Greek for entrance to college, and two years later Alexander Miller of Hanover Square made a specialty of getting young Presbyterians ready for the College of New Jersey. Cadwallader Colden endorsed an "Academy of the Liberal Arts" run by William Adams from the University of Aberdeen which, after several moves, settled down in Harlem.

Newport children could attend either a religious or a public institution. The Trinity Church School looked after poor Anglicans, the Moravians maintained a primary school for their people, and finally, in 1772, the Congregationalists opened nondenominational charity classes on Thursday and Saturday afternoons; beginning with 32 pupils, Messrs. Pemberton and Dennison soon had 134 poor children in attendance, using books and paper supplied "through the liberality of several Gentlemen and Ladies." In that same year the Bray Associates started a school in Newport at the house of Widow Mary Brett, who taught about thirty Negroes "of all societies" to read, write, and sew. Support must have been uncertain, for the *Newport Mercury* spoke of it in 1773 as if it had been closed for a time, and then again in 1774 announced that it was to be reopened. Newport's town school records are so sparse that about all that is known is that one existed. At the end of the previous period some cultivated men had urged the establishment of additional schools, but apparently the stagnation of trade, the inability to collect taxes, and competition coming from Providence made Newporters loath to initiate new projects. William Rogers, Jr., undertook to teach Latin and Greek at the insistence of several gentlemen interested in relieving "the great Want of Grammar Schools." Here again the private schools filled the gap.

The superiority of Boston's tax-supported school system remained unchallenged. Because of its excellence and also because of careful scrutiny by the Selectmen of all applications from aspiring teachers, there were fewer private schools than in the other cities. Carefully supervised by the authorities, the writing schools provided the kind of instruction most boys needed, while the grammar schools prepared students for Harvard or the professions. Twenty-eight lads began their studies in 1766 at the South Grammar (Boston Latin) School, from which they graduated seven years afterwards; in time two became judges, one a British admiral, another a British general, one a member of Parliament, one an architect, and among the rest were three baronets, two American colonels, two clergymen, thirteen merchants, five masters of arts, two Fellows of the American Academy of Arts and Sciences, and two poetasters. Throughout this period the five Boston public schools annually trained more than nine hundred boys—nearly six per cent of the entire population.

In all the towns, private schools or masters qualified youths for various trades, the countinghouse, or the sea by offering courses in almost anything—geography, surveying, "plating and Designs for Architecture in all its Branches," foreign languages, navigation, bookkeeping, and so on. These schools naturally drew most of their patronage from city populations, but an increasing number of boys and young men came in from the country to attend them. Evening schools specialized in trade subjects, but they also offered classical studies. So many of them abounded in Philadelphia that, "To prevent Trouble," in October 1767 eleven of the principal pedagogues jointly advertised that they would start evening classes on October 12, and that their fees would be twelve shillings sixpence per quarter for reading and writing (pens, ink, and fire included), and for mathematics "the usual Price." Others entered into the agreement the next year, which suggests that cutthroat competition had become so fatal that the schoolmasters were forced to reach some agreement on hours and fees.

The number of schools offering courses in written and spoken English implies that there must have been a growing insistence that urban youth should be able to write and "speak their own Language" if they were to get ahead in the world. Thomas Byerley opened an English Grammar School in New York in 1773 with five classes, beginning with reading and pronunciation, and progressing through grammar to syntax and advanced prose to poetry. A former Boston teacher coupled proficiency in English with the ability to learn other languages, but most of them, like Hugh Hughes, merely advertised that "just Pronounciation" was taught in their night school "for respectable people." Apparently the instructors of young women did not put much emphasis on grammar, for in Benjamin Franklin's reply to his sister's apology for incorrectnesses in her writing, the kindly brother told her that she wrote better than most Americans of her sex.

Girls and young ladies who essayed any branch of learning beyond the elementary still had to resort to private masters for instruction. This was true even at Boston, where the publicly paid masters charged a fee for private classes for teaching English, French, and Latin to girls; and Philadelphia, with so many schools for boys, had no "proper boarding schools" for girls before the seventies. "Female embellishments" were all that were supplied in this man's century even if the colonial cities did do more to educate their women than contemporary English communities. In a *Boston Gazette* of 1773 "Clio" deplored the universal neglect of women's education: "But few of the Fair Sex have been sufficiently instructed in their own Language to write it with Propriety and Elegance: and many have passed through Life unknown, who with an Education would have adorned Humanity, added to the Treasures of Literature, and with new born Rays extended the Beam of Knowledge."

Here was the problem formulated, but no solution could come as long as such a man as John Adams could write with obvious ambivalence to his cultured Abigail: "Your sentiments of the importance of education in women are exactly agreeable to my own. Yet the *femmes savantes* are contemptible characters."

Varying motives—sectarian requirements, available wealth, civic pride and intercity rivalries, even nascent patriotism—prompted a universal interest in higher education after the end of the last French War. As early as 1761 Ezra Stiles began to assemble data and to lay plans for a college at Newport which, in keeping with the enlightened spirit of the times, would embrace all religious denominations. The Reverend Morgan Edwards of Philadelphia and other leaders of the Baptists, desiring an institution to train their clergy, sent James Manning to sound out their brethren of Rhode Island in 1763 about locating a college in that province. Joining forces with Newport's liberal Baptists, the Congregationalists, under Stiles and William Ellery, drew up a charter giving the Baptists "the lead" on the board of trustees and the Congregationalists on the board of fellows. Passage of the charter was held up in the Assembly by Daniel Jenckes, a Providence Baptist, and when it was finally issued in October 1765, the instrument retained all of Stiles's liberal provisions but gave control of both boards to the Baptists. A struggle immediately commenced between Newport and Providence to obtain the college, which had been temporarily located at Warren. In retrospect, Newport had every asset: a large city renowned for its culture and the Redwood Library, cheaper boarding for students, a healthful climate, greater wealth to tap, and ease of communications with other colonies; on the other hand, Providence could only claim that, being smaller, youths would be exposed to fewer temptations. In February 1770, in the face of a larger financial offer by the older town, Providence won the contest. This decision to locate Rhode Island College at Providence signalized the transfer of power to the younger, smaller, but more vigorous community. The War for Independence merely gave Newport the *coup de grâce*.

What Mr. Stiles had termed "College Enthusiasm" had repercussions in other cities. The Harvard Corporation stifled one in Hadley, persuading Governor Bernard to rescind a royal charter for "Queen's College" by demonstrating the harm a rival would do to the Cambridge institution. Boston clergy and merchants were also hostile to Eleazar Wheelock's scheme for educating Indians, which culminated in the founding of Dartmouth College in New Hampshire, largely because they believed that one man ought not to handle such large funds without being held accountable. One of the opponents signing himself "Phil-Africanus" inquired pertinently why there was so much concern about the Indian and nothing being done for the Negroes. The Reformed Dutch of Manhattan turned away from Episcopalian King's College and supported the establishing of their own Queen's, which opened in New Brunswick in 1771. At the College of Philadelphia, although the spirit of Enlightenment revealed more of itself than in any other institution, sectarian jockeying for control shook it to its foundations and made it a central issue in Pennsylvania politics. With Provost Smith aspiring to a "pair of lawn sleeves," and Vice-Provost Alison heading the opposition to a bishopric, the College could not but suffer; yet it played perhaps a more vital part in Philadelphia's cultural ferment than Harvard did at Boston.

It looked for a time as if Charlestonians who wanted higher education made available in their city might be successful when, in 1764, a committee was designated to draw up a bill for "a public College," which reached a second reading in the next session only to lose out during the Stamp Act excitement. In his *Gazette* in 1769 Peter Timothy expressed the sentiments of all but the very rich when he pointed out that since the "mother Country seems unfriendly," boys now sent to college at Philadelphia ought to be kept at home, both to save money and to attach them to their native province. The Northern colonies have their own colleges, cried "Carolinacus," "Why cannot we imitate so successful an example?" From "a Native" promptly came an incisive reply: "From want of a College among us, youth of moderate fortunes are reduced to the necessity of a common confined education . . . many of whom would, otherwise, have been an honour and a credit to their country and friends. The Rich, indeed, may be indifferent about such an establishment which might deprive their sons of the only advantage of being distinguished among their Countrymen, by an education superior to theirs acquired at great expence."

Lavish contributions made by wealthy Charlestonians to solicitors from Rhode Island College, the College of Philadelphia, and the College of New Jersey again focused public opinion on the need for a local institution, and in 1770 Governor William Bull asked the Assembly to establish a college as the citizens concurrently petitioned for one. In March, John Rutledge introduced a bill embodying Bull's ideas and providing for a "very extensive" scheme for provincial education with a first-rate college at the head. In spite of opposition from aristocrats who warned that "learning would become cheap and too common, and every man would be for giving his son an education," the measure went through two readings and would have become a law had not the Governor and Assembly reached an impasse over the notorious Wilkes Fund. Supporters of the college did not give up hope, for in 1772–3 John Mackenzie of Broom Hall left it £1,000 sterling and over eight hundred books; John Pine, a cabinetmaker, bequeathed it about £2,000 sterling, and Miles Brewton a similar sum. Had not the War for Independence intervened, it seems certain that not only would a college have been founded, but Charles Town would have been the center of the first broadly conceived experiment in public education in America.

In the realm of medical education, two of the cities outdistanced those of England, and one of them, Philadelphia, rivaled Edinburgh itself. Fresh from the grand tour and "flushed with honors" from the *cognoscenti* of Europe, Dr. John Morgan came home to Philadelphia and delivered his famous discourse on the founding of medical schools in America at the College commencement in 1765. The following November, Morgan and Dr. William Shippen, Jr., began lecturing on medicine, anatomy, and surgery, and in 1766 "a compleat and regular" medical curriculum went into effect at the College. Soon, also, Dr. Thomas Bond commenced giving clinical lectures at the Pennsylvania Hospital for the benefit of the medical students. The College granted the first degrees to ten bachelors of medicine in June 1768 and conferred its first doctors' diplomas in the summer of 1771.

The idea for the New York school of medicine originated in a letter that Samuel Bard wrote from Edinburgh to his father, Dr. John Bard, in December 1762. Young Bard was describing the plans of Dr. William Shippen, Jr., for a medical school in Philadelphia, which "will have the start of us by several years. I own I feel a little jealous of the Philadelphians, and should be glad to see the College of New York at least upon an equality with theirs." Six or more Manhattan physicians started a medical society, and, led by Dr. Samuel Clossy, who had instituted medical lectures in 1763, they proposed the formation of a medical school at King's College in August 1767. The trustees readily agreed, and in November the institution opened with a faculty of six able medicos, of whom Dr. Bard was the most eminent. Two years later Robert Tucker and Samuel Kissam became bachelors of medicine, and in 1770 and 1771 received the doctor's degree. By 1774 nine other bachelor's degrees had been awarded, and though the New York school did not fulfill young Bard's hope of equaling that of its neighboring city, when the war came, these two medical schools sent both faculty and students to the medical service of the Continental Army.

III

The number of bookstores and the extent to which the American colonists, particularly those living in or near the cities, purchased or borrowed and read books offer conclusive evidence of their maturity. Importations were large enough to have played an increasingly important part in both overseas and intercolonial trade. Philadelphia had seventy-seven bookshops between 1761 and 1776, or one less than the total of the first ten provincial cities of England; Boston with thirty-one and New York with twenty-seven may be compared with Newcastle, Liverpool, and Bath, whose total was thirty-one. Even Newport with ten and Charles Town with six would have rated high in the English list. Taken together, the five colonial cities had 151 such establishments in contrast with 104 for the sixteen leading cities of England outside of London.

Certain booksellers rose to prominence as importers and wholesalers, supplying other shops in city or country and operating on an intercolonial scale as well as retailing or auctioning books, magazines, pamphlets, and broadsides locally. Some of the more enterprising also ventured into publishing. The absence of any copyright law permitted Robert Bell of Philadelphia, easily the foremost American bookman, to reproduce numbers of English works in cheap reprints, thereby encouraging the purchase of good literature and forcing his competitors into similar undertakings. A buyer of private libraries and the first important dealer in second-hand books, Bell carried the auction to its highest point. Occasionally he traveled to other cities to sell his books, but achieved his success principally through newspaper advertising; in the gazettes from Portsmouth to Savannah, he informed the public of his holdings—Tissot on *Health,* Robertson's *History of Charles V,* Blackstone's *Commentaries,* and so forth. In 1776 he earned the distinction of publishing the first issue of Thomas Paine's *Common Sense.*

Book shops must have been profitable enterprises for the leaders of the trade, judging from the degree of affluence and influence reached by some of them. The largest stock of books in the South was commanded by Robert Wells, who regularly and promptly imported the latest British publications. His high prices shocked Rivington of New York, but they explain how Wells and his rival Nicholas Langford could afford to take their families to Newport in the summer. After opening shops at New York, Philadelphia, and Boston, the erratic James Rivington, son of the well-known London publisher Charles Rivington, settled down at Manhattan. The steadying influence and social prestige of Elizabeth Van Horne, whom he married in 1769, together with his English connections enabled him to rise rapidly both as a member of the local gentry and as a book merchant. His "London Bookstore" in Hanover Square was one of the most frequented in the colonies, but not so profitable but that every variety of patent medicine was sold as well as the "handsomest Shaving Equipages, fit for Persons of the first Rank," dice, and "Racquets for Tennis and Fives." Acquiring a printing office, he also went into publishing, claiming in 1768 that he had 2,200 advance subscriptions for his edition of the poems of Charles Churchill. Having given up his interest in the Boston store, Rivington supplied Newport dealers and Henry Knox of Boston from New York. Knox also acted as agent for Maredant's Drops, Keyser's Female Pills, and *Rivington's New York*

Gazetteer. A Scot, John Mein, had bought out Rivington & Miller of Boston in 1765, and within a year had imported about 1,200 volumes and had a stock of 10,000 volumes. He claimed "the most extensive trade of any person on the American Continent," with profits estimated at £40 to £60 a week; and he might be credited with making novel, drama, and magazine readers out of New Englanders.

Through hawkers and country storekeepers, city booksellers, like the merchants, augmented their sales in rural America. Henry Knox opened his Cornhill shop in 1771, and stocked large numbers of books, pamphlets, and magazines from Henry Longmans of London, which he in turn distributed to Nathaniel Bird of Newport, as far eastward as Boothbay, and inland to Worcester; occasionally he got orders from distant St. Croix and Essequibo in Dutch Guiana. Rivington recommended his own one-shilling reprint of Hervey's *Meditations* "in strong paper" because, as at New York, "many poor people will readily purchase this who cannot afford to buy the whole at once and the Pedlars will sell great numbers of it." Bell of Philadelphia used broadsides to advertise in the country, and Richard King of Charles Town solicited inland orders by sending out catalogues. His competitors George Wood and Robert Wells featured "good allowances to schoolmasters, or others, that take a quantity." From Philadelphia, G. C. Reinholt and Henry Miller shipped books imported from Germany all over the back country of "Greater Pennsylvania." Both Henry Knox and William Woodhouse of Philadelphia catered also to "those Gentlemen in the Country who are actuated with the most genuine Principles of Benevolence in their Exertions to Exterminate Ignorance and Darkness by the Noble Medium of Social Libraries."

Although the likes of John Donaldson, who advertised "the only Shop for Cheap Books" at New York, existed in all cities, many persons who wanted to read books could not afford them. For such as these the circulating library had proved a boon. All of the cities save Boston had libraries, but their restrictions or charges encouraged new ones. In August 1763 George Wood established a lending library which supplied Charlestonians with histories, travels, biographies, memoirs, novels, and plays until 1767, when he offered his collection of over one thousand volumes for sale. Not until 1772 did Samuel Gifford open another library, "on the same Terms as in London," which turned out to be one pound sterling a year, with the privilege of borrowing only one book at a time. Several New Yorkers tried library ventures: Garrat Noel started a lending library of several thousand volumes in his New York bookstore in 1763, because sundry gentlemen had "for a long Time been desirous of seeing such a Thing established in this City"; it closed down in 1765 but reopened again in 1768; in 1771 Ebenezer Hazard became his partner. Samuel Loudon undertook a circulating library in 1774, and he soon discovered that Manhattan ladies "are his best customers and shew a becoming delicacy of taste in their choice of books." John Mein's lending library at Boston started out in 1765 with twelve hundred volumes, from which country customers might withdraw two books at a time upon paying double the subscription fee of £1. 8s. lawful money and the "Expence of Carriage." The venture apparently did not succeed, for no record survives beyond the year of founding. Philadelphians had access to three circulating libraries. Beginning modestly in 1767, in two years Lewis Nicola had five hundred volumes of "the most approved Authors in History, Poetry, Novels, and other works of entertainment, likewise some well chosen French Books." In this year Thomas Bradford's library opened on Second Street near Arch, and, not to be outdone in anything pertaining to books, Robert Bell established a "Universal Library" in 1774.

The multiplication of libraries at Philadelphia narrowed the resources and memberships of the separate institutions. Convinced that consolidating the collections and memberships of small libraries having common aims would improve services, the Union reduced the price of its shares in 1766, to facilitate absorbing the less affluent members of the Amicable; in 1769 it merged with the Association, and finally the Union itself was incorporated into the Library Company. The combined collections had more than eight thousand titles, and the enlarged membership with dues of ten pounds currency made it a very strong institution. This did not mean that it was a rich man's club, for in 1772 the Reverend Jacob Duché reported that "the librarian assured me, that for one person of distinction and fortune there were twenty tradesmen that frequented the library." The same held true for the Loganian Library, where, as Du Simitière noted, its few but regular readers were "composed of some obscure mechanicks who have a turn for mathematics."

The other libraries, founded prior to 1760, retained their separate entities, growing larger and wealthier through contributions and bequests; and a few new ones opened up. The Philadelphia Baptist Association appointed the Reverend Morgan Edwards and Isaac Jones as librarians in charge of the books donated by Thomas Hollis of London for use of ministers; in 1770 it established "the Trustees for promoting Learning amongst the Baptist Churches" to accept contributions, some of which were spent on books. The growing Lutheran School Library, first catalogued in 1763, had the best choice of German works of any in America, and the library of the College of Philadelphia added a great many new volumes to its holdings, bringing them up to two thousand by 1776. The choicest of these special collections, however, was started with a gift of books and anatomical drawings to the Pennsylvania Hospital by Dr. John Fothergill of London in 1763, and, augmented by several special bequests, it became a truly outstanding medical library.

No merger of New York's libraries took place in this period, but the Corporation Library of almost two thousand volumes and the New York Society Library both enjoyed the services of a schoolmaster named Thomas Jackson as librarian and both were housed in the same room in City Hall. There was, apparently, room for another, for in 1771 Walter Franklin, Garret Rapalje, and Lindley Murray headed the 140 subscribers of influence and position who formed the Union Library Society with "near 1000 volumes" and three times the membership of the Society Library—anyone could afford the Union's low rate of thirty shillings. Curiously enough, after May 1776 the library of King's College was shelved in the same room in City Hall, each collection being separated by a mere partition.

When Josiah Quincy viewed the Charles Town Library Society in 1773, he described it as "a handsome, square, spacious room, containing a large collection of very valuable books." In 1767, at his departure, Lord Charles Hope had presented nearly two hundred well-chosen books to the library; in 1772 the catalogue and supplement listed 886 titles. About the same time John Mackenzie bequeathed an admirable collection of more than eight hundred volumes to the Library Society "for the use of a college when erected." Incorporated by the Assembly in 1770, the trustees of the Library Society ambitiously contemplated supporting professors of arts and sciences and promoting "a full and accurate Natural History" of South Carolina, for which they "fitted up a Museum" with Charles Cotesworth Pinckney, Thomas Heyward, and two prominent physicians as curators. Unlike the Library Company of Philadelphia or the Union Library of New York, however, the trustees made no gesture toward including the lower orders in their undertaking. Although no other subscription library was established, the Provincial Library of 1700 was still in existence in 1762.

Under the librarianship of the Reverend Ezra Stiles from 1756 to 1775, the Redwood Library not merely prospered but served as the focus of all of Newport's cultural activities, but it was not going according to plan. "This set out as a Quaker affair; Mr. Redwood being a Friend," Stiles wrote in 1771, describing his efforts to make the membership more representative, but politics eventually frustrated the design. "Thro' the Blindness of Mr. Redwood and [Thomas] Ward and [John] Callender (the 2 last Men of great Learning and Penetration) the Episcopalians slyly got into and obtained a majority which they are careful to keep. At first of 46 but 18 were Episcopalians. Since this they are become a majority. . . . The Founder has often told me of it, and said it was contrary to his Intention; and that this was one Reason of his refusing to sit in the Director's Meetings." Yet the lending of books went on, and the gift of Mrs. Catharine Macaulay through Henry Marchant of a set of her Whiggish history to the Redwood, because she so admired the librarian's sermon on *Christian Union,* must have given Mr. Stiles hope for the cause of liberty. Since only members had access to the collection, Stiles and neighboring clergymen in 1763 began to assemble the works of the Church Fathers, which in time became a much-consulted and valuable "Ecclesiastical Library" for Congregational ministers in New England.

The Bostonians still remained strangely indifferent to the subscription library movement. Such lawyers as Benjamin Pratt, Jeremiah Gridley, and John Adams and citizens like James Bowdoin and Joseph Harrison built up really outstanding personal libraries, which probably outnumbered and rivaled in taste all but the celebrated collections of John Dickinson and the Philadelphians or a few private libraries at Charles Town. Harvard graduates had access to the books at the College, to which Thomas Hollis so liberally contributed after the fire of 1764. Andrew Eliot put his finger on one prime reason for the paucity of circulating libraries in 1770, when he explained to Hollis why Bostonians were so heedless of what was being said for and against them in England: "Few of our merchants are readers, and others are out of the way of procuring. Our accounts of things are chiefly by private correspondence." Whatever the cause, bookish Boston lagged far behind the other cities in library collections, and its less affluent citizens must have been hard put to it for books to read.

IV

Depressions, mobs, and politics changed the content of the public prints as local news replaced foreign; and these years, already pregnant with the strained relationships between the colonies and the mother country, saw the printers emerge as civic leaders and molders of public opinion. After 1764 neither the lawyers, nor the physicians, nor the clergy counted so heavily in urban activities as the men who put out the weekly journals and scores of pamphlets; yet in comparison with the aforesaid groups they were fewer in number. One printing house, operated by the Widow Franklin, then by Samuel Hall, and ultimately by Solomon Southwick, accommodated Newport; four throve at Charles Town, and elsewhere six or more establishments found business enough to prosper.

If they are viewed merely as business enterprises and if the intangible force they represented is ignored, these printing establishments do not seem so impressive as many an artisan's workshop or certain urban manufactories. There were occasions when Peter Timothy did not even have an assistant because of the shortage of labor in Charles Town; on the other hand, some printing shops became fairly large for the times, each using a number of presses and employing numerous journeymen and apprentices. In Philadelphia twenty-three printers, operating between 1770 and 1776, trained many of the journeymen who set up as master printers in such smaller towns as Baltimore, Lancaster, New Haven, New Bern, and Savannah. There were a number besides Benjamin Franklin who made money out of the craft. Franklin's own partner David Hall prospered, rose to prominence at Philadelphia, was able to send his wife to Bristol Springs with the quality, while he joined library and fire companies. His chief rival, William Bradford, invested printing profits in publishing, bookselling, insurance, a coffeehouse, and allied activities; he became influential in Pennsylvania politics, and one of his sons went to college in the city and another to the College of New Jersey, where he became a fast friend of James Madison. Significant, too, was the success of Henry Miller, the first Philadelphia printer successfully to challenge and break the monopoly of printing and publishing in German hitherto regarded by the Saurs of Germantown as their prerogative. His bookstore and print shop in Second Street flourished from its opening in 1761 as he went out after the business of the Lutherans and German Reformed, leaving Saur to traffic with the proportionately much smaller number of "the plain people."

The houses profited and expanded as a result of the movement for colonial manufactures as well as the growth in population. Of the 5,862 titles listed by Evans for the years 1761–76, 4,121 or seventy per cent came from the presses of the five cities:

City	English	Foreign Language
Philadelphia	1,458	122
Boston	1,278	0
New York	1,111	18
Newport	195	0
Charles Town	74	0
Total	4,116	140

The primacy in publishing that Boston had enjoyed since the seventeenth century, it lost to Philadelphia after 1764; New York, too, made great strides, and Newport, with its one printing house, moved well ahead of Charles Town, where the market for books evidently did not warrant many publishing ventures.

The number and variety of new titles issued in this period is impressive in its coverage, indicating that colonial printers kept their readers well abreast of the best literary offerings of the Old World. Such publishers as Bell and James Humphreys of Philadelphia, Rivington of New York, and Edes & Gill of Boston reprinted editions "in home-made garb" of European and British authors and sold them cheaper than they could be imported. Appealing to "the Lovers of Literary Amusement, and the Encouragers of American Manufactures," in 1772 William Mentz advertised an "American Edition" of *The Vicar of Wakefield,* printed on Pennsylvania paper and neatly bound, for four shillings sixpence when the English one retailed at eight shillings. In 1768 Bell brought out Johnson's *Rasselas,* then issued Lady Montagu's *Works,* Blackstone's *Commentaries,* Sterne's *Sentimental Journey,* Robertson's *History of Scotland,* Defoe's *Robinson Crusoe,* and in 1775 James Burgh's influential *Political Disquisitions,* together with books of travel, plays, and verse. His competitors were also active: Dunlap proposed to print a twenty-four-volume edition of Voltaire in English translation; Robert Aitken got out the first American edition of the New Testament and one of Gray's *Elegy* in 1773; and James Humphreys published Sterne in five volumes and Chesterfield's *Letters* in four. The presence of the American Company of Comedians at Philadelphia and New York undoubtedly popularized play-reading and stimulated the reprinting of many English plays. Rivington not only sold quantities of reprinted plays at New York, but his correspondent Knox of Boston marketed them for him through Nathaniel Bird at Newport. In 1774, also through Knox, Rivington sought the services of Paul Revere for engraving two plates for a travel work. Boston reprints ran the gamut from practical works to ephemera of such deceptive titles as *Look E'er You Leap; or a History of Lewd Women:* Chapter iii told of "Women consider'd in the three-fold Capacity of Maid, Wife, and Widow—with Directions how to choose a good Wife." John Fleeming proposed bringing out in two volumes "the First Bible ever printed in America." In 1772 John Boyle promised Montesquieu's *Spirit of the Laws* for ten shillings eightpence instead of the twenty shillings charged for the English edition, because it "ought to be in Every man's Hands." Inasmuch as the publishers of all these books controlled the newspapers, they naturally advertised them widely in the journals and gave them an intercolonial distribution through booksellers everywhere.

The size of the printings or sales of particular books is not known, but early in 1773 John Dunlap wrote some "Observations relative to the Manufactures of Paper and Printed Books in the Province of Pennsylvania" to show the benefits to be derived from encouraging the local paper industry and to point out that a publisher had to print three thousand copies of a large work to meet the costs of paper, presswork, and binding. That publishers felt their sales could attain this figure for as many books as they issued seems quite remarkable. Apparently a satisfactory market existed for books that could never be classed as light literature, such as Jared Eliot's *Essays on Field Husbandry* (Boston, 1761); Anthony Benezet's *Some Historical Account of Guinea* (Philadelphia, 1771); Bernard Roman's *Concise Natural History of East and*

West Florida (New York, 1775; 2nd ed., 1776); or Jacob Duché's *Observations on a Variety of Subjects* (Philadelphia, 1774); or for the reprinting of five hundred copies, in one volume, of John Wise's *Church's Quarrel Espoused* and *Vindication of the Government of the New England Churches* (Boston, 1772)—"The cheapest Book of the size ever printed in America." Yet these and many more books sold well along with an increasing number of colonial textbooks.

For years, sermons and religious tracts had made up a very large part of the publishing business, but they now gave way before the secular trend to the pamphlet. Whenever a debatable issue arose—social, religious, economic, political—the presses deluged the public with these ephemera, which were generally lively and partisan, sometimes satirical or witty, bumptious or scurrilous, and seldom dignified or reasonable. They served as the editorial or, better, as the columnistic writings of their time; and a people nourished in the great age of English pamphleteering avidly devoured their contents. The torrid Quaker-Presbyterian conflict in Pennsylvania, the Stamp Act, and each successive attempt of the British government to tighten the colonial system brought forth its crop of pamphlets, and the printers grew rich on the work. As Dr. Robert Honyman arrived in each city on his way from Virginia to New England in 1775, he customarily "went out and bought some pamphlets." At New York on March 13 he dropped into Rivington's shop, "lookt over the Titles of a number of Pamphlets," intending on his return "to get a compleat set," for "he is the only man to furnish me with both sides of the question."

The number of newspapers was never large, but the five cities published 47.5 per cent of all colonial newssheets and clearly set the standard for colonial journalism. Twenty-nine were established to compete with the twelve already existing in 1760, and in 1775 nineteen still remained in business—six in Philadelphia, five at Boston, four at New York, three in Charles Town, and one at Newport. In 1768–9, the *Massachusetts Gazette* appeared on Mondays and Thursdays as a part of the *Boston Post Boy* and *Boston Newsletter* alternately, and the next year Mein and Fleeming introduced biweekly publication with their *Boston Chronicle,* January 2, 1769. At Philadelphia on January 24, 1775 Benjamin Towne's *Pennsylvania Evening Post* became the first local evening paper and the first colonial triweekly. Indeed, the following year Penn's city had access to seven newspapers: five came out on weekday mornings, the *Evening Post* on Tuesday, Thursday, and Saturday evenings, and Henry Miller's *Philadelphische Staatsbote* every Tuesday and Thursday.

Newspaper printings ran from 700 to more than 3,600 copies for each weekly issue; probably the *Boston Newsletter's* 1,550 approached the average. But these rag-paper journals were read by many people other than subscribers and listened to by as many more, and the circulation was by no means limited to their immediate locality. Mein's biweekly *Boston Chronicle* had forty-nine subscribers in Newport; Ezra Stiles received half a dozen other sheets by the post. Henry Knox of Boston and Moses Michael Hays at Newport acted as agents for *Rivington's New York Gazetteer*. In each community, moreover, coffeehouses and taverns carried a variety of newspapers for the use of patrons. Thrifty Ezra Collins wrote in 1773 to his brother Stephen at Philadelphia that he had not sent him the *Boston Evening Post* because he "well remembered that thou frequently attended the Coffee House, where all the Boston news papers lay open for perusal free of Expence."

Most inland settlements received one or more newspapers. Peter Timothy listed in his *South Carolina Gazette* in 1764 fifty or more subscription agents located from Brunswick in North Carolina southward to St. Augustine, along the Gulf to Pensacola and Mobile, and westward in the upcountry to the Congarees, Ninety-Six, and Augusta. Robert Wells merely stated that his "Circulated through all the Southern Colonies." Bradford's *Pennsylvania Journal* went by special postriders to the Lower Counties, Maryland, Virginia, New Jersey, and eastern Pennsylvania, and all parts of the province east of the Susquehanna; in addition, he had seventeen subscribers in Jamaica, eight in Barbados, four in Antigua, four in St. Kitts, eighteen in Dominica, three in England, and one at Bordeaux. Through the efforts of thirty-eight agents, Goddard's *Pennsylvania Chronicle* covered much the same area and also went to Halifax, Quebec, and parts of New England as well; Miller's *Staatsbote* reached nearly every German settlement as far south as the Savannah River. The Manhattan papers, on the other hand, circulated widely in Connecticut and Rhode Island. In 1766 when the General Court was told that since the *Boston Newsletter* did not circulate widely in the country and that therefore public notices need not appear in it, the Drapers branded this a falsity, affirming that it "circulates mostly in the Country, especially on the Great Western Road to Worcester, Springfield, Northampton, Hartford, New Haven" by riders, and that only one other Boston paper enjoyed a larger distribution.

John Holt of the *New York Journal* published the following apostrophe to "The Newspaper," which Solomon Southwick clipped for his *Newport Mercury:*

> *'Tis truth (with deference to the College)*
> *News-papers are the spring of knowledge,*
> *The general source throughout the nation,*
> *Of every modern conversation.*
> *What could this mighty people do,*
> *If there, alas! were nothing new?*

. . . .

> *Our services you can't express,*
> *The good we do you hardly guess;*
> *There's not a want of human kind,*
> *But we a remedy can find.*

Self-praise such as this was actually merited. By printing the shipping news, prices current, occasional letters from merchants, and public notices, and by giving a variety of government and commercial items, "both foreign and domestick," the printers kept the trading community alive to world as well as provincial happenings. Their advertising columns lengthened as retailers and wholesalers alike used them to notify the public of their wares. Competitive advertising gained ground during the years of the depression as every retailer claimed to sell cheaper than his fellows. "Timothy Fagwell" of New York, annoyed at such absurdities, advertised accordingly:

> *None of your Cents, nor under Cents,*
> *But* GOODS *given away* GRATIS.

This, Timothy insisted, was absolutely the best offer ever made the public. Advertising did improve in attractiveness, often featuring one or two articles instead of listing the whole stock of a shop. Printers then as now published letters to the editors; one to John Holt praised the wide circulation of newspapers, "in which I observe with Pleasure, Advertisements, particularly addressed to Ladies and Gentlemen of *Taste*," because they "communicate this to distant Regions and prove presumptively that such Persons reside among us."

In addition to beating the drum for home industries, the press gave actual encouragement by adopting American-made type. The divines Ezra Stiles and Charles Chauncy used their "Influence with some Generous Patriots" in 1769 to procure patronage for the first American movable types, cast at Killingworth, Connecticut, by Abel Buell and sold as cheaply as those imported; Southwick of Newport pulled the first sheets from them. About the same time William Goddard of Philadelphia bought a mahogany press constructed by Isaac Doolittle at New Haven. From its first issue in April 1775, Story and Humphreys' *Pennsylvania Mercury* was printed with Buell's type, and Jacob Bay of Germantown announced that he could henceforth supply printers with "Long Primer Roman Type," of which his advertisement in the *Pennsylvania Packet* was a sample. Edes & Gill printed their *Boston Gazette* on paper made at Milton, with American type, and ink manufactured locally by the stonecutter Henry Christian Geyer.

The publishers of the colonial newspapers had learned gradually during the years since 1742 that the primary function of a newspaper was to discover and reflect public opinion, and that by a further extension, they could form and even manipulate it for desired ends. Through various forms of interchange over the years, especially the practice of clipping each other's journals, urban publishers had also developed a sense of common purpose equal to if not exceeding that of the colonial merchants. They had contended for the freedom of the press in several towns, and after 1760 it was free in fact if not in law. The acute developments of the imperial crisis of 1764–5 did not take the publishers by surprise. Although some of the more successful of them—Benjamin Franklin, Draper, Wells—had assiduously steered clear of politics, others such as Parker, Bradford, Timothy, and James and Ann Franklin had contended for local civic and social reforms and had occasionally taken sides in provincial controversies.

Reflections of the marked decline in trade appeared in all newspapers after 1763, and their owners could not but feel its reaction upon their circulation and advertising. With the passage of Grenville's measures the following year, the press of the Northern cities was filled with letters, essays, and proposals pointing out the actual and probable results of a bad policy. But the Stamp Act hit the printers directly and they struck back immediately; John Holt's *New York Gazette* of June 6, 1765 lashed out fiercely at what James Parker branded "the fatal Black Act"; the *Boston Evening Post* of June 24 gave all of the first page, two columns on the last, and part of its July 1 issue to reprinting the law. "This Piece first gave the greatest Alarm about the Stamp Act," wrote Harbottle Dorr, an artisan, on the margin of his copy of that issue. The almost unanimous opposition of the colonial newspapers to the measure fully justified John Watts's exclamation: "The Printers are all mad." They not only resented its effect upon themselves but gave full expression to the "People's Antipathy," condemning with relentless vigor, sarcasm, and not infrequently invective the unconstitutionality and injustice of the law; and, too, more than any other agency, they promoted active popular disregard of the Stamp Act and incited much of the violence accompanying it. As all foreign-language documents and newspapers had to pay a double tax, Henry Miller's *Wochentliche Philadelphische Staatsbote* told the Germans that in the absence of any economic justification for such an imposition, it could be considered an attack on their cherished mother tongue and argued them into making common cause with English colonists. At Charles Town, Peter Timothy's profitable sinecure at the post office imposed a discreet though galling silence on his newspaper; at the same time Robert Wells privately expressed one of the few dissident opinions: "I wish to be under the jurisdiction of a British Parliament and not our little Provincial Senates aping the greatest Assembly in the World without knowledge, skill, power or any other requisite." Thus the way opened for Charles Crouch, a former apprentice of Timothy, to establish the *South Carolina Gazette, and Country Journal* in December 1765, with substantial local support. Manhattan newspapers may have taken the first step, but those of Boston, led by Edes & Gill's *Gazette,* quickly earned for their town the reputation of being the hotbed of revolution. As a member of the "Loyal Nine," Benjamin Edes participated in the direction of the city's popular resistance to authority and worked with Samuel and John Adams and other manipulators in guiding opinion during succeeding crises.

Popular approval and gratitude accompanied newspaper support of the cause of liberty. "The press hath never done greater service since its first invention," one Son of Liberty declared; "Mr. Holt has gained very great popularity," Parker admitted. The owners of the journals thrilled with the satisfaction of having stood together and demonstrated the power of popular sentiment as they had focused it on the Stamp Act. A revolution in colonial journalism had taken place.

Although such unanimity was never known again, a very large majority of the newspapers in all five cities opposed the Townshend Acts, reprinted John Dickinson's "Farmer's Letters," which appeared initially in Bradford's *Pennsylvania Journal,* urged non-importation, together with encouragement of colonial industries, and carried pieces on the controversy over an Anglican episcopate. No propaganda device dreamed up by these "Trumpeters of Sedition" more effectively served the opposition's purpose than a column headed "A Journal of the Times" or a "Journal of Occurrences," which, though composed at Boston by Samuel Adams and his assistants, always came out in Holt's *New York Journal* and was then copied a week later by three Boston sheets as well as by most of the newspapers up and down the coast and in several English journals. Aimed at stirring up "a general Clamour" against quartering troops in Boston in peacetime, this "Journal" with its "impudent, virulent, and Seditious Lies, Perversions of Truth and Misrepresentations" as Governor Bernard not inaccurately described it, powerfully aided the cause of its authors. As a result of the constant vigilance of the newspapers and unfailing appearance of the "Journal," Americans everywhere began to get the idea that what had happened at Boston might also happen to them.

Testimony to the astounding success of such men as the Fleets and Edes & Gill of Boston, Southwick of Newport, Holt of New York, Bradford in Philadelphia, and Timothy at Charles Town not only in opposing British policy but also in championing the cause of the middle class came from enemies as well as friends. Outstanding recognition of this fact was the effort of the Boston conservatives to counteract the *Gazette* and *Evening Post* by capturing the *Newsletter* and *Post Boy* with grants of official printing in 1768, and the subsidizing of John Mein's *Boston Chronicle* by the Customs Commissioners to expose clandestine importations by Massachusetts merchants in 1769, making it a "paid government organ" with perhaps the largest intercolonial circulation until the tension relaxed in 1770. Ezekiel Russell's anti-faction paper, *The Censor* (1771), and Mills & Hicks's continuation of the *Post Boy* in 1773 at Boston, the *New York Gazetteer* of James Rivington, and Wells's *South Carolina and American General Gazette* were Tory newspapers, and there is some reason to suspect that the first two may have received some support from secret government funds.

The city newspapers prepared the public mind for revolution. They told the citizens what their liberties were, what they ought to be, and, above all, how they were threatened by ministerial and regal policies. They focused attention upon vanishing British liberty by reprinting accounts of the Wilkes troubles in contemporary London and of the plight of the English poor. They took every opportunity to draw the colonies together from 1765 onward. A subtle campaign was carried on to stimulate a martial spirit in the people by featuring military intelligence, emphasizing the large number of men of fighting age in each province, and depreciating British power as compared with colonial ardor and accomplishment since the conquest of Louisburg in 1745. "There is nothing so much neglected in this land as the art of war," a "Military Countryman" (William Heath of Roxbury) warned in a series of letters to the *Boston Gazette* in 1772, as he eloquently urged his fellow provincials to "be wise in time." Virtually every one of the celebrated political pamphlets made a prior appearance in a newspaper, and these, together with many an essay that never achieved separate publication, contained the arguments that impelled first the cities, then the country, to revolt. Commencing in the 1740's to discuss and judge public issues, by 1776 the newspapers governed, for better or for worse, a now dominant public opinion.

V

The excitement of the controversies being waged in the press and the social changes all too apparent even to contemporaries generated discussion, and men felt an irresistible urge to communicate their beliefs and sentiments to others. Old ideas and loyalties were being challenged, new concepts not wholly ripe needed to be elucidated, circulated, and defended, and practical problems, also, called out a spate of vigorous, expository, and practical prose writings. Then, too, the aspiration of some of the leisured gentry to imitate current English literary modes supplied an added stimulant to the development of a native literature in the cities. Vehicles for publication were available in the local presses, and an eager public was ready and waiting to hear what they had to say. One senses in this urban prose the steady inexorable shifting of the American mind within the short span of fifteen years from a willing colonial subordination and pride in the British connection to a nascent nationalism and a determination to be independent.

Of the five towns, the colonial metropolis alone enjoyed a small success in imitating the classical and poetical writings of Georgian England. Provost William Smith's literary circle, which included Nathaniel Evans, Jacob Duché, Thomas Coombe, and Francis Hopkinson, continued to produce graceful and correct yet unimaginative society verse. Thomas Godfrey soared somewhat higher in his *Prince of Parthia* (1765), a minor contribution to the few experiments with the closet drama in the English language. In 1767, as mentioned before, the American Company performed this tragedy at the Southwark Theater; but it was a substitute for *The Disappointment, or the Force of Credulity,* a rollicking farce mercilessly pillorying middle-class hunters of buried treasure, written by Thomas Forrest. It included some dramatic lyrics and introduced the first stage Irishman, Scot, and German, with their dialects. This play marked the beginning of American drama, and so realistically did it mirror the native scene that one of those whom it lampooned was quoted as saying "that it might begin in a Comedy, but that he would make it end in a Tragedy."

Many Philadelphians devoted their creative talents to producing literature valid for its day and more lasting, because it dealt with native themes and issues. In this spirit Provost Smith published an excellent work of current history in his *Historical Account of the Expedition against the Ohio Indians* (1764), Benjamin Rush and Anthony Benezet wrote with accuracy and fervor against the slave trade, and the latter's *Thoughts on the Nature of War* (1766, 1776) and a tract on Indian intemperance mark him as an early American reformer. The partisan writings arising from the march of the Paxton Boys and other local issues of 1764–5, which culminated in the attack on the propietary government and the attempt to have Pennsylvania made a royal province, gave Philadelphia a dress rehearsal for the great revolutionary debate when Franklin, David James Dove, Isaac Hunt, Hugh Williamson, and their fellows published more than thirty poems, dramatic skits, satirical sketches, and serious essays, notable for liveliness, abuse of opponents, and pungent prose. Above all else, such pieces dramatized the serious social cleavage in the colony. In the *Letters from a Farmer in Pennsylvania to the Inhabitants of the British Colonies,* directed at the Townshend Acts, John Dickinson achieved an unprecedented dignity for a controversialist and elevated the newspaper and pamphlet essay to the plane of literature, eliciting warm applause from Burke and Voltaire; he thereby inaugurated the career that eventually won him the sobriquet "Penman of the American Revolution." The culmination of this literature of controversy was, of course, *Common Sense,* written by a recently arrived hack, Thomas Paine, for Aitken's *Pennsylvania Magazine.*

The seriousness with which these literary men took the craftsmanship of the written word is evidenced in an entry in William Bradford's memorandum book for May 4, 1776: "in the Evening I went to Society. This is a social institution formed for literary purposes which I have attended with pleasure and I trust not without advantage. I read a piece on the Florid Stile, the necessity of Diligence in forming a stile, and some directions for this purpose. After the exercises were over, the general Dispute was whether stealing of Property should be punished with Death. The decision was in the Negative."

Boston fell far behind Philadelphia in the volume of its literary output, but, through the polemical Jonathan Mayhew and Charles Chauncy, maintained its reputation for influential clerical discourses; and in James Otis, Samuel and John Adams, and Josiah Quincy, Jr., made invaluable contributions to colonial political theory. Publication in 1770 of an *Elegiac Poem on the Death of the Celebrated Divine . . . George Whitefield* by Phillis, a seventeen-year-old slave of John Wheatley, a tailor, created a sensation, which spread to London, where in 1773 appeared a bound volume of her *Poems on Various Subjects, Religious and Moral.* Not only was the youthful Negress precocious, but her echoes of Pope and Gray, though lacking in originality, were as successful as anything produced in the colonies and so acknowledged in Philadelphia. *The History of the Colony of Massachusetts Bay* (Boston, 1764; London, 1765, 1768) by Thomas Hutchinson represented the first true fusion of authority and readability by a colonial historian. "The Puritan Hutchinson," wrote J. Franklin Jameson, "was in his way a member of the school of Montesquieu, Turgot, and Voltaire—a disciple, consciously or unconsciously, of the *Essai sur les Mœurs.*" His performance ranks with those of Hume and Robertson and was one of the very few American literary contributions to the Enlightenment. Because of its accuracy and its astonishing display of moderation, it remains today a fundamental authority on its subject.

The cultural passivity of the Charlestonians was less marked in letters than in other branches of the arts, though most practitioners were outsiders who merely tarried in the city for a time. Notwithstanding a visit of the compiler of *Fingal* and the poems of Ossian in 1765, no local bard endeavored to celebrate the "gothick" and "romantick" qualities of the red man which William Bartram of Pennsylvania was currently recording in Georgia and Carolina and would ultimately incorporate in his *Travels.* Three years later Timothy tried to find subscribers for James Adair's *History of the American Indians,* a first-rate performance, but not until 1775 did the author bring it out in London. *An Historical Account of the Rise and Progress of the Colonies of South Carolina and*

Georgia (1779) also came from London presses, but because the author, the Reverend Alexander Hewat had fled from Carolina because of Tory sentiments. In preparing his work, between 1763 and 1775, the author adhered to the historical canons of the Enlightenment and gave a careful description of the life and manners of the people. At Charles Town in 1771 Nathaniel Tucker penned a long nostalgic poem about his birthplace, Bermuda, in the manner of *The Deserted Village*. Publication of *The Bermudian* at Edinburgh and Williamsburg in 1773 seems less of a tribute to Tucker's feeble muse than the enterprise of his brother, St. George Tucker. Robert Wells's *Gazette* alone of the Charles Town papers printed excerpts from London reviews of the poem.

The literati of Newport and New York shone by promise, not performance. John Maylem's doggerel on "The Boston Sabbath" and his lines on the town of Newport were the best either community could achieve by versifying. Ezra Stiles was a tireless promoter of things literary, but his activities in this sphere kept him from completing his contemplated Ecclesiastical History of New England and of British North America before the war broke out. He filled "perhaps two quire of paper" in 1769, but did not get back to writing again until 1772, when he would spend twelve hours a day in composition. Although the Literary Society formed at King's College in 1766 by a cultured coterie of faculty and students had ample funds to encourage learning and letters as well as to award premiums, about all it produced was a stilted pseudoclassical piece called "The Furies, a Fable, Imitated from the German of Mr. Lessing," which Rivington printed in his newspaper in 1773. It did, however, indicate an early awareness at Manhattan of the *Sturm und Drang* literature of Germany. The bookseller Ebenezer Hazard, whom John Adams rated a genius, issued a prospectus in 1774 for a volume to be known as "Hazard's State Papers," which was to include documents bearing on American history since the time of Hakluyt. Support for the project came from many quarters, but the collection was another war casualty and did not come out until 1792.

No discussion of urban literary efforts can omit the vital cultural contribution of the newspapers in fostering belles-lettres as well as ordinary prose. Isaiah Thomas of the *Massachusetts Spy,* the proprietor of the *Newport Mercury,* James Rivington, William Goddard of the *Pennsylvania Chronicle,* and Timothy and Wells of the Charles Town press were but a few of the printers who made an effort to put out well-written newspapers and to fill their columns with palatable literary fare. Newporters who took the *Providence Gazette* in 1762 read, with some dismay perhaps, the installments of Stephen Hopkins's readable "Planting and Growth of Providence"; Timothy perennially sought to elevate his fellow Charlestonians by publishing essays such as "The Power, Effects, and Improvement of Taste." In 1768 Bradford instituted a "Poet's

Corner" in his *Pennsylvania Journal,* and the next year in Goddard's *Chronicle* "Timothy Sobersides" attempted to rally Philadelphians for promoting the cause of the Muses concurrently with that of home manufactures. Phillis Wheatley's elegy on two Nantucket sailors first appeared in the *Newport Mercury,* while the Boston journals of the sixties offered their readers such pieces as frank and unflattering London reviews of the Harvard verses, *Pietas et Gratulatio,* presented to George III, Bishop Berkeley's as yet unhackneyed "Westward the Course of Empire," samples of William Collins's *Eclogues,* and an excerpt from Voltaire on History translated from Diderot's great *Encyclopédie,* "now publishing in Paris" (1768).

At a time when grammar schools were multiplying and private masters were offering courses in pronunciation, the newspapers reflected the genuine public concern over American speech, whose grammatical purity many citizens felt was being corrupted by non-English elements as well as by ignorance. Henry Miller commenced printing English lessons by the use of phonetics in his *Philadelphische Staatsbote* in 1762, explaining as best he could how to reproduce the English sounds of *th, v,* and *ch.* About the same time Parker's *New York Gazette* condemned the bad grammar of "pretending men" who said "lay" for "lye," "set" for "sit," and "wrote" for "written." In the *Boston Gazette,* "Spellarius" called on the printing fraternity to foster orthographical uniformity and pointed to the already noticeable divergence of British and American speech seventeen years before Noah Webster published his *Grammatical Institutes.* Isaiah Thomas, of the *Royal American Magazine,* addressing himself to "the Literati of America" in January 1774, predicted that since "the dispensations of Providence, and the present aspect of the World, make it evident, that America will soon be the seat of science, and the grand theatre where human glory will be displayed in its brightest colours," the present generation ought to prepare for the future by an assiduous study of language, the foundation science and medium of communication. He proposed to organize the "Fellows of the American Society of Language" to publish annual observations on language, "to correct, enrich, and refine it, until perfection stops their progress and ends their labour." Thus America can make "swifter advances to the summit of learning." It would be difficult to cite a more vivid example of the influence of the Enlightenment on letters.

Popular literary taste, as in all ages, naturally ran to human-interest stories. Criminals, dead or alive, fascinated all ranks, and pamphlets or broadsides about them sold faster than anything else. In 1762 Benjamin Mecom arranged to cover Boston's gallows history with *A Serious & Comicall imaginary Dialogue between the famous Dr. Seth Hudson and the noted Joshua How . . . containing . . . a Touch on TOM BELL.* Weyman made a huge success at New York with his *Life of Godfried*

Swan, now in the New Gaol . . . for the Murder of his only Child. At Philadelphia in 1770 Bradford had difficulty in keeping up with the demand for the *Life and Confessions of Herman Rosencrantz, executed . . . on the 5th of May for counterfeiting:* "the sale of 2,000 of this interesting piece has made it necessary, that a new impression should be struck off, which are sold with good allowance to Hawkers, Pedlars, and others that buy to sell again." Broadside verses on Gunpowder Night, such as *South End Forever, North End Forever,* with a woodcut of the pope and the devil in their car, appealed as much to Bostonians as a ballad on *Election Expences* did to Newporters. David James Dove mirrored the already serious social rift at Philadelphia in 1762 in his satire on certain men and women of fashion, *The Manners of the Times,* which the populace eagerly lapped up. In fact, evidences of class resentment as well as emerging patriotism can be distinguished in nearly all provincial popular literature after the mid-sixties, and much of it was shot full of broad sly native humor.

VI

"The people here have a growing taste for the arts, and are becoming more and more fond of encouraging their progress amongst them. I fondly flatter myself they will here find patronage, and an Asylum, when oppression and tyranny shall perhaps banish them from seats where they now flourish." This profession of faith, made by Charles Willson Peale in 1771 to his friend Mr. Franklin, then in England, elicited one of the sage's most famous statements: "The Arts have always travelled westward, and there is no doubt of their flourishing hereafter on our side of the Atlantic, as the number of wealthy inhabitants shall increase, who may be able and willing suitably to reward them; since, from several instances, it appears that our people are not deficient in genius."

During the fifteen years preceding independence the citizens of well-to-do homes enriched their lives with songs and music. Many an evening passed delightfully in impromptu musicales, such as the occasion at the Rowe mansion in Boston when David Propert, "Professor of Musick," accompanied Mr. Lane's singing with "a fine hand" on Miss Sucky Rowe's spinet. Sally Franklin played the harpsichord "so well" that Francis Hopkinson advised her absent father in 1765 to buy her a new and better one. Those unable to perform on the harpsichord, spinet, or chamber organ might own the equivalent of a player-piano: an organ set to play as many as "sixteen of the newest and most celebrated tunes" then in vogue. At Philadelphia, where music was most widely cultivated, new town houses of the rich contained specially planned music rooms. Michael Hillegas and other devotees gathered in such mansions to talk "perpetually of the forte and piano, of Handel, &c., and song and tunes." Often during the tea hour, as Pierre Duponceau recalled, the gentlemen at Edward Shippen's sang hunting songs and the ladies trilled Scottish ballads and popular airs unaccompanied.

Accounts of those days give the impression that people of all ranks sang at all times and anywhere, and taverns reverberated with songs— boisterous, bawdy, cheerful. "The School of Anacreon seems of late to be on the decline," Rivington lamented as he reported in 1773 the deaths of "Poor Dr. John Levine," and "Mr. James Yeoman," watchmaker, whose "song and story ever set the table in a roar." In the less reputable pubs of Manhattan and Philadelphia in 1765, bibulous companions paid their respects to the notorious bawd Kitty Crow by shouting the words of "A new Song. About Miss Kitty leaving the Country, to the Tune of Derry down, down, down, Derry down." Traditional English ballads and collections of well-known songs and tunes of the mother country were as popular as ever; from the New York press issued two books: the *American Cock Robin,* "a choice collection of English songs, both old and new, being such as are generally esteemed, and agreeable to the North-American taste," and *The Masque* (1767). During the seventies, at two shillings, "Miss Ashmore's Favorite Collection of Songs, as sung at the Theatres and Public Gardens, in London and Dublin," could be purchased at Newport and Boston, where citizens were denied hearing the members of the American Company render the songs from *Lionel, Clarissa, The Padlock,* and other current London ballad operas.

Adroit sponsors of the revolutionary movement saw an opening in the vogue for ballads and popular tunes like "Derry down" and "Hearts of Oak," and introduced them on every possible occasion. As John Adams said, "This is cultivating the sensations of freedom." John Dickinson's *Liberty Song* of 1768 was published with music on a broadside; Newporters had a song celebrating the victory at Havana; and Peter Franklin sent Benjamin a Boston ballad ridiculing "expensive foppery and encouraging industry and frugality" with the hope that it might also catch on at Philadelphia. Verses about Johnston, Moffatt, and Howard, sung at the gallows during the Newport Stamp Act protest, achieved recognition at Boston, as did a *Song about the Gaspee.* But the most catching of all was the "Yankee Song":

> *Corn stalks twist your hair off,*
> *Cart-wheel frolic round you,*
> *Old fiery dragon carry you off,*
> *And mortar pessel pound you.*

With woodcuts and words less runic, this soon came out at Boston as the famous *Yankee Doodle.*

Acceptance by all religious societies of the value of music in worship had done much to encourage popular interest in the musical art. New books of psalmody, hymnals, and new collections, often having engraved notes, appeared. James Lyon's *Urania* (1761, 1767) and a *Collection of Psalm Tunes* (1763) by Francis Hopkinson, both published at Philadelphia, are the best-known, and they supplemented or replaced the works of Wesley and Watts in many churches. Benjamin Yarnold and Peter Valton, organist of St. Philip's at Charles Town, composed several anthems for special occasions, as did William Tuckey of Manhattan. Many churches now utilized instrumental music in their services, but the tale of the "Violins, Bass Viols, French Horns, Flutes, Hautboys, &c. used in the Musick in public Worship at the Consecration of the Chapel" of New York's Trinity in 1766 outdid anything Ezra Stiles had ever heard about.

All the seaports save Newport supported music dealers and instrument-makers; sheet music, books of instruction, and all sorts of musical instruments and supplies might be had at any time. Newporters procured their music and instruments from either Boston or Manhattan, though they, too, as in other Northern cities, had the opportunity in 1763 of selecting the best yet offered the colonists when a Londoner stopped there on his tours. The "Catalogue of Music" and the instruments kept in stock by James Rivington make it appear that the New Yorker eventually surpassed Michael Hillegas of Philadelphia as the largest dealer. Philadelphia's excellent organ-builders, John Klem, David Tannenberger, and Philip Fyring, also had to meet the competition of Thomas Johnston of Boston, John Scheiuble of New York (formerly of the Quaker City), and John Speissigger of Charles Town. By 1775 colonial crafts could produce any instrument then in use in Europe. John Harris of Boston made harpsichords and spinets; James Joan produced violins as good as the average imported fiddle; while Jacob Trippell advertised that for nine years he had "worked with the best Hands in London" since he left Germany and could turn out any kind of violin, guitar, or harp; and in 1775 John Behrent of Philadelphia completed the first pianoforte to be made in the colonies.

The harvest reaped by music teachers in previous years attracted many more to the profession, and singing schools grew very popular at Charles Town, Newport, and Boston for people who wanted to sing "catches, glees, canons, songs and Church Music with sobriety and ease." Benjamin Yarnold guaranteed to teach the science of music to the young ladies of Charles Town in from twelve to eighteen months for twenty-five pounds a year. Giving up the dying trade of tanner at Boston, William Billings, untutored but undaunted, set out to be a singing teacher and choir trainer at Brattle Street and Old South churches; he introduced the pitch pipe and viol to ensure a more exact pitch and seemed to have improved rhythmic singing. From this he progressed to composition, writing many tunes for choirs that caught the public's fancy; Edes & Gill brought out his *New England Psalm-Singer,* which contained music engraved by Paul Revere, in 1770. Similarly, Francis Hopkinson, who served as organist at Christ Church, Philadelphia, turned composer and, in addition to hymns, wrote the first important piece of colonial secular music, *My Days Have Been So Wondrous Free.* At least twenty-five musicians gave lessons at Philadelphia before 1776, and although fewer were available in other communities, their inhabitants were well served by day or night music schools.

Patronage of music and attendance at performances were approved social activities of an aristocracy and account for the considerable development of concert life in four of the towns. Under the ægis of Francis Hopkinson, Philadelphia led the other cities in chamber and concert music, and nearly every winter subscription concerts drew the gentry to the Assembly Room. When the American Company was in town, its members put on special concerts of vocal and instrumental music just as they did at Charles Town and New York. Occasionally the College gave musical entertainments, and a group of gentlemen, including Hillegas, John Penn, and David Franks, met regularly for amateur musicales. On occasion these gentlemen played for the American Company when it staged ballad operas. Yet it was Boston that never let a year pass without a musical entertainment. Ordinarily Stephen Deblois promoted subscription affairs at his Concert Hall, which boasted the finest organ in America in 1763. Opening in November, the season of 1766–7 consisted of a concert "every Tuesday evening for Eight Months." To further home manufactures in 1770, in a benefit concert for Mr. Joan, the musical-instrument-maker, all the violins used were of his own make. On such gala occasions the gentry turned out en masse, and, as might be suspected, to be seen rather than to listen. Once in 1771 a real music-lover complained in the *Newsletter* of "a perpetual talking among some of the Audience," as well as of some very obnoxious "volunteer vocal performers" who tried to aid the orchestra by humming and whistling the airs. After the Boston Port Bill went into effect, William Turner advertised the Concert Hall and a superb collection of sheet music for sale at sterling cost; thenceforth all concerts were Tory affairs.

New Yorkers were spared the admission that music suffered from the neglect accorded other cultural activities. Subscription concerts were given nearly every year, and, in addition, one could attend weekly pop concerts in the gardens of Ranelagh and Vauxhall or at the King's Arms. In 1767 the Royal American Band played for a benefit at Burns's New Assembly Room, and amateurs, calling themselves the Harmonic Society, assisted at several benefit concerts in 1773 and 1774. To William Tuckey, teacher and organist at Trinity Church, goes the credit for introducing choral concerts of church music in America on October 28, 1766, with pieces of his own composition. Mr. Tuckey also gave the first colonial rendering of Handel's *Messiah* in 1770, when he directed the overture and the singing of sixteen other pieces from the oratorio. Good music had come to the gentlemen of New York, but some of them, too, had yet to learn proper concert manners, for it was said that "instead of a modest and becoming silence nothing is heard during the whole performance, but laughing and talking very loud, squalling, overturning the benches, etc. Behaviour more suited to a broglio than a musical entertainment."

The founding of the St. Cecilia Society at Charles Town in 1762 was a cultural event of the same magnitude as the opening of the Library Society, for it revived the interest in and patronage of the concert life that had been dormant since the thirties. Filling the membership with gentlemen subscribers at twenty-five pounds each took time, and this probably accounts for the absence of any reference to concerts until 1766. Meanwhile in 1765 Thomas Pike directed a concert "performed by the Gentlemen of the place," played the French horn and bassoon himself, and threatened to prosecute any ruffian who climbed over the fence to interrupt the music. The high point of Peter Valton's harpsichord concert at the theater in Queen Street that year was the first American appearance of the Misses Wainwright and Hallam. These and the musicales of the St. Cecilia were open to subscribers only, and the ordinary people of the city never got to hear the superb musicians whom the gentry imported at fancy salaries. The officers advertised in the Northern press in 1771 for two violin-players, two hautboys, and one bassoon-player to come to Charles Town on a three years' contract. Josiah Quincy of Boston attended a St. Cecilia concert as the guest of David Deas in March 1773. It was for him a brilliant social gathering: "The music was good. The two bass-viols and French horns were grand. One Abercrombie, a Frenchman just arrived, played a first fiddle, and a solo incomparably better than any I ever heard: I have several times heard John Turner and Morgan at Boston play a solo. Abercrombie cannot speak a word of English, and has a salary of 500 guineas a year from the St. Cecilia Society. Hartley [formerly of Boston] was here, and played as I thought badly in the harpsichord. The capital defect of this concert was want of an organ." The Orpheus Society, probably a company of amateurs, of which William Packrow was "first musician," held quarterly meetings prior to 1772.

When the outstanding musical event of the colonial period occurred at Philadelphia in 1769–70, it is doubtful if even Francis Hopkinson or Michael Hillegas was aware of it. Giovanni (John) Gualdo was a wine merchant who had failed during the hard times of the non-importation agreements and turned to his avocation as a means of support. The Italian opened a music store, adapted music for all instruments, copied music for customers, and gave lessons on the flute. On October 18, 1769 he gave his first concert, "after the Italian Method," for Master Billy Crumpto, a seven-year-old prodigy with the violin. More impressive was the concert of November 16, during which instrumental music composed in America was played for the first time: a violin trio, a flute and violin concerto, and "a new symphony after the present taste," all by Maestro Gualdo himself. At his next performance the Genoese played more of his own works in the excellent company of Geminiani, Barbella, Campioni, Zanetti, Pelligrino, Abel, Bach, and the Earl of Kellie. In succeeding concerts Gualdo employed all known instruments, including the then rare clarinet, and played more compositions of his own, among them six minuets. Financial worries proved too much for this able Latin, the foremost colonial composer and musical director, and he died in chains in the insane ward of the Pennsylvania Hospital in 1772.

VII

Artists of all times and places, those of the English colonies included, were governed by the wishes of aristocratic patrons and of the urban gentry in particular. "A taste of painting is too much Wanting to affoard any kinds of helps; and was it not for preserving the resembla[n]ce of perticular persons, painting would not be known in this plac[e]. The people generally regard it no more than any other usefull trade, as they sometimes term it, like that of a Carpenter, tailor, or shew maker, not as one of the most noble Arts in the World." This contemptuous judgment of his countrymen made by John Singleton Copley in self-defense against certain English criticisms of the works he exhibited at London in 1767 was not devoid of truth, but he spoke only of Boston, where he admitted making "a pretty living" of some three hundred pounds a year, and where gentlemen and ladies meekly accepted his insistence upon painting them as he saw them and not as they might wish to be viewed. In 1770 John Wilkes could thank Nathaniel Barber for sending over a Copley painting of his son: "I was very happy to Observe to what a degree of excellence the most elegant art of Painting is arrived at in New England, and as you rival us in every essential good, so you now equal us in the refinements of Polished Life"; and by 1776 the London *cognoscenti* ranked West, Copley, Benbridge, Pratt, and Peale high among British painters, and the populace acclaimed each new exhibit of Patience Wright's waxworks.

The few well-to-do gentlemen who made a beginning at art-collecting were now followed by the growing crop of wealthy aristocrats, and a number possessed pictures by well-known artists. Martin Howard of Newport had one by Sir Peter Lely, and one of the many counts against Dr. Thomas Moffatt was his unwillingness to admit owning a portrait of the Duke of Cumberland "in the habit of a butcher with a cleaver in his hand," and the Pretender's picture, which Jacobite relics the Stamp Act mob destroyed with the physician's "other choice pieces of painting." When Pierre du Simitière visited Newport in 1769, he admired a portrait of Tsar Peter I by Kneller or a disciple at Isaac Hart's, and John Banister's pictures of Charles I and his Queen; and Catherine of Braganza, and a bust in oils of himself, by Van Dyke himself, "very fine, with Several more of lesser note." Among Charles Paxton's most cherished possessions were a number of valuable Italian paintings. Three pictures at Peter Harrison's mansion attracted attention: a "Large Roman painting," a "savior on the Cross," and a St. Francis, "both Spanish paintings valued at 100 guineas." Among Charlestonians, only Judge Egerton Leigh, who died in 1774, assembled "some of the First Masters"—Paul Veronese, Carladolsi, Giordano, Ghisoli, Correggio, and Guido Reni— and several "excellent Miniature Pictures, particularly one of Queen Elizabeth, done in the year 1574." The Hancock mansion at Boston housed some fine paintings, two of which Copley believed "either a copy or genuine Vanduyck and also a Reubens." Peter Chardon also owned a number of much-admired pictures.

Spurred by collections viewed in England and wonders seen on the grand tour, wealthy Philadelphians hastened to collect works of art for their town and country houses. Bush Hill, the seat of the Hamiltons, already famous for its gardens and statuary, boasted a Murillo and some historical pictures by Richard of Paris. In 1763 James Hamilton and William Allen acquired some good copies of celebrated Italian paintings, among them Titian's *Venus* and Correggio's *Holy Family,* a Giorgione, and Reni's *Herodias,* executed by Benjamin West, who also sent Colonel Joseph Shippen his copy of Mengs' *Holy Family.* Samuel Powel and Dr. John Morgan brought home from Italy many original drawings and two Raphael cartoons in addition to numerous copies of the masters painted for them by one named Companions at Rome. John Penn, William Peters, and William Hamilton also made a start at collecting before 1774. This assembling of pagan and Roman Catholic art in the Quaker City provided an introduction to taste for many and an inspiration to such ambitious daubers as Henry Pelham, who gratefully reported in detail to his half-brother the "three hours very entertaining and instructive Conversation on painting and Art" he had had with Governor Hamilton and Judge Allen, "who had been in Rome."

After the departure of West for Italy and fame in 1758, Philadelphia's artistic activity lapsed for nearly a decade. Matthew Pratt crossed to London in 1764, studied with West for a year, exhibited his ambitious

American School at the Spring Gardens with great success, and made a good living in portraiture at Bristol before he decided to return to Philadelphia in 1768. Thereafter he had "full employ" in painting likenesses of many of the Pennsylvania, New York, and Virginia gentry. His striking and individual full-length portrait of Cadwallader Colden marks Pratt as one of the ablest of the colonial painters. A young Marylander, fleeing from his creditors in July 1765, ventured into the color shop of John Moffatt at Boston. There he viewed the copies of the Italian masters and some "groups of figures"; he next made the acquaintance of the already famous Copley. "The sight of Mr. Copley's picture room was a great feast to Peale," his autobiography tells us. "Mr. Copley treated him very civilly, and lent him [a portrait head painted by] candle light to copy." But it was with Philadelphia that Charles Willson Peale identified himself by making annual visits there after 1769. His superb portrait of David Rittenhouse and the charming informality of his *Cadwalader Family* (1772) proved him a better draftsman than Pratt. "My reputation is greatly increased by a Number of New Yorkers haveing been here, who have given me the character of being the best painter in America—that I paint more certain and handsomer Likenesses than Copley," this enthusiastic man informed a patron in 1772. In this same year, in spite of the sensational triumph of his full-length portrait of the Corsican patriot Pasquale Paoli (commissioned by James Boswell), Henry Benbridge chose "from affection to return and settle in Philadelphia." There he devoted his uncommon technical skill to portraiture until asthma forced him southward early in 1772. He returned for a short time to claim his bride, Charles Willson Peale's pupil, the miniaturist Letitia Sage. These three talented artists and the twenty-one other face-painters, limners, and amateurs who worked in the city, along with the gentlemen "conosurs," gave Philadelphia such a reputation for things artistic that John Singleton Copley went over there from New York for a week in 1771 because he regarded it as a "place of too much importance not to visit."

Boston had forfeited its leadership in painting to Philadelphia just as it had its commercial supremacy, but in John Singleton Copley the city reared a painter whose genius was so evident that few limners cared to contend with him. George Mason from London, however, lingered about town for nearly three years after 1765; one How came there in 1774; and Christian Remick, "lately from Spain," worked in water colors, essayed sea pieces, landscapes, and coats of arms; his famous *Perspective View of the Blockade of Boston Harbor* (1768) is the work of a mere journeyman, not a master painter. The death in 1773 of Shrimpton Hutchinson, Jr., probably deprived the Boston aristocracy of its contribution to the fine arts, for even the *Gazette,* always hostile to his family, described him as "a young Gentleman of an uncommon Genius for

Painting; and it is thought by good judges, had his Life been spared a few Years, he would have equalled, if not excelled most, in that Art."

This dearth of limners left the sitters to Copley, who turned out a remarkable number of excellent portraits in these years, for he made great strides as a draftsman and colorist as he matured his style. After repeated urging by Captain R. G. Bruce, he permitted the mariner to take his painting of his half-brother, Henry Pelham (*The Boy with the Squirrel*), to the exhibition of the Society of Arts at London in 1766. It was "universally allowed to be the best Picture of its kind that appeared on that occasion," and Sir Joshua Reynolds remarked to Captain Bruce "that in any Collection of Painting it will pass for an excellent Picture, but considering the Dissadvantages 'I told him' you had laboured under, that *it was a very wonderfull Performance,*" surpassing "any Portrait that Mr. West ever drew." West himself generously acclaimed his fellow colonial, urged him to exhibit again, and procured his election to the Society of Arts. Transatlantic recognition brought Copley more commissions at home, and in 1771 he went to New York for a most profitable stay. His brief visit to Philadelphia resulted in Mr. and Mrs. Thomas Mifflin's sitting for him at his studio in Boston in 1773, whereby he had "the Honour of furnishing Philadelphia with one of the best Pictures it has to boast"; in fact, this painting marked the greatest perfection of his American style. Copley's decision to go to Italy and England in 1774, conditioned in part by his mildly Tory sympathies and dislike of public contention, left portraiture in his native town to Henry Pelham, whose own Toryism attracted few sitters and drove him away forever after the siege of Boston.

The artistic tradition founded at Newport by Robert Feke fell into the inadequate hands of Samuel King, who painted stiff likenesses of local worthies or made miniatures. Ezra and Mrs. Stiles sat for each kind, and the parson also commissioned King to do portraits of other members of his family. The Rhode Islander to attain the greatest fame in the arts, Gilbert Stuart, was born in Narragansett in 1755. At an early age he evinced talent by copying pictures and attempting pencil portraits; he must have taken some of his inspiration from viewing the collections of Dr. Moffatt (his father's employer) and John Banister, who sat for him. Cosmo Alexander was impressed by the lad, whom he met when he came to paint Dr. William Hunter, who had asked the boy to paint pictures of his two dogs. Accompanying Alexander to Scotland in 1772, Stuart was left almost destitute at his mentor's death but managed to work his way back to Newport. He had little knowledge or interest in the concerns of his own sort in America, and when his business ended with the outbreak of war, he had enough money saved to sail for London and there to start on his great artistic career.

A hearty welcome and generous patronage from the gentry and not a few of the middle class always awaited the face-painter at Charles Town, for this city had no local artists on whom to rely. In all, sixteen limners offered their services, but of those who sought aristocratic patronage, John Wollaston was the only one who really competed with Jeremiah Theus during the short time he was in Charles Town in the sixties; after the death of Theus in 1772, Henry Benbridge came down from Pennsylvania and his portraits seem to have won lasting fame. Many of the wealthiest Carolinians still could not be satisfied with anything less than a portrait done in London or on the Continent; amusingly enough, Mr. and Mrs. Ralph Izard were painted by Copley when they were in Rome —the background may have been classical, but the artist was an American. Unknown to most South Carolinians, in August 1765 John Bartram, the Philadelphia botanist, was staying at Thomas Lamboll's and arranging his specimens; his son Billy was drawing a fine old locust. Little did his host surmise that some day young William Bartram's collection of water colors and ink drawings would be one of the prized possessions of the British Museum.

Manhattan's gentry apparently would pay handsomely for the best in portraiture and encouraged such practitioners as Pratt and Du Simitière to make prolonged and profitable visits. If they desired to sit for Copley they would travel to Boston, as did President Myles Cooper of King's College, unless they were lucky enough to get some of his time in 1771 when the "Beau Monde" lured him to New York for a summer. In spite of good fees to be won, no artist of the caliber of West or Copley ever emerged from the numerous limners that set up their easels in New York. Abraham Delanoy, in spite of a few important commissions, never earned wide popularity there or at Charles Town, where he went in 1768; nor did John Mare, who executed a portrait of George III for the Corporation, persuade any of the gentry to sit for him, and in 1772 he took off for Albany; nor the Connecticut painter John Durand, who tarried only a short time and then, like the others, departed.

Ownership of oil paintings was pretty well restricted to men of means, but through engravings and mezzotint maps and pictures the colonials cultivated a taste for the currently fashionable works of art. Awareness of artists and art further proved their growing maturity, and retailers in every city, quick to sense a new market, carried sizable stocks of prints and engravings. Few of them did as large a business as Robert and Thomas Kennedy at the sign of West's Head in Philadelphia, who displayed a variety of prints from the "most Capital paintings in England by the ablest artists," selected by Benjamin West, unless it was Nicholas Brooks, also of Philadelphia, who ran an exhibit of "occular entertainment" of "Pictures and Maps" for "all gentlemen and ladies who delight in the fine arts." It included cartoons on glass by Raphael, Rosalba's *Four Seasons* (a perennial favorite), "landskips," hunting scenes, sea pieces, Le Brun's "passions of the soul," and a variety of engravings and mezzotints by the "greatest artists in Rome and London."

A greater attention to the prints and engravings made by Americans paralleled the movement for domestic manufactures and the rising tide of resentment against the mother country. An advertisement of prints of "elegant gardens, landscapes and AMERICAN VIEWS, fit for GENTLEMEN FARMERS, Lovers of art and their country" illustrates this nicely. As a brother member of the Society for the Encouragement of Arts, Manufactures, and Commerce at London, James Bowdoin had been invited to subscribe for the engravings selected by West but refused because of the colonial policy of non-importation. Beginning with an engraving of the Pennsylvania Hospital by James Claypoole, Jr., in 1761, prints of such colonial buildings as the Zion Lutheran Church (1763) and the House of Employment and surrounding structures (1769) at Philadelphia, Thomas You's *View of St. Michael's* (1765), at Charles Town, and Paul Revere's *View of a Part of the Town of Boston* (1770) began to displace their English counterparts in the offerings of the print shops. Patriotism impelled Nathaniel Hurd of Boston to change over from engraved portraits of George III, Pitt, and Wolfe, which he had offered before the Peace of Paris, to mezzotints of Jonathan Mayhew and Joseph Sewall. Canny Robert Bell naturally capitalized on an "elegant engraved Copperplate Print of the Patriotic American Farmer" (John Dickinson) and another of John Wilkes. Reproduction of portraits of public figures by engravers sold in proportion to the subject's popularity. In 1773 Samuel Okey, twice a mezzotint premium-winner at the Society of Arts, moved to Newport and set up as a printseller, paperhanger, and engraver. Within a few years he had produced portraits of the Reverend James Honeyman, Dr. Samuel Cooper, the Reverend Thomas Hiscox, and Samuel Adams. Pierre Du Simitière executed a fine engraving of Bevan's William Penn in 1774. With the issuing of the familiar *Bloody Massacre Perpetrated in King Street, Boston March 5, 1770,* by Paul Revere, and Amos Doolittle's *Exact View of the Late Battle at Charlestown* (1775), depicting the village in flames from British gunfire, the engraver's art of pictorial representation was turned with good effect to the production of war propaganda.

VIII

A correspondent of Purdie and Dixon's *Virginia Gazette* wrote in 1773 that he had "often Reflected with Concern on the slow Progress which Science" had made in the Old Dominion. "I believe it may be with Truth asserted, that there has not been a single Production which has occasioned our Name even to be known in the Republick of Letters. This

I have always imputed to the Want of that Intercourse and Association which is necessary to the Perfection of every Power of Man, whether mental or bodily. . . . Among the necessary Means of the Association, whose Influence we have attempted to establish, are *populous Cities,* where Men of genius, from Motives of Amusement or Business, reside together; of these we have a very distant Prospect Indeed." This rural "Academicus" clearly perceived what a recent immigrant, Thomas Paine, saw in a flash in 1775: that "a country whose reigning character is the love of science" could cultivate and nourish that spirit only through urban institutions. If this period's contributions to scientific knowledge did not equal those of the preceding one, its achievement was none the less significant and charged with future import. These were the years of organization and integration, of popularizing the wonders of natural philosophy, and, above all, of effecting on an intercolonial scale that collective action by many scattered individuals so essential to the advancement of science.

The largest contribution toward laying the groundwork for scientific co-operation came from European-trained physicians and their disciples. Medical men now developed a professional pride, and as more of them came back from Edinburgh, London, Leyden, and Paris, they strove to raise professional standards in their cities. Schools of medicine opened at Philadelphia and New York, patterned on Edinburgh, the alma mater of so many of the colonial practitioners; at Boston in 1765 Dr. William Lee Perkins delivered public lectures on anatomy, and students of the classes of 1770–2 at Harvard, headed by John Warren, formed an Anatomical Society. The two largest cities also had medical societies, and New York and Charles Town physicians, albeit without success, endeavored to procure provincial legislation requiring the licensing of all practitioners to prevent the abuses of those who, as John Rowe said, had "made an Apothecary Shop in my Stomach."

Professional demands, willing acceptance of charitable and civic responsibilities, and the energy expended in taking sides on burning political issues absorbed so much of the time of these doctors that it is remarkable that they found even a few hours for medical research and writing. Most of the colonial medical publications were written in cities having a large number of European-trained doctors, and for this reason Boston and Newport produced nothing of consequence, though each contained some able practitioners. Dr. John Morgan of Philadelphia somehow found time to write an essay on inoculation, as did Thomas Ruston, recently from Edinburgh. Dr. Benjamin Rush began his long career of medical publication with a pioneer popular work on personal hygiene in *Sermons to Gentlemen upon Temperance and Exercise* (1772), a treatise on mineral springs (1773), and a study of Indian medicine (1774). At Philadelphia, too, Dr. John Kearsley, Jr., brought out some admirable observations on the *Angina Maligna* in 1769, which won him acclaim and republication in London. The stirring Philadelphia *Discourse upon the Institution of Medical Schools in America* by Dr. John Morgan was matched at New York in Dr. John Bard's *Discourse on . . . the Necessity of a Public Hospital* for persuasiveness and forthright exposition to a popular audience of the medical needs of the day. Dr. Bard's *Inquiry in Angina Suffocativa* (1771) was a thoroughly scientific piece for the time, as was Dr. John Jones's *Plain, Concise Practical Remarks on the Treatment of Wounds and Fractures,* published by Bell in 1776. Following the precedent of Old World universities, graduates of the first class of the Medical School at Philadelphia presented four theses, which were printed. In the opinion of Dr. Peter Fayssoux of Charles Town, "few places have the Science of Medicine on a worse footing than this; it is sufficient for a Man to call himself a Doctor" to find "fools to employ him. Yet we have some . . . Men of Letters and Candour." One of these was Dr. Lionel Chalmers, whose *Essay on Fevers,* published at Charles Town in 1767, was reprinted serially in the *Pennsylvania Chronicle* by order of the American Society at Philadelphia and as a pamphlet in 1768 and 1769, as well as in extract form in Nicola's *American Magazine.* Dr. Chalmers incorporated this essay with much new material and some other studies in two volumes he issued at London in 1776 as *Essays on the Weather and Diseases of South Carolina*—the finest general medical work written during the colonial period.

The press also aided in spreading medical knowledge by printing essays concerning public health or the defenses issued by physicians against their critics. Dr. Rush inserted a piece about the Philadelphia epidemic of hives in the *Pennsylvania Journal* in 1769, reviewing its history and differing from the accepted views on the cause of the ailment; the following year this was run in two issues of the *New York Gazette.* At Boston, and later in Philadelphia, the ardent patriot Dr. Thomas Young frequently sent "Medical Observations" for public use to both magazines and newspapers. The reprinting of European works of medicine, and such useful treatises as William Cadogan's *Essay upon Nursing, and the Management of Children* (Bradford, Philadelphia, 1773); the *Lectures on Medicine* of Professor William Cullen of Edinburgh (Bell, Philadelphia, 1775); and the first great modern classic on pathology, Dr. Alexander's translation of John Baptist Morgagni's *Seats and Causes of Diseases Investigated by Anatomy* (Rivington, New York, 1774), must have done much to make colonial practitioners aware of the latest European medical thought.

The most successful effort at intercolonial co-operation before the meeting of the First Continental Congress was achieved in the intellectual sphere by the founding of the American Philosophical Society at Philadelphia. It all began in 1750 with the weekly discussion meetings of a society of Charles Thomson, William Franklin, and other young men, chiefly Quakers, calling themselves the Junto after Benjamin Franklin's earlier group. In the summer of 1761 Thomson, Isaac Paschall, and Edmund Physick reorganized the society to make it "more useful to the Publick." The addition of vigorous new members, among them Samuel Powel, Dr. Cadwalader Evans, the bookseller Lewis Nicola, Owen Biddle, the instrument-maker, and two sons of John Bartram, brought the total up to thirty; in 1766 Dr. John Morgan was admitted to the group. On December 13 of that year the name The American Society for Promoting and Propagating Useful Knowledge, Held at Philadelphia (hereafter called the American Society) was adopted, and it was proposed by Charles Thomson that they extend the group's activities, "fabricated on a plan from that of the Royal Society and the Society of Arts," and invite the participation of a number of public-spirited gentlemen in other colonies and abroad. Goddard's *Pennsylvania Chronicle* published a complete prospectus of the American Society on March 7, 1768.

Patriotism symbolizing a rising nationalism as well as scientific motives animated the reorganization of the American Society. On January 1, 1768 Charles Thomson had told his fellow members: "As Philadelphia is the Centre of the Colonies, as her Inhabitants are remarkable for encouraging laudable and useful undertakings, why should we hesitate to enlarge the plan of our Society, call to our Assistance Men of Learning and Ingenuity from every Quarter and unite in one generous, notable attempt not only to promote the Interest of our Country, but to raise her to some eminence in the rank of polite and learned nations." His hope, revealed in this speech, was to effect an intercolonial cultural union of wealthy patrons, men of learning, natural philosophers, skilled craftsmen, and farmers as part of the rising forces of liberty. Not for nothing was he known as "the Sam Adams of Philadelphia."

Projects for an intercolonial scientific body were in the air at this time. They all had their origin, of course, in the original proposals of 1743 made by Benjamin Franklin for his now defunct society. As early as 1765 Ezra Stiles of Newport drafted the first of three constitutions for an American Academy of Sciences to "collect all the curious Things in Science, especially in America, and maintain a correspondence over all the World." The Council of Associates "shall ever have Two Thirds of the Associates Presbyterians or Congregationalists. The number is thus limited to defeat episcopal Intrigue by which this Institution would be surreptitiously caught into an anti-American Interest. It being designed that this shall be for the Honor of American Literature, contemned by Europeans. Therefore let the Associates be all Americans, and if born in America of the 2d Generation, it shall be indifferent whether of English, Scotch, Irish, French, or German Blood, all the Distinctions being lost in American Birth." With the Associates all sound men, Stiles would leave to them the election of Fellows from "Men of Genius and Literature" in Europe and America. He elaborated his scheme in later drafts, but before it could be put into operation, the American Society at Philadelphia elected him a corresponding member. In South Carolina, Dr. Garden had hoped for some kind of a co-ordinating scientific body; in 1768 the *Providence Gazette* reprinted Franklin's proposals of 1743; and some Virginians founded a philosophical society in 1773 under the patronage of the Royal Governor and dedicated to "the Advancement of Useful Knowledge." But as "Academicus" foresaw, this body soon languished because the Old Dominion, even though the largest and most populous colony, lacked the essential support of "populous cities."

Although the Society at Philadelphia enjoyed an immediate success in 1768, Pennsylvania politics intruded itself when the proprietary group, headed by Dr. Thomas Bond, the Shippens, and Francis Alison, revived the old American Philosophical Society, which had died out by 1748. Their claim of revival was specious indeed, but five of the original members still lived. Here were materials for a wasteful competition, but fortunately the local squabble faded before the larger issues raised by the Townshend Acts. After some prodding from public opinion, men of wisdom and patriotism in each body merged the two societies in 1769, and the members elected Benjamin Franklin, who had been absent from the city since 1764, the first president of the American Philosophical Society, Held at Philadelphia, for Promoting Useful Knowledge; Vice-President Thomas Bond, however, guided the learned society for the remainder of the colonial period. With a distinguished roster of 144 local members, 90 from other colonies, and 17 foreign correspondents of the first eminence, it started its long and useful career.

The American Philosophical Society encouraged that union of minds among widely separated men so fundamental to eventual political agreement through its work of fostering natural philosophy. As early as January 8, 1768 the Reverend John Ewing headed a committee to observe the transit of Venus across the sun predicted for June 2, as a part of a world-wide co-operative effort solicited by the Royal Astronomer of Great Britain. Local members arranged to collect data at Philadelphia, Norriton, and Cape Henlopen, and the Society gave all possible support to distant members and correspondents undertaking similar observations in the colonies. Among these were Professor John Winthrop of Cambridge, Ezra Stiles at Newport, Robert Harpur at New York, and Dr. Alexander Garden in Charles Town. Papers reporting the results were read at meetings and formed the most valuable part of Section I ("Mathematical and Astronomical Papers") in the first volume of the *Transactions of the American Philosophical Society,* published at Philadelphia in 1771, a handsomely printed and illustrated volume which received wide distribution in the colonies by booksellers who were proud to show customers what their fellow Americans could accomplish. From Old World savants came fulsome though sincere tributes, which were collected by Jean Bernoulli of the Royal Academy at Berlin in his *Recueil pour les Astronomes* (1772) as he commended the American philosophers for publishing "not only the conclusions from their observations, but also the data on which they are based, so that others may examine the evidence and judge for themselves; a practice worthy of imitation by those European astronomers who are so sparing of detail and who speak only in general terms of their instruments and their observations."

Regardless of wealth, social status, or occupation, individual votaries of science dwelling in or near Philadelphia enjoyed the patronage as well as membership of the American Philosophical Society. Owen Biddle served as curator and later as librarian, was on several committees, and read his papers at the meetings. John Bartram, who had first conceived the idea of such a learned body in 1739, was accorded the honors of an elder statesman. But it was the astronomer David Rittenhouse whom the Philosophical Society regarded as the most promising young natural philosopher on the continent, and he indeed became "one of the luminaries of the eighteenth century." This man of great native genius, self-education, and humble birth typified the faith of enlightened men in putting science to work for human betterment. He completed the first of his orreries, or planetaria, in 1771, saying: "I would have my Orrery really useful, by making it capable of informing us truly, of the astronomical phenomena for any particular point of time; which I do not find that any Orrery yet made can do." Urged by the Society, the Pennsylvania Assembly granted three hundred pounds to Rittenhouse in honor of his invention, and importuned by the same body in 1775, the legislators were on the verge of making him "Public Astronomer," but the war broke out and this philosopher-democrat served on the Committee of Public Safety and helped frame the Pennsylvania constitution of 1776 instead.

In the view of many men, the work of the American Philosophical Society in supporting and propagating useful knowledge took precedence over natural science as the breach with England widened. Papers on improving agriculture from Georgia, Virginia, Maryland, New Jersey, and Pennsylvania together with accounts of useful inventions went into the *Transactions* along with medical and miscellaneous contributions. The merchant members of Philadelphia not only financed but displayed a real interest in a series of surveys to determine the best routes for a canal to connect Delaware and Chesapeake bays, and the most feasible routes for new roads between their city and the Susquehanna Valley in order to divert the down-river trade from Baltimore to Philadelphia. The leader in these projects was Thomas Gilpin, a Quaker from the Lower Counties, who admirably combined the qualities of a farmer, merchant, and scientific investigator by performing experiments on the wheat fly, writing the life history of the locust, inventing a horizontal windmill, and devoting knowledge of European canals learned in travel to the problem of internal improvements. These surveys occupy a prominent place in the first volume of the *Transactions*.

Each of the other cities, except New York, had its devotees of natural philosophy who followed the leadership of an outstanding personage. The ablest scientist of the late colonial period was Professor John Winthrop of Harvard, a member of the Royal Society as well as of the American body. Although he lived in suburban Cambridge, the people of Boston regarded him as their own, and such dilettantes as James Bowdoin, Joseph Harrison, and the Reverend Samuel Stillman bowed to his authority on matters of natural phenomena. Winthrop won a popular audience by publishing in the newspapers before he issued his essays in pamphlet form. In April 1761 he ran an article in the *News-letter* and *Post Boy* about the transit of Venus due on June 6, explaining its rarity and importance to astronomy. Plans were under way to observe it in Europe, he declared, and "it were greatly to be wished, that America also might bear a part," but the phenomenon would not be visible on this continent. Public interest encouraged the General Court to listen "to the still [small] Voice of the Sciences" amid "the Tumults of War," and to send him with two students in the province sloop to Newfoundland, where the transit could be seen; on his return he brought out a detailed report of it, *Relation of a Voyage from Boston to Newfoundland* (Edes & Gill, 1761). The next year he spelled out in the *Newsletter* the relation between thunder, lightning, and electricity to allay popular fears and prejudices aroused by recent accidents during storms. Banking on James Bowdoin's love of science and influence in high places, Winthrop planned an expedition from Harvard in 1769 to observe the transit of Venus in Canada and at Michilimackinac and arranged to borrow Joseph Harrison's telescope and chronometer for the trip. General Gage indicated his willingness to aid the project, but thought he and the Council were "unauthorized" to act. Bowdoin's subscription also failed; so Winthrop confined his activity to a successful observation at Cambridge, which the American Philosophical Society later published.

Ezra Stiles personified the Enlightenment in Yankee New England; his insatiable curiosity ranged over things natural and human as well as things supernatural. In 1761 this Rhode Island divine commenced a series of chemical experiments and undertook studies of the North American Indians that may be considered as a venture in cultural anthropology. In June of this year he took time out to observe the transit of Venus. The present of a Fahrenheit thermometer from his friend Franklin three years later led to temperature and meteorological recordings that ended only two days before his death in 1798, and that he began to publish in the *Newport Mercury* in 1765. As the best scientist among the three Newport members of the American Philosophical Society, he naturally superintended the observation of the transit of Venus in 1769 with the reflecting telescope and sextant furnished for the occasion by Abraham Redwood. Assisting him in the observation of a comet in September 1769 were Henry Marchant and Henry Thurston; later William Ellery joined him in observing a comet. On other occasions this universal man lectured to the young men of his church about "scripture geography" and investigated the Greenland ice sheet and the flora and fauna of the Falkland Islands, found time to read the *Principia* of Newton "often" as well as Voltaire's *Philosophical Dictionary,* to decide that Réamur was "not a Man of true Greatness," and to measure the humidity of Rhode Island with Dr. John Bartlett's hygrometer. Stiles and his friends formed the nucleus of a cultured group at Newport that kept itself well informed about the doings of the scientific world.

Doctors Chalmers, Garden, and Milligen, John Deas, John Himili, Ralph Izard, and Henry Laurens made up the Carolina membership of the American Philosophical Society, but beyond their undoubted distinction as public men, only the first two furthered the cause of science. In 1773 the Royal Society recognized Dr. Alexander Garden's contribution to the science of botany at Charles Town by electing him to membership. He succeeded in persuading Justice Thomas Lamboll and Governor Arthur Dobbs of North Carolina to exchange seeds, and he did all he could to assist Bartram in his journey to Florida in 1765, but in spite of the value of a public botanical garden for colonial self-sufficiency the Assembly failed to act on Garden's petition for a small grant of land in Charles Town. Even the weather conspired against him; it was cloudy the day he and others arranged to observe the transit of Venus in 1769. In March 1773 the Library Society, including natural philosophy in its province, made a public appeal for contributions, "either Animal, Vegetable, or Mineral, with Accounts of the various Soils, Rivers, Waters, Springs," and other natural features of South Carolina, and appointed a committee to receive and arrange such specimens in a room fitted up in the Library. Charlestonians were content, however, to be passive observers, not investigators of nature, and the coming of the war put an end to the scheme.

Museums furnished one of the effective means by which the inhabitants of colonial towns kept informed on the wonders of the new science, and Philadelphia, always enthusiastic about education and science, had more collections than the other cities. Miscellaneous as they were, such displays were the goal of visitors; John Adams managed to take in the anatomical exhibits of Dr. Abraham Chovet in Vidal's Alley during his visit in 1774 and reported on it in his typically exuberant fashion. The Library Company added to its cabinet of curiosities (the forerunner of the museum), and an ill-arranged but interesting assortment of Indian relics opened at the Society of Fort St. David. By 1770 the Philosophical Society had assembled many specimens and Pierre Eugène Du Simitière had made the beginning of his important and systematic collection of exhibits in the "American Museum."

The public lecture on natural philosophy, which reached more people than the museums, won popular support as both entertainment and education. When advertising for a journeyman in 1770, an apothecary stated that "he may be allowed time to attend lectures, or for any useful improving studies." Ebenezer Kinnersley of Philadelphia continued his lecture tours of the towns to perform his electrical experiments. A high point in his career must have been the November night in 1772 at Philadelphia when Kayashuta, the Seneca chief, who had been entertained by experiments on a previous visit, requested with Iroquois gravity to see "Thunder and Lightning produced by human Art." Perhaps an even greater favorite in this line was William Johnson, who also sold a printed syllabus of his course on electricity. In 1765 he used the Library Room at Charles Town for his lectures, which, he hoped, "to the more Polite and sensible Part of the Town, at least, will prove as agreeable an Entertainment as a Puppet Shew." At Boston the Selectmen agreed that he might lecture at Concert Hall; and in New York he appeared in Burns's City Arms Tavern. Settling finally at Charles Town in 1767, Johnson opened a school, but his "ingenious lectures and experiments" were continued until his death two years later. D. Eccleston lectured on natural philosophy at Boston and New York in 1770; and the immigrant Christopher Colles delivered an excellent series on engineering subjects when he went over from Philadelphia to Manhattan to install the first city waterworks.

IX

The cultural accomplishments of the last years of British rule in America were overwhelmingly urban in their attributes. This fact is strikingly demonstrated by a comparison of the arts and sciences at Newport with those of the Old Dominion. Virginia was the oldest, largest, and most populous of the thirteen colonies; it was also predominantly rural, having in Norfolk a population of about 5,000 and in Williamsburg about 1,500 out of its total of more than 400,000 people, who were distributed over 359,480 square miles of territory. The arresting feature of Virginia life between 1743 and 1776 was the absence of native talent in cultural fields in contrast with a plenitude of legal and political genius. Its aristocratic leaders were men of action, not intellectuals or artists; they lived a gracious existence above and apart from the rest of society. Virginia uncovered no local painter to match Robert Feke, Gilbert Stuart, or even Samuel King; and the masters of the great tidewater plantations made no attempt to acquire paintings other than family likenesses to rival the collections of Banister, Hart, and Hunter. Williamsburg had its press, but no such library as the Redwood; prior to Thomas Jefferson it produced no such Nestor as Ezra Stiles to preside over its arts and sciences; no such Mæcenas as Redwood or Collins appeared. It had its beautiful mansions, but no architect of the stature of Peter Harrison, and because of its established church it lacked the sweet reasonableness of Newport's tolerant citizens, who allowed all to worship as they saw fit and applauded the Anglican who designed a pagan temple for the members of an Oriental faith. On the other hand, Newport could show no playwright like Robert Munford and no two scientists equal in talent to John Clayton and Dr. John Mitchell (a temporary resident). In music neither society figured prominently. Yet in the end the balance tips slightly in the favor of the twelve thousand inhabitants of the little island city.

Through constant communication and interchange, the five cities had moved with rapid strides toward the integration of colonial culture, a culture that had diverged sufficiently from the English standard by 1776 to be recognized as American. To this end, since 1761, many individuals had been more or less unwittingly directing their talents and energy, but as each new political crisis arose, the word *American* was pronounced more often and with growing conviction. In 1766 the Reverend Charles Chauncy assured Ezra Stiles that he was not so afraid of bishops as many others were because "Tis without all doubt the design of providence that there should arise in North America one or more of the most considerable empires that have been in the world." Benjamin Franklin had posited this concept of a manifest destiny as early as 1750, and now many Europeans perceived it too, as did Edmund Burke and his prescient associates, albeit with great reluctance. As the realization of nationality spread, the citizens pronounced it good, and their collective self-confidence soared. The founding of the American Philosophical Society provided these Americans with the outward and visible sign of their maturing culture, and they realized, with Thomas Paine, that this body, "by having public spirit for its support, and public good for its object, is become a treasure we ought to glory in. . . . We may justly say, that no nation ever struck out in so short a time, and with so much spirit and reputation, into the labyrinth of art and science; and that not in the acquisition of knowledge only, but in the happy advantages flowing from it. The world does not in this day exhibit a parallel, neither can history produce its equal."

Cities in Revolt:
Conclusion

B ETWEEN THE FOUNDING OF NEW AMSTERDAM in 1625 and the
year 1742, five towns were established in the English colonies
and gradually grew into small cities, together constituting a genuine urban society. Within this period of little more than a hundred years,
chronicled in *Cities in the Wilderness,* there emerged an *urban section*
along the Atlantic seaboard which was sharply differentiated from the
settled *rural areas* of the agricultural countryside or the newer, wilder,
and sparsely populated districts of the *back country.* Throughout the remainder of the colonial period, by means of their particular form of
urban imperialism, the cities, in effect, came to dominate the other two
sections.

Constant communication, arising out of the needs of commerce, served
to forge these communities into an integrated urban society—the only
segment of colonial population so fused. In each of the cities certain
common physical, economic, cultural, and social characteristics accentuated the homogeneity whereas the other two sections exhibited vivid
differences, north and south, in crops, architecture, people, and customs.
The achievement of the integration of urban elements was an essential
prelude to independence. Otherwise the meeting of the First Continental
Congress appears as a cataclysmic event not subject to historical explanation.

In this volume it is evident that two persistent themes run through
the history of the colonial cities, 1743–76. The first is the astonishing
expansion of all the activities of urban existence, for in spite of and because of war conditions for almost half the period, population mounted
and the residents clamored for and secured municipal services, and outwardly the evolution of an urban society went on apace and undisturbed.
Nevertheless the towns were in revolt, and this constitutes the second
theme. On all sides the citizens were coming face to face with new situations and the new ideas of what we know as the Enlightenment. Gradually, almost imperceptibly, familiar ways of doing things, inherited be-

liefs, old loyalties gave way before novel methods, exciting or unsettling new ideas, and strange gods. In the brief passage of time between the return of the survivors from the British expedition to Carthagena and the Declaration of Independence, the inhabitants discarded forever their seventeenth-century traditions and fatefully and irrevocably accepted the symbols and ways of modernity. In so doing, moreover, they transformed their communities from English colonial into American cities. These communities represented the fact, the constructive accomplishment of the age, not merely its dreams, its theories or its attacks on outworn institutions; in 1776 the achievements of the American cities stood as the great triumph of the Enlightenment just as their leading citizen, Benjamin Franklin, personified it.

The spectacular physical growth of the five cities naturally attracted the attention of foreign visitors first. Although every community expanded its area, compactness if not congestion typified them all, even Newport; and this living together in close proximity, in the environment, was the marrow of urban existence. Under the pressure of growing numbers, agencies for maintaining life and services devised in former years needed enlarging or revamping, and new municipal responsibilities were thrust upon civic authorities. Housing and its accompaniment, building regulations, and fire-fighting and water supply posed problems perennially. Rapid growth created pressing demands for new streets, drainage, paving, traffic laws, wharves, and ferries; and in the train of urban expansion came a critical increase of the poor, criminals, moral laxity, each intensified by wartime conditions, to impose a heavy expense and police burden on each city. Public health also became a matter of concern for city fathers.

Inasmuch as the cities had ample wealth to meet their civic requirements, the success attending efforts to solve the problems of urban living depended upon the willingness of local governments to levy taxes and of the inhabitants to pay for the solutions. The town meetings of the two New England cities ordinarily responded to reasonable demands with generous grants of funds; the elected Corporation of New York usually complied, but that of Philadelphia had to be supplemented by bodies with taxing authority; while at Charles Town an assembly of planters interested in other concerns too frequently turned a deaf ear to the citizens' petitions. As a group, the townsmen quickly became more aware of public issues and of ways and means than their rural brethren; they grew more alert and well informed about local political matters, an advantage they improved when the time came for them to play politics on a provincial or imperial scale.

These five seaports were above all else commercial centers. Overseas, coastal, or internal trade determined the economic well-being of the inhabitants. As colonials their merchants had to conduct trade according to the rules laid down in the Navigation Acts. For seventy years they succeeded in accommodating themselves to the British colonial policy, but when rigid observance of the Molasses Act of 1733 was ordered, which would mean ruin for many of them, these same individualistic merchants did not hesitate to resort to illicit trading and manufacturing in defiance of Parliamentary prohibitions. Furthermore, they prospered —more so in fact than the farms or plantations.

An inevitable conflict of interests was inherent in the subordinate status in which the mother country kept these city states—for their unprecedented growth had made them the equals, in some cases the superiors, of all the cities of Britain save London. It is not here asserted that no resolution of these differences was possible; rather that the British government, failing to perceive the nature of the issues, never attempted to resolve them. Economically the cities and the colonies they served had so matured by 1760 that the attempts of British authorities to impose restrictions on them brought on a series of political explosions that impelled the citizenry to re-examine the entire connection.

One inherited concept to which the citizens offered little challenge before 1760 was a belief in a hierarchy of classes based on status. A mercantile aristocracy had rooted itself in the cities and, grown rich and powerful, presumed to control in its own interest public policy, organizations of many kinds, religious bodies, and social life as well as most of the external relations with the provinces and the British Isles. Through patronage it exercised a determining influence on education and the entire range of urban intellectual activities, and, on the whole, had evolved a very promising and fruitful culture. In the five cities one could glimpse these aristocracies in action, and one could also detect the rise of their Nemesis, the up-and-coming middle class.

The craftsmen and shopkeepers, men of middle rank, shared in the new prosperity, and as their class moved upward in numbers and strength, they came to sense their importance as a group and to entertain ambitions for political power commensurate with their economic status. They had no wish to overthrow the gentry, but rather they desired to move up into their ranks and share the power and prestige. Economic and political freedom concerned them much more than the social equality bred to the westward; the career open to talent was the goal, and the past history of the cities offered an abundance of success stories to sustain their hopes. The average person believed that he carried the civilian equivalent of a marshal's baton in his knapsack; he had no need of a Bonaparte to tell him so.

Citizens of the lower class—seamen, day laborers, Negroes—composed a much smaller fraction of city populations, save at Charles Town, than one might suppose. Lacking the franchise, they had little to say in municipal affairs, but one thing is certain, their white members were not a depressed group. Many of them rose to middle-class standing and not a few became property-owners. Along with the tradesmen and artisans they had hopes of improving their status and their fortunes.

City life wrought changes in attitudes and behavior that set the residents farther than ever apart from the inhabitants of the rural and back-country sections. Worldliness, which was insidiously making its way against traditional piety as townspeople increasingly cultivated all sorts of amusements and recreations, was far more the outgrowth of urban life than of the advance of science. The English, Scots, Scotch-Irish, and Germans more readily discarded extreme provincial or national traits and assumed a more tolerant attitude toward strangers once they came under the cosmopolitanism of the cities. Furthermore, with the exception of Newport, the seaports grew less English as their populations mounted.

Despite the distances that separated the two continents and the demands made on the new arrivals to establish themselves, the commercial and cultural bonds joining European and American peoples were such that probably not until after our first war with Germany was the average citizen of the New World again so much aware of his membership in the Atlantic community. Thousands of immigrants arrived at most of the ports each year: Englishmen of all conditions, but notably skilled artisans and craftsmen eager to exchange the low wages and insecurity of London and Bristol for higher pay and surer employment at Philadelphia, New York, or Charles Town; Palatines lured by promotion literature; and Scotch-Irish bitter against the Britons and in desperate need of a new start. These newcomers contributed intelligence and skills as well as brawn to the building of the cities. Conversely, more colonials were making the long voyage back to Europe—home, as many said of England. Masters and their crews were, of course, familiar with the ports of the Old World, and merchants too. Now young men began to travel to complete their education in the universities of England, Scotland, and Europe or to make the grand tour before they settled down in counting-houses or the professions.

Ideas as well as persons and material goods took passage with every vessel and helped to batter down provincialism and force colonials to sharpen their wits. In the American cities, less bound by tradition and superstition than those of the Old World and bourgeois to the very core, the seminal ideas of the Age of Reason found a warm reception; no accumulated rubbish of the past had to be cleared out before the revolutionary and liberating forces of the Enlightenment could be released. Changing from old ways to new did not entail such a wrench in the New World, where the experimental temper of the people, continually facing new situations in a new environment, nourished a new philosophy. The Protestantism of the colonials, their very dissent from the established church, prepared the ground for these new concepts; the psychological change had been in progress for over thirty years before the shot heard round the world gave notice of the fact.

The people, living in congested cities and in constant contact with one another, could not fail to acquire a host of traits that collectively comprised the urban character—a character quite as American as that which Crèvecœur discovered in the inland farmers. The average townsman seemed, to travelers, to be more intelligent than his European opposite, or perhaps gave that impression because the life he led was more untrammeled. By their public acts the citizens showed themselves outstanding humanitarians, and in their good works offered models to Europeans. Individually most of them were ambitious and energetic, assertive and often grasping, generally thrifty, and independent. Doubtless many immigrants failed to adjust to the strange new world, and frustration and pessimism must have gripped many others; still, experience apparently confirmed the optimism and hope of most of the citizens. In short, the colonial urban temperament had in it a mixture of imported theory and native experience. Above all, in such figures as Benjamin Franklin, Ezra Stiles, Charles Willson Peale, James Parker, and Henry Laurens, the cities produced leaders, men who became not only great citizens but great Americans, because they grasped the essentials of their own existence and that of their fellows and set their sights on fixed and attainable goals.

With very few exceptions, the culture of the late colonial period was of urban origin. In the cities alone could the necessary conditions for a vital intellectual life be found: wealth and leisure for patronage, talent for performance, and an audience to enjoy, applaud, and encourage further efforts. The commercial aristocrat far more than the gentleman planter met the requirements for the patron, and he displayed the willingness to gather in the trophies produced by local talent. Passive in his attitudes toward the arts, he never became a professional, or, at the most, indulged in the dilettantism of a Francis Hopkinson. Nowhere save in these cities did there exist a vigorous middle class from whose "ingenious craftsmen" the practitioners of the arts and sciences might be recruited—a Franklin, a Copley, a Timothy, or a Harrison. The city offered better education and opportunities for persons of like minds to convene, discuss, and practice their arts amid friendly surroundings. Harvard, King's, and the College of Philadelphia did much to foster interest in the sciences. Finally, the cosmopolitan urban center served as the seedbed for the ideas of the Enlightenment, and in the long run, the social change, call it revolution, first took hold in the cities and their environs and proved more far-reaching and permanent than that begun in France and spread over continental Europe.

For the times, the accomplishments of the colonial urban centers were noteworthy and were admired abroad as well as applauded at home.

The press, a purely urban phenomenon, enjoyed greater freedom than that of any other country, including England, and, in its role of formulating and swaying public opinion, was the fundamental fact of American culture. Through its support and encouragement, a vigorous prose style evolved, which culminated in the magnificent controversial literature and impressive state papers of the Revolution—a political literature almost unsurpassed in history. At least seven painters from the four Northern towns won foreign recognition after having succeeded in their craft on this side of the water. In architecture Peter Harrison and Robert Smith earned intercolonial reputations, and the work of many gentlemen amateurs, like Robert Crommelin, revealed a well-developed taste in this art. No musician of permanent worth appeared in the colonial towns, but a wide interest and participation in singing and playing testified to a forming taste, and a few such as Gualdo and Billings portended later accomplishment. The most significant performances came in science with the first-rate achievement of Franklin in electricity, the minor though sound astronomical work of John Winthrop and David Rittenhouse, and the botanical contribution of John Bartram. With the formation of the American Philosophical Society, scientific investigation on this continent entered into that co-operative phase which has characterized all subsequent investigation. The record of intercolonial and international traffic in culture by these new communities is impressive.

The Enlightenment took different forms in different parts of the Western World according to the nature of the society or the needs of its people. That which was universal in it was a corpus of ideas; votaries borrowed such of them as suited their peculiar wants. One could hardly expect, therefore, that the Enlightenment would take the same form in the cities as it did in the British Isles or in France. It had to be an American variant. What happened was that with discriminating selectivity the citizens took the ideas of the Old World as refurbished by the philosophers of the Enlightenment and, working out their own responses to such forces of modernity as intimately affected their existence in their own communities, translated them into action. Here were five points at which ideas became facts and thereby created history. The novel element, "the American thing," was not the philosophy or the system but the synthesis. In their indefeasible loyalty to the Enlightenment, the townsmen in their civic as well as their cultural undertakings insisted upon performance rather than talk or thought (perhaps too much so); they determined to set ideas in motion. By 1776 they had proved beyond all cavil their collective greatness by their capacity to borrow, not merely to imitate but successfully to adapt, to transform, and ultimately to assimilate current and older European elements. In so doing the people of these cities ceased to be colonials; they became Americans.

In 1743 the average citizen, when he thought about it at all, loved his native community for its age, its local traditions and associations, and as the place he called home. Nationalism in the modern sense did not then exist, even in England or in France; local patriotism absorbed the loyalties of most people. A series of negative reactions to imperial policies, however, served to arouse colonial pride concurrently with resentment of the mother country: the fiasco of Carthagena and the heedless loss of nine out of ten colonials, the return of hard-won Louisburg to France in 1748, the brutal activities (no matter how legal) of the press gang, the ill-concealed contempt of the British military for "Americans," Parliamentary prohibition of vitally needed paper money, the course and aftermath of the wars in general, and the detestation of placemen. These and other irritants played a prominent part in the growing realization that, as Goethe would later say:

> *Amerika, du hast es besser*
> *Als unser Continent. . . .*

Prior to 1763 such sentiments as these seldom rose to the surface of colonial thinking but remained, for the most part, in "the deep well of unconscious cerebration."

All of these issues between the colonials and the mother country hinged on attitudes toward overseas authority and the actions of its local representatives. A minority of American conservatives consistently supported British officialdom; they were now branded Tories. The Whig, or liberal majority view, stressed provincial rights. Both sides sought to guide public opinion through the press, but gradually the latter, with the support of the printers, won out. The newspapers began to single out anything "American" for unrestrained praise, which stimulated the burgeoning pride of the citizens. In 1760 Benjamin Franklin, a loyal British subject, welcomed the accession of George III; only fifteen years later he spoke with contempt of "that noble China-vase, the British Empire" —so far had loyalties shifted under provocation and self-stimulus. The contest of the sixties forced the citizens to a recognition of the differences between Englishmen and Americans, to list their own strengths and virtues, to discount or overlook their weaknesses and defects, and above all to feel their own maturity as a society. The colonial world was a new place, it *was* different. Most people had come to live in it by choice, and they were, as Crèvecœur said, a new breed.

Notwithstanding their status as colonials and therefore somewhat restricted by British policy, the citizens had lived in a free society, the freest then known anywhere. During the war years and after 1763, suspicions that hard-won liberties were to be abridged or lost aroused fear and resentment, and at the same time there welled up a strange, new, but exhilarating emotion—Americanism. A majority of citizens determined to preserve these freedoms at any cost; and as the issues clarified with each new crisis, they proceeded from protest to opposition, from opposition to revolt, and ultimately, in 1776, to independence. This shift of loyalties and birth of nationalism occurred before Lexington; it was upon a sure knowledge of this powerful sentiment that Thomas Paine could, in *Common Sense,* make the great emotional appeal for independence. Provincial attachments had long been and would again continue to be foremost in the thoughts of rural inhabitants, especially in Virginia, but decades before independence the cities became the birthplace of American nationality.[1] Thinking men like John Adams saw this clearly: "The Revolution was effected before the war commenced. The Revolution was in the minds and hearts of the people. . . . This radical change in the principles, sentiments, and affections of the people was the real American Revolution."

The primary role of the cities in the attaining of American independence was preparatory. They provided five centers where the essential conjunction of people, leadership, and events could occur and give concrete expression to what Thomas Jefferson with his customary felicity called "the unquestionable republicanism of the American mind." Revolt would never have succeeded—nay, it would hardly have been attempted—had there not been this silent social and intellectual preparation which sustained the sense of American nationality so evident in the cities after 1764. These communities composed a dynamic society, one bursting with pent-up forces which have often been thought to be the result of the War for Independence, whose true role was not to generate but to release them. When the final break came, the city dwellers succeeded in carrying their fellows of the rural and frontier sections with them. From this point of view, the uprising against Great Britain is seen as the culmination of a deeper, more subtle change that encompassed the entire colonial urban experience as the cities, so completely in harmony with the ideas of the Enlightenment, silently and persistently revolted against the tyranny of the past and cast their lot with modern times.

[1] No disparagement of the great and vital contribution of the Virginia planters to the revolutionary movement is here implied. Even in the Old Dominion the village of Williamsburg assumed during "publick times" certain urban attributes and exerted an influence similar to that of the large cities, as I have pointed out in *Seat of Empire* (Williamsburg, 1950), pp. 29, 33.

NOTES AND REFERENCES

T HE FOLLOWING references, together with an occasional note, were originally planned as footnotes to *Cities in Revolt*, but were omitted from the volume because of high publication costs. Because so many citations are needed in a work of social history, it was thought best to group them at the end of each paragraph, as in *Cities in the Wilderness*.

At the left-hand side of each page is noted the *page* and *paragraph* on that page for every set of references. Thus, "170:4" indicates that the references belong to paragraph 4 of page 170.

Below is a list of the *abbreviations* used for authorities cited frequently. The first citation of every reference, save those listed in the abbreviations, gives the name of the author, title of the work, place, and date of publication.

PRINCIPAL ABBREVIATIONS USED IN THE NOTES

Bos. Rec. Com.—Report of the Record Commissioners of the City of Boston, containing minutes of the Selectmen and Town Meeting.

Cities, I—Cities in the Wilderness: The First Century of Urban Life in America, 1625–1742, by Carl Bridenbaugh.

C.O.—Colonial Office documents in Public Record Office, London, or in transcripts at the Library of Congress.

Col. Soc. Mass.—Colonial Society of Massachusetts.

Edwards, *New York—New York as an Eighteenth Century Municipality,* by George William Edwards.

*Extra—*Extraordinary or supplementary issue of a newspaper.

Franklin, *Works* (Sparks)—Benjamin Franklin's *Works* or *Writings* in the editions of Jared Sparks, John Bigelow, or A. H. Smyth.

HSP—Historical Society of Pennsylvania, Philadelphia.

HL—Henry E. Huntington Library, San Marino, Calif.

LC—Library of Congress.

Mass. Acts—Acts and Resolves of the Province of Massachusetts Bay.

MHS—Massachusetts Historical Society, Boston.

NEHG Reg.—New England Historical and Genealogical Register.

NHS—Newport Historical Society, Newport, R.I.

Newp. T.C., T.M., Recs.—Newport Town Council, Town Meeting Records, in NHS and Newport City Hall (trans.).

Newsletter—Boston Newsletter.

N.Y. Gaz.—New York Gazette, or the Weekly Post Boy, 1747–1773; also *New York Gazette,* 1743–1744.

NYHS—New York Historical Society, New York City.

N.Y.M.C.C.—Minutes of the Common Council of the City of New York.

NYPL—New York Public Library.

Pa. Col. Recs.—Minutes of the Provincial Council of Pennsylvania.

Pa. Mag.—Pennsylvania Magazine of History and Biography.

Pa. Statutes—Statutes at Large of the State of Pennsylvania.

Pa. Votes—Votes and Proceedings of the House of Representatives of the Province of Pennsylvania (Philadelphia, 1752–1776, editions).

P.M.C.C.—Minutes of the Common Council of the City of Philadelphia.

PRO—Public Record Office, London.

R.I. Acts—Acts and Laws of the Colony of Rhode Island and Providence Plantations (1744, 1752, 1767, 1772 editions).

R.I. Arch.—Rhode Island State Archives, in the Capitol, Providence.

R.I. Col. Recs.—Records of the Colony of Rhode Island and Providence Plantations in New England, edited by J. R. Bartlett in 10 vols., must be checked from originals in R.I. Arch. on all crucial points, which are cited as R.I. Col. Recs. (MS).

S.C.A.G. Gaz.—South Carolina and American General Gazette.

S.C. Commons, Journal—Commons House of Assembly (South Carolina), Journals, South Carolina Historical Commission, Columbia.

S.C. Council, Journal—Governor's Council (South Carolina), Journals, South Carolina Historical Commission, Columbia.

S.C. Country Jour.—South Carolina Gazette and Country Journal.

SCHG Mag.—South Carolina Historical and Genealogical Magazine.

S.C. Pub. Recs.—Public Records of South Carolina, South Carolina Historical Commission, Columbia.

Stokes, *Iconography*—I. N. Phelps Stokes, *Iconography of Manhattan Island.*

Sup.—Supplement.

Trans.—Transcript, either by hand or typewriting.

NOTES

CHAPTER I

3:1 *N.Y. Merc.,* Oct. 8, 1753; Lois Mulkearn, ed., Thomas Pownall, *Topographical Description of the United States of America* (Pittsburgh, 1949), 42.

3:2 Rufus R. Wilson, ed., Andrew Burnaby, *Travels through North America* (New York, 1904), 133; Adolph S. Benson, ed., *The*

America of 1750: Peter Kalm's Travels in North America (New York, 1937), I, 33.

5:3   The growth of the total colonial population, which was overwhelmingly rural, was impressive: in 1743 it was under 800,-000; by 1760 it approximated 1,695,000. These figures and those in the tables are, except when indicated, estimates based on data in Evarts B. Greene and Virginia D. Harrington, *American Population before the Federal Census of 1790* (New York, 1932); and Stella H. Sutherland, *Population Distribution in Colonial America* (New York, 1936); and additional references.

6:3   For the earlier history of city governments see *Cities*, I, 6, 144, 304.

7:1   *Bos. Post Boy,* May 2, 1743; 14 *Bos. Rec. Com.,* 2; Robert F. Seybolt, *Town Officials of Colonial Boston* (Cambridge, 1939), 229; 16 *Bos. Rec. Com.,* 1.

7:2   14 *Bos Rec. Com.,* 49, 309, 319; 19 *Bos. Rec. Com.,* 93.

7:3   14 *Bos Rec. Com.,* 12, 197, 256, 296; 16 *Bos. Rec. Com.,* 29; *Mass. Acts,* IV, 20, 398; Gertrude S. Kimball, ed., *Correspondence of William Pitt with Colonial Governors* (New York, 1906), I, 362; MHS *Colls.,* 74, p. 7.

7:4   Newp. T.M. Recs., 337; *R.I. Col. Recs.,* V, 54, 59, 66; *R.I. Acts* (1745), 262.

8:1   Newp. T.M. Recs., 356, 374, 378, 390, 438, 590, 617; Petitions to the Rhode Island Assembly (R. I. Archives), IV, 106.

8:2   Between 1743–60 freedoms were granted to 1,326 men. NYHS *Colls.,* 1885, p. 145; Edwards, *New York,* 13, 46; McAnear, *N.Y. History,* XXI, 427.

9:1   *Pa. Statutes,* II, 414; Edward P. Allison and Boies Penrose, *Philadelphia, 1681–1887* (Baltimore, 1887), 28.

9:2   *P.M.C.C.,* 463, 470, 480, 498, 504, 505, 522, 550, 666; Biddle, *Pa., Mag.,* XIX, 65.

9:3   The initial stimulus to urban growth in England was an increase in trade, which was felt in the seaports about 1750; new industrial developments did not drastically augment populations much before 1776. The Webbs regard parliamentary action authorizing the election of commissioners for Liverpool in 1748 as the beginning of "local acts" for municipal betterment. Not until after the Peace of Paris in 1763, however, did most English cities seek such authority. Sidney and Beatrice Webb, *English Local Government: Statutory Authorities for Special Purposes* (London, 1922), 10, 242; *P.M.C.C.,* 420, 422; *Pa. Statutes,* V, 111.

10:1   Ernest S. Griffith, *History of American City Government: The Colonial Period* (New York, 1938), 246; *Cities,* I, 145, 304.

10:2   All civil functions were retained by St. Philip's parish in 1751 when St. Michael's parish was set off from it. St. Philip's Vestry, Minutes, I, 1, 102, 137, 142, 150, 162; II, 5, 14; *S. C. Gaz.,* Apr. 19, 1742; Apr. 2, 1744; Apr. 18, 1748; Apr. 15, 1751; Apr. 23, 1753; Apr. 22, *Sup.,* 1756; Albert E. McKinley, *The Suffrage Franchise in the Thirteen English Colonies in America* (Philadelphia, 1905), 155.

11:1   William Simpson, *Practical Justice of the Peace and Parish Officer of His Majesty's Province of South Carolina* (Charles Town, 1761); *S. C. Gaz.,* Mar. 28, Apr. 15, 1743,; Apr. 15, 1745; Mar. 30, 1747; May 1, Nov. 4, 1756; May 12, 1759.

11:3   14 *Bos. Rec. Com.,* 12; Edwards, *New York,* 35; McAnear, *Journal of Political Economy,* XLVIII, 63; *Journal of the Legislative Council of the Colony of New York* (Albany, 1861), II, 916.

11:4   Petitions to R. I. Assembly, VII, 133; Gertrude S. Kimball, ed., *Correspondence of the Governors of Rhode Island* (Providence, 1902), I, xxxii, xxxix, Ward Papers (RIHS), Box I, Apr. 19, 1757.

12:1   Edwards, *New York,* 35; *Pa. Votes,* IV, 211; *P.M.C.C.,* 647; Lincoln, *Pa. Mag.,* XXIII, 30*n.*

12:2   Carl Bridenbaugh, *Myths and Realities: Societies of the Colonial South* (Baton Rouge, 1952), 163.

12:3   William Douglass, *Summary, Historical and Political . . . of the . . . British Settlements in North America* (Boston, 1755), I, 535; Charles F. Adams, ed., John Adams, *Works* (Boston, 1856), X, 241.

13:1   *Pa. Gaz.,* Aug. 16, 23, 1744; *N. Y. Wkly. Jour.,* Dec. 7, 1747; *N.Y. Eve. Post.* Sept. 26, 1748; *Independent Reflector,* July 5, 1753; Franklin B. Dexter, ed., *Itineraries and Other Miscellanies of Ezra Stiles* (New Haven, 1916), 103.

14:1   *P.M.C.C.,* 441; *Pa. Chronicle,* Jan. 15, 1770; *Pa. Gaz.,* June 30, 1743; Apr. 2, 1761; Jan. 18, 1770; Carl Bridenbaugh, ed., *Gentleman's Progress: The Itinerarium of Dr. Alexander Hamilton, 1744* (Chapel Hill, 1948), 18; Israel Acrelius, *History of New Sweden* (Philadelphia, 1874), 142.

14:2   In 1748 about 120 dwellings, warehouses, and stores were built. *London Magazine,* 1749, p. 344; *American Magazine and Monthly Chronicle,* Dec., 1757, p. 116; Kalm, *Travels,* I, 19, 20, 33; Acrelius, *New Sweden,* 141; *Some Cursory Remarks Made by James Birket* (New Haven, 1916), 66; Carl T. Eben, ed., Gottlieb, Mittelberger, *Journey to Pennsylvania in 1750* (Philadelphia, 1898), 49, 74; *Pa. Gaz.,* Sept. 29, 1748.

14:3   *Pa. Jour.,* Oct. 31, 1754.

15:1 *Maryland Gaz.,* June 7, 1749; *Pa. Mag.,* XVIII, 212; Joseph Jackson, *Cyclopedia of Philadelphia* (Harrisburg, 1932), III, 682; Lawrence H. Gipson, *Lewis Evans* (Philadelphia, 1939), 98; Nicholas Scull, *Plan of the Improved Part of the City . . . of Philadelphia* (Philadelphia, 1762).

15:2 Carl and Jessica Bridenbaugh, *Rebels and Gentlemen: Philadelphia in the Age of Franklin* (New York, 1942), 199; *Pa. Mag.,* VIII, 120; XVIII,, 515; XXXVIII, 243; Burnaby, *Travels,* 88, 91; Lewis B. Walker, *Burd Papers: Extracts from Chief Justice William Allen's Letter Book* (n.p., 1897), 14; T. G. Tappert and J. W. Doberstein, *Journals of Henry Melchior Muhlenberg* (Philadelphia, 1942), I, 87.

15:3 Bridenbaugh, *Gentleman's Progress,* 21; Mittelberger, *Journey,* 120; Franklin, *Works* (Smyth), II, 93.

16:1 Most craftsmen heated their shops with "charcoal fires in open pots." Franklin, *Works* (Sparks), VI, 35; Carl Van Doren, *Benjamin Franklin's Autobiographical Writings* (New York, 1945), 720; *Pa. Mag.,* XXXIX, 223; *Newsletter,* July 20, 1749; *N.Y. Post Boy,* Nov. 19, 1744.

16:2 Stokes, *Iconography,* IV, 607, 613; Bridenbaugh, *Gentleman's Progress,* 44; William Smith, *History of the Late Province of New York* (NYHS *Colls.,* IV, 1829), I, 254; Pownall, *Topographical Description,* 44; *Newsletter,* Feb. 18, 1762.

16:3 Stokes, *Iconography,* IV, 575; Bridenbaugh, *Gentleman's Progress,* 44; Birket, *Cursory Remarks,* 43; Kalm, *Travels,* I, 132; Pownall, *Topographical Description,* 43; *Pa. Mag.,* XII, 440.

17:1 *N.Y. Eve. Post,* Oct. 20, 1746; *Pa. Mag.,* XII, 446; Ontario Archives, *Second Report* (Toronto, 1905), I, 115; Edwards, *New York,* 147; Pownall, *Topographical Description,* 45; NYHS *Colls.,* 1895, p. 229.

17:2 Birket, *Cursory Remarks,* 28; Stiles, *Itineraries,* 24; Ezra Stiles, Miscellaneous Papers (LC), Sept. 13, 1761.

17:3 Birket, *Cursory Remarks,* 28; *Newp. Merc.,* May 22, Aug. 14, Nov. 20, 1759.

17:4 MHS *Colls.,* IV, 189; Birket, *Cursory Remarks,* 20.

18:1 *N.Y. Wkly Jour.,* Jan. 17, 1742/3; *Newsletter,* Sept. 13, 1753.

18:2 *Bos. Eve. Post,* Aug 1, 1743; *Newsletter,* Dec. 6, 1744; Mar. 30, 1749; *American Magazine and Historical Chronicle,* Dec., 1744, I, 691; George F. Dow, *Holyoke Diaries, 1709–1756* (Salem, 1911), 7, 15, 24.

18:3 *Bos. Post Boy* Mar. 24, 31, 1760.

19:1 *S.C. Gaz.,* May 16, 1743; June 17, 1745; Oct. 31, 1748; July 22, 1751; S.C. Pub. Recs., XXIV, 328.

19:2 *S.C. Gaz.,* Sept. 19, 27, Oct. 3, 1752; *Bos. Post Boy* Oct. 16,

Nov. 13, 1752; *American Gazetteer* (London, 1762), I, article on "Charlestown."

20:1 Walter Ison, *Georgian Buildings of Bristol* (London, 1952), 21, 99, 105, 108, and especially plates 4, 14, 18, 19, 22, 34; John Corry, *History of Liverpool* (Liverpool, 1810), 98, 117, and plates; John Summerson, *Georgian London* (New York, 1946).

20:2 Carl Bridenbaugh, *Peter Harrison: First American Architect* (Chapel Hill, 1949), 45, 88, 98, and figures 7, 11, 15, 27, 30, 36; Burnaby, *Travels,* 120; Birket, *Cursory Remarks,* 27, 29; Douglass, *Summary,* II, 100.

21:1 *S.C. Gaz.,* Oct. 23, 1751; Feb. 22, Mar. 23, 1752; July 2, 1753; Bridenbaugh, *Peter Harrison,* 63; Chapman J. Milling, *Colonial South Carolina: Two Contemporary Descriptions* (Columbia, 1952), 143, 145.

21:2 Bridenbaugh, *Peter Harrison,* 54; Samuel G. Drake, *History and Antiquities of Boston* (Boston, 1856), 641; Journal of a Captive, 1745–48 (LC); MHS *Colls.,* III, 253; *Providence Gaz.,* Jan. 28, 1769; Birket, *Cursory Remarks,* 21; Pownall, *Topographical Description,* 87.

22:1 2 MHS *Procs.,* VII, 341; Edward P. Cheyney, *History of the University of Pennsylvania* (Philadelphia, 1940), 23, 37, 53; Society of Architectural Historians, *Journal,* XI, 23; Bridenbaugh, *Rebels and Gentlemen,* 199, and illustrations facing pp. 58, 223; Birket, *Cursory Remarks,* 65; Burnaby, *Travels,* 90.

22:2 Bridenbaugh, *Gentleman's Progress,* 44; James G. Wilson, *Memorial History of the City of New York* (New York, 1892), II, 279, 302 (illustrations); Morgan Dix, *History of the Parish of Trinity Church in New York City* (New York, 1898), I, 247, 261; Pownall, *Topographical Description,* 44; Birket, *Cursory Remarks,* 44; *N.Y. Col. Laws,* IV, 126, 202, 355; Minutes of the Governors of King's College (Columbia University Archives), May 12, July 13, 1756; Burnaby, *Travels,* 112; *Pa. Mag.,* XII, 446; *N.Y. Post Boy,* June 30, 1760.

23:1 *S.C. Statutes,* III, 606, 608; *Pa. Gaz.,* June 23, 1743; *Memoirs of Peter Henry Bruce* (Dublin, 1783); *Pa. Jour.,* Aug. 22, 1745; S.C. Pub. Recs., XX, 496; XXI, 22; Plowden C. J. Weston, *Documents Connected with South Carolina* (pr. pr., 1856), 93; *S.C. Gaz.,* May 6, 1756; B. R. Carroll, ed., *Historical Collections of South Carolina* (New York, 1836), II, 487.

23:2 Bridenbaugh, *Gentleman's Progress,* 156; Bridenbaugh, *Peter Harrison,* 18, 20, 90, and figures 10, 11.

24:1 Birket, *Cursory Remarks,* 19, 22; *Jour. Legis. Council of N.Y.,* II, 849, 879, 907; James Lyne, *Plan of the City of New York from Actual Surveys* (G. Duyckinck edn.,); *P.M.C.C.,* 488; *Pa.*

Gaz., Nov. 26, Dec. 12, 1747; *Pensylvanische Berichte,* Jan. 16, 1748; *S.C. Gaz.,* Dec. 10, 1747; July 25, 1748; J. Thomas Scharf and Thompson Westcott, *History of Philadelphia, 1609–1884* (Philadelphia, 1884), I, 215.

24:2   Here again, the colonial cities led the exodus to the country. The suburban movement began at Bristol about 1760, as it did at Edinburgh; it came later at Liverpool and other provincial cities. John Latimer, *Annals of Bristol in the Eighteenth Century* (Bristol, 1893), 343; Henry G. Graham, *Social Life of Scotland in the Eighteenth Century* (London, 1937), 85; Francis Bamford and Sacheverell Sitwell, *Edinburgh* (London, 1938), 233, 245; Burnaby, *Travels,* 88; Franklin, *Works* (Smyth), II, 322.

25:1   Franklin, *Works* (Smyth), III, 13; *Pa. Gaz.,* Mar. 21, 1743/4; May 15, 1746; July 17, 1755; May 22, 1760; *Pa. Jour.,* Aug. 4, 1748; June 15, 1749; Feb. 19, 1754; 1 *Pa. Archives,* I, 675; *P.M.C.C.,* 443, 446.

25:2   Arthur Browne, *Miscellaneous Sketches* (London, 1798), II, 196*n;* Lillie, Cambridge Historical Society, *Pubs.,* XXVI, 48; Birket, *Cursory Remarks,* 17.

25:3   Birdenbaugh, *Gentleman's Progress,* 103, 153; Birket, *Cursory Remarks,* 27, 40; *N.Y. Post Boy,* Sept. 2, 1744; *Pa. Mag.,* XII, 444; *N.Y. Gaz.,* Jan. 29, 1759; Bridenbaugh, *Myths and Realities,* 69, 76.

26:1   Douglass, *Summary,* II, 68; Birket, *Cursory Remarks,* 20; 17 *Bos. Rec. Com.,* 125; 14 *Bos. Rec. Com.,* 123.

26:2   14 *Bos. Rec. Com.,* 118, 123; 16 *Bos. Rec. Com.,* 26; 17 *Bos. Rec. Com.,* 160, 168; *Bos. Post Boy,* July 13, 1747; Jan. 21, 1760; *Bos. Eve. Post,* Sept. 8, 1746; May 9, 1757; *Newsletter,* Sept. 13, Dec. 27, 1744; *Mass. Acts,* IV, 177.

27:1   *Pa. Mag.,* XII, 437; *Newsletter,* Jan. 5, 1758; *N.Y. Gaz.,* Feb. 9, 1747; Jan. 14, 1760; Kalm, *Travels,* I, 135; Stokes, *Iconography,* I, 306.

27:2   Franklin, *Works* (Sparks), VI, 35, 44; Kalm, *Travels,* I, 50; *Pa. Gaz.,* Jan. 10, 1760; *Pa. Jour.,* Jan. 7, 21, 1752.

27:3   *S.C. Gaz.,* Mar. 19, 1744; Feb. 12, 1753; Feb. 1, 1759; *SCHG Mag.,* XX, 11; XXVI, 93; Newp. T.M. Recs., 438, 670, 676, 682; *Newp. Merc.,* Dec. 26, 1758; Apr. 22, 1760; *Newsletter,* Nov. 21, 1745.

28:1   14 *Bos. Rec. Com.,* 51, 250; Newp. T.M. Recs., 350, 354, 462, 528, 532, 613; Edwards, *New York,* 162; *P.M.C.C.,* 500, 627; St. Philip's Vestry, Minutes, I, 102; S.C. Pub. Recs., XXI, 414; *S.C. Statutes,* VII, 76. For contemporary problems in England, *see* Webb, *Statutory Authorities,* 235; *S.C. Gaz.,* July 9, 1750.

28:2   *Mass. Acts,* III, 78; Newp. T.M. Recs., 462, 478; *R.I. Acts*

(1767), 142; *Ind. Reflector,* Dec. 14, 1752; Simpson, *Practical Justice of the Peace,* 55; *S.C. Statutes,* IV, 73.

29:1   Webb, *Statutory Authorities,* 57; 17 & 19 *Bos. Rec. Com., passim; N.Y.M.C.C.,* IV, 103; V, 191, 199, 229, 265, 370; *Ind. Reflector,* Nov. 22, 1755; 1 *Pa. Archives,* II, 3; Court Papers, Phila. County (HSP), II, Oct. 1749; July, 1750; *P.M.C.C.,* 620; Alexander Graydon, *Memoirs of a Life . . . in Pennsylvania* (Edinburgh, 1822), 36; *S.C. Statutes,* III, 405, 694; IV, 112; S. C. Pub. Recs., XXIII, 216; *S. C. Gaz.,* July 9, 1750; *N.Y. Post Boy,* May 5, 1746.

30:1   John Spranger, *A Proposal . . . for the Better Paving, Cleansing and Lighting the Streets of Westminster. . . .* (London, 1754); Jonas Hanway, *A Letter to Mr. Spranger on His Excellent Proposal. . . .* (London, 1754); Webb, *Statutory Authorities,* 242, 274, 299; Latimer, *Bristol in the 18th Century,* 277; *Journal of a Captive,* Boston, 1748; 14 *Bos. Rec. Com.,* 112, 279; *Newsletter,* Apr. 14, May 12, 1757; *N.Y.M.C.C.,* V, 293, 306; VI, 14, 17, 97; *N.Y. Col. Laws,* III, 844; Birket, *Cursory Remarks,* 21, 44; Burnaby, *Travels,* 133; Smith, *New York,* I, 255.

30:2   Newp. Hist. Soc., *Bulletin* (Jan., 1912), 5; *R.I. Col. Recs.,* V, 342; VI, 105; *R.I. Acts* (1767), 202; Newp. T. M. Recs., 500, 522.

30:3   Kalm, *Travels,* I, 19; Court Papers, Phila. Co., Oct., 1749; July, 1750; *Pa. Mag.,* XVIII, 212; *Pa. Votes,* IV, 786; Thompson Westcott, *Hist. of Philadelphia* (clippings, HSP), chap. CXLV.

31:1   *Cities,* I, 321; Spranger, *A Proposal,* preface; *N.Y.M.C.C.,* V, 122; *N.Y. Post Boy,* Feb. 27, 1743/4; Jan. 6, 1745/6; Mar. 2, 1746/7; *N.Y. Col. Laws,* III, 996; 14 *Bos. Rec. Com.,* 140; *Newsletter,* July 23, 1752.

31:2   *S.C. Gaz.,* Nov. 5, 1744; June 18, July 9, *Sup.,* 1750; Mar. 19, 1754; May 8, 1755; June 9, 1757; Dec. 1, 1758; *S.C. Statutes,* III, 723; IV, 42; Simpson, *Practical Justice of the Peace,* 243.

32:1   Newport's fragmentary records give no evidence of concern about dirty streets for the balance of the colonial period, though they did in previous years. Since all kinds of other grievances were aired there and in the *Newport Mercury,* I conclude that by some means, by now unknown, the streets were kept reasonably clean. *Pa. Gaz.,* July 12, 1750; Jan. 8, 1750/1; Dec. 26, 1754; Court Papers, Phila., Co., IV, Feb. 14, 1754; *Pa. Mag.,* XXXII, 433.

32:2   *R.I. Acts* (1745) 306; *R.I. Acts* (1767), 144, 146; Newp. T.M. Recs., 418, 458; *Pa. Gaz.,* Sept. 27, 1744; *S.C. Gaz.,* Nov. 5, 1744; *S.C. Statutes,* VII, 76; *N.Y.M.C.C.,* VI, 152; *N.Y. Post Boy,* Aug. 27, 1744.

33:1 Newp. T.C. Recs., IX, 40; *Pa. Votes,* IV, 210; *Ind. Reflector,* Jan. 18, 1753.

33.2 Burnaby, *Travels,* 89, 91, 112; 17 *Bos. Rec. Com.,* 71, 252; Kalm, *Travels,* I, 19, 131; *Pa. Mag.,* XVIII, 212.

34:1 Birket, *Cursory Remarks,* 67; Albert C. Myers, ed., *Hannah Logan's Courtship: Diary of John Smith, 1736–1752* (Philadelphia, 1904), 263; *Pa. Statutes,* V, 111; *P.M.C.C.,* 647; *Pa. Gaz.,* Oct. 3, 1751; James B. Hedges, *Browns of Providence Plantations* (Cambridge, 1952), 92.

34:2 *Bos. Post Boy,* Oct. 7, 1751; R.I. Col. Recs., (MS, R.I. Archives), VI, 235; *R.I. Acts* (1752), 96; *R.I. Acts* (1767), 162; *N.Y. Col. Laws,* III, 855; *N.Y. Gaz.,* Dec. 23, 1751; Feb. 3, 1752; Dec. 30, 1754; *Mass. Acts,* III, 645.

34:3 *N.Y. Gaz.,* July 12, 1756; *Pa. Jour.,* July 21, 1743.

35:1 *Pa. Mag.,* VI, 305; Birket, *Cursory Remarks,* 58; *Cities,* I, 324; S.C. Commons, Jour., XXV, 252; *N.Y. Gaz.,* Sept. 3, 1750; *S.C. Gaz.,* July 9, *Sup.,* 1750; June 9, 1757; *Newp. Merc.,* Jan. 23, 1759.

35:2 *Bos. Post Boy,* Aug. 11, 1746; Newp. T.M. Recs., 382; S.C. Commons, Jour., XXV, 252.

36:1 Bridenbaugh, *Rebels and Gentlemen,* 12; *Mass. Acts,* III, 360, 467; *Bos. Post Boy,* Oct. 19, 1747; Adams, *Works,* II, 65.

36:2 *Cities,* I, 21, 170, 325; 14 *Bos. Rec. Com.,* 231; 19 *Bos. Rec. Com.,* 4; Bridenbaugh, *Gentleman's Progress,* 46; Pownall, *Topographical Description,* 43; *Pa. Jour.,* July 17, 1746; June 22, Oct. 26, 1749.

37:1 For a list of ferries, see *Gentleman's Progress,* index under Ferries; Birket, *Cursory Remarks,* 16, 17, 31, 47.

37:2 *Pa. Votes.,* IV, 103, 107, 108; V, 107; *P.M.C.C.,* 619, 658; *Pa. Mag.,* XVIII, 212; *R.I. Acts* (1767), 108; *Mass. Acts,* III, 465; Edwards, *New York,* 178; *N.Y.M.C.C.,* V, 270; *S.C. Gaz.,* Mar. 2, 1747; *R.I. Col. Recs.,* V, 504

38:1 Adverse tides or lack of wind delayed ferries everywhere as often as rough water. *Pa. Jour.,* Dec. 13, 1748; *N.Y. Wkly. Jour.,* Aug. 21, 1749; *N.Y. Merc.,* Mar. 15, 1756.

38:3 Birket, *Cursory Remarks,* 22, 73; 17 *Bos. Rec. Com.,* 221; *Newsletter,* July 9, 1747; Apr. 4, 1760; *Bos. Eve. Post,* Apr. 5, 1756; Ontario Archives, *Second Report,* I, 637.

39:1 Birket, *Cursory Remarks,* 29; Stiles, *Itineraries,* 23; Misc. MSS, Malbone, Apr. 30, 1755 (NYHS); Plan of Long Wharf in 1760 (MHS), probably by Stiles; Records of the Proprietors of Long Wharf (Newport, The Proprietors); *Newp. Merc.,* Jan. 23, 1759; George C. Mason, *Reminiscences of Newport* (Newport, 1884, extra. illus. copy NYPL), II, 123.

39:2 James Mease, *Picture of Philadelphia* (Philadelphia, 1811), 25;

P.M.C.C., 422, 428, 491, 558, 617; Scull, *Improved Part of Philadelphia;* Thomas Richie, Account Book, 1755–1758 (LC).

39:3   James Lyne, *Plan of the City of New York from Actual Surveys* (G. Duyckinck edn.); *N.Y. Col. Laws,* III, 437, 993; IV, 23; Edwards, *New York,* 151; Stokes, *Iconography,* IV, 308, 311, 607; *N.Y.M.C.C.,* VI, 81; Birket, *Cursory Remarks,* 43; Isaac Norris, Journal, Sept. 30, 1745 (HL: HM 3057); *American Gazetteer,* III, article on New York.

40:1   In January 1751 the highest tides "in the Memory of Man" caused extensive damage to wharves, shipping, and merchandise at Newport, amounting to between seventy and eighty thousand Rhode Island pounds; and back in 1743 Boston suffered heavily from a violent storm and high tides that overflowed the wharves and drove vessels ashore or up against the piers. *Bos. Eve. Post,* Jan. 28, 1751; *Bos. Post Boy,* Oct. 24, 1743; S.C. Pub. Recs., XXIV, 313; *Cities,* I, plate 10; *S.C. Gaz.,* Dec. 3, *Sup.,* 1744; May 25, 1745; May 25, 1747; Oct. 7, Nov. 8, 1751; Jan. 29, *Sup.,* May 6, July 22, 1756; *Pa. Jour.,* Nov. 9, 1752; *Charleston Yearbook, 1884,* map (frontispiece).

40:2   S.C. Commons, Jour., XXV, 251; Edwards, *New York,* 152, 156; *P.M.C.C.,* 498, 651; *N.Y. Col. Laws,* III, 753; *S.C. Gaz.,* Mar. 30, 1747; Mar. 5, 1753; 2 *Pa. Archives,* II, 3.

41:1   *Cities,* I, 172; *Bos. Post Boy,* Apr. 29, 1751; July 30, 1753; Reports to the General Assembly, 1751–1765 (R.I. Archives), 25; Figure 11 in Bridenbaugh, *Peter Harrison,* shows Beaver Tail Light; R.I. Col. Recs., (MS), VI, 172; *Pa. Gaz.,* Aug 2, 1753; *N.Y. Gaz.,* July 9, 1753; S.C. Commons, Jour., XXV, 15.

42:1   Corry, *Liverpool,* 117; Wilson, *Mem. Hist. N.Y.,* II, 314.

CHAPTER II

43:1   *Pa. Votes,* IV, 2; *Pa. Jour.,* Apr. 27, 1758.

43:2   Earlier stages of urban economic development are discussed in *Cities,* I, 26, 175, 330; for colonial shipping statistics for 1743, C.O. 5, vol. V, 299.

44:1   Samuel Powel, Letter Book (HSP), III, 61; John Reynell, Letter Books, 1743–1760 (HSP), *passim;* Thomas W. Balch, *Letters and Papers Relating Chiefly to the Provincial History of Pennsylvania* (Philadelphia, 1855), 176, 181, 184; Anne Bezanson et al., *Prices in Colonial Pennsylvania* (Philadelphia, 1935), *passim; Pa. Mag.,* IV, 509.

44:2   *S.C. Gaz.,* Apr. 30, 1753; Powel, Letter Book, II, 243, 297, 365, 401, 466, 521, 576, 580, 604; III, 14, 61; *Pa. Gaz.,* Nov. 19, 1747; *Pa. Jour.,* Mar. 7, 1748/9.

45:1   1 *Pa. Archives,* II, 708; Powel, Letter Book, III, 87.

45:2   *Pa. Jour.,* Apr. 27, 1758; Mittelberger, *Journey,* 51; Burnaby, *Travels,* 93; Robert Proud, *History of Pennsylvania* (Philadelphia, 1798), II, 272; *Bos. Post Boy,* Aug. 4, 1760.

45:3   Adam Anderson, *The Origins of Commerce* (Dublin, 1790), V, 42; Smith, *New York,* I, 281; Alexander Papers, 1717–1756 (NYHS), I, 13; Gerardus G. Beekman, Letter Book, 1752–1770 (NYHS); *N.Y. Col. Docs.,* VI, 393, 510; Virginia D. Harrington, *The New York Merchant on the Eve of the Revolution* (New York, 1935), 164; *S.C. Gaz.,* Apr. 30, 1753.

46:1   *N.Y. Merc.,* Feb. 25, 1754; *Ind. Reflector,* Nov. 22, 1755; *N.Y. Col. Docs.,* VI, 1016.

46:2   *Charleston Year Book, 1880,* 246; *S.C. Gaz.,* Oct. 8, 22, 29, Dec. 10, 1744; King's MSS (LC), 206:54.

46:3   S.C. Pub. Rec., XXIII, 36, 123, 230; *S.C. Gaz.,* Aug. 23, 1746; Carroll, *Historical Collections of S. C.,* II, 221, 229; Weston, *Documents,* 82.

46:4   William B. Weeden, *Economic and Social History of New England* (Boston, 1890), II, 644.

47:1   John Banister, Letter Book, 1739 (NHS), Banister to John Thomlinson, June 1, 1739; Bridenbaugh, *Peter Harrison,* 7, 9, 81; William Redwood, Journal, 1749–1760 (HSP); Letters to George Whitefield (NYPL), David Van Horne to Whitefield, Nov. 12, 1750; Gerardus G. Beekman, Letter Book, 1746–1750 (NYHS), Box 43.

47:2   Philip Cuyler, Letter Book, 1755–1760 (NYPL), Cuyler to John Tweedy, Mar. 27, 1758; to Richards and Coddington, Apr. 10, 1759; Burnaby, *Travels,* 124.

47:3   *S.C. Gaz.,* July 25, 1748; Nov. 17, 1759.

48:2   The statements by the Town Meetings on Boston's decline are most vivid and significant: 14 *Bos. Rec. Com.,* 99, 100, 180, 220, 238, 280; Douglass, *Summary,* I, 532; Boston *Independent Advertiser,* Feb. 8, 1748; Feb. 27, 1749; *N.Y. Eve. Post,* Nov. 20, 1749, Birket, *Cursory Remarks,* 23; *Pa. Gaz.,* Apr. 28, 1757; Kimball, *Pitt Correspondence,* I, 362; Burnaby, *Travels,* 142.

49:1   Lawrence H. Gipson, *British Empire Before the American Revolution* (Caldwell, Idaho, 1936), III, 10*n*; *Virginia Gaz.,* Mar. 2, 1753; *S.C. Gaz.,* Apr. 2, 1753; Ruth Crandall, "Wholesale Commodity Prices at Boston," *Rev. Economic Statistics,* XVI, 117.

50:1   *Cities,* I, 334; Reynell, Letter Books, especially Ledger A, 157; Ledger D, 171; *Pa. Gaz.,* Dec. 11, 1760.

50:2   *New Amer. Mag.,* (Woodbridge, N.J.), July, 1758, p. 157; John

Lownes, Letter Book, 1760–1769 (LC); Stephen Collins Papers (LC), I, 26th 4th, 1760; 16th 5th, 1761; Penn Land Grants, 1681–1806, Penn MSS (HSP), IX, 125.

50:3 Davey and Carson, Letter Book, 1745–1750 (LC), June 5, 1746; Birket, *Cursory Remarks,* 53, 67; Edward Hocker, *Germantown* (Germantown, 1933), 78; Acrelius, *New Sweden,* 143; Pownall, *Topographical Description,* 102.

51:1 Carl Bridenbaugh, *Colonial Craftsman* (New York, 1950), 115; Acrelius, *New Sweden,* 143; *Lancastersche Zeitung,* Jan. 29, June 16, 1752; *Pa. Gaz.,* June 19, Sept. 18, Nov. 6, 1760; *Hoch Teutsche und Englische Zeitung,* Jan. 1, 1752; Balch, *Letters,* 35, 38, 184, 186; MHS *Colls.,* VII, 177.

51:2 Four new counties were formed out of the Philadelphia hinterland in this period: York, 1749; Cumberland, 1750; Northampton, 1752; Berks, 1752. *Genealogical Map of the [Pa.] Counties* (Harrisburg, 1936); *Pa. Jour.,* Feb. 26, 1745; *Pa. Gaz.,* June 7, 1753; Bridenbaugh, *Myths and Realities,* 138; Gipson, *Lewis Evans,* 94 and maps; Mittelberger, *Journey,* 102; Schaper, "Sectionalism and Representation in South Carolina," Amer. Hist. Assoc., *Annual Report,* 1900, I, 318.

52:1 *New London Summary,* Mar. 6, 1751; Mar. 27, 1761; *Newsletter,* Feb. 6, 1752; Nov. 14, 1754; May 18, Oct. 12, 1758; William T. Baxter, *House of Hancock* (Boston, 1945), 22, 24, 216; Bridenbaugh, Amer. Antiquarian Soc., *Procs.,* LVI, 38.

52:2 *Ind. Reflector,* Nov. 22, 1755; *N.Y. Merc.,* Apr. 25, 1757; Jacobus and William Van Gaasbeck, Account Book, Ulster Co., N.Y., 1736–1775 (NYHS); James Beekman, Letter Book (NYHS, White transcript), Nov. 4, 1750; Nov. 16, 1751; Dec. 15, 1756; Oct. 12, 1757; Nov. 21, 1759; Cuyler, Letter Book, I, Dec. 12, 1757; Birket, *Cursory Remarks,* 46; Robert Rogers, *Concise Account of North America* (London, 1765), 76; Harrington, *N.Y. Merchant,* 164; *New Amer. Mag.,* Mar. 1759, p. 50.

53:1 G. Beekman, Letter Book, Feb. 8, 1749; Jan. 30, 1754; Sept. 26, 1755; Feb. 14, July 25, 1760; Cuyler, Letter Book, I, June 2, 30, 1755; June 10, July 21, 1760; Harrington, *N.Y. Merchant,* 122, 206, 212, 214; Stiles, *Itineraries,* 83.

53:2 *Ind. Reflector,* Jan. 18, 1753.

53:3 *R.I. Col. Recs.,* V, 12; William Ellery Ledger, 1726–1753 (NHS), 52; *Bos. Gaz.,* Sept. 26, 1757; *Bos. Eve. Post,* May 30, 1757; *New London Summary,* Aug. 10, 1759; Douglass, *Summary,* II, 98.

54:1 Bridenbaugh, *Myths and Realities,* 54; *S.C. Gaz.,* Feb. 7, *Post.,* 21, 1743; Jan. 12, 1759.

54:2   *S.C. Gaz.*, Aug. 18, 1759; Aug. 30, 1760; Robert L. Meriwether, *Expansion of South Carolina* (Kingsport, 1940), 94, 100, 106.

54:3   *S.C. Gaz.*, Feb. 6, 1744; July 29, *Sup.*, 1756; Gipson, *British Empire*, IV, 53, 166.

55:2   An advertisement for a coach to carry "Ladies and Gentlemen" from the Falmouth boat up to Exeter or London ran in New York papers in 1759, indicating the growing volume of transAtlantic passenger traffic. *N.Y. Merc.*, Feb. 16, 1756; *N.Y. Gaz.*, June 25, 1759; Pownall *Topographical Description*, 45; *Newp. Merc.*, Dec. 26, 1758; Jan. 23, Oct. 30, 1759; *N.Y. Post Boy*, Sept. 9, 1745; *New London Summary*, Sept. 5, 1760; *S.C. Gaz.*, Feb. 20, 1744; Mar. 7, 1748; *Pa. Mag.*, IV, 408.

56:1   Drake, *Hist. of Boston*, 623; Pownall, *Topographical Description*, 110, 128; Kalm, *Travels*, I, 322; Gipson, *Lewis Evans*, 98; *Pa. Gaz.*, June 13, July 4, Aug. 8, 1751; *Pa. Jour.*, May 27, 1756.

56:3   *Cities*, I, 333; *Newsletter*, Aug. 8, 1745; May 26, 1757; *Bos. Eve. Post*, Aug. 19, *Sup.*, 1745; Aug. 29, 1748; Gertrude S. Kimball, *Pictures of Rhode Island in the Past, 1642–1833* (Providence, 1900), 40.

57:1   Bridenbaugh, *Gentleman's Progress*, 170; Isabel S. Mitchell, *Roads and Road-Making in Colonial Connecticut* (Tercentenary Pamphlet, XIV, New Haven, 1933), 20; Stiles, *Itineraries*, 481; *N.Y. Post Boy* Oct. 14, 1745; *Pa. Jour.*, June 22, 1749.

57:2   *Pa. Jour.*, June 17, 1744; Apr. 7, May 26, Dec. 8, 1757; *N.Y. Gaz.*, Oct. 22, 1750; Aug. 12, 1751; Mar. 16, 1752; Feb. 23, 1756; Oct. 8, 1759; *N.Y. Merc.*, Oct. 2, 1752; Oct. 8, 1753; Aug. 19, 1754; *Pa. Gaz.*, June 16, 1757; Sept. 13, 1759; Mar. 13, 1760; *Md. Gaz.*, Apr. 14, 1757; Wheaton J. Lane, *From Indian Trail to Iron Horse* (Princeton, 1939), 79.

57:3   Joshua Fry and Peter Jefferson, *Map of the Improved Part of Virginia. . . .* (London, 1751); Bridenbaugh, *Myths and Realities*, 128, 147.

58:1   Gipson, *Lewis Evans*, 100; Burnaby, *Travels*, 98; *London Mag.*, Aug., 1749, p. 344; *Pa. Mag.*, XVII, 269; *New Amer. Mag.*, Mar., 1758, p. 52; James T. Flexner, *America's Old Masters: First Artists of the New World* (New York, 1939), 25; *DAB*, XIII, 166; *Pa. Berichte*, May 1, 1749.

59:1   Harkness, *Miss. Valley Hist. Rev.*, XXXVII, 61; *Pa. Gaz.*, Jan. 4, 1742/3; *Newsletter*, Sept. 17, 1741; July 22, Dec. 9, 16, 30, 1742; Kimball, *R. I. Governors*, I, 261, 354, 360, 367.

59:2   *Amer. Mag. & Hist'l Chron.*, II, 314.

59:3   Powel, Letter Book, II, 410.

59:4 In 1747–1749 French and Spanish privateers raided with impunity and devastating effect off the entrance to Charles Town's harbor and well up into Delaware Bay. G. Beekman, Letter Book, June 19, 1748; *Pa. Jour.,* Jan. 10, Feb. 12, 1748/9; Aug. 8, 1751; June 14, 1753; *N.Y. Gaz.,* June 11, 1750; S.C. Pub. Recs., XXIII, 123; *S.C. Gaz.,* Mar. 14, 1748; Mar. 9, May 11, Aug. 17, 1752.

60:1 *Bos. Ind. Advertiser,* Feb. 8, 1748; *Pa. Jour.,* Sept. 7, 1749.

60:2 *Pa. Jour.,* July 25, Sept. 12, 19, 26, 1754; July 24, 31, Dec. 25, 1755; Mar. 4, 11, 25, Apr. 29, 1756; *Pa. Berichte,* Mar. 16, 1756; Dec. 24, 1757; *Pa. Gaz.,* Dec. 14, 1758; *S.C. Gaz.,* July 21, 1757.

61:1 Mason, *Reminiscences of Newport* (NHS), IV, 283A; Champlin Papers (NHS), I, 49; Gardiner, RIHS *Pubs.,* n.s., VI, 167, 172; Francis Bernard, *Select Letters on the Trade and Government of America* (London, 1774), 31; *Newsletter,* Oct. 14, 28, 1756; July 28, 1757; *Bos. Eve. Post,* May 16, 1757; Nov. 12, 1759; on the bankruptcies, *Bos. Eve. Post,* Nov. 21, 1757–July 10, 1758; *Acts Privy Council,* IV, 388.

62:1 Stokes, *Iconography,* IV, 576; *N.Y. Post Boy,* Aug. 6, Sept. 17, 1744; Nov. 4, 1745; Howard M. Chapin, *Privateering in King George's War* (Providence, 1928), 121, 172; *Pa. Jour.,* Mar. 20, 1753; *Newsletter,* June 23, 1748.

62:2 Stuyvesant Fish, *New York Privateers, 1756–1763* (New York, 1945), 54; *N.Y. Merc.,* Nov. 22, 1756; *Md. Gaz.,* Oct. 28, 1756; July 7, 1757; Cuyler, Letter Book, I, Feb. 22, Mar. 31, 1757; Dec. 15, 1758; *Newp. Merc.,* Dec. 18, 1775; NYHS *Colls.,* 1897, p. 21; Harrington, *N.Y. Merchant,* 308.

63:1 *Pa. Gaz.,* Mar. 17, 1742/3; July 19, 26, Sept. 13, 1744; Maritime Papers, Colonial Wars, 1723–1766 (R.I. Archives); Public Notary Records (R.I. Archives), V, VI; *Pa. Jour.,* June 21, 1744; May 23, 30, 1745; *S.C. Gaz.,* Oct. 29, 1744; *Md. Gaz.,* 3, 17, 1745; *Bos. Eve. Post,* Oct. 17, 1757; *Amer. Mag. & Hist'l Chron.,* I, Jan., 1744, p. 219; Letters to the Governors, 1742–1745 (R.I. Archives), 116; Douglass, *Summary,* II, 99.

63:2 Public Notary Records (R.I. Archives), V, VI; Burnaby, *Travels,* 129; Ward Papers, Box I, Feb. 19, 1758; *R.I. Col. Recs.,* VI, 264; John Austin Stevens, "Newport in the Revolutionary Period" (Typescript NYHS, 1897), 4.

63:3 *N.Y. Post Boy,* Aug. 27, 1744; Chapin, *Privateering,* 25, 59; a search in the *Newsletter* and *Bos. Eve. Post* 1754–1760 uncovered only six privateers at Boston; Clifford K. Shipton, *Biographical Sketches of Those Who Attended Harvard College* (Cambridge, 1951), VIII, 467.

63:4   Chapin, *Privateering,* 185; *Pa. Gaz.,* Aug. 30, Nov. 15, 1744;
       Jan. 19, 1744/5; Sept. 25, Nov. 10, 1745; May 27, 1746; Davey
       and Carson, Letter Book, May 27, 1746.

64:1   *Pa. Gaz.,* Dec. 15, 1757; May 4, July 6, Aug. 17, 1758; Mar. 8,
       Apr. 5, 19, May 10, June 28, July 12, Nov. 1, 1759; May 8,
       July 10, Oct. 2, 1760; *History of the Life, Strange Adventures,
       and Works of Captain John MacPherson* (Philadelphia, 1789),
       (LC).

64:2   Chapin, *Privateering,* 25; *S.C. Gaz.,* Jan.–Feb. 1743; Sept. 3,
       1744; *Pa. Jour.,* May 26, 1757; *Pa. Gaz.,* Jan. 19, 1758.

64:3   The whole matter of patriotism in the 18th century before the
       American and French revolutions gave rise to modern national-
       ism needs investigation. Richard Pares, *War and Trade in the
       West Indies, 1739–1761* (Oxford, 1936), 403, 410.

65:1   Bruce M. Bigelow, Commerce between Rhode Island and the
       West Indies before the Revolution (Thesis, Brown University
       Library), Pt. I, chap. VI, 5.

65:2   Bigelow, Commerce between R. I. and West Indies, Pt. I, chap.
       VI; *R. I. Col. Recs.,* V, 258; Banister, Letter Book, 1748–50
       (NHS), Feb. 27, 1747/8; Frank W. Pitman, *Development of
       the British West Indies* (New Haven, 1917), 289.

66:1   C.O. 5, V, 291; Powel, Letter Book, II, 569; *N.Y. Post Boy,*
       Nov. 5, 1744; June 6, 1748; *Bos., Eve. Post,* June 20, 1748; *Pa.
       Jour.,* Oct. 20, 1743; *S.C. Gaz.,* Apr. 15, 1745; June 25, *July*
       13, 1747; June 15, 1748; Bos. *Ind. Advertiser,* Sept. 19, 1748;
       G. Beekman, Letter Book, Nov. 29, 1747.

66:2   *Pa. Jour.,* Nov. 24, 1748; *Pa. Gaz.,* Jan. 3, 1748/9; Birket, *Cur-
       sory Remarks,* 30; *Newp. Hist. Mag.,* II, 123, 124; Pitman,
       West Indies, 401, 417; C. O. 137: 25, f. 113; John Stamper,
       Letter Book, 1751–1770 (HSP), to Fogo & Co., Mar. 17, 1758.

67:1   George L. Beer, *British Colonial Policy, 1754–1765* (New
       York, 1922), 74; *N.Y. Col. Docs.,* VII, 226; *R.I. Col. Recs.,* V,
       516; VI, 11, 264; Pitman, *West Indies,* 57, 314, 315, 326; *Acts
       Privy Council,* IV, 444; Moses Brown Papers (RIHS), I, 24.

67:2   Pitman, *West Indies,* 316; G. Beekman, Letter Book, Oct. 17,
       1759; *N.Y. Gaz.,* Apr. 16, 1759; *N.Y. Col. Docs.,* VII, 271,
       273; Harrington, *N.Y. Merchant,* 223, 260, 308; William Smith,
       Papers (NYPL), II, 408.

68:1   Beer, *British Colonial Policy,* 91; Chalmers Papers, Pennsyl-
       vania (NYPL), I, Peters to Monckton, July 24, 1760; Ward
       Papers, Box I, Greene to Assembly, Sept. 23, 1757; *R.I. Col.
       Recs.,* V, 173; Cuyler, Letter Book, I, letters to John and William
       Tweedy, Richards and Coddington, and Joseph Wanton, 1759–
       60.

68:2   James & Drinker, Letter Book, 1758–1762 (HSP), II, June 26, July 10, 1760; *Colden Letter Book* (NYHS *Colls.,* 1876), I, 27; *Commerce of Rhode Island* (MHS *Colls.,* 69), I, 83.

68:3   Baxter, *House of Hancock,* 95; Alexander Papers, I, *passim;* Harrington, *N.Y. Merchant,* 292.

69:1   Harrington, *N.Y. Merchant,* 115, 292; *N.Y. Col. Docs.,* VI, 1016; Amer. Jewish Hist. Soc., *Pubs.,* XI, 182; Franklin, *Works* (Smyth), III, 336; *Letter Book of John Watts* (NYHS *Colls.,* 1928), 26; Burnaby, *Travels,* 118.

69.2   Ward Papers, Box I, Henry to Samuel Ward, Feb. 19, 1758; *R.I. Col. Recs.,* VI, 212; Burnaby, *Travels,* 129; Pares, *War and Trade,* 467.

70:2   Harrington, *N.Y. Merchant,* 13, 19, 53; Charles P. Keith, *Provincial Councillors of Pennsylvania* (Philadelphia, 1883), 318; Thomas W. Balch, *Willing Letters and Papers* (Philadelphia, 1922), 2; Bridenbaugh, *Peter Harrison,* 23, 28; Bridenbaugh, *Rebels and Gentlemen,* 184; *S.C. Gaz.,* Dec. 3, 1750; Jan. 24, 1751; Donnan, *Amer. Hist. Rev.,* XXXIII, 815; *Bos. Eve. Post,* Aug. 4, 1746.

71:1   *S.C. Gaz.,* Feb. 20, 1744; *Papers of the Lloyd Family of Lloyd's Neck* (NYHS *Colls.,* 1926), II, 520, 523; *Newp. Hist. Mag.,* II, 89; *Commerce of R.I.,* I, 118.

71:2   David D. Wallace, *Henry Laurens* (New York, 1915), 8; Baxter, *House of Hancock,* 4, 67, 80, 95, 204, 224, 304.

72:1   Bridenbaugh, *Peter Harrison,* 83; For the mode of life and extracurricular activities of the Philadelphia group, see Frederick B. Tolles, *Meeting-House and Counting House: The Quaker Merchants of Colonial Philadelphia* (Chapel Hill, 1948), 109; and Bridenbaugh, *Rebels and Gentlemen.*

72:2   Davey & Carson, Letter Book, Feb. 15, 1746/7; Scull and Heap, *Man of Philadelphia; American Gazetteer,* III (under Philadelphia); Gipson, *Lewis Evans,* 102; *Pa. Mag.,* XXIV (ship registers, 1743–60); XXXVIII, 137 (launching); *Pa. Jour.,* Feb. 19, 1754.

73:1   John Banister, Account Book, 1739–44 (NHS), 111, 124, 172, 183, 214; Banister, Letter Book, 1739, pp. 4, 35; Banister, Letter Book, 1748–50, Mar. 30, 1747; Elizabeth Donnan, *Documents Illustrative of the History of the Slave Trade to America* (Washington, 1932), III, 134, 137, 140, 143; *N.Y. Post Boy,* May 20, 1745; *Bos. Eve. Post,* Sept. 28, 1747; Bridenbaugh, *Peter Harrison,* 10; Bridenbaugh, *Colonial Craftsman,* 92.

73:2   In April 1743, Newbury shipwrights launched six ships that had been on the stocks only nine months and laid keels of ten more "to be launched in half the time." *Bos. Eve. Post,* Apr. 11, 1743;

14 *Bos. Rec. Com.,* 13, 99; Albert B. Hart, ed., *Commonwealth History of Massachusetts* (New York, 1928), II, 400; John Custis, Letter Book (Typescript, LC), 173, 181.

73:3   *N.Y. Gaz.,* Oct. 29, 1744; NYHS *Colls.,* 1885, *passim;* Kalm, *Travels,* I, 95; S.C. Commons, Jour., XXV, 15; Meriwether, *Expansion of South Carolina, 29n;* D. P. Coke, *Royal Commission on the Losses and Services of American Loyalists* (Oxford, 1915), 267; Leila Sellers, *Charleston Business on the Eve of the Revolution* (Chapel Hill, 1934), 62.

74:1   On Dec. 23, 1749, Peter Kalm learned of a man at Philadelphia who, by a secret process, made spermaceti candles that Benjamin Franklin was using. Kalm, *Travels,* II, 664; Newp. T.M. Recs., 492; *Pa. Jour.,* Jan. 30, 1753; *Commerce of R.I.,* I, 65, 92; *Newp. Merc.,* Apr. 10, 1759; Cuyler, Letter Book, Dec. 5, 1759; Shipton, *Biographical Sketches,* VII, 109; VIII, 467; Hedges, *Browns of Providence,* 89.

74:2   14 *Bos. Rec. Com.,* 12, 100; Justin Winsor, ed., *Memorial History of Boston . . . 1630–1880* (Boston, 1880), II, 447; *Pa. Jour.,* Aug. 22, 1751.

74:3   Stiles, Miscellaneous Papers, Sept. 13, 1761; Petitions to R.I. Assembly, VI, 13; G. Beekman, Letter Book, Sept. 3, 1748; Redwood, Journal, Sept. 7, 28, 1751; Samuel Freebody, Distilling-House Ledger, 1756–68 (NHS), Jan. 29, 1757.

75:1   The earliest suggestion of whiskey I have found is an advertisement of 1747 at Philadelphia for a man "who perfectly understands the Distilling of Grain," by which, of course, is meant rye, not corn. *Pa. Jour.,* Aug. 13, 1747; Mar. 28, May 9, 1751; *N.Y. Col. Docs.,* VI, 511; Stokes, *Iconography,* IV, 631; Pownall, *Topographical Description,* 44; *N.Y. Merc.,* Nov. 26, 1753; *Pa. Mag.,* XVII, 265; *Pa. Gaz.,* Sept. 14, 1758; July 31, 1760; *Pa. Jour.,* Mar. 5, 1745; *Md. Gaz.,* Mar. 15, 1753; *S.C. Gaz.,* Jan. 1, 1750; Feb. 22, 1752; July 1, 1756.

75:2   Nehemiah Allen, Account Book (HSP), II; *Pa. Gaz.,* Dec. 19, 1752; July 8, 1756; May 26, 1757; Bridenbaugh, *Colonial Craftsman,* 61, 74; Joseph Richardson, Letter Book, 1732–1757 (HSP), Mar. 1, 1757; Arthur C. Bining, *Pennsylvania Iron Manufacture in the Eighteenth Century* (Harrisburg, 1938), 49, 188; Laubach, Bucks County Hist. Soc., *Papers,* I, 234; 1 *Pa. Archives,* II, 53.

76:1   Bridenbaugh, *Colonial Craftsman,* 72, 82; Cuyler, Letter Book, I, Sept. 17, 1759; Isaac Stelle, Ledger (RIHS), June, 1744; John Stevens, Account Book, (privately owned); G. Beekman, Letter Book, Sept. 10, 1746; Oct. 5, 1747; loose paper *ca.* Feb. 1748; *Bos. Post Boy,* Aug. 23, 1742; *Newp. Merc.,* May 8,

1759; *N.Y. Post Boy,* June 4, 1744; S.C. Pub. Recs., XXIV, 310; *S.C. Gaz.,* Feb. 13, 1744; Feb. 17, 1759.

76:2   14 *Bos. Rec. Com.,* 12, 99.

76:3   The urban artisan is treated in detail in my *Colonial Craftsman.*

77:1   *Pa. Mag.,* XXVIII, 31; *Bos. Eve. Post,* Jan. 23, 1744; *Lloyd Papers,* II, 565.

77:2   *S.C. Gaz.,* July 6, 1747; Mar. 30, 1752; Nov. 11, 1756; Arthur H. Hirsch, *Huguenots of South Carolina* (Durham, 1928), 228; *N.Y. Merc.,* Oct. 1, Dec. 24, 1753; NYHS *Colls.,* 1885, p. 145; *Bos. Eve. Post,* June 14, 1756; *Pa. Gaz.,* Jan. 1, 1754.

77:3   William Beekman of New York who had sold both by wholesale and retail since 1749 announced in 1756 that he "intends for the future to sell by wholesale only. *N.Y. Gaz.,* July 26, 1756; *Bos. Wkly Advertiser,* Sept. 26, 1757; *Newsletter,* Oct. 12, 1758; *Pa. Jour.,* Apr. 21, Sept. 8, 1743; Jan. 8, 1745; *Bos. Eve. Post,* Nov. 26, 1759.

78:1   R.I. Col. Recs. (MS), V, 286; *Pa. Jour.,* Dec. 2, 9, 16, 1746; 17 *Bos. Rec. Com.,* 88, 106; *Newsletter,* June 9, 1748; *Bos. Post Boy,* Nov. 6, 1752; Newp. T.C. Recs., IX, 362; *Newp. Merc.,* Apr. 10, Oct. 9, 1759; *N.Y. Gaz.,* Nov. 10, 1755; *S.C. Gaz.,* May 22, *Sup.,* 1756; Apr. 19, 1760; Dec. 23, 30, 1760.

78:2   Mrs. Elizabeth Schuyler, Account Book, 1773–69 (NYHS); *Bos. Eve. Post,* July 25, 1748; May 1, 1758; *Bos. Wkly Advertiser,* Mar. 12, 1759.

79:1   Harrington, *N.Y. Merchant,* 88; *Pa. Jour.,* Apr. 10, 24, 1746; *N.Y. Merc.,* July 3, 1758; Mar. 26, 1759; Pownall, *Topographical Description,* 45; *Newsletter,* Aug. 18, 1743; Apr. 18, 1746; Jan. 18, 1759; *Bos. Wkly. Advertiser,* Jan. 15, Feb. 12, 1759; *Bos. Post Boy,* May 28, 1753.

79:2   *R. I. Acts* (1745), 240, 253; *R. I. Acts* (1752), 6, 25; *R.I. Col. Recs.,* VI, 94; *S.C. Gaz.,* Aug. 10, 17, 1747; S.C. Commons, Jour., XXV, 252; *S.C. Statutes,* III, 734; *Pa. Votes,* IV, 206; *Pa. Gaz.,* Feb. 4, June 20, 1755.

80:1   *London Mag.,* Mar. 1749, pp. 115, 161; *S.C. Gaz.,* Mar. 30, 1752; Christopher C. Crittenden, *Commerce of North Carolina* (New Haven, 1936), 30, 89n; *Md. Gaz.,* Mar. 29, 1753; Simpson, *Practical Justice of the Peace,* 114; *N.Y.M.C.C.,* V, 292; James Beekman Notes (by Philip White, NYHS), Box 16, folder 1, receipts of Robert Gregg, peddler; *Bos. Eve. Post,* Jan. 19, 1756.

80:2   14 *Bos. Rec. Com.,* 4, 20, 99, 141, 159.

81:1   Simpson, *Practical Justice of the Peace,* 132, 138; *S.C. Gaz.,* Apr. 23, 1737; Feb. 19, 1750; Apr. 5, 1760; Milling, *Colonial South Carolina,* 145; S.C. Commons, Jour., XXXIII, 160, 176,

177, 187; Charles Fraser, *Reminiscences of Charleston* (Charleston, 1854), 33; Newp. T. M. Recs., 482, 502, 510, 512, 528, 530, 666; Bridenbaugh, *Peter Harrison,* 105; Records of the Proprietors of Long Wharf (Transcript, 1857, Newport, R.I.), 273; *Newp. Merc., Mar.* 11, 1760.

81:2 "Our oysters are a considerable article in support of the poor. Their beds are within view of the town; a fleet of two hundred small craft are often seen there, at a time, when the weather is mild in winter; and this single article is computed to be worth annually 10 or £12,000." Smith, *New York,* I, 255; Moses Brown Papers (RIHS), I, 21; Birket, *Cursory Remarks,* 45; *Newp. Merc.,* Apr 17, 1759.

82:1 Bridenbaugh, *Gentleman's Progress,* 88; *P.M.C.C.,* 443, 446, 644, 658; I *Pa. Archives,* I, 675; *Pa. Gaz.,* Sept. 8, 1748; Mittelberger, *Journey,* 65, 70; *Pa. Mag.,* XVII, 266; Kalm, *Travels,* I, 30; Birket, *Cursory Remarks,* 66, 69; Burnaby, *Travels,* 90.

82:2 S.C. Commons, Jour., XXI, 357; Newp. T.M. Recs., 404, 406, 665; Court Papers, Phila. Co., IV, Feb. 14, 1754; *N.Y.M.C.C.,* V, 85.

83:1 *Bos. Eve. Post,* Feb. 1, 1748; *Bos. Post Boy,* Apr. 13, 1747; *Newsletter,* July 12, 1744; Jan. 26, 1758; Nov. 8, 1759; *N.Y. Eve. Post,* Nov. 7, 1748; July 31, 1749.

83:2 14 *Bos. Rec. Com.,* index under "Grain," "Granary"; *S.C. Gaz.,* Apr. 2, 11, 18, 23, 1753; *Newp. Merc.,* Jan. 1, 1760.

83:3 For earlier municipal regulations of economic affairs, see *Cities,* I, 49, 198.

84:1 *Bos. Post Boy,* Mar. 25, 1754; 19 *Bos. Rec. Com.,* 57; *S.C. Gaz.,* Nov. 5, 1744; Apr. 9, 16, 1750; *S.C. Statutes,* III, 715; *N.Y. Eve. Post,* Nov. 14, 1748; Oct. 7, 1752; Bos. *Ind. Advertiser,* Sept. 26, 1748.

84:2 *N.Y. Gaz.,* Oct. 22, 1750; *Jour. of Legis. Council of N.Y.,* II, 1127; *N.Y. Post Boy,* Jan. 28, 1745; *N.Y. Gen. Assembly Jour.,* II, 294; Stokes, *Iconography,* IV, 623; *N.Y. Col. Laws,* III, 788; *Ind. Reflector,* May 10, 1753; *S.C. Gaz.,* Dec. 19, 1748.

85:1 *Ind. Reflector,* Nov. 22, 1755; Tavern Keepers Licences, 1756–66, (NYHS); 14 *Bos. Rec. Com.,* 11, 313, 325; 17 *Bos. Rec. Com.,* 13, 54; 15 *Bos. Rec. Com.,* 334; S. C. Commons, Jour., XXV, 251; *S.C. Gaz.,* July 9, 16, 1750; May 15, 1755; *Pa. Votes,* V, 57; Birket, *Cursory Remarks,* 59.

85:2 In 1750 Liverpool authorities were still prosecuting "foreigners being not free of this burrough." James A. Picton, *Municipal Archives and Records* (Liverpool, 1886), 120, 122; McAnear, *N.Y. History,* XXI, 423, 425.

86:1 Bridenbaugh, *Colonial Craftsman; N.Y. Gaz.,* Mar. 19, 1753;

R.I. Col. Recs., V, 289; 364; Col. Soc. Mass., *Pubs.,* XXXV, 101.

86:2 St. Philip's Vestry, Minutes, I, 73, 75, 94, 121, 130, 158, 190; II, 17; Simpson, *Practical Justice of the Peace,* 16, 18.

87:2 NYHS, *Colls.,* 1868, p. 360; 1896, pp. 35, 332; *N.Y. Col. Docs.,* V, 511; Edwards, *New York,* 62; *R.I. Col. Recs.,* VI, 379; *Newsletter,* Dec. 23, 1742; *N.Y. Merc.,* Aug. 7, 1758.

87:3 Mittelberger, *Journey,* 26; *Pa. Gaz.,* Nov. 9, 1752; *Pa. Jour.,* Jan. 13, 1757; Muhlenberg, *Journals,* I, 304.

88:1 With evident exaggeration, Muhlenberg estimated slaves at "fifteen to every white man" in 1742, *Journals,* I, 58; Col. Soc. Mass., *Pubs.,* VIII, 245; Greene and Harrington, *American Population,* 22, 66, 67, 101; 2 MHS *Colls.,* III, 95; Donnan, *Amer. Hist. Rev.,* XXXIII, 807; Donnan, *Slave Trade,* III, 147*n,* 150.

89:1 Wilson, *Mem. Hist. N.Y.,* II, 314; Col. Soc. Mass., *Pubs.,* XXV, 253; *Newp. Merc.,* Jan. 16, 1759; S. C. Commons, Jour., XIX, 144, 159; S. C. Council, Jour., XII, 6, 7, 8, 9; *S.C. Gaz.,* Nov. 5, 1744; June 18, 1750; May 13, 1751; Aug. 26, 1756; Bridenbaugh, *Colonial Craftsman,* 122, 138.

89:2 Smith, *New York,* I, 277; *American Gazetteer,* III (under New York); Burnaby, *Travels,* 127; Bridenbaugh, *Gentleman's Progress,* 44, 107; *N.Y. Merc.,* Mar. 4, 1754; *Newsletter,* Mar. 29, 1750; *Bos. Post Boy,* June 8, 1747.

90:1 Baxter, *House of Hancock,* 11, 185; Bridenbaugh, *Peter Harrison,* 86; *Pa. Gaz.,* Oct. 18, 1753; Oct. 30, Nov. 13, Dec. 11, 1760; *Md. Gaz.,* Apr. 23, 1761.

90:2 Interest from currency lent out by Pennsylvania's Loan Office paid all the regular expenses of the province from about 1730 paid all the regular expenses of the province from about 1730 to 1754, relieving the people from annual direct taxes—a matter of great significance in explaining Philadelphia's rapid economic growth. Ferguson, 3 *W. & M. Quart.,* X, 157, 159, 161, 163, 169; *Pa. Votes,* IV, 38, 96; *S.C. Gaz.,* Dec. 11, 1749; *SCHG Mag.,* XXXV, 125; *Pa. Gaz.,* July 26, 1753; Thomas Pownall, *Administration of the Colonies* (London, 1768), 185.

91:1 Gipson, *British Empire,* III, 70; *Amer. Mag. & Hist'l Chron.,* I, 264, 307; Petitions to R. I. Assembly, VII, 133; *R. I. Col. Recs.,* V, 311, 315, 329, 331; Letters to George Whitefield, 1738–69 (NYPL), Van Horne to Whitefield, Nov. 12, 1750; Leo F. Stock, *Proceedings and Debates of the British Parliament respecting North America* (Washington, 1941), V, xi, 464, 465, 511; Kimball, *R. I. Governors,* I, 291*n; Bos. Eve. Post,* July 15, 1751.

91:2 Pownall, *Administration of the Colonies,* 220; Bos. *Ind. Adver-*

tiser, Mar. 28, 1748; *Newsletter,* July 7, 1748; *Lloyd Papers,* I, 372, 380, 399; Andrew M. Davis, *Currency and Banking in the Province of the Massachusetts Bay* (New York, 1900), 233, 234, 242, 250, 251; *Acts Privy Council,* IV, 81; *Pa. Jour.,* Oct. 5, 1749; *Mass. Acts,* III, 544.

92:1   Davis, *Currency and Banking in Mass.,* 234; *Lloyd Papers,* I, 450, 484; *Pa. Jour.,* May 3, June 7, 1750.

92:2   *Lloyd Papers,* I, 462, 476, 483; Baxter, *House of Hancock,* 112; *Pa. Jour.,* Aug. 2, 1750.

92:3   As early as July 7, 1748, a citizen wrote for the *Boston News-letter* a judicious proposal for "a gradual Consumption of Old Tenor," which "will give us time to look about us, and wisely and maturely consider the Best Methods to be used, for the Good of the Public." *Newsletter,* July 7, 1748; but cf. Thomas Hutchinson, *History of the Province of the Massachusetts Bay* (Cambridge, 1936), II, 333; For the 1780's, see Oscar and Mary F. Handlin, *Commonwealth* (New York, 1947), 13.

93:1   Donnan, *Slave Trade,* III, 147, 168; *Commerce of R. I.,* I, 72, 73; G. Beekman, Letter Book, G. B. to Peleg Thurston, May 6, 1747; Cuyler, Letter Book, I, P. Cuyler to John Tweedy, June 18, July 12, 1758; June 30, July 14, 1760; Harrington, *N.Y. Merchant,* 154, 155, 161; Redwood, Journal, II, 1756–1759; James & Drinker, Letter Book, 1759–62, II, James & Drinker to Samuel Franklin, May 1, 1760; Hedges, *Browns of Providence,* 72; on Charles Town factors, see advertisements for Glen & Cooper, William Gibbes, John Benfield, Hutchins & Pole in *S.C. Gaz.,* Nov. 13, 1751; Sept. 17, 1753; Feb. 17, 1759; Dec. 6, 1760.

93:2   *Newsletter,* June 2, 1743; Nov. 21, Dec. 26, 1745; *Bos. Eve. Post,* Oct. 28, 1745; Mar. 14, 1748; Dec. 10, 1749; Sept. 6, 1756; Harrington, *N.Y. Merchant,* 154; *N.Y. Gaz.,* Aug. 21, 27, Sept. 17, 1759; *Pa. Gaz.,* Aug. 13, 1752; Sept. 13, 1759; *Pa. Jour.,* May 7, Aug. 20, 1752; Sept. 30, 1756; Harrold E. Gillingham, *Marine Insurance in Philadelphia, 1721–1800* (Philadelphia, 1933), 11, 18, 31, 42, 52, 55, 64, 103, 110.

94:1   *Bos. Eve. Post,* July 1, 1745; *N.Y. Post Boy,* May 6, 1745; *N.Y. Gaz.,* Jan. 19, 1756; *Pa. Gaz.,* Jan. 2, 1749; *Pa. Jour.,* Mar. 11, 1755.

94:2   *Pa. Jour.,* Aug. 12, Sept. 30, 1756; Feb. 16, 1758; *Pa. Gaz.,* July 3, 1755.

94:3   *Lloyd Papers,* II, 563, 569, 586; Stiles, *Itineraries,* 72; *Newp. Merc.,* Apr. 10, 1759; Harrington, *N.Y. Merchant,* 126, 131; James & Drinker, Letter Book, May 9, 1760; Philip Syng, Account Book, 1759–83 (LC).

95:1   *S.C. Gaz.,* Feb. 1, Aug. 23, 1746; Jan. 1, *Sup.,* Mar. 9, Aug. 10, 1752; July 29, 1756.

96:1   Hart, *Commonwealth Hist. of Mass.,* II, 172, 181; Shipton, *Biographical Sketches,* IV, 375; VII, 520; *Lloyd Papers,* I, 450, 453, 462, II, 522; E. Alfred Jones, *American Members of the Inns of Court* (London, 1924); Col. Soc. Mass., *Pubs.,* XXXV, 98; *Ind. Reflector,* July 30, 1753; *Pa. Jour.,* Feb. 7, 1748/9; Jan. 17, 1754; Oct. 2, 1755; Alexander Papers, I, 32; *S.C. Gaz.,* Sept. 25, 1755. For legal training in America, see Paul M. Hamlin, *Legal Education in Colonial New York* (New York, 1939).

96:2   Ruth Butler, *Benjamin Franklin, Postmaster General* (New York, 1928); B. Franklin, *Directions to the Deputy Post Masters for Keeping their Accounts* (Broadsides, Ab. vol. V, 631, HSP); *Pa. Gaz.,* July 5, 1753; Feb. 11, Mar. 25, 1755; Aug. 21, 1760.

96:3   Riders carried letters, newspapers and parcels from Charles Town to Pon Pon and Jacksonborough. *S.C. Gaz.,* Mar. 7, May 16, 1743; Feb. 8, 1748; July 4, Dec. 5, 1754; Aug. 19, 26, 1756.

97:1   *Pa. Mag.,* XXI, 104; *Pa. Jour.,* May 26, 1757; *Pa. Gaz.,* Sept. 3, 1747; Feb. 19, 1751; Apr. 19, 1759; *N.Y. Eve. Post,* Dec. 17, 1744; *Bos. Wkly. Advertiser,* July 17, Aug. 14, 1758; Nov. 12, 1759.

CHAPTER III

98:1   The development of urban problems is traced in *Cities,* I, chaps. III, VII, XI.

99:1   *N.Y. Gaz.,* Apr. 24, Sept. 11, 1749; 17 *Bos. Rec. Com.,* 17, 18, 220, 221, 239; *Mass. Acts,* III, 429; IV, 378.

99:2   *S.C. Gaz.,* May 16, 1743; Apr. 1, 1745; July 30, 1753; July 31, 1755; *Bos. Eve. Post,* Aug. 25, 1755; *Philosophical Transactions of the Royal Society of London* (London, 1809), X, 522.

99:3   14 *Bos. Rec. Com.,* 53, 62; *Bos. Wkly. Advertiser,* Nov. 13, 1758; Newp. T.M. Recs., 370, 372; *S.C. Gaz.,* Nov. 5, 1744.

100:1   *S.C. Gaz.,* July 31, 1755; Court Papers, Phila. Co., V, 1760; *N.Y.M.C.C.,* VI, 116; *R.I. Col. Recs.,* V, 4; *R.I. Acts* (1767), 113; Newp. T.M. Recs, 512, 518, 562; S.C. Commons, Jour., XXX, 640; *Pa. Gaz.,* Jan. 10, 1760.

100:2   14 *Bos. Rec. Com.,* 30, 230; 16 *Bos. Rec. Com.,* 44; 17 *Bos. Rec. Com.,* 184; 19 *Bos. Rec. Com.,* 76, 78; *N.Y. Gaz.,* Mar. 12, 1753.

101:1   *Pa. Jour.,* Nov. 17, 1743; Jan. 1, 1744/5; *Bos. Post Boy,* Sept. 21, Dec. 14, 1747; July 30, 1753.

101:2   MHS *Colls.,* III, 270; *Bos. Post Boy,* Mar. 24, 1760.

102:1   29 *Bos. Rec. Com.,* contains documents on the fire and its after-math including detailed losses of each family and the distribution of charity money. See also 16 *Bos. Rec. Com.,* 40, 41; 19 *Bos. Rec. Com.,* 129; Stiles, *Itineraries,* 120; 1 *Pa. Archives,* III, 714.

102:2   Thompson Westcott, *History of the Philadelphia Fire Department* (Clippings, HSP), chaps., VII, X, XI, XIII; *Pa. Gaz.,* Jan. 13, 1742/3; NYHS *Quart. Bulletin,* XX, 71.

103:1   Myers, *Hannah Logan's Courtship,* 205; Elizabeth Drinker, Diary (HSP), Sept. 24, 1760; Union Fire Co., Minutes (LCP), 22, 38, 90, 105, 151, 211; *Pa. Gaz.,* Nov. 29, 1744.

103:2   *Pa. Gaz.,* Jan. 13, 1742/3; Balch, *Letters,* Dec. 9, 1757.

103:3   *Bos. Post Boy,* June 27, 1748; Union Fire Co., Minutes, 117, 118, 151; Nicholas B. Wainwright, *A Philadelphia Story* (Philadelphia, 1952), 21; *Pa. Gaz.,* July 25, 1751.

104:1   *Pa. Gaz.,* Feb. 4, 1752; *Pa. Jour.,* June 11, 1752; *Bos. Post Boy,* Jan. 7, 1754; *Pa. Votes,* IV, 78, 101; Wainwright, *Philadelphia Story,* 26.

104:2   Edwards, *New York,* 133, 137; *N.Y. Eve. Post,* June 24, 1745; Feb. 26, 1750; *N.Y. Gaz.,* Jan. 19, 26, 1746/7; Feb. 5, 1750; *Ind. Reflector,* Jan. 12, 1753.

105:1   *Bos. Eve. Post,* Feb. 7, 1743; *Newsletter,* Apr. 21, 1743; Engine No. 1, Minutes (NHS), I; Newp. T. M. Recs., 382, 392, 418, 445, 446, 449, 480, 486, 576, 580, 617; R.I. Col. Recs. (MS), VI, 193; *R.I. Hist. Mag.,* VI, 76.

105:2   *S.C. Gaz.,* Jan. 23, 1744; Nov. 7, 1754; May 6, June 17, 1756; *S. C. Statutes,* IV, 72, 143.

106:1   *Mass. Acts,* IV, 378.

106:2   In 1743 the first two public wells were sunk at Liverpool. Picton, *Municipal Archives,* 137; Bridenbaugh, *Gentleman's Progress,* 21; Kalm, *Travels,* I, 25; *Pa. Statutes,* V, 111, 224, 284; Union Fire Co., Minutes, 156.

106:3   *S. C. Gaz.,* Jan. 1, 1752; May 6, *Sup.,* 1756; June 30, 1759; Nov. 15, 1760.

107:1   Birket, *Cursory Remarks,* 44; *N.Y.M.C.C.,* V, 219, 223, 234, 291; *N.Y. Gaz.,* Nov. 5, 1750; Muhlenberg, *Journals,* I, 307; *Ind. Reflector,* Jan. 12, 1753; *N.Y. Col. Laws,* III, 942.

107:2   In 1749 Liverpool received authority to erect a night watch. Corry, *Liverpool,* 117; Latimer, *Bristol in 18th Century,* 340, 355.

108:1   Seybolt, *Town Officials of Colonial Boston,* 229, 238, 251, 273, 290; *Newp. Hist. Mag.,* I, 251; *N.Y. Eve. Post,* Feb. 18, Apr. 15, 1745; *Pa. Mag.,* XL, 120; Simpson, *Practical Justice of the Peace,* 84.

108:2   Newp. T.M. Recs., 382, 438, 560, 562, 590; *R.I. Col. Recs.,* VI, 51; *N.Y. Gaz.,* Oct. 1, 1744; Mason, *Reminiscences of Newport* (NHS copy), IV, 282A.

108:3   *Cities,* I, 375; *Bos. Eve. Post,* Feb. 22, 1742; July 1, 1745; *N.Y. Eve. Post,* Nov. 25, 1745; 14 *Bos. Rec. Com.,* 117; 17 *Bos. Rec. Com.,* 21, 26.

109:1   Edwards, *New York,* 123; *Ind. Reflector,* Dec. 14, 1752.

109:2   *P.M.C.C.,* 418, 425, 512, 522; *Pa. Votes,* III, 526; IV, 5, 176; *Pa. Gaz.,* June 6, 1751; *Pa. Statutes,* V, 111; VI, 309.

110:1   *S.C. Statutes,* III, 683; S.C. Commons, Jour., XVIII, 586; XXI, 305; XXXIII, 28; *S.C. Gaz.,* Nov. 5, 1744; Apr. 15, 1745; Mar. 13, 1749; May 28, 1754; S.C. Pub. Recs., XIII, 39.

110:2   *Pa. Gaz.,* Apr. 11, Sept. 5, 1751; *Ind. Reflector,* Mar. 15, 1753.

111:1   *Pa. Gaz.,* June 16, 1743; Jan. 3, 1743/4; Aug. 14, Sept. 18, 1746; *Bos. Post Boy,* Mar. 7, 1743; *Bos. Eve. Post,* Dec. 19, 1743; *N.Y. Eve. Post,* Mar. 25, 1745; Sept. 4, 1749; *Pa. Jour.,* Feb. 28, 1748/9; *Va. Gaz.,* July 17, 1752; *S.C. Gaz.,* July 18, Aug. 8, 1754; *N.Y. Gaz.,* Oct. 9, 1752; *Pa. Mag.,* III, 145.

112:1   *Bos. Post Boy,* Sept. 4, 1749; Aug. 12, Sept. 16, 1751; *Pa. Jour.,* Aug. 30, 1744; *Bos. Eve. Post,* Apr. 12, Oct. 9, 1752; *Bos. Gaz.,* May 24, 1756; *Pa. Gaz.,* Aug. 9, 1744; *N.Y. Gaz.,* May 10, 1756.

112:2   Bridenbaugh, *Gentleman's Progress,* 116; *Pa. Gaz.,* Sept. 5, 1751; *Bos. Post Boy,* Feb. 25, 1760; Bos. *Ind. Advertiser,* Jan. 16, 1749; *N.Y. Post Boy,* May 5, 1746; *N.Y. Gaz.,* Sept. 4, 1760.

112:3   *S.C. Gaz.,* Apr. 6, 1752; July 4, 1754; Dec. 29, 1759.

113:1   Court Papers, Phila., Co., IV, V; *P.M.C.C.,* 466-669; *Pa. Jour.,* Dec. 10, 1747; Oct. 26, 1749; *Md. Gaz.,* Feb. 15, 1758; *Bos. Post Boy,* Feb. 25, 1751.

113:2   Bos. *Ind. Advertiser,* Jan. 9, 1749; *Pa. Jour.,* Oct. 3, 1751; *N.Y. Post Boy,* Mar. 12, 1750; *N.Y. Gaz.,* Aug. 19, 1754; Feb. 20, 1758; Feb. 11, 1760; *N.Y. Merc.,* Dec. 27, 1756; *Newp. Merc.,* Jan. 23, 1759.

114:1   A. S. Turberville, ed., *Johnson's England* (Oxford, 1933), I, 221; Morris Craig, *Dublin, 1660–1860* (New York, 1952), 88.

114:2   *Bos. Eve. Post,* May 7, 1744; Nov. 11, 1745; 17 *Bos. Rec. Com.,* 102; *Pa. Jour.,* Nov. 21, 1745; *Bos. Post Boy,* Nov. 5, 1750; *Mass. Acts,* III, 647, 997.

115:1   Admiral Sir Peter Warren thought the act forbidding impressment in the colonies was still in force. Stock, *Debates of British Parliament,* V, 236; MHS *Procs.,* XVIII, 370, 371; 15 *Bos. Rec. Com.,* 315; Letters of Admiral Warren, P.R.O., Admiralty I (LC Transcript), 480:78; *Newsletter,* Nov. 14, 1745; *Bos.*

Post Boy, Nov. 25, 1745; Mar. 24, 1746; 14 *Bos. Rec. Com.,* 84, 86; *N.Y. Post Boy,* Dec. 2, 1745.

116:1 Col. Soc. Mass., *Pubs.,* III, 214, 216; Charles H. Lincoln, ed., *Correspondence of William Shirley* (New York, 1912), I, 406, 412; *Bos. Post Boy,* Nov. 23, 1747.

116:2 In 1750 the General Court of Massachusetts reached the significant conclusion that in any future war Great Britain should be requested to require each of the American colonies "to bear their respective Proportions of such a War, both as to Men and Money," and that Massachusetts be freed from any "impresses" by the Royal Navy. *Journals of the House of Representatives of Massachusetts, 1749–1750* (Boston, 1951), XXIV, 212; XXVI, 165; *Bos. Post Boy,* Dec. 21, 1747; Jan. 4, 1748; *Shirley Correspondence,* I, 406; *Bos. Ind. Advertiser,* Jan. 4, 1748; 17 *Bos. Rec. Com.,* 116, 125.

117:1 *Shirley Correspondence,* I, 418; *Bos. Ind. Advertiser,* Feb. 8, 1748; May 30, 1748.

117:2 *Mass. Acts, II,* 544; *Newsletter,* Oct. 28, 1756; Drake, *History of Boston,* 627; 19 *Bos. Rec. Com.,* 97.

118:1 Kimball, *R. I. Governors,* 235, 240; Newp. T. C. Recs., IX, 1; *N.Y. Post Boy,* Sept. 24, 1744; July 15, 1745; *N.Y. Wkly Jour.,* May 16, 1743; *N.Y. Gaz.,* Sept. 16, 1751; Jan. 26, 1754; Myers, *Hannah Logan's Courtship,* 69, 76; *N.Y. Col. Docs.,* VI, 471; Muhlenberg, *Journals,* I, 301; G. Beekman, Letter Book, June 23, 1747; Sept. 23, 1748; Julian P. Boyd, *Susquehannah Company Papers* (Wilkes-Barre, 1930), I, xiii; John C. Long, *Lord Jeffery Amherst* (New York, 1933), 124.

118:2 R.I. Col. Recs. (MS), V, 560; *N.Y.M.C.C.,* V, 253; Birket, *Cursory Remarks,* 44; Edwards, *New York,* 102; S.C. Pub. Recs., XX, 97; *S.C. Gaz.,* Apr. 15, 1745; Dec. 13, 1751; Fulham Palace MSS (LC Trans.), S.C., 91.

118:3 Drake, *Hist. of Boston,* 635; *N.Y. Gaz.,* Mar. 11, 18, 1751; Court Papers, Phila. Co., II, Oct. 29, 1744; *S.C. Gaz.,* Dec. 1, 1758.

119:1 *R.I. Acts* (1767), 211; *N.Y. Eve. Post,* Jan. 22, 1750; *Jour. of Legis. Council of N.Y.,* II, 2032; Court Papers, Phila., Co., V, Oct. 1751.

119:3 Latimer, *Bristol in 18th Century,* 263; *Bos. Wkly Advertiser,* Nov. 14, 1757; *N.Y. Eve. Post,* Mar. 2, 1747; Newp. T.M. Recs., 437; *Pa. Statutes,* V, 42.

120:1 Latimer, *Bristol in 18th Century,* 306, 336; *Pa. Gaz.,* Jan. 3, 1749; Dec. 11, 1760; 17 *Bos. Rec. Com.,* 29, 76; *Bos. Wkly Advertiser,* June 19, 1758; *Newsletter,* June 12, 1746; Mar. 28,

1754; Sept. 11, 1760; Newp. T.M. Recs., 372, 568; *S.C. Gaz.,* Jan. 5, 19, Mar 30, 1747.

120:2   NHS *Bulletin,* I, 3; *R.I. Acts* (1767), 132; Stokes, *Iconography,* IV, 606; *N.Y. Eve. Post,* Apr. 29, 1745; *N.Y.M.C.C.,* VI, 204; *S.C. Statutes,* III, 729; *Pa. Statutes,* V, 445; *Sophia Hume's Exhortation and Epistles to the People of South Carolina* (London, 1752), 43.

121:1   *S.C. Gaz.,* Jan. 3, Nov. 7, 1743; *N.Y. Wkly Jour.,* Jan. 2, 1748/9; Bridenbaugh, *Gentleman's Progress,* 88.

121:2   Newp. T.C. Recs., IX, 7, 21, 271; Bridenbaugh, *Gentleman's Progress,* 151; R.I. Monthly Meeting, Minutes, 121, 146, 154, 180; Muhlenberg, *Journals,* I, 58; *S.C. Gaz.,* Mar. 28, 1743; Shipton, *Biographical* Sketches, VII, 577.

121:3   Bridenbaugh, *Gentleman's Progress,* 46; *N.Y. Post Boy,* July 25, 1743; *Newsletter,* Feb. 24, 1743; *Mass. Acts,* IV, 178; *N.Y. Gaz.,* Aug. 13, 1750; Feb. 4, 1750/1.

122:1   Newp. T.C. Recs., IX, 7; Col. Soc. Mass., *Pubs.,* XXXIV, 14, 15; *Md. Gaz.,* June 28, Aug. 9, 1753; Drake, *Hist. of Boston,* 633; *P.M.C.C.,* 445, 561; Graydon, *Memoirs,* 47.

122:2   *N.Y. Merc.,* July 23, 1753; *N.Y. Gaz.,* Aug. 11, 1755; *Newsletter,* Oct. 30, 1760; *Colden Letter Book,* I, 43.

123:1   R.I. Col. Recs., (MS) VI, 509; *Ind. Reflector,* Dec. 28, 1752; Myers, *Hannah Logan's Courtship,* 152.

123:2   17 *Bos. Rec. Com., passim;* 19 *Bos. Rec. Com., passim.*

124:1   St. Philip's Vestry, Minutes, I, 152, 155, 179; II, 1757–60; S.C. Commons, Jour., XXIX, 79, 80, 200; XXXII, 32; XXXIII, 10; S.C. Council, Jour., XXII, 85.

124:2   Boston had 1200 widows in December, 1742, "one Thousand whereof are in low Circumstances and a great Number of other Persons so poor that they are not Taxed." 15 *Bos. Rec. Com.,* 369; *Pa. Jour.,* Sept. 5, 1751; At Newport, out of 397 Congregational and Episcopal families in 1760, there were 59 widows. Stiles, *Itineraries,* 13; Newp. T.C. Recs., IX, 244; St. Philip's Vestry, Minutes, I, 193, 245; II, 12; III, 22; *Pa. Mag.,* X, 481.

124:3   *N.Y. Gaz.,* June 11, 1750; Newp. T.M. Rec., 554, 674; Newp. T.C. Rec., IX, 117; *R.I. Acts* (1767), 197.

125:1   At Glasgow in 1750, "every child was at work, and not a begger was to be seen," Graham, *Social Life of Scotland,* 129; *Industry and Frugality Proposed as the Surest Means to make us a Rich and Flourishing People and the Linen Manufacture Recommended . . . with Some Cursory Remarks on Charity* (Boston, 1753), 7, 8, 10, 13; *NEHG Reg.,* XLIV, 100; *Pa. Jour.,* Sept. 5, 1751; *Bos. Post Boy,* Feb. 19, Mar. 12, July 30, 1753; King's MSS., 206:4; Hart, *Hist. of Mass.,* II, 408.

125:2 17 *Bos. Rec. Com.,* 20, 23, 37; 19 *Bos. Rec. Com.,* 56, 107; *N.Y.M.C.C.,* V, 171, 466; VI, 143; S.C. Commons, Jour., XX, 173; *S.C. Gaz.,* Nov. 26, 1753; St. Philip's Vestry, Minutes, I, 196; II, April 30, 1759; July 21, 1760; Newp. T.C. Recs., IX, 21, XII, 9.

126:1 Newp. T.M. Recs., 366, 478, 674, 676; St. Philip's Vestry, Minutes, I, 164, 204, 215; *S.C. Statutes,* VII, 79; George S. Brookes, *Friend Anthony Benezet* (Philadelphia, 1937), 64; *Pa. Votes,* IV, 705, 708; *Mass. Acts,* III, 108; *R.I. Acts* (1767), 197.

126:2 14 *Bos. Rec. Com.,* 89; St. Philip's Vestry, Minutes, I, 248; S.C. Commons, Jour., XXX, 150; *Pa. Votes,* IV, 175; *R.I. Acts* (1744), 249.

126:3 St. Philip's Vestry, Minutes, I, 121, 197, 251; II, 2, 18, 23; *S.C. Statutes,* IV, 49; 16 *Bos. Rec. Com.,* 57; *N.Y.M.C.C.,* VI, 167; *Pa. Votes,* IV, 6, 7; *Pa. Statutes,* V, 79; Westcott, *Hist. of Philadelphia,* II, chap. CXLV.

127:1 R.I. Monthly Meeting, Minutes, 58, 93, 122; *Newsletter,* June 4, 1752; *Bos. Post Boy,* Sept. 23, Oct. 7, 1754; Mar. 31, Aug. 11, 1760; *N.Y. Col. Laws,* IV, 454; Stiles, *Itineraries,* 112; St. Philip's Vestry, Minutes, I, 217.

127:2 Wilmarth S. Lewis and Ralph M. Williams, *Private Charity in England, 1747–1757* (New Haven, 1938); M. Dorothy George, *London Life in the Eighteenth Century* (London, 1925), 19, 320; *Constitution and By-Laws of the Charitable Scots Society of Boston* (Cambridge, 1867), 47, 63, 106, 128; Bridenbaugh, *Gentleman's Progress,* 133; Episcopal Charitable Society in New England (MS in MHS); *Constitution and By-Laws of the Charitable Irish Society of Boston* (Boston, 1876), 26; *Newsletter,* Mar. 1, 1750; *Mass. Acts,* III, 708; Mason, *Reminiscences of Newport* (RIHS copy in MS), II, 104; R.I. Land Recs. (R.I. Arch.), VI, 365; *Historical Catalogue of the St. Andrew's Society of Philadelphia* (Philadelphia, 1913), I, 14, 28, 36; *Pa. Jour.,* Feb. 13, 1749/50; *Records of the Presbyterian Church* (Philadelphia, 1841), I, 215; *Pa. Gaz.,* June 5, 1760; George A. Morrison, *History of the St. Andrew's Society of the State of New York* (New York, 1906), 7.

128:1 List of "Publick" Societies, *S.C. Almanack, 1763; S.C. Statutes,* VIII, 106; J. H. Easterby, *History of the St. Andrew's Society of Charleston* (Charleston, 1929), 20, 34, 43; *Centennial Celebration of the South Carolina Society* (Charleston, 1837), vi. 18, 59; *St. George's Society of Charleston* (Charleston, 1898), 3.

128:2 The incidence of the terrible contagion of 1735–1740 was much greater in rural New England than in the cities. Ernest M. Caulfield, *A True History of the . . . Throat Distemper* (New Haven, 1939); Ernest M. Caulfield, *The Infant Welfare Movement in the Eighteenth Century* (New York, 1931); Turberville, *Johnson's England,* I, 209; M. C. Buer, *Health, Wealth, and Population in the Early Days of the Industrial Revolution* (London, 1926), 102, 104.

129:1 John Bonner and William Price, *A New Plan of the Great Town of Boston* (Boston, 1743); 14 *Bos. Rec. Com.,* 120, 257; 17 *Bos. Rec. Com.,* 23, 38; 19 *Bos. Rec. Com.,* 39; *Mass. Acts,* III, 898; *N.Y. Post Boy,* Jan. 2, 9, 1743/4; *Colden Papers,* III, 46, 95; *N.Y.M.C.C.,* V, 113, 117, 118; *P.M.C.C.,* 487, 494; *S.C. Gaz.,* Nov. 5, 1744; Mar. 10, 1757; *S.C. Statutes,* III, 773; Muhlenberg, *Journals,* I, 281, 307.

129:2 *Mass. Acts,* III, 124, 476; *Bos. Post Boy,* Feb. 10, 1746; Nov. 25, 1751; Jan. 13, Feb. 10, Mar. 23, Apr. 13, June 8, July 6, Aug. 10, 17, 1752; 17 *Bos. Rec. Com.,* 277, 283; *Pa. Geschichtschreiber,* July 1, 16, 1752; *Pa. Jour.,* July 16, 1752; *Va. Gaz.,* May 29, 1752.

130:1 Some accounts placed Negro deaths as high as five hundred. *N.Y. Eve. Post,* Nov. 18, 1745; *S.C. Gaz.,* June 13, 1743; *S.C. Statutes,* III, 694, 720; S.C. Commons, Jour., XIX, 128, XXIV, 458.

130:2 J. E. Smith, *A Selection of the Correspondence of Linnaeus and other Naturalists* (London, 1821), I, 473, 483; Harriott P. Holbrook, *Journal and Letters of Eliza Lucas* (Wormsloe, Georgia, 1850), 16; *Newp. Merc.,* Feb. 26, 1760; *New London Summary* Mar. 7, 1760; *S.C. Gaz.,* Mar. 1, 1760.

130:3 *S.C. Gaz.,* Mar. 22, Apr. 19, 26, Nov. 8, Dec. 6, 1760; *Newp. Merc.,* Apr. 22, 1760; *Pa. Gaz.,* June 26, 1760.

131:1 *Pa. Statutes,* IV, 382; *Pa. Votes,* III, 519; IV, 121; 1 *Pa. Archives,* I, 769, III, 82; *Pa. Gaz.,* July 26, 1759; *Pa. Mag.* VII, 21, XXXVI, 476; *N.Y. Gaz.,* Mar. 5, 1744; June 22, 1747; *N.Y. Col. Laws,* III, 1071; IV, 76.

131:2 Most Newport and Providence people who wished to be inoculated joined New York acquaintances for treatment by Dr. Barnard of Elizabeth Town in New Jersey, Brown Papers, Misc., Letters (JCB), L 60 M; Sept. 15, 1760. *R.I. Acts* (1745), 274; Newp. T.M. Recs., 370, 442, 504, 524, 590, 645; *R.I. Acts* (1752), 38, 54; *Newp. Merc.,* Dec. 4, 1759; Jan. 1, 1760.

132:1 *Pa. Statutes,* V, 128; Bridenbaugh, *Rebels and Gentlemen,* 244; 1 *Pa. Archives,* 87; *Pa. Geschichtschreiber,* June 16, 1751; *Pa. Gaz.,* July 4, 1751; *A Continuation of the Account of the Pennsylvania Hospital* (Philadelphia, 1760), 42.

132:2 *Pa. Geschichtschreiber,* May 1, 1752; Sept. 1, 1754; *Pa. Gaz.,*

Mar. 24, 1752; Aug. 8, 1754; Burnaby, *Travels,* 100; *Pa. Votes,* IV, 639; V, 64, 149; Bridenbaugh, *Rebels and Gentlemen,* 245; *Continuation of the Account of the Pennsylvania Hospital,* 62.

CHAPTER IV

134:2 Franklin, *Works* (Sparks), II, 311, 325.

135:1 Latimer, *Bristol in the 18th Century,* 153; *Pa. Jour.,* Dec. 6, 1750; June 7, 1753; *Pa. Gaz.,* May 9, 1751; *N.Y. Eve. Post,* Dec. 17, 1750; Bridenbaugh, *Colonial Craftsman,* 68.

135:2 Kalm, *Travels,* I, 32; Proud, *Hist. of Pennsylvania,* II, 273; Cheesman A. Herrick, *White Servitude in Pennsylvania* (Philadelphia, 1926), 214; *Pa. Jour.,* Sept. 14, 1749; Feb. 6, 1749/50; Dec. 6, 1750; Mittelberger, *Journey,* 37.

135:3 A number of Jewish families settled in Philadelphia before 1760. Jacob R. Marcus, *Early American Jewry* (Philadelphia, 1953), II, 6; Franklin, *Works* (Sparks), VII, 72; Knauss, Pa. Ger. Soc., *Procs.,* XXIX,, 69; 1 *Pa. Archives,* II, 217; *Pa. Mag.,* XVI, 120.

136:1 Muhlenberg, *Journals,* I, 63; *S.C. Gaz.,* Jan. 7, 1745; Feb. 1, 1746; Dec. 25, 1749; Feb. 12, Apr. 1, 15, 1756; Charles Reznikoff, *Jews of Charleston* (Philadelphia, 1950), 14; Hirsch, *Huguenots of S.C.,* 102n.

136:2 *N.Y. Gaz.,* Nov. 19, 1750; *Pa. Jour.,* Aug. 23, 1753; *N.Y.M.C.C.,* V, 476.

136:3 *Bos. Post Boy,* Oct. 1, 1750; *Pa. Jour.,* Sept. 20, 1750; *N.Y. Gaz.,* Oct. 2, 1752; *R.I. Col. Recs.,* V, 317, 340, 403, 472; VI, 262; *New London Summary,* Nov. 7, 14, 1760; *Pa. Mag.,* LI, 263.

137:2 *R.I. Hist. Mag.,* VI, 167.

137:3 Shipton, *Biographical Sketches,* VII, 229.

138:2 Stiles, *Itineraries,* 1.

139:1 Winsor, *Mem. Hist. of Boston,* II, 533; William H. Whitmore, *Massachusetts Civil Lists for the Colonial and Provincial Periods* (Boston, 1870); Col. Soc. Mass., *Pubs.,* XXVIII, 39, 42; E. Alfred Jones, *Loyalists of Massachusetts* (London, 1930), 249; plates, XVII, XLV; *Lloyd Papers,* I, 381, 482; II, 388; Elias Nason, *Sir Charles Henry Frankland* (Albany, 1865), 10, 12, 25n; 6 MHS *Colls.,* IX, 149n.

139:2 Shipton, *Biographical Sketches,* VII, 209; Birket, *Cursory Remarks,* 24.

140:1 The Philadelphia gentry are treated at length in Bridenbaugh, *Rebels and Gentlemen,* especially Chap. VI. See, in addition,

Keith, *Provincial Councillors of Pa.,* 89, 130; *Pa. Mag.,* I, 326, 457; VI, 108, XI, 130; Drinker, Diary, Sept. 26, 1759; Thomas W. Balch, *Philadelphia Assemblies* (Philadelphia, 1916), 36.

140:2 *Amer. Mag. & Hist'l Chron.,* I, 176; *Commerce of R.I.,* I, 52, 77; Bridenbaugh, *Peter Harrison,* 7, 16, 25; Journal of a Captive, 1745–1748 (LC).

141:1 In 1759 only one New York merchant served in the Provincial Council. E. B. O'Callaghan, *Documentary History of the State of New York* (Albany, 1849), IV, 1037; Carl L. Becker, *History of Political Parties in the Province of New York* (Madison, 1909), 8, 16; Smith, Papers, II, 414; NYHS *Colls.,* 1885, p. 145; Harrington, *N.Y. Merchant,* 11, 14, 39; Alexander, Papers, I, 13; *N.Y. Col Docs.,* VI, 471.

141:2 Harriet H. Ravenel, *Eliza Pinckney* (New York, 1896), 17; Bidenbaugh, *Myths and Realities,* 76; *S.C. Gaz.,* May 30, 1743; June 20, Dec. 31, 1744; Mar. 18, 1745; Aug. 4, 1746; Nov. 6, 1749; Jan. 22, 1750; Apr. 30, May 14, 1753.

142:1 Wallpapers were first introduced at Boston about 1730; they became common in fine town and country houses after 1750. Edinburgh's first wallpapers appeared in 1745. Graham, *Social Life of Scotland,* 57; *Bos. Post* Boy, Feb. 22, 1748; Kalm, *Travels,* I, 132; *Pa. Gaz.,* July 14, 1746; Dec. 17, 1751; *S.C. Gaz.,* May 6, 1751; Bridenbaugh, *Colonial Craftsman,* 75; *N.Y. Gaz.,* Sept. 25, 1758.

142:2 MHS *Procs.,* XVIII, 344; *Old-Time New England,* XVII, 7; *Newsletter,* Mar. 10, 1743.

142:3 Wilson, *Mem. Hist. N.Y.,* II, 305, 373, 403; Stokes, *Iconography,* IV, 630.

143:1 Kenneth Clark, *Newport (White Pine Series,* VIII, St. Paul, 1922), 4; Antoinette F. Downing and Vincent J. Scully, Jr., *The Architectural Heritage of Newport, Rhode Island* (Cambridge, 1952), 129, 179, 181, 188; plates, 75, 82, 88, 89, 97, 111, 117.

143:2 Frank Cousins and Phil M. Riley, *Colonial Architecture of Philadelphia* (Boston, 1920), plate IX.

144:1 S.C. Pub. Recs., XXIV, 308; Alice R. and D. E. Huger Smith, *Dwelling Houses of Charleston* (Philadelphia, 1917), 361; *S.C. Gaz.,* July 4, 1743; May 6, 1751.

144:3 An appraisal of the Royall property in 1740 listed the mansion at £50,000 and the real estate at £37,000, which, even in Massachusetts currency, was a very large sum. *Medford Historical Register,* III, 133, 149; XXIX, 1; MHS Procs., XVIII, 349; Thomas Weston, *History of the Town of Middleborough* (Boston, 1906), 362; Cordingley, *Old-Time New England,* XII, 53; Francis S. Drake, *Town of Roxbury* (Roxbury, 1878), 121;

Hugh S. Morrison, *Early American Architecture* (New York, 1952), 484; Bridenbaugh, *Gentleman's Progress,* 120, 239; *NEHG Reg.,* L, 57; Birket, *Cursory Remarks,* 20.

145:1 Bridenbaugh, *Gentleman's Progress,* 103, 153, 232; Birket, *Cursory Remarks,* 27; J. Clarence Webster, *Journals of Jeffery Amherst* (Chicago, 1931), 95.

145:2 Birket, *Cursory Remarks,* 40; *N.Y. Gaz.,* Jan. 29, 1759; *Pa. Mag.,* XII, 444, 446; Burnaby, *Travels,* 107.

145:3 Harold D. Eberlein and Horace M. Lippincott, *The Colonial Houses of Philadelphia and Its Neighborhood* (Philadelphia, 1912), 319; *Pa. Mag.,* V, 10; XII, 447; XVI, 375; XVII, 267; XXVIII, 28, 37; *Pa. Gaz.,* Feb. 16, June 29, 1758; Kalm, *Travels,* I, 49; Thompson Westcott, *Historic Mansions and Buildings of Philadelphia* (Philadelphia, 1877), 468; Bridenbaugh, *Rebels and Gentlemen,* 186, 191; and for excellent photographs, Philip H. B. Wallace and M. Luther Miller, *Colonial Houses, Philadelphia, Pre-Revolutionary Period* (New York, 1931).

146:1 Bridenbaugh, *Myths and Realities,* 72; *SCHG Mag.,* XXVI, 103; Samuel G. Stoney, *Plantations of the Carolina Low Country* (Charleston, 1938).

146:2 Ward Papers, Box I, Receipt dated July 1, 1746; *Pa. Gaz.,* Mar. 24, 1752.

146:3 A "good Riding Chair" cost £22–25 at Boston in 1760. Cuyler, Letter Book, I, Sept. 17, 1759; Feb. 21, 1760; Franklin, *Works* (Smyth), II, 379; Hart, *Hist. of Mass.,* II, 217; Mease, *Picture of Philadelphia,* 335; S. C. Pub. Recs., XXIV, 308; *Lloyd Papers,* II, 497; *Commerce of R.I.,* I, 23, 33; 2 MHS *Procs.,* IX, 6.

147:1 S.C. Pub. Recs., XXIV, 318; NYHS *Colls.,* 1897, pp. 51, 414; Norris S. Barratt, *Outline of the History of Old St. Paul's Church, Philadelphia* (Philadelphia, 1917), 30n.

147:2 *N.Y. Eve. Post,* Dec. 21, 1747; *Bos. Gaz.,* Dec. 8, 1747; *Pa. Mag.,* IX, 358.

148:1 *Old-Time New England,* XXX, 1; Bridenbaugh, *Colonial Craftsman,* chap. V; *N.Y. Post Boy,* May 6, 1745; *Pa. Gaz.,* Jan. 31, 1748/9; *N.Y. Gaz.,* May 8, 1758; William Darlington, *Memorials of John Bartram and Humphrey Marshall* (Philadelphia, 1849), 199.

148:2 Adams, *Works,* II, 64; *Pa. Mag.,* XVI, 120; Samuel McKee, Jr., *Labor in Colonial New York* (New York, 1935), 22; *S.C. Gaz.,* June 30, 1758; Newp. T.C. Recs., XII, 203; NYHS *Colls.,* 1895, p. 254; *DAB,* XII, 21; *Burd Papers,* 43.

149:1 Acrelius, *New Sweden,* 157; *Bos. Eve. Post,* Sept. 17, 1759; *S.C. Gaz.,* Mar. 14, 1748; *N.Y. Post Boy,* Jan. 18, *Sup.* 1747/8; *Colden Papers,* III, 326.

149:2 Mittelberger, *Journey,* 107; N. M. Tiffany, *Letters of James Murray, Loyalist* (Boston, 1901), 103, 105, 107, 108, 109.

149:3 *N.Y. Gaz.,* Mar. 5, 1753; *N.Y. Eve. Post,* June 3, 1751; *American Gazetteer,* III (article on New York); Bridenbaugh, *Gentleman's Progress,* 44, 89, 102, 140, 155; *Bos. Eve. Post,* Dec. 10, 1744.

150:1 *N.Y. Eve. Post,* Sept. 16, 1751; *N.Y. Gaz.,* Jan. 5, 1756; *Pa. Jour.,* July 16, 1747; *Bos. Gaz.,* Dec. 17, 1759.

150:2 Bridenbaugh, *Gentleman's Progress,* 77, 135, 150; *N.Y. Merc.,* May 5, 1755; Ralph Davol, *Two Men of Taunton* (Taunton, 1912), 164.

151:2 *Christian History,* July 16, 1753; Feb. 9, 16, 1744/5; Bridenbaugh, *Gentleman's Progress,* 145.

151:3 *Bos. Eve. Post,* Oct. 29, Dec. 3, 1744; Mar. 25, June 3, 1745; Oct. 14, 1754; *S.C. Gaz.,* Feb. 18, 1745; Jacob C. Meyer, *Church and State in Massachusetts* (Cleveland, 1930), 74; *Pa. Gaz.,* Sept. 3, 1747; *NEHG Reg.,* XXXV, 29; Letters to George Whitefield, D. Van Horne to G. W., Nov. 12, 1750; *Pa. Jour.,* Dec. 5, 1754.

152:1 *Pa. Jour.,* Sept. 12, 1745; Sept. 25, 1746; Apr. 2, 1752; Sept. 5, Dec. 5, 1754; *Pa. Gaz.,* Sept. 25, 1746; Apr. 23, 1747; *N.Y. Merc.,* July 29, Sept. 9, 1754; *S.C. Gaz.,* Nov. 11, 1745; Jan. 26, 1747.

152:2 *Records of the Presbyterian Church in the U.S.,* 164, 233, 276, 284.

152:3 Bridenbaugh, *Peter Harrison,* 54, 80; MHS *Colls.,* III, 259, 264; Adams, *Works,* II, 127; Stiles, *Itineraries,* 15; Stiles, *Literary Diary,* I, 56n; Abiel Holmes, *The Life of Ezra Stiles* (Boston, 1798), 29, 40.

153:1 Dix, *Trinity Church,* I, 260, 261, 271, 276; Birket, *Cursory Remarks,* 45; Smith, *New York,* I, 256, 257; William S. Perry, *Historical Collections Relating to the American Colonial Church* (Hartford, 1871), II, 271, 536; *Pa. Mag.,* XLVII, 350; LVIII, 5; Gertrude Foster, Documentary History of Education in South Carolina (Thesis, Univ. S.C., 1931), VIII, chap. XI, 14; Frederick Dalcho, *Historical Account of the Protestant Episcopal Church in South Carolina* (Charleston, 1820), 165; Benjamin Dorr, *Historical Account of Christ Church,* Philadelphia (Philadelphia, 1859), 89, 102, 111.

153:2 Perry, *Colonial Church,* II, 268; Hugh Hastings, *Ecclesiastical Records of the State of New York* (Albany, 1906), V, 3427, 3456.

154:1 John W. Thornton, *Pulpit of the American Revolution* (Boston, 1860), 39–104; *Newsletter,* Mar. 1, 22, 1750; *Bos. Eve. Post,*

June 18, 1750; *Bos. Gaz.,* Apr. 3, 1750; Rev. Henry Caner to Bishop of London, Jan. 31, 1750; June 8, 1751, Fulham Palace MSS, Mass. (LC), Box II, nos. 193, 195; Ezra Stiles, *Discourse on the Christian Union* (Boston, 1761).

154:2   Stiles, *Itineraries,* 235; Muhlenberg, *Journals,* I, 57; *N.Y. Post Boy,* Feb. 1, 1742/3; *Charleston Year Book, 1884,* p. 262; Reznikoff, *Jews of Charleston,* 17; *Bos. Eve. Post,* Feb. 21, Mar. 20, 1743; George P. Disosway, *Earliest Churches of New York and Its Vicinity* (New York, 1865), 214.

154:3   Rufus M. Jones, *Quakers in the American Colonies* (New York, 1911), 129n; Birket, *Cursory Remarks,* 27, 73; Amelia M. Gummere, *Journal and Essays of John Woolman* (Philadelphia, 1922), 241; Bridenbaugh, *Rebels and Gentlemen,* 16; Edmund Peckover, Journal (NYPL), I, 16, 118; II, 8; *Pa. Mag.,* XVI, 219; *N.Y. Eve. Post,* Feb. 29, 1747/8; *Eccles. Recs. of N.Y.,* IV, 2955; 2956.

155:1   Meyer, *Church and State in Mass.,* 33n; I. Woodbridge Riley, *American Philosophy from Puritanism to Pragmatism* (New York, 1915), 63.

155:2   *N.Y. Wkly Jour.,* May 30, 1743; *S.C. Gaz.,* Mar. 28, 1743; Stiles, *Itineraries,* 105; Mittelberger, *Journey,* 32; *N.Y. Gaz.,* Apr. 27, May 4, Aug. 3, 1752; Muhlenberg, *Journals,* I, 301; *N.Y. Post Boy,* July 21, 1746; *Pa. Jour.,* Sept. 5, 1751.

156:1   Meyer, *Church and State in Mass.,* 21; *London Mag.,* Apr. 1749, p. 184; Graydon, *Memoirs,* 6, 135; Bridenbaugh, *Gentleman's Progress,* 157; Weston, *Documents,* 196; Perry, *Colonial Church,* II, 236; *N.Y. Eve. Post,* Apr. 13, 1747; 2 MHS *Procs.,* VII, 339, 342; 1 *Pa. Archives,* III, 144; *Pa. Gaz.,* Aug. 21, 1755.

156:2   Stephen B. Weeks, *The Southern Quakers and Slavery* (Baltimore, 1896), 102, 111; Guy S. Klett, *Presbyterians in Colonial Pennsylvania* (Philadelphia, 1937), 134; H.M.J. Klein, *History of the Eastern Synod of the Reformed Church in the United States* (Lancaster, 1943), 3, 28, 38, 47; *Eccles. Recs. of N.Y.,* IV, 2973; Kalm, *Travels,* I, 129; *Minutes of the Philadelphia Baptist Association* (Philadelphia, 1851), 46.

157:2   New York City, Tavern Keepers' Licenses, 1756–66 (NYHS); *N.Y.M.C.C.,* V, 118, 369; VI, 180; *Pa. Mag.,* XXII, 497; Gipson, *Lewis Evans,* 128; *Pa. Votes,* IV, 655; 14 *Bos. Rec. Com.,* 220; Newp. T.C. Recs., IX, 21, 27, 35, 164, 285, 289; Adams, *Works,* II, 85; On billeting, see Scharf & Westcott, *Hist. of Phila.,* I, 212; *P.M.C.C.,* 601.

157:3   Acrelius, *New Sweden,* 163; *Newp. Merc.,* Jan. 23, 1759; 8 *Pa. Archives,* V, 3645; *Pa. Votes,* IV, 282; *Pa. Gaz.,* July 26, 1759; Andrew Elliott to John Brown, July 27, 1757 (HL: H.M. 9857).

158:1   *Pa. Votes,* IV, 210; *Pa. Gaz.,* Oct. 18, 1753; *S.C. Gaz.,* Nov. 14, 1743; Apr. 15, June 1, 1745; *Newsletter,* July 7, 1748.

158:2   2 MHS *Procs.,* VII, 340; *Pa. Mag.,* XVII, 263.

158:3   *Bos. Eve. Post,* Jan. 18, 1748; *S.C. Gaz.,* Mar. 12, Nov. 19, 26, 1744; Feb. 12, 1753; June 3, 1756; Sept. 8, 1759; *N.Y. Gaz.,* May 28, Dec. 31, 1750; Jackson, *Cyclopedia of Philadelphia,* IV, 973.

159:1   *Pa. Mag.,* II, 433; XII, 444, 445; Birket, *Cursory Remarks,* 39; *Pa. Jour.,* Nov. 24, 1757; Jackson, *Cyclopedia of Philadelphia,* II, 407; Stokes, *Iconography,* IV, 607; *S.C. Gaz.,* Feb. 27, Apr. 23, 1744; Feb. 29, 1748.

159:2   Bridenbaugh, *Gentleman's Progress,* 18, 20, 150.

159:3   Stokes, *Iconography,* IV, 625; *Bos. Post Boy,* May 2, 1743; *Pa. Gaz.,* July 23, 1747; Dec. 6, 1750; Birket, *Cursory Remarks,* 40; *N.Y. Gaz.,* June 3, 1751; *Newsletter,* Dec. 31, 1747; *Pa. Jour.,* Feb. 5, 26, 1751.

160:1   *Pa. Mag.,* XXII, 497; *S.C. Gaz.,* Mar. 28, 1743; Apr. 15, 1745; May 1, 1756; *N.Y. Wkly Jour.,* Nov. 21, 1743; *Pa. Votes,* IV, 129.

160:2   Bridenbaugh, *Gentleman's Progress,* 19, 43, 106; *S.C. Gaz.,* May 26, 1759; *Bos. Eve. Post,* Mar. 15, 1756; *Newsletter,* Sept. 16, 1756; *Newp. Merc.,* June 5, 1759; *N.Y. Gaz.,* Jan. 29, 1759; *Pa. Mag.,* XVII, 263.

161:1   Adams, *Works,* II, 85; *Newsletter,* July 5, 1750; 16 *Bos. Rec. Com.,* 20; *S.C. Statutes,* III, 581; *S.C. Gaz.,* Nov. 5, 1744; Mar. 30, 1747; *Pa. Col. Recs.,* V, 428; *Pa. Votes,* IV, 134; *R.I. Acts* (1745), 291; *R.I. Acts* (1767), 90, 151; *An Act to Prevent Keeping of Disorderly Houses* (Newport, 1753, Broadside, RIHS).

161:2   Samuel A. Drake, *Old Boston Taverns and Tavern Clubs* (Boston, 1917), 62; 106, 116; Bridenbaugh, *Gentleman's Progress,* 89, 151, 154, 176; *Newp. Merc.,* Apr. 22, 1760; *N.Y. Post Boy,* Jan. 16, 1743/4; *N.Y. Gaz.,* Jan. 1, 1749/50; May 7, 1750; May 20, 1751; *N.Y. Merc.,* Feb. 4, 1754; *S.C. Gaz.,* Mar. 28, May 16, 1743; Nov. 20, 1753; Oct. 10, 1754.

162:1   *Pa. Jour.,* Mar. 22, 1743; Nov. 29, 1744; May 25, 1749; Apr. 11, July 4, 18, 1754; Feb. 4, 1755; May 27, 1756; *Pa. Gaz.,* May 22, 1746; Apr. 25, 1751; Oct. 5, 1752; John W. Wallace, *Colonel William Bradford* (Philadelphia, 1884), 48.

163:1   *American Gazetteer,* III (article on New York); Stokes, *Iconography,* IV, 624; *Pa. Mag.,* I, 245; 409; *SCHG Mag.,* XXVI, 26.

163:2   Melvin M. Johnson, *Beginnings of Freemasonry in America* (Washington, 1924), 333, 369, 380, 382; *Bos. Post Boy,* Jan. 1, 1750; June 29, 1752; *Newp. Merc.,* Jan. 2, June 26, 1759; *N.Y.*

Merc., Dec. 31, 1753; *Pa. Jour.,* Jan. 10, 1754; *Pa. Mag.,* XVII, 273; XX, 116, 121; XXXI, 19; Balch, *Letters,* 32; Stiles, *Itineraries,* 224; *S.C. Gaz.,* Jan. 3, 1742/3.

163:3 Charlestonians delighted in societies with comical names and purposes: the Laughing Club, Smoking Club, Amicable Society, and the Brooms, whose meetings were "sweeps." The Loyal and Grand Candlestick Club "held every Night" at the King of Prussia wanted six dozen large Bermuda straw hats and a "very large Size for the President." In 1759 it had £3,550 "to Let." Bridenbaugh, *Myths and Realities,* 79; *S.C. Gaz.,* Feb. 14, 1743; Feb. 27, 1744; Aug. 14, 1749; Jan. 30, 1755; Apr. 28, 1759; *Pa. Mag.,* XXI, 417; *Charleston Year Book, 1886,* p. 28; *Newsletter,* July 14, 1743; *Md. Hist. Mag.,* XXXVIII, 167, 226; *Pa. Jour.,* Apr. 3, 1755; Myers, *Hannah Logan's Courtship,* 80; *Md. Gaz.,* Mar. 24, 1747.

164:1 *Md. Gaz.,* Jan. 5, 1758; *S.C. Gaz.,* Nov. 7, 1743; Oct. 23, 1751; *SCHG Mag.,* XX, 59, 60, 61; *Pa. Gaz.,* Nov. 16, 1752; *Pa. Mag.,* V, 352; *Newsletter,* Oct. 18, 1759; *N.Y. Merc.,* Dec. 15, 1755.

164:2 R.I. Hist. Soc., Scrapbook, No. 30, p. 52; RIHS *Colls.,* XXIII, 56.

164:3 *Cities,* I, 439; Bridenbaugh, *Gentleman's Progress,* 22, 23; Balch, *Philadelphia Assemblies,* 18, 51; *Pa. Gaz.,* Sept. 27, 1750; Oct. 3, 1751; Oct. 2, 1755.

165:1 *SCHG Mag.,* XXVI, 95; Bridenbaugh, *Myths and Realities,* 87; *N.Y. Merc.,* Mar. 20, Nov. 27, 1758; *NEHG Reg.,* L, 56.

165:2 Mason, *Reminiscences of Newport,* 101; Bridenbaugh, *Gentleman's Progress,* 89; Davey & Carson, Letter Book, July 21, 1748; *Pa. Mag.,* XXIV, 405; Burnaby, *Travels,* 97, 117; Wilson, *Mem. Hist. N.Y.,* II, 458; Birket, *Cursory Remarks,* 59.

166:1 *NEHG Reg.,* L, 53; Shipton, *Biographical Sketches,* VII, 309.

166:2 Drinker, Diary, 1759–60; *Pa. Mag.,* X, 115; XII, 437; *Commerce of R.I.,* I, 58; Stiles, *Itineraries,* 80; *Pa. Gaz.,* Jan. 6, 1746/7; J. Smith Futhey and Gilbert Cope, *History of Chester County, Pennsylvania* (Philadelphia, 1881), 202; *Burd Papers,* 19; Darlington, *Memorials of John Bartram,* 338.

167:1 *Bos. Post Boy,* Dec. 17, 1750; *S.C. Gaz.,* Feb. 14, 1743; Oct. 1, 1750; Apr. 10, 1755; Bridenbaugh, *Myths and Realities,* 81; *N.Y. Wkly. Jour.,* Sept. 26, 1743; Jan. 30, 1743/4; *N.Y. Gaz.,* June 4, 1750; Mar. 24, 1755; Weyman's *N.Y. Gaz.,* Apr. 16, 1759.

168:1 *Newsletter,* Apr. 14, 1743; May 6, 20, 27, 1756; *Pa. Jour.,* Oct. 18, 1744; Nov. 17, 1748; Jan. 15, 1756; *Pa. Gaz.,* Dec. 18, 1755; Jan. 22, 1756; *S.C. Gaz.,* May 30, 1743; July 2, 1753;

June 11, 1754; *SCHG Mag.,* XX, 58; *Bos. Eve. Post,* May 26, 1744; *Bos. Post Boy,* Oct. 21, 1751; *N.Y. Merc.,* Sept. 10, 1753; *N.Y. Eve. Post,* Sept. 8, Dec. 29, 1746; Sept. 11, 1749; *N.Y. Gaz.,* Aug. 28, 1749.

168:2   Some kind of a play was given by local talent in Philadelphia in 1748. *Pa. Mag.,* VII, 16; Bridenbaugh, *Rebels and Gentlemen,* 137; *P.M.C.C.,* 523; John Smith, Diary (LCP), VII, Aug. 22, 1749; Joseph Addison, *Cato,* Act. II, Scene iii, 10; *N.Y. Gaz.,* Feb. 26, 1749/50; Mar. 12, 26, Sept. 24, Nov. 5, Dec. 10, 1750; Jan. 21, Apr. 22, Dec. 23, 1751; George C. Odell, *Annals of the New York Stage* (New York, 1927), I, 32, 68; *Mass. Acts,* III, 500; Drake, *Hist. of Boston,* 631.

169:1   *N.Y. Merc.,* July 2, Sept. 17, 1753; Stokes, *Iconography,* IV, 642; *N.Y. Gaz.,* Mar. 18, 25, 1754; *Pa. Gaz.,* Mar. 9, 26, Apr. 25, July 13, 1754; Bridenbaugh, *Rebels and Gentlemen,* 138; *SCHG Mag.,* XX, 59; *S.C. Gaz.,* Sept. 5, Oct. 3, 1754; Bridenbaugh, *Myths and Realities,* 92.

169:2   *N.Y. Merc.,* Jan. 1, 1759; Odell, *N.Y. Stage,* I, 75, 78; 1 *Pa. Archives,* III, 656, 659; *Pa. Votes,* V, 51; *Pa. Statutes,* V, 445; *Pa. Gaz.,* June 21–Dec. 27, 1759; Jan. 10, 1760.

170:1   New York beat a London team in a "great Cricket Match." *N.Y. Gaz.,* Apr. 29, May 6, 1751; *N.Y. Eve. Post,* Nov. 25, 1751; 14 *Bos. Rec. Com.,* 5; Petitions to R.I. Assembly, VII, 30; VIII, 91; *Newp. Merc.,* Aug. 14, 1759; Jackson, *Cyclopedia of Philadelphia,* I, 77; *N.Y. Post Boy,* Feb. 25, 1745; *S.C. Gaz.,* Feb. 19, 1756; *Newsletter,* Feb. 21, 1754; Graydon, *Memoirs,* 19; *Pa. Mag.,* XII, 433; Mittelberger, *Journey,* 112; Shipton, *Biographical Sketches,* VII, 191.

170:2   Bridenbaugh, *Gentleman's Progress,* 88, 102, 199; Balch, *Letters,* 11; *Pa. Mag.,* XXXVI, 162.

171:1   Burnaby, *Travels,* 96; Benjamin Rush, *David Rittenhouse* (1796) 33.

CHAPTER V

173:1   *Cities,* I, 121, 280, 442; Bridenbaugh, *Rebels and Gentlemen,* 29.

173:2   The South Grammar School was the celebrated Boston Latin School. 17 *Bos. Rec. Com.,* 20, 71, 139, 266; 19 *Bos. Rec. Com.,* 27, 52, 160, 219; 16 *Bos. Rec. Com.,* 11, 26, 46, 78; 14 *Bos. Rec. Com.,* 197.

173:3   The "Public School" maintained by the Society of Friends was open to all sects in this period. Zora Klain, *Educational Activi-*

ties of New England Quakers (Philadelphia, 1928), 36, 60; Newp. T.M. Recs., 360, 433, 546; Stiles, *Itineraries,* 24.

174:1 Bridenbaugh, *Rebels and Gentlemen,* chap. II; James Mulhern, *History of Secondary Education in Pennsylvania* (Philadelphia, 1933), 35, 42, 44, 47, 54, 61, 104; Pa. Ger. Soc., *Procs.,* XXXVIII, 61; XL, 175; Scharf & Westcott, *Hist. of Philadelphia,* II, 1308; III, 1922; *Minutes of Phila. Baptist Assoc.,* 74.

174:2 S.C. Commons, Jour., XVIII, 388; XXIV, 339; *S.C. Gaz.,* Sept. 21, 1748; Jan. 30, 1749; Mar. 9, 1752; Dec. 17, 1753; Dec. 19, 1754; Oct. 30, 1755; St. Philip's Vestry, Minutes, I, 121, 215; II, 5, 7.

174:3 *N.Y. Wkly Jour.,* Feb. 13, 1748/9; *Ind. Reflector,* Nov. 8, 1753; William H. Kilpatrick, *Dutch Schools of New Netherland and Colonial New York* (Washington, 1912), 152, 153; *Eccles. Recs. of N.Y.,* IV, 2828, 3024; V, 3203; Smith, *New York,* I, 278; William W. Kemp, *Support of Schools in Colonial New York* (New York, 1913), 57.

175:1 Commissary Roger Price advised the S.P.G. in 1754 to drop plans for a Catechetical Charity School at Boston where there were already schools aplenty. Foster, Doc. Hist. Educ., S.C., V, 705; VIII, 8:43; VIII, 9:14, 19; VIII, 10:22, 36; VIII, 13.6; Stokes, *Iconography,* IV, 612, 615; St. Philip's Vestry, Minutes, II, 13; *Pa. Mag.,* LVIII, 3, 7; LXIII, 285; *N.Y. Merc.,* Sept. 15, 1760.

175:2 Garrat Noel and Benjamin Leigh taught "a new invented Short Hand" at New York in 1751. *N.Y. Gaz.,* Jan. 7, 1750/1; *N.Y. Merc.,* Nov. 17, 1760.

176:1 *N.Y. Eve. Post,* Sept. 9, 1751; *S.C. Gaz.,* Sept. 3, 1744; *Newsletter,* July 17, 1755; Franklin, *Works* (Smyth), III, 230; Bridenbaugh, *Rebels and Gentlemen,* 36.

176:2 Occasionally a rural teacher like Charles Peale of Kent County, Md., drew students from Philadelphia. *Pa. Gaz.,* Mar. 12, 1744/5; Aug. 30, 1759.

176:3 *Pa. Mag.,* XXX, 349, 351, 427; *Newsletter,* Sept. 13, 1753; Oct. 1754; *N.Y. Eve. Post,* July 27, 1747; May 27, 1751; *Pa. Gaz.,* Nov. 10, 1743; Nov. 25, 1756; *S.C. Gaz.,* Oct. 29, 1744; Aug. 18, 1746; *N.Y. Gaz.,* July 31, 1758.

177:1 *S.C. Gaz.,* Oct. 11, 1746; July 6, 1747; *Pa. Gaz.,* July 27, 1749; Aug. 29, 1751; May 10, 1753; Mar. 23, 1758; *Newp. Merc.,* May 22, 1759; *Bos. Eve. Post,* Apr. 14, 1755; *N.Y. Eve. Post,* Apr. 23, 1750; *N.Y. Gaz.,* July 8, 1751; Apr. 5, 1756.

177:2 *Newp. Merc.,* Dec. 19, 1758; May 8, 1759; Alice M. Earle, *Home Life in Colonial America* (New York, 1899), 291; *Bos. Eve. Post,* Mar. 25, 1751; *Murray Letters,* 110.

178:1   Morison, *Rice Institute Pamphlet,* XXIII, 262; Bridenbaugh, *Rebels and Gentlemen,* 42; *Pa. Gaz., Aug.* 24; 1749; Franklin, *Works* (Smyth), II, 386.

178:2   *Pa. Gaz.,* Dec. 25, 1750; Jan. 8, 1750/1; Sept. 12, 1751; Mar. 11, 1755; Aug. 12, 1756; Franklin, *Works* (Smyth), II, 390; III, 92, 127, 353; Cheyney, *History of the University of Pennsylvania,* Chap. II; *P.M.C.C.,* 526; Bridenbaugh, *Rebels and Gentlemen,* 40, 55.

179:1   The charter of the Charles Town Library Society, issued in 1754, mentions as one of its purposes "raising a Fund for an Academy" and, at Newport, several gentlemen headed by Ezra Stiles, had begun to draw up plans for a college in Rhode Island. *S.C. Gaz.,* Feb. 19, Aug. 6, 13, 1750; July 7, 1759; Stiles, *Itineraries,* 423; for King's College, see *Pa. Jour.,* Apr. 26, 1753; *N.Y. Col. Laws,* III, 607, 679, 731, 899; *N.Y. Eve. Post,* May 18, Aug. 7, 1747; Nov. 28, 1748; *N.Y. Gaz.,* Nov. 25, 1751; June 3, 1754; *Eccles. Recs. of N.Y.,* IV, 3505, 3612; V, 3339, 3354, 3359, 3487; *Ind. Reflector,* Mar. 22, 29, Apr. 5, 12, 19, 26, 1755; *Minutes of the Governors of the College of the Province of New York . . . and of the Corporation of King's College* (Facsimile, New York, 1932), May 7, 1755–June 26, 1760; McAnear, Bibliographical Society of America, *Papers,* XLIV, 301; *N.Y. Merc.,* Mar. 24, 1755.

179:2   H. R. Plomer, et. al., *Dictionary of the Printers and Booksellers who were at Work in England, Scotland and Ireland from 1726 to 1775* (Oxford, 1932); Isaiah Thomas, *History of Printing in America* (Albany, 1874); H. Glenn and Maud O. Brown, *Directory of the Book-Arts and Book Trade in Philadelphia to 1820* (New York, 1950); George L. McKay, *Register of Artists, Engravers, Booksellers . . . and Publishers in New York City* (New York, 1942); and the contemporary newspapers; *Pa. Mag.,* VII, 21; *Burd Papers,* 12, 24, 36.

179:3   *Newp. Merc.,* Feb. 26, 1760; Moses Brown Papers (RIHS), I, 11; *N.Y. Merc.,* Nov. 13, 1752; *Pa. Gaz.,* June 6, 1754.

180:1   *Newp. Merc.,* Nov. 20, 1759; *Pa. Gaz.,* Oct. 26, 1758; Oct. 2, 1760; *Pa. Jour.,* Mar. 19, 28, 1751; *Bos. Eve. Post,* Jan. 9, July 9, 1744; Bridenbaugh, *Gentleman's Progress,* 112, 116; *S.C. Gaz.,* Aug. 30, 1748; Feb. 5, 1753; George L. McKay, *American Book Auction Catalogues* (New York, 1937), 42.

180:2   Christopher Saur of Germantown, Pa., sold most of the books printed in German, though Franklin and his partner, David Hall, also made a specialty of this trade after 1750. *N.Y. Merc.,* June 23, *Sup.,* 1755; Dec. 24, 1759; Oct. 6, 1760; *N.Y. Gaz.,* Jan. 22, 1759; *Pa. Jour.,* Feb. 26, 1754; *Pa. Gaz.,* Feb. 22, *Extra,*

1759; *S.C. Gaz.,* Aug. 10, 1752; Bridenbaugh, *Gentleman's Progress,* 99.

181:1   *Bos. Post Boy,* June 20, 1748; Jan. 7, 1751; Aug. 4, 1760; Bos. *Ind. Advertiser,* Dec. 12, 1748; Bridenbaugh, *Peter Harrison,* 43, 73, 164, 168; NYHS *Colls.,* 1895, p. 339; Wilson, *Mem. Hist. N.Y.,* IV, 114; *Newsletter,* Aug. 12, 1756; *S.C. Gaz.,* May 22, 1742; Apr. 15, 1756; *Bos. Eve. Post,* Sept. 12, 1743.

181:2   *Cities,* I, 458; Bridenbaugh, *Pa. Mag.,* LXV, 17, 24; *N.Y. Gaz.,* Mar. 24, 1760; Kalm, *Travels,* II, 638; John Latimer, *Annals of Bristol in the Seventeenth Century* (Bristol, 1900), 52; Minute Book of the Company of the Redwood Library (The Library, Newport); George C. Mason, *Annals of the Redwood Library* (Newport, 1891), 7, 27; *R.I. Col. Recs.,* V, 227; Bridenbaugh, *Peter Harrison,* 45.

181:3   *S.C. Gaz.,* July 31, 1749; Apr. 1750; Jan. 15, May 14, 1754; Sept. 16, 1756; *S.C. Statutes,* VIII, 107; Gregorie, S.C. Hist. Assoc., *Procs.,* 1935, p. 10.

182:1   *N.Y.M.C.C.,* V, 142, 299; *N.Y. Post Boy,* June 16, 1746; *N.Y. N.Y. Merc.,* Apr. 8, May 6, Oct. 14, 21, 1754; May 12, 1755; Smith, *New York,* I, 261; Smith, Papers, II, 359; Austin B. Keep, *The Library in Colonial New York* (New York, 1909).

182:2   *Cities,* I, 131, 290; Col. Soc. Mass., *Pubs.,* XIX, 130; MHS *Colls.,* IV, 76; Shipton, *Biographical Sketches,* V, 360.

182:3   Louis Shores, *Origins of the American College Library* (New York, 1935), 15, 32, 37; *Pa. Mag.,* LXV, 22, 23; MHS *Procs.,* XVIII, 426; Dorr, *Christ Church,* 103; Mulhern, *Secondary Education in Pa.,* 54; *Recs. of the Presbyterian Church,* 219; *Pa. Gaz.,* Nov. 7, 1751; Oct. 16, 1760; Du Simitiere Papers, Pa., N.E. (LCP), sub Loganian Library; Tolles, *Meeting House and Counting House,* 144, 161.

183:1   Thomas, *History of Printing;* Lawrence C. Wroth, *The Colonial Printer* (Portland, 1938); *Bibliographical Essays: A Tribute to Wilberforce Eames* (Cambridge, 1924), 339; *Bos. Wkly Advertiser,* July 24, 1758.

183:2   James Franklin, Jr., Ledger, 1750–1762 (NHS); George S. Eddy, *Account Books Kept by Benjamin Franklin* (New York, 1929), II; 2 MHS *Procs.,* XVI, 186.

184:1   New London, New Haven, Williamsburg, Germantown, and Annapolis accounted for the bulk of the books not published in the five largest cities. Lawrence Wroth has calculated that Evans's figures should be multiplied by 4.7 to approximate the actual number of issues of the colonial press, in which case, the five cities published 12,915 titles in this period. Lawrence C. Wroth, *American Bookshelf, 1755* (Philadelphia, 1934);

Charles Evans, *American Bibliography* (Chicago, 1903–55), II–IV; Charles R. Hildeburn, *Century of Printing: Issues of the Pennsylvania Press* (Philadelphia, 1885), I; John E. Alden, *Rhode Island Imprints* (New York, 1949); Hildeburn, *Pa. Mag.*, XIII, 208.

185:1 Lyon N. Richardson, *History of Early American Magazines* (New York, 1931), 105, 364; List of subscribers to the *American Magazine,* 1757, Bradford Papers (HSP). For example: 109 subscriptions to *American Magazine* came from the North Carolina low country, 95 from New Jersey, 57 from the Lower Counties on the Delaware, and 12 from Suffolk in Virginia. Georgia was the only continental colony without an agent. *Pa. Gaz.,* Feb. 19, 1756; Nov. 24, 1757.

185:2 Subscription receipts in Ward Papers, Box I, 1748, 1759; "the List for the New York Gazet. What's due to July 1st, 1757" (RIHS) reports 66 for Newport and Providence; Clarence S. Brigham, *History and Bibliography of American Newspapers* (Worcester, 1947), I–II; *N.Y. Post Boy,* Apr. 1, 1745; *Pa. Berichte,* Nov. 1, 1753.

185:3 Eddy, *Franklin's Account Books,* II; 2 MHS *Procs.,* XVI, 186; *SCHG Mag.,* XXXV, 124; *Pa. Gaz.,* Feb. 2, 1747/8; Aug. 22, 1751; May 9, 1754; *Pa. Mag.,* LXII, 569; Carl Van Doren, ed., *Letters of Benjamin Franklin and Jane Mecom* (Princeton, 1950), 48, 55; Harrington, *N.Y. Merchant,* 84.

186:1 *Pa. Gaz.,* June 4, 1752; *N.Y. Gaz.,* July 2, *Sup.,* 1753; *Pa. Jour.,* Feb. 19, 1756.

186:2 *Occasional Reverberator,* Sept. 7–Oct. 5, 1753; "Watch-Tower" articles, *N.Y. Merc.,* Nov. 25, 1754–Nov. 17, 1755; *John Englishman,* April 1–July 5, 1755; Paul L. Ford, ed., *Journals of Hugh Gaine, Printer* (New York, 1902), I, 6; II, 3; Wilson, *Mem. Hist. N.Y.,* IV, 135; Clyde A. Duniway, *Development of the Freedom of the Press in Massachusetts* (Cambridge, 1906), 112, 115, 122*n;* Thomas, *Hist. of Printing,* I, 133; *Pa. Berichte,* May 16, 1756.

187:1 Only one month after the passage of the Stamp Act, Governor Shirley wrote to Sir Thomas Robinson (Feb. 4, 1755) proposing parliamentary stamp duties "so diffused as to be in a manner insensible," for raising defense revenues, but the strenuous opposition of the Massachusetts agent prevented action. John S. Barry, *History of Massachusetts* (Boston, 1855), II, 252; *Mass. Acts,* III, 793, 834, 947; *Bos. Eve. Post,* May 5, 1755; Apr. 4, 1757; *Pa. Gaz.,* Apr. 21, 1757; Col. Soc. Mass., *Pubs.,* IX, 424, 468; Duniway, *Freedom of Press in Mass.,* 119; *NEHG Reg.,* XIV, 267.

187:2   *Pa. Gaz.,* Mar. 11, 1755; *Pa. Jour.,* Feb. 23, Mar. 2, 9, 16, 30, Apr. 6, 1758; *S.C. Gaz.,* June 20, 1744.

190:1   Shipton, *Biographical Sketches,* VIII, 42; Barbara N. Parker and Anne B. Wheeler, *John Singleton Copley* (Boston, 1939), plate 126B, for portrait; *Magazine of History,* 1917, Extra no. 57, part 2; Wroth, Col. Soc. Mass., *Pubs.,* XXXII, 87.

190:2   Bridenbaugh, *Rebels and Gentlemen,* 103; Alfred F. Gegenheimer, *William Smith* (Philadelphia, 1943), 95; *American Magazine,* Oct. 1757, p. 44.

191:1   Nothing apparently came of a proposal in the *S.C. Gaz.,* Aug. 25, 1757, for printing by subscription of "A Collection of Poems on various subjects, by a Resident of South Carolina." Also: *S.C. Gaz.,* June 17, 1745; Mar. 20, *Post,* 1749; *Gentleman's Magazine,* XIX, 424.

191:2   Samuel Cooper, Mr. Pope's Messiah Imitated, c. 1745 (HL: 6074); Alden, *Rhode Island Imprints,* 27; *Bos. Eve. Post,* Nov. 7, 1748; Thomas, *Hist. of Printing,* II, 254; Worthington C. Ford, comp., *Massachusetts Broadsides* (MHS *Colls.,* 75, 1922), No. 1011; Evans, *American Bibliography,* No. 6613.

192:2   *N.Y. Gaz.,* Mar. 12, 1753; Edward Field, *State of Rhode Island and Providence Plantations* (Boston, 1902), I, 214*n;* Mass. *Broadsides,* Nos. 833, 913, 915, 1000, 1003, 1004, 1012, 1155, 1156; Muhlenberg, *Journals,* I, 320.

193:1   *Spectator* (June 16, 1711), No. 93; Edward Channing and Archibald C. Coolidge, eds., *Barrington-Bernard Correspondence and Illustrative Matter* (Cambridge, 1912), 12.

193:2   Newport does not seem to have had any music teachers; those desiring to learn to play or sing had to go to Boston. *N.Y. Merc.,* July 2, 1753; *Pa. Gaz.,* July 12, 1744; Mar. 28, 1748; Apr. 11, 1754; *N.Y. Post Boy,* Sept. 9, 1745; Bridenbaugh, *Gentleman's Progress,* 84, 138; *MHS Colls.,* 71, pp. 6, 15; *Bos. Eve. Post,* May 30, 1743; *S.C. Gaz.,* Sept. 9, 1745; Tpr. 6, 1746; Nov. 8, 1751; Oct. 29, 1753; St. Philip's Vestry, Minutes, I, 219.

193:3   *Pa. Gaz.,* Dec. 27, 1759; Hillegas to Stiegel, May 5, 1760, Michael Hillegas, Letter Book, 1757–1760 (HSP); *Pa. Mag.,* XXVII, 118; *German American Annals,* n.s., VI, 165, 166; Bridenbaugh, *Rebels and Gentlemen,* 154; Ellis to Rev. Alexander Garden, Feb. 14, 1745/6, Robert Ellis, Letter Book, 1736–1748 (HSP), 470; Stokes, *Iconography,* IV, 578; *N.Y. Merc.,* Feb. 3, 1755; Mar. 8, 1756; *S.C. Gaz.,* Jan. 8, 1754; Apr. 22, 1756.

194:1   *Pa. Mag.,* II, 43; *German Amer. Annals,* n.s., VI, 163; *NEHG Reg.,* XLII, 197; *Bos. Eve. Post,* June 25, Sept. 24, 1744; Muhlenberg, *Journals,* I, 300; Mittelberger, *Journey,* 114; *N.Y.*

Merc., Mar. 11, 1754; *S.C. Gaz.,* Mar. 6, 1749; Nov. 6, 1752; Nov. 13, 1755; *Pa. Jour.,* Dec. 6, 1759; May 15, 1760; *Pa. Gaz.,* July 11, 1754; Oct. 23, 1760.

195:1 Bridenbaugh, *Gentleman's Progress,* 48, 191; *Pa. Mag.,* I, 416; *Pa. Gaz.,* Jan. 20, 27, 1757; Dec. 27, 1759; May 15, 1760.

195:2 Pa. Soc. Colonial Dames, *Church Music and Musical Life in Pennsylvania in the Eighteenth Century* (Philadelphia, 1947), III, i, 71, 81; *S.C. Gaz.,* Nov. 8, 1751; Feb. 13, 1754; Oct. 11, 1760; *Newp. Merc.,* Apr. 22, 1760; Oscar G. Sonneck, *Early Opera in America* (Boston, 1915), 15, 21, 26, 28, 29, 65; *Pa. Gaz.,* Jan. 20, 1757.

195:3 Handel's *Messiah* was performed "in the New Musick Room" at Bristol on Jan 14, 1756; *Judas Maccabaeus* and the *Messiah* on Mar. 2–3, 1757. This city's advanced concert life may be traced in part to the flocking of fashion to the Hot Well where, in 1759, four concerts were given weekly. Latimer, *Bristol in the 18th Century,* 244, 308; Corry, *Liverpool,* 142; *N.Y. Post Boy,* Jan. 7, 1745; *N.Y. Merc.,* Dec. 8, 1755; *N.Y. Gaz.,* Jan. 14, 1760; 17 *Bos. Rec. Com.,* 87, 88, 89, 90, 159; Shipton, *Biographical Sketches,* VII, 255; *NEHG Reg.,* XXIV, 54; *Newsletter,* Jan. 2, 1755; Apr. 1, 1756; Jan. 27, 1757; Mar. 9, 1758.

196:2 MHS *Procs.,* 49, p. 36; *Newsletter,* Apr. 4, 1751; Nov. 11, 1756; Henry W. Foote, *John Smibert, Painter* (Cambridge, 1950), 50, 57, 81; Henry W. Foote, *Robert Feke* (Cambridge, 1930), 72, 74; Alan Burroughs, *John Greenwood in America* (Andover, 1943), 13, 17, 32, 45, 53; Park, MHS *Procs.,* 51, p. 158; Park, Amer. Antiquarian Soc., *Procs.,* XXXII, 273; Virgil Barker, *American Painting* (New York, 1950), 85, 110, 118, 132.

197:1 Foote, *Smibert,* 52n; Parker and Wheeler, *Copley,* 4, 5; Plates, 1–23, 128.

197:2 Foote, *Feke,* 67, 71; Bridenbaugh, *Rebels and Gentlemen,* 164; *Pa. Mag.,* XIX, 461; XXXIV, 192; LXII, 433; Myers, *Hannah Logan's Courtship,* 289; *Pa. Jour.,* Jan. 13, 1763; Darlington, *Memorials of John Bartram,* 420; Barker, *Amer. Painting,* 98, 113, 128; Flexner, *Mag. of Art,* XXXVII, 242, 276.

197:3 Rutledge, 3 *W. & M. Quart.,* VI, 637; Anna Wells Rutledge, *Artists in the Life of Charleston* (Philadelphia, 1950), 128, figures 2–5, 8; *SCHG Mag.,* XX, 128; XXXI, 277; XXXIV, 170, 171; *SC. Gaz.,* Oct. 22, 1744; Barker, *Amer. Painting,* 102.

198:1 *N.Y. Post Boy,* May 19, 1746; *N.Y. Gaz.,* May 13, July 8, 1754; Oct. 2, 1758; *N.Y. Merc.,* Sept. 30, 1754; Aug. 28, 1758; Disosway, *Earliest Churches of N.Y.,* 216; Philip Cuyler to Copley, Oct. 19, Dec. 6, 1757, Cuyler, *Letter Book,* I; Stokes, *Iconography,* IV, 703, 710.

198:2 Inventories, Newp. T.C. Recs., IX, 82, 134, 135, 184, 189, 246, 365, 371, 379; G. H. Richardson Collection (NHS), 971:27; Bridenbaugh, *Myths and Realities,* 111; Drinker, Diary, Nov. 1, 1759; Bridenbaugh, *Rebels and Gentlemen,* 194, 213; Shippen to Alexander Ray, Apr. 5, 1760, Edward Shippen Papers, 1724–1783 (LC).

199:1 MHS *Procs.,* 49, p. 36; *Bos. Post Boy,* Aug. 11, 1746; Newp. T.C. Recs., IX, 135, 196, 226, 246, 365, 371; XII, 196; *N.Y. Wkly Jour.,* Oct. 16, 1749; *N.Y. Merc.,* Dec. 17, 1753; *Pa. Jour.,* July 25, 1754; Hirsch, *Huguenots of S.C.,* 162.

200:1 Unfortunately space does not permit further treatment of the interesting and important role of the medical profession in the five cities. See *Cities,* I, 88, 242, 402. Dr. John Mitchell of Virginia also wrote a treatise on yellow fever to which Colden's second paper was addressed. *Colden Papers,* III, 77; *Amer. Med. & Philos. Register,* I (1811), 304, 310; IV (1814), 378; *Amer. Museum,* III (1788), 53; John Lining, *Description of the American Yellow Fever which prevailed At Charlestown in South Carolina in the Year 1748* (Charles Town, 1753; Philadelphia, 1799); John Carter Brown Library, *Report* (1952), 53; Aldredge, *Charleston Year-Book* (1940), 209.

200:2 *Pa. Gaz.,* Nov. 29, 1750; Mar. 5, 1750/1; June 27, 1751; *Pa. Jour.,* Dec. 13, 20, 1750; Jan. 1, 1750–1; Apr. 18, *Sup.,* 1751; Bridenbaugh, *Rebels and Gentlemen,* 248, 265; Michael Kraus, *The Atlantic Civilization* (Ithaca, 1949), 211, 212; Middleton, *Annals of Medical History,* VIII, 218; *Bos. Post Boy,* Apr. 20, 1752.

201:1 Attempts to establish a "Course of Anatomy" at Bristol in 1746 failed. Latimer, *Bristol in the 18th Century,* 264; Stephen Wickes, *History of Medicine in New Jersey* (Newark, 1879), 51; *Phil. Trans.,* X, 28; Bridenbaugh, *Rebels and Gentlemen,* 267, 271; *Bos. Eve. Post,* Mar. 26, 1744; Aug. 7, 1749; Jan. 20, 27, Feb. 3, 1755; *Bos. Wkly Advertiser,* May 14, 1759; *N.Y. Merc.,* July 3, 1758; Col. Soc. Mass., *Pubs.,* XIX, 283; G. H. Richardson Collection, 970:180.

201:2 Of the twenty-five contributions from Norwich, sixteen came from one FRS; the rural areas of America and the West Indies made fifteen in all, Ireland nineteen, and Scotland five, 1743–1760. At Boston in 1749 there were, however, those who made fun of the kind of communications read to the Royal Society. *Phil. Trans.,* IX–XI; *R.I. Col. Recs.,* V, 497, 512; Bridenbaugh, *Rebels and Gentlemen,* 319; *Pa. Gaz.,* Nov. 5, 1747; Jan. 31, 1748/9; Dec. 19, 1749; Apr. 13, 1758; *Pa. Jour.,* July 7, 1748; *N.Y. Merc.,* June 11, 1752.

202:1 Wroth, *American Bookshelf,* 148; Gipson, *Lewis Evans,* 5, 9,

11, 17, 23, 56, and maps; *Pa. Mag.,* LIX, 280, 295; LXXIV, 90; *Bos. Eve. Post,* Sept. 8, 1746; *Pa. Mag.,* Apr. 14, 1757; June 4, 1759; *Newsletter,* Jan. 1, 1756; *S.C. Gaz.,* Feb. 5, 1756; Lawrence C. Wroth, *Some American Contributions to the Art of Navigation* (Providence, 1947), Fisher Chart, p. 22; 1 *Pa. Archives,* II, 592; *Pa. Jour.,* Jan. 19, 1758; Oct. 11, 1759.

202:2   Kalm, *Travels,* I, 155; Penn MSS, Private Correspondence (HSP), IV, 93; Penn MSS, Official Correspondence (HSP), VI, 79; Thomas Jefferys, *The Great Probability of a North West Passage* (London, 1768), xi, xii, 131, 132, 145, 146, 151, 153; *Pa. Jour.,* Nov. 1, 15, 1753; May 2, Oct. 24, 1754; *Pa. Gaz.,* Nov. 15, 1753; Jan. 1, May 2, 1754; *Newsletter,* Dec. 27, 1753; Bridenbaugh, *Rebels and Gentlemen,* 329; Balch, *Pa. Mag.,* XXXI, 419; Solis-Cohen, *Pa. Hist.,* XIX, 148.

203:1   *N.Y. Post Boy,* Mar. 19, 1743/4; *Amer. Mag. & Hist'l Chron.,* I, 202, 207; *N.Y. Gaz.,* Apr. 16, 1759; Stiles, *Itineraries,* 422, 595; *Bos. Wkly Advertiser,* July 2, 1759; *Pa. Geschichtschreiber,* June 16, 1744; *Pa. Berichte,* Dec. 16, 1754; Dec. 1, 1755; *Amer. Mag.,* Dec. 1757, p. 112; *Phil. Trans.,* X, 666, 667; XI, 62.

203:2   Journal of a Captive, c. 1748; *Newp. Merc.,* Mar. 20, 1759; Mason, *Reminiscences of Newport* (NHS copy), II, 189A for two copies of horoscopes.

204:1   Young Bromfield was versatile, having constructed an organ and several microscopes, ground lenses, made several maps, and drawn pen and ink landscapes. *Pa. Jour.,* July 7, 1748; *Pa. Gaz.,* Dec. 20, 1748; Jan. 3, 1749; May 23, 1751; Apr. 5, May 3, Sept. 6, 1753; *N.Y. Merc.,* Sept. 10, 1753; Isabel W. Calder, ed., *Letters and Papers of Ezra Stiles* (New Haven, 1933), 1, 5; *Phil. Trans.,* X, 414; Myers, *Hannah Logan's Courtship,* 265; Kalm, *Travels,* I, 140.

204:2   Bridenbaugh, *Gentleman's Progress,* 156, 158; *Amer. Mag. & Hist'l Chron.,* I, 369; III, 548; *Phil. Trans.,* VII, 683, IX, 110, 514; X, 400; Weston, *Documents,* 73; A. Wolf, *History of Science, Technology and Philosophy in the Eighteenth Century* (New York, 1939).

205:1   Darlington, *Memorials of John Bartram,* 160, 193, 195, 197, 202, 371, 393, 412; *Phil. Trans.,* IX, 70, 123, 699; X, 4, 28; *Colden Papers,* 3, 6, 12, 31, 35, 40, 45, 47, 62; John Bartram, *Observations on the Inhabitants, Climate, Soil, Rivers, Productions, Animals and other Matters of Notice, made . . . in . . . Travels from Pensilvania. . . .* (London, 1751); Conway Zirkle, *Beginnings of Plant Hybridization* (Philadelphia, 1935), 145.

205:2 George Roupel of the customs service "showed an excellent genius" at drawing specimens for Dr. Garden, many of them being engraved for publication in London. Smith, *Correspondence of Linnaeus,* I, 284, 286, 288, 342, 344, 355, 357, 363, 366, 377, 382, 386, 407, 431, 446, 452, 461, 476, 507; II, 299, 308; *Phil. Trans.,* XI, 508.

206:2 Dr. Spencer's Boston period commenced in March, or earlier, and lasted until late in August, 1743. *Newsletter,* Apr. 4, 1743; *Bos. Eve. Post,* May 30, June 6, Aug. 1, 1743; Mar. 3, Dec. 29, 1746; *N.Y. Wkly Jour.,* Oct. 24, 1743; Jan. 23, 1743/4; *Pa. Gaz.,* Apr. 26, July 26, 1744; *Pa. Mag.,* I, 246; Bridenbaugh, *Gentleman's Progress,* 189; *Va. Gaz.,* Jan. 9, 1746; I. Bernard Cohen, ed., *Benjamin Franklin's Experiments* (Cambridge, Bridenbaugh, *Rebels and Gentlemen,* 323.

207:1 Cohen, *Franklin's Experiments,* is essential and exhaustive; Carl Van Doren, *Benjamin Franklin* (New York, 1933), 156; *Gentleman's Magazine,* Sept. 1753, p. 431; *N.Y. Gaz.,* July 15, 1754; *Pa. Jour.,* Aug. 9, 1753; *Phil. Trans.,* X, 189, 289, 295, 301, 302, 303, 372, 522, 629, 632; XI, 189, 435; Bridenbaugh, *Rebels and Gentlemen,* 324.

207:2 *Amer. Mag. & Hist'l Chron.,* II, 530; III, 96; *Bos. Eve. Post,* Mar. 3, Dec. 29, 1746; *Amer. Mag.,* 1758, pp. 164, 272, 374, 424, 470, 475, 528; *New Amer. Mag.* (Woodbridge, N.J.), Apr. 1759, p. 422.

208:1 I. Bernard Cohen, *Some Early Tools of American Science* (Cambridge 1950); *Bos. Eve. Post,* Aug. 24, Sept. 7, Oct. 5, 12, 1747; Oct. 7, Nov. 4, 18, 1751; *N.Y. Post Boy,* May 2, 1748; *S.C. Gaz.,* Oct. 31, 1748; Mar. 2, 1752; *Pa. Gaz.,* Apr. 11, May 2, 1751; Sept. 14, 1752; Dec. 27, 1759; *Pa. Mag.,* XIII, 248; *A Course of Experiments, etc., May 16, 1752* (Broadside, Brown Univ.); Cohen, *Franklin's Experiments,* 409; *N.Y. Merc.,* May 18, 1752; *N.Y. Gaz.,* July 22, 29, Aug. 5, 1751; June 26, 1766.

208:2 Darlington, *Memorials of John Bartram,* 132, 159, 162, 203, 325; *Colden Papers,* III, 34, 60, 69, 82, 83, 159, 180, 182, 330, 357; *Pa. Hist.,* VI, 17; Bartram to Colden, Apr. 7, 1745 (Bos. Pub. Library); Bridenbaugh, *Rebels and Gentlemen,* 321; Kalm, *Travels,* I, 31.

209:1 Franklin, *Works* (Smyth), II, 94, 228.

CONCLUSION—PART I

210:1 Pownall, *Topographical Description,* 130; *Pa. Mag.,* VIII, 228; XII, 434; *N.Y. Wkly Jour.,* Feb. 19, 1749/50.

211:1   Ralph May, *Early Portsmouth History* (Boston, 1926), 223;
        Nathaniel Adams, *Annals of Portsmouth* (Portsmouth, 1825),
        205; *N.H. Gaz.,* Oct. 7, 1756; Birket, *Cursory Remarks,* 15;
        James D. Phillips, *Salem in the Eighteenth Century* (Boston,
        1937), 189, 257; Gertrude S. Kimball, *Providence in Colonial
        Times* (Providence, 1912), 210, 221; Arthur J. Weise, *History
        of the City of Albany* (Albany, 1884), 256, 309, 328, 330, 350;
        Pa. Gaz., Feb. 26, 1750/1; Mar. 13, 1760; *Lancastersche Zeit-
        ung,* Jan. 29, 1752; Joseph M. Levering, *History of Bethlehem*
        (Bethlehem, 1903), 191, 202, 205; *Pa. Mag.,* VIII, 118; E. S.
        Riley, *The Ancient City* (Annapolis, 1887), 118, 146.

211:2   M. Dorothy George, *England in Transition* (London, 1921),
        54, 75, 87, 92, 102; George, *London Life in the Eighteenth
        Century,* 269.

211:3   Darlington, *Memorials of John Bartram,* 203.

CHAPTER VI

215:1   *Md. Gaz.,* Nov. 4, 1773.

216:3   These estimates are compiled from the following and many other
        statistics. Mease, *Picture of Philadelphia,* 31; NYHS *Colls.,*
        1881, pp. 409, 447; Carl Bridenbaugh, ed., Patrick M'Robert,
        Tour through Part of the North Provinces of America (Philadel-
        phia, 1935), 31; 1 *Pa. Archives,* IV, 597; Stokes, *Iconography,*
        IV, 871, 930; Stiles, *Literary Diary,* I, 88, 104, 592; MHS
        Procs., VIII, 406; Chalmers Papers relating to S. C., II, 45; *R.I.
        Hist. Mag.,* VII, 47; *Newp. Hist. Mag.,* I, 122; Edward Peterson,
        History of the Island of Rhode Island and Newport (New York,
        1853), 247; Philip Padelford, ed., *Colonial Panorama: Dr. Rob-
        ert Honyman's Journal* (San Marino, 1939), 36; *Newp. Merc.,*
        Dec. 4, 1775.

217:1   Population figures for the cities of the British Isles are far less
        reliable than for colonial towns, being remarkably exaggerated,
        and must therefore be used with care. In 1775 Bristol's popula-
        tion was said to be 35,440; Liverpool's was c. 34,407, Birming-
        ham's 30,804, and Manchester's, 27,246 (1773). David Mac-
        pherson, *Annals of Commerce* (London, 1805), III, 222; Lati-
        mer, *Bristol in the 18th Century,* 420; Corry, *Liverpool,* 149;
        Phil. Trans., XIII, 679.

218:1   *Newp. Merc.,* June 13, 1763; June 22, 1772; 18 *Bos. Rec. Com.,*
        217; Seybolt, *Town Officials,* 339; Edwards, *New York,* 34, 201.

218:2   *Pa. Statutes,* VI, 195, 196; VII, 9, 75, 143; Griffith, *Amer. City
        Govt.,* 253.

218:3   *Pa. Chron.,* Jan. 15, 1770; *Pa. Statutes,* VI, 43, 214; VIII, 25, 172; Griffith, *Amer. City Govt.,* 256; *Pa. Votes,* VI, 43.

219:1   S.C. Commons, Jour., XXXIV, 37, 43; XXXV, 51; *S.C. Gaz.,* Jan. 25, 1770; Feb. 7, 1771; Feb. 22, May 24, Oct. 25, 1773; Oct. 31, 1774; Rind's *Va. Gaz.,* May 26, 1768; *S.C.A.G. Gaz.,* Apr. 24, 1771; Jan. 29, July 16, 1772; *N.Y. Jour.,* July 16, 1772; MHS *Procs.,* 49, p. 454; S.C. Pub. Recs., XXXII, 366, 404.

219:2   Edwards, *New York,* 38, 197; Stokes, *Iconography,* IV, 825; *S.C. Statutes,* IV, 253; S.C. Commons, Jour., XXXVIII, 277, 279; Benjamin F. Stevens, *Facsimiles of Manuscripts in European Archives Relating to America, 1773–1783* (London, 1889–95), no. 2086.

220:2   Newp. T.M. Recs., 690, 820, 864, 870, 892, 900, 914, 916, 1038, 1042; Kimball, *R.I. Governors,* II, 324.

221:1   Governor Bernard declared in 1765 that it was the wrong time to tax the colonies: "But it should be considered, that the American governments themselves, have in the prosecution of the late war, contracted very large debts; which it will take some years to pay off, and in the mean time, occasion very burdensome taxes for that purpose only. . . ." Massachusetts "raises every year £37,500 sterling for sinking their debt," and it will take at least four years more to effect. He does not mention local taxes, nor has this aspect of the problem received much consideration. Bernard, *Select Letters,* 30; 16 *Bos. Rec. Com.,* 92, 200; 18 *Bos. Rec. Com.,* 162.

221:2   Charles Town had only six representatives until 1771, when another was added, out of a total of forty-eight in the Commons House, and Philadelphia had two compared with Philadelphia County's eight. *S.C. Gaz.,* Oct. 19, 1767; June 13, 1768, May 28, 1772, Jan. 23, 1775; *S.C. Country Jour.,* Mar. 28, 1769; Schaper, Amer. Hist. Assn., *Annual Report,* 1900, I, 345; Fulham Palace MSS, S.C. (LC Trans.), No. 72; Charles H. Lincoln, *Revolutionary Movement in Pennsylvania* (Philadelphia, 1903), 45.

222:1   Among the members of the Caucus were Lawyer John Ruddock, William Story of the Vice Admiralty Court, William Cooper, town clerk for forty-nine years, Assessor William Fairfield, Samuel Adams, "and a *rudis indigestaque moles* of others." John Rowe, John Hancock, Thomas Cushing, James Otis, and Josiah Quincy were prominent in the Merchant's Club. Adams, *Works,* II, 144; Colegrove, Col. Soc. Mass., *Pubs.,* XXI, 418.

222:2   Colegrove, Col. Soc. Mass., *Pubs.,* XXI, 420; *Bos. Eve. Post,* May 14, 1764; Oct. 28, 1765; MHS *Procs.,* 55, p. 249*n,* 265;

Peter Oliver, Origin and Progress of the American Rebellion, Egerton MSS (LC Trans.), 2671:74; Original Minute Books of the Boston Committee of Correspondence, 1772–1774 (NYPL), 1, 5; 18 *Bos. Rec. Com.,* 93.

223:1   *Newp. Merc.,* Apr. 16, 1764; *R.I. Col. Recs.,* VI, 549; *Providence Gaz.,* Mar. 19, Apr. 9, 1768; Henry Ward to John Comstock, Apr. 13, 1770, Ward Papers, Box I; Newp. T.M. Recs., 1044.

223:2   4 MHS *Colls.,* X, 587; Watts, *Letter Book,* 138; Lewis B. Walker, ed., *The Burd Papers. Selections from Letters Written by Edward Burd, 1763–1828* (Pottsville, Pa., 1899),72; McAnear, *N.Y. History,* XXI, 423, 426, 430; Edwards, *New York,* 48, 51; *N.Y. Gaz.,* Feb. 15, 1768; *N.Y. Col. Laws,* V, 228; *N.Y.M.C.C.,* VII, 313.

223:3   *Burd Papers,* 56, 63; Muhlenberg, *Journals,* II, 123, 273; *P.M.C.C.,* 704; Bridenbaugh, *Rebels and Gentlemen,* 13, 15, 121; McKinley, *Suffrage Franchise,* 286, 288, 290; Hindle, 3 *W. & M. Quart.,* III, 477; *Pa. Mag.,* V, 60; *S.C. Gaz.,* Oct. 3, 10, 1768; Feb. 7, 1771.

224:1   Chalmers, Papers relating to S.C., I, 165.

224:3   *Pa. Gaz.,* Apr. 2, 1761; Jan. 18, 1770; *N.Y. Gaz.,* Jan. 22, 1770; Edward H. Tatum, ed., *American Journal of Ambrose Serle* (San Marino, 1940), 266*n;* Stevens, *Facsimiles,* no. 2085; Pollard to Swaine, May 6, 1773; Misc. Papers, Phila. Co.; Proud, *History of Pennsylvania,* II, 277; *P.M.C.C.,* 795; *Pa. Mag.,* XLVIII, 235, 237.

225:1   Proud, *History of Pennsylvania,* II, 277; *Pa. Mag.,* XVII, 454; XLVIII, 235, 237, 238.

225:2   *Pa. Mag.,* XV, 36; Graydon, *Memoirs,* 56; *Pa. Gaz.,* Feb. 13, 1766; Oct. 19, 1769; *Pa. Packet,* May 29, 1775.

225:3   Drinker, *Diary,* Sept. 3, 1770; Mar. 1771; *Pa. Chron.,* Mar. 16, 1767; June 27, 1768; Ontario Archives, *Second Report,* i, 670; Stevens, *Facsimiles,* no. 2086.

226:1   Newton D. Mereness, ed., *Travels in the American Colonies* (New York, 1916), 414; *N.Y. Merc.,* Dec. 2, 1765; *Amer. Hist. Rev.,* XXXII, 82; Stokes, *Iconography,* IV, 801; N.Y. Public Library, *Bulletin,* XXXV, 149; MHS *Colls.,* 71, p. 117; Thomas Anburey, *Travels Through the Interior Parts of America* (London, 1789), II, 530; M'Robert, *Tour,* 3.

226:2   *N.Y. Merc.,* Jan. 17, 1763; Apr. 11, 1768; *Bos. Post Boy,* Feb. 13, 1764; *N.Y. Gaz.,* Mar. 15, 1764; Aug. 20, 1767; Peterson and Edwards, *New York* (illustrated edn.), 427.

227:1   Serle, *Journal,* 271; *Newp. Hist. Mag.,* I, 122; J. F. D. Smyth, *Tour in the United States of America* (London, 1874), II, 370;

Contract for a House on the Point (Isham Collection, RIHS); Census of the Colony of Rhode Island, 1774 (R.I. Archives); *R.I. Hist. Mag.,* VI, 167n.

227:2 Newp. T.M. Recs., 742; Bridenbaugh, RIHS *Colls.,* XXVI, 7; *Newp. Merc.,* May 20, 1765; Feb. 15, 1768.

227:3 Weston, *Documents,* 195; Stiles, *Itineraries,* 58; Milling, *Colonial South Carolina,* 141; *S.C. Gaz.,* May 4, 1769; Oct. 11, *Sup. Ex.,* 1770; Aug. 6, 1772; Mar. 7, 1773; Feb. 14, 1774; *Newp. Merc.,* Sept. 14, 1767; King's MSS (LC Trans.), 210:28; L. Clarkson to D. Van Horne, Feb. 17, 1774, Clarkson Letters (LC); *Pennsylvania Magazine* (1776), II, 269.

228:1 *S.C. Gaz.,* Mar. 8, July 5, 1773; Sept. 26, 1774; Feb. 20, 1775.

228:2 19 *Bos. Rec. Com.,* 197; 20 *Bos. Rec. Com.,* 144; 16 *Bos. Rec. Com.,* 148; MHS *Colls.,* IV, 190; *Bos. Post Boy,* Dec. 15, 1760; Jones, *Loyalists of Mass.,* 158, 185, 220; MHS *Procs.,* VIII, 340.

228:3 *Bos. Gaz.,* July 18, 1763; *Murray Letters,* 132; 4 MHS *Colls.,* I, 268; *Pa. Mag.,* XXXV, 113.

229:1 Cheyney, *Hist. of University of Pa.,* 55; University of Pennsylvania, Treasurer's Ledger, 1749–1779; *Pa. Gaz.,* Jan. 31, 1765; Bridenbaugh, *Rebels and Gentlemen,* 201; Peterson, Amer. Phil. Soc., *Trans.,* n.s., XLIII, 96; *Pa. Mag.,* XLVII, 348; Philip B. Wallace, *Churches and Meeting Houses in Pennsylvania, New Jersey, and Delaware* (New York, 1931), 28, 31, 81, 82; Barratt, *Old St. Paul's,* 37, 41, 43.

229:2 *P.M.C.C.,* 804, 806; M'Robert, *Tour,* 30.

230:1 *S.C. Statutes,* IV, 257; *S.C.A.G. Gaz.,* Sept. 23, 1768; Weyman's *N.Y. Gaz.,* May 11, 1767; *S.C. Gaz.,* Sept. 14, Oct. 12, 1767; Jan. 26, 1769; Jan. 17, 1771; Jan. 31, 1774; Carroll, *Historical Collections,* map showing "A Plan of Charles Town," 1775; *Charleston Year-Book, 1898,* pp. 357, 370; *1881,* frontispiece; Mereness, *Travels,* 398; MHS *Procs.,* 49, pp. 441, 444, 447; Hector St. John De Crevecoeur, *Letters from an American Farmer* (New York, 1912), 158.

230:2 Dix, *Trinity Church,* I, 316; *Crayon,* IV, 180; Muhlenberg, *Journals,* II, 239; Stokes, *Iconography,* IV, 776; Du Simitiere Papers (LCP); N.Y. Pub Library, *Bull.,* XXXV, 149, 150; *N.Y. Merc.,* Apr. 13, 1772; *N.Y. Jour.,* Mar. 2, 1775; Edwards, *New York,* 103; M'Robert, *Tour,* 3; Adams, *Works,* II, 346; Serle, *Journal,* 109.

231:1 Bridenbaugh, *Peter Harrison,* 1, 102, 106, 111; Newp. T.M. Recs., 786, 862, 962, 966, 1002, 1004; Friedman, *Old-Time New England,* XXXVI, 52; *Bos. Post Boy,* Jan. 19, 1761; *Mass. Acts,* IV, 425; Abram E. Brown, *Faneuil Hall and Faneuil Hall*

Market (Boston, 1900), 96, 97, 99; *Mass. Gaz.,* Mar. 13, 1769; Col. Soc. Mass., *Pubs.,* XXI, 418; *R.I. Hist. Mag.,* VI, 164*n.*

231:2 Balch, *Letters,* 173; *Pa. Gaz.,* Mar. 19, 1761; Jan. 18, 1770; *Pa. Chron.,* Mar. 16, June 8, 22, 1767; NYHS *Colls.,* 1886, p. 28.

231:3 *Pa. Col. Recs.,* VIII, 694; *Pa. Gaz.,* Apr. 8, 1762; Muhlenberg, *Journals,* I, 593; II, 6; 1 *Pa. Archives,* IV, 312; *Pa. Statutes,* VI, 214; VIII, 25.

232:1 S.C. Commons, Jour., XXXVII, 215, 281; Wallace, *Henry Laurens,* 33.

232:2 Charles Blaskowitz, *Plan of the Town of Newport in Rhode Island* (London, 1777); Newp. T.M. Recs., 742; *Newp. Merc.,* Sept. 9, 1771; *New England Magazine,* XII, 348; *N.Y.M.C.C.,* VI, 287, 333; Richard Frothingham, *History of Charlestown* [Mass.] (Boston, 1845); Winsor, *Mem. Hist. Boston,* II, 362; Mereness, *Travels,* 184.

232:3 Darlington, *Memorials of John Bartram,* 245.

233:1 *Cities,* I, 313; *Newp. Merc.,* Nov. 3, 1761; Jan. 24, Oct. 31, 1763; May 7, Oct. 29, 1764; Feb. 4, 1765; Mar. 7, May 30, 1768; June 22, 1772; Newp. T.M. Recs., 800, 860; *Bos. Post Boy,* Feb. 18, 1765; *Bos. Gaz.,* Nov. 5, 1764; *S.C. Gaz.,* Nov. 19, 1764.

233:2 *Prov. Gaz.,* Feb. 16, 1765; Weyman's *N.Y. Gaz.,* Nov. 30, Dec. 7, 1767; *Newp. Merc.,* Oct. 17, 1768; June 24, 1771; Newp. T.M. Recs., 956, 1108, 1110; Stiles, *Literary Diary,* I, 662; Serle, *Journal,* 274, 276; *R.I. Col. Recs.,* VIII, 637, 638.

234:1 *Colden Letter Book,* I, 61; *Lloyd Papers,* II, 731; *N.Y. Gaz.,* Jan. 22, 1761; *N.Y. Merc.,* Feb. 17, 1766; *N.Y. Jour.,* Feb. 20, 1772; *N.Y.M.C.C.,* VI, 320; *Bos. Post Boy,* Nov. 24, 1766; *S.C. Country Jour.,* Apr. 6, 1773.

234:2 16 *Bos. Rec. Com.,* 77; *Bos. Post Boy,* Jan. 14, 1765; Aug. 3, 1772; Jan. 16, 1775; Weyman's *N.Y. Gaz.,* Feb. 16, 1767; *Bos. Gaz.,* June 15, 1772; June 20, 1774; *Newsletter,* Mar. 24, Aug. 4, 1768; Treasury 1, Bundle 442, f. 265, P.R.O. (LC Trans.); 23 *Bos. Rec. Com.,* 91, 142; MHS *Procs.,* LVIII, 425.

235:1 *S.C. Gaz.,* June 20, Nov. 14, 1761; Mar. 5, 1763; Feb. 18, Nov. 12, 1764; Feb. 2, Oct. 31, 1765; May 2, 1768; Feb. 28, 1771; Nov. 12, 1772; *S.C. Country Jour.,* Sept. 17, Oct. 15, 1771; St. Philip's Vestry, Minutes, II, May 2, 1768.

235:2 *Pa. Votes,* V, 354; *Pa. Gaz.,* Jan. 7, 1762; *Pa. Chron.,* Apr. 13, 1767; Jan. 15, 22, 1770; *Pa. Mag.,* I, 42.

236:1 For the extent of the highway systems in the cities, consult: Blaskowitz, *Plan of Newport;* Ezra Stiles, Map of Newport (MHS); John Montresor, *Plan of the City of New York & its*

Environs . . . survey'd in the Winter of 1775 (London, 1776); John Reed, *Map of the City and Liberties of Philadelphia* (Philadelphia, 1774); Carroll, *Historical Collections,* map showing "A Plan of Charles Town," 1775; *N.Y. Col. Laws,* IV, 838; V, 655; *Pa. Statutes,* VIII, 25; Whitelaw, Vermont Hist. Soc., *Procs.,* 1905–6, p. 123; Jackson, *Cyclopedia of Philadelphia,* IV, 1099, 1237; MHS *Procs.,* 49, p. 477.

236:2   For a map of Boston in 1774, see insert in *Map of the Most Inhabited Parts of New England* (Boston, 1774); 19 *Bos. Reac. Com.,* 189; 20 *Bos. Rec. Com.,* 215; 18 *Bos. Rec. Com.,* 165, 197; *Mass. Acts,* V, 226.

237:1   *Cities,* I, 12; *S.C. Statutes,* VII, 85, 89, 92, 93; *S.C. Country Jour.,* May 5, 1767; *S.C. Gaz.,* Aug. 24, 1769; May 24, 1773; Robert Mills, *Statistics of South Carolina* (Charleston, 1826), 393; St. Philip's Vestry, Minutes, II, Feb. 27, Dec. 15, 1770.

237:2   Corry, *Liverpool,* 144; 19 *Bos. Rec. Com.,* 161; 20 *Bos. Rec. Com.,* 254.

237:3   *N.Y.M.C.C.,* VII, 181; Court Papers, Phila. Co., IV, Apr. 1768; *Pa. Statutes,* VI, 230; *Pa. Chron.,* Nov. 13, 1769; *Pa. Votes,* IV, 121.

238:1   Newport alone still depended upon the force of gravity to carry off waste water and rain. *S.C. Gaz.,* Aug. 25, 1764; May 25, 1765; Apr. 11, 1768; Sept. 24, *Sup.,* 1772; *S.C.A.G. Gaz.,* June 20, 1766; Lionel Chalmers, *Account of the Weather and Diseases of South Carolina* (London, 1776), I, 16, 32.

238:2   19 *Bos. Rec. Com.,* 249; 20 *Bos. Rec. Com.,* 220, 258; 23 *Bos. Rec. Com.,* 223; MHS *Procs.,* VIII, 337; Winslow C. Watson, ed., *Men and Times of the Revolution: or the Memoirs of Elkanah Watson* (New York, 1856), 68; *N.Y.M.C.C.,* VI, 249, 330; VII, 15, 19, 30, 116, 124, 178, 323; *N.Y. Gaz.,* Mar. 5, 1763; *N.Y. Jour.,* June 16, 1774; Edwards, *New York,* 167.

239:1   *Pa. Statutes,* VI, 196, 305; VII, 163, 277; *Pa. Votes,* V, 236, 476; *Pa. Gaz.,* Apr. 1, 15, 1762; Mar. 3, 1768; Apr. 12, June 28, 1770; Feb. 23, 1774; *P.M.C.C.,* 668, 672, 683, 729, 774; *Pa. Mag.,* IX, 484; XL, 366; XLVIII, 60; *Pa. Chron.,* May 18, 1767; Mar. 27, Sept. 18, Oct. 2, Dec. 11, 1769.

239:2   Freebody Papers (RIHS, MSS), XVI, 99; *R.I. Col. Recs.,* VI, 268, 287, 532, 536; VII, 48, 53; *Newp. Merc.,* May 19, 1761; June 18, 1764; Jan. 12, Apr. 6, July 20, 1767; Nov. 11, 1771; May 4, Oct. 19, 1772; Apr. 25, 1774.

239:3   *S.C. Gaz.,* Aug. 25, Oct. 22, 1764; Oct. 12, 1769; *S.C.A.G. Gaz.,* Oct. 10, 1766; Webster, Southern Hist. Assn., *Pubs.,* II, 135; Andrew J. Morrison, ed., Johann D. Schoepf, *Travels in the Confederation* (Philadelphia, 1911), II, 164.

240:1   Bristol did not have flagstone footways until 1771, shortly after
         they had been introduced at London, and then only in front of
         the Exchange. Latimer, *Bristol in the Eighteenth Century,* 377,
         396; Webb, *Statutory Authorities,* 238, 242, 274, 282; Buer,
         Health, Wealth, and Population, 29, 83, 86, 87; A. D. Bayne,
         A Comprehensive History of Norwich (London, 1869), 280,
         290, 570; *Newp. Merc.,* July 23, 1770; Schoepf, *Travels,* II,
         195; *S.C. Gaz.,* Nov. 14, 1761; Aug. 25, 1764; June 14, 1773;
         S.C. Commons, Jour., XXXV, 6, 50, 91; *S.C. Statutes,* IV, 112,
         181; *S.C.A.G. Gaz.,* Feb. 5, 1771.

241:1   Drinker, Diary, Jan. 20, 1760; *Pa. Statutes,* VI, 196, 234; VII,
         277; *Pa. Gaz.,* Mar. 24, 1763; Apr. 11, 1765; Apr. 24, 1766;
         Jan. 5, 1769; *Pa. Chron.,* Mar. 27, 1769; *Paving Proclamation,*
         Broadsides (HSP), Ab. V, 641.

241:2   Mereness, *Travels,* 415; *N.Y. Merc.,* May 30, 1768; *N.Y. Jour.,*
         May 28, 1772; Sept. 8, 1774; Adams, *Works,* II, 347; *Bos.
         Gaz.,* June 13, 1763; *Mass. Acts,* IV, 724; 20 *Bos. Rec. Com.,*
         130, 283; 16 *Bos. Rec. Com.,* 236; 18 *Bos. Rec. Com.,* 12, 76;
         23 *Bos. Rec. Com.,* 156; *Newp. Merc.,* July 23, 1770.

242:1   *Pa. Votes,* V, 449, 513; VI, 269, 663; *Pa. Statutes,* VII, 5; VIII,
         96; *P.M.C.C.,* 759; *N.Y. Col. Laws,* IV, 533; *N.Y.M.C.C.,* VI,
         276, 278, 334, 343; VII, 211, 279, 429; Weyman's *N.Y. Gaz.,*
         Feb. 8, 1762; Stokes, *Iconography,* IV, 722; Dasch and Ellis,
         bills for lamps and globes, 1762 (NYHS, MSS), VIII, nos. 18,
         23; *N.Y. Gaz.,* Feb. 3, 1763; Dec. 13, 1764; *Bos. Post Boy,*
         July 28, 1766; *N.Y. Merc.,* Dec. 2, 1771.

242:2   Robert Beard, "Tin-Man," lighted lamps by the quarter or year
         in 1771. *S.C. Gaz.,* Apr. 23, 1763; Nov. 9, 1767; Mar. 29,
         1770; Oct. 10, 1771; July 2, 1772; Feb. 22, 1773; *S.C.A.G.
         Gaz.,* Mar. 26, 1770; Feb. 5, 1771; S.C. Commons, Jour.,
         XXXVIII, 340; *Acts of the Assembly* (Charlestown, 1770), 22.

243:1   Graham, *Social Life in Scotland,* 140; Picton, *Municipal Ar-
         chives,* 154; *Buer, Health, Wealth, and Population,* 84, 86;
         Bayne, *Norwich,* 290; *Newsletter,* Feb. 27, 1772; Mar. 3, 1774;
         18 *Bos. Rec. Com.,* 72, 115, 128,135, 163, 196; 23 *Bos. Rec.
         Com.,* 212, 219, 226, 233; Anne R. Cunningham, ed., *Letters
         and Diary of John Rowe* (Boston, 1903), 239, 243, 249, 260,
         264; *Bos. Gaz.,* Sept. 13, 1773; MHS *Procs.,* VIII, 327; XV,
         348, 349; *Bos. Post Boy,* Feb. 28, 1774; Arthur W. H. Eaton,
         The Famous Mather Byles (Boston, 1914), 124.

243:2   16 *Bos. Rec. Com.,* 55; 18 *Bos. Rec. Com.,* 35, 37; 23 *Bos. Rec.
         Com.,* 30, 240; *Newsletter,* Aug. 6, 1761; Apr. 19, *Sup.,* 1765;
         Bos. Post Boy, May 9, 1763; MHS *Colls.,* 72, p. 31; *Bos. Gaz.,*
         May 9, 1763; Feb. 25, 1765; Sept. 1, 1766.

244:1   *Pa. Mag.,* XXXIX, 273; XLVIII, 237; Graydon, *Memoirs,* 46;

Pa. Statutes, VI, 65, 249; VII, 28, 81, 356; Pa. Gaz., Mar. 26, Apr. 16, 1761; Dec. 16, 1762; Oct. 11, 1770; Jan. 23, 1772; Pa. Votes, V, 289, 312, 451, 518.

244:2 S.C. Gaz., Aug. 25, Oct. 8, Dec. 31, 1764; May 3, 1770; Oct. 29, 1772; July 26, 1773; S.C. Commons, Jour., XXXVII, 93; S.C.A.G. Gaz., Apr. 24, 1771; S.C. Country Jour., Apr. 6, 1773.

244:3 Bos. Post Boy, June 14, 1762; Apr. 23, 1764; Aug. 26, 1771; Nov. 22, 1773; 20 Bos. Rec. Com., 57, 231; Mereness, Travels, 449; 18 Bos. Rec. Com., 46; 23 Bos. Rec. Com., 213, 222. MHS Colls., III, 247.

245:1 John Bartram saw the public square at Savannah in 1765, thought it "a fine ornament, and much wanted in Philadelphia." Bartram, Amer. Philos. Soc., Trans., n.s., XXXIII, 31; Stokes, Iconography, IV, 771; Adams, Works, II, 346; Pa. Votes, V, 284; Pa. Chron., July 11, 1768.

245:2 Wilton's marble Pitt and the only other colonial statue, Lord Botetourt, still survive at Charleston and Williamsburg. N.Y. Merc., July 12, 1762; Aug. 20, Sept. 10, 1770; S.C. Statutes, IV, 253; S.C. Gaz., Dec. 1, 1766; May 31, 1770; SCHG Mag., XV, 18; XXVIII, 79, 91; MHS Procs., 49, pp. 456, 480; N.Y. M.C.C., VII, 212, 220; N.Y. Col. Laws, V, 457; Adams, Works, II, 346.

246:1 N.Y. Gaz., June 28, 1764; Feb. 19, 1770; N.Y.M.C.C., VI, 388; VIII, 7; Edwards, New York, 186; MHS Colls., 71, p. 128; Westcott, History of Philadelphia, II, Chaps. CXLVII, CLVII; Pa. Eve. Post, May 11, 1775; S.C. Gaz., Jan. 19, 1765; Sept. 14, Nov. 2, 1769; Feb. 22, 1773; S.C. Statutes, IX, 208, 209, 235; S.C.A.G. Gaz., Apr. 24, 1771; MHS Procs., 49, p. 452. An agitation for making the Schuylkill ferry at High Street free, see Pa. Votes, VI, 117, 354; P.M.C.C., 738.

246:2 Pa. Berichte, June 5, 1761; S.C. Country Jour., May 20, 1766; S.C. Gaz., Dec. 7, Sup., 1767; June 27, 1768; Jan. 5, June 22, 1769; Mar. 7, 1774.

247:1 S.C. Gaz., Nov. 12, 1764; June 8, 1765; Nov. 9, 1767; Apr. 26, 1773; Mar. 7, 1774; Feb. 13, 1775; S.C. Statutes, II, 755; IV, 286; S.C.A.G. Gaz., Apr. 1, 10, 24, 1771.

247:2 16 Bos. Rec. Com., 58, 89, 101; Bos. Gaz., Aug. 10, 1772; Mass. Acts, V, 200; Blaskowitz, Plan of Newport; Commerce of R.I., I, 112; R.I. Hist. Mag., VI, 44; Montresor, Map of New York; N.Y.M.C.C., VI, 410; VII, 32; N.Y. Jour., Apr. 23, 1772; Edwards, New York, 153, 158; Reed, Map of Philadelphia; P.M.C.C., 680, 712, 729, 746, 774; Westcott, History of Philadelphia, II, Chap. CLXX; Pa. Votes, V, 238, 394; VI, 15, 21; Pa. Statutes, VI, 234, 409.

248:1 The Corporation of Liverpool erected a lighthouse on Bidston

Hill overlooking the Mersey in 1771; since 1763 vessels had been guided by the light on Holyoke Head. Picton, *Municipal Archives,* 242; *Pa. Statutes,* VII, 19; VIII, 58; *Pa. Mag.,* XXXVIII, 241; George R. Putnam, *Lighthouses and Light Ships of the United States* (Boston, 1917), 2, 11, 17; *Prov. Gaz.,* Dec. 13, 1766; *Newp. Merc.,* June 25, 1764; July 20, 1767; *Doc. Hist. N.Y.,* I, 704; *N.Y. Gaz.,* June 24, 1764; *S.C. Gaz.,* Oct. 15, 1764; July 6, 1765; Dec. 1, 1766; Jan. 31, 1774; Jan 28, 1775; *S.C. Country Jour.,* June 28, 1768; Aug. 14, 1770; *S.C.A.G. Gaz.,* Nov. 28, 1766; *Bos. Post Boy,* Dec. 30, 1771.

248:2   Honyman, *Journal,* 13, 20, 22, 32, 36, 39, 42, 72; Mereness, *Travels,* 449; M'Robert, *Tour,* 1, 6, 11, 13, 29, 32; Gregory, *New England Mag.,* XII, 344; Smyth, *Tour,* II, 82; Chalmers, *Weather and Diseases of South Carolina,* I, 33; Coates to William Logan, Sept. 26, 1770, Samuel Coates, Letter Book (HSP); A. G. Bradley, ed., *Journal of Nicholas Cresswell, 1774–1777* (New York, 1928), 158; Lyman H. Butterfield, ed., *Letters of Benjamin Rush* (Philadelphia, 1951), I, 31.

CHAPTER VII

251:1   For postwar depression, see Arthur M. Schlesinger, *Colonial Merchants and the American Revolution* (New York, 1918), 56; Andrews, Col. Soc. Mass., *Pubs.,* 159, 181, 379; Harrington, *N.Y. Merchant,* 313, 316; Stoker, Cornell Agr. Sta., *Memoirs, CXLII,* 203; Berg, *Pa. History,* XIII, 187; Taylor, *Jour. of Econ. and Bus. Hist.,* IV, 358, 365; Sachs, *Jour. Econ. Hist.,* XIII, 274; *Charleston Yearbook, 1880,* 246.

251:2   Schlesinger, *Colonial Merchants,* 50, 52, 57; Harrington, *N.Y. Merchant,* 316, 322, 333; 16 *Bos. Rec. Com.,* 121; Col. Soc. Mass., *Pubs.,* XIX, 379; Memorial of Merchants of N.Y. vs. Sugar Act, NYHS Misc., VIII; Bernard, *Select Letters,* 9, 10, 31; *R.I. Col. Recs.,* VI, 378; *Newp. Merc.,* Feb. 6, 13, 1764; June 10, 1765; Bezanson, *Prices in Colonial Philadelphia,* chart XXIX; *Bos. Post Boy,* June 3, 1765.

252:1   Ezra Collins to Stephen Collins, Nov. 8, 1772, Collins Papers, XIV; Clarkson to Van Horne, June 12, 27, Oct. 20, 1774, Clarkson Letters.

252:2   *Pa. Chron.,* Nov. 16, 1767; Collins Papers, especially III, May 12, June 6, 1763; Plummer, *Pa. Mag.,* LXVI, 385.

253:1   Watts, *Letter Book,* 66, 79; J. Beekman, Letter Book, May 4, 1768, July 22, 1769; Apr. 21, 1770; June 19, 1773; *Burd Papers,* 66, 67, 77, 78; *Pa. Votes,* V, 233; *Pa. Mag.,* XX, 205,

208; Collins Papers, XIV, May 15, 1772; XVIII, Feb. 22, 1775; XIX, Oct. 23, 1775; MHS *Procs.*, 343; *Bowdoin Temple Papers,* I, 139.

253:2   *S.C. Gaz.,* July 9, Nov. 5, 1763; Feb. 9, 1767; Mar. 2, 1769; Dec. 27, 1770; Feb. 28, 1771; Laurens to Brown, Nov. 5, 1763, Henry Laurens, Letter Book, 1762–1771 (HSP); cf. Andrews, Col. Soc. Mass., *Pubs., XIX,* 187*n; Bos. Chron.,* Mar. 30, 1769.

253:3   Watts, *Letter Book,* 228, 368; Collins Papers, II, March, 1763; Petitions to R.I. Assembly, XIII, 36, 128; *Pa. Chron.,* Aug. 3, 31, 1767; *S.C. Country Jour.,* May 15, 1770.

254:1   Rome's letter to Moffatt was published in the press and printed separately. *Prov. Gaz.,* June 26, 1773; R.I. Land Recs., VII, 465, 466, 541, 543; VIII, 11; Petitions to R.I. Assembly, XIV, 7; XV, 80; Stiles, *Literary Diary,* I, 92; Coke, *Amer. Loyalists,* 262; *R.I. Col. Recs.,* VI, 212.

255:1   *Bos. Gaz.,* Nov. 2, 1767; *Newletter,* Feb. 25, Mar. 3, 1768; *Burd Papers,* 67; J. Beekman, Letter Book, Nov. 26, 1766; Collins Papers, VII, Mar. 17, 1768; X, Nov. 6, 18, 1769; XII, July 20, 1771.

255:2   *Newp. Hist. Mag.,* II, 58; *Newp. Merc.,* Jan. 23, 1769; *Bos. Post Boy,* Jan. 16, 1764; Dec. 25, 1769; Collins Papers, V, Aug. 23, Sept. 2, 1765; *Pa. Chron.,* Feb. 23, 1767; Dec. 25, 1769; Dec. 31, 1770.

256:1   Adams & Griffin to Vernons, July 4, 25, Sept. 20, Nov. 12, 1763; Jan. 28, 1764; Dec. 6, 1768; Jan. 10, 1770, Slave Box, I (NYHS); *Newsletter,* Sept. 12, 1763; Colonial Exports and Imports, 1768–72, P.R.O., Customs 16/1; Donnan, *Slave Trade,* III, 194, 207, 211, 214; *Newp. Merc.,* Apr. 30, 1764; July 10, 1765; Feb. 10, 1766; *Bos. Eve. Post,* Oct. 28, 1765; Weyman's *N.Y. Gaz.,* Aug. 24, 1767.

256:2   MHS *Procs.,* 58, p. 422; Harrington, *N.Y. Merchant,* 201; Collins Papers, X, Nov. 18, 1769; *Bos. Gaz.,* June 3, 1771; *Pa. Gaz.,* May 21, *Sup.,* 1761.

256:3   New York maintained twelve whalers, and in 1774 the United Whaling Company was established. Other colonies also tried whaling. In 1768 the sloop *Sally* cleared from New Berne, North Carolina, her "whole apparatus having been imported from Boston." 4 Force *Amer. Archives,* I, 1650; *Rivington's N.Y. Gaz.,* May 26, 1774; *Bos. Chron.,* May 2, July 18, 1768; July 27, 1769; May 24, 1770; *Newsletter,* Aug. 8, 22, 1765; Gov. Palliser to Board of Trade, 1764, King's MSS (LC Trans.), 205; 636, 637, 643; *Prov. Gaz.,* Oct. 4, 1766; *S.C. Gaz.,* June 1, 1767; *Conn. Jour.,* Mar. 29, 1775; *R.I. Col. Recs.,* VII, 213; Mason, *Reminiscences of Newport,* 38.

257:1 Shipping and trade statistics in P.R.O., Customs 16/1; Harrington, *N.Y. Merchant,* Appendices F, G; *Pa. Chron.,* Jan. 26, Mar. 16, 23, 1767; *Pennsylvania Mag.,* I (1775), 72; Stevens, *Facsimiles,* 2087; George Chalmers, Papers relating to Philadelphia (NYPL), II, 63; *Pa. Eve. Post,* Mar. 4, 1775; Proud, *Hist. of Pennsylvania,* II, 265n; Smyth, *Tour,* II, 307; *Bos. Chron.,* Jan. 30, 1769.

257:2 The new customs regulations of 1764 requiring bonds, fees, entry, and clearance for all coasters evoked bitter complaints. Apparently orders were relaxed in 1768, and little was heard of the problem after 1773. Morison, Amer. Antiquarian Soc., *Procs.,* XXXII, 24, 43, 50; Bigelow, R.I. Commerce, I, vii; 11, 12, 13; Annapolis Port Entries, Treas. 1, Bundles 406, 414, 435 (LC Trans.); Donnan, *Slave Trade,* III, 195; *Burd Papers,* 65; MHS *Colls.,* 71, p. 173; Receipt, Oct. 25, 1763, Vernon Papers, 1762–63 (NHS); *Bos. Chron.,* Dec. 19, 1768; Samuel and Jonathan Smith, Letter Book (LC), July 27, Aug. 23, 1765; Oct. 28, 1766; *Newp. Merc.,* Feb. 1, 1773; *S.C. Gaz.,* Dec. 10, 1764; Aug. 20, *Sup.,* 1770.

258:1 *Pa. Chron.,* Mar. 16, 1767; *S.C. Gaz.,* Oct. 21, 1768; Oct. 26, 1769; Harrington, *N.Y. Merchant,* 242; Collins Papers, I, July 30, 1761; Feb. 3, 1762; II, May 30, June 4, 8, 1762; IV, Feb. 6, Apr. 19, 1765; XIV, July 25, 1772.

258:2 Lownes, Letter Book, Apr. 1, 1761; Harrington, *N.Y. Merchant,* 238; Morison, Amer. Antiquarian Soc., *Procs.,* XXXII, 43; *Mass. Gaz.,* Apr. 3, 1766.

259:1 Reese in *Cambridge History of the British Empire* (New York, 1927), I, 585; Morison, Amer. Antiquarian Soc., *Procs.,* XXXII, 26; Dickerson, *Miss. Valley Hist. Rev.,* XXXII, 517; Br. Mus., Add. MSS, 15,484: 4, 7, 8, 27; *N.Y. Col. Docs.,* VII, 584; MHS *Colls.,* I, 80; Harrington, *N.Y. Merchant,* 263, 268, 275.

259:2 Gipson, *British Empire,* I, 75; *R.I. Col. Recs.,* VI, 380; Samuel G. Arnold, *History of Rhode Island* (Providence, 1853), II, 246; Stiles, *Itineraries,* 204; Edmund S. and Helen M. Morgan, *Stamp Act Crisis* (Chapel Hill, 1953), 23, 40; *Prov. Gaz.,* Dec. 22, 1764; *S.C.A.G. Gaz.,* Dec. 5, 1768; Bigelow, R.I. Commerce, II, iii, 5, 8, 9, 16, 17, 19, 22, 24; Duties Collected in America, 1765–66, PRO: Treas. 1, Bundle 442, folio 30; Petitions to R.I. Assembly, XIII, 100; *Newsletter,* Sept. 21, 1769; Br. Mus. Add. MSS, 15,484: 3; *Newp. Merc.,* Jan. 30, 1764.

260:1 Colonial Exports and Imports, 1768–1772, P.R.O., Customs 16/1; Gilman Ostrander, Molasses Trade of the Thirteen Colonies (MA Thesis, Univ. of California, Berkeley), Tables I–VI; Adams, *Works,* X, 345.

260:2   *Pa. Chron.,* May 16, 1768.

261:1   James & Drinker, Letter Book, II, June 19, 1761; Collins Papers, I, Nov. 14, 1761; II, May 15, 1762, Sept. 15, 1762; III, Oct. 22, 1763; IV, Aug. 29, Nov. 23, 1764; V, June 9, 1766; VI, Nov. 18, 1766; NYHS *Colls.,* 1886, p. 56; *Pa. Chron.,* Nov. 16, 1767; Yearly exports of produce from several inlets on the western shore of the Delaware, 1770–1774, Chalmers, Papers relating to Philadelphia, II; and for a mass of information, G. W. Walters, The Commerce of Colonial Philadelphia (Ph.D. Thesis, Yale University, 1933).

261:2   Whitelaw, Vermont Hist. Soc., *Procs.,* 1905–6, p. 137; Perry, *Collections . . . Amer. Colonial Church, Pa.,* II, 277; Collins Papers, IV, Jan. 15, 1765; V, May 2, 1768; VIII, Aug. 14, 1768; XVI, Sept. 16, 1773.

261:3   Albert T. Volweiler, *George Croghan and the Westward Movement in Pennsylvania* (Cleveland, 1926), 40, 150, 151, 189, 190, 203, 233; *Pa. Chron.,* May 16, 1768; *Pa. Eve. Post,* Mar. 2, 1775.

262:1   Bridenbaugh, *Myths and Realities,* 121, 126, 128, 150; Sellers, *Charleston Business,* 31, 34, 88, 89; *S.C. Gaz.,* July 6, 1769; Dec. 5, 1771; S.C. Pub. Recs., XXXII, 395, 402; Alexander Gregg, *History of the Old Cheraws* (New York, 1867), 118; *Bos. Chron.,* Dec. 12, 1768; Laurens, Letter Book, Dec. 3, 1763; *Md. Gaz.,* July 21, 1768; *S.C.A.G. Gaz.,* Jan. 30, Nov. 20, 1767; Mereness, *Travels,* 399; Crittenden, *Commerce of North Carolina,* 30, 32, 75, 76, 88, 89, 92; Adelaide R. Fries, ed., *Records of the Moravians in North Carolina* (Raleigh, 1922–25), I, 235, 277; II, 762, 820, 868.

262:2   King's MSS (LC Trans.), 205:594; *S.C. Gaz.,* July 18, 1761; Mar. 21, 1768; Mereness, *Travels,* 393; *American Museum,* IV, 278; Sellers, *Charleston Business,* 45, 47; Wallace, *Henry Laurens,* 50; *S.C.A.G. Gaz.,* Oct. 7, 1768.

263:1   *Newsletter,* Oct. 13, 1763; Feb. 16, 1764; *New London Summary,* Oct. 8, 1762; *Newp. Merc.,* Nov. 21, 1763; *Essex Gaz.,* Dec. 6, 1768; Jan. 31, Mar. 7, 1769; Jan. 9, 1770; *Bos. Gaz.,* July 13, 1761; May 17, 1762; *New Hampshire Gaz.,* Aug. 4, 1769; MHS *Colls.,* 71, p. 281.

263:2   Rogers, *Concise Account of North America,* 53; Harrington, *N.Y. Merchant,* 166, 169, 255; Samuel Loudon, Letters, 1763–1774 (NYHS), Nov. 26, 1763; Dec. 17, 1771; Mitchell, *Roads and Road Making in Connecticut,* 23; Adams, *Works,* II, 276, 341; *Connecticut Journal,* Aug. 17, 1770; *Albany Gaz.,* Aug. 3, 1772; *American Chronicle* (NY), May 31, 1762; *New Amer. Mag.,* March, 1758, p. 52.

264:1 Stiles, *Itineraries,* 89; *Journal of John Lees of Quebec, Merchant* (Detroit, 1911), 11; *R.I. Hist. Mag.,* VI, 46; *Commerce of R.I.,* I, 344, 347, 356, 367; Serle, *Journal,* 280; Lownes, Letter Book, Dec. 15, 1766; Jan. 12, 1768; Harrington, *N.Y. Merchant,* 69, 70.

264:2 The *Boston Chronicle* of Feb. 5, 1770 remarked that "Providence, which was the other day but a struggling village, does now bid fair to rival this town in greatness." *Bos. Eve. Post,* Feb. 8, 1768; Kimball, *R.I. Governors,* II, 273; Brown Papers, Misc. Letters, 1760 (John Carter Brown Library), L60M; *Prov. Gaz.,* Apr. 16, 1763; Mar. 10, 1764; Jan. 11, 1772; *Newp. Merc.,* Jan. 19, June 1, 1767; Watson, *Men and Times of the Revolution,* 67; and in general, Kimball, *Providence in Colonial Times,* and Hedges, *Browns of Providence Plantations.*

265:1 *Bos. Gaz.,* Feb. 1, 1762; *Pa. Gaz.,* July 9, 1761; *Pa. Chron.,* Feb. 22, 1768; *Cape Fear Mercury,* Jan. 13, 1773; *N.Y. Col. Laws,* IV, 925; V, 68; Licences for Pedlars, 1763–1774, Secretary's Office, Ledger A (HSP).

265:2 Mereness, *Travels,* 411; *Amer. Hist. Rev.,* XXVII, 79; Crevecoeur, *Letters of an American Farmer,* 75; Jacob Duché, *Observations on a Variety of Subjects* (Philadelphia, 1774), 69; Schoepf, *Travels,* I, 22.

265:3 S.C. Pub. Recs., XXXII, 282, 393; Sellers, *Charleston Business,* 31, 34, 35; *S.C. Gaz.,* Jan. 25, 1770; Dec. 5, 1771; *S.C. Country Jour.,* Aug. 7, 1770; Whitelaw, *Vermont Hist. Soc., Procs.,* 1905–6, p. 143.

266:1 John Hughes, Papers (HSP), Sept. 7, 1769; *Commerce of R.I.,* I, 240, 246, 437; Harrington, *N.Y. Merchant,* 258; *R.I. Col. Recs.,* VI, 545; Petitions to R.I. Assembly, XIII, 21; *Prov. Gaz.,* Mar. 14, 1772.

266:2 Mouzon, *Map of North and South Carolina;* Bartram, Amer. Phil. Soc., *Trans.,* n.s., XXXIII, 23; Weston, *Documents relating to S.C.,* 178; Charles Woodmason to Bishop of London, Fulham Palace MSS, S.C., no. 62; *S.C. Gaz.,* Mar. 2, 1765; May 9, 1768; *S.C.A.G. Gaz.,* July 10, 1767.

267:1 *Pa. Chron.,* Mar. 30, 1767; *Albany Gaz.,* Dec. 16, 1771; June 22, 1772; NYHS *Colls.,* 1871, p. 117; *Bos. Post Boy,* June 25, 1764; Mitchell, *Roads and Road Making in Connecticut,* map.

267:2 *N.Y. Merc.,* Aug. 26, 1771; *S.C. Gaz.,* Jan. 18, 1770; Jan. 7, 1773.

267:3 Moale's Baltimore in James T. Adams, *Provincial Society* (New York, 1927), 202; *Pa. Votes,* V, 291, 495; VI, 346, 558, 560; *Pa. Chron.,* Jan. 26, Feb. 16, Mar. 16, 1767; Jan. 8, 1770; *Pa. Mag.,* XLIX, 306; *Pa. Gaz.,* Apr. 3, 1760; Mar. 19, 1761; Jan.

4, 1770; 1 *Pa. Archives,* IV, 360, 362, 442; Bridenbaugh, *Rebels and Gentlemen,* 347.

268:1　*Bowdoin and Temple Papers,* I, 158.

268:2　Even Jamaica had its Society for the Encouragement of Arts, Agriculture and Commerce. *Georgia Gaz.,* May 16, 1765. On the movement for domestic manufactures, see Schlesinger, *Colonial Merchants,* 77, 86, 107, 109, 122, 130, 151, 243; *N.Y. Merc.,* Dec. 3, 10, 1764; *Bos. Gaz.,* Sept. 27, 1762; Sept. 24, 1764; *Bos. Post Boy,* May 26, 1766; *Pa. Mag.,* XVIII, 262; XLIX, 309; *Pa. Eve. Post,* Jan. 31, 1775; Nathan G. Goodman, *Benjamin Rush, Physician and Citizen* (Philadelphia, 1934), 46; William Duane, ed., *Extracts from the Diary of Christopher Marshall* (Albany, 1877), 14, 36n; *Newp. Merc.,* Feb. 25, 1765; Nov. 30, 1767; June 5, 1769; Stiles, *Literary Diary,* I, 107, 108; *S.C. Gaz.,* Jan. 31, 1771; 4 Force, *Amer. Archives,* I, 344n.

269:1　Bridenbaugh, *Colonial Craftsman,* 60, 92, 97; *Pa. Gaz.,* Apr. 9, 1761; Jan. 5, 1769; *Pa. Chron.,* June 8, Dec. 7, 1767; Jan. 18, 1768; Oct. 30, 1769; Oct. 22, 1770; Mar. 4, 1771; *Amer. Hist. Rev.,* XXVII, 79; Lownes, Letter Book, Sept. 19, 1761; Coke, *Amer. Loyalists,* 326; *Pa. Mag.,* XXIV, *passim; 3 Pa. Archives,* XIV, lists shipbuilders taxed; Proud, *Hist. of Pennsylvania,* II, 265, 267, 269; Bining, *Pa. Iron Manufacture,* 132, 178; Arthur C. Bining, *British Regulation of the Colonial Iron Industry* (Philadelphia, 1933), 122.

269:2　John Penn had Edward Shippen send over some Philadelphia bottled beer in 1772: "I intend to surprize some of our English Folks with it, who think that there is nothing Good in America." Edward Shippen Papers (LC), Oct. 18, 1772; Mar. 1, 1773; Proud, *History of Pennsylvania,* II, 265, 267, 269; Du Simitiere Papers, Pa., N.E., July, 1772; *Pa. Gaz.,* Apr. 2, Dec. 3, 10, 1761; Mar. 4, 1762; Apr. 2, 1767; Feb. 6, 1772; *Pa. Jour.,* Nov. 11, 1772; Jan. 27, 1773; Dec. 7, 1774; *Pa. Chron.,* Mar. 27, 1769; Jan. 1, 1770; *Pa. Merc.,* July 7, 1775; *Pa. Packet,* Apr. 13, 1771; May 29, 1775; *Pa. Mag.,* XI, 492; *N.Y. Gaz.,* Sept. 17, 1772; Mar. 15, 1773; *N.Y. Jour.,* Nov. 17, 1774.

270:1　King's MSS, 205:41, 55; MHS *Colls.,* I, 81; MHS *Procs.,* VIII, 362, 390; XV, 344; 58, p. 424; Rowe, *Diary,* 80; *Bos. Eve. Post,* Mar. 7, 1769; June 3, 1771; *Bos. Chron.,* Dec. 28, 1767; May 22, 1769; *Bos. Gaz.,* Oct. 6, 1766; Feb. 22, Nov. 14, 1768; Mar. 12, June 4, *Sup.,* Nov. 12, 1770; Feb. 25, Dec. 16, 1771; Dec. 13, 1773; Bernard, *Select Letters,* 10; Jones, *Loyalists of Massachusetts,* 7, 55, 175, 181; Coke, *Amer. Loyalists,* 238; *Murray Letters,* 116, 152, 155; A List of Rolls and Estates . . .

Boston, 1771 (Mass Archives), I, 147; *Amer. Gazetteer,* I, article on Boston.

270:2   Stiles, *Itineraries,* 23, 490; Bigelow, R.I. Commerce, II, i, 29; Letters from the Governors (R.I. Archives), II, 2; Samuel Freebody, Distilling House Ledger, 1756–68 (NHS), Jan. 29, 1757; *R.I. Col. Recs.,* VI, 380; Memoirs of 1766–1767, Stiles MSS (Yale), 13; G. H. Richardson Collection, 970:62; John Lord Sheffield, *Observations on the Commerce of the American States* (London, 1784), 96.

271:1   Channing-Ellery Papers (RIHS), I, 61, 63; United Company Agreements, Mason, *Reminiscences of Newport* (NHS copy), I, 40A, 44A, 49A; *Commerce of R.I.,* 88, 92, 97, 114, 130, 137; S. Broches, *Jews in New England* (New York, 1942), II, 46; Hedges, *Browns of Providence* supersedes all accounts of this first intercolonial business agreement.

271:2   *N.Y. Merc.,* Oct. 19, 1767; July 18, 1768; May 13, 1771; Mar. 15, 1773; June 13, 1774; *Rivington's N.Y. Gaz.,* Apr. 22, Sept. 2, *Sup.,* 1773; Oct. 20, *Sup.,* 1774; Mar. 30, 1775; *N.Y. Jour.,* June 25, 1767; June 4, *Sup.,* July 14, Nov. 17, 1768; May 24, 1770; Harrington, *N.Y. Merchant,* 270, 274; *N.Y. Col. Docs.,* VII, 888; *Journal of John Lees,* 12; Stokes, *Iconography,* IV, 746; Weyman's *N.Y. Gaz.,* Sept. 28, 1767; *Bos. Chron.,* Aug. 28, 1769; *S.C. Gaz.,* Apr. 10, 1775; NYHS *Bull.,* XXIX, 78; *N.Y. Gaz.,* Feb. 11, 1771; NYHS MSS, Misc. 1775, no. 11.

272:1   King's MSS, 205:56; *S.C. Gaz.,* Mar. 26, Apr. 23, Sept. 17, 1763; Sept. 28, Oct. 31, 1765; Dec. 29, 1766; June 27, 1768; Oct. 4, 18, 1770; Jan. 17, 31, 1771; Oct. 25, 1773; Feb. 21, 1774; *Prov. Gaz.,* Mar. 24, 1764; Thomas Griffith, Diary, Sept. 21, 1767 (Copy in N.C. Archives, Raleigh); Webster, Southern Hist. Assn., *Pubs.,* II, 135; *S.C. Country Jour.,* Jan. 21, 1766; Feb. 16, 1773; *Newsletter,* Nov. 7, 1765; Clarkson Letters, Apr. 20, Dec. 12, 1773.

272:2   This subject is treated at length in Bridenbaugh, *Colonial Craftsman,* 65–100. See also, 3 *Pa. Archives,* XIV, 385; NYHS *Colls.,* 1885; *Pa. Chron.,* Jan. 10, 1769.

273:1   Bridenbaugh, *Colonial Craftsman,* 75; *Bos. Chron.,* Aug. 8, 1768; *N.Y. Jour.,* Aug. 17, *Sup.,* 1769; *N.Y. Merc.,* Mar. 18, 1765; Weyman's *N.Y. Gaz.,* Jan. 14, 1765; *Pa. Packet,* Dec. 13, 1773; *S.C. Gaz.,* Nov. 16, 1769.

273:2   Edward Shippen Papers (LC), May 18, 1771; Stiles, *Literary Diary,* I, 259; *Newsletter,* Aug. 13, 1767; *Bos. Post Boy,* Aug. 10, 1767; Jan. 29, 1770; *Newp. Merc.,* Aug. 29, Sept. 5, 1768; Nov. 9, 1772; *Pa. Gaz.,* Oct. 9, 1766; *Bos. Gaz.,* Jan. 18, 25, 1768; Aug. 22, 1774; *N.Y. Merc.,* Sept. 2, 1765; July 10, 1776;

Pa. Chron., Mar. 16, 1767; Thomas Morgan, Ledger A, 1771–1802 (HSP).

273:1   *Bos. Chron.,* June 6, 1768; *N.Y. Jour.,* Dec. 7, 1767; *Pa. Gaz.,* Feb. 6, 1766; *S.C. Gaz.,* Oct. 31, 1765; July 23, 1772.

274:2   Webster, Southern Hist. Assn., *Pubs.,* II, 135; Bridenbaugh, *Colonial Craftsman,* 122; *S.C. Gaz.,* Feb. 2, Oct. 19, 1765; *Md. Gaz.,* Feb. 19, 1767; *Pa. Chron.,* July 13, 1767; *S.C. Country Jour.,* Jan. 19, 1773; *Newp. Merc.,* May 3, 1773; *SCHG Mag.,* XXXV, 13.

274:3   Bridenbaugh, *Colonial Craftsman,* chaps. III, IV; Clarence E. Carter, ed., *Correspondence of General Thomas Gage* (New Haven, 1933), II, 616.

275:1   19 *Bos. Rec. Com.,* 223.

275:2   *N.Y. Jour.,* Aug. 20, 1772; Drinker, Diary, May 4, 14, June 26, 1759; Jan. 26, 1760; Sept. 19, 1769; *Pa. Mag.,* VII, 24; *Newp. Merc.,* Dec. 26, 1763.

276:1   *Pa. Chron.,* Mar. 16, 1767; *Commerce of R.I.,* I, 423; Collins Papers, XVI, Oct. 2, 1773; J. Beekman, Letter Book, Aug. 3, 1768; Col. Soc. Mass., *Pubs.,* XIX, 175, 182.

276:2   *Bos. Gaz.,* Apr. 11, 1768; May 4, *Sup.,* 1772; *Newsletter,* May 19, 1763; May 9, 1771; Jan. 9, 1772; *S.C. Country Jour.,* May 27, 1766; July 21, 1767; *N.Y. Merc.,* Apr. 1, 1771; Harrington, *N.Y. Merchant,* 62; *N.Y. Gaz.,* July 19, 1764; *N.Y. Jour.,* June 18, *Sup.,* 1767; *Pa. Chron.,* Sept. 21, 1767.

276:3   *Bos. Post Boy,* June 13, 1774; *S.C. Country Jour.,* Apr. 15, June 3, 1766; Apr. 11, 1769; *Bos. Chron.,* Feb. 29, 1768; *Pa. Gaz.,* June 4, 1761; *Pa. Chron.,* July 31, 1769; *Pa. Jour.,* July 5, 1770; *N.Y. Merc.,* July 29, 1771; Feb. 8, 1773; *Pa. Mag.,* I, 69.

277:1   Collins Papers, XIII, Feb. 28, 1772; XV, Dec. 12, 1772; Watts, *Letter Book,* 115, 381; Scharf & Westcott, *History of Philadelphia,* I, 891.

277:2   *Bos. Post Boy,* Feb. 17, 1766; Mar. 15, 1772; July 26, 1773; *Mass. Acts,* V, 248, 300, 357, 360; *Acts Privy Council,* V, 393; 23 *Bos. Rec. Com.,* 169, 178, 184; *Bos. Gaz.,* Apr. 11, 1774; MHS *Procs.,* VIII, 323; *N.Y. Col. Laws,* V, 547; *N.Y. Gaz.,* May 2, 1768; *Pa. Gaz.,* Sept. 7, 1774; *Pa. Votes,* VI, 449; Marshall, *Diary,* 43; *Newp. Merc.,* June 8, 1767; May 30, 1768.

278:1   *Newsletter,* Jan. 15, 1761; 19 *Bos. Rec. Com.,* 133, 226; Winsor, *Mem. Hist. Boston,* II, 266; *Newp. Merc.,* May 4, 1772; Stiles, *Literary Diary,* I, 130; Newp. T.M. Recs., 798, 902, 1002, 1004, 1028, 1054, 1058, 1086; Edwards, *New York,* 71, 74, 76; *S.C. Gaz.,* May 21, 1763; Oct. 15, 1764; Feb. 1, 1768; Jan. 25, 1770; *Acts of Assembly,* S.C., 1770, 18.

278:2   *Pa. Mag.,* X, 115, XI, 240; *P.M.C.C.,* 683, 684, 699, 711, 778,

781, 783; *Pa. Gaz.,* June 23, July 14, 1773; NYHS *Colls.,* 1886, pp. 12, 14; Westcott, *Hist. of Philadelphia,* II, chap. CCV; *Pa. Votes,* VI, 215, 378, 386.

279:1 18 *Bos. Rec. Com.,* 20; *Newsletter,* Apr. 1, 1762; *Bos. Chron.,* July 11, 1768; *Newp. Merc.,* Jan. 3, 1763; June 21, 1773.

279:2 *N.Y. Merc.,* Nov. 26, 1770; *Newp. Merc.,* Nov. 12, 1764; June 29, 1767; *S.C. Gaz.,* May 7, Dec. 17, 1763; Dec. 9, 1764; Apr. 13, 1767; Jan. 5, 1769; *N.Y. Gaz.,* Feb. 29, 1768; *S.C. Country Jour.,* Apr. 11, 1769; Nov. 23, 1773; *Bos. Post Boy,* Jan. 14, 1771; Dec. 26, 1774; *Pa. Packet,* Dec. 7, 1772.

280:1 *N.Y. Merc.,* Apr. 18, 1768; *S.C. Gaz.,* Sept. 17, 1763, Oct. 8, 1764; June 15, 1767; Sept. 26, 1774; Bernard, *Select Letters,* 2, 3; *Mass. Gaz.,* Sept. 18, 1769; Weyman's *N.Y. Gaz.,* July 13, 1767; *American Gazetteer,* III, article on New York; *Newp. Merc.,* Aug. 15, 1763; Feb. 8, 1773; *N.Y. Jour.,* Apr. 26, 1770; *N.Y. Gaz.,* July 28, 1763; *Pa. Gaz.,* Sept. 24, 1761.

280:2 *Newp. Merc.,* Oct. 16, 1768; *Newsletter,* Oct. 8, 1761; Dec. 1, 1763; *Bos. Post Boy,* Aug. 9, 1762; *Bos. Gaz.,* Nov. 28, 1763; Apr. 2, 1764; *N.Y.M.C.C.,* VI, 260; *P.M.C.C.,* 775; *S.C. Gaz.,* Nov. 12, 1772.

280:3 *Newp Merc.,* May 7, 1765; Sept. 30, 1765; Nov. 24, 1766.

281:1 18 *Bos. Rec. Com.,* 170; *Newp. Merc.,* Oct. 6, 1766; *S.C. Country Jour.,* July 22, Aug. 12, 1766; *S.C. Gaz.,* May 7, 1772; Apr. 18, 1774; Jones, *Loyalists of Massachusetts,* 130.

281:2 Stiles, Miscellaneous Papers (LC), Valuation of estates in Newport, Sept. 13, 1761.

281:3 *Burd Papers,* 37, 43, 47; *Lloyd Papers,* II, 639, 641, 653, 742, 745; Stiles, *Itineraries,* 81; Stiles, *Literary Diary,* I, 94; Collins Papers, V, July 22, Aug. 21, 1765; Mar. 24, May 8, 1766; *DAB,* XI, 33.

282:1 Bridenbaugh, *Peter Harrison,* 121, 127, 130, 140.

282:2 Schlesinger, *Colonial Merchants,* 27, 50, 91, 157, 197; Andrews, Col. Soc. Mass., *Pubs.,* XIX, 160, 163n; Wiener, *N.E. Quarterly,* III, 464; *N.Y. Merc.,* Apr. 2, 1770.

284:1 *Bos. Gaz.,* Sept. 23, 1765; Apr. 9, 1770; *Pa. Gaz.,* June 19, 1766; Abiel Holmes, *The Life of Ezra Stiles* (Boston, 1798), 162; *SCHG Mag.,* XXXV, 20.

284:2 *Bos. Gaz.,* Sept. 24, Oct. 1, 1764; *Articles and Regulations of the Friendly Society of Tradesmen, House-Carpenters, in the City of New York* (Broadside, 1767, NYPL); *N.Y. Jour.,* Apr. 13, 1769; Schlesinger, *N.E. Quarterly,* VIII, 68; Hutchinson Correspondence, II, Mass Archives XXVI, 391; *N.Y. Merc.,* Nov. 18, 1771; Crevecoeur, *Letters from an American Farmer,* 58.

284:3 NYHS *Colls.,* 1897, pp. 18, 120, 245.

285:1 *Rush Letters,* I, 18; Stokes, *Iconography,* IV, 602; *N.Y. Jour.,*
Apr. 7, 1768; Wroth, *Colonial Printer,* 166; *Murray Letters,*
122, 132; Adams, *Works,* X, 260; *Georgia Gaz.,* Mar. 28, 1770.

285:2 *Bos. Post Boy,* May 9, Oct. 31, 1763; *Pa. Mag.,* XI, 492.

286:1 Boston had eighteen free negroes in 1762. 19 *Bos. Rec. Com.,*
195; Stiles, *Literary Diary,* I, 409; McKee, *Labor in Colonial
New York,* chap. III; *Newp. Merc.,* Jan. 24, 1763; Aug. 5, Sept.
16, 1771; *S.C. Gaz.,* June 13, 1768; Mar. 15, 1770; Oct. 25,
1773; S.C. Pub. Recs., XXXII, 387.

286:2 *Rush Letters,* I, 85; *N.Y. Merc.,* June 1, 1772.

287:1 *Bos. Post Boy,* Feb. 1, 1762; *Pa. Chron.,* Jan. 26, July 6, Nov.
9, 1767; *Bos. Gaz.,* May 7, 1764; July 25, 1768; Feb. 5, 1770;
Newsletter, July 23, 1765; July 21, 1768; *Newp. Merc.,* May 17,
24, Sept. 6, Nov. 29, 1773; *N.Y. Merc.,* Apr. 11, 1763; Sept. 5,
1774; *Pa. Gaz.,* Dec. 13, 1770; *Pa. Eve. Post,* May 30, 1776;
Rivington's N.Y. Gaz., Sept. 2, Sup., 1773; Mar. 24, Sept. 8,
1774; *S.C.A.G. Gaz.,* Feb. 5, Mar. 19, 1771; *S.C. Country Jour.,*
May 12, *Sup.,* 1772; *S.C. Gaz.,* Dec 27, 1773; Jan 23, 30, 1775.

287:2 Gillingham, *Marine Insurance,* 34, 52, 55, 104; John Kidd &
William Bradford, Maritime Insurance Accounts, Book A and
Journal of Underwriters, Philadelphia Insurance Co., 1768–
1774, Bradford Papers (HSP); *Pa. Chron.,* Mar. 9, 1767; *Bos.
Gaz.,* Feb. 26, *Sup.,* 1770; July 8, 1771; Nov. 1, 1773; *Newp.
Merc.,* Mar. 23, 1762; Nov. 29, 1773; G. Beekman, Letter
Book, May 7, 1761; *S.C. Gaz.,* Jan. 19, 1769.

288:1 *Newsletter,* Aug. 13, 1761; Society for Encouraging Trade and
Commerce (Boston), Rules and Letters (MHS); *N.Y. Gaz.,*
Nov. 29, 1764; Oct. 24, 1765; John A. Stevens, ed., *Colonial
Records of the New York Chamber of Commerce,* 1768–1784
(New York, 1867), 3, 8, 11, 17, 21, 30; *S.C. Gaz.,* Dec. 13,
1773; Feb. 28, 1774.

288:2 Evidence of excessive usury during the currency crisis can be
found in a rigorous Rhode Island law of 1767 fixing a limit of
six per cent for interest and providing for the forfeiture of both
principal and interest in cases of violation. *R.I. Acts* (1772), 3;
Scharf & Westcott, *History of Philadelphia,* III, 2086; *S.C. Gaz.,*
June 4, 1772; A list of Rolls and Estates . . . Boston, 1771
(Mass. Archives), I, 92, 134, 135, 137, 147; *Lloyd Papers,* II,
596; Philip Syng, Account Book, 1759–1788.

289:1 Hamlin, *Legal Education,* 135, 142, 145, 163, 201, 204; Stokes,
Iconography, IV, 815; Stiles, *Itineraries,* 24; *Rivington's N.Y.
Gaz.,* Oct. 6, 1774; Adams, *Works,* II, 146; MHS *Procs.,* XIX,
147; Jackson, *Cyclopedia of Philadelphia,* III, 825; *S.C. Gaz.,*

Nov. 7, 1771; Col. Soc. Mass., *Pubs.,* VI, 385; S.C. Pub. Recs., XXXII, 378.

289:2 Coke, *Amer. Loyalists,* 86, 119, 310; MHS *Procs.,* 49, p. 447; *The Burd Papers,* 17; *Pa. Mag.,* IX, 181, 183; Adams, *Works,* II, 378.

290:1 *Newp. Merc.,* Aug. 10, 1762; Apr. 15, 1765; Nov. 16, 1767; Oct. 2, 1769; Apr. 23, 1770; Mar. 14, 1774; *N.Y. Jour.,* Feb. 5, 1767; *New London Gaz.,* Apr. 7, June 16, 1769; *Prov. Gaz.,* July 18, 1767; *N.Y. Gaz.,* Nov. 21, 1768; *Pa. Chron.,* Apr. 13, July 20, Oct. 26, 1767; June 6, Oct. 31, 1768; *S.C. Gaz.,* Feb. 23, *Sup.,* 1765; Dec. 17, 1772; Nov. 22, 1773.

290:2 Col. Soc. Mass., *Pubs.,* XI, 34; *Journal kept by Hugh Finlay, Surveyor of the Post Roads. . . . 1773–1774* (Brooklyn, 1867); MHS *Procs.,* 50, p. 170; *Bos. Post Boy,* Jan. 16, 1764; *Bos. Gaz.,* Jan. 27, 1772; *S.C. Gaz.,* Oct. 31, *Sup.,* 1765; Butler, *Benjamin Franklin: Postmaster General,* 61, 85, 90.

291:1 Post Office Accounts, Newport, R.I., 1771–1774 (NYPL); *Newp. Merc.,* Mar. 28, 1774; July 3, 31, 1775; 4 Force, *Amer. Archives,* I, 500; *Bos. Gaz.,* Mar. 21, Apr. 11, 25, 1774; Stiles, *Literary Diary,* I, 437, 439, 550; *Bos. Post Boy,* May 2, 1774; *R.I. Col. Recs.,* VII, 352, 367; *Pa. Merc.,* Oct. 13, 1775.

CHAPTER VIII

293:1 *N.Y. Col. Laws,* IV, 571, 869, 1047; Stokes, *Iconography,* IV, 852; *Bos. Post Boy,* June 14, 1762; *Mass. Acts,* IV, 599; *S.C. Gaz.,* Nov. 14, 1761; Oct. 12, Dec. 28, 1769; *S.C.A.G. Gaz.,* Jan. 1, 1771.

293:2 MHS *Procs.,* XV, 12; Milling, *Colonial South Carolina,* 128; *S.C. Gaz.,* Nov. 30, 1767; Oct. 1, 1772; *Pa. Statutes,* VIII, 171; 18 *Bos. Rec. Com.,* 47, 55; *Rivington's N.Y. Gaz.,* Jan. 20, 27, Apr. 7, 1774.

294:1 16 *Bos. Rec. Com.,* 167; 20 *Bos. Rec. Com.,* 206, 271; *Newp. Merc.,* Apr. 19, 1773; *Newsletter,* Apr. 16, May 14, Aug. 20, 1772; *N.Y. Gaz.,* July 31, 1769; *N.Y. Merc.,* Apr. 20, 1767; *N.Y. Jour.,* June 18, Sup., 1767; *Pa. Chron.,* Mar. 16, 1767; Oct. 24, 1768; *N.Y. Gaz.,* Apr. 15, 1771; Newp. T.M. Recs., 938; S.C. Commons, Jour., XXXVII, 124.

294:2 *Mass. Acts.,* IV, 661; 20 *Bos. Rec. Com.,* 120, 278; 18 *Bos. Rec. Com.,* 87; 23 *Bos. Rec. Com.,* 159, 162, 216, 236; Newp. T.M. Recs., 716, 896, 912, 928, 930, 934; *Newp. Merc.,* Jan. 18, 1768; *N.Y.M.C.C.,* VI, 250, 314; VII, 144, 387; *N.Y. Col. Laws,* IV, 673, 1048; V, 456; *S.C. Gaz.,* Sept. 28, 1768; July 30, Oct. 1, 8, 29, 1772; Feb. 22, 1773.

294:3 Westcott, *Hist. Phila. Fire Dept.; Pa. Mag.,* XVIII, 431; *Pa. Gaz.,* Oct. 27, 1768; Scharf and Westcott, *Hist. of Philadelphia,* III, 1886; Jacob C. Parsons, ed., *Extracts from the Diary of Jacob Hiltzheimer of Philadelphia, 1765–1798* (Philadelphia, 1893), 20, 32; *P.M.C.C.,* 673, 745, 746; Drake, *History of Boston,* 665; *Newsletter,* June 8, 1769; *Prov. Gaz.,* Dec. 29, 1770; *N.Y. Jour.,* Feb. 9, 1767; *N.Y. Merc.,* Nov. 6, 1769; *S.C. Gaz.,* Nov. 9, 1767; Jan. 25, July 19, 1770; *S.C.A.G. Gaz.,* Feb. 5, 1771.

295:1 Westcott, *Hist. Phila. Fire Dept.,* Chap. VII; *Pa. Gaz.,* Feb. 28, Mar. 7, 14, 1765; *Newp. Merc.,* Mar. 11, 18, 1765; *Bos. Gaz.,* Aug. 11, 1766; *Bos. Chron.,* June 5, July 10, 1769; Col. Soc. Mass., *Pubs.,* XXXII, 414; Weyman's *N.Y. Gaz.,* Mar. 4, 1765.

295:2 *Cities,* I, 372; *Pa. Statutes,* VII, 174; *S.C. Gaz.,* Sept. 28, 1765; *Newp. Merc.,* Mar. 1, 1773.

296:1 18 *Bos. Rec. Com.,* 119; 19 *Bos. Rec. Com.,* 169; *Bos. Post Boy,* Jan. 30, 1769; Chalmers, *Weather and Diseases,* I, 34; Carroll, *Historical Collections of S.C.,* II, 482; *S.C.A.G. Gaz.,* Aug. 22, 1766; Sept. 24, 1770; Feb. 5, 1771; *S.C. Gaz.,* Oct. 6, 1766; Nov. 9, 1767; July 23, 1772; Feb. 28, 1774; S.C. Commons, Jour., XXXIV, Mar. 21, 1774.

296:2 *Pa. Gaz.,* Mar. 31, 1763; Jan. 27, 1773; Mar. 9, *Sup.,* 1774; *Pa. Chron.,* May 23, 1768; *Pa. Votes,* VI, 271, 285; *Pa. Jour.,* Jan. 24, 1771; *Pa. Statutes,* VIII, 96, 464.

296:3 *N.Y.M.C.C.,* VI, 268; VII, 142; VIII, 26, 41, 43, 62; *N.Y. Merc.,* Aug. 1, Sept. 5, 1774; Adams, *Works,* II, 353; Wilson, *Mem. Hist. N.Y.,* II, 477; *Rivington's N.Y. Gaz.,* Feb. 16, 1775; Peterson and Edwards, *New York* (Illustrated edn.), 232; Bridenbaugh, *Colonial Craftsman,* 56; *Newsletter,* Sept. 3, 1772.

297:1 Shipton, *Biographical Sketches,* VII, 184.

297:2 *Newp. Merc.,* Dec. 17, 1764; Nov. 14, 28, 1774; Feb. 20, May 8, 1775; Newp. T.M. Recs., 734, 806, 922.

298:1 *Pa. Statutes,* VIII, 96, 464; Court Papers, Phila. Co., IV, 1766, Oct., 1770; Westcott, *Hist. of Philadelphia,* II, Chap. CLXVII; *Pa. Gaz.,* July 16, 1772; *Pa. Chron.,* May 11, 1772; *N.Y. M.C.C.,* VI, 278; VII, 462; VIII, 15, 29, 137; Stokes, *Iconography,* IV, 870; *N.Y. Merc.,* Jan. 3, 1774.

298:2 16 *Bos. Rec. Com.,* 62; *Mass. Acts,* IV, 462; 19 *Bos. Rec. Com.,* 154, 167; *Bos. Gaz.,* July 20, 1761; 20 *Bos. Rec. Com.,* 172, 317; 23 *Bos. Rec. Com.,* 3, 39, 42, 45, 57, 171; 18 *Bos. Rec. Com.,* 118, 194; Stiles, *Literary Diary,* I, 512.

299:1 *S.C. Gaz.,* June 20, 1761; July 11, 18, Aug. 1, 1761; Oct. 12, Nov. 9, 1767; Aug. 2, 1770; Sept. 3, 1772; May 24, 1773; Feb. 28, 1774; S.C. Pub. Recs., XXXII, 387; *N.Y. Jour.,* July 16,

1772; *S.C.A.G. Gaz.,* Jan. 29, 1772; June 9, 1775; *S.C. Country Jour.,* June 13, 1775.

299:2   19 *Bos. Rec. Com.,* 214, 217; 20 *Bos. Rec. Com.,* 100; Rowe, *Diary,* 177; *Pa. Chron.,* June 12, 1769; Muhlenberg, *Journals,* II, 526; *Rivington's N.Y. Gaz.,* Sept. 23, 1773.

300:1   Charles Woodmason, "Journal," in Richard J. Hooker, *Carolina Backcountry on the Eve of the Revolution,* 27, 218*n;* Bridenbaugh, *Myths and Realities,* 164; *S.C. Gaz.,* Aug. 3, 1767; *Bos. Post Boy,* Nov. 13, 1769; *Newsletter,* Dec. 21, 1769; *Newp. Merc.,* Sept. 7, 1767.

301:1   *Newp. Merc.,* Mar. 16, Dec. 13, 1762; Nov. 19, 1764; Mar. 9, Aug. 31, Oct. 12, 1767; May 9, 1768.

301:2   *Bos. Post Boy,* Mar. 1, 1762; Dec. 7, 1767; *Newp. Merc.,* Dec. 19, 1763; Jan. 23, 1764; *Newsletter,* Mar. 10, 1768; Jan. 4, 1770; Aug. 13, 1772; *Weyman's N.Y. Gaz.,* July 13, 1767; Rowe, *Diary,* 252; *Mass. Broadsides,* Nos. 1640–1648.

302:1   *Bos. Post Boy,* Feb. 18, 1765; *Bos. Chron.,* Mar. 13, 1769; *Newp. Merc.,* Nov. 18, 1771.

302:2   *Pa. Mag.,* VIII, 410; XXIV, 409; XLVIII, 240; *Pa. Gaz.,* Aug. 23, 1764; Oct. 3, 1765; *P.M.C.C.,* 679, 705, 710, 711, 742; Drinker, Diary, Apr. 30, 1774; May 4, 1776; Court Papers, Phila. Co., IV, Aug. 28, 1766; *Pa. Chron.,* Aug. 15, 1768.

303:1   *N.Y. Gaz.,* Jan. 21, Mar. 11, 1762; Apr. 9, 1770; *N.Y. Col. Laws,* IV, 669, 777; V, 10; *N.Y. Merc.,* Nov. 1, 7, 1773; Nov. 28, 1774; *Newsletter,* Sept. 5, 1765; May 16, 1771; *N.Y.M.C.C.,* VII, 435.

303:2   *S.C. Gaz.,* Mar. 30, 1765; Dec. 22, 1766; Apr. 13, June 15, 1767; May 11, 1769; Aug. 22, Oct. 10, Nov. 7, 1771; Nov. 15, 1773; *Bos. Gaz.,* Sept. 11, 1769; *S.C.A.G. Gaz.,* Apr. 24, 1771.

304:1   Hooker, *Carolina Backcountry,* 236; *Pa. Votes,* VI, 200; *N.Y. Jour.,* Feb. 6, 1772; *Pa. Chron.,* Jan. 22, 1770.

304:2   *Newp. Merc.,* June 8, 1767; Petitions to R.I. Assembly, XIII, 112; *Bos. Post Boy,* Sept. 25, 1769; Dec. 24, 1770; *N.Y. Merc.,* Jan. 7, 1771; *Bos. Gaz.,* May 19, 1766; Bridenbaugh, *Rebels and Gentlemen,* 250; *S.C. Gaz.,* Nov. 12, 1764.

305:1   *Bos. Post Boy,* July 28, 1766; Feb. 2, Sept. 28, 1767; *Bos. Chron.,* June 27, 1768; Feb. 2, 6, May 1, 1769; *Bos. Gaz.,* Mar. 21, 1774; G. H. Richardson Collection, 972:53; *Newp. Merc.,* Jan. 6, 1772; *S.C. Gaz.,* Nov. 9, 1767; May 10, 1770; *S.C.A.G. Gaz.,* June 10, 1771; *N.Y. Jour.,* Nov. 12, 1767; *N.Y.M.C.C.,* VIII, 82; NYHS *Quart. Bull.,* XXIX, 80; Edwards, *New York,* 102.

305:2   *Pa. Votes,* VI, 432, 438; *Pa. Statutes,* VIII, 300, 417; *NYHS Colls.,* 1886, p. 24; Honyman, *Journal,* 15; *Pa. Mag.,* XI, 239;

Bridenbaugh, *Rebels and Gentlemen,* 249; Westcott, *Hist. of Philadelphia,* II, Chap. CCXXV.

307:1   19 *Bos. Rec. Com.,* 149; 20 *Bos. Rec. Com.,* 101; John Rowe, Diary (MS, MHS), Nov. 5, 1764.

307:2   Bernard, *Select Letters,* 37; Anderson, Col. Soc. Mass., *Pubs.,* XXVI, 30, 31, 35, 38, 40, 42, 43; Thomas Hutchinson, *History of the Colony of Mass. Bay,* III, 87, 90, 101; Rowe, *Diary,* 88; Peter Oliver, Origin and Progress of the American War to 1776, Br. Mus., Egerton MSS, 2671 (LC Trans.), 77, 160; Morgan, *Stamp Act Crisis,* 123, 126; *Murray Letters,* 154, 156; *Bos. Gaz.,* Sept. 2, 1765; *Newsletter,* Nov. 7, 1765; *Bos. Post Boy,* Nov. 11, 1765; 4 MHS *Colls.,* IV, 406.

308:1   For evidence that "British Revenue Racketeers" attempted to frame Hancock and failed, see Dickerson, *Miss. Valley Hist. Rev.,* XXXII, 517; and *W. & M. Quart.,* IV, 501; Rowe, *Diary,* 111; Francis Bernard, Letters (Force Transcripts, LC), 69, 97, 99, 101, 126, 132; Adams, *Works,* X, 204, 206; MHS *Procs.,* IV, 8; XX, 8; 55, pp. 250n, 254, 283; *Bowdoin-Temple Papers,* Pt. I, 176, 211; Seventy-Six Society, *Papers Relating to Public Events in Massachusetts* (Philadelphia, 1876), 64.

309:1   Hutchinson, *Hist. of Mass. Bay,* III, 186, 187, 193, 194; Oliver M. Dickerson, *Boston Under Military Rule* (Boston, 1936); Hutchinson Correspondence, XXVI, Oct. 19, 1769 (Mass. Archives); for the "Journal of Occurrences," see *Bos. Post Boy,* Mar. 12, 1770; Nov. 22, Dec. 20, 1773; Jan. 31, May 2, June 6, 1774; Jan. 23, 1775; *Prov. Gaz.,* Feb. 22, 1772; *Bos. Gaz.,* July 25, 1768; Jan. 31, Apr. 4, 1774; *Bos. Chron.,* Aug. 22, 1768; Col. Soc. Mass., *Pubs.,* VIII, 93; XXVI, 52, 54n.

309:2   Bernard, *Select Letters,* 89; Bernard Papers (Sparks MSS, IV, Harvard), X, 238; *Barrington-Bernard Correspondence,* 44; Ezra Stiles, Papers (Bancroft Trans., NYPL), 1761–1776, p. 29.

310:1   *R.I. Col. Recs.,* VI, 428; VII, 58; Treasury 1, Bundle 442, folios 207, 211; Misc. Court Papers (R.I. Archives), Folder 1750–1769, July 9, 1764; *Newp. Merc.,* July 16, 1764; June 10, 1765; Ward Papers, Box 1, July 12, 1765.

310:2   Dr. Thomas Moffatt, Recollections of the Stamp Act Riots at Newport, Chalmers, Papers Relating to R.I. (NYPL), 99; Br. Mus. Add. MSS, 33030, folio 78; Treasury 1, Bundle 442, folio 241; MHS *Procs.,* 55, p. 235; Letters to the Governors, 1763–1775 (R.I. Archives), 26, 28; *Newp. Merc.,* Sept. 9, 1765; Morgan, *Stamp Act Crisis,* 144, 193; *Prov. Gaz.,* Aug. 24, *Extra,* 1765; Newp. T.C. Recs., 802.

311:1   Chalmers, Papers Relating to R.I., Moffatt to J. Harrison, Oct.

16, 1765; Treasury 1, Bundle 442, folio 252; *R.I. Col. Recs.,* VI, 456, 477; *Bos. Post Boy,* Nov. 11, 1765; *Newp. Merc.,* Apr. 7, May 19, 26, 1766; Dec. 7, 1767; June 5, 1775; Newp. T.M. Recs., 846, 1088; Papers concerning Newport, June 15, 1770 (RIHS); Stiles, *Literary Diary,* 242, 324, 329; Coke, *Amer. Loyalists,* 307.

311:2   Watts, *Letter Book,* 89, 92, 100.

312:1   *Bos. Post Boy,* June 23, 30, 1764; *N.Y. Gaz.,* July 12, 1764; Feb. 5, 12, 1770; *N.Y. Col. Docs.,* VII, 771, 773, 776; Morgan, *Stamp Act Crisis,* 152; 4 MHS *Colls.,* X, 560, 563; Montresor, Journals, NYHS *Colls.,* 1881, pp. 335, 338, 339; NYHS MSS, Misc. IX, no. 23; X, no 27; *N.Y. Jour.,* Mar. 29, May 10, 1770; *Colden Letter Books,* II, 347; *Rivington's N.Y. Gaz.,* Mar. 7, 1775; Becker, *Political Parties in Province of New York,* 22, 26, 30, 76, 79.

313:1   *S.C. Gaz.,* Feb. 16, Oct. 31, 1765; Jan. 11, 1767; Nov. 7, 1768; Laurens, Letter Book, 1762–1768 (HSP), Oct. 11, 22, 1765; Wallace, *Laurens,* 116; Fulham MSS, S.C., No. 230 (Oct. 20, 1765); Samuel Adams, Papers (NYPL), CI, Adams to Gadsden, Dec. 11, 1766; Morgan, *Stamp Act Crisis,* 156, 163, 181; Chalmers, Papers Relating to Carolina, I, 175.

313:2   Laurens, Letter Book, 1762–1768, Jan. 29, 1766; *Bos. Chron.,* Nov. 7, 1768; *S.C.A.G. Gaz.,* Sept. 24, 1770; *SCHG Mag.,* XXVII, 126, 129, 135; Oliver M. Dickerson, *Navigation Acts and the American Revolution* (Philadelphia, 1951), 224, 230, 254.

313:3   *Pa. Statutes,* VI, 325; Collins Papers, III, Jan. 15, 1764; Hindle, 3 *W. & M. Quart.,* III, 475, 477; *Pa. Mag.,* V, 60.

314:1   Adams, *Works,* II, 173; *N.Y. Gaz.,* Nov. 21, 1765; Chalmers, Papers Relating to Philadelphia (NYPL), II, 59; *Pa. Gaz.,* Oct. 12, 1769.

314:2   Graydon, *Memoirs,* 47; Lincoln, *Revolutionary Movement in Pa.,* 77; William Bradford Jr., Letters (HSP), Jan. 4, 1775; *Pa. Mag.,* XV, 35; XXI, 481, 484; *Pa. Merc.,* May 26, 1775.

314:3   Rind's *Va. Gaz.,* Oct. 13, 1774; *Newp. Merc.,* Sept. 26, 1774.

315:1   *Rush Letters,* I, 7; *R.I. Acts* (1772), 13; *Bos. Post Boy,* Feb. 9, 1761; *Bos. Gaz.,* Sept. 10, 1764; *Newsletter,* Sept. 13, 1764; *S.C. Gaz.,* June 8, 1765; Feb. 22, 1773; Schoepf, *Travels,* II, 222.

316:1   *Pa. Statutes,* VI, 184; *Pa. Gaz.,* Aug. 20, 1761; Bridenbaugh, 3 *W. & M. Quart.,* 171; Newp. T.M. Recs., 922; *S.C. Statutes,* IV, 158; *S.C. Gaz.,* Feb. 1, 1768; Oct. 5, 1769.

316:2   Watts, *Letter Book,* 6; *Newp. Merc.,* Sept. 5, 1763; Nov. 12, 1764; Apr. 25, 1768; *Bos. Post Boy,* Dec. 16, 1771.

317:1 *N.Y. Merc.,* Mar. 23, 1761; Jan. 7, 1771; *N.Y. Gaz.,* June 4,
1767; Mar. 28, Apr. 4, 11, 1768; *N.Y. Jour.,* Oct. 23, 1766;
Oct. 22, Nov. 5, 1767; *Bos. Post Boy,* Nov. 16, 1767; *Pa.
Chron.,* Mar. 7, *Post,* 1768; M'Robert, *Tour,* 3, 5.

317:2 Drake, *History of Boston,* 755; *Bos. Post Boy,* Nov. 13, 1769;
Feb. 27, 1775; Rowe, *Diary,* 218; *Mass. Spy,* July 25, 1771;
23 *Bos. Rec. Com.,* 134; MHS *Procs.,* VIII, 333, 382; Col. Soc.
Mass., *Pubs.,* XXXIV, 22; Stiles, *Literary Diary,* I, 619, 628.

318:1 *Bos. Chron.,* June 26, 1769; *P.M.C.C.,* 678, 760, 794; Samuel
Coates, Letter Book, Coates to Logan, Sept. 26, 1770; *Pa. Gaz.,*
Apr. 5, 1772.

318:2 Pitman, *West Indies,* 28; *S.C. Gaz.,* Oct. 29, Nov. 12, 1764;
June 2, 1766; Feb. 1, 1768; Nov. 7, 1771; *S.C. Statutes,* II, 755.

318:3 *Newp. Merc.,* May 7, 1764; Feb. 27, 1769, Mar. 6, 1771; *Bos.
Post Boy,* Apr. 22, 1771; Stiles, *Literary Diary,* I, 158; *Bos.
Chron.,* May 9, 1768.

319:1 Watts, *Letter Book,* 201; *Bos. Gaz.,* July 26, 1762; Muhlenberg,
Journals, II, 89; Coates, Letter Book, Logan to Coates, 1767;
Emmett Collection (NYPL), 4061; W. Logan to Dr. Fothergill,
May 5, 1768; *N.Y. Merc.,* May 21, 1764; NYHS MSS, Misc.
VIII, No. 62, James Magra, July 29, 1765; *N.Y. Gaz.,* Sept. 25,
1769; 16 *Bos. Rec. Com.,* 273, 274; 18 *Bos. Rec. Com.,* 19;
S.C. Gaz., Nov. 9, 1767.

320:1 16 *Bos. Rec. Com.,* 91, 126, 139, 184, 275; 20 *Bos. Rec. Com.,*
86, 99, 112, 117, 135, 194, 201, 219, 235, 236, 305; 23 *Bos.
Rec. Com.,* 3, 5, 11, 14, 76, 107, 159; 18 *Bos. Rec. Com.,* 87;
Mass. Acts, V, 177.

320:2 *Bos. Post Boy,* Oct. 10, 1763; Dec. 1, 1766; Sept. 13, 1773; *Bos.
Gaz.,* Feb. 27, 1764; Dec. 10, 1770; Aug. 17, 1772; Rowe,
Diary, 65, 80.

321:1 18 *Bos. Rec. Com.,* 177, 179, 181, 184, 186, 188, 189; *Bos.
Gaz.,* June 1, 1774; Col. Soc. Mass., *Pubs.,* XXXIV, 39.

321:2 Philadelphia's handling of its poor is traced in detail in Briden-
baugh, *Rebels and Gentlemen,* Chap. VII; see also, Adams,
Works, II, 380, 395; *Pa. Votes,* V, 295, 447, 451, 519, 549;
VI, 21, 43, 131; *Pa. Statutes,* VII, 9, 75, 143, 197, 310; VIII,
75; Allinson and Penrose, *Philadelphia,* 38; *P.M.C.C.,* 712, 718;
NYHS *Colls.,* 1886, p. 23; Honyman, *Journal,* 17.

321:3 *Pa. Votes,* VI, 45, 50, 128, 135, 664, 681; Misc. Papers, Phila.
Co., 1767–1802 (HSP), W. Pollard to John Priestly, Feb. 24,
1772; *Pa. Gaz.,* May 1, 1766; May 24, 1770, Jan. 9, 16, 1772;
Proud, *History of Pennsylvania,* II, 282.

322:1 *Pa. Mag.,* XXIV, 248; Bridenbaugh, *Rebels and Gentlemen,*
231, 235; *Newp. Merc.,* Aug. 15, 1763; *Pa. Gaz.,* Jan. 24, 31,

1765; Feb. 4, 18, 1768; Mar. 15, 1770; Mar. 26, 1772; *Pa. Chron.,* Jan. 22, 1770; May 10, 1773; Muhlenberg, *Journals,* II, 248.

322:2   *Wochentliche Philadelphische Staatsbote,* Dec. 17, 31, 1764; Jan. 14, Aug. 31, 1765; *Pa. Mag.,* LX, 26; William Gordon, *Plan of a Society for making Provision for Widows, by Annuities, for the Remainder of Life, and for Granting Annuities to Persons after certain Ages* (Boston, 1772), i, ii, iv, 2, 14, 93; Harry W. Pfund, *History of the German Society of Pennsylvania* (Philadelphia, 1944), 9; Westcott, *History of Philadelphia,* II, Chaps. CLXXX, CXLVIII; *Pa. Votes,* VI, 124; *Pa. Jour.,* Apr. 4, 1771; Feb. 13, 1772; May 25, 1774; John H. Campbell, *History of the Friendly Sons of St. Patrick and of the Hibernia Society* (Philadelphia, 1892), 23; Theodore C. Knauff, *History of the Society of the Sons of St. George* (Philadelphia, 1923), 15, 23; *Pa. Chron.,* May 4, 11, 1772; May 10, 1773.

323:1   St. Philip's Vestry, Minutes, II, June 29, 1763; Aug. 6, Dec. 17, 1764; Sept. 29, Dec. 7, 15, 22, 1766; Jan. 2, June 5, 1769; June 27, 1772; Mar. 4, Sept. 17, 1773; *S.C. Statutes,* VII, 90; S.C. Commons, Jour., XXXVII, 342; *S.C.A.G. Gaz.,* Feb. 5, 1771; *S.C. Gaz.,* June 8, 1765; June 29, Nov. 9, 1767; Jan. 25, 1770; Feb. 22, May 10, 1773.

323:2   David Ramsay, *History of South Carolina* (Newberry, S.C., 1858), II, 386; *S.C. Gaz.,* Apr. 10, Sept. 18, 1762; Mar. 29, 1770; Jan. 10, Mar. 28, Apr. 4, 1771; July 9, 1772; Jan. 21, 28, Apr. 19, 1773; Mar. 13, 1775; Mills, *Statistics of S.C.,* 431; J. H. Easterby, *Rules of the South Carolina Society* (Baltimore, 1932), vi; George Gongaware, *History of the German Friendly Society of Charleston, South Carolina* (Richmond, 1936), 1, 5, 7, 9, 11; S.C. Commons, Jour., XXXVII, 177; Muhlenberg, *Journals,* II, 538.

324:1   Newp. T.C. Recs., XV, 37; Newp. T.M. Recs., 712, 724, 728, 732, 740, 852; *Newp. Merc.,* Dec. 12, 1763; Jan. 2, Dec. 17, 1764; July 8, 1765; Aug. 17, Nov. 30, 1767; *R.I. Acts* (1767), 198.

324:2   Newp. T.M. Recs., 1082, 1101, 1104, 1113; *R.I. Col. Recs.,* VII, 381; *Newp. Merc.,* Nov. 13, Dec. 25, 1775.

325:1   *NY.M.C.C.,* VII, 55, 61, 103; *N.Y. Gaz.,* Apr. 4, 1765; Feb. 11, 1771; Jan. 13, 1772; *Newsletter,* Apr. 9, *Sup.,* May 21, 1772; *N.Y. Jour.;* Jan. 7, 14, 21, 28, Feb. 4, 11, 1768; *N.Y. Merc.,* Dec. 25, 1769; Aug. 12, 1771; Mar. 15, 1773; *N.Y. Col. Laws,* V, 659.

325:2   *N.Y. Gaz.,* Aug. 27, 1761; Feb. 4, 1762; Jan. 31, 1765; Nov. 26, 1770; *N.Y. Merc.,* Nov. 3, 1766; Dec. 11, 1769; Weyman's

N.Y. Gaz., Nov. 3, 10, 1766; *N.Y. Jour.,* Dec. 17, 24, 31, 1767; Feb. 4, 11, 1768; Mar. 29, 1770; *Bos. Post Boy,* Mar. 15, 1772; Jan. 24, 1774; Stokes, *Iconography,* IV, 801; *Newsletter,* July 2, 1772.

325:3   Cecil K. Drinker, *Not so long Ago: A Chronicle of Medicine and Doctors In Colonial Philadelphia* (New York, 1937); Muhlenberg, *Journals,* II, 566, 597; Scharf and Westcott, *Hist. of Philadelphia,* II, 889; Bartram, Amer. Phil. Soc., *Trans.,* n.s., XXXIII, 21, 50; *Pa. Mag.,* XI, 282; *Pa. Chron.,* May 9, 1768.

326:1   Waring, *Annals of Medical History,* n.s., IV, 288; George C. Mason, *Annals of Trinity Church, Newport* (Newport, 1890), 1st ser., 148; Newp. T.M. Recs., 768; *N.Y.M.C.C.,* VII, 119.

326:2   Bridenbaugh, 3 *W. & M. Quart.,* III, 151; *Bos. Post Boy,* July 23, 1764; *Bos. Gaz.,* June 1, Aug. 17, 31, 1767; *Bos. Eve. Post,* June 20, Aug. 8, 15, 1768; *Bos. Chron.,* Aug. 15, 1768; *Rivington's N.Y. Gaz.,* June 17, 24, 1773.

326:3   Graydon, *Memoirs,* 35; *Pa. Mag.,* V, 63; Muhlenberg, *Journals,* II, 258; Drinker, Diary, May 27, 1774; Chalmers, *Weather and Diseases,* II, 207; *S.C. Gaz.,* July 30, 1772; *Bos. Post Boy,* Sept. 28, 1767; *Mass. Gaz.,* Oct. 9, 1769; Caulfield, Col. Soc. Mass., *Pubs.,* XXXV, 53; Franklin, *Works* (Bigelow), III, 251; NYHS *Colls.,* 1886, p. 31; Schoepf, *Travels,* II, 172.

327:1   MHS *Procs.,* IV, 325; *Newsletter,* Mar. 5, 1761; 20 *Bos. Rec. Com.,* 7, 13, 32; *Mass. Acts,* IV, 668; 16 *Bos. Rec. Com.,* 103, 109; *Bos. Post Boy,* Feb. 13, 20, 27, Mar. 5, 12, 19, May 28, 1764.

327:2   20 *Bos. Rec. Com.,* 57, 64, 80, 87; Benjamin Gale, "Historical Memoirs relating to the Practice of Inoculation for the Smallpox, in the British American Provinces, particularly in New England," in *Phil. Trans.,* XII, 229; *Bos. Post Boy,* June 11, July 2, 1764.

327:3   *Bos. Post Boy,* Feb. 6, 1764; *Newsletter,* Mar. 8, 1764; May 28, *Sup.,* 1772; *Bos. Gaz.,* Apr. 29, Nov. 18, 1771.

328:1   Boston's population 1742–1775 averaged about 15,500; and the total deaths during epidemic years were: 1747 (measles), 777; 1752 (smallpox), 645; 1772 (measles), 517. Deaths in normal years averaged 400–600; the year of the Louisburg expedition (1745), when many troops were in town, was very sickly, producing 780 deaths without any epidemic. *Bos. Post Boy,* Jan. 11, 1773; 18 *Bos. Rec. Com.,* 246; MHS *Procs.,* 63, p. 395.

329:1   *Bos. Post Boy,* Nov. 21, 1763; *Prov. Gaz.,* Nov. 26, 1763; Dec. 18, 1773; *Newp. Merc.,* July 18, 1763; Apr. 2, 9, 1764; Sept. 14, 1772; Apr. 12, 19, May 10, June 7, July 5, 1773; Feb. 7, Mar. 28, Apr. 4, 1774; Mar. 20, 1775; *N.Y. Jour.,* Oct. 13, 1768; Stiles, *Itineraries,* 487; Stiles, *Literary Diary,* I, 299, 300,

303, 322; *N.Y. Merc.,* Nov. 19, 1770; Jan. 7, 1771; *Bos. Gaz.,* Oct. 18, 25, 1773; *Colden Letter Books,* I, 210.

329:2   *S.C. Gaz.,* Mar. 26, May 7, 14, 21, 28, June 4, 11, 18, 1763; Webster, Southern Hist. Assn., *Pubs.,* II, 143; *S.C.A.G. Gaz.,* May 4, 1772.

329:3   *Pa. Packet,* Jan. 4, 1773; Feb. 7, 1774; 1 *Pa. Archives,* IV, 59; Whitelaw, Vermont Hist. Soc., *Procs.,* 1905–6, p. 122; *Pa. Gaz.,* June 6, 1765; Feb. 2, 16, 23, 1774; *Pa. Votes,* VI, 511; *Bos. Post Boy,* Feb. 21, 1774.

330:1   Newp. T.M. Recs., 702, 704, 776, 998, 1000, 1008; Petitions to R.I. Assembly, XI, 71; *Bos. Post Boy,* Mar. 19, 1764; *Newp. Merc.,* June 10, 1765; June 9, 1766; Aug. 31, 1772; Mar. 20, 1775; *Newp. Hist. Mag.,* I, 126; Stiles, *Literary Diary,* I, 271, 297, 298, 352; Collins Papers, XIV, Sept. 8, 1772; *Prov. Gaz.,* Oct. 24, 1772; *R.I. Col. Recs.,* VII, 199; R.I. Col. Recs. (MS), X, 6.

330:2   Bridenbaugh, *Rebels and Gentlemen,* 246; Bond, *Jour. Hist. Medicine and Allied Sciences,* II, 10; Thomas G. Morton and Frank Woodbury, *The History of the Pennsylvania Hospital, 1751–1895* (Philadelphia, 1897), 242; *Pa. Gaz.,* July 11, 1765; Francis N. Mason, ed., *John Norton & Sons* (Richmond, 1937), 262; MHS *Procs.,* 49, p. 475; Adams, *Works,* II, 359, 382; Benjamin Rush, *Oration on Indian Medicine* (Philadelphia, 1774), 99, 101; Honyman, *Journal,* 15.

331:1   *N.Y. Jour.,* May 25, 1769; Sanuel Bard, *Discourse upon the Duties of a Physician, With Some Sentiments upon the Usefulness and Necessity of a Public Hospital* (New York, 1769), iii, v, 13, 16; *N.Y.M.C.C.,* VII, 200, 364; *N.Y. Col. Laws,* V, 367; Adams, *Works,* II, 402.

CHAPTER IX

333:1   F. R. Diffenderfer, *German Immigration into Pennsylvania* (Lancaster, 1900), 45; Muhlenberg, *Journals,* II, 11, 123, 423; *Rush Letters,* I, 14; *Philadelphische Staatsbote,* Mar. 22, May 4, 1762; Drinker, Diary, June 14, 1760; Hiltzheimer, *Diary,* 9.

333:2   Marshall, *Diary,* 5, 7, 9, 29; *Pa. Chron.,* Nov. 16, 1767; *NEHG Reg.,* LXII, 250, 326; LXIII, 63; 4 MHS *Colls.,* X, 711.

334:1   S.C. Pub. Recs., XXXII, 388; *S.C. Gaz.,* Jan. 28, 1764; July 14, 1766; Jan. 4, 1768; June 11, Oct. 1, 22, 1772; July 4, 1774; *Newp. Merc.,* Apr. 2, 1764; *S.C.A.G. Gaz.,* Oct. 10, 1766; Oct. 21, 1771; *S.C. Country Jour.,* Dec. 29, *Sup.,* 1772; Aug. 24, 1773; Mar. 8, 1774; *SCHG Mag.,* XXVII, 134, 136.

334:2   4 MHS *Colls.,* X, 711; *N.Y. Gaz.,* Feb. 3, 10, 1772.

335:1   Serle, *Journal,* 296; Stiles, *Literary Diary,* I, 375; Stiles, *Itineraries,* 217; *Burd Papers,* 42; Hutchinson, *Hist. Mass. Bay,* III, 211, 214; *Bowdoin-Temple Papers,* I, xiii, xiv, xv, xvi.

335:2   *History of the Life, Very Strange Adventures and Works of Captain John MacPherson;* Jackson, *Cyclopedia of Philadelphia,* III, 854; *Pa. Mag., XXIII,* 56; Westcott, *Historic Mansions of Philadelphia,* 214; *Bos. Chron.,* Nov. 20, 1769; MHS *Colls.,* 71, p. 136.

336:1   Bridenbaugh, *Peter Harrison,* 121, 127, 132, 135n; *Bos. Chron.,* Jan. 11, Mar. 14, 1768; *Bos. Gaz.,* Dec. 24, 1770; MHS *Colls.,* 74, p. 77.

337:1   Uhlendorf, *Siege of Charlestown,* 91; Carolina Art Association, *This is Charleston* (Charleston, 1944), 61, 74, 95, 96, 104, 106; Smith, *Dwelling Houses of Charleston,* 93, 103, 119; *S.C.A.G. Gaz.,* Aug. 23, 1769; *Historical Magazine,* IX, 342.

337:2   NYHS, *Quart. Bull.,* XXIII, 94; Downing and Scully, *Architectural Heritage of Newport,* plates, 111, 113, 115; M. Bowler to W. Vernon, Apr. 20, 1773; Emmett Coll. (NYPL), 180; *Newp. Merc.,* June 17, 1765; Bridenbaugh, *Rebels and Gentlemen,* 209, 211; Adams, *Works,* II, 358, 361; *Pa. Mag.,* XVIII, 38; Wallace and Miller, *Colonial Houses, Philadelphia,* 178, 180, 182, 186, 196, 229; Coke, *Amer. Loyalists,* 231.

337:3   *Newsletter,* Apr. 23, 1762; *Pa. Chron.,* Dec. 12, 1768; Charles L. Sellers, *Artist of the Revolution: The Early Life of Charles Willson Peale* (Hebron, Conn., 1939), 107; List of Planned Drawings of North America, Du Simitiere Papers (LCP); Bridenbaugh, *Rebels and Gentlemen,* 216.

338:1   The excellent, authentic scale-model of Cambridge of 1775 made by the Theodore B. Pitman Studios, now in the Widener Library of Harvard College, recovers the beauty and uniqueness of the village as does nothing else. Henry Pelham, a pioneer in landscaping, made an excellent Plan of Boston in New England (1775), which locates all of the principal estates. See also, Lillie, Cambridge Hist. Soc., *Pubs.,* XXVI, 48; Fulham Palace MSS, Mass., Box II, No. 213; Samuel Eliot Morison, *Three Centuries of Harvard* (Cambridge, 1936), 94, 96, 98; Bridenbaugh, *Peter Harrison,* 116; Samuel Chamberlain, *Fair Harvard* (New York, 1948), 13–25, for photographs; *Murray Letters,* 180, 183.

338:2   *Bos. Gaz.,* Oct. 23, 1769; Mar. 10, 1775; *Bos. Chron.,* Mar. 20, 23, 1769; *Murray Letters,* 109, 120, 122; Winsor, *Mem. Hist. Boston,* II, 342, 344; Drake, *Roxbury,* 351, 429; *Old-Time New England,* XXVIII, 85; A. K. Teele, *History of Milton, Mass., 1640–1887* (Boston, 1888), 136.

339:1   The village of Germantown had several estates in its neighborhood of which the Chew Mansion (1764) was notable for academic proportions and superb use of Pennsylvania field stone construction. Wallace and Miller, *Colonial Houses, Philadelphia,* 139–72; Serle, *Journal,* 290; *Pa. Jour.,* Dec. 29, 1763; J. Kent, trans., Marquis Francois Jean de Chastellux, *Travels in North America* (London, 1787), I, 174, 176; Burnaby, *Travels,* 43; Edward Shippen Papers (LC), Shippen to John Penn, June 29, 1771; Mar. 15, 1773; May 11, 1776.

339:2   Mercantile Library Association, *New York City During the American Revolution* (New York, 1861), 29; Harrington, *N.Y. Merchant,* 23; John Edward Pryor, Jr., Account Book, 1762–1767, and Building Accounts, 1759–1768 (NYHS); Exhibition of Country Houses on Manhattan (NYHS, 1952); NYHS *Quart. Bull.,* 1933, p. 113; Mereness, *Travels,* 453; NYPL *Bulletin,* XXXV, 141, 145, 147; M'Robert, *Tour,* 6; Honyman, *Journal,* 32.

340:1   William P. and Julia R. Cutler, Life, *Journals and Correspondence of the Reverend Manasseh Cutler* (Cincinnati, 1888), I, 68; Peterson, *Rhode Island,* 88; Mason, *Reminiscences of Newport,* 38; Alice G. Lockwood, *Gardens of Colony and State* (New York, 1931), I, 211, 215, 219; *Newp. Hist. Mag.* I, 67; R. T. H. Halsey and Charles O. Cornelius, *Handbook of the American Wing* (New York, 1942), 93; RIHS *Colls.,* XXIII, 10; Honyman, *Journal,* 65.

340:2   Webster, Southern Hist. Assoc., *Pubs.,* II, 137; Bartram, Amer. Phil. Soc., *Trans.,* n.s., XXXIII, 13, 14, 21, 30; *S.C. Gaz.,* Oct. 22, 1763; *SCHG Mag.,* XXXVI, 109; MHS *Procs.,* 49, p. 443.

341:1   Drinker, Diary, Aug. 19, 1763; Nov. 8, 1767; Jan. 21, 1769; Sept. 8, 1771; J. Beekman, Letter Book, Nov. 7, 1769; *Murray Letters,* 121, 142.

341:2   Du Simitiere, Papers relating to Pa., N.E., June–July, 1772, No. 9, and Papers relating to New York, Nos. 67, 70 (LCP); George L. Houghton, *Coaches of Colonial New York* (Pamphlet, New York, 1890), 17, 24, 26, 27; *Pa. Mag.,* IV, 171; XXIV, 406; XXVII, 375; XXXIII, 326; NYHS *Colls.,* 1886, pp. 14, 28; 1897, p. 346; Watts, *Letter Book,* 233; *Bos. Gaz.,* Nov. 9, 1767; Weyman's *N.Y. Gaz.,* Dec. 14, 1767.

342:1   *Historical Magazine,* IX, 343; *S.C. Gaz.,* Aug. 3, 1765; S.C. Pub. Recs., XXXII, 392; Coke, *Amer. Loyalists,* 11; Houghton, Coaches, 27; Rowe, *Diary,* 103; Hutchinson, *Hist. Mass. Bay,* III, 146; *Bos. Gaz.,* Aug. 17, 1767; Jan. 24, 1770; Susan B. Brayton, Henry Marchant's Friends (MS privately owned).

342:2   Adams, *Works,* II, 353, 358, 361, 369, 370, 378, 381, 386, 428; John and Abigail Adams, *Familiar Letters during the Revolution*

(Boston, 1876), 43; *Pa. Mag.*, XIX, 531; MHS *Colls.*, 49, p. 443, 448, 471, 473, 479.

343:1 MHS *Colls.*, 72, p. 17; Adams, *Works,* II, 353.

343:2 *Bos. Gaz.*, Jan. 7, 1765; July 20, 1772; Rowe, Diary (MS), July 16, 1772; Watson, *Men and Times of the Revolution,* 56.

344:1 *Newp. Hist. Mag.*, VI, 46; *Burd Letters,* 27; Hooker, *Carolina Backcountry,* 273; *SCHG Mag.*, XXXVI, 6.

345:1 The first American actress to marry a title had her bliss cut short when a previous marriage of Lord Rosehill's came to light in August 1770; she returned to the American Company. G. E. Cockayne, *Complete Peerage* (London, 1910–1940), III, 4; VI, 573; IX, 696; Mereness, *Travels,* 397; *Connecticut Courant,* Sept. 15, 1766; *Georgia Gaz.*, Jan. 10, 1770; *N.C. Col. Recs.,* VIII, 210; *Newsletter,* Oct. 25, 1770; *S.C. Gaz.*, Apr. 23, 1763; *Pa. Chron.*, Aug. 29, Sept. 19, Dec. 12, 1768; July 9, 1770; Mason, *Reminiscences of Newport,* 385; *N.Y. Gaz.*, Dec. 30, 1762; *Bos. Post Boy,* Apr. 9, 1770.

345:2 Collins Papers, IV, May 28, 1765; V, June 15, 1765; VI, Sept. 20, 1766; *Pa. Packet,* Nov. 22, 1773; May 23, 1774.

346:1 Sarah Wilson built her title on what was common knowledge in every city: that the Duke of Gloucester had married his paramour, the Countess of Waldegrave and an illegitimate daughter of a son of Sir Robert Walpole in January, 1771; and that a year later the King's sister, Carolina Mathilda, was imprisoned for adultery. Wallace, *Henry Laurens,* 186; *S.C. Gaz.*, July 30, Dec. 17, 1772; *Newp. Merc.*, Sept. 14, 1772; May 31, Nov. 29, 1773; July 17, 1775; *Rivington's N.Y. Gaz.*, May 13, 1773; *Newsletter,* Dec. 9, 1773; *Prov. Gaz.*, Mar. 29, 1773; Jan. 22, Apr. 2, 1774.

346:2 Watts, *Letter Book,* ix, x; *Pa. Mag.*, I, 170; *N.Y. Jour.*, May 7, 1767; *S.C. Gaz.*, Oct. 4, 1770; *Pa. Gaz.*, Jan. 14, 1768; *Newp. Merc.*, July 8, 1765; Aug. 22, 1774; *Burd Letters,* 54.

347:1 "The Governor of Penna has married Miss Masters," wrote William Patterson to John MacPherson in London in 1772. "Doubtless you know his Rib. Some say she is handsome, some passably, and some quite homely. Thirty thousand Pounds are thirty thousand Charms." W. J. Mills, *Glimpses of Colonial Society* (Philadelphia, 1903), 94; *Pa. Chron.*, Jan. 25, Aug. 14, 1768; Aug. 14, 1769; *Pa. Mag.*, XXIII, 56; *Newp. Merc.*, May 10, 1773; July 11, 1774; *Bos. Chron.*, Mar. 27, May 8, 1769; *Murray Letters,* 183n; MHS *Procs.*, 49, p. 448.

348:1 Rowe, Diary (MS), Sept.–Dec., 1764; *Bos. Gaz.*, Aug. 10, 1772; *S.C. Gaz.*, Nov. 16, 1767; *Bos. Chron.*, Oct. 23, 30, 1769; Mar. 26, 1770; *Newp. Merc.*, June 28, Sept. 6, 1773; Drinker,

Diary, Feb. 27, Aug. 17, 1766; Jan. 1, 1772; *Pa. Mag.,* V, 200; X, 115, 205; XII, 448; Hughes, Papers, Sept. 7, 1769; Apr. 13, 1771; Davol, *Two Men of Taunton,* 158, 160; Maine Hist. Soc., *Colls.,* VII, 235; *Burd Letters,* 49.

348:2   *Bowdoin-Temple Papers,* I, 19, 51; *Murray Letters,* 137; Chalmers, Papers Relating to Philadelphia (NYPL), II, 55; *S.C. Gaz.,* May 17, 24, 1773; *Pa. Chron.,* Apr. 13, 1767.

348:3   *The Journal of Dr. John Morgan, 1764* (Philadelphia, 1907); *Burd Papers,* 38, 40; Bridenbaugh, *Rebels and Gentlemen,* 193; Watts, *Letter Book,* 110, 205, 282, 386, 390; Stiles, *Literary Diary,* I, 117; *Bos. Gaz.,* Oct. 18, 1773.

349:1   Bridenbaugh, *Rebels and Gentlemen,* chap. X; French, MHS *Procs.,* 63, p. 27; 4 MHS *Colls.,* IV, 454; MHS *Colls.,* 74, pp. xxi, 77; Shipton, *Biographical Sketches,* VIII, 742; Harriet K. Leiding, *Charleston: Historic and Romantic* (Philadelphia, 1931), 43.

349:2   Serle, *Journal,* 48; Fulham Palace MSS, Mass., Box II, May 12, 1768; *Amer. Hist. Rev.,* XLVI, 865.

350:1   Serle, *Journal,* 157.

351:1   Bridenbaugh, *Colonial Craftsman,* 158; Chandler, *Harvard Graduates Magazine,* X, 529; *S.C. Gaz.,* Mar. 1, 1773.

351:2   *S.C. Gaz.,* Oct. 1, 1763; Jan. 10, 1771; July 16, 1772; June 28, 1773; July 13, 1774; *Bos. Gaz.,* June 3, 1771.

351:3   *N.Y. Merc.,* Oct. 10, 1763; *Newp. Merc.,* Dec. 14, 1772; Hughes, Papers, Sept. 7, 1769; Mereness, *Travels,* 451.

352:1   Graydon, *Memoirs,* 31, 74; William Henry Drayton, *Letters of Freeman* (London, 1771), 60; Mary Cochrane Rogers, *Glimpses of an Old Social Capital* (Boston, 1923), 49; *Pa. Gaz.,* Sept. 27, Dec. 20, 1770; Sept. 22, 1773; I. Minis Hays, *Calendar of the Papers of Benjamin Franklin in . . . American Philosophical Society* (Philadelphia, 1908), II, 52; *Pa. Eve. Post,* Apr. 27, 1776; *Newsletter,* Feb. 20, 1766.

352:2   Benjamin Vaughan told Franklin in 1779 that Joseph Galloway "said that at the taking up of arms, only 1/5 were for independence; but that the party had begun in the chief towns, ever since 1754. . . ." Franklin, *Writings* (Smyth), I, 21. In 1769, General Mackay wrote to General Gage from Boston: "At present from the Information I have, I believe the Country [Mass.] is peaceably Inclined; but the danger is, that when the Assembly is Dissolved, those factious Men may go among their Constituents, and poison their Minds by false Representation, as they have already the bulk of the lower people in the Maritime Towns." Clements Library: Gage Papers, Amer. ser., LXXXVI, July 4, 1769.

352:3 "In every major port—Boston, Salem, Providence, [Newport] New London, New York, Philadelphia, Charleston, and even Bermuda—the hostility of the seamen and mechanics toward the whole revenue system was far more pronounced than among the merchants or any other group of the population"; Dickerson, *Navigation Acts,* 219; *SCHG Mag.,* XXVII, 131; *Pa. Gaz.,* Sept. 27, Dec. 20, 1770.

353:1 Stiles, *Itineraries,* 101; Stiles, *Literary Diary,* I, 230, 279; Lewis B. Namier, *England in the Age of the American Revolution* (London, 1930), 279; *Rush Letters,* I, 7; Proud, *Hist. of Pennsylvania,* II, 339.

353:2 Barratt, *Old St. Paul's,* 52; Letters to George Whitefield, 1763–1769 (LC); *Newp. Merc.,* Feb. 6, Oct. 29, 1764; June 12, 1769; Aug. 13, 1770; Perry, *Historical Collections . . . Amer. Colonial Church,* II, 354, 365, 461; *Pa. Mag.,* XII, 200; XVIII, 37; Fulham Palace MSS, Pa. (LC), No. 132; MHS *Procs.,* 49, pp. 455, 476; *Mass. Gaz.,* July 10, 1769; *S.C. Gaz.,* Mar. 3, 1764; June 22, 1767; Feb. 9, 1769; Feb. 8, 1773; *SCHG Mag.,* XXVIII, 181; Annie H. Thwing, *The Crooked and Narrow Streets of the Town of Boston* (Boston, 1925), 61; *DAB,* XIII, 361; Samuel A. Seaman, *Annals of New York Methodism* (New York, 1892), 14, 17, 25, 41, 53.

354:1 Bridenbaugh, *Rebels and Gentlemen,* 255; Brookes, *Friend Anthony Benezet,* 80, 93, 106; *Rush Letters,* I, 77, 81; *Pa. Chron.,* May 23, Nov. 28, 1768; Gummere, *Journal of John Woolman,* 64, 66; Stiles, *Literary Diary,* I, 174, 450, 486; Elsbree, *N.E. Quart.,* VIII, 534, 542; Klett, *Presbyterians in Colonial Pennsylvania,* 196; *Newp. Merc.,* June 13, 1774.

354:2 *Journal of the Life . . . of John Griffiths* (Philadelphia, 1780), 358, 397; Phila. Baptist Assoc., *Minutes,* 72, 84, 88, 93, 101, 128, 141; Muhlenberg, *Journals,* I, 434, 529, 668, 673, 685; II, 258, 271, 303, 306; Ezra S. Tipple, *Heart of Asbury's Journal* (Cincinnati, 1904), 49, 51.

354:3 S.P.G. MSS, Pa. (LC), Aug. 31, 1761; Stiles, *Literary Diary,* I, 31; Herbert M. Morais, *Deism in Eighteenth Century America* (New York, 1934), 86, 88, 91; Duché, *Observations,* 46; MHS *Procs.,* 49, p. 476; Bridenbaugh, *Myths and Realities,* 97; Hooker, *Carolina Backcountry,* 75.

355:1 Drake, *History of Boston,* 665; *N.Y. Gaz.,* July 21, 1766.

355:2 Perry, *Historical Collections . . . Amer. Colonial Church, Pa.,* II, 394; S.P.G., MSS, series B, II, 15; Arthur L. Cross, *The Anglican Episcopate and the American Colonies* (Cambridge, 1924) 147, 150, 151.

356:1 Dora M. Clark, *British Opinion and the American Revolution*

(New Haven, 1930), 184; S.P.G., MSS, series B, II, 203, 204, 231; Fulham Palace MSS., Mass., No. 150.

356:2   Cross, *Anglican Episcopate,* chaps. VII–IX; Fulham Palace MSS., Mass., No. 147, Sept. 25, 1769; No. 216, May 12, 1768; Foster, Doc. Hist. Educ., S.C., IX, 18:7; 4 MHS *Colls.,* IV, 431, 436; *Bos. Gaz.,* Dec. 16, 1771; Ezra Stiles, Papers (Bancroft Trans., NYPL), 1761–76, pp. 165, 181, 193; Stiles, *Itineraries,* 435, 443; *Pa. Mag.,* XI, 284.

357:1   *Recs. of Presbyterian Church,* 355–453; *Minutes of the Convention of Delegates from the Synod of New York and Philadelphia and from the Consociation of Connecticut* (Hartford, 1843), plan of union, p. 10; Stiles, *Itineraries,* 427, 429, 466; Stiles, *Letters and Papers,* 15; 2 MHS *Colls.,* I, 140; S.P.G., MSS., series B, II, 147.

358:1   S.P.G. MSS., series B, II, 137; Osgood, *Amer. Hist. Rev.,* VI, 498; *Pa. Chron.,* Oct. 9, 1769; *Pa. Packet,* Aug. 9, 1773; Stiles, *Literary Diary,* I, 344, 415; Stiles, *Letters and Papers,* 39; *N.Y. Merc.,* Nov. 8, 1773; *Bos. Post Boy,* Apr. 4, 1774.

358:3   23 *Bos. Rec. Com.,* 28, 225; Newp. T.C. Recs., XV, 174; XVI, 1; *Newp. Merc.,* Mar. 6, 1771; Mar. 15, 1773; List of Taverns kept at Newport, 1774, Papers concerning Newport, RIHS MSS; Tavern Licences, Secretary's Office, Ledger A (HSP); *Pa. Mag.,* XXII, 126; Public House Permits, Phila. Co., Court Papers, Phila. Co., IV: *S.C.A.G. Gaz.,* Apr. 24, 1767; Apr. 24, 1771; May 4, 1772; *N.Y.M.C.C.,* VII, 2, 420; *N.Y. Merc.,* July 20, 1767; *Bos. Post Boy,* Apr. 5, 1773.

359:1   *S.C.A.G. Gaz.,* Aug. 12, 1771; *N.Y. Merc.,* July 26, 1762; Stokes, *Iconography,* IV, 814; NYHS *Colls.,* 1886, p. 12; *Pa. Packet,* Mar. 21, 1774; *Newsletter,* Apr. 21, 1774; Adams, *Works,* II, 358, 361.

359:2   MHS *Procs.,* 49, p. 441; *S.C. Gaz.,* July 23, 1772; Graydon, *Memoirs,* 56, 58, 60, 63, 71; *Pa. Mag.,* XLVIII, 241; NYHS *Colls.,* 1886, p. 45; *Newp. Merc.,* Aug. 8, 1768; July 5, 1773.

360:1   *S.C. Gaz.,* Aug. 22, 1761; Dec. 25, 1762; Nov. 26, 1763; Apr. 27, 1767; *S.C.A.G. Gaz.,* May 29, 1767; *S.C. Country Jour.,* Nov. 22, 1768; *Pa. Gaz.,* May 6, 1762; June 26, 1766; *Pa. Packet,* July 5, 1773; Sept. 4, 1775; *Pa. Chron.,* Nov. 1, 1773; *N.Y. Gaz.,* July 17, 1766; *Mass. Gaz.,* Aug. 14, Sept. 14, 1769; *Bos. Post Boy,* Jan. 1, Mar. 12, 1770.

360:2   Turberville, *Johnson's England,* I, 188; *N.Y. Merc.,* June 3, 17, 1765; July 17, 1769; Oct. 25, 1773; *N.Y. Gaz.,* May 16, 1765; July 25, 1768; *Rivington's N.Y. Gaz.,* July 15, *Sup.,* 1773; *N.Y. Jour.,* May 25, *Sup.,* 1775.

361:1   *Newp. Merc.,* Aug. 12, 1765; Nov. 17, 1766; May 11, 1767; May 22, 29, Oct. 30, 1769; Oct. 29, 1770; June 29, Sept. 21,

1772; Jan. 4, Apr. 19, Nov. 8, 1773; May 23, Aug. 29, Sept. 5, 1774; 23 *Bos. Rec. Com.,* 69; *Bos. Post Boy,* Dec. 10, 1770; *Rivington's N.Y. Gaz.,* Oct. 25, 1770; Nov. 29, Dec. 6, 1777.

362:1 *Pa. Gaz.,* Aug. 4, 1763; Sept. 15, 1768; Rowe, *Diary,* 67, 142; 20 *Bos. Rec. Com.,* 111; *Newp. Merc.,* Aug. 20, 1764; *S.C. Country Jour.,* Apr. 28, 1767; July 5, 1774; *Pa. Chron.,* Sept. 25, 1769; *S.C. Gaz.,* Jan. 31, 1771; *N.Y. Gaz.,* Aug. 5, 1771; *Prov. Gaz.,* Oct. 16, 1773; *Pa. Packet,* Aug. 22, 1774; *N.Y. Jour.,* Mar. 17, 1774; Adams, *Familiar Letters,* 271.

363:1 Rowe, *Diary,* 66, 67, 156, 172, 203, 211, 229, 250; Stokes, *Iconography,* IV, 780; *S.C. Country Jour.,* Aug. 5, 1766; *Pa. Mag.,* XI, 282; *Newp. Merc.,* June 2, 1766; Stiles, *Literary Diary,* I, 6, 42, 182, 472; 16 *Bos. Rec. Com.,* 175, 205; *Bos. Gaz.,* Aug. 8, 1768; *Bos. Chron.,* Sept. 5, 1768; Schlesinger, *N.E. Quart.,* XXV, 435; Adams, *Works,* II, 218.

363:2 *Bos. Post Boy,* Jan. 5, 1761; Rowe, Diary (MS), Dec. 19, 1764; Rowe, *Diary,* 71, 72, 92, 141, 180, 230; *Bos. Chron.,* Nov. 28, Dec. 12, 1768; *Bos. Gaz.,* Aug. 14, 1769; June 29, Aug. 31, 1772; Weyman's *N.Y. Gaz.,* June 30, 1766; *Newp. Merc.,* Dec. 23, 1765; *S.C.A.G. Gaz.,* Apr. 1, 1771; Collins Papers, XVIII, June 3, 1774.

363:3 *History of the Schuylkill Fishing Company of the State in Schuyl-kill* (Philadelphia, 1889), 356, 401; *Pa. Mag.,* VIII, 203; XXVII, 88, 90; Balch, *Letters and Papers,* xxn, xxi; *Pa. Chron.,* Apr. 20, 27, 1767; Feb. 15, 1773; Hiltzheimer, *Diary,* 26, 32.

364:1 *Pa. Chron.,* May 16, 1768; *Pa. Gaz.,* June 2, 1768; Aug. 19, 1772; William Eddis, *Letters from America* (London, 1792), 115; *Pa. Mag.,* V, 29; MHS *Procs.,* 49, p. 472; *At a Meeting at the Philosophical Society's Hall on Friday, June 10th [1774] . . . from all Societies. . . .* (Broadside, LCP), no. 4675; *N.Y. Merc.,* Apr. 2, 1770; *Mass. Gaz.,* Mar. 20, 1766; Philip Davidson, *Propaganda and the American Revolution* (Chapel Hill, 1941), 99.

365:1 *Bos. Post Boy,* Sept. 29, 1760; Aug. 19, Sept. 16, 1765; *Mass. Gaz.,* Sept. 21, 1769; *Newp. Merc.,* Mar. 28, May 9, 1763; May 6, Dec. 23, 30, 1765; *S.C. Gaz.,* Feb. 11, 18, Mar. 24, 1764; Feb. 1, 1768; *S.C. Country Jour.,* Feb. 11, 1772; MHS *Procs.,* 49, p. 451; *Pa. Gaz.,* Aug. 13, 1761; Aug. 30, 1764; Briden-baugh, *Myths and Realities,* 81; Pa. Mag., IX, 180; Register of the Jockey Club, 1766–1774 (HSP); *Pa. Chron.,* Aug. 19, 1767; June 13, Oct. 3, 10, 1768; May 31, 1773; *Burd Letters,* 44, 45; *Pa. Packet,* Mar. 8, May 31, 1773; *N.Y. Merc.,* Apr. 4, Sept. 5, 1768; *N.Y. Gaz.,* Oct. 1, 22, 1767; Mar. 26, Sept. 30, 1770; *Rivington's N.Y. Gaz.,* Sept. 16, 30, Oct. 14, 1773.

365:2 The Gloucester Hunt is the first organized fox-hunting club in either England or America of which a definite record survives. J. Blau Van Urk, *The Story of American Fox Hunting* (New York, 1940), I, 26, 27, 65, 70, 84, 85; Hiltzheimer, *Diary,* 9, 10, 14; Hunt Club records in *Schuylkill Fishing Company,* 406, 407, 409; Wilson, *Mem. Hist. N.Y.,* II, 458, 459; *S.C. Gaz.,* June 20, 1761; *Newp. Merc.,* Aug. 13, 1770; *Pa. Mag.,* IX, 173.

366:1   Weyman's *N.Y. Gaz.,* Sept. 26, 1763; *Rivington's N.Y. Gaz.,* June 30, July 28, 1774; *Commerce of R.I.,* I, 166; Hiltzheimer, *Diary,* 17, 20; *S.C. Gaz.,* Mar. 28, Apr. 4, 1768; *N.Y. Jour.,* Apr. 29, 1773; *Pa. Mag.,* XLIV, 74.

366:2   Graydon, *Memoirs,* 76; *Newp. Merc.,* Sept. 28, 1762; Sept. 11, 1769; *Bos. Post Boy,* Jan. 30, 1775; *Pa. Packet,* Oct. 31, 1774.

366:3   *Pa. Mag.,* XI, 277, 281, 286; XL, 200; Graydon, *Memoirs,* 49, 53, 62; Hiltzheimer, *Diary,* 28, 29; *R.I. Hist. Mag.,* VI, 169; Peterson, *Rhode Island,* 104.

367:1   Jared Sparks, *Life of Gouveneur Morris* (Boston, 1832), I, 21; *Pa. Mag.,* XI, 280, 283; XXIV, 410; *Newp. Merc.,* Oct. 15, 1764; *S.C. Country Jour.,* Mar. 31, 1772; May 2, 1775; *SCHG Mag.,* XXXVI, 73; *N.Y. Gaz.,* Apr. 29, 1762; Oct. 24, 1765; Apr. 17, Oct. 23, 1766; *Bos. Post Boy,* Feb. 2, 1767; *S.C.A.G. Gaz.,* Apr. 10, 1771; Rowe, *Diary,* 150, 181, 182, 184, 185, 224, 238; *Bos. Chron.,* Dec. 26, 1768.

368:1   Mullett, *Public Baths and Health in England,* 20; Bridenbaugh, 3 *W. & M. Quart.,* III, 151; Samuel Peters, *General History of Connecticut* (London, 1782), 174, 240; *Conn. Courant,* Sept. 20, 1765; *Prov. Gaz.,* Nov. 1, 1766; July 18, 1767; *Newsletter,* July 2, 1767; *N.Y. Jour.,* July 31, Sept. 18, 25, 1766; *S.C. Country Jour.,* May 16, 1769.

368:2   Bridenbaugh, 3 *W. & M. Quart.,* III, 164; Edward Shippen Papers (LC), July 11, 19, 1766; Aug. 12, 1776.

369:1   Bridenbaugh, RIHS *Colls.,* XXVI, 3; Gertrude S. Kimball, *Pictures of Rhode Island in the Past, 1642–1833* (Providence, 1900), 110; *R.I. Hist. Mag.,* VI, 45, 165*n;* Watson, *Men and Times,* 67; *S.C. Gaz.,* May 31, 1770; Hooker, *Carolina Backcountry,* 229; RIHS *Pubs.,* n.s., II, 177; *S.C.A.G. Gaz.,* June 8, 1770; *Newp. Merc.,* June 18, 1770; June 12, 1775.

370:1   In defiance of the law, a performance of Otway's *The Orphan* took place at a Boston tavern in December 1763. It "was neither a Credit to the Actors or the Company" of 210, and therefore the players were "in no danger of incurring the Penalties in the Law for preventing Theatrical Entertainments as this could not be any Ways denominated entertaining." In 1775 some British officers and ladies formed a Society for Promoting Theatrical Amusements and gave several plays at Faneuil Hall. *Newp. Merc.,*

Nov. 3, 1761; Aug. 10, 1762; Dec. 12, 1763; Aug. 31, 1767; Charles Blake, *An Historical Account of the Providence Stage* (Providence, 1868), 18, 20; Newp. T.C. Recs., 710; *Bos. Post Boy,* Sept. 21, 1761; *Bos. Gaz.,* Sept. 21, 1761; *R.I. Acts* (1767), 242; Drake, *Hist. of Boston,* 756; *Newsletter,* Mar. 5, 1767; Nov. 30, 1775; Gov. Wm. Tryon, N.C., to Gov. Sam Ward, June 15, 1768; Misc. Letters (R.I. Archives); Mason, *Reminiscences of Newport,* 123.

370:2   On the English theater, see Sybil M. Rosenfeld, *Strolling Players and Drama in the Provinces* (Cambridge, 1939). *N.Y. Merc.,* Aug. 17, 1761; Dec. 7, 1767; Du Simitiere, Papers relating to Pa., N.E., No. 3, p. 96; *N.Y. Gaz.,* Nov. 26, 1761; Eola Willis, *The Charleston Stage in the XVIII Century* (Columbia, S.C., 1924), 43; *Newp. Merc.,* Jan. 13, 1766; *S.C. Gaz.,* July 26, Dec. 13, 1773; *Pa. Jour.,* Oct. 30, 1766; *Pa. Mag.,* XXIII, 267.

370:3   Dougald MacMillan, *Drury Lane Calendar* (Oxford, 1938), 134; List of plays given at the John Street Theatre, 1773 (NYHS), Box I, 1771–1774; *Pa. Chron.,* Nov. 6, 1769; *Pa. Gaz.,* Apr. 23, 1767; Thomas C. Pollock, *Philadelphia Theatre in the Eighteenth Century* (Philadelphia, 1933), 73–100; Willis, *Charleston Stage,* 73.

371:1   *Advice and Caution from the Monthly Meeting of Friends in Philadelphia* . . . Sept. 23, 1768 (Broadsides, HSP), V, No. 647; 2 MHS *Procs.,* XVI, 225; *N.Y. Merc.,* May 3, 10, 1762; *Colden Papers,* VI, 281; *N.Y. Gaz.,* May 8, 1766; Aug. 20, 27, Dec. 3, 10, 17, 1767; Feb. 1, 1768; *Burd Papers,* 18; *Bos. Post Boy,* May 19, 1766; *Pa. Votes,* V, 524, 526; *Pa. Gaz.,* July 31, 1766; Feb. 16, Mar. 5, Aug. 13, 1767; *Pa. Chron.,* Feb. 16, Mar. 2, 1767; *Pa. Mag.,* XI, 494; *S.C.A.G. Gaz.,* July 31, 1769.

371:2   *N.Y. Merc.,* May 3, 10, 1773; *Pa. Jour.,* Jan. 18, Feb 1, 1770; *S.C. Gaz.,* Nov. 15, 1773; Worthington C. Ford and Gaillard Hunt, *Journals of the Continental Congress* (Washington, 1904), I, 78.

372:1   *N.Y. Gaz.,* Aug. 13, 20, 1767.

375:4   Samuel E. Morison, *Sources and Documents Illustrating the American Revolution* (Oxford, 1929), 169.

CHAPTER X

375:1   *S.C. Gaz.,* Sept. 17, 1763; Oct. 1, 1764; Mar. 9, *Sup.,* 1765; Aug. 3, 24, 1769; Oct. 29, *Sup.,* 1772; Mar. 15, 1770; Feb. 28, 1774; Wallace, *Henry Laurens,* 177; St. Philip's Vestry, Minutes, II, Feb. 1, 1774; S.C. Pub. Recs., XXXII, 390; Webster, Southern Hist. Assoc., *Pubs.,* II, 135; *S.C. Country Jour.,* Apr. 11,

1769; *S.C.A.G. Gaz.,* May 30, 1766; Feb. 12, 1772; Foster, Doc. Hist. Educ. S.C., I, 228*e;* V, 798; IX, 15:11.

375:2   Cheyney, *Univ. of Pa.,* 59; Bridenbaugh, *Rebels and Gentlemen,* 254; Thomas Woody, *Early Quaker Education in Pennsylvania* (New York, 1920), 64; Muhlenberg, *Journals,* II, 94, 199; Scharf and Westcott, *Hist. of Philadelphia,* III, 1922; Pa. Ger. Soc., *Procs.,* XXXVIII, 68; *Phila. Staatsbote,* Jan. 12, 1773; Graydon, *Memoirs,* 85; Mulhern, *Secondary Education in Pa.,* 35, 42, 51, 123; *Pa. Jour.,* Sept. 26, 1771; June 23, 1773; *S.C.A.G. Gaz.,* Feb. 12, 1772.

376:1   Foster, *Doc. Hist. Educ., S.C.,* IX, 15:17, 19; 16:27; 17:10, 16; 18:14, 19; Weyman's *N.Y. Gaz.,* Apr. 5, 1762; *N.Y. Gaz.,* May 27, 1762; Nov. 29, 1764; *N.Y. Merc.,* Oct. 11, 1762; May 2, 1768; June 11, 1770; Kilpatrick, *Dutch Schools,* 157; *Bos. Gaz.,* Aug. 8, 1763.

376:2   Stiles, *Literary Diary,* I, 152, 159, 174, 195, 200, 216; *Newp. Merc.,* Apr. 11, 1763; Oct. 2, 1769; June 1, 22, Aug. 3, Nov. 9, 1772; Apr. 5, 1773; Mar. 14, 1774.

376:3   MHS *Procs.,* XVII, 217; 4 MHS *Colls.,* IV, 436; 18 *Bos. Rec. Com.,* 23, 25, 54, 79, 131, 167; Adams, *Works,* IV, 199.

377:1   S.C. Pub. Recs., XXXII, 392; *S.C. Country Jour.,* May 27, 1766; Oct. 18, 1768; Sept. 19, 1769; *Pa. Chron.,* Oct. 5, 1767; Sept. 26, 1768.

377:2   Graydon, *Memoirs,* 16; *Rivington's N.Y. Gaz.,* July 1, 1773; *N.Y. Merc.,* Aug. 23, 1773; *Bos. Chron.,* Apr. 20, 1769; *N.Y. Jour.,* Feb. 16, 1769; Van Doren, *Franklin Mecom Letters,* 139, 273.

378:1   *Bos. Post Boy,* Nov. 28, 1774; *Pa. Gaz.,* Nov. 17, 1773; Dec. 6, 1775; *Pa. Packet,* Oct. 17, Nov. 21, 1774; *Pa. Chron.,* Oct. 26, 1767; *Bos. Gaz.,* Mar. 22, 1773; Adams, *Familiar Letters,* 218.

378:2   Stiles, *Literary Diary,* I, 22*n,* 23*n,* 31, 39, 46, 49, 108; *R.I. Col. Rec.,* VI, 384; *Newp. Merc.,* Nov. 20, 1769; Jan. 15, 29, Feb. 12, Mar. 12, 1770; *New London Gaz.,* Feb. 20, 1770; Walter C. Bronson, *History of Brown University* (Providence, 1914), 8–50.

379:1   Stiles, *Literary Diary,* I, 45, 46; MHS *Procs.,* XX, 47; *Bos. Chron.,* June 27, 1768; 4 MHS *Colls.,* IV, 415; *N.Y. Jour.,* Oct. 24, 1771; Apr. 30, 1772; Nov. 3, 1774; William S. Demarest, *History of Rutgers College* (New Brunswick, 1924), 82, 89; Stiles, *Itineraries,* 428, 431; Bridenbaugh, *Rebels and Gentlemen,* 59.

379:2   Foster, Doc. Hist. Educ., S.C., I, 267, 278; S.C. Commons, Jour., XXXVII, 30, 59, 66, 75; *S.C. Gaz.,* Aug. 24, Nov. 9, 30, 1769: *S.C.A.G. Gaz.,* Nov. 14, 20, 1769.

380:1 *S.C. Gaz.,* Oct. 26, 1769; Jan. 8, Feb. 15, Mar. 8, 15, Apr. 12, 19, 1770; May 30, 1771; *SCHG Mag.,* XLV, 189; XLVIII, 95; Newp. T.C. Recs., XVI, 160; J. H. Easterby, *History of the College of Charleston* (Charleston, 1935), 8, 10, 12, 13, 14; Wallace, *Henry Laurens,* 177; S.C. Commons, Jour., XXXVIII, 368.

380:2 John Morgan, *Discourse upon the Institution of Medical Schools in America* (Baltimore, 1937); Bond, *Jour. Hist. Medicine,* II, 10; *Pa. Gaz.,* Nov. 11, 1762; May 9, Sept. 26, 1765; Dec. 11, 1766; June 30, 1768; July 4, 1771; *Pa. Chron.,* Oct. 5, 1767; Aug. 8, 1768; Aug. 14, 1769; *Pa. Packet,* Oct. 10, Nov. 28, 1774; Bridenbaugh, *Rebels and Gentlemen,* 285.

380:3 Betsy C. Corner, *William Shippen, Jr., Pioneer in American Medicine* (Philadelphia, 1951), 95; Wickes, *Hist. of Medicine in New Jersey,* 52; John H. Van Amringe, *A History of Columbia University* (New York, 1904), 308, 312; *N.Y. Merc.,* Nov. 9, 1767; Aug. 29, 1768.

381:1 These figures are for booksellers who were already in business or who started during the years 1761–1776; of course all of them did not continue, either in the colonies or in England. London had 245 booksellers, and its preponderance undoubtedly kept down the number of provincial shops. Brown, *Directory of the Book Arts in Philadelphia;* McKay, *Register of Booksellers in New York;* McCulloch, Amer. Antiquarian Soc., *Procs.,* n.s., XXXI, 89; Boston, Newport, and Charles Town newspapers; Plomer, *Dictionary of Printers and Booksellers in England.*

381:2 *Pa. Chron.,* Apr. 11, May 2, June 13, 1768; Feb. 11, 1771; *Pa. Packet,* Oct. 28, 1771; Sept. 6, 1773; *S.C. Country Jour.,* May 25, 1773; *Newp. Merc.,* Jan. 6, 1772; Nov. 8, 1773; *N.Y. Merc.,* Oct. 31, 1768; *Bos. Post Boy,* Nov. 29, 1773; Bridenbaugh, *Rebels and Gentlemen,* 84, 295.

382:1 *S.C.A.G. Gaz.,* Aug. 22, 1766; Jan. 30, 1767; *S.C. Gaz.,* Aug. 28, 1768; *Pa. Gaz.,* Sept. 3, 1761; *NY. Gaz.,* Feb. 18, 1762; Sept. 4, 1766; *N.Y. Merc.,* Nov. 21, 1768; Col. Soc. Mass., *Pubs.,* XIX, 227n; XXXIV, 578; MHS *Procs.,* 61, p. 255, 263, 275.

382:2 MHS *Procs.,* 61, p. 229; *Bos. Chron.,* Feb. 1, 1768; *N.Y. Merc.,* June 10, 1771; *Mass. Gaz.,* Apr. 22, 1773; *Pa. Chron.,* Sept. 19, 1772; *S.C. Gaz.,* May 14, 1763; July 20, 1767; Hildeburn, *Issues of the Pa. Press,* 1769, no. 2428.

383:1 *Rivington's N.Y. Gaz.,* Sept. 16, Dec. 30, 1773; Nov. 17, 1774; *S.C. Gaz.,* Aug. 13, 1763; July 20, 1767; Nov. 12, 1772; Weyman's *N.Y. Gaz.,* Aug. 29, Sept. 12, 1763; Keep, *Library in Col. New York,* 105, 107; *N.Y. Merc.,* Aug. 29, 1768; Oct. 28,

1771; Nov. 7, 1774; *Newsletter,* Oct. 31, 1765; *Bos. Post Boy,* Nov. 4, 11, 1765; *Pa. Jour.,* Jan. 2, Sept. 21, Dec. 14, 1769; *Pa. Gaz.,* Sept. 21, 1769; Feb. 9, 1774; *Pa. Packet,* Mar. 14, 1774.

383:2   *Pa. Gaz.,* June 14, 1764; Apr. 3, 10, 1766; Jan. 14, Mar. 24, 1768; Jan. 19, Feb. 16, Mar. 13, Sept. 28, 1769; Sept. 8, 1773; *Pa. Chron.,* Mar. 21, Dec. 26, 1768; Jan. 9, Feb. 13, 1769; *Pa. Jour.,* Apr. 27, 1769; Bridenbaugh, *Rebels and Gentlemen,* 86, 89, 90.

383:3   Phila. Baptist Assoc., *Minutes,* 82; *Pa. Gaz.,* Aug. 30, Sept. 20, 1770; *Pa. Chron.,* Sept. 9, 1771; Muhlenberg, *Journals,* I, 607, 611; II, 247; Scharf and Westcott, *Hist. of Philadelphia,* II, 1194, 1195; *Pa. Mag.,* XLII, 217; Klett, *Presbyterians in Col. Pa.,* 217, 218*n*; Joseph T. Wheeler, Literary Culture in 18th Century Maryland (MS Thesis, Brown University), 19.

384:1   *N.Y.M.C.C.,* VI, 427; VIII, 24; *N.Y. Gaz.,* Sept. 19, 1765; *N.Y. Merc.,* Dec. 30, 1771; Apr. 13, 1772; *N.Y. Jour.,* Jan. 14, 1773; Keep, *Library in Col. New York,* 81.

384:2   MHS *Procs.,* 49, p. 447; Weyman's *N.Y. Gaz.,* May 25, 1767; Frederick P. Bowes, *Culture of Early Charleston* (Chapel Hill, 1942), 60, 62, 64,; S.C. Pub. Recs., XXXII, 391; *S.C. Gaz.,* Mar. 22, 1773; Ravenel, *Eliza Pinckney,* 229.

385:1   Stiles, *Literary Diary,* I, 166; Holmes, *Life of Ezra Stiles,* 95, 104; MHS *Colls.,* X, 166; *Newp. Merc.,* Nov. 9, 1772.

385:2   *Bos. Gaz.,* Jan. 18, 1768; MHS *Colls.,* 72, p. 117; Audit Office 13, vol. 46, bundle 41 (PRO, London); Jones, *Loyalists of Mass.,* 13, 77, 160, 230; MHS *Procs.,* 51, p. 362; *Bos. Post Boy,* Nov. 28, 1763; Brayton, *N.E. Quart.,* VIII, 277; 4 MHS *Colls.,* IV, 451.

386:1   *S.C. Gaz.,* Mar. 31, 1764; Mar. 16, 1769; 3 *Pa. Archives,* XIV; *Pa. Gaz.,* Sept. 24, 1761; Jackson, *Cyclopedia of Philadelphia,* I, 48; William C. Wells, *Two Essays* (London, 1818), xxx; *Pa. Jour.,* Apr. 30, 1761; July 8, 1762; *Phila. Staatsbote,* Jan. 18, 1762; Dapp, *German Amer. Annals,* n.s., XIV, 118.

386:2   Figures for Newport corrected by data from Alden, *Rhode Island Imprints.*

387:1   *Pa. Packet,* Mar. 2, Nov. 2, 1772; Apr. 25, 1774; Hildeburn, *Issues of the Pennsylvania Press,* I, vii-viii; Evans, *American Bibliography; Pa. Gaz.,* Aug. 18, 1773; *Newsletter,* May 13, 1762; Dec. 7, 1770; *Bos. Post Boy,* Oct. 19, 1772; MHS *Procs.,* 61, pp. 258, 290, 298.

388:1   *Pa. Packet,* Jan. 26, 1773; *Bos. Post Boy,* Mar. 2, 1772.

388:2   Honyman, *Journal,* 31, 53, 54, 68; Bridenbaugh, *Rebels and Gentlemen,* 73.

388:3   Brigham, *Hist. and Bibliography of Amer. Newspapers,* I, II; *Bos. Chron.,* Jan. 2, Mar. 23, 1769; *Pa. Eve. Post,* Jan. 24, 1775.

389:1   *Calendar of Franklin Papers,* II, 69; *Rivington's N.Y. Gaz.,* Oct. 13, 1774; Jones, *Loyalists of Mass.,* 122; *Newp. Hist. Mag.,* I, 230; *Newp. Merc.,* Mar. 1, 1773; Collins Papers, XVI, Aug. 23, 1773; Honyman, *Journal,* 16.

389:2   *S.C. Gaz.,* Aug. 25, 1764; *S.C.A.G. Gaz.,* Oct. 31, 1765; List of subscribers to Col. Wm. Bradford's Newspaper *The Pennsylvania Journal,* 1764 (HSP); *Pa. Mag.,* XIV, 445; *Pa. Chron.,* Aug. 17, 1767; Oct. 28, 1771; J. W. Wayland, *German Element of the Shenandoah Valley of Virginia* (Charlottesville, 1907), 141; *N.Y. Merc.,* Mar. 15, 1762; *Rivington's N.Y. Gaz.,* Sept. 9, 1773; *Newsletter,* July 3, 1766.

390:1   *Newp. Merc.,* May 14, 1770.

390:2   *N.Y. Merc.,* Nov. 11, 1771; *N.Y. Jour.,* Jan. 9, 1772.

390:3   Stiles, *Letters and Papers,* 17; *N.Y. Merc.,* Aug. 21, 28, 1769; *Bos. Gaz.,* Jan. 16, 1775; *Newp. Merc.,* Aug. 21, 1769; Stiles, *Literary Diary,* I, 549; *Pa. Merc.,* Apr. 7, 1775; *Pa. Packet,* Dec. 5, 1774.

392:1   2 MHS *Procs.,* XVI, 198; *Bos. Eve. Post,* June 24, July 1, 1765 (Dorr copies, MHS); Watts, *Letter Book,* 386, 399; *Phila. Staatsbote,* Aug. 20, 1764; Oct. 28, 1765; *Arthur D. Graeff, The Relations between The Pennsylvania Germans and the British Authorities* (Norristown, Pa., 1939), 223; Letter of R. Wells, Aug. 13, 1765, South Carolina MSS (NYPL), Box 2; Oliver, Origin and Progress of the American Rebellion, Egerton MSS (LC Trans.), 2671, 77; Schlesinger, *N.E. Quart.,* VIII, 63; Adams, *Works,* III, 457.

392:2   2 MHS *Procs.,* XVI, 211; *Newsletter,* Mar. 8, 1770; Schlesinger, *N.E. Quart.,* VIII, 81; *Bos. Post Boy,* Mar. 24, 1766.

392:3   *Bos. Chron.,* Mar. 16, 1769; Sparks MSS (Harvard Coll. Lib.), VIII, 123, 148; the "Journal of the Times" is printed by Oliver M. Dickerson, *Boston Under Military Rule* (Boston, 1936); Schlesinger, *Pa. Mag.,* LX, 309; *S.C. Country Jour.,* Oct. 11, 1768; Philip Davidson, *Propaganda in the American Revolution* (Durham, 1941), chaps. XII, XIII; Greenough, Amer. Antiquarian Soc., *Procs.,* n.s., XLV, 288.

393:1   Col. Soc. Mass., *Pubs.,* XXXII, 396; XXXIV, 582; *The Censor,* Nov. 23, 30, 1771; May 2, 1772; Dickerson, *N.E. Quart.,* XXIV, 453.

393:2   "Massachusettensis," *Bos. Post Boy,* Dec. 12, 1774; *Bos. Gaz.,* June 29, Dec. 9, 1771; Jan. 27, Sept. 21, 1772; *Bos. Chron.,* Aug. 29, 1768; MHS *Colls.,* 72, p. 51; *S.C.A.G. Gaz.,* June 2,

1775; Van Doren, *Franklin Mecom Letters,* 106; *Pa. Gaz.,* Jan. 7, 1768; Sept. 29, 1773; Serle, *Journal,* xxi.

394:2   There is a detailed account of Philadelphia literature in Briden-baugh, *Rebels and Gentlemen,* chap. III.

395:1   Philadelphia's and America's greatest writer, Benjamin Franklin, was absent from the city all but the two years 1762–64. The "Farmer's Letters" first appeared in the *Pa. Journal* and ultimately in twenty-one of the twenty-five newspapers; and in at least eight editions in the colonies as well as in Dublin, London (several printings), and Amsterdam (in French). Moses C. Tyler, *Literary History of the American Revolution* (New York, 1899), I, 236.

395:2   William Bradford, Memorandum Book, May 4, 1776, Bradford MSS (HSP).

395:3   Charles F. Mullett, "Some Political Writings of James Otis," *University of Missouri Studies,* IV, 261, 363; H. A. Cushing, *Writings of Samuel Adams* (New York, 1904–8); Adams, *Works,* III, IV; Josiah Quincy, *Observations on the Act of Parliament* (Boston, 1774); *DAB,* XX, 36; *Newsletter,* Oct. 11, 1770; *Bos. Post Boy,* Apr. 19, 1773; *Bos. Gaz.,* Jan. 31, 1774; J. Franklin Jameson, *History of Historical Writing in America* (New York, 1891), 79; *Bos. Chron.,* Jan. 2, 1769.

396:1   *N.Y. Gaz.,* May 6, 1762; *S.C. Gaz.,* July 20, 1765; Oct. 5, 1769; *Pa. Chron.,* June 19, 1769; Bowes, *Culture of Early Charleston,* 72, 76; Alexander Hewatt's "Account," *Carroll, Historical Collections, S.C.,* I, lxxii, 501; Lewis Leary, *The Literary Career of Nathaniel Tucker* (Durham, 1951); Percival C. Turrentine, Nathaniel Beverley Tucker (MS Thesis, Harvard Univ.), I, 26; Bridenbaugh, *Myths and Realities,* 44, 106; *S.C.A.G. Gaz.,* Oct. 7, Nov. 14, 1774.

396:2   *Newp. Merc.,* May 19, 1761; Stile's manuscript is in the MHS; Stiles, *Literary Diary,* I, 3, 199; Stiles, *Letters and Papers,* 36, 40, 41; Stiles, *Itineraries,* 516; Adams, *Works,* II, 352; *N.Y. Jour.,* June 19, 1766; May 7, 1767; Sept. 1, 1774; Literary Society instituted 1766, Minutes (NYHS MSS), VIII, no. 95; *Rivington's N.Y. Gaz.,* Aug. 26, 1773.

397:1   *Prov. Gaz.,* Oct. 20, 1762; *S.C. Gaz.,* Mar. 8, 1773; *Pa. Chron.,* Feb. 30, 1769; *Newp. Merc.,* Dec. 21, 1767; *Newsletter,* Nov. 3, 1763; *Bos. Chron.,* Feb. 8, June 27, Dec. 19, 1768.

397:2   English travelers usually commended the purity of speech they discovered prevailing from the Chesapeake country north to Philadelphia, where, remarked Lord Adam Gordon, "the propriety of Language here surprized me much, the English tongue being spoken by all ranks, in a degree of purity and perfection, surpassing any, but the polite part of London." From New York to Portsmouth the Yankee dialect and idiom in many local variations, diverged widely from the norm, like that of many regions of Old England. "She is not as the New England Men say dredfull handsome," John Watts wrote of a slave to a Virginian in 1763. Mereness, *Travels,* 411; Watts, *Letter Book,* 126; Smyth, *Tour,* II, 363; *Phila. Staatsbote,* July 5, 1762; *N.Y. Gaz.,* Jan. 29, 1761; *Bos. Gaz.,* Mar. 4, 1765; *Royal Amer. Mag.,* Jan., 1774, p. 6.

398:1 *Newsletter,* Apr. 1, 1762, *Weyman's N.Y. Gaz.,* July 15, 1765; *Pa. Jour.,* May 31, 1770; *Mass. Broadsides,* nos. 1348, 1456, 1467, 1469, 1502, 1631, 1635, 1808, 1922; *Newp. Merc.,* Aug. 29, 1768; Philadelphiensis [David J. Dove] *The Manners of the Times: A Satire* (Philadelphia, 1762), lines 31–32, 73–78; *Pa. Gaz.,* Oct. 19, 1774; Evans, *American Bibliography,* IV, nos. 9963, 10848, 10849; MHS *Procs.,* VIII, 371.

398:2 Sellers, *Artist of the Revolution,* 99; *Crayon,* I, 82.

399:1 Rowe, *Diary,* 213; *Calendar of Franklin Papers,* II, 52; *Bos. Post Boy,* Apr. 13, 1767; *Pa. Gaz.,* July 5, 1770; *Pa. Packet,* Oct. 28, 1771; Graydon, *Memoirs,* 69; Wallace and Miller, *Colonial Houses of Philadelphia,* 180; Adams, *Works,* II, 429; *Pa. Mag.,* LXIII, 336.

399:2 Very little indication of popular songs and singing exists for Charles Town. *Rivington's N.Y. Gaz.,* May 20, 1773; Hildeburn, *Issues of Pa. Press,* no. 4659; Evans, *American Bibliography,* III, 9569; IV, 10674; *Newp. Merc.,* Jan. 19, 1767; Sept. 5, 1774; *Newsletter,* Nov. 28, 1771.

399:3 Adams, *Works,* II, 218; Tyler, *Lit. Hist. Amer. Revolution,* I, 239; *Newp. Merc.,* Sept. 14, 1762; Franklin, *Works* (Bigelow), III, 392; *Bos. Eve. Post,* Sept. 2, 1765; Alden, *Rhode Island Imprints,* 195; RIHS *Colls.,* XXX, 36.

400:1 In 1768 Peter Valton published six sonatas for harpsichord and violin by subscription. Bridenbaugh, *Rsbels and Gentlemen,* 153; Wroth, *Colonial Printer,* 248; Hildeburn, *Issues of Pa. Press; S.C. Gaz.,* Feb. 20, 1762, Oct. 10, 1768; *S.C. Country Jour.,* Oct. 18, 1774; *N.Y. Jour.,* Mar 28, 1771; Stiles, *Itineraries,* 225; Adams, *Works,* II, 364, 379, 395, 401.

400:2 *N.Y. Gaz.,* Feb. 4, 1762; *Rivington's N.Y. Gaz.,* Oct. 14, 1773; *Pa. Gaz.,* Dec. 23, 1762; Aug. 4, 1763; Aug. 23, Sept. 20, 1770; June 11, 1772; May 11, 1774; *Bos. Post Boy,* June 25, 1764; July 31, 1769; *Bos. Gaz.,* June 27, 1763; Sept. 18, 1769; *Newp. Merc.,* Oct. 31, 1763; May 4, 1767; *N.Y. Merc.,* Mar. 18, 1765; June 18, Sept. 17, Oct. 8, 1770; Dec. 16, 1771; Mar. 30, 1772; Oct. 10, 1774; *S.C. Gaz.,* May 23, 1761; Feb. 24,

Aug. 10, 1767; *Pa. Packet,* Mar. 13, 1775; Bridenbaugh, *Colonial Craftsman,* 56.

401:1   *S.C.A.G. Gaz.,* Apr. 21, 1775; *S.C. Gaz.,* Oct. 30, 1762; *DAB,* II, 269; *Bos. Gaz.,* Dec. 10, 1770; Bridenbaugh, *Rebels and Gentlemen,* 152.

401:2   *Pa. Mag.,* XXXIX, 277; *Pa. Gaz.,* Apr. 4, 18, 1765; Jan. 9, 1766; Feb. 5, Nov. 19, 1767; Sept. 30, 1772; Bridenbaugh, *Rebels and Gentlemen,* 156; *Newsletter,* May 19, 1763; Jan. 31, 1771; Oct. 21, 28, 1773; July 14, 1774; *Bos. Post Boy,* Feb. 19, 1770.

402:1   Newporters gave occasional concerts after 1767 but only when "a Number of the first Performers" came down from Boston in 1772 did they hear anything like "a Grand Concert of Vocal and Instrumental Musick." *Newp. Merc.,* Aug. 24, 1767; May. 4, 1772; Aug. 1, 1774; Stiles, *Literary Diary,* I, 46; Weyman's *N.Y. Gaz.,* May 24, Oct. 11, 1762; Apr. 20, 1767; *N.Y. Gaz.,* May 27, 1762; Dec. 27, 1764; Jan. 1, 1770; *Rivington's N.Y. Gaz.,* May 6, 1773; Apr. 14, 1774.

402:2   *S.C. Gaz.,* Sept. 14, Oct. 31, 1765; Apr. 9, 1772; June 7, 1773; *S.C.A.G. Gaz.,* Oct. 10, 1766; Apr. 17, 1771; *Newp. Merc.,* June 24, 1771; *S.C. Country Jour.,* Mar. 9, 1774; *SCHG Mag.,* I, 223; MHS *Procs.,* 49, p. 441.

403:1   *Pa. Chron.,* Feb. 6, Oct. 16, Nov. 27, 1769; Oct. 8, Nov. 19, 1770; *Pa. Jour.,* Sept. 21, Nov. 9, 16, 23, 30, 1769; Sept. 27, Nov. 8, 1770; Jan. 31, 1771; Oct. 7, 1772; *Pa. Gaz.,* Jan. 24, 1771; Bridenbaugh, *Rebels and Gentlemen,* 157.

403:2   The English themselves paid very little attention to anything except portrait painting; and the London press for many years slighted exhibitions of the work of contemporary painters. William T. Whitley, *Artists and Their Friends in England, 1700–1799* (London, 1928), I, 167, 187; MHS *Colls.,* 71, pp. 31, 63, 65, 68, 95.

404:1   *R.I. Col. Rec.,* VII, 201, 216; Newp. T.C. Recs., XV, 14, 27, 42, 43, 108, 123; *Newp. Merc.,* July 19, 1773; RIHS *Colls.,* XII, 50; Jones, *Loyalists of Mass.,* xxi, 230; Bridenbaugh, *Peter Harrison,* 78; MHS *Colls.,* 71, pp. 27, 240, 245, 250, 251; *S.C. Gaz.,* June 6, 1774; *S.C.A.G. Gaz.,* Sept. 9, 1774.

404:2   Adams, *Works,* II, 397; *Burd Papers,* 51; Balch, *Letters,* lxix, lxxi; Allen to Thomas Penn, Mar. 11, 1765, Penn MSS, Official Correspondence, X, 1 (HSP); MHS *Colls.,* 71, pp. 163, 272, 293, 341, 393; Bridenbaugh, *Rebels and Gentlemen,* 212.

405:1   William Sawitzky, *Matthew Pratt* (New York, 1942), 9, 15, 17, 20, 29, 35; Sellers, *Artist of the Revolution,* 61, 63, 94, 95, 110, 111, 113; Adams, *Familiar Letters,* 215, 216; Whitley, *Artists* and Their Friends, I, 187; Pa. Jour., Sept. 21, 1769; Rutledge, Amer. Phil. Soc., Trans., n.s., XXXIX, 122; MHS Colls., 71, p. 163; Bridenbaugh, Rebels and Gentlemen, 169, 173.

406:1 Bos. Post Boy, Nov. 18, 1765; June 13, 1774; Newsletter, Jan. 7, 1768; Bos. Gaz., Oct. 16, 1769; July 5, 1773.

406:2 MHS Colls., 71, pp. 26, 41, 43, 45, 48, 55, 250, 288, 361; Collins Papers, S. Eliot to Wm. Barrell, Aug. 24, 1773; Whitley, Artists and Their Friends, I, 262; Parker and Wheeler, John Singleton Copley 24–129.

406:3 King's greatest service to American art was the instruction and encouragement he was to give to Washington Allston and Edward G. Malbone, the miniaturist, in the nineties. DAB, I, 224; X, 401; XII, 216; Newp. Merc., Nov. 7, 1763; Jan. 28, 1766; June 7, 1773; Stiles, Literary Diary, I, 52, 131, 144, 367; Stiles, Itineraries, 384; William T. Whitley, Gilbert Stuart (Cambridge, 1932), 3, 5, 6.

407:1 Rutledge, Amer. Phil. Soc., Trans., n.s., XXXIX, 123; S.C. Gaz., Nov. 3, 1766; Feb. 2, Apr. 27, June 1, 1767; Nov. 14, 1768; Mar. 8, 15, 1770; Mar. 26, May 14, 1772; Apr. 5, Jan. 9, Dec. 12, 1774; Jan. 2, 1775; Ravenel, Eliza Pinckney, 231; Bartram, Amer. Phil. Soc., Trans., n.s., XXXIII, 19; XXXIX, 536.

407:2 John Durand, probably an itinerant limner from Connecticut, was in and out of New York briefly between 1763 and 1770 before going to Virginia, where he painted what seems to have been the earliest American nude. Thorne, 3 W. & M. Quart., VI, 565; N.Y. Gaz., May 13, 1762; Apr. 25, 1768; MHS Colls., 71, pp. 71, 76, 94, 113; N.Y. Merc., June 8, 1763; July 31, 1769; Jan. 7, 1771; NYHS Quart. XXXV, 355; Albany Gaz., Jan. 27, 1772; S.C. Gaz., Nov. 14, 1768; Rivington's N.Y. Gaz., Aug. 4, 1774.

408:1 Pa. Jour., May 31, 1770; Nov. 21, 1771; Pa. Gaz., Apr. 2, 1761; Apr. 22, 1762; Apr. 28, 1773; S.C.A.G. Gaz., Mar. 13, 1767; S.C. Country Jour., May 15, 1770; Oct. 15, 1771; N.Y. Merc., Dec. 23, 1771.

408:2 Pa. Chron., Oct. 24, Dec. 12, 1768; Bowdoin Temple Papers, I, 86; MHS Colls., 71, pp. 264, 265; Pa. Gaz., Oct. 29, Nov. 5, 1761; Feb. 2, 1769; Phila. Staatsbote, June 6, 1763; S.C. Gaz., Oct. 31, Sup., 1774; S.C. Country Jour., Dec. 17, 1765; Aug. 7, 1770; Bos. Gaz., July 21, 1766; Apr. 16, 1770; Bos. Eve. Post, Dec. 27, 1762; Pa. Packet, Sept. 12, 1774; Sept. 18, 1775; Newp. Merc., Sept. 27, 1773; Apr. 4, 1774; Jan. 30, Feb. 6, 13, 1775; N.Y. Gaz., Oct. 14, 1762.

409:1 Purdie & Dixon, Virginia Gaz., Aug. 5, 1773; Pennsylvania Mag., I (1775), 9.

409:2   *Bos. Gaz.,* Nov. 25, 1765; Col. Soc. Mass., *Pubs.,* XIX, 287*n*;
XX, 12, 13*n*, 14; Morison, *Three Centuries of Harvard,* 167;
Pa. Packet, Nov. 1, 1773; *Wickes, Hist. Medicine in New Jersey,*
52; *S.C. Gaz.,* Feb. 16, *Sup.,* 1765; *Old-Time New England,*
XIII, 18; S.C. Commons, Jour., XXXVII, 32; *N.Y. Gaz.,* Feb.
26, May 21, 28, 1767.

410:1   Bridenbaugh, *Rebels and Gentlemen,* 295; Goodman, *Benjamin
Rush,* 36, 453, 404; *Amer. Mag.,* June, 1769, p. 164; Stiles,
Itineraries, 195; Dr. Peter Fayssoux, Letters (SCHS), Aug. 4,
1770; *S.C.A.G. Gaz.,* May 15, 1767; *Pa. Chron.,* Dec. 12, 1768.

410:2   *Rush Letters,* I, 51, 66; *Pa. Jour.,* Dec. 14, 1769; *N.Y. Gaz.,*
Jan. 15, 22, 1770; *Royal Amer. Mag.,* Feb. 1774, p. 47; *Bos.
Eve. Post,* June 3, 1771; *Pa. Gaz.,* July 26, Oct. 18, 1775;
Hildeburn, *Issues of the Pennsylvania Press,* no. 3188; *Pennsylvania Magazine,* I (1775), 25; *Rivington's N.Y. Gaz.,* Jan. 13,
1774; *Newp. Merc.,* Apr. 10, 1775; *Pa. Chron.,* Dec. 19, 26,
1768.

411:1   Thomson, NYHS *Colls.,* 1878, p. 19; Junto Minutes (Amer.
Phil. Soc., Phila.); *Pa. Chron.,* Mar. 7, 1768; *Pa. Gaz.,* Jan. 28,
Mar. 17, 1768; *Calendar of Franklin Papers,* II, 17, 44, 102,
201; V, 203; Bridenbaugh, *Rebels and Gentlemen,* 334.

411:2   Junto Minutes, Jan. 1, 1768.

412:1   American Academy of Sciences, Aug. 15, 1765, Nov. 24, 1766,
and the Institution of the Selden Academy of Sciences in New
England in America, Jan. 5, 7, 1767, both in Stiles MSS (Yale
Univ. Library, used by permission); *Prov. Gaz.,* Feb. 20, 1768;
Purdie & Dixon, *Virginia Gaz.,* May 13, July 22, Aug. 5, Oct.
28, Nov. 11, 1773; June 16, 1774.

412:2   Bridenbaugh, *Rebels and Gentlemen,* 322; *Pa. Chron.,* Nov. 14,
Dec. 19, 1768; Jan. 9, 1769; *Pa. Gaz.,* Dec. 29, 1768.

413:1   Bridenbaugh, *Rebels and Gentlemen,* 342, 349; *N.Y. Gaz.,* June
12, 26, 1769; Jean Bernoulli, *Receuil pour les Astronomes*
(Berlin, 1772), II, 305.

413:2   *Early Proceedings of the American Philosophical Society for the
Promotion of Useful Knowledge* (Philadelphia, 1884); Briden-
baugh, *Rebels and Gentlemen,* 342, 351, 353; *Pennsylvania
Magazine,* I (1775), 141; *Pa. Chron.,* May 16, 1768; William
Barton, *Memoir of the Life of David Rittenhouse* (Philadelphia,
1813), 155, 162, 193, 194, 223; Adams, *Works,* II, 429; X, 90.

414:1   The *Pennsylvania Magazine* carried numerous esays on useful
inventions and applied science; Amer. Phil. Soc., *Trans.,* I, 118,
205, 218, 235, 239; *Pa. Mag.,* XLIX, 292; Gilpin MSS (HSP);
Early Proceedings of the Amer. Phil. Soc., 51, 53, 84, 97;
Bridenbaugh, *Rebels and Gentlemen,* 347.

414:2   *Newsletter,* Mar. 5, Apr. 2, July 9, *Post.,* July 30, Aug. 13, Dec. 4, 1761; Sept. 9, 1762; *Bowdoin Temple Papers,* I, 21, 116, 119, 127, 129, 130; *Bos. Gaz.,* Nov. 9, 1767; May 16, 1768; May 8, June 5, *Sup.,* 1769; Apr. 20, 1772; Col. Soc. Mass., *Pubs.,* VII, 327.

415:1   Holmes, *Ezra Stiles,* 102, 134; Stiles, *Itineraries,* 106, 448, 473, 476; Stiles, *Letters and Papers,* 11, 15, 21; Stiles, *Literary Diary,* I, 10, 12, 14, 21, 24, 28, 57, 70, 85, 93, 106, 131, 132, 201, 357, 502; *Newp. Merc.,* Jan. 7, 1765; June 5, 1769; Feb. 21, 1774; Mar. 20, 1775; *Essex Gaz.,* June 20, 1769.

415:2   Stearns, 3 *W. & M. Quart.,* III, 231, 243, 244, 246, 249, 258; Darlington, *Memories of John Bartram,* 265; *S.C. Country Jour.,* Mar. 8, 1774; *S.C. Gaz.,* Aug. 31, 1765; Mar. 2, 1769; Mar. 3, Apr. 5, 12, 1773; *S.C.A.G. Gaz.,* June 12, 1769; Charleston Museum, *Quarterly,* I, 3, 4, 6, 11; Smith, *Correspondence of Linnaeus,* I, 530, 537; Bridenbaugh, *Myths and Realities,* 106.

416:1   *Pennsylvania Magazine,* I (1775), 53; Adams, *Works,* II, 397; Bridenbaugh, *Rebels and Gentlemen,* 353.

416:2   *Pa. Gaz.,* Mar. 12, 1761; Apr. 18, 1765; Dec. 25, 1766; Sept. 13, 1770; *Pa. Chron.,* Nov. 14, 1772; Dec. 12, 1773; *S.C. Gaz.,* Apr. 13, May 4, 1765; Feb. 16, 24, 1767; 20 *Bos. Rec. Com.,* 171; *N.Y. Merc.,* Oct. 24, 1763; Nov. 7, 1774; *Prov. Gaz.,* Jan. 28, 1769; *Bos. Post Boy,* June 11, 1770; *Pa. Packet,* Jan. 13, 27, Mar. 2, 1772; Mar. 22, 1773; Feb. 7, 1774; *Rivington's N.Y. Gaz.,* Mar. 10, 1774; *N.Y. Gaz.,* Oct. 15, 1770; *S.C.A.G. Gaz.,* Mar. 25, 1768.

417:1   Bridenbaugh, *Myths and Realities,* chap. I.

417:2   Stiles, *Itineraries,* 443; *Pennsylvania Magazine,* I (1775), 57; *Pa. Eve. Post,* Mar. 16, 1775.

CONCLUSION

424:1   *Goethes Samtliche Werke* (Munich, 1909), V, 39, p. 106.

BIBLIOGRAPHICAL NOTE

S O VAST is the corpus of materials pertaining to the history of the five cities and cognate subjects that the investigator is faced with a problem of selection in his research, and then with one of taking notes on his notes. It has therefore seemed best in this essay on authorities to describe the several kinds of available sources, their locations, and to single out for comment some that proved of the greatest value in the preparation of this volume. There is nothing esoteric about these materials; nor have I made a major "bibliographical find."

The best introduction to the subject is through the card catalogues and printed guides to the manuscript collections and printed materials in historical societies and certain great research libraries: the Massachusetts Historical Society at Boston; the American Antiquarian Society at Worcester; the Rhode Island Historical Society at Providence; the Newport Historical Society; the New York Historical Society; the Historical Society of Pennsylvania at Philadelphia; the South Carolina Historical Society at Charleston; and the Harvard College Library at Cambridge; the great John Carter Brown Library of Americana at Providence; the New York Public Library; the Library Company of Philadelphia (Franklin's library); the Library of Congress; the libraries of the College of William and Mary and of the Institute of Early American History and Culture at Williamsburg, Va.; the Charleston Library Society; the Henry E. Huntington Library at San Marino; and the University of California Library at Berkeley.

I. CITY RECORDS

The Town Meeting and Selectmen's minutes for Boston are printed in the *Reports of the Record Commissioners* of that city, Vols. 12, 14–20, 23, 29 (1885–1900); for New York there are the *Minutes of the Common Council,* Vols. IV–VIII (1905); and for Philadelphia the rare *Minutes of the Common Council of Philadelphia* (1856). The records of the Town Meeting and Town Council of Newport, lost temporarily in a shipwreck off Hell Gate during the War for Independence, are badly water-stained and rendered still more difficult to read by repair between two sheets of transparent silk. They are in Vault B of the Newport Historical Society. Charleston, lacking a city government, naturally has no records, but the minutes of the Church Wardens and Vestry of St. Philip's Church (in the parish house on Church Street) are invaluable.

II. PROVINCE RECORDS

Provincial assemblies and officials had much to do with the cities, and their journals are full of information. Rhode Island, New York, and Pennsylvania have published their records in full; but Massachusetts has only the *Journal of the House of Representatives* down to 1753. Rare colonial records of the House and Council must be consulted at the Massachusetts Historical Society or the Massachusetts Archives (State House, Boston). South Carolina is only now beginning to publish its Assembly's proceedings, but at Columbia in the Historical Commission the Commons House journals are in excellent condition and readily available. (The Library of Congress and the University of North Carolina have microfilmed all of the legislative proceedings of the thirteen colonies, and many libraries possess copies.) The collections of printed statutes of the five colonies are, of course, of prime importance. In the Rhode Island Archives (State House, Providence) are many manuscript materials bearing on Newport and in cases requiring unusual accuracy the originals of the Assembly Records must be consulted because J. R. Bartlett's edition of them is so faulty. A wonderful WPA index makes this archive a joy to work in.

III. NEWSPAPERS

The newspapers of the thirteen colonies, especially those of the five cities, furnished the basic source for this work. Forty-one papers were issued in the five towns, and these, together with twenty-one others from Portsmouth, Salem, Providence, Norwich, New London, Hartford, New Haven, Albany, Germantown, Lancaster, Baltimore, Annapolis, Williamsburg, Norfolk, New Bern, Wilmington, N.C., and Savannah, have been searched issue by issue from 1743 to 1776. Often local news of one city was printed more completely in the newspaper of another. Of particular significance are the advertisements, which cast light upon educational, artistic, musical, literary, religious, recreational, and allied activities, as well as upon economic matters. Much of the science of the day reached a public first in newspaper essays; in fact, there was scarcely any activity that the press did not mention either in advertising or news columns. Increasingly political and social questions were debated in the press as the Revolution approached. Clarence S. Brigham's *History and*

Bibliography of American Newspapers, 1690–1720 (Worcester, 1947) gives all essential data and the locations of these newspapers. The University of California has nearly all of them in reproductions.

IV. MANUSCRIPTS

Much useful material is still in manuscript, particularly merchants' journals, ledgers, and letter books; also the records of organizations, such as fire companies, charitable societies, social clubs, and churches, as well as personal materials. Two excellent guides to these are Greene and Morris, *Guide to the Sources for Early American History in New York City* (2nd edn., New York, 1953); and the *Guide to the Manuscript Collections of the Historical Society of Pennsylvania* (2nd edn., Philadelphia, 1949). Transcripts of important documents from the Public Record Office, London, are listed by the late Grace G. Griffin in *Guide to Manuscripts Relating to American History in British Depositories Reproduced for the Library of Congress* (1946). The Historical Records Survey performed a very great service by making guides and calendars of state, local, and church records, but unfortunately no complete list of them was ever issued.

V. PRINTED SOURCES

In evaluating city life, letters, diaries, journals, and other compilations by individuals not only yielded much information but supplied a needed human touch. Among these are the *Letters of James Murray, Loyalist* (Boston, 1901); Henry M. Mühlenberg, *Journals* (Philadelphia, 1942–5); William Darlington, *Memorials of John Bartram and Humphry Marshall* (Philadelphia, 1849); *Journal Kept by Hugh Finlay, Surveyor of the Post Roads . . .* (Brooklyn, 1867); Anne R. Cunningham, *Letters and Diary of John Rowe* (Boston, 1903); and the extraordinarily useful compendia of the Rev. Ezra Stiles, *Literary Diary* (New York, 1901), and *Itineraries and other Miscellanies* (New Haven, 1916), both edited by Franklin B. Dexter. Among unofficial published records are several collections dealing with the churches: *Records of the Presbyterian Church in the United States of America* (Philadelphia, 1841–1904); William S. Perry, *Historical Collections relating to the American Colonial Church* [Anglican] (Hartford, 1870–8); and the hitherto unnoticed *Minutes of the Convention of Delegates from the Synod of New York and Philadelphia, and from the Associations of Connecticut, Held Annually from 1765 to 1775, Inclusive* (Hartford, 1843).

VI. MAGAZINES, PAMPHLETS, BROADSIDES

Virtually all of what might be called colonial literature issued from the presses of the five cities or those of their lesser satellites; and besides being a mirror of the public mind, it is crammed with facts and curious sidelights relating to the urban scene. Lyon N. Richardson's *Early American Magazines, 1741–1789* (New York, 1931) analyzes this genre and provides a complete bibliography of all issues, which are now on microfilm. Pamphlets dealt with all subjects, including the flood of sermons, and may be traced, along with other printed items, in the great bibliographical works of Joseph Sabin, *Bibliotheca Americana. Dictionary of Books Relating to America* (New York and Portland, 1868–1936), and Charles Evans, *American Bibliography* (Chicago, 1903–34), which have been little used by historians. In addition, John E. Alden, *Rhode Island Imprints* (New York, 1949) and Charles R. Hildeburn, *A Century of Printing. Issues of the Pennsylvania Press* (Philadelphia, 1885) are still indispensable.

VII. PUBLICATIONS OF LEARNED SOCIETIES

Many nuggets lie buried in the collections of historical societies, which contain much source material and also valuable articles on special topics: Colonial Society of Massachusetts, *Publications;* Massachusetts Historical Society, *Collections* and *Proceedings* (see *Handbook of Publications,* 1934); Rhode Island Historical Society, *Proceedings* and *Rhode Island History;* New-York Historical Society, *Collections* and *Bulletin;* Historical Society of Pennsylvania, *Collections* and *Pennsylvania Magazine of History and Biography* (the oldest and best journal of any society, for which a superb index to the first 75 volumes was published, 1954); and the *South Carolina Historical and Genealogical Magazine,* published by the South Carolina Historical Society. The *William and Mary Quarterly,* 3rd ser., (1944–) is excellent, as is the *New England Quarterly;* and for particular topics such magazines as *Antiques, Annals of Medical History, Magazine of Art, Journal of the Society of Architectural Historians,* and *Transactions* of the American Philosophical Society are among the more important journals.

VIII. TRAVEL ACCOUNTS

Travelers are often unreliable and inaccurate, but their reports are priceless for physical descriptions of cities and of people and manners. I have scrupulously never used a traveler for any date beyond the time of his visit to a community. The best of such accounts are: *Gentleman's Progress: the Itinerarium of Dr. Alexander Hamilton, 1744* (edited by Carl Bridenbaugh, Chapel Hill, 1948); and the well-known travels of Peter Kalm, James Birket, Rev. Andrew Burnaby, Lord Adam Gordon, John Bartram, Dr. Robert Honyman, Patrick M'Robert, and Nicholas Cresswell. In the forthcoming Bibliography of Southern Travel, edited by Thomas D. Clark, Lester Cappon will cover the period of this volume.

IX. MAPS, ENGRAVINGS, PAINTINGS

Historians have long neglected graphic materials in their work, but for the cities such sources are as important as any written documents. The best guide to maps is P. Lee Phillips, *List of Maps of America in the Library of Congress* (Washington, 1901), and Louis C. Karpinski, *Early Maps of Carolina and Adjoining Regions* (2nd edn., Charleston, 1937). But many maps must be searched for in the great depositories. Excellent maps exist for all of the cities; that of John Reed, *Map of the City and Liberties of Philadelphia* (1774), gives the most detail, though John Montrésor's map of New York and Charles Blaskowitz's Newport are both interesting. I. N. Phelps Stokes and Daniel C. Haskell's *American Historical Prints* (New York, 1932) concentrates on views of cities, which depict all sorts of useful details. Very useful is Boies Penrose: "Prints and Drawings in the Collections of the Historical Society of Pennsylvania," *Pa. Mag. Hist. & Biog.,* LX, LXI. Similarly the Boston Museum of Fine Arts, the historical societies of Massachusetts, Rhode Island, New York, and Pennsylvania, the Redwood Library of Newport, and the Gibbes Art Gallery in Charleston contain the bulk of the extant portraits of colonial worthies by such craftsmen as Smibert, Feke, Blackburn, Copley, Wollaston, West, Peale, Benbridge, and Theus.

X. PHYSICAL REMAINS

The graphic sources mentioned in the section above are best comprehended after a careful survey of the remains of the colonial period in the five towns. It is possible to become familiar with the lay of the land, the nature of the waterfront and harbor, the plan, and much of the architecture as well as to recover through the imagination something of the "feel" of each of the five cities. New York has few buildings left and the shoreline is greatly altered; but Newport has changed very little, and will give any visitor the best possible idea of what a colonial town was like—even better than restored Williamsburg—and in Antoinette F. Downing and Vincent J. Scully's beautifully printed *Architectural Heritage of Newport*

(Cambridge, 1952) he will find a superb guide. For Charleston, the next-best-preserved city, there are numerous architectural studies and a handy guide, *This is Charleston* (1944). The *Catalog* of the Historic American Buildings Survey (Washington, 1941) lists photographs of buildings in each city which are now to be had from the photographic service of the Library of Congress for twenty-five cents each.

XI. SECONDARY AUTHORITIES

Nearly all of the historical studies of the colonies, 1743–76, in some fashion have a bearing on the five cities; and that I have drawn heavily on them any professional reader will at once perceive. I wish there were space to thank old and new colleagues individually. Nobody can write on this subject without recourse to the great city histories of Boston by Samuel G. Drake and Justin Winsor; of New York by I. N. Phelps Stokes and James G. Wilson; of Philadelphia by Thompson Westcott; and George C. Mason's unsatisfactory *Reminiscences of Newport,* of which copies exist at the Newport and Rhode Island Historical Societies and the New York Public Library with three different sets of very important original documents bound in. These works need to be supplemented, however, for formerly local historians wrote genteel narratives about members of their own upper class. Among the many special studies on urban history, the following are outstanding: Ernest S. Griffith, *History of American City Government. The Colonial Period* (New York, 1938); Virginia D. Harrington, *The New York Merchant on the Eve of the Revolution* (New York, 1935); Thomas C. Pollock, *The Philadelphia Theatre in the Eighteenth Century* (Philadelphia, 1933); George C. Mason, *Annals of the Redwood Library* (Newport, 1891); Robert F. Seybolt, *The Town Officials of Colonial Boston* (Cambridge, 1939); and Stuyvesant Fish, *New York Privateers, 1756–1763.* In several other volumes, I have dealt in more detail with certain subjects originally planned for this book: *The Colonial Craftsman* (New York, 1950); *Myths and Realities: Societies of the Colonial South* (Baton Rouge, 1952); *Seat of Empire: The Political Role of Eighteenth-Century Williamsburg* (Williamsburg, 1950); and with Jessica Bridenbaugh, *Rebels and Gentlemen: Philadelphia in the Age of Franklin* (New York, 1942), a volume that deals in detail with the intellectual and cultural life of the colonial metropolis. Unpublished studies that I have used freely are: Bruce M. Bigelow, The Commerce of Rhode Island with the West Indies Before the Revolution (thesis, Brown University, by permission); Gertrude Foster, Documentary History of Education in South Carolina (thesis, University of South Carolina); Constance Morrison, Windham County, Conn. (seminar paper, Brown University, 1939); George W. Houghton, The Coaches of Colonial New

York (typescript, New York Hist. Soc.); Gaines W. Walters, The Commerce of Colonial Philadelphia (thesis, Yale University, by permission); and Gilman Ostrander, The Molasses Trade of the Thirteen Colonies (M.A. thesis, Univ. California, Berkeley, to be published in *Agric. History*). I am grateful for the opportunity to thank these authors for the use of their meaty researches. Among biographies, of which there are all too few for this period, are several in the first class: James B. Hedges, *The Browns of Providence Plantations* (Cambridge, 1952) stands by itself; Henry Wilder Foote's studies of *John Smibert* and *Robert Feke* (Cambridge, 1930, 1950); George S. Brookes's *Friend Anthony Benezet* (Philadelphia, 1937); David D. Wallace's *Henry Laurens* (New York, 1915); and William T. Baxter's *The House of Hancock* (Cambridge, 1944) supply larger studies than the invaluable *Dictionary of American Biography* and Clifford K. Shipton's charming and learned *Biographical Sketches of Those Who Attended Harvard College,* IV–VIII (Cambridge, 1933–51). Two population studies have aided me at every turn: Stella M. Sutherland, *Population Distribution in Colonial America* (New York, 1936), and Evarts B. Greene and Virginia D. Harrington, *American Population Before the Federal Census of 1790* (New York, 1932).

XII. ENGLISH CITIES

A large number of good books treat the history of English cities, to which Stanley Pargellis and D. J. Medley, *Bibliography of British History: The Eighteenth Century* (Oxford, 1951) provides the best introduction. Especially useful were John Latimer, *Annals of Bristol in the Eighteenth Century* (Bristol, 1893); Walter Ison, *Georgian Buildings of Bristol* (London, 1952); Sir James A. Picton, [Liverpool] *Municipal Archives and Records* (Liverpool, 1886); John Corry, *History of Liverpool* (Liverpool, 1810); William Hutton, *History of Birmingham* (Birmingham, 1781); M. Dorothy George, *London Life in the Eighteenth Century* (London, 1925); John Summerson, *Georgian London* (New York, 1946); Maurice Craig, *Dublin* (New York, 1952); Francis Bamford and Sacheverell Sitwell, *Edinburgh* (London, 1938). The following books on certain topics or general works were of real value: M. C. Buer, *Health, Wealth, and Population in the Early Days of the Industrial Revolution* (London, 1926); Charles Burney, *General History of Music* (London, 1935); Ernest Caulfield, *Infant Welfare Movement in the Eighteenth Century* (New York, 1931); Henry Grey Graham, *Social Life of Scotland in the Eighteenth Century* (London, 1937); J. R. Hutchinson, *Press-Gang Afloat and Ashore* (London, 1913); Richard Pares, *War and Trade in the West Indies* (Oxford, 1938); E. R. Plomer, G. H. Bushnell, and E. R. M. Dix, *Dictionary of Printers and Booksellers who were at* work in England . . . *1726 to 1775* (Oxford, 1932); Sybil M. Rosen-feld, *Strolling Players and Drama in the Provinces* (Cambridge, 1939); A. S. Turberville, *Johnson's England* (Oxford, 1933); Sidney and Bea-trice Webb, *English Local Government: Statutory Authorities for Special Purposes* (London, 1922); William T. Whitely, *Artists and Their Friends in England, 1700–1799* (London, 1928).

XIII. FURTHER REFERENCES

The reader is also directed to the Bibliography in *Cities in the Wilder-ness: The First Century of Urban Life in America, 1625–1742* for addi-tional information and also for the same kind of documentation that was prepared for this work but omitted because of lack of space. Copies of the notes to *Cities in Revolt* are available at the Harvard College Li-brary, Historical Society of Pennsylvania, Library of Congress, State Historical Society of Wisconsin, and the University of California Library at Berkeley.

Index

Index